故宫博物院藏品大系

善本特藏編

8

滿文古籍

故宫博物院 編

故宫出版社

图书在版编目（CIP）数据

故宫博物院藏品大系．善本特藏编．满文古籍 / 故宫博物院编．— 北京：故宫出版社，2014.8
ISBN 978-7-5134-0545-4

Ⅰ．①故… Ⅱ．①故… Ⅲ．①故宫博物院－历史文物－北京市－图集②满语－古籍－善本－汇编－中国－清代
Ⅳ．① K870.2 ② Z424.9

中国版本图书馆 CIP 数据核字 (2013) 第 315669 号

故宫博物院藏品大系

善本特藏编 滿文古籍

撰稿統籌：張　榮
主　　編：春　花
編　　委：李　英　阮衛萍　嚴　勇　郭文通
攝影統籌：馮　輝
攝　　影：李　凡
資料提供：周耀卿
翻　　譯：李紹毅
編輯統籌：陳麗華　王亞民　趙國英　劉　輝
責任編輯：江　英　宋　歌
裝幀設計：李　猛
出版發行：故宫出版社
地址：北京東城區景山前街 4 號　郵編：100009
電話：010-85007808　010-85007816　傳真：010-65129479
郵箱：ggcb@culturefc.cn
網址：www.culturefc.cn
印　　刷：北京雅昌藝術印刷有限公司
開　　本：787 × 1092 毫米　1/8
印　　張：42.25
字　　數：40 千字
圖　　版：452 幅
版　　次：2014 年 8 月第 1 版第 1 次印刷
印　　數：1~1,000 册
書　　號：ISBN 978-7-5134-0545-4
定　　價：760.00 元

故宮博物院藏品大系

編輯出版委員會

總目

滿文古籍部分概述 9
本卷凡例 14
圖版目録 17
圖版 21
圖版索引 313

故宫博物院藏品大系

《故宫博物院藏品大系·善本特藏編》

滿文古籍部分概述

春花　李英

清廷是由滿族作爲統治民族的統一的多民族政權，明萬曆二十七年（一五九九）創製滿文，开始以滿文撰拟朝廷軍政紀要，同時以滿文翻譯了一些漢籍。順治元年（一六四四）清軍入關後，除了大量翻譯漢文典籍之外，還以滿文纂修本朝歷史及政策、法規等。爲有效地統治蒙、藏民族，清廷对其實施了提倡信奉佛教的政策，并以滿文翻譯了大量的佛經。因各民族间相互學習、交流需要，編纂了很多滿文及多語合璧辭書。總之，清廷执政期間留下很多滿文古籍文獻，根據内容，可分爲翻譯文獻、創作文獻兩種。

一　翻譯文獻

（一）漢籍的滿文翻譯：清統治者崇尚漢文化，早在入關前就由文館以滿文翻譯《明會典》、《素書》、《資治通鑒》、《孟子》、《三國演義》、《金史》等漢文典籍。清軍入關後，順治帝大力提倡尊孔、崇儒并積極推行學習漢文化的活動，還下令以滿文翻譯《洪武要訓》、《範行恒言》、《表忠録》、《詩經》等，以促使『滿漢聯合』民族政策的实施，也爲康乾盛世時期文化的蓬勃發展奠定了基礎。

康熙帝大力推崇漢文化的結晶——儒家思想、程朱理學等，并敕令以滿文翻譯、注釋、刊刻《御製日講四書解義》、《御纂性理精義》、《御批通鑒綱目》等儒家典籍。此外，民間還以滿文翻譯《西厢記》、《西漢演義》、《西游記》、《金瓶梅》、《隋唐演義》、《列國志》等文學作品。從而使孔子和朱熹的學説逐漸成爲清代正統的官方思想。

雍正帝也尊崇儒家思想和漢文化，他在位期間，創辦各種官學，推行普及旗民教育。乾隆帝繼續發揚博學鴻儒活動，并以規範後的滿文重新翻譯、刊行『四書』、『五經』等。

（二）佛經的滿文翻譯：早在入關前文館的达海巴克什曾以滿文翻譯《大乘經》，清軍入關後，對蒙、藏民族有效實施信奉佛教政策，清前期諸帝敕修很多滿文佛經。如康熙年《金剛經》、雍正年《摩訶般若波羅蜜多心經》，尤其乾隆帝敕修《清文全藏經》、《救度佛母贊》、《無量壽佛祈禱文》、《讀咒法》等大量的滿文佛經及《御製滿漢蒙古西蕃合璧大藏全咒》、《御譯大雲輪請雨經》、《白傘蓋儀軌經》等四體合璧佛經。清前期諸帝信佛及敕修滿文佛經的舉措，促進了臣子之間佛教传播的蔓延，如巴林公德勒克抄寫《文殊師利贊》及《文殊師利菩薩贊佛法身禮》、永瑢抄寫《金剛壽命經》等，均是敬獻乾隆帝的藏滿蒙漢四體合璧經文。

清代經過一百多年的推崇學習漢族儒家文化和提倡信奉藏传佛教以及滿文翻譯儒家經典和佛經等活動，促使了『滿漢聯合』、『滿蒙聯盟』政策的有效實施，同時也强烈地刺激了編印滿文及多語合璧辭書的啓蒙、發展。

（三）滿文詞典的問世及發展演變：清軍入關後，隨著各民族语言间翻譯需要，康熙帝敕纂《御製清文鑒》，康熙四十七年（一七〇八）刊行。後把該詞典譯成蒙文和漢文，刊行滿蒙合璧的《御製清文鑒》和滿漢合璧的《音漢清文鑒》、《一學三貫清文鑒》等。

乾隆帝爲規範滿文中的漢語音譯借詞，曾下令内府及各部院、衙門等編纂《欽定清語》、《新定清語》、《清文鑒外新語》、《御製兼漢清文鑒》等，并以滿文意譯詞替代《御製清文鑒》中的漢語借詞，再增補新詞、古詞。最後彙編成《御製增訂清文鑒》，乾隆三十六年（一七七一）刊行。該詞典成了編纂滿文詞典的典範。後乾隆帝爲存留、發展、規範各民族語言音韻，又敕令以《御製增訂清文鑒》爲準，纂修《御製滿洲蒙古漢文三合切音清文鑒》、《御製四體清文鑒》、《御製五體清文鑒》等多語合璧詞典。乾隆帝曾在『御製增訂清文鑒序』中以遼、金、元三史爲例，强調互注切音的重要性，同時命以滿文標注三史人名、地名、官名等，編成《欽定遼金元三史語解》，乾隆四十五年（一七八〇）刊行。

以上所述清代皇帝敕修滿文詞典均为按类编排的詞典，民间纂修滿文音序詞典也緊跟著官修分類詞典的發展步伐，如《大清全書》、《滿漢同文全書》、《清文彙書》等早期編纂的滿漢合璧音序詞典，收入大量的漢語音譯借詞方面與《御製清文鑑》基本一致。而《御製增訂清文鑑》問世後，宗室宜興彙集七千九百餘條欽定的新滿文詞語，以《清文彙書》體例編成了《清文補彙》，乾隆五十一年（一七八六）刊行。後由荆州八旗駐防翻譯總學教習志寬、培寬二人組織學生，編《清文彙書》、《清文補彙》词语成《清文總彙》，光緒二十三年（一八九七）刊行。

總之，清代編纂衆多滿文及多語合璧詞典，標志著滿文詞語空前繁榮發展，這些詞典爲進一步鞏固『滿漢聯合』政策以及各民族文化的傳播與交流提供了最有效的橋梁，也爲强化『國語』及宏揚各民族文化起了巨大的促進作用。

二　創作文獻

（一）本朝史地文獻的纂修：自康熙年开始設立方略館、國史館和武英殿修書處等，皇帝欽命以滿、漢、蒙三種文字編纂刊行了大量的本朝史地方面的書籍。

首先，在國史館編纂《實録》、《聖訓》、《方略》、《傳記》等本朝歷史資料。清代每朝皇帝駕崩，後任皇帝即位，立即敕命恭纂《實録》、《聖訓》，自太祖至德宗十二朝，《實録》、《聖訓》各纂有十二種，還有天聰九年修成的滿蒙漢合璧《太祖武皇帝實録》。各朝滿文《實録》、《聖訓》均有大、小紅綾本和小黄綾本，《聖訓》還有武英殿刻本。

此外，康熙四十九年（一七七〇）在國史館敕纂《欽定國史功臣列傳》，至乾隆年編成。此書的問世成了編修本朝大臣、忠烈傳記的開端。如雍正十三年（一七三五）敕纂《八旗滿洲氏族通譜》，乾隆九年（一七四四）刊行。乾隆年不僅續修《欽定國史功臣列傳》，爲更詳細地記述本朝人物功勳，分門别類立傳列表，編成了《宗室王公功績表傳》、《恩封宗室王公表》、《欽定外藩蒙古回部王公表傳》、《欽定國史大臣列傳》、《欽定國史功臣列傳》、《欽定國史忠義列傳》、《昭忠祠列傳》等，後幾朝不斷續纂完善。

其次，康熙年又開設了撰著清朝戰争史實的方略館，先後以滿漢兩種文字刊行了《平定三逆方略》、《親征平定朔漠方略》、《平定准噶爾方略》、《平定西北方略》、《平定金川方略》、《平定兩金川方略》等涉及平定邊疆少數民族戰争始末的書籍。此外，乾隆帝爲宣示清初開國事迹，敕修《皇清開國方略》。

其三，清代編纂本朝地理資料較多，但以滿文翻譯的只有《欽定滿洲源流考》、《欽定八旗通志初集》、《欽定清涼山志》、《欽定國子監志》等幾種。

（二）本朝政策、法規的彙集整理：清廷爲維護社會秩序，鞏固國家統一，開設律例館，以滿、漢文編印很多有關本朝政策、法規方面的書籍。康熙九年（一六七〇）刊行的《大清律解附例》爲流傳至今最早的滿文法律全書，爲解決八旗圈地導致人民逃亡問題，歷朝編製修訂了《督捕則例》。此外，編訂《欽定六部現行則例》，康熙十九年（一六八〇）刊行。

雍正帝即位後立即敕命對舊律刪繁就簡，加以規範，編成了集解、附例齊全的《大清律集解》，并改稱《欽定大清律》。其中新條例附於律，結束了康熙以來例、律分開及以例代律的情况。乾隆朝修律時，去掉總注及條例中原、增、欽定的區別，并稍加删改，大量增補條例，編成了《大清律例》，乾隆五年（一七四〇）刊行，後該體例成了清律的定性。因『五年一小修，十年一大修』，其修訂原則是『律文歷代相因，例條不斷增改』，以至後期的《大清律續纂條例》卷次增多，條例增加。

此外，清廷爲維護皇族特權，編訂《宗人府則例》，爲維持皇宫秩序，編纂《内務府現行則例》。還針對不同問題，專門製定了《八旗則例》、《軍器則例》、《中樞政考》、《處分則例》、《白塔信炮章程》、《銓選則例》、《品級考則》、《處分則例》、《欽定户部旗務則例》、《欽定太常寺則例》、《欽定國子監則例》等很多『子則例』，其纂修也遵循『五年一小修，十年一大修』的慣例。

清廷一向重視安撫邊疆少數民族并不斷加强对他们的日常管理問題，爲治理蒙古，早在天聰七年（一六三三）頒行《盛京定例》，這是清代最早製定的民族區域法。崇德元年（一六三六）設立『蒙古衙門』，三年（一六三八）改稱『理藩院』，八年（一六四三）頒布《蒙古律書》。順治十四年（一六五七）增修條例，康熙六年（一六六七）再刊。後又屢經修訂，至乾隆五十四年（一七一五）以滿蒙漢三種文字頒行《蒙古律例》。自嘉慶十六年（一八一一）開始對有關蒙古的律例、成案進行全面清理，并增加《西藏通志》、《回疆則例》及有關喇嘛教事務和俄羅斯事務等内容，歷時三年以滿、蒙、漢三種文字編成《理藩院則例》。

可見，清廷製定的法律、法規，內容豐富，種類繁多。爲此早在康熙二十三年（一六八四）開設會典館，彙總這些法律、法規，編成《大清會典》，康熙二十九年（一六九〇）刊行，是清代第一部綜合性的大綱、大法，後續修四次。乾隆朝第三次續修時，修成《會典》、《則例》兩部分，嘉慶朝第四次續修時，附加圖。

總之，《大清會典》和《律例》、《則例》等形式多樣的法律、法規交錯在一起形成了較爲完備的行政法規體系，以維護各種特權的同時，保障多民族統一國家的穩定局面。

（三）滿族人以滿文創作的文學作品：隨著滿漢文化的深入接觸和影響，自康熙年涌現出衆多滿族作家，但其中衹有少數作家用滿文創作少量作品。如《御製避暑山莊詩》、《御製盛京賦》、《御製全韻詩》、《太宗皇帝大破明師於松山之戰書事文》、《隨軍紀行》、《異域録》、《出使交址紀事》等，其中《御製避暑山莊詩》是康熙帝唯一一部滿文詩集。至乾隆八年（一七四三）乾隆帝抵盛京謁陵祭祖時所撰《御製盛京賦》是最著名的一篇詩賦，後命臣工肇三十二體滿文篆字，并用滿漢文篆字編寫《御製盛京賦》，於乾隆十三年（一七四八）刊行。滿漢合璧《御製全韻詩》也是乾隆帝創新之作，乾隆四十四年（一七七九）刊刻。此外《隨軍紀行》、《異域録》、《出使交址紀事》等是『紀行』、『紀事』體散文。

總之，以滿文譯寫或創作的多數作品，後來由蒙文翻譯，也有些譯成了法文、德文、英文等。

本卷凡例

一　收録範圍：本文主要介紹故宫舊藏清代滿文及滿文與漢、蒙、藏、維等各民族語言合璧的珍貴書籍，其中多數爲滿漢合璧或滿漢蒙三體合璧書籍，含有維語或藏語的多語合璧書籍較少。

二　分類排列：本文大體以古籍經、史、子、集的分類順序編排，每類先排官修書籍，後排非官修書籍，并按成書時間先後爲序。

三　書名：滿文及多語合璧書籍具有一書多名的特點，如有『書名頁題名』、『卷端題名』、『牌記題名』、『封面題名』、『書口題名』、『書簽題名』、『文獻中記載』、『聯合目録所著書名』、『别名』、『擬名』、『譯名』等很多，這些名稱大同小異。本文主要采用『卷端題名』，若無『卷端題名』，則依次采用『書名頁題名』、『牌記題名』或『封面題名』、『書口題名』等。但不是説所有書名的選定，都一律遵循這一規則，有些書名是根據具體情况而定，選擇了最能完整地反映書籍基本特徵的書名。在清代滿文及多語合璧書籍書名前通常冠有『欽定』、『御製』、『翻譯』、『滿漢合璧』、『合璧』、『滿漢文』等字節，這些均予保留，以存真相。本文書名只采用漢文一種文字書名。

四　語種、文種：清代滿文書籍以多語合璧書籍爲主，有雙語合璧、三體合璧、四體合璧、五體合璧等，且語種、文種的組合形式豐富多樣。如《蒙古托忒彙集》是蒙托忒滿漢等四種文字合璧的音序詞典，由於托忒蒙古文是衛拉特方言區使用的一種蒙古文，按語種來説，該詞典是一部蒙漢滿三體合璧詞典；此外，《御製滿蒙文鑒》、《滿蒙藏維四體字書》、《滿蒙藏嘉戎維語五體字書》等均是多語合璧詞典，其中蒙語、藏語、嘉戎語、維吾爾語等语言詞語部分均由滿文字母轉寫而成，这些多語合璧字書文種只有滿文一種。還如《滿蒙漢字書》是滿蒙漢三體合璧詞典，其蒙語部分全由滿文字母轉寫而成，該字書的文種只有漢文、滿文兩種。可見，這些多語合璧字書的『文種』比『語種』少。可見，每部書所包含的語種、文種的多寡并不完全統一，本文主要以語種數量爲依據，并以書内各語言實際排列爲序，叙述多語合璧書籍的語種。

圖版目録

1 《日講易經解義十八卷》—— 22
2 《日講書經解義十三卷》—— 26
3 《詩經二十卷》—— 28
4 《御製翻譯禮記三十卷》—— 30
5 《律呂纂要二卷》—— 34
6 《律呂節要五卷》—— 38
7 《太上皇帝筵宴慶隆舞樂章一卷》—— 40
8 《緬甸獻琛抒悃樂章一卷》—— 42
9 《御製翻譯春秋六十四卷綱領一卷》—— 44
10 《日講春秋解義六十四卷總說一卷》—— 46
11 《翻譯孝經一卷》—— 48
12 《女孝經一卷》—— 52
13 《聖孝鑒十卷》—— 54
14 《四書十三卷》—— 56
15 《御製清文鑒二十卷首一卷
後序一卷總綱四卷》—— 60
16 《御製滿蒙文鑒二十卷首一卷總綱八卷》—— 64
17 《御製滿蒙文鑒二十卷首一卷》—— 66
18 《御製滿蒙文鑒總綱八卷》—— 68
19 《御製兼漢清文鑒不分卷》—— 70
20 《御製增訂清文鑒三十二卷首二卷總綱八卷
補編四卷補編總綱一卷》—— 72
21 《御製滿州蒙古漢字三合切音清文鑒
三十一卷首一卷》—— 74
22 《御製四體清文鑒三十二卷補編四卷》—— 76
23 《御製五體清文鑒三十二卷補編四卷》—— 78
24 《音漢清文鑒二十卷》—— 80
25 《清文鑒擇録八卷》—— 84
26 《實録内摘出舊清語十四卷》—— 86
27 《清文彙書十二卷》—— 88
28 《蒙古托忒彙集八卷》—— 90
29 《清文補彙八卷》—— 92
30 《清文總彙十二卷》—— 94
31 《欽定西域同文志二十四卷》—— 98
32 《欽定遼金元三史語解四十六卷》—— 100
33 《滿蒙漢字書不分卷》—— 104
34 《滿蒙藏維四體字書一卷》—— 106
35 《滿蒙藏嘉戎維語五體字書不分卷》—— 108
36 《集要二卷》—— 110
37 《四體阿禮嘎禮字一卷》—— 114

38 《欽定同文韻統六卷》 116
39 《欽定清漢對音字式一卷》 120
40 《蒙文指要四卷》 122
41 《一百條四卷》 126
42 《重刻清文虛字指南編二卷》 128
43 《滿蒙漢三文合璧教科書八卷》 132
44 《三國志六十五卷》 134
45 《遼史八卷》 136
46 《金史八卷》 138
47 《元史十五卷》 140
48 《明史九十七卷》 142
49 《通鑒彙纂八十卷》 144
50 《大清開國方略三十二卷》 146
51 《平定三逆方略六十卷》 148
52 《蒙古源流八卷》 150
53 《欽定滿州源流考二十卷首一卷》 152
54 《宗室王公功績表傳五卷首二卷》 154
55 《欽定續纂外藩蒙古回部王公傳十二卷》 156
56 《大清國史大臣列傳》（擬訂） 158
57 《大清國史功臣列傳》 160
58 《欽定國史忠義列傳十九卷》 162
59 《昭忠祠列傳續編一百二十卷》 164
60 《順天鄉試題名一卷》 166
61 《進士登科録一卷》 168
62 《古今列女傳六卷》 170
63 《大清會典一百六二卷首一卷》 172
64 《欽定滿洲祭神祭天典禮六卷》 176
65 《欽定宗人府則例三十一卷首一卷》 178
66 《欽定八旗則例十二卷》 180
67 《八旗通志初集二百五十卷目録二卷》 182
68 《欽定回疆則例八卷首一卷》 184
69 《欽定理藩院則例六十三卷首三卷》 186
70 《欽定國子監則例三十卷首二卷》 188
71 《欽定軍器則例十二卷》 190
72 《御製人臣敬心録一卷》 194
73 《大清太祖高皇帝聖訓四卷》 196
74 《清涼山志十卷》 200
75 《明洪武寶訓六卷》 202
76 《二十四孝圖説不分卷》 204
77 《養正圖解四卷》 208
78 《御製資政要覽三卷後序一卷》 212
79 《御製牛戒一卷》 214

80 《三合聖諭廣訓四卷》 216
81 《御纂性理精義十二卷》 220
82 《翻譯大學衍義四十三卷首一卷》 224
83 《素書一卷》 228
84 《三略一卷》 230
85 《六韜二卷》 232
86 《雷公炮製書十六卷》 236
87 《醫藥治症通書三卷》 238
88 《壽世保元二十二卷》 242
89 《王叔和脉訣四卷》 244
90 《西洋藥書不分卷》 246
91 《馬經全書八卷》 248
92 《幾何原本七卷》 250
93 《天文星宿記考一卷》 254
94 《光緒十年八月十七日戊子望月食圖》 256
95 《琴譜六卷》 258
96 《三國志演義二十四卷》 262
97 《列國志一百八回》 266
98 《西游記一百則》 268
99 《後西游記四十回》 270
100 《平山冷燕十六卷》 272
101 《清文翻譯全藏經一百八卷目録一卷》 274
102 《御製滿漢蒙古西番合璧大藏全咒八十卷目录八卷》 278
103 《佛説盂蘭盆經》 282
104 《摩訶般若波羅蜜多心經》 284
105 《大乘首楞嚴經十卷》 288
106 《御譯大雲輪請雨經八卷》 292
107 《白傘蓋儀軌經》
（又名：《薄伽梵白傘蓋佛母成就發悉地甘露寶瓶》） 296
108 《丹書克經》 298
109 《諸佛事略圖説》 300
110 《無量壽佛經》（又名《佛説大乘聖無量壽决定光明王
如來陀羅尼經》） 302
111 《御製避暑山莊詩二卷》 306
112 《御製盛京賦三十二卷》 310

圖版

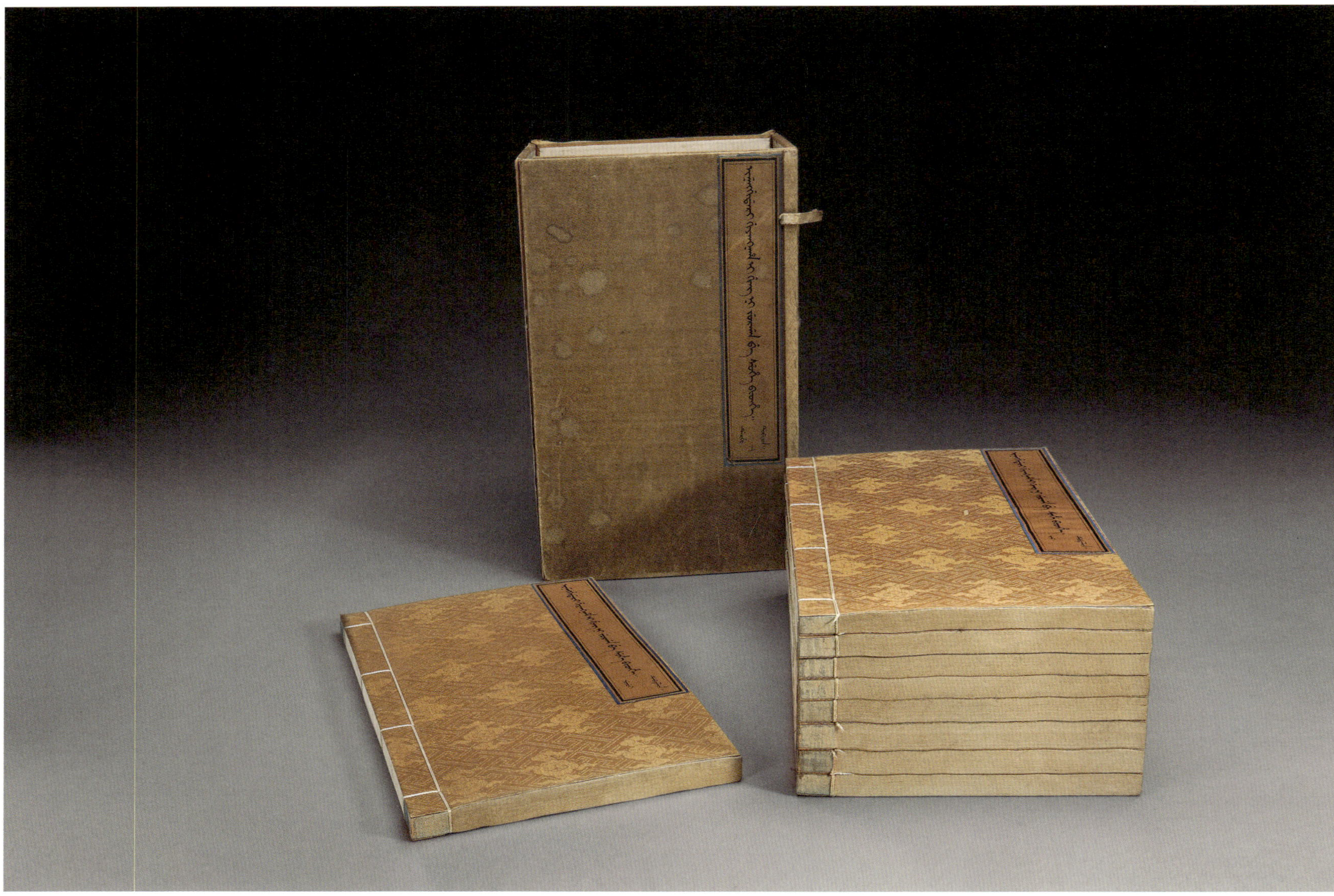

絳色曲水雲紋暗花綾書面
Brown twill-weave silk cover with veiled swastika and cloud pattern

書21723
《日講易經解義十八卷》
清 牛鈕等撰
清康熙二十三年（1684）內府刻滿文本
開本 縱37厘米 橫21.7厘米
版框 縱25.9厘米 橫18.6厘米
十八冊 二函
附："筮儀一卷朱子圖說"

I

Inventory number: Shu 21723
Everyday Textbook: Interpretation of the Book of Changes
Eighteen chapters
Compiled by Niuniu et al., Qing dynasty (1644-1911)
Printed in Manchu in 1684 by the Qing court
Format: 37 × 21.7 cm
Frame: 25.9 × 18.6 cm
Eighteen volumes in two cases
Appendix: one chapter on rites for divination and illustrated text by Zhu Xi

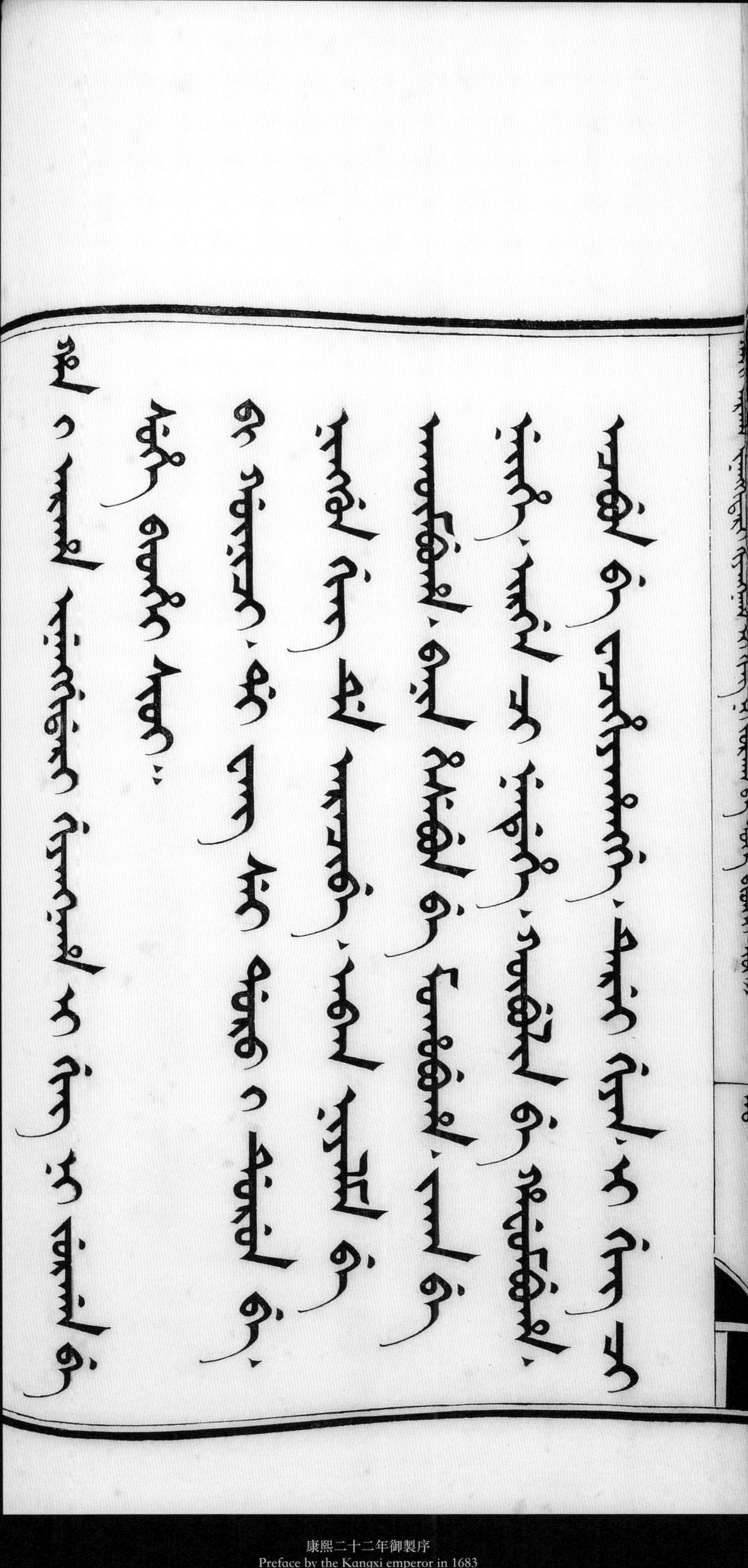

康熙二十二年御製序

Preface by the Kangxi emperor in 1683

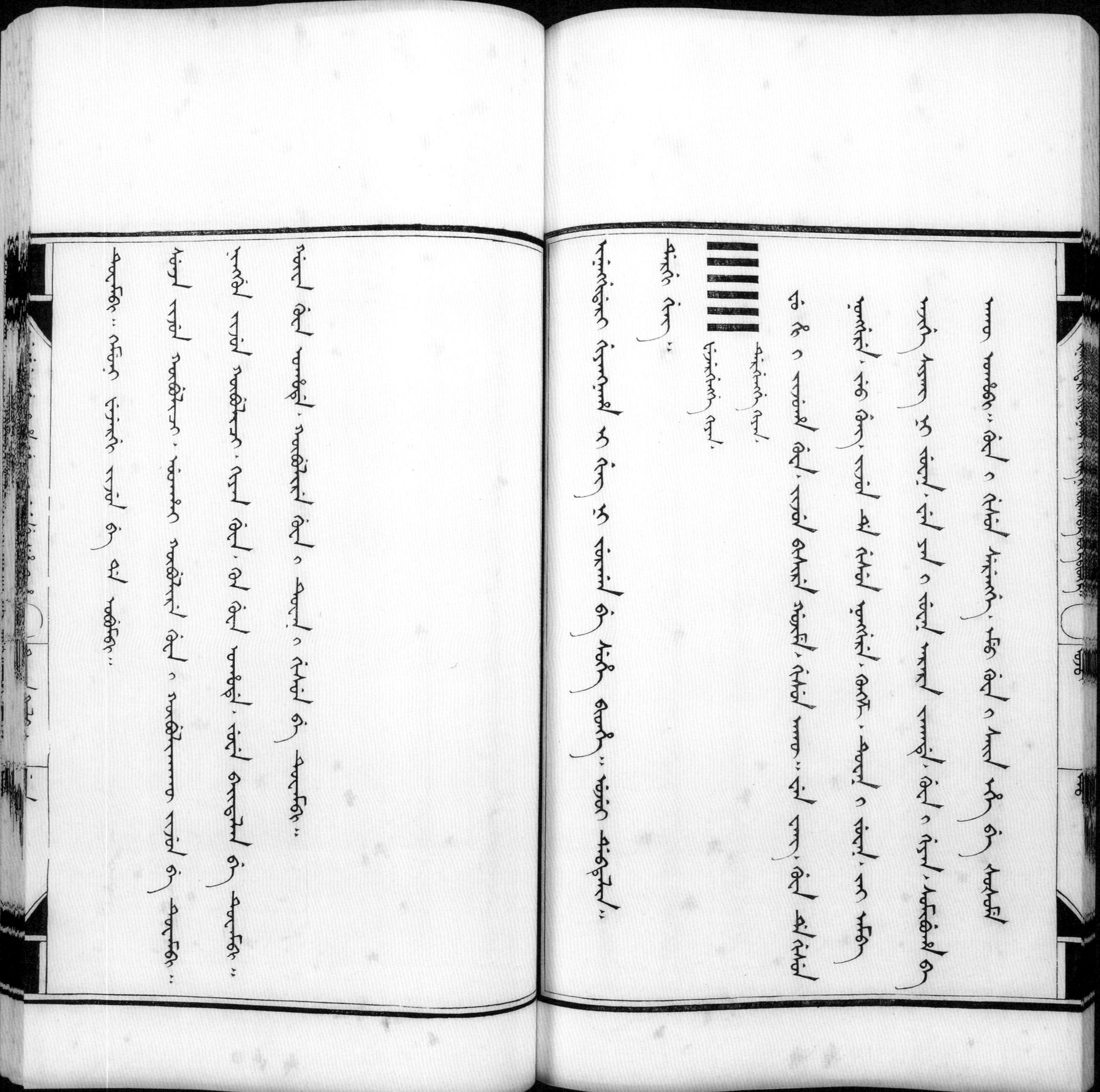

卷端
Beginning

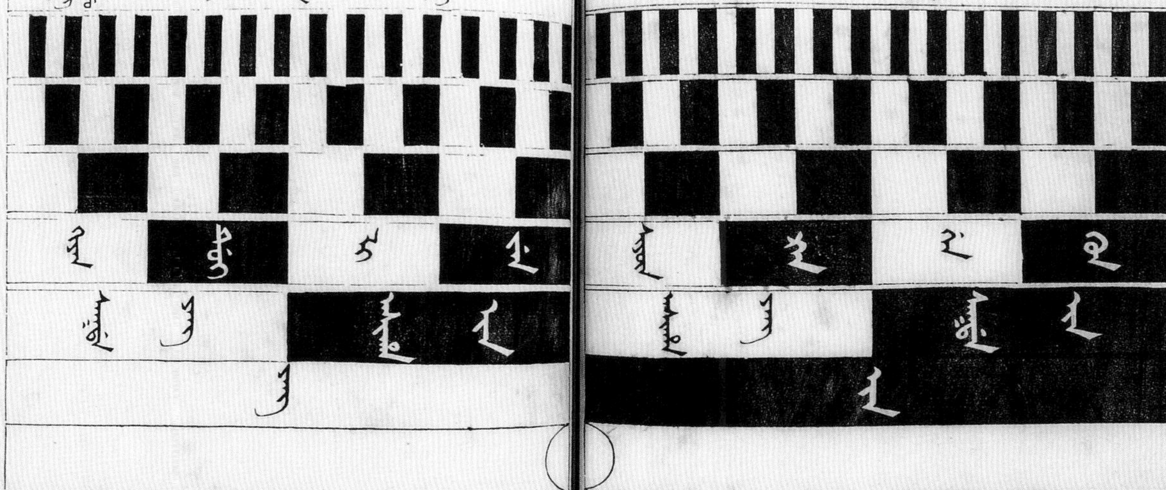

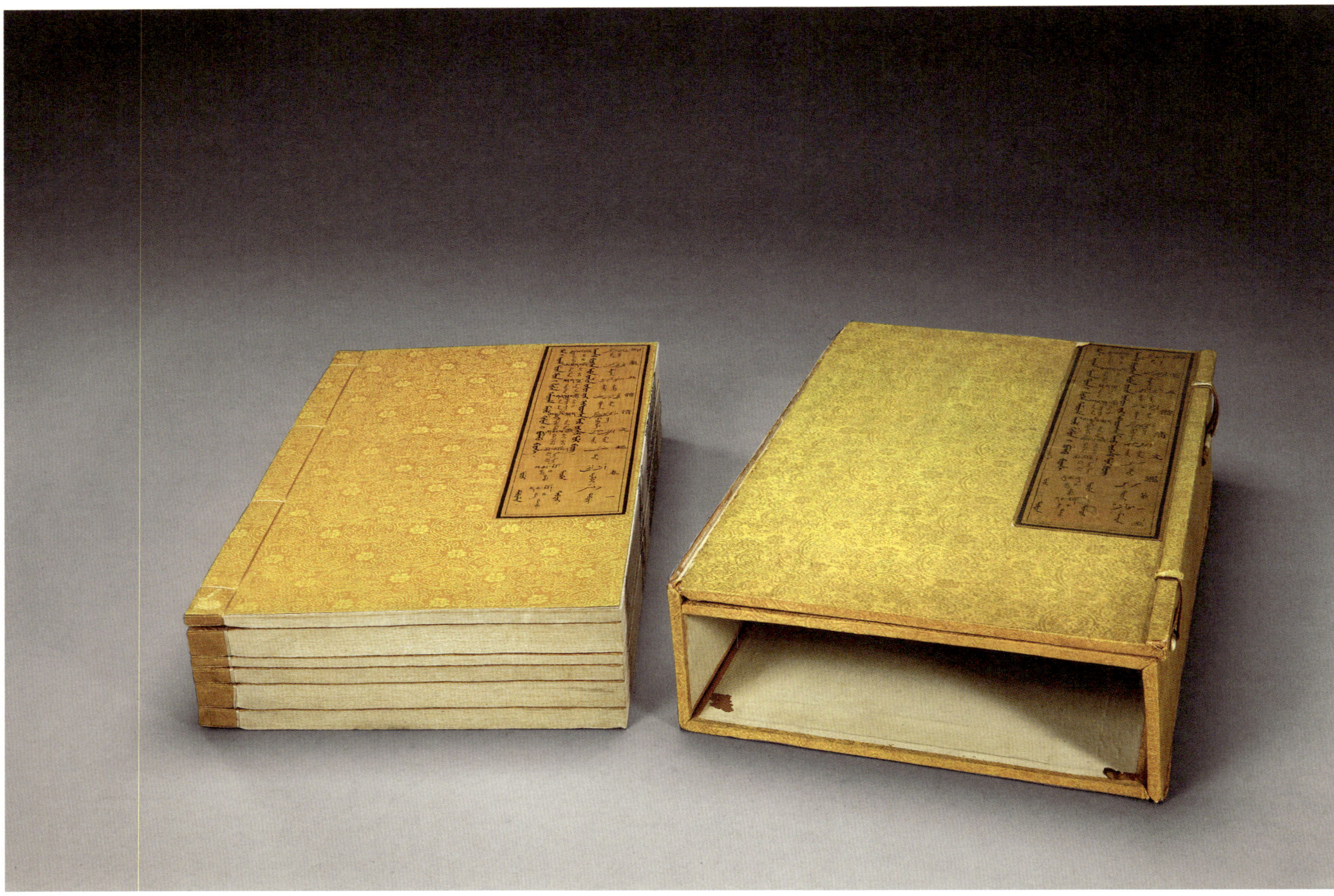

明黄色萬字曲水朵花紋暗花綾書函
Bright yellow twill-weave silk case with veiled swastika and floral pattern

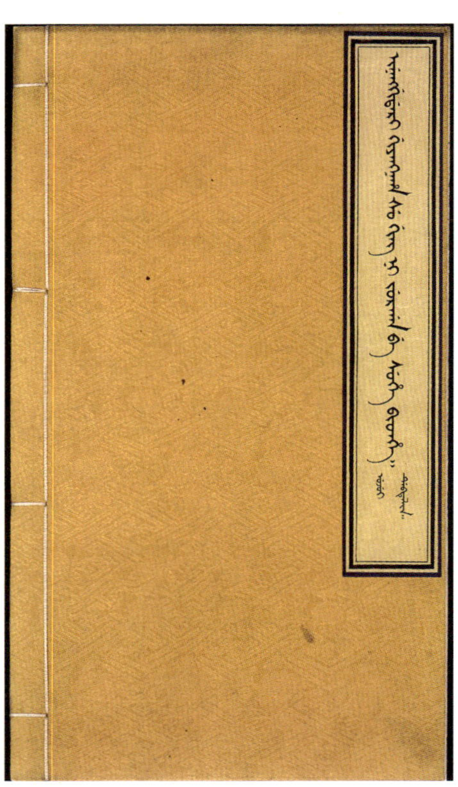

明黄色萬字曲水蘭菊紋暗花綾書面
Bright yellow twill-weave silk cover with veiled orchid and chrysanthemum pattern on continuous swastika ground

書21726
《日講書經解義十三卷》
清　庫勒納等奉敕撰
清康熙十九年（1860）内府刻滿文本
開本　縱37.5厘米　横22厘米
版框　縱26厘米　横18.8厘米
十三册　二函

2

Inventory number: Shu 21726
Everyday Textbook: Interpretation of the Book of History
Thirteen chapters
Compiled by imperial order by Kulena et al., Qing dynasty (1644-1911)
Printed in Manchu in 1680 by the Qing court
Format: 37.5 × 22 cm
Frame: 26 × 18.8 cm
Thirteen volumes in two cases

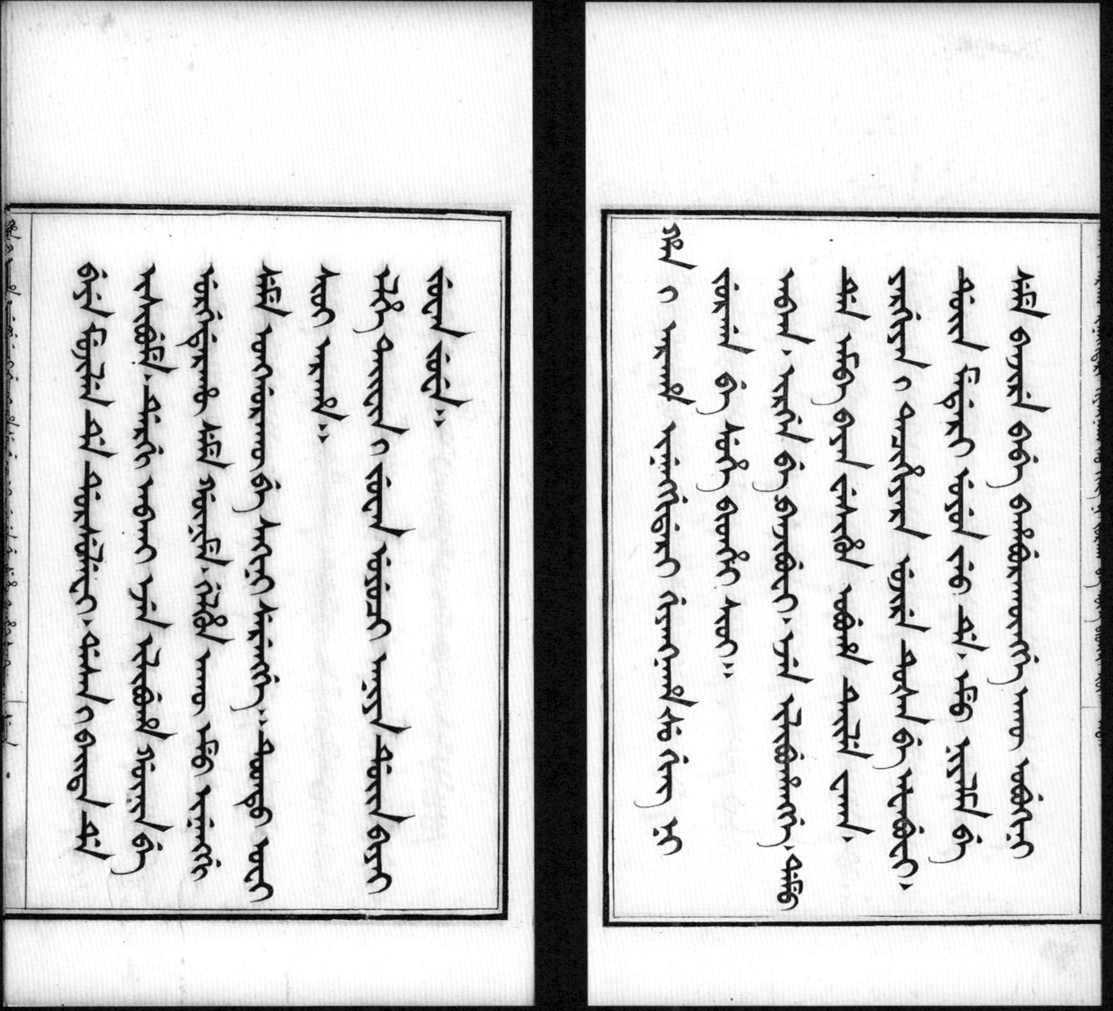

康熙十九年御製序
Preface by the Kangxi emperor in 1680

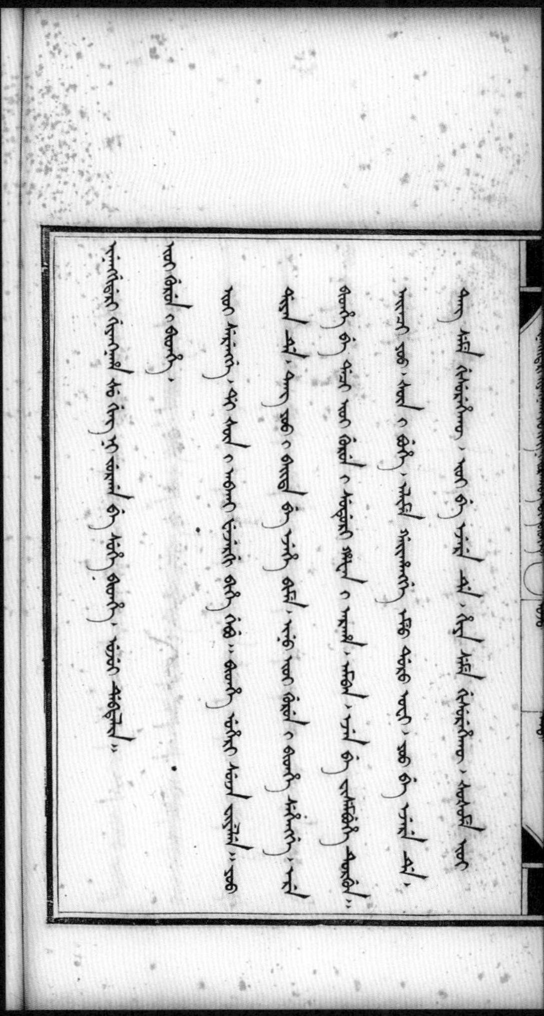

卷端
Beginning

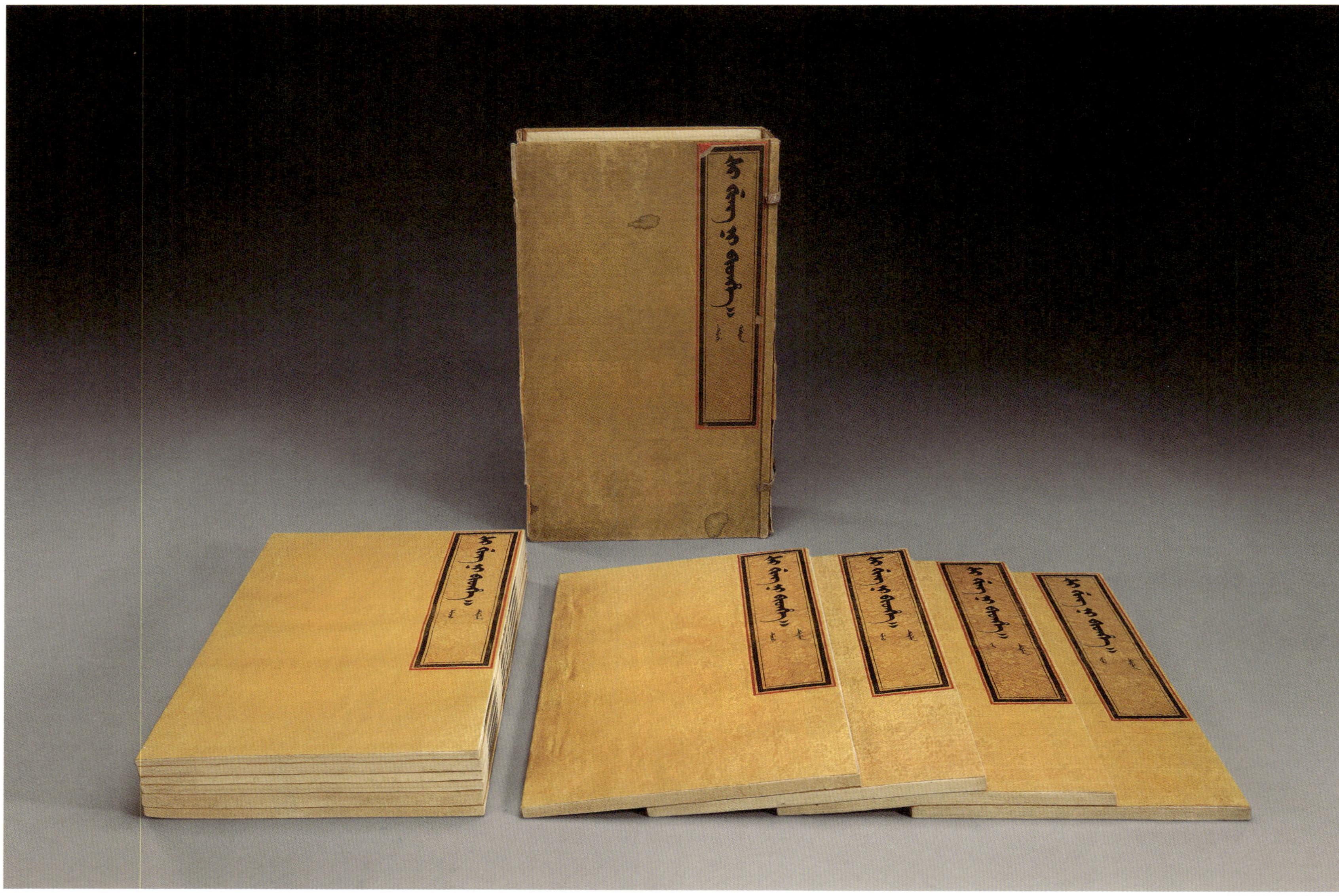

黄色萬字曲水朵菊紋暗花綾書面
Yellow twill-weave silk cover with veiled swastika and chrysanthemum pattern

3

書21730
《詩經二十卷》
宋　朱熹集注　清　佚名譯
清順治十一年（1654）內府刻滿文本
開本　縱36.3厘米　橫21.5厘米
版框　縱23.6厘米　橫17.2厘米
二十册　二函

Inventory number: Shu 21730
Book of Odes
Twenty chapters
Annotated by Zhu Xi
Compiler unknown, Qing dynasty (1644-1911)
Printed in Manchu in 1654 by the Qing court
Format: 36.3 × 21.5 cm
Frame: 23.6 × 17.2 cm
Twenty volumes in two cases

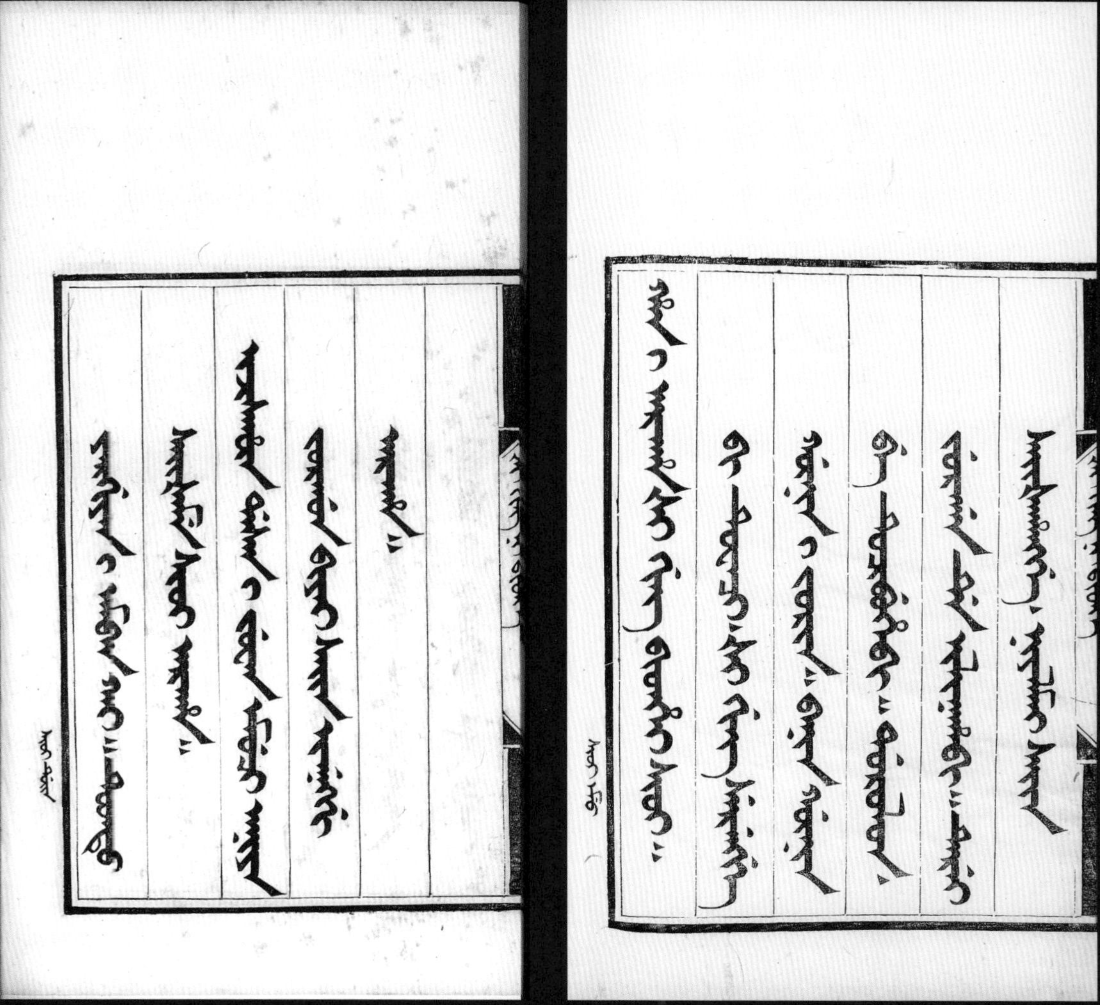

顺治十一年御製序
Preface by the Shunzhi emperor in 1654

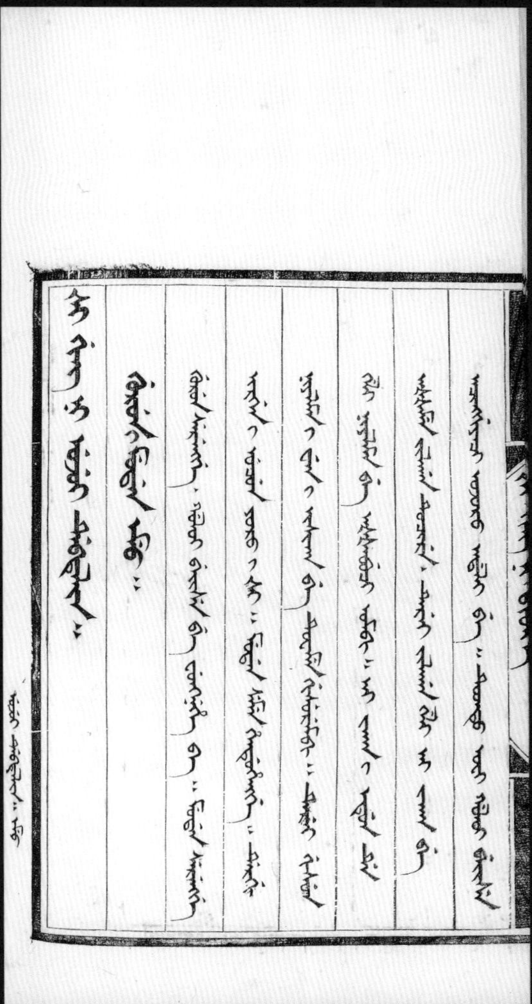

卷端
Beginning

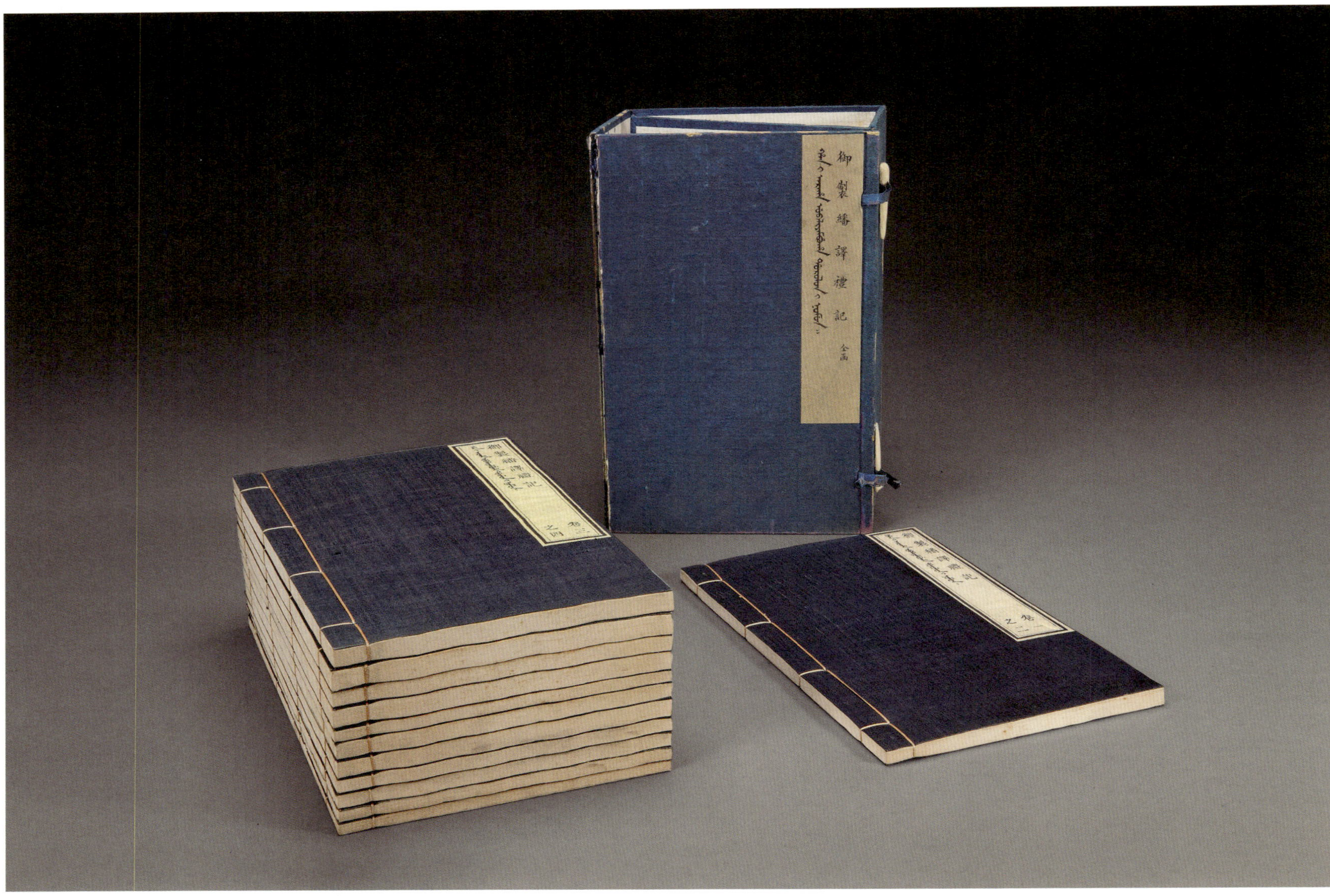

藍色素綢書面
Blue silk cover

書21735
《御製翻譯禮記三十卷》
西漢　戴聖編纂　清　高宗弘曆敕譯
清乾隆四十八年（1783）武英殿刻滿漢合璧本
開本　縱26.8厘米　橫16.9厘米
版框　縱18厘米　橫14厘米
十二冊　一函

4

Inventory number: Shu 21735
Translated Version of the Book of Rites
Thirty chapters
Compiled by Dai Sheng, Western Han dynasty (206 BCE -25 CE)
Translated at the order of the Qianlong emperor (r.1736-1795)
Printed in Manchu and Chinese in 1783 at the Hall of Martial Valour
Format: 26.8 × 16.9 cm
Frame: 18 × 14 cm
Twelve volumes in one case

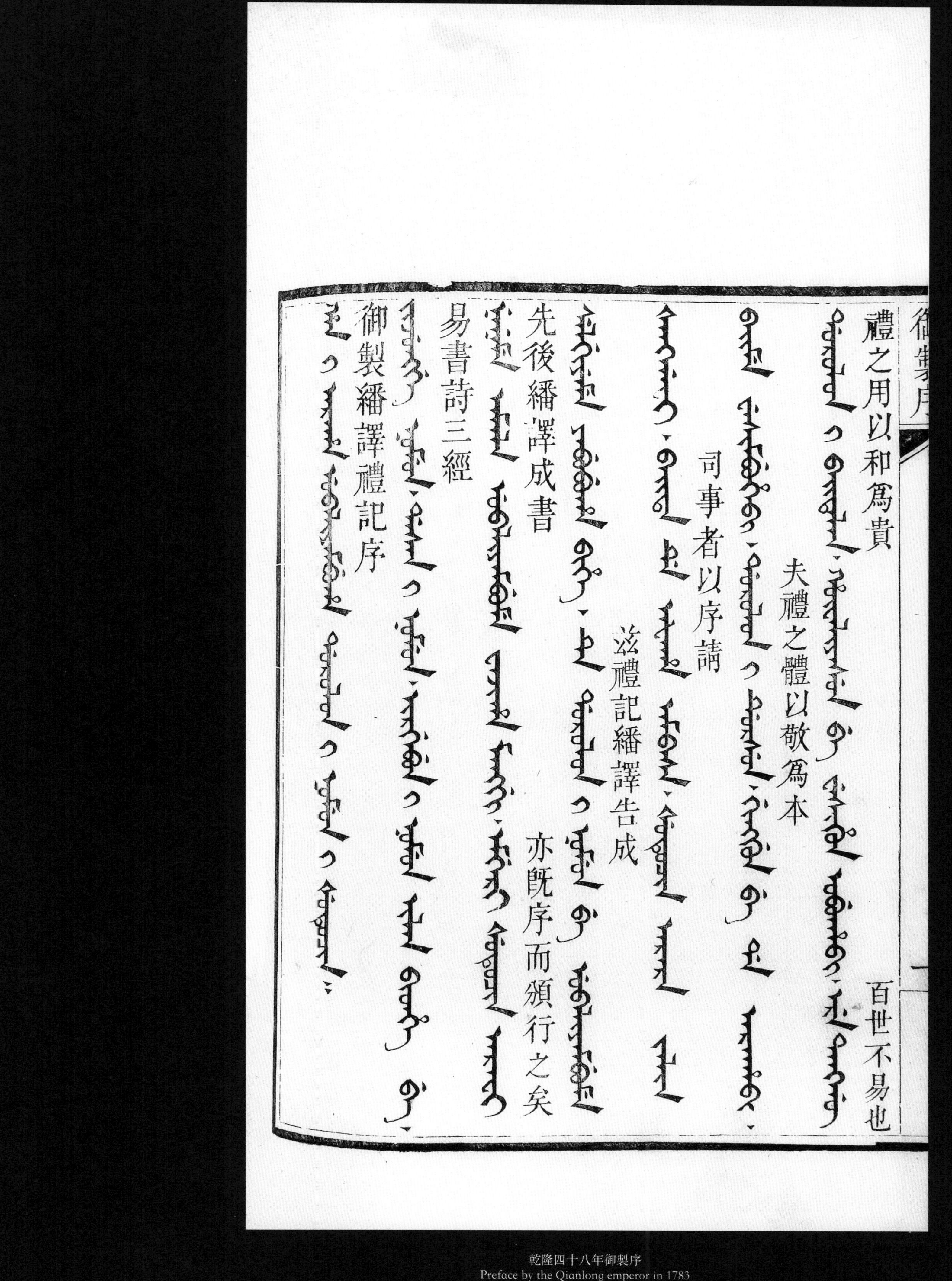

禮之用以和爲貴

百世不易也

夫禮之體以敬爲本

司事者以序請

茲禮記繙譯告成

先後繙譯成書

亦既序而須行之矣

易書詩三經

御製繙譯禮記序

乾隆四十八年御製序

Preface by the Qianlong emperor in 1783

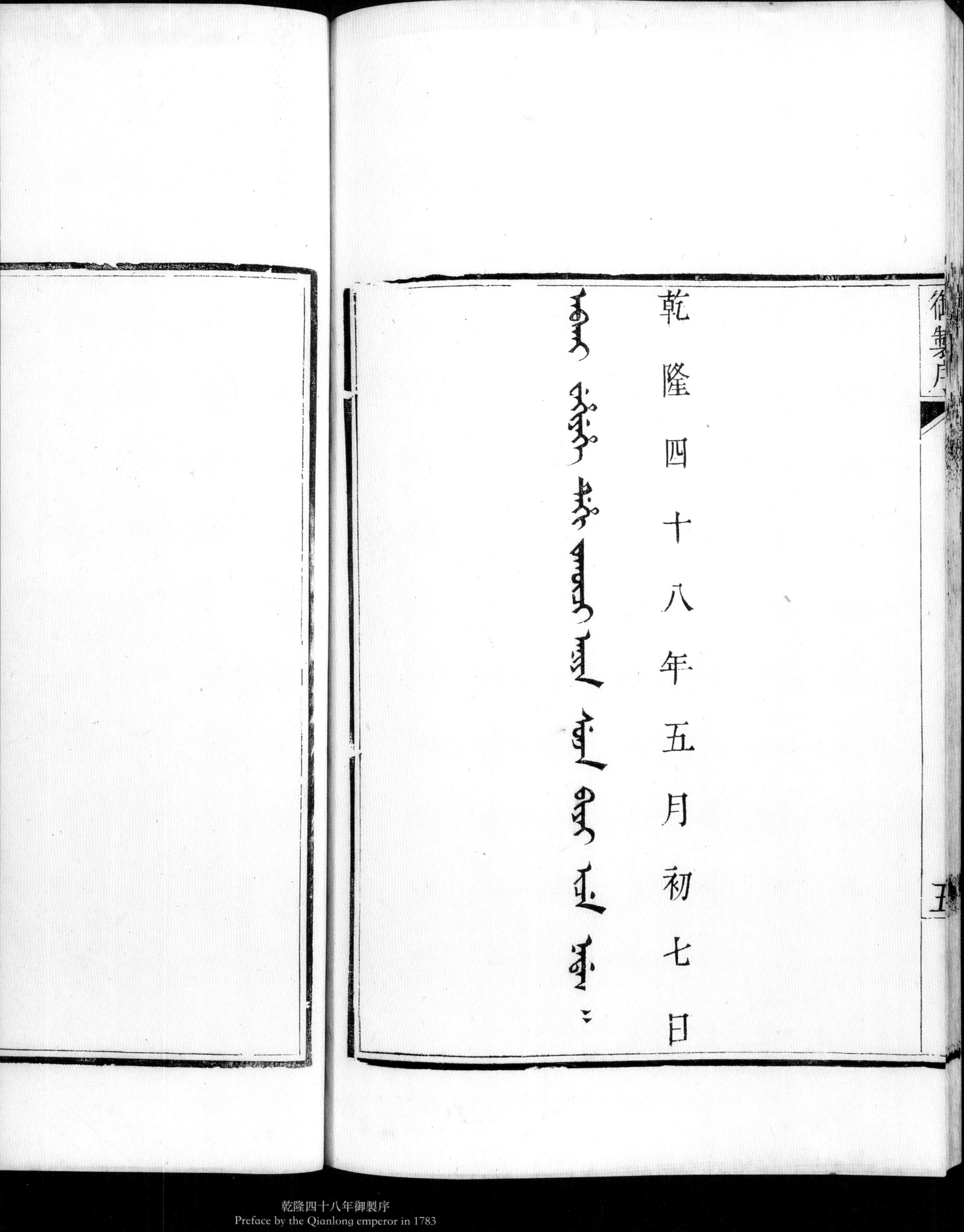

乾隆四十八年五月初七日

乾隆四十八年御製序
Preface by the Qianlong emperor in 1783

因書以爲序

以和爲用者　其亦有所發明歟

聖人循天秩之自然

萬物散殊而禮行焉

則高卑定位而禮立焉

僞貌飾情之具也　原其所起

皆人性所固有　而非

禮者　所以經天地　理人倫

禮記卷之一

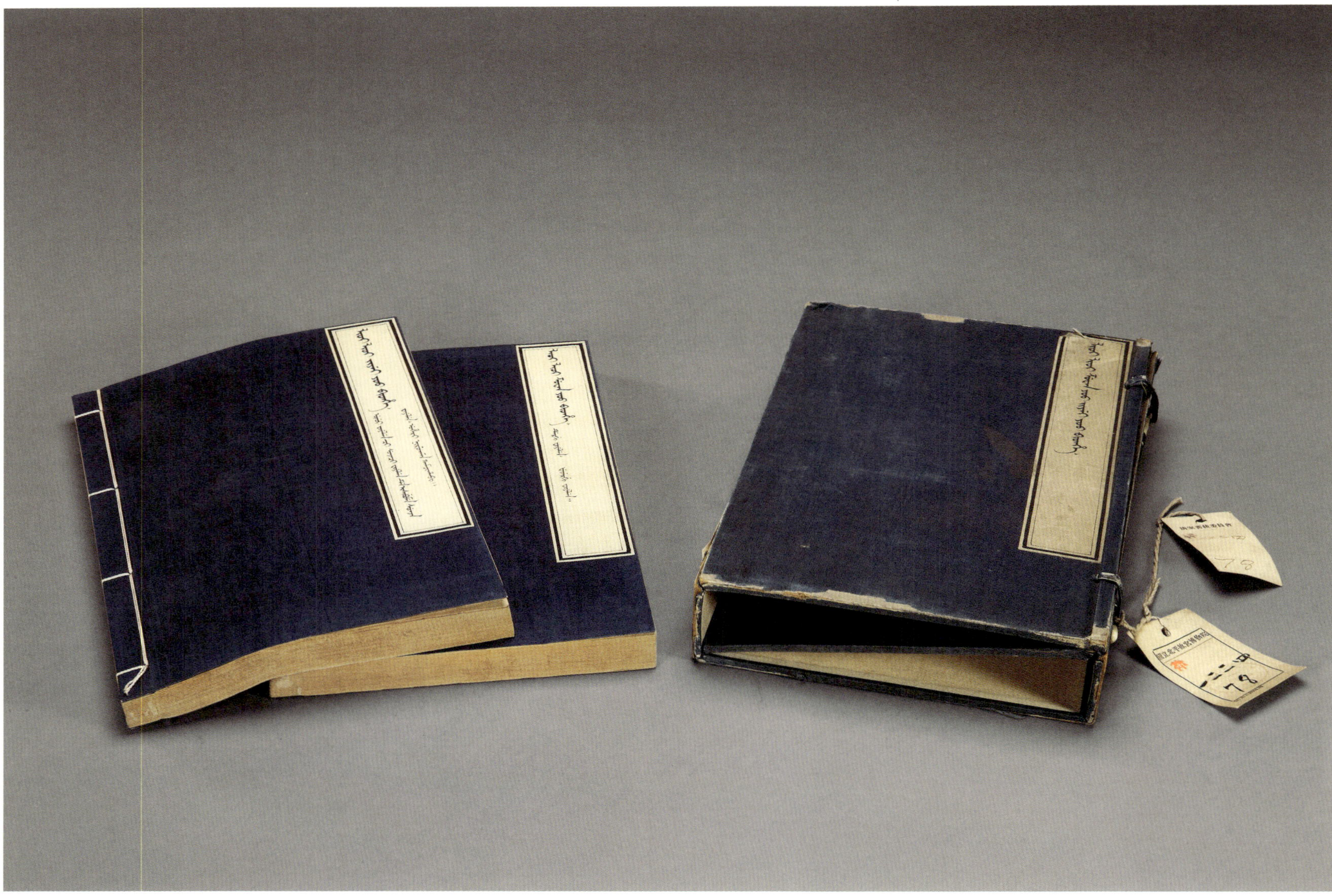

藍色素絹書函
Lake blue silk case

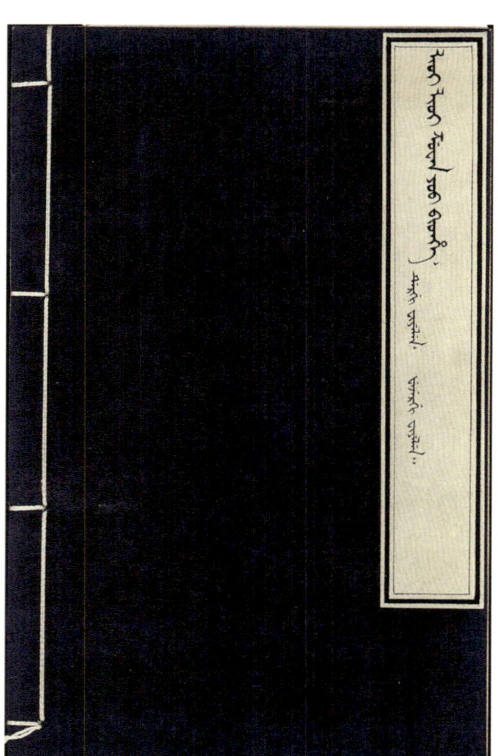

藍色素絹書面
Lake blue silk cover

5

書21782
《律吕纂要二卷》
清 佚名輯
清康熙年内府精寫滿文本
開本 縱26.4厘米 横17厘米
版框 縱20.5厘米 横14.8厘米
二册 一函（與書21783合函）

Inventory number: Shu 21782
Elements of Music
Two chapters
Anonymous, Qing dynasty (1644-1911)
Transcribed in Manchu by the Qing court
Format: 26.4 × 17 cm
Frame: 20.5 × 14.8 cm
Two volumes in one case, sharing the same case with Shu 21783

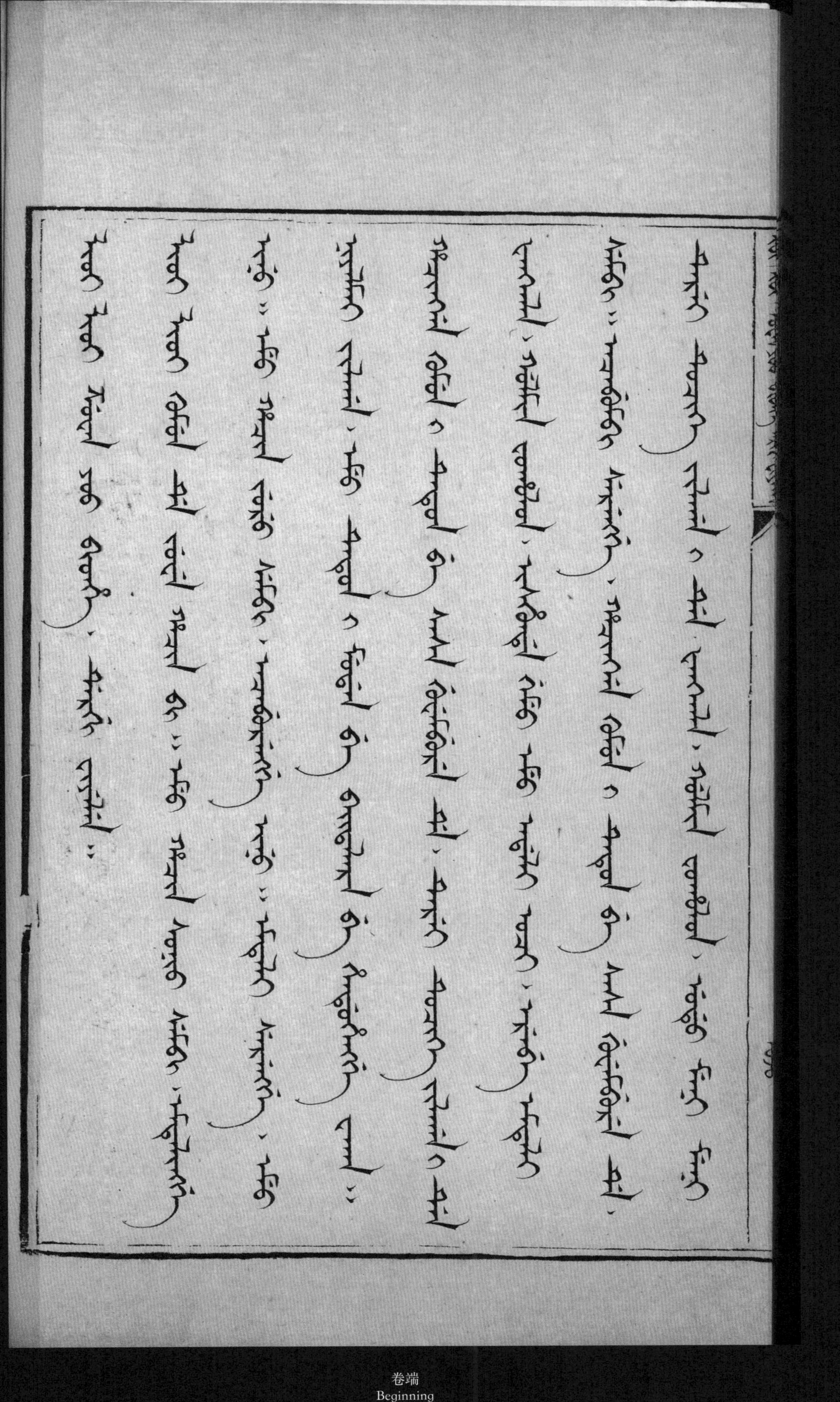

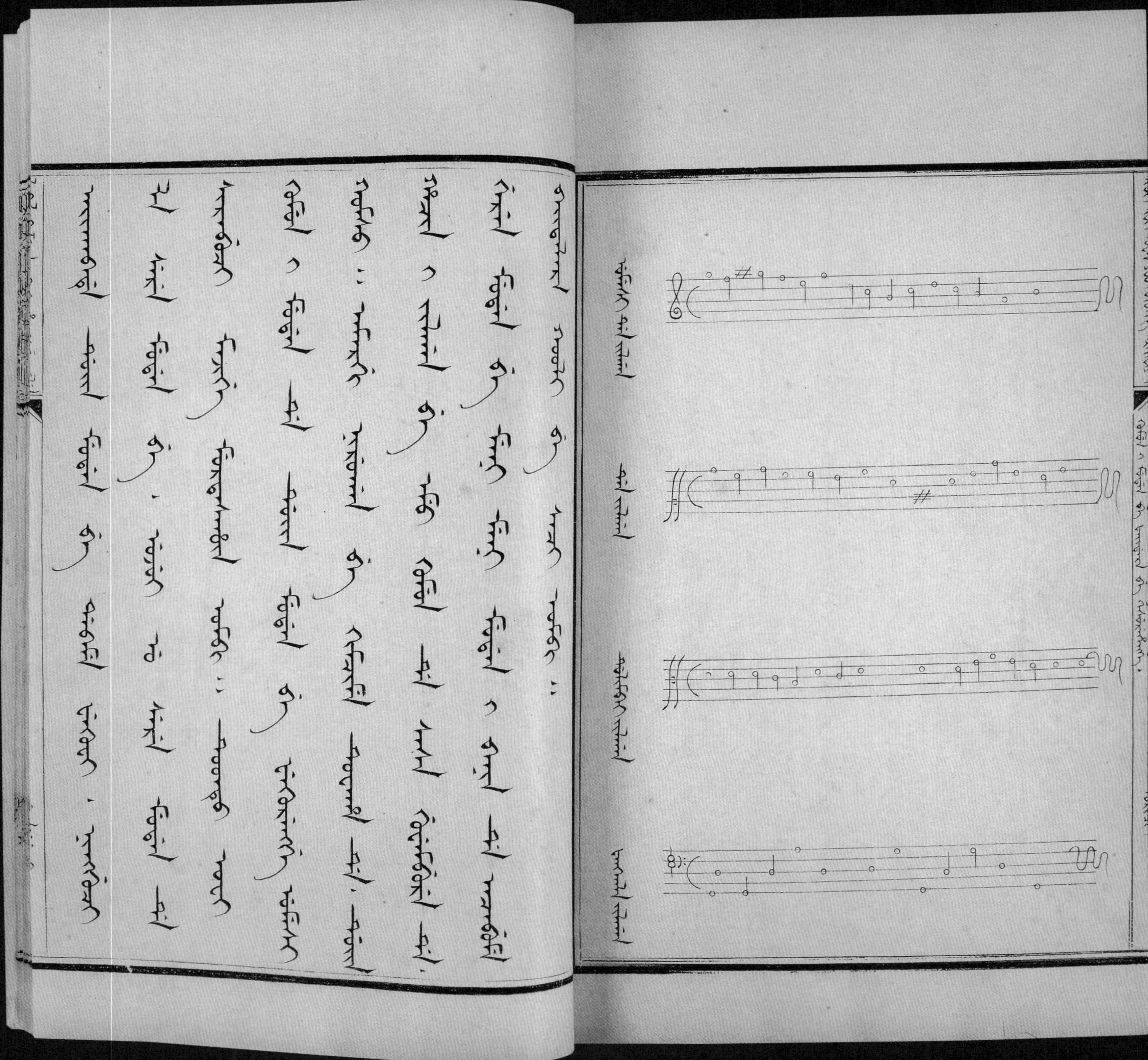

正文 1
Text I

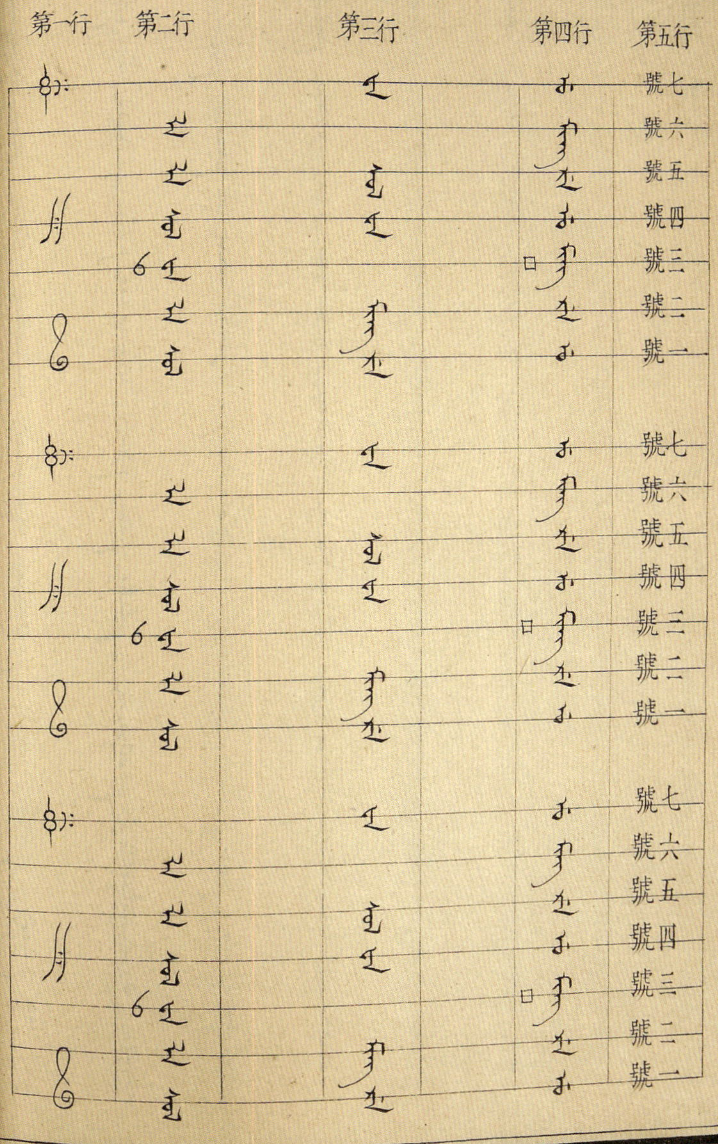
第一行
第二行
第三行
第四行
第五行
號七
號六
號五
號四
號三
號二
號一
6
號七
號六
號五
號四
號三
號二
號一
6
號七
號六
號五
號四
號三
號二
號一
6

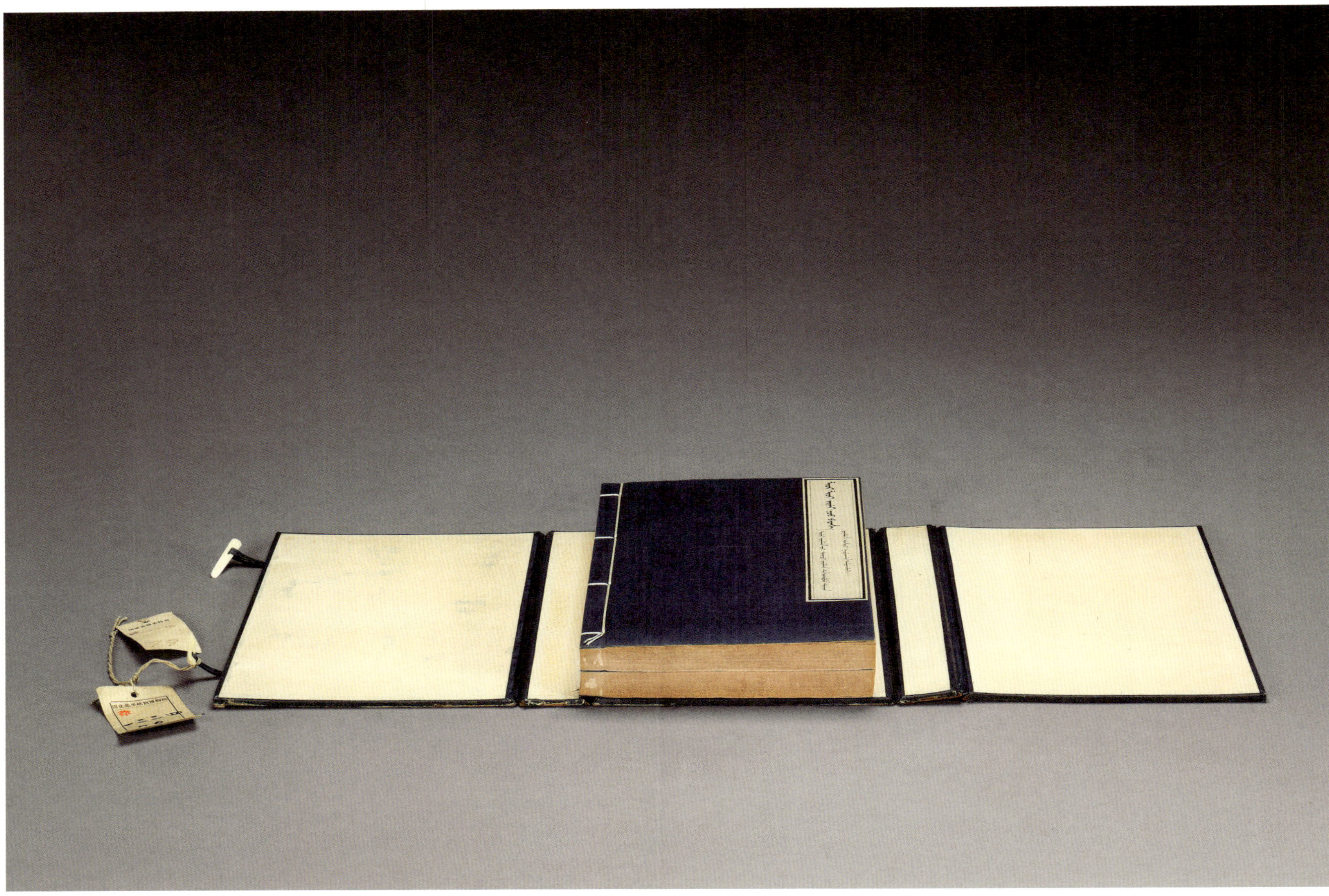

藍色素絹書函
Blue silk case

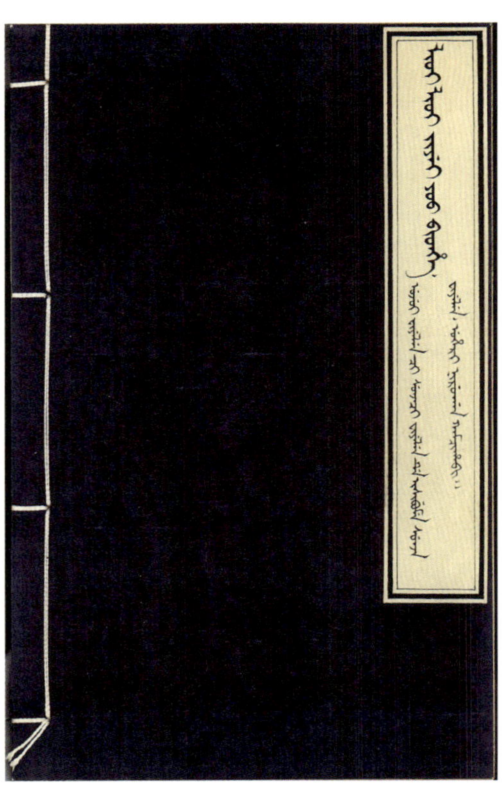

藍色素絹書面
Blue silk cover

書21783
《律吕節要五卷》
清 佚名輯
清康熙年内府精寫滿文本
開本 縱26.4厘米 橫17厘米
版框 縱20.5厘米 橫14.8厘米
一册 一函（與書21782合函）

6

Inventory number: Shu 21783
Essentials of Music
Five chapters
Anonymous, Qing dynasty (1644-1911)
Transcribed in Manchu by the Qing court
Format: 26.4 × 17 cm
Frame: 20.5 × 14.8 cm
One volume in one case, sharing the same case with Shu 21782

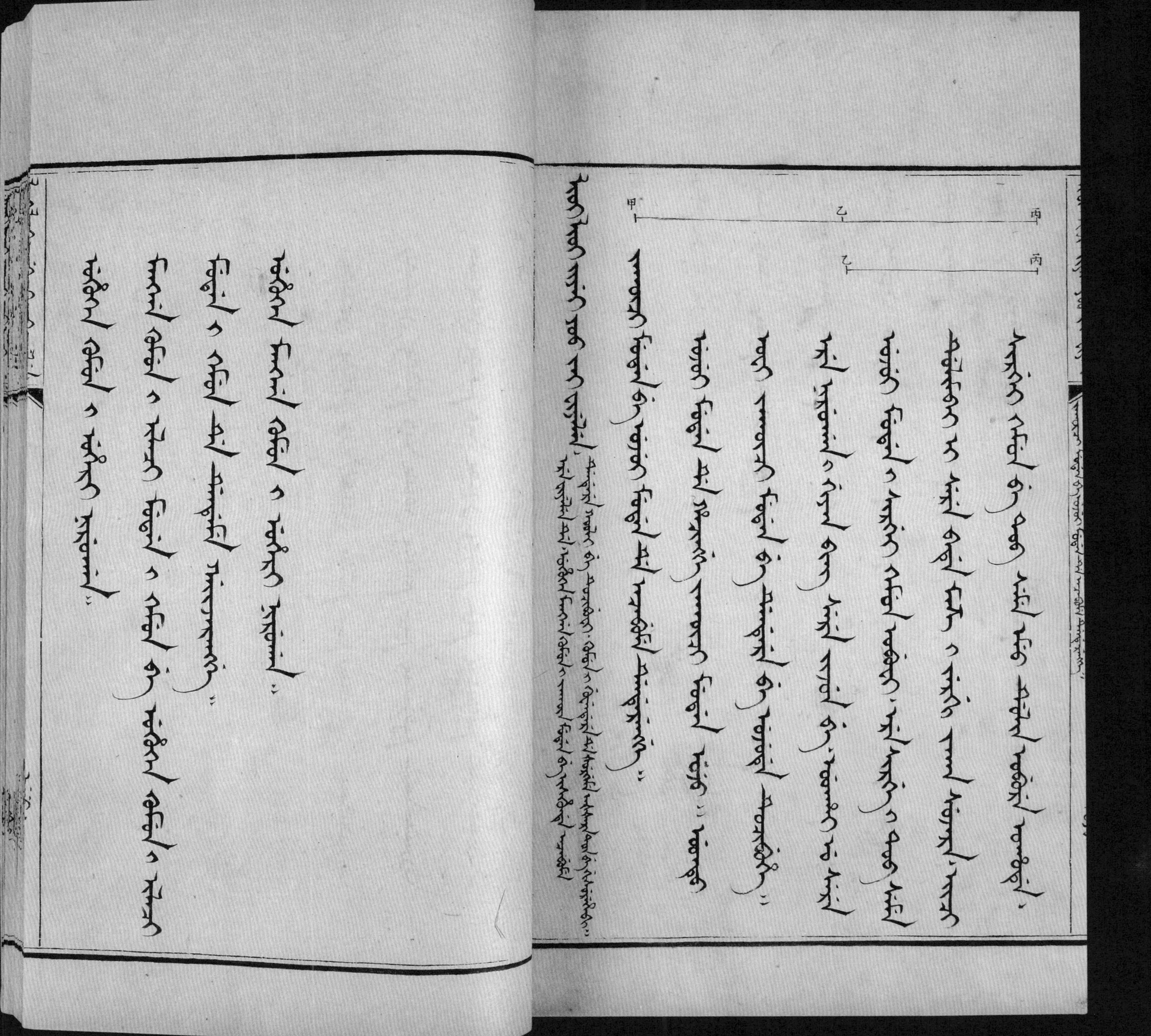

卷端
Beginning

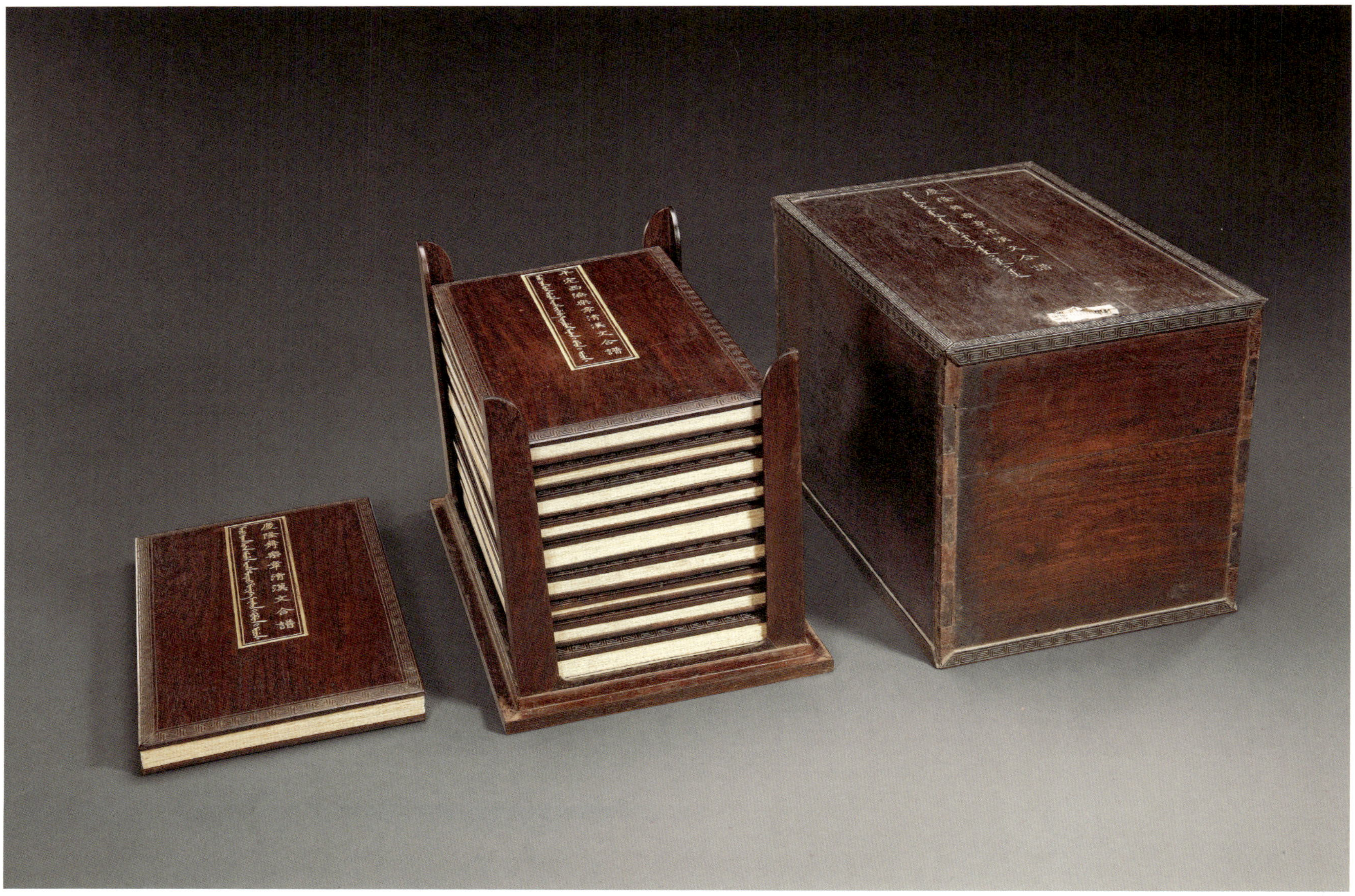

紫檀木書盒
Red sandalwood case

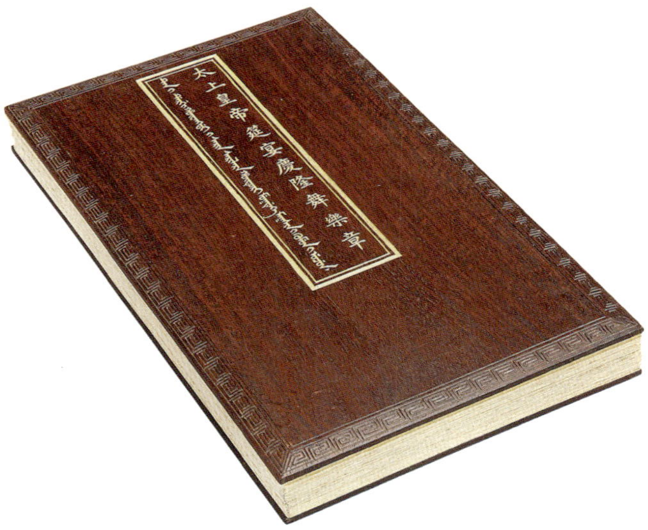

紫檀木書面
Red sandalwood cover

7

書6568
《太上皇帝筵宴慶隆舞樂章一卷》
清　佚名譯
清嘉慶元年（1796）泥金寫滿漢合璧進呈本
開本　縱29.1厘米　橫17.4厘米
版框　縱28.3厘米　橫34.1厘米
一冊　一函（与書6569合函）

Inventory number: Shu 6568
Music of Banquet Dance Presented to the Super-sovereign
Translator unknown, Qing dynasty (1644-1911)
Transcribed with powdered gold in Manchu and Chinese and presented to the Qing court in 1796
Format: 29.1 × 17.4 cm
Frame: 28.3 × 34.1 cm
One volume in one case, sharing the same case with Shu 6569

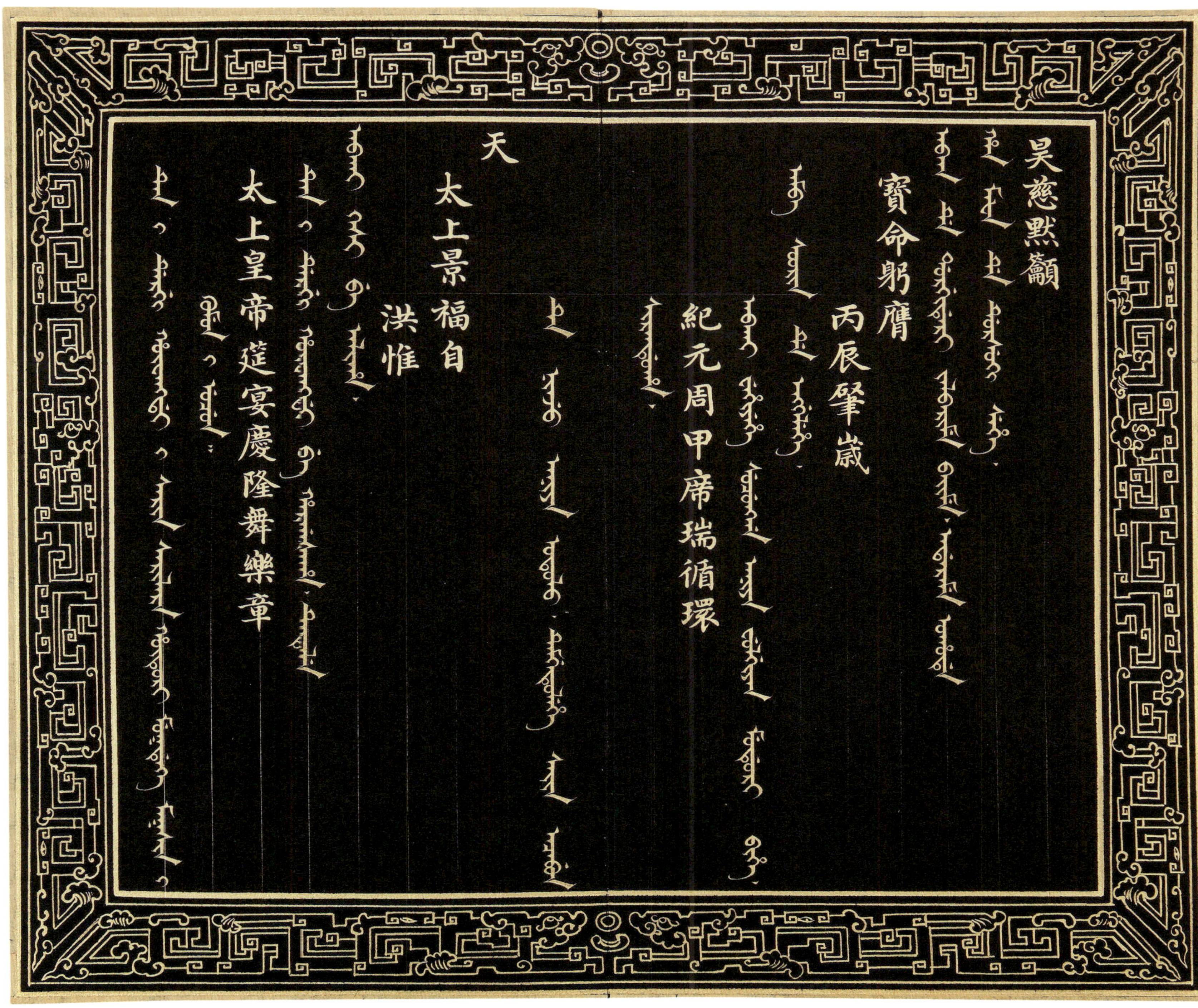

卷端
Beginning

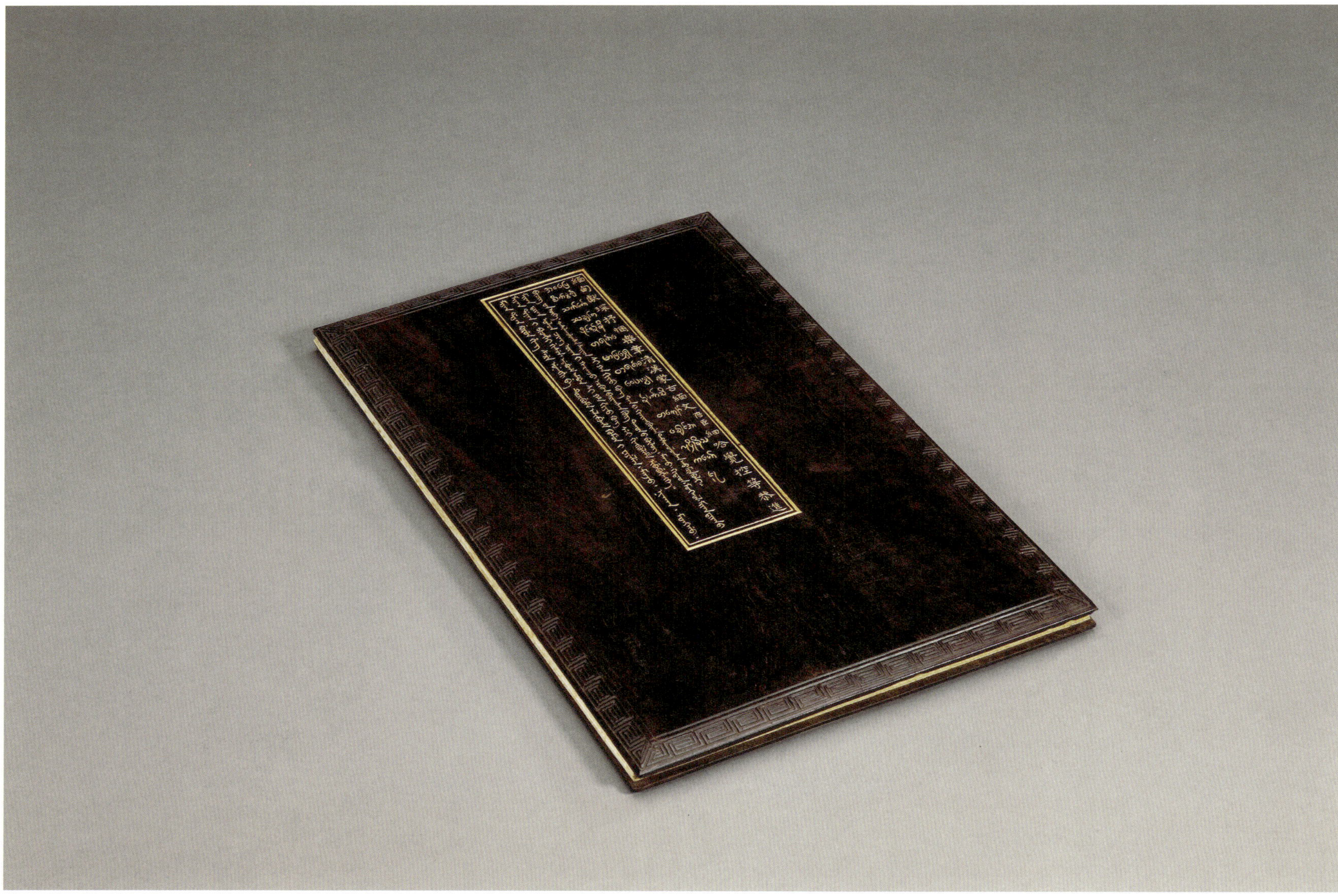

紫檀木書面
Red sandalwood cover

書6569
《緬甸獻琛抒悃樂章一卷》
緬甸　細哈覺控等進　清　佚名譯
清嘉慶元年（1796）泥金寫滿蒙緬漢合璧進呈本
開本　縱29.1厘米　橫17.4厘米
版框　縱28.3厘米　橫34.1厘米
一册　一函（与書6568合函）

8

Inventory number: Shu 6569
Music Respectfully Presented by Envoys of Burma
Translator unknown, Qing dynasty (1644-1911)
Transcribed with powdered gold in Mongolian, Manchu, Burmese and Chinese and presented to the Qing court in 1796
Format: 29.1 × 17.4 cm
Frame: 28.3 × 34.1 cm
One volume in one case, sharing the same case with Shu 6568

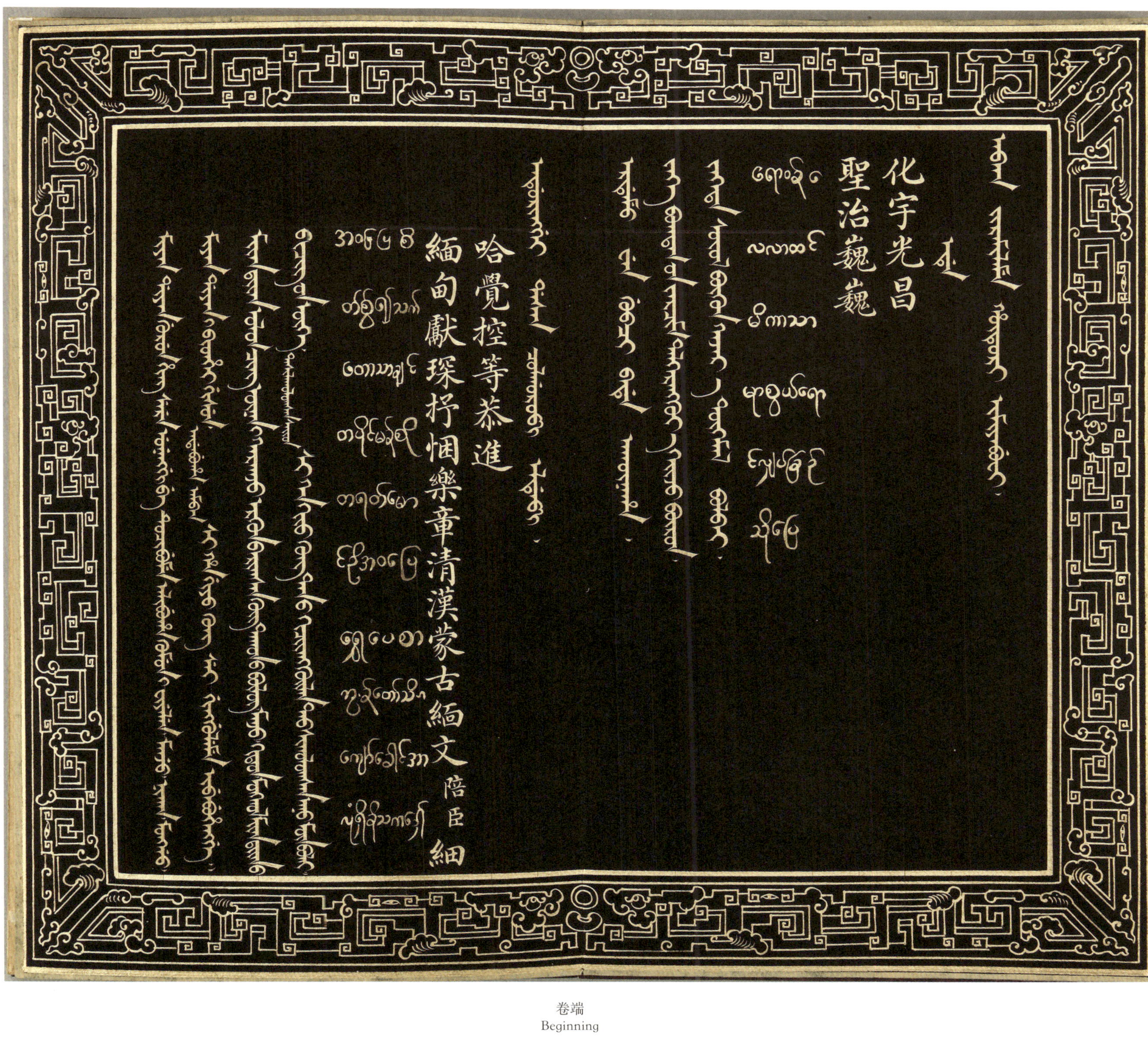

化宇光昌
聖治巍巍

緬甸獻琛抒悃樂章清漢蒙古緬文陪臣細
哈覺控等恭進

卷端
Beginning

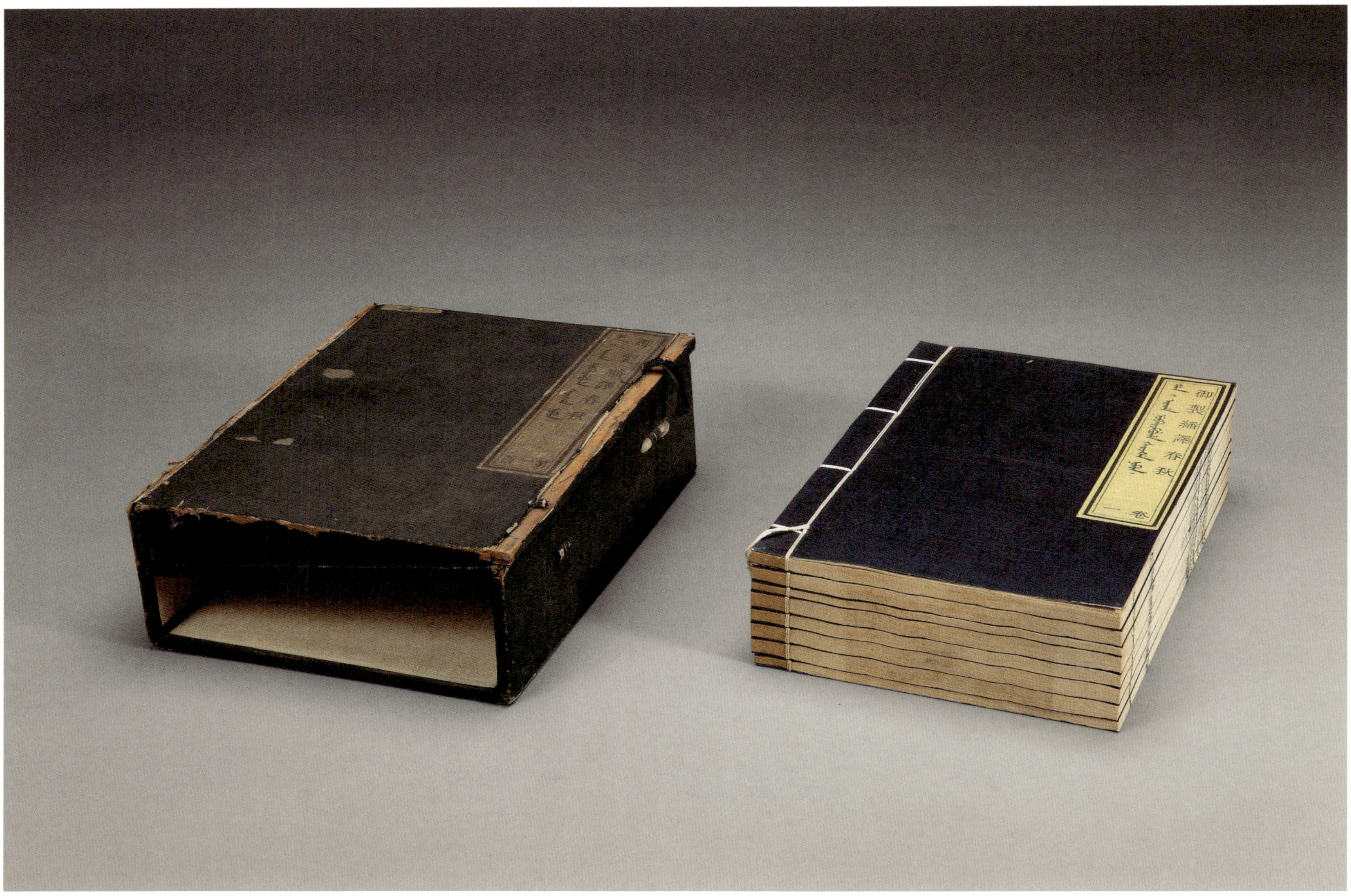

藍色素綢書函
Blue silk case

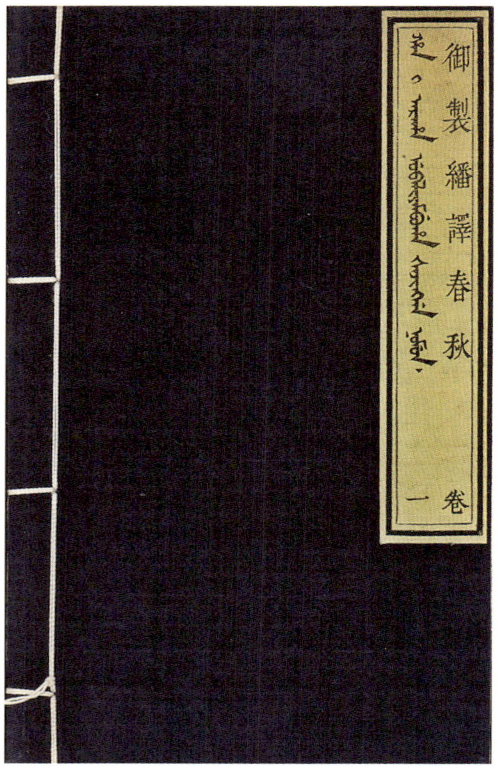

藍色素綢書面
Blue silk cover

9

書21739
《御製翻譯春秋六十四卷綱領一卷》
春秋　孔子撰　清　高宗弘曆敕譯
清乾隆四十九年（1784）武英殿刻滿漢合璧本
開本　縱26.5厘米　橫16.9厘米
版框　縱17.6厘米　橫14厘米
四十八册　六函

Inventory number: Shu 21739
Translated Version of the Spring and Autumn Annals
Sixty-four chapters as text, one chapter as guiding principle
Written by Confucius
Translated at the order of the Qianlong emperor (r.1736-1795)
Printed in Manchu and Chinese in 1784 at the Hall of Martial Valour
Format: 26.5 × 16.9 cm
Frame: 17.6 × 14 cm
Forty-eight volumes in six cases

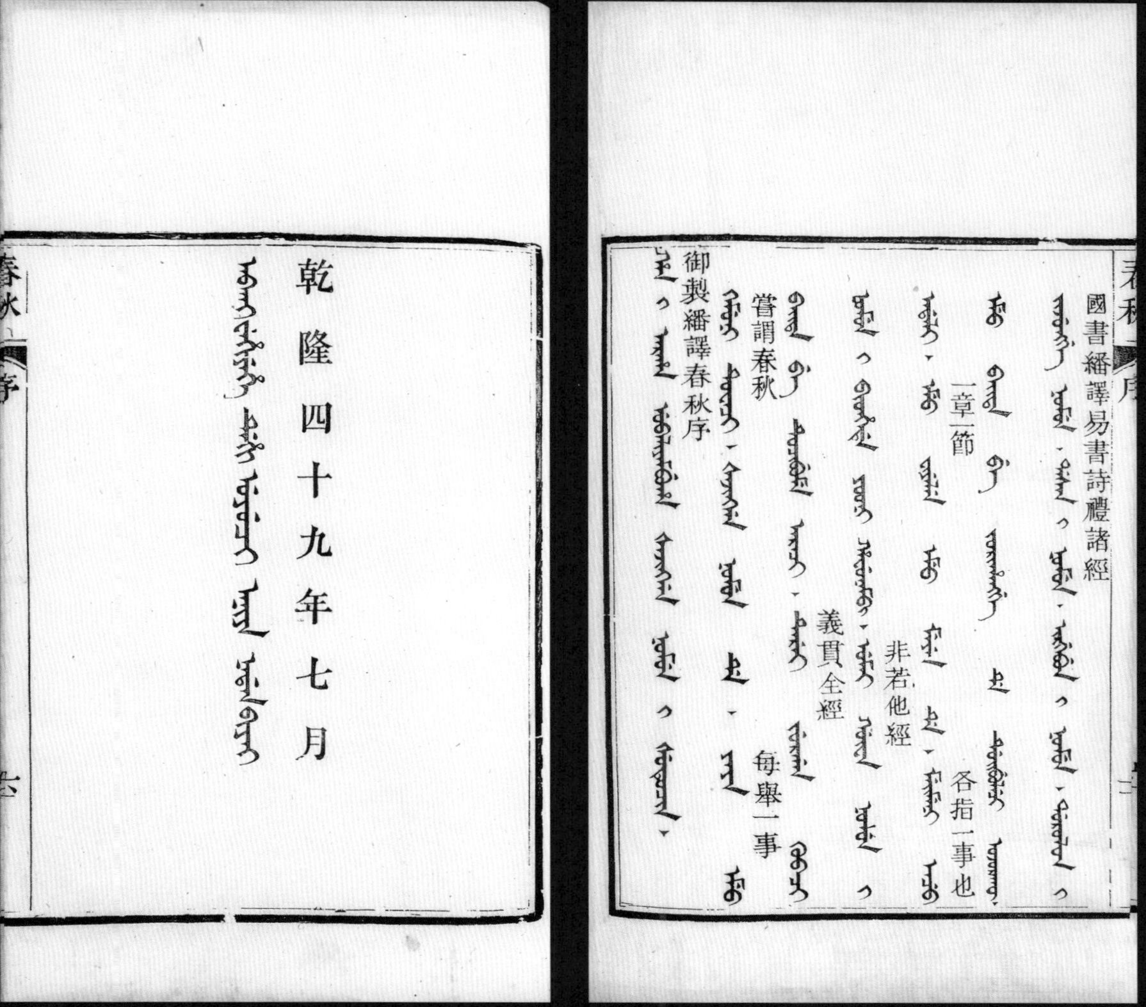

乾隆四十九年御製序
Preface by the Qianlong emperor in 1784

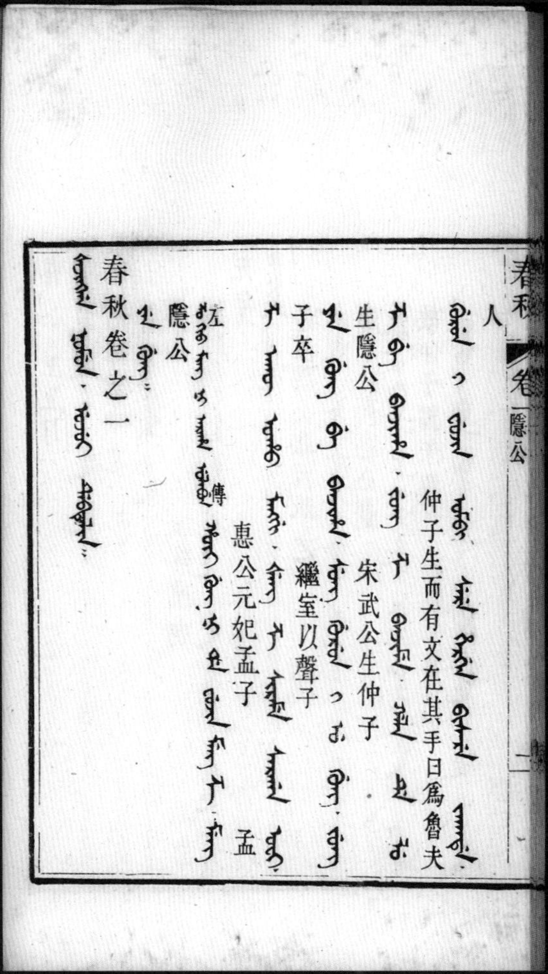

卷端
Beginning

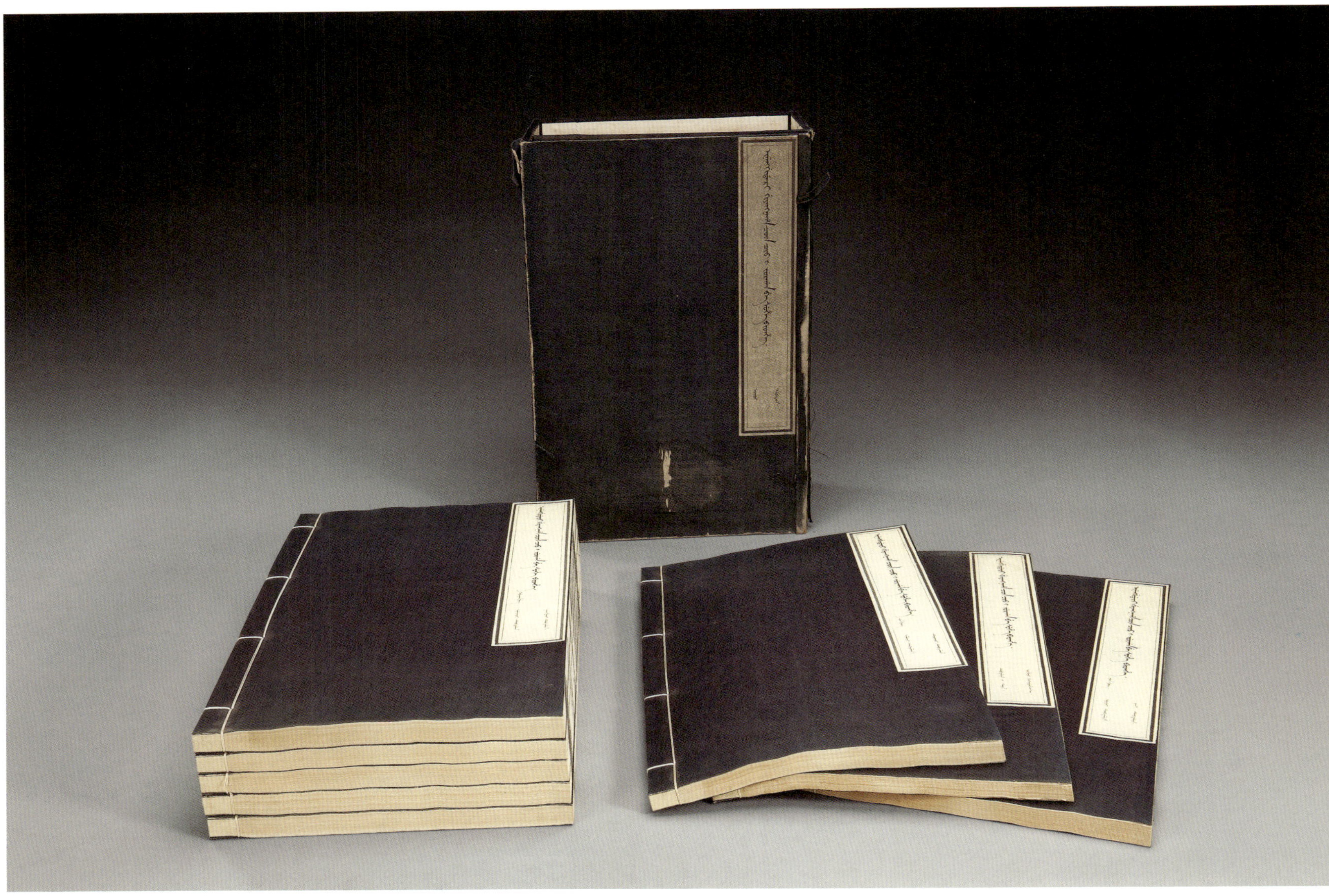

藍色素絹書面
Blue silk covers

書21746
《日講春秋解義六十四卷總說一卷》
清　庫勒納等奉敕撰
清乾隆二年（1737）武英殿刻滿文本
開本　縱34厘米　橫21.7厘米
版框　縱26厘米　橫18.5厘米
三十二册　四函

10

Inventory number: Shu 21746
Everyday Textbook: Interpretation of the Spring and Autumn Annals
Sixty-four chapters as text, one chapter as introduction
Compiled by imperial order by Kulena et al., Qing dynasty (1644-1911)
Printed in Manchu in 1737 by the Qing court
Format: 34 × 21.7 cm
Frame: 26 × 18.5 cm
Thirty-two volumes in four cases

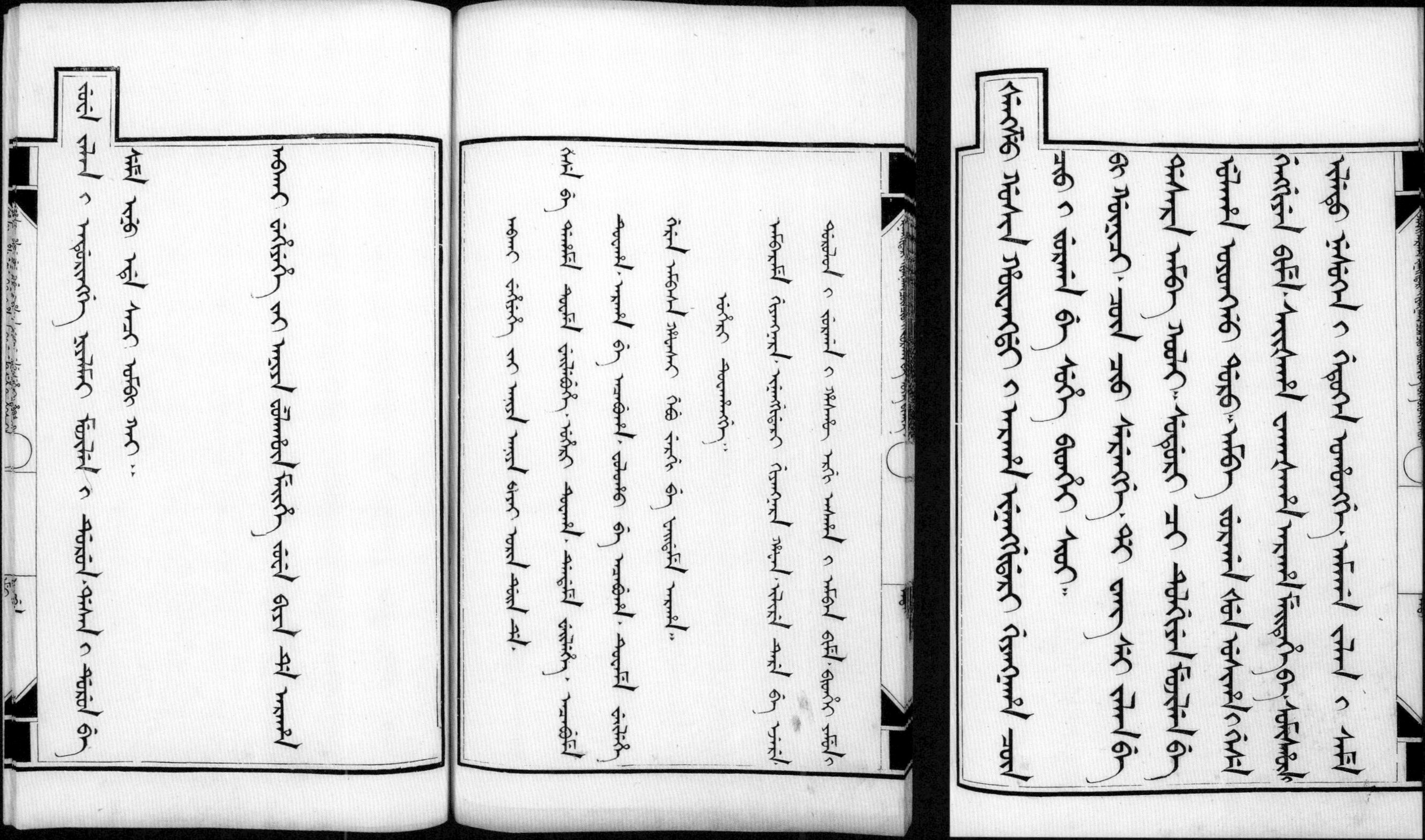

乾隆二年御製序
Preface by the Qianlong emperor in 1737

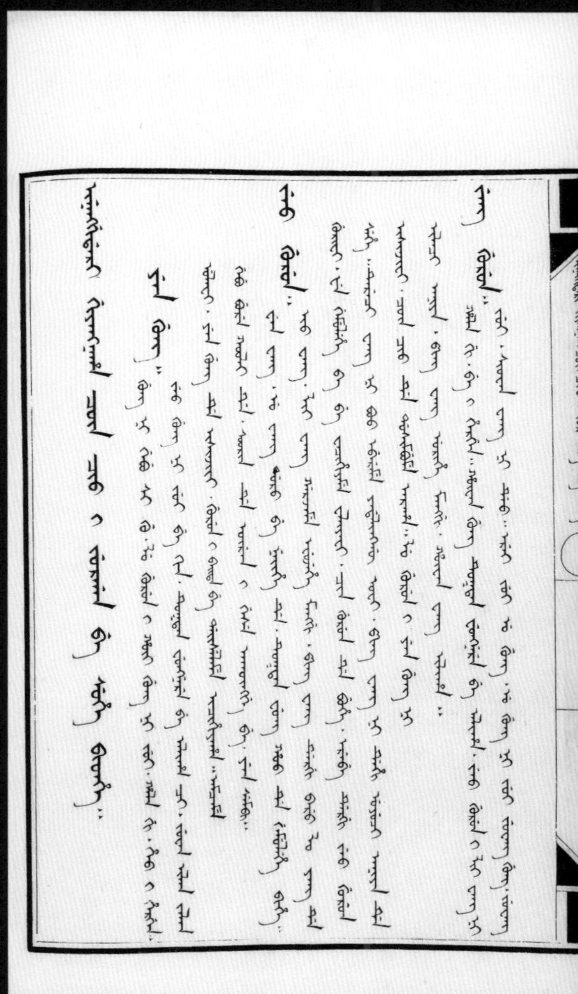

卷端
Beginning

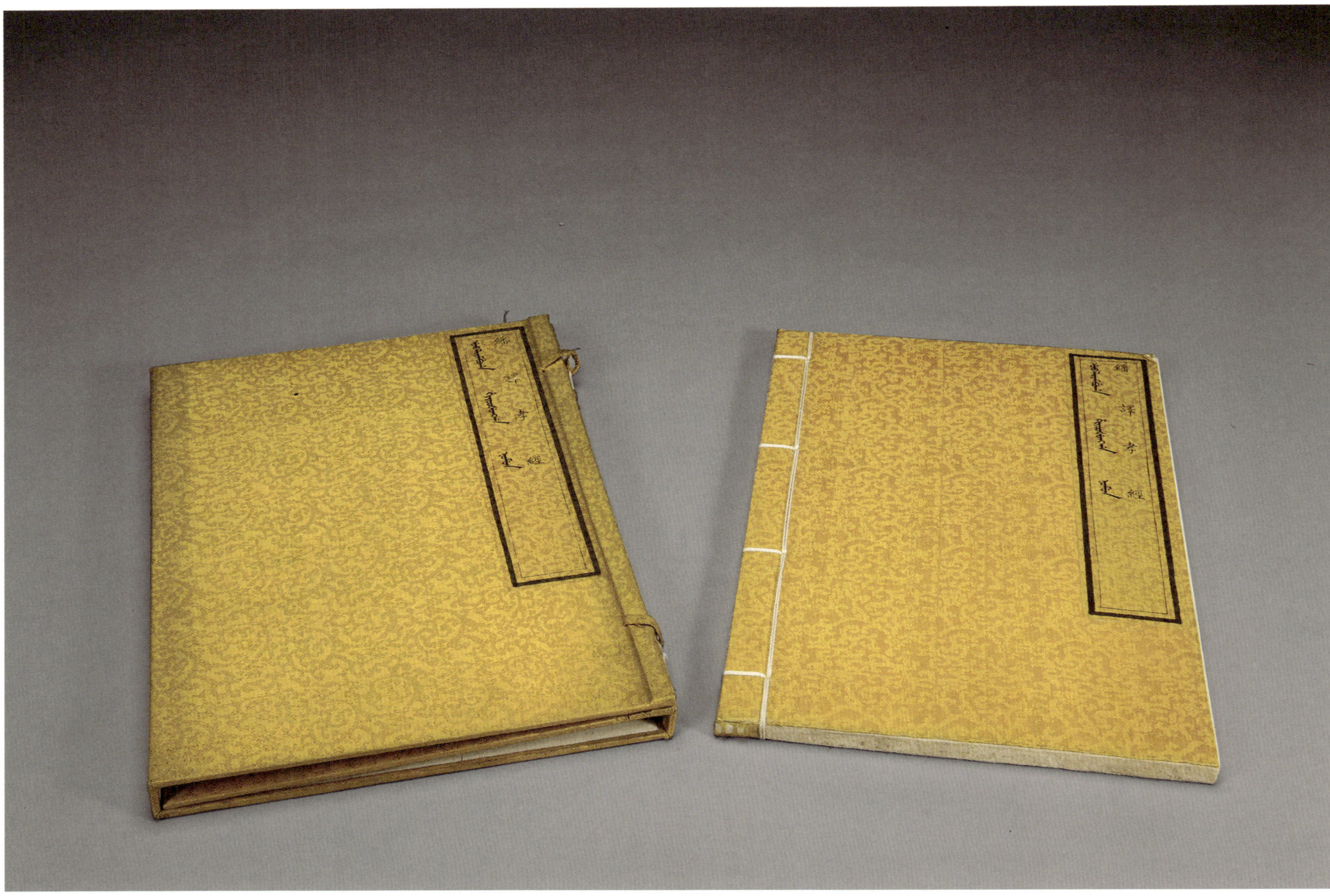

明黃色纏枝花紋暗花綾書函
Bright yellow twill-weave silk case with veiled pattern of floral scrolls

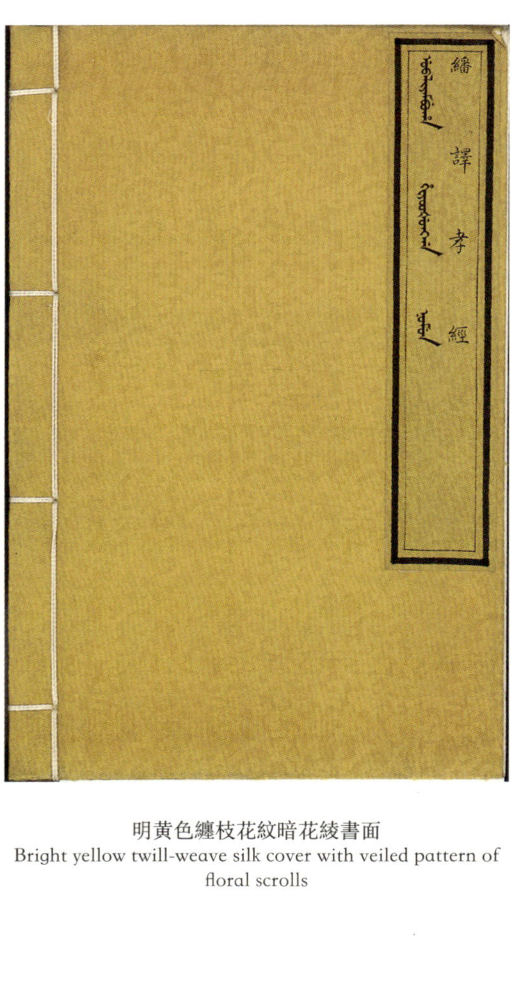

明黃色纏枝花紋暗花綾書面
Bright yellow twill-weave silk cover with veiled pattern of floral scrolls

11

書21571
《翻譯孝經一卷》
清　世宗胤禛敕譯　文宗奕詝校
清咸豐六年（1856）武英殿刻滿漢合璧本
開本　縱32.6厘米　橫21.6厘米
版框　縱21.2厘米　橫18.3厘米
一冊　一函

Inventory number: Shu 21571
Translated Version of the Classic of Filial Piety
One chapter
Translated by the Yongzheng emperor (r.1723-1735)
Proofread by the Xianfeng emperor (r.1851-1861)
Printed in Manchu and Chinese in 1856 at the Hall of Martial Valour
Format: 32.6 × 21.6 cm
Frame: 21.2 × 18.3 cm
One volume in one case

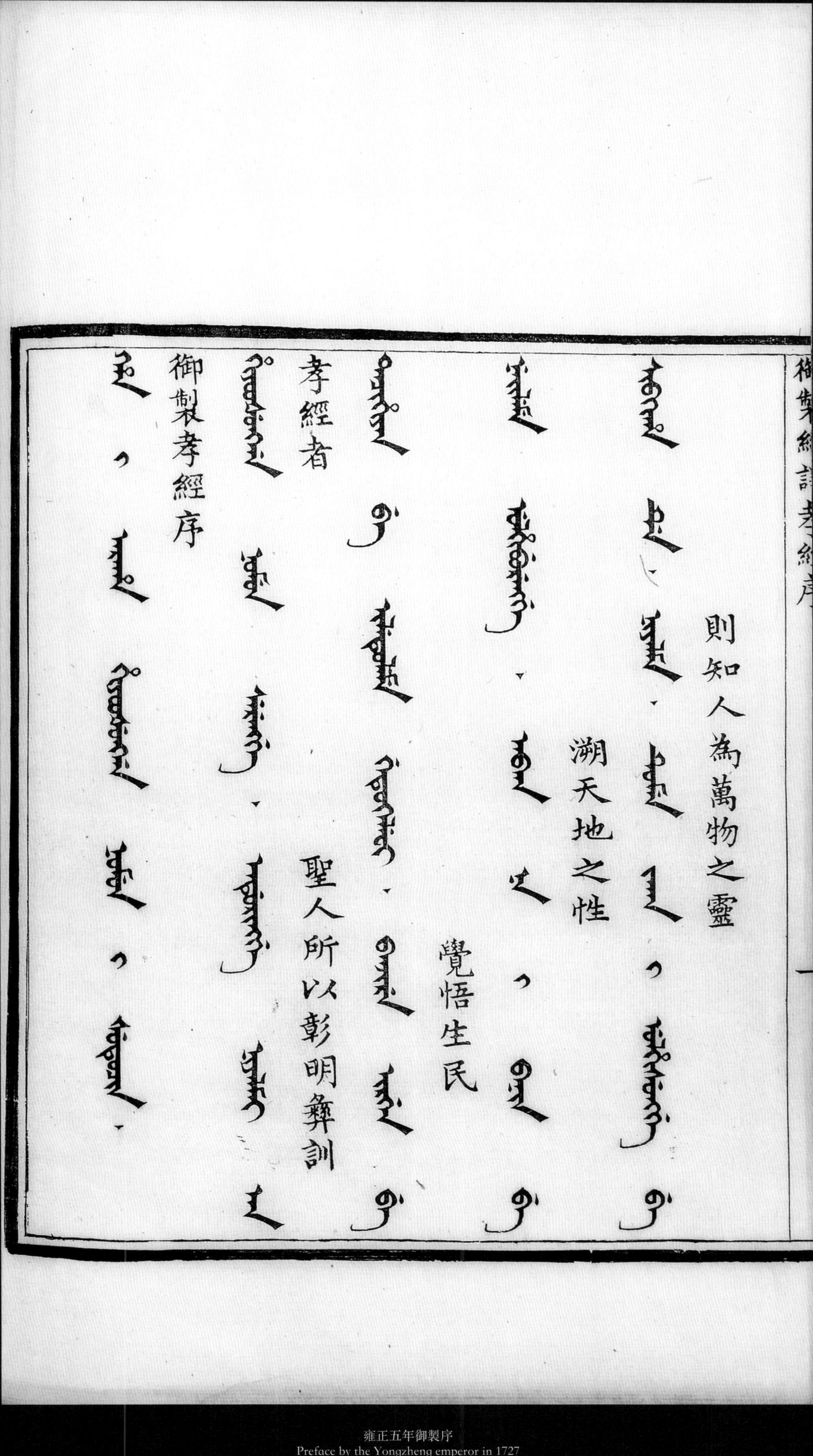

御製孝經序

孝經者聖人所以彰明彝訓覺悟生民溯天地之性則知人為萬物之靈

雍正五年御製序
Preface by the Yongzheng emperor in 1727

雍正五年十二月初三日

咸豐六年七月二十三日奉

上諭

繙譯孝經

係雍正年間編輯

為八旗各項考試命題之本

孝經

開宗明義章第一

仲尼居　曾子侍

子曰　先王有至德要道

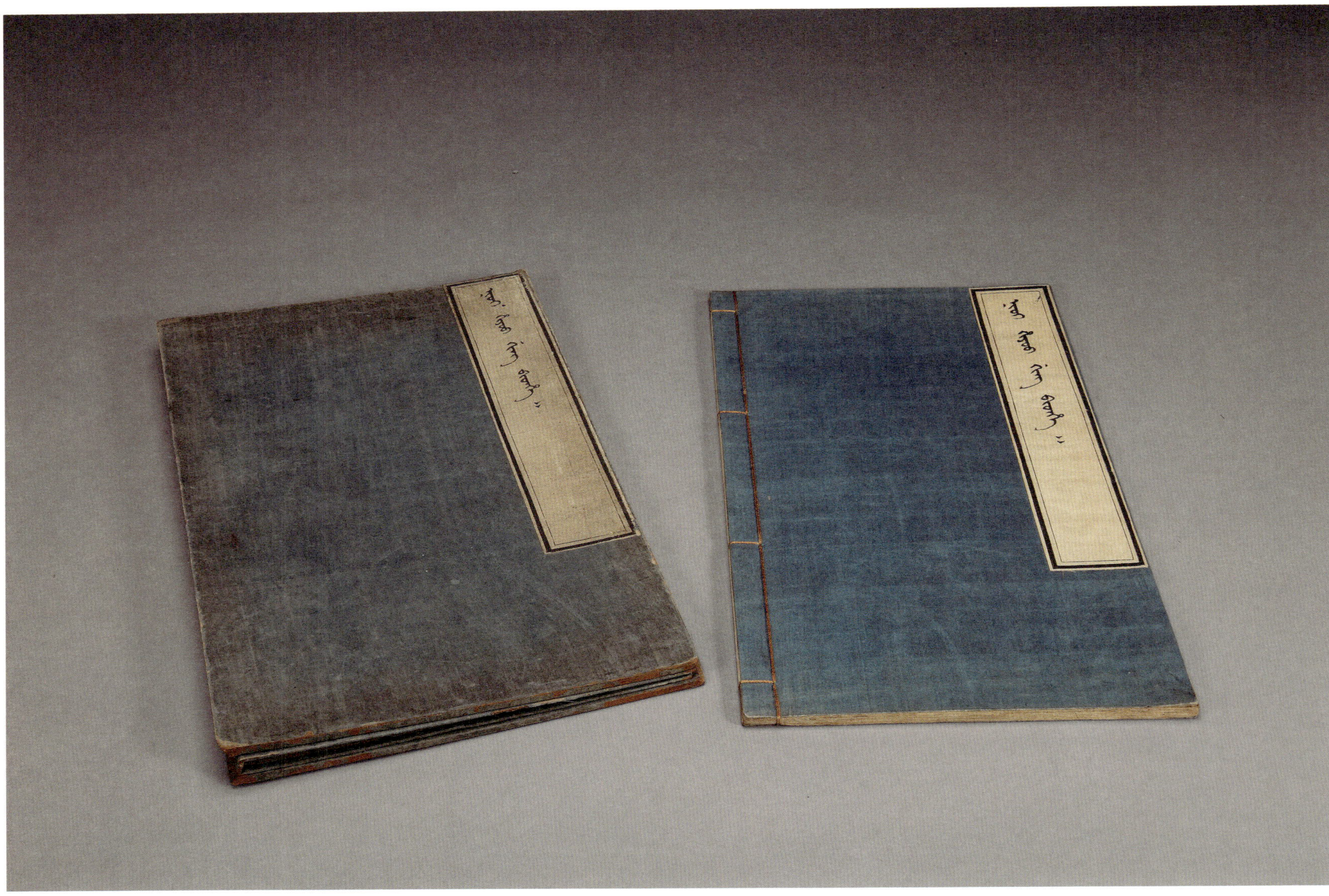

湖色素絹書函
Lake blue silk case

書21759
《女孝經一卷》
唐　陳邈妻鄭氏撰
清内府精寫滿文本
開本　縱33.4厘米　橫19.5厘米
版框　縱24.2厘米　橫16.7厘米
一册　一函

12

Inventory number: Shu 21759
Classic of Female Filial Piety
One chapter
Written by Madame Zheng, wife of Chen Miao, Tang dynasty (618-907)
Transcribed in Manchu by the Qing court
Format: 33.4 × 19.5 cm
Frame: 24.2 × 16.7 cm
One volume in one case

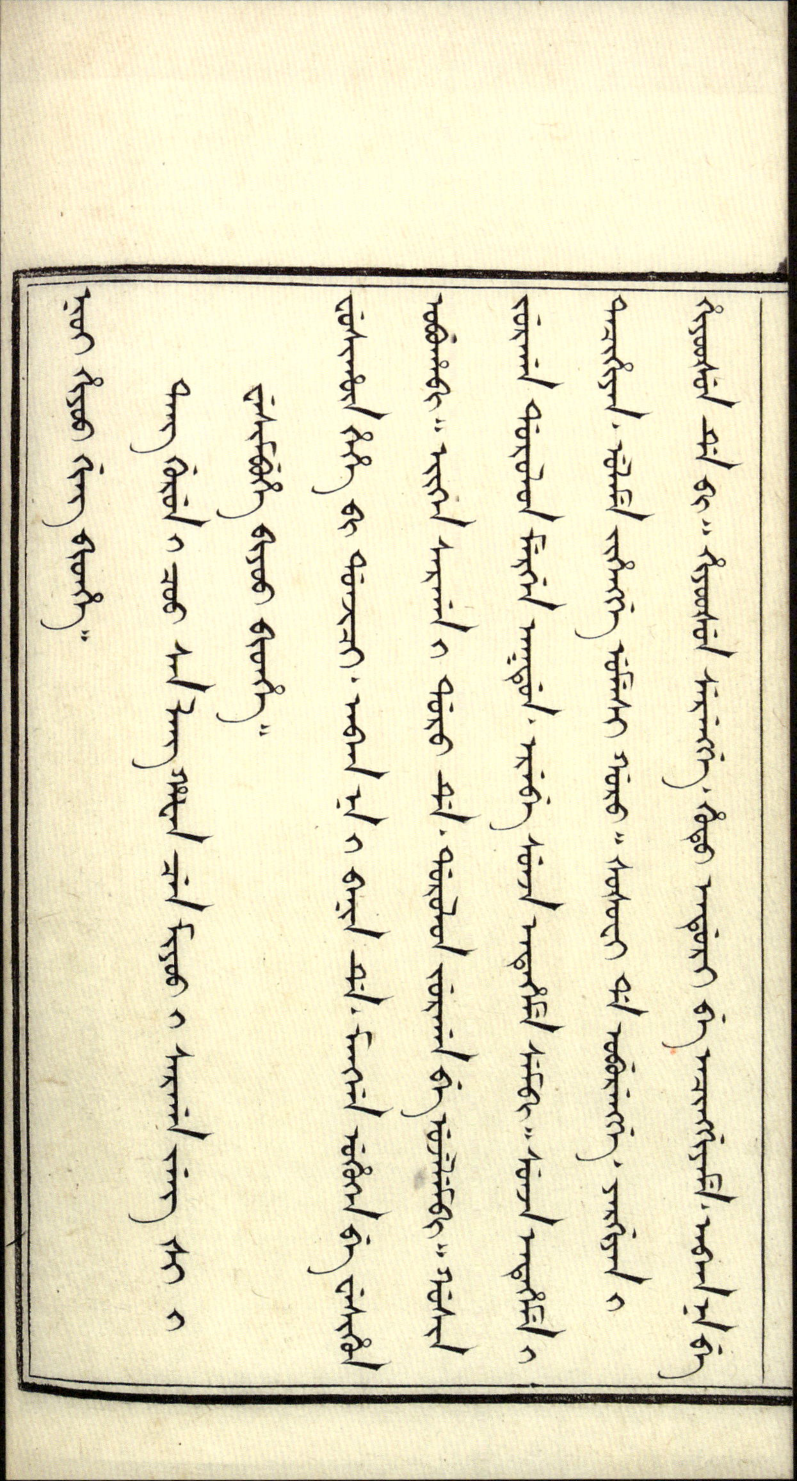

卷端
Beginning

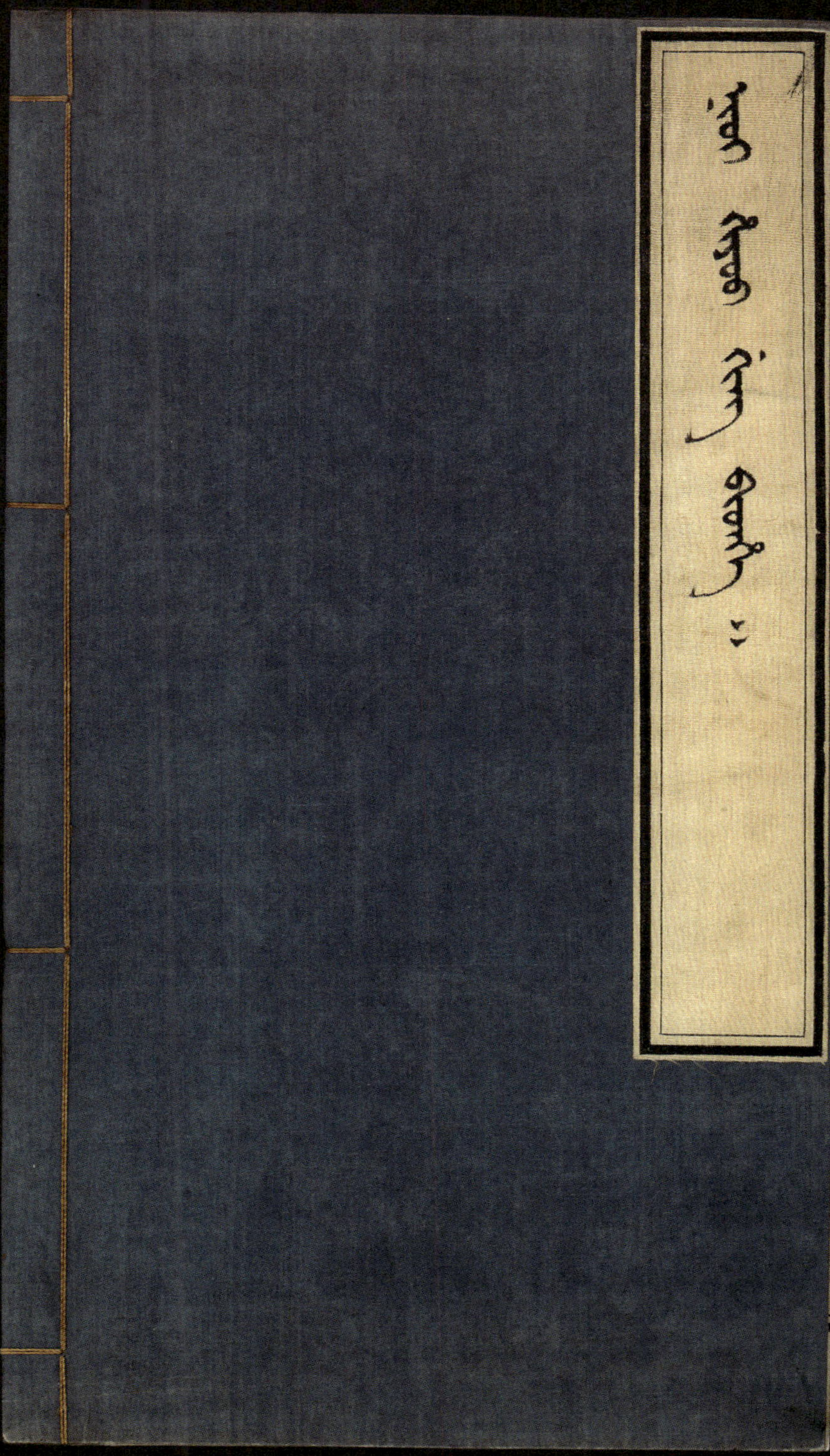

湖色素絹書面
Lake blue silk cover

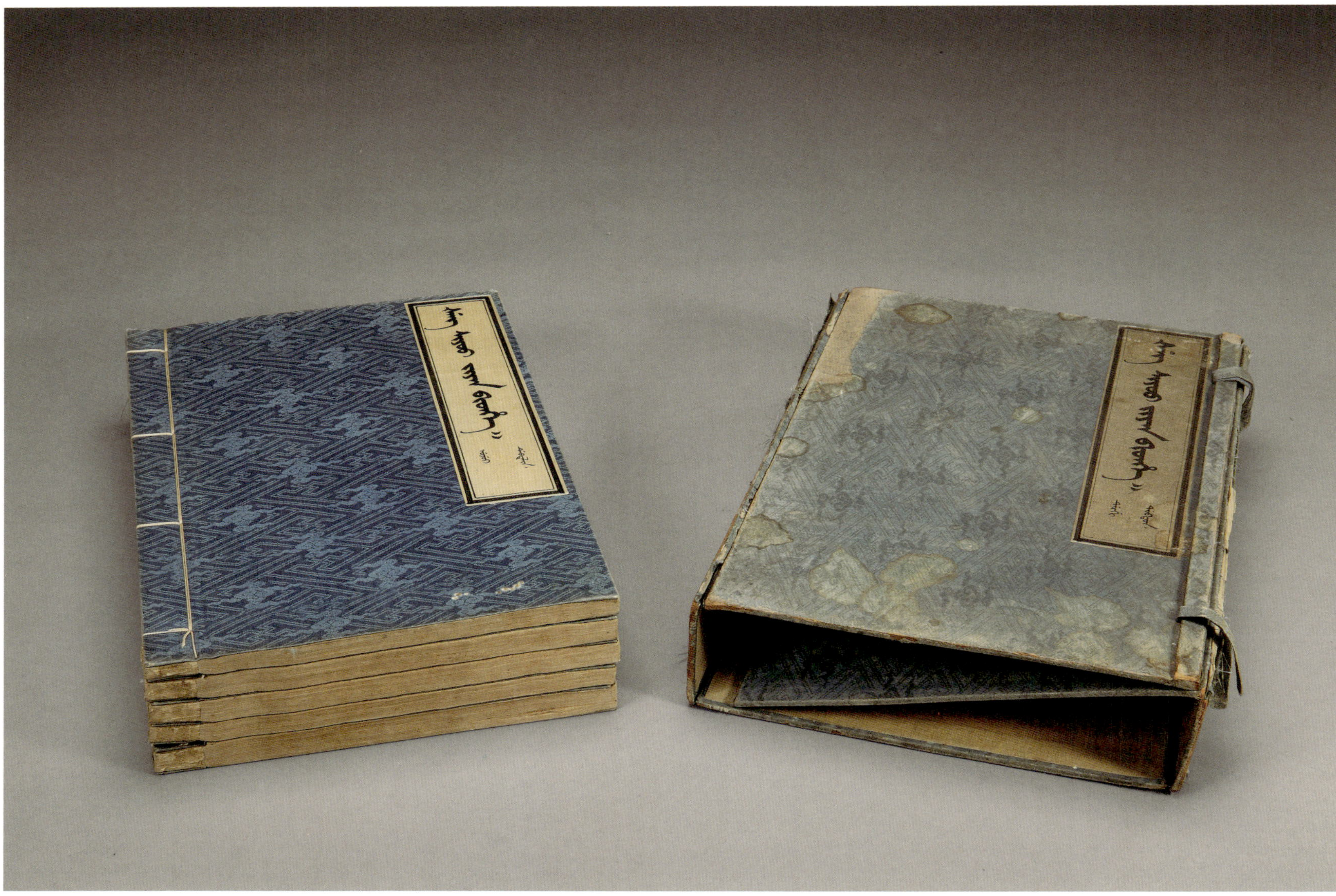

湖色萬字曲水雲紋暗花綾書函
Lake blue twill-weave silk case with veiled swastika and cloud pattern

13

書21763
《聖孝鑒十卷》
清初 佚名輯
清內府精寫滿文本
開本 縱31厘米 橫20.1厘米
十冊 二函

Inventory number: Shu 21763
Mirror for Imperial Filial Piety
Ten chapters
Anonymous, early Qing dynasty (1644-1911)
Transcribed in Manchu by the Qing court
Format: 31 × 20.1 cm
Ten volumes in two cases

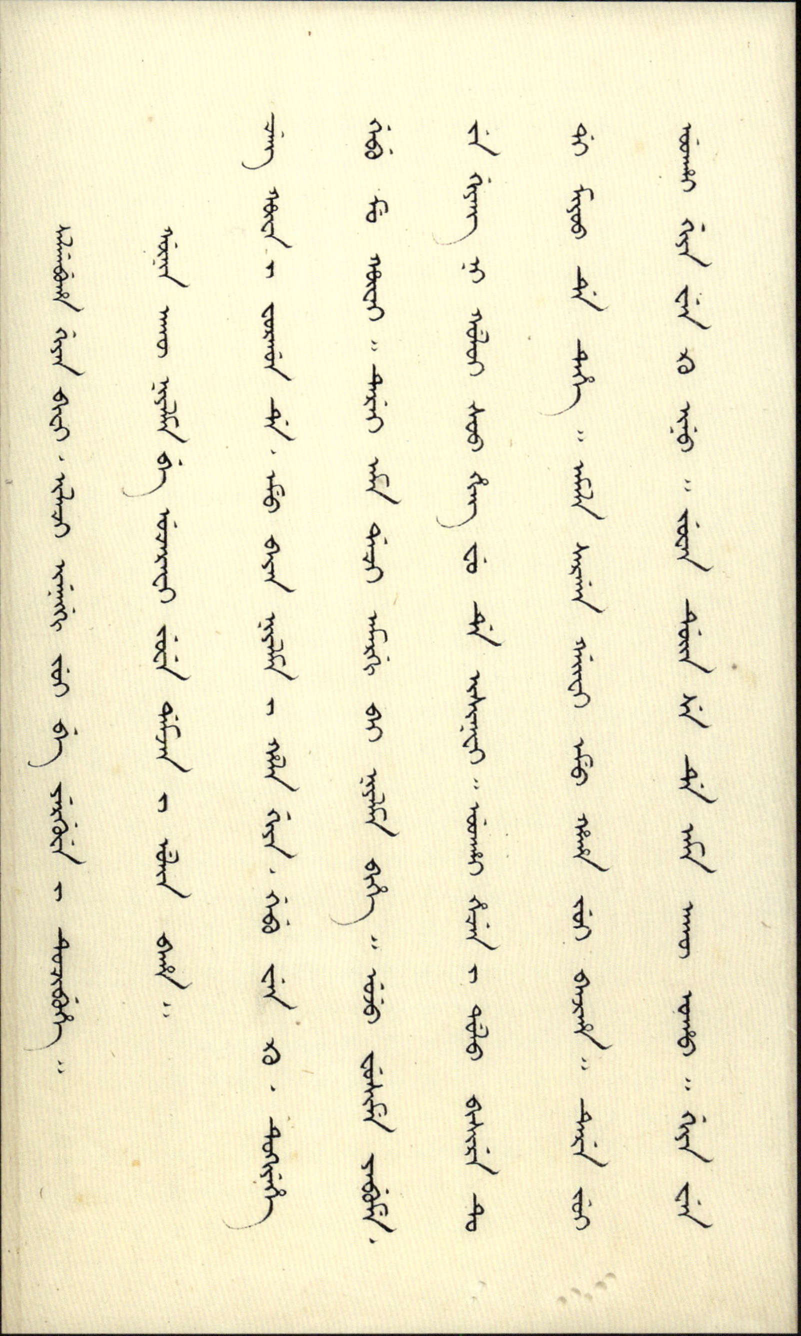

卷端
Beginning

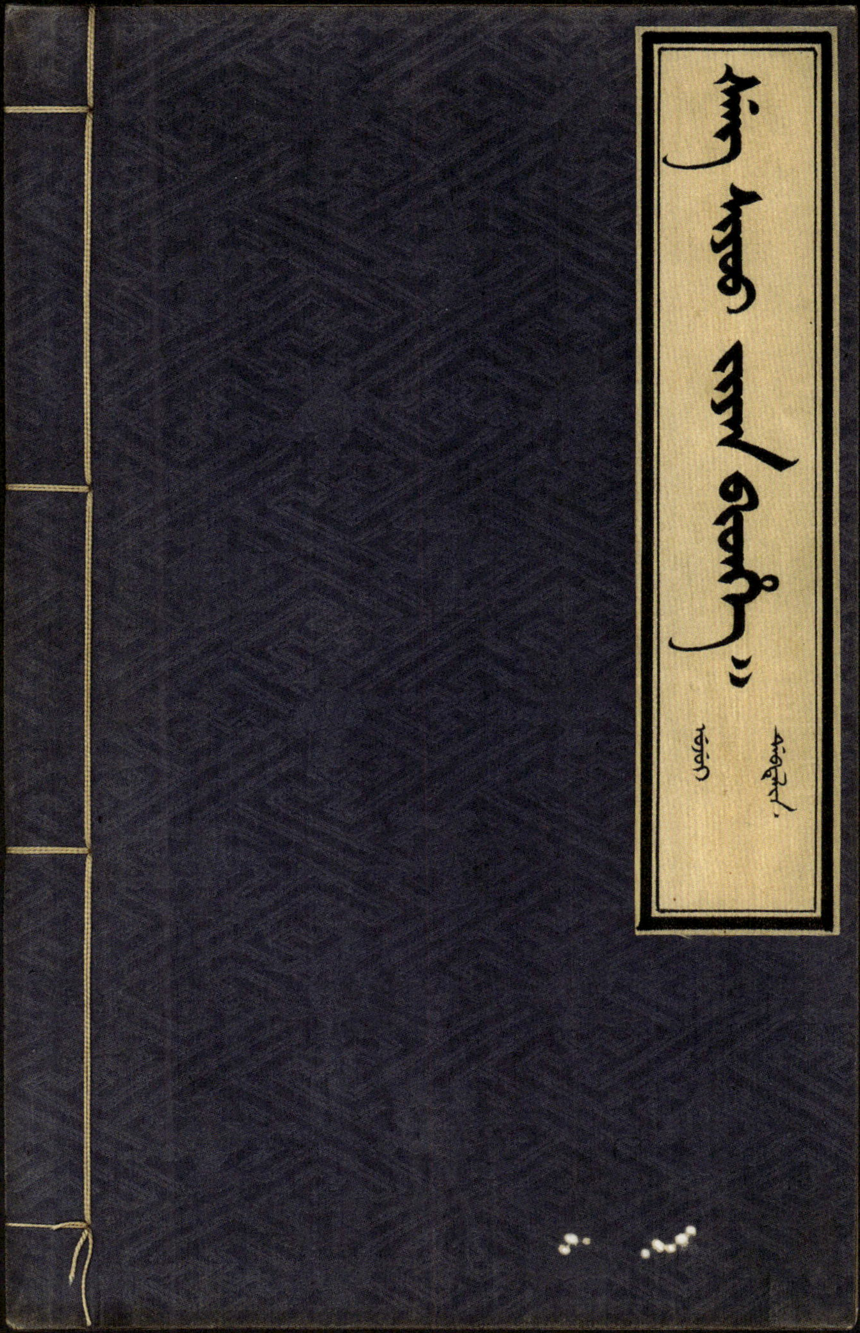

湖色萬字曲水雲紋暗花綾書面
Lake blue twill-weave silk cover with veiled swastika and cloud pattern

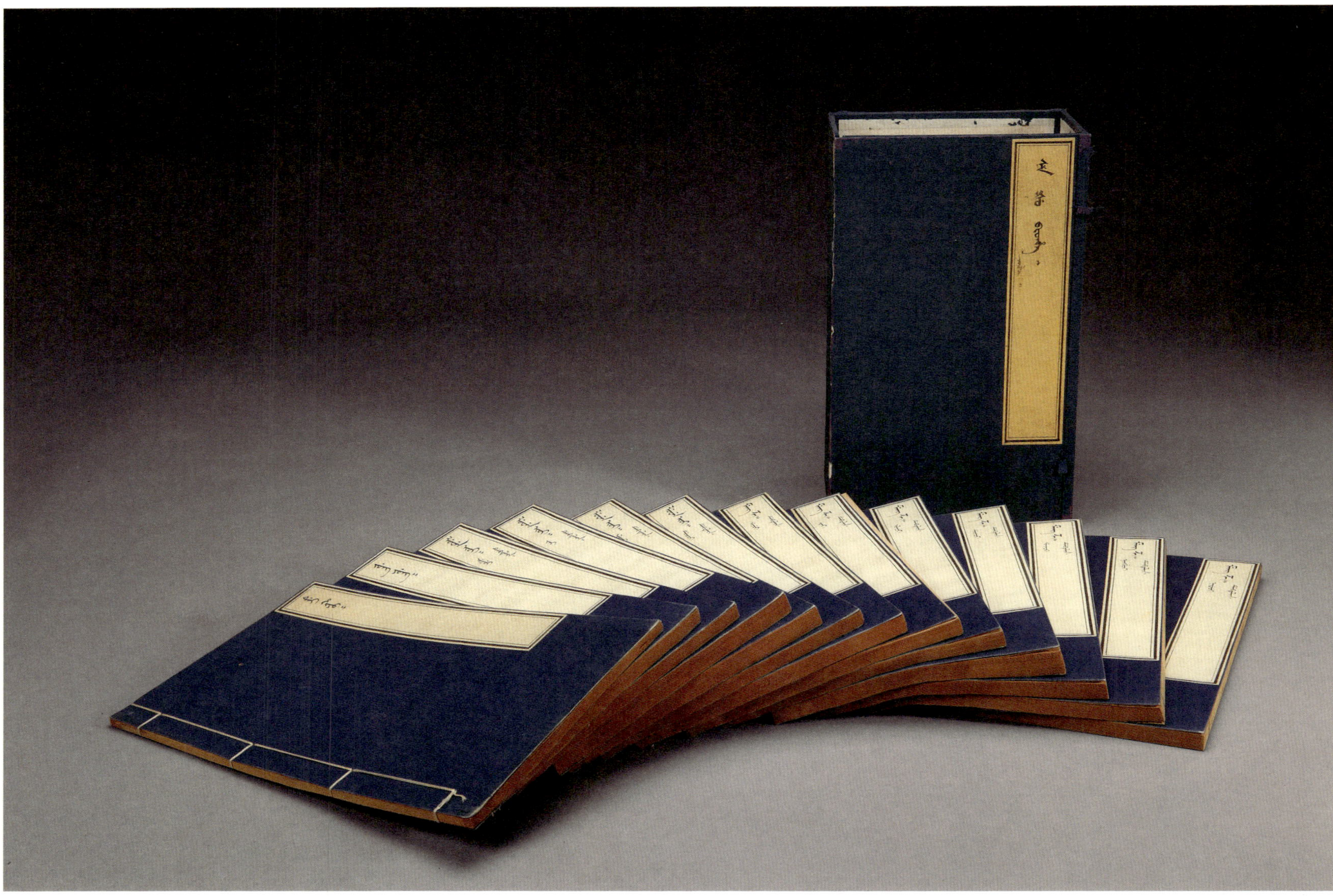

湖色素絹書函
Lake blue silk case

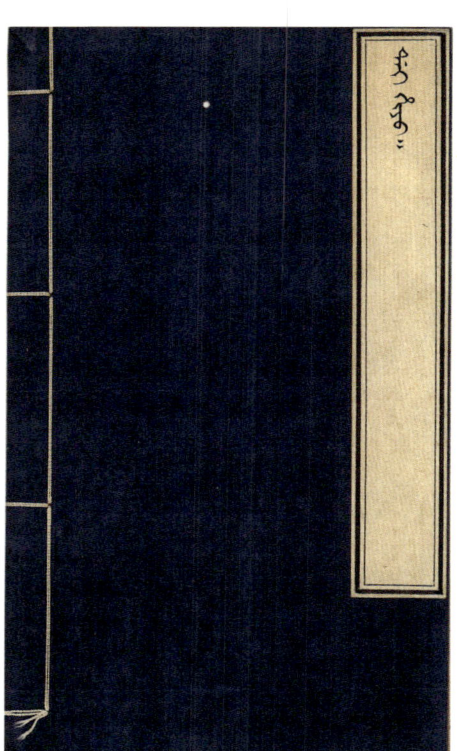

藍色素絹書面
Lake blue silk cover

書21764
《四書十三卷》
宋　朱熹著　清　佚名譯
清內府精寫滿文本
開本　縱27厘米　橫16厘米
版框　縱20.7厘米　橫12.7厘米
十三冊　一函

14

Inventory number: Shu 21764
Four Books
Thirteen chapters
Annotated by Zhu Xi
Translator unknown, Qing dynasty (1644-1911)
Transcribed in Manchu by the Qing court
Format: 27 × 16 cm
Frame: 20.7 × 12.7 cm
Thirteen volumes in one case

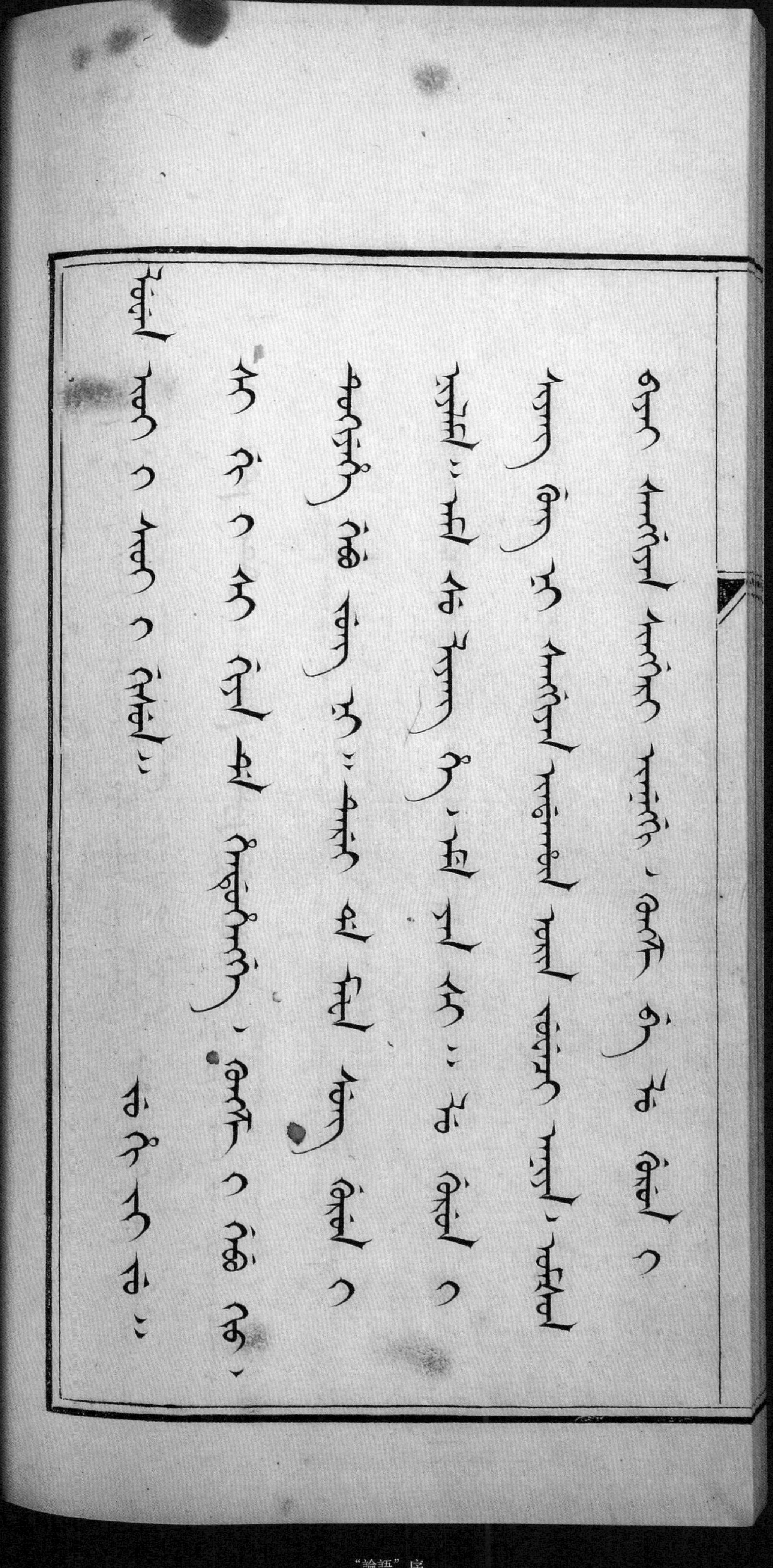

“論語”序
Preface to *Analects*

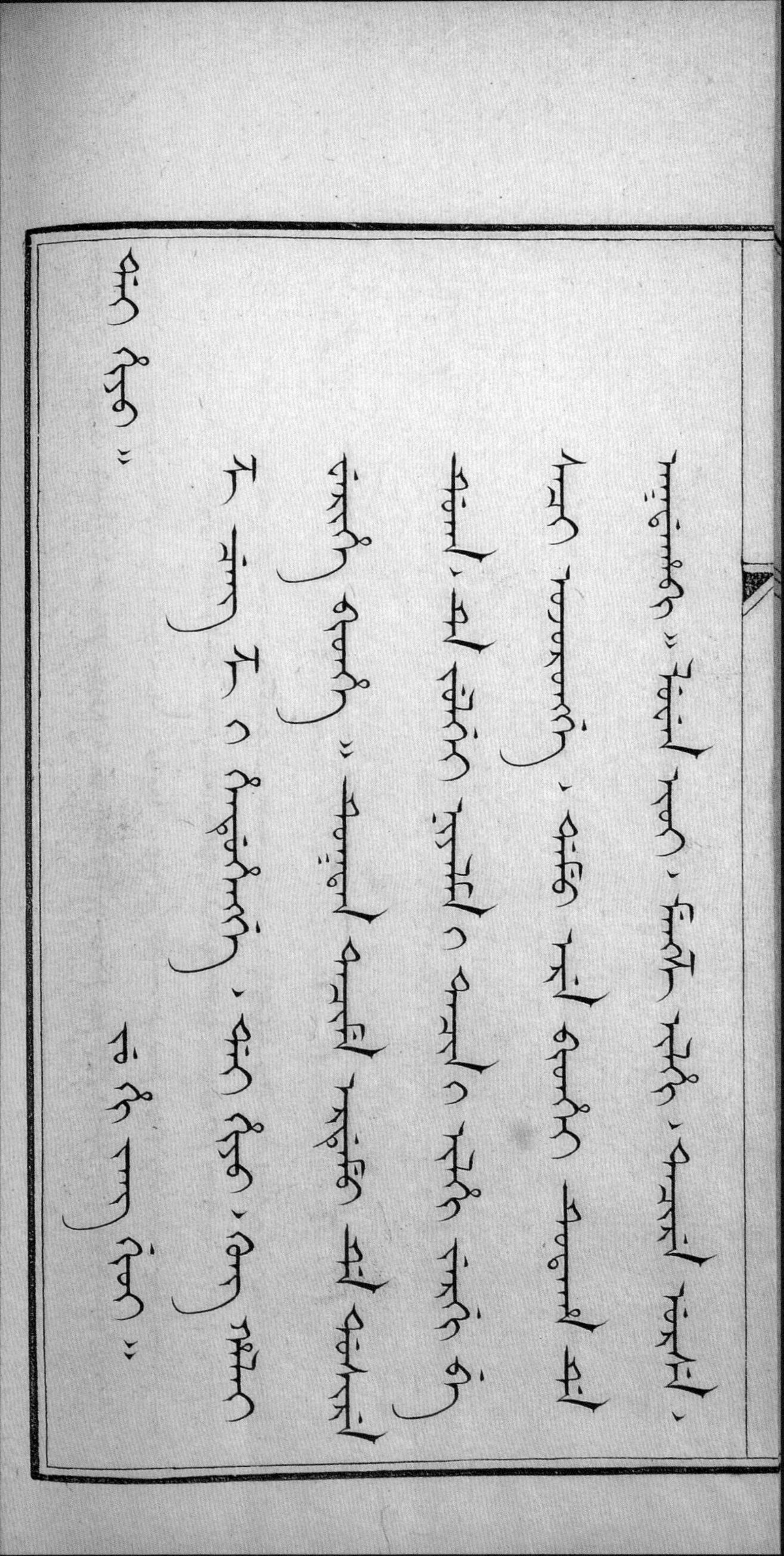

"大學"卷端
Beginning of *The Great Learning*

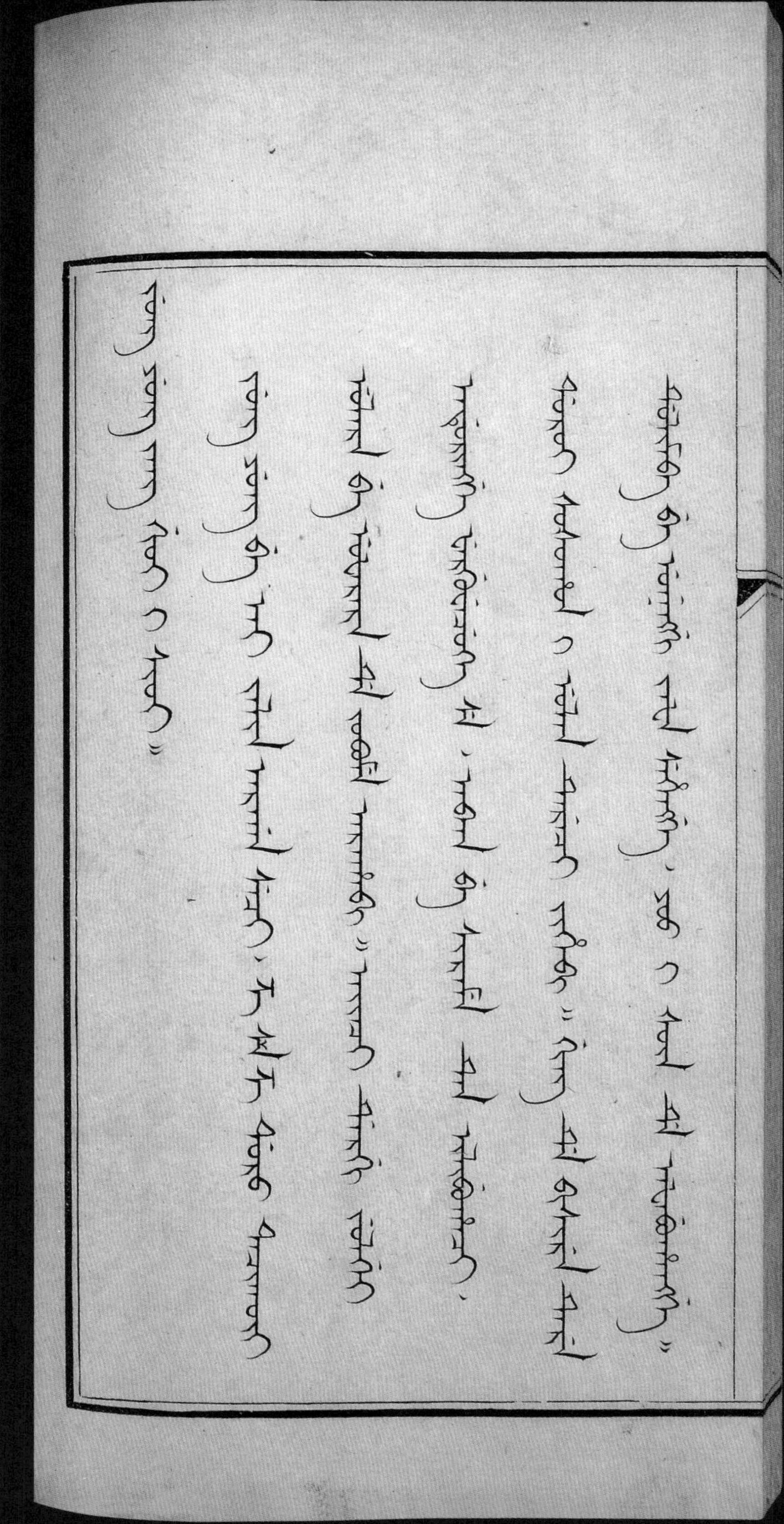

"中庸"序
Preface to *Doctrine of the Mean*

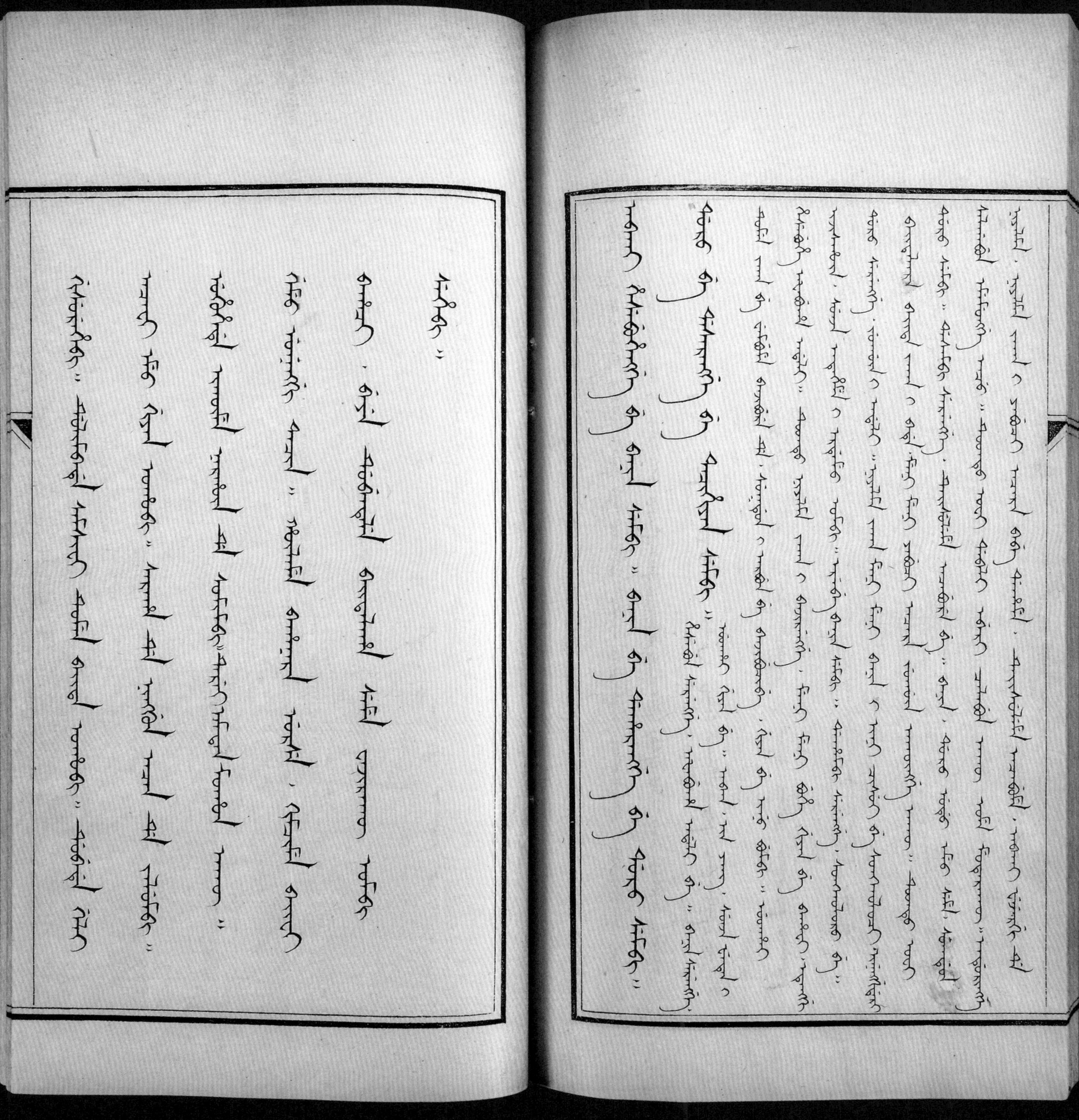

“孟子”正文
Text of *The Mencius*

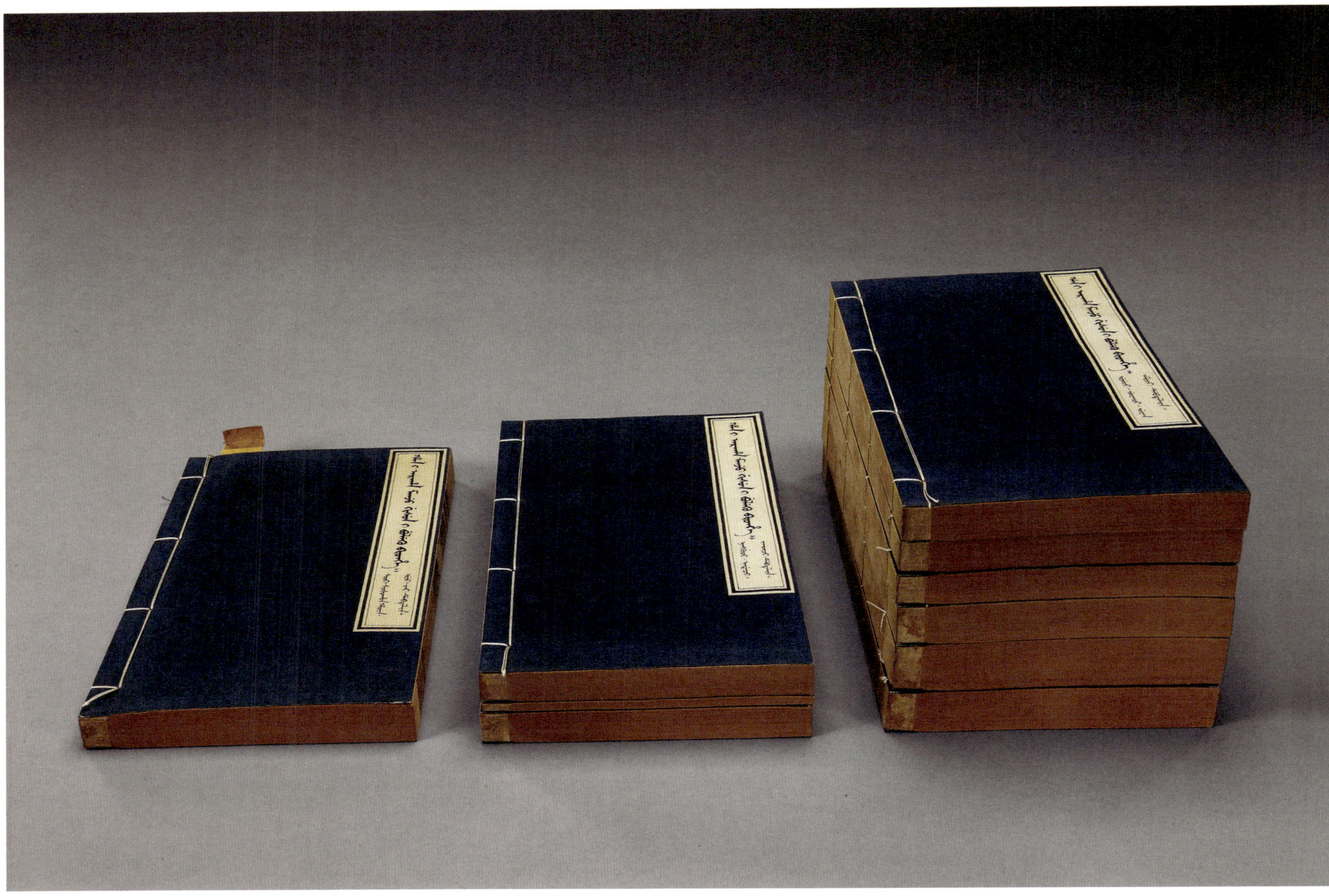

藍色素絹書面
Blue silk cases

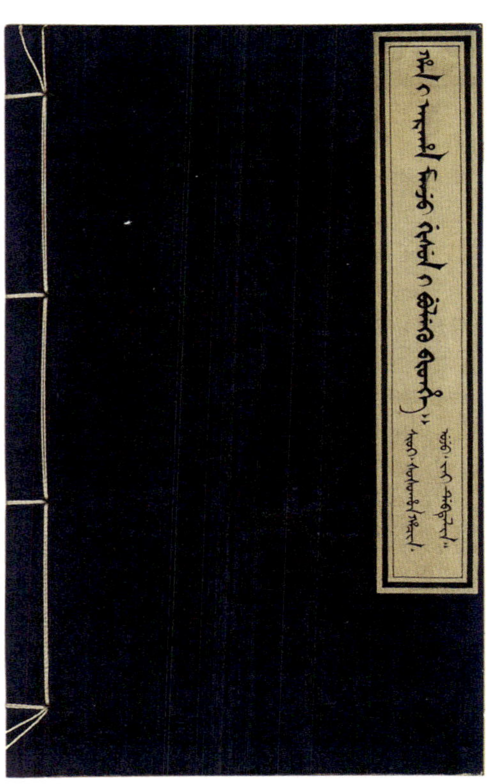

藍色素絹書面
Blue silk cover

書21842
《御製清文鑒二十卷首一卷後序一卷總綱四卷》
清　聖祖玄燁敕撰
清康熙四十七年（1708）內府精寫滿文本
開本　縱22.7厘米　橫14.7厘米
版框　縱17.4厘米　橫12.2厘米
十冊　一函

15

Inventory number: Shu 21842
Dictionary of the Qing Language
Twenty chapters as text, one chapter as preliminary remarks, four chapters as general principles, one chapter as postscript
Compiled at the order of the Kangxi emperor (r.1662-1722)
Transcribed in Manchu in 1708 by the Qing court
Format: 22.7 × 14.7 cm
Frame: 17.4 × 12.2 cm
Ten volumes in one case

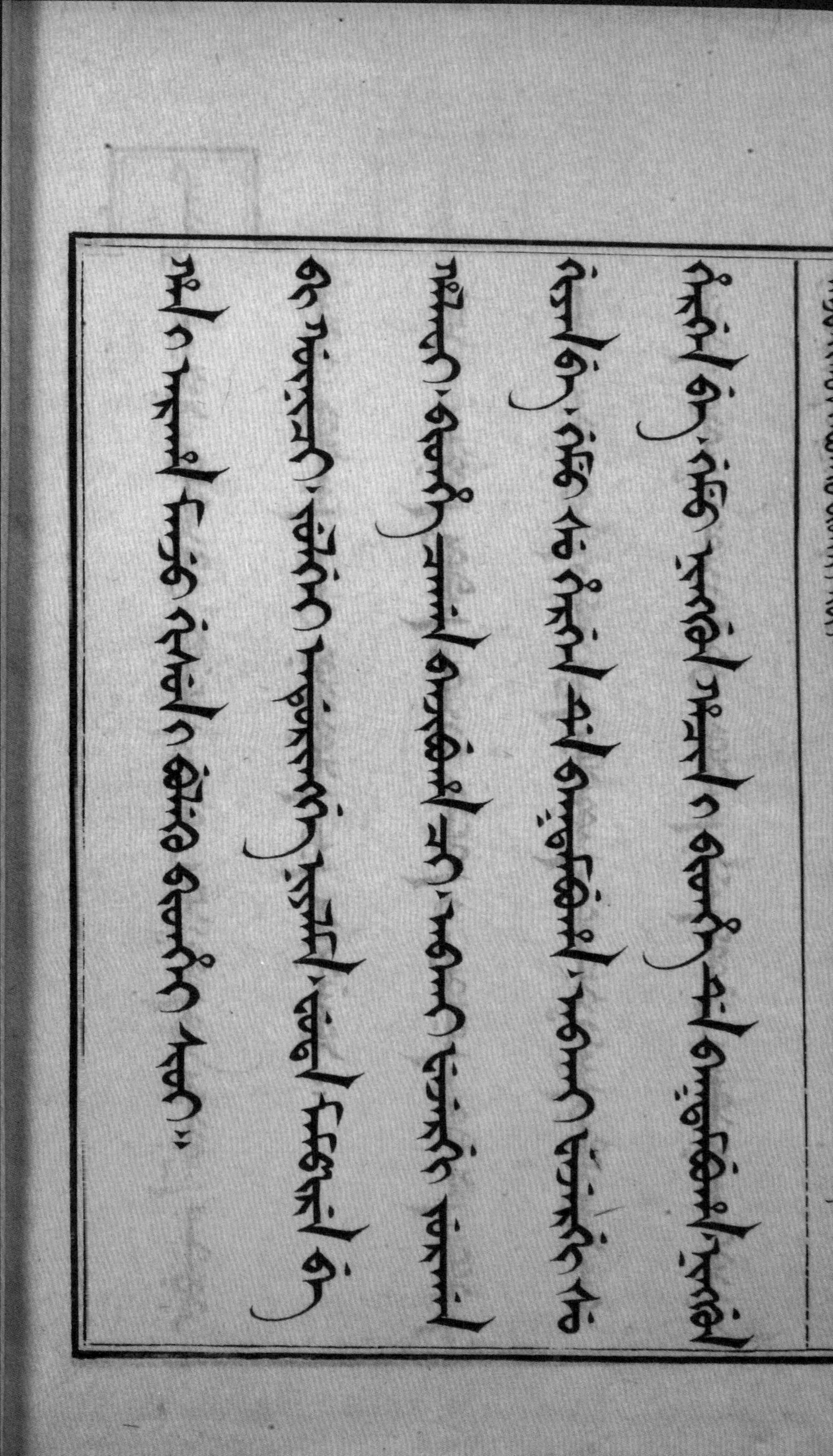

康熙四十七年御製序
Preface by the Kangxi emperor in 1708

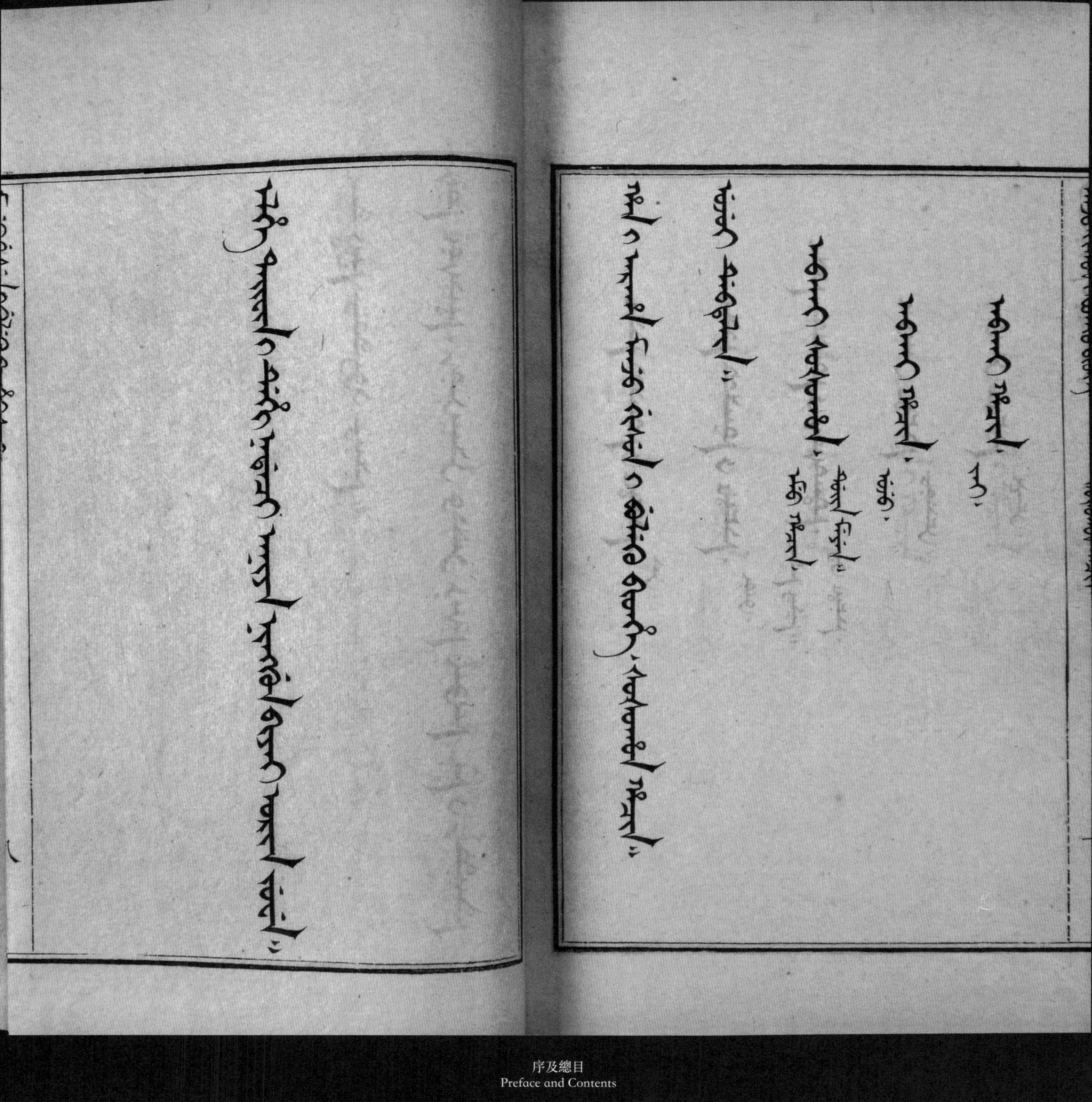

[illegible]

[illegible]

[illegible]

[illegible]

[illegible]

[illegible]

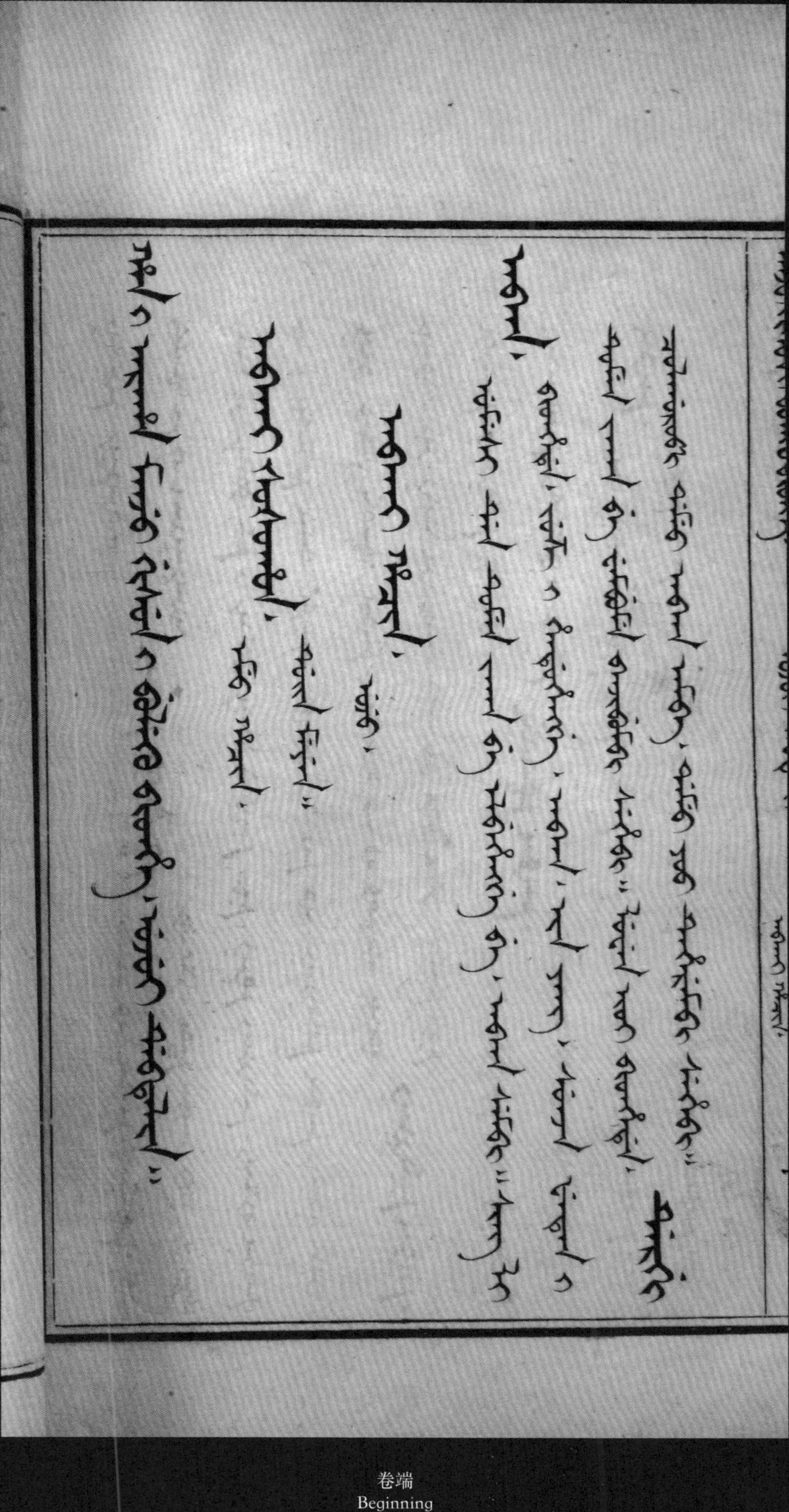

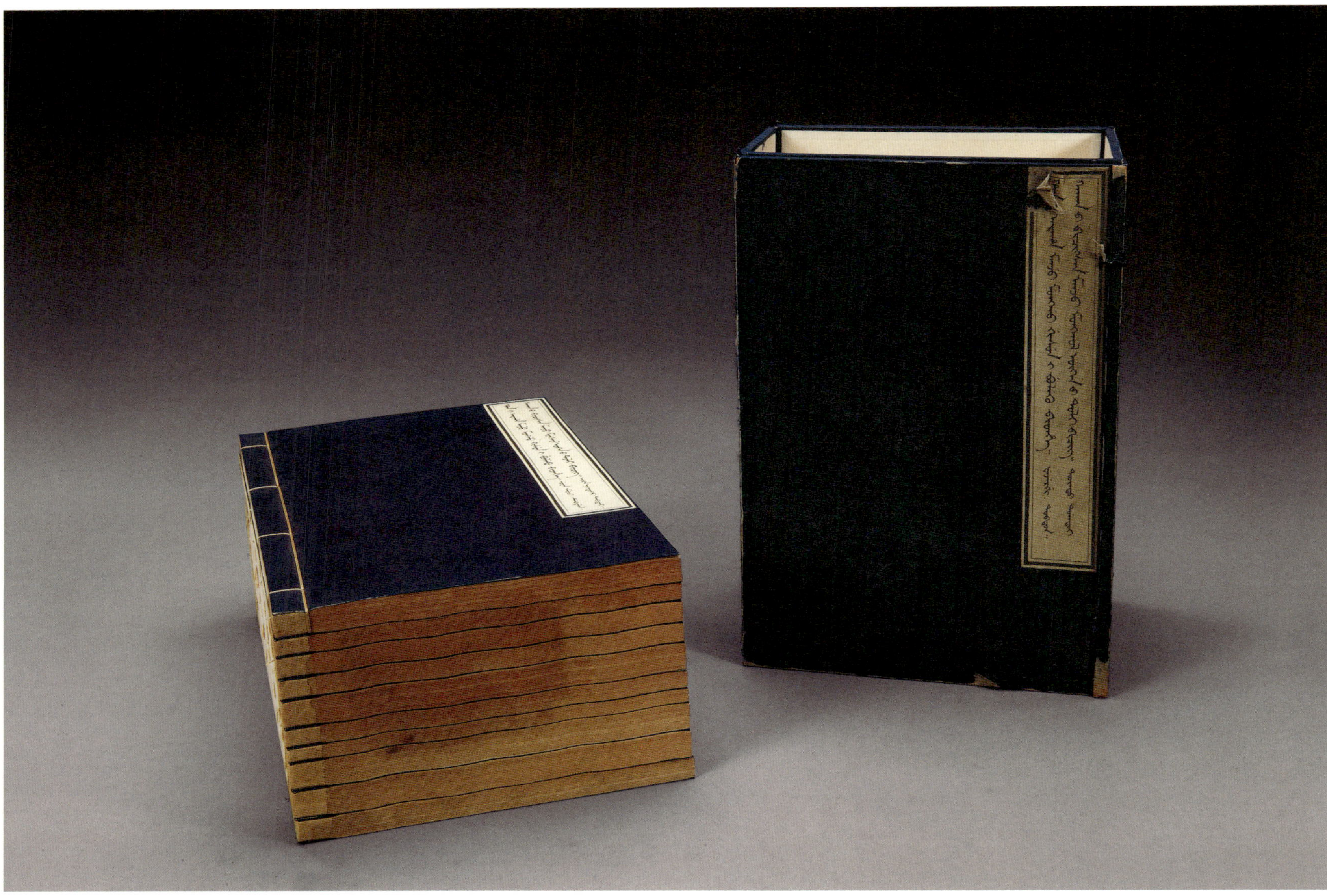

藍色素絹書函
Blue silk case

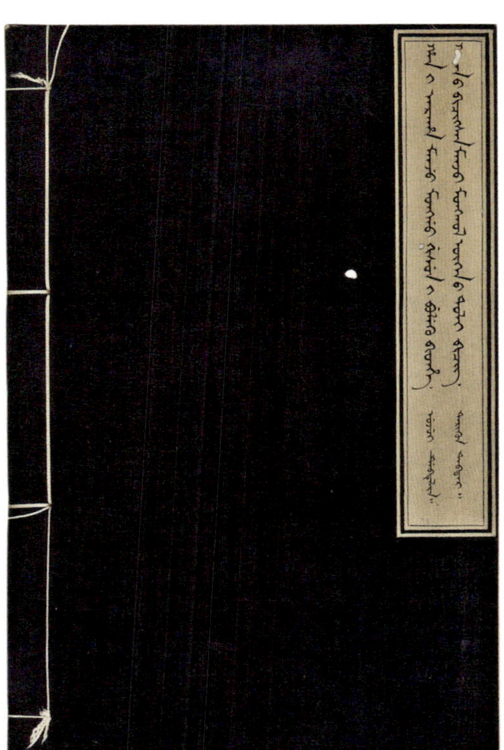

藍色素絹書面
Blue silk cover

書21866

《御製滿蒙文鑑二十卷首一卷總綱八卷》

清　聖祖玄燁敕撰　拉錫等編譯
清康熙五十六年（1717）武英殿刻滿蒙合璧本
開本　縱29.6厘米　橫19.5厘米
版框　縱21.2厘米　橫16.5厘米
存十册　一函（又一部全書二十九册三函）

16

Inventory number: Shu 21866

Manchu-Mongolian Dictionary

Twenty chapters as text, one chapter as preliminary remarks
Compiled and translated at the order of the Kangxi emperor (r.1662-1722) by Laxi et. al.
Printed in Manchu and Mongolian in 1717 at the Hall of Martial Valour
Format: 29.6 × 19.5 cm
Frame: 21.2 × 16.5 cm
Ten volumes in one case

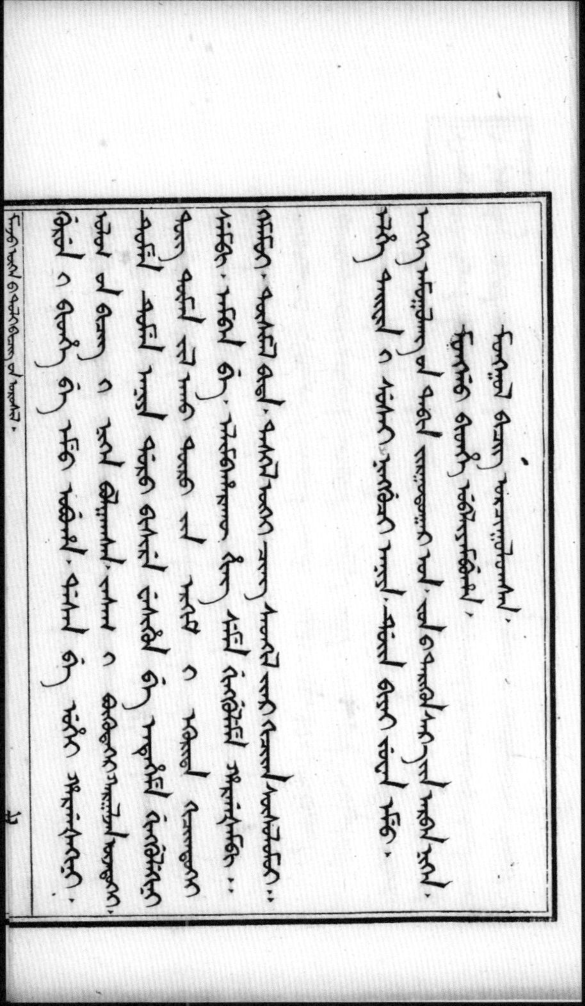

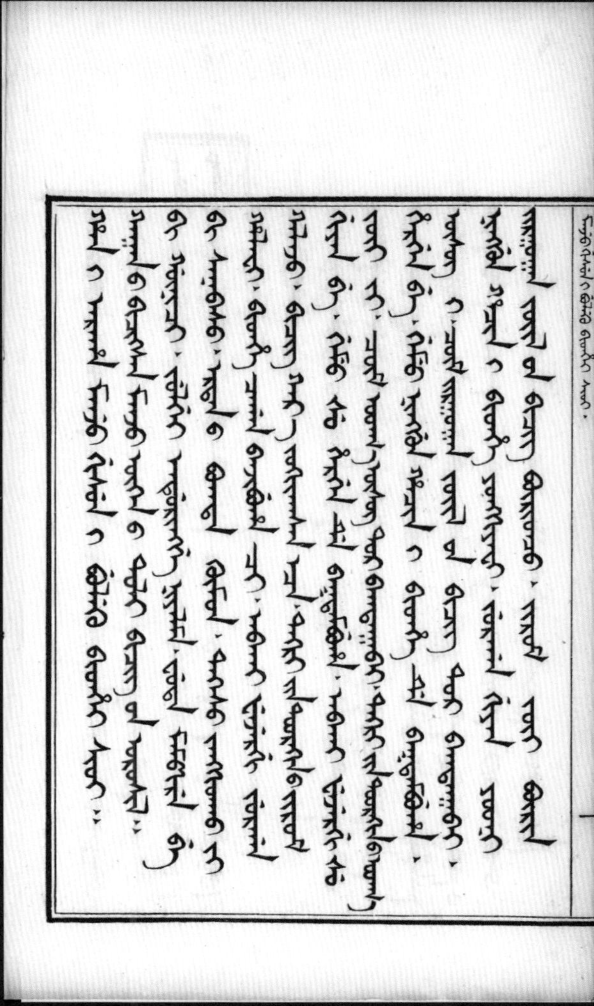

康熙五十六年御製序
Preface by the Kangxi emperor in 1717

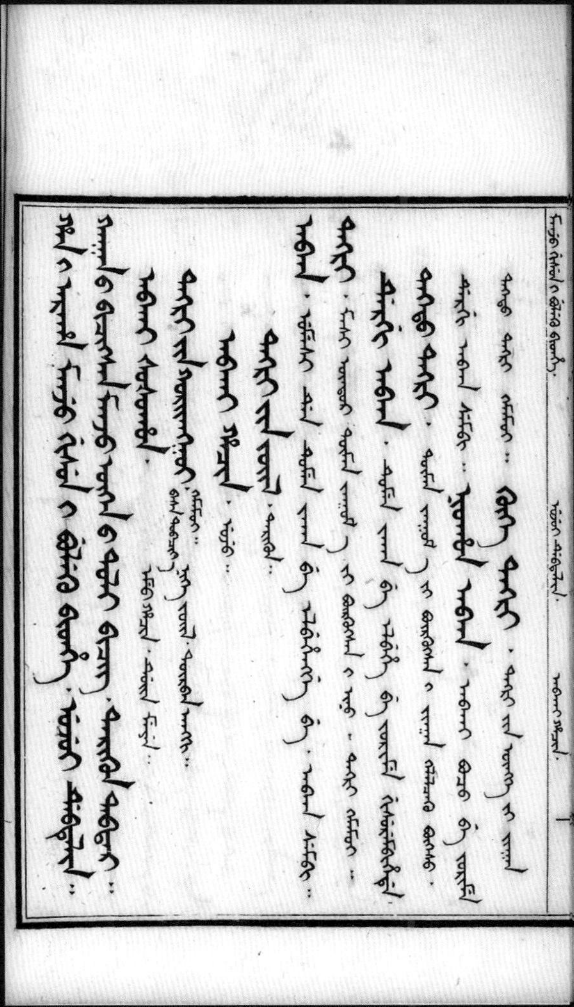

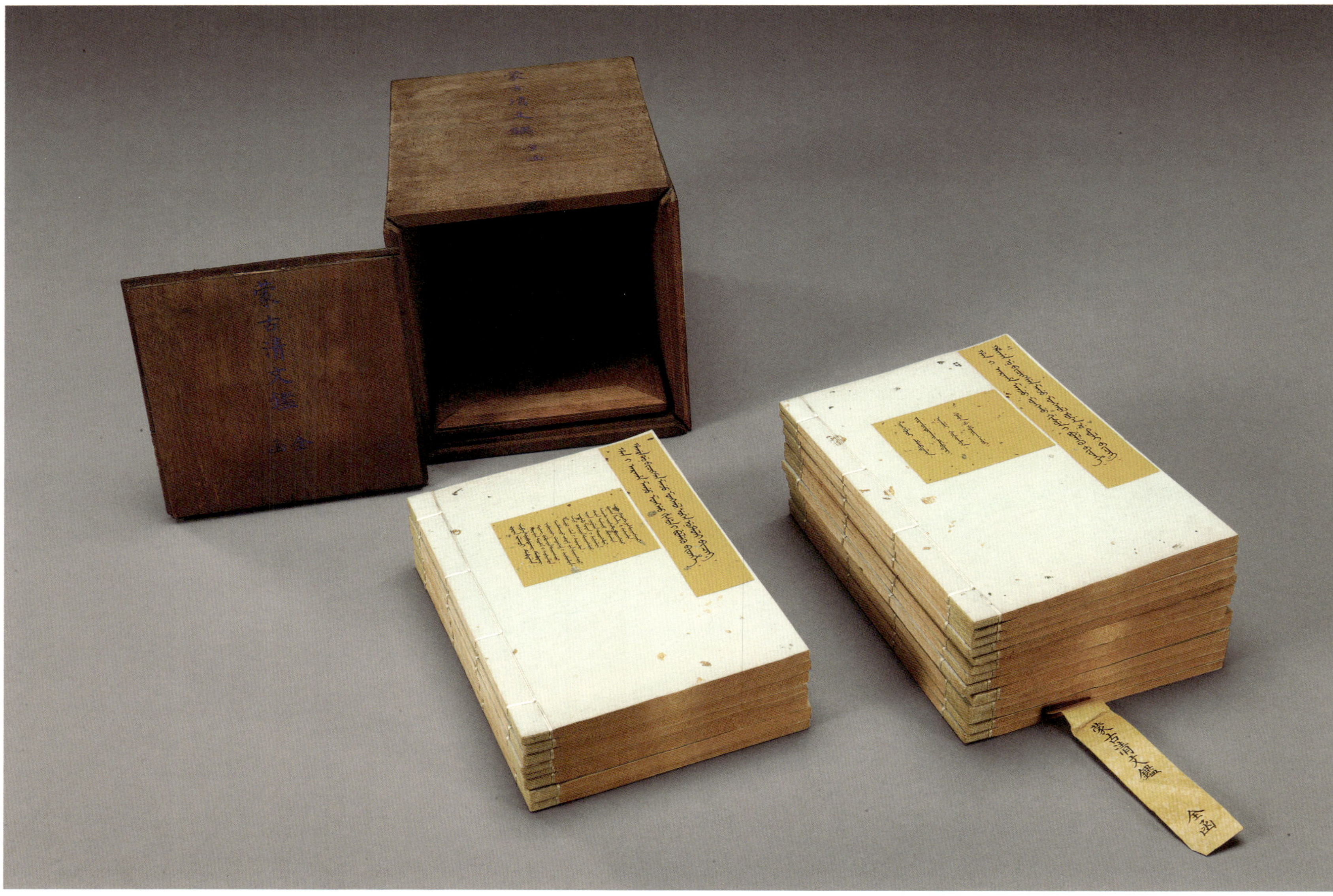

花梨木書盒
Rosewood case

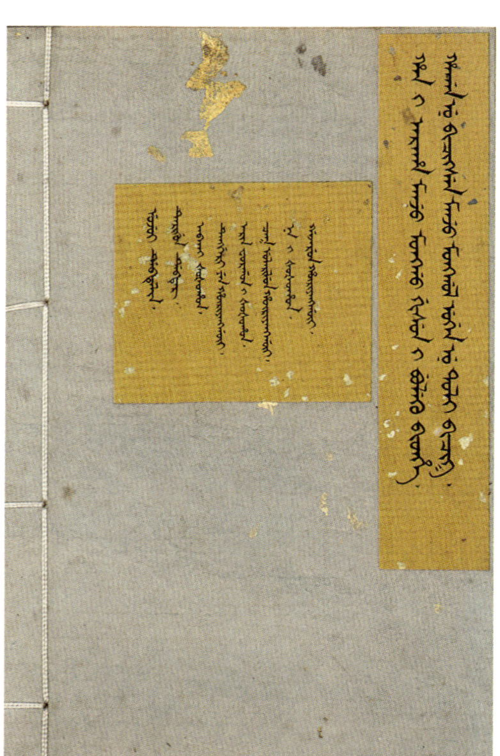

淺綠色撒金紙書面
Light green cover made of gold-sprinkled paper

書21867
《御製滿蒙文鑒二十卷首一卷》
清　聖祖玄燁敕撰　拉錫等編譯　高宗弘曆敕纂　班第等編
清乾隆八年（1743）內府朱墨精寫滿蒙合璧本
開本　縱17.2厘米　橫11.4厘米
版框　縱12.3厘米　橫8.9厘米
二十一册　一木盒

17

Inventory number: Shu 21867
Manchu-Mongolian Dictionary
Twenty chapters as text, one chapter as preliminary remarks
Compiled and translated at the order of the Kangxi emperor (r.1662-1722) by Laxi et. al.
Transliterated at the order of the Qianlong emperor (r.1736-1795) by Bandi et. al.
Transcribed with red ink in Manchu and Mongolian in 1743 by the Qing court
Format: 17.2 × 11.4 cm
Frame: 12.3 × 8.9 cm
Twenty-one volumes in one wood case

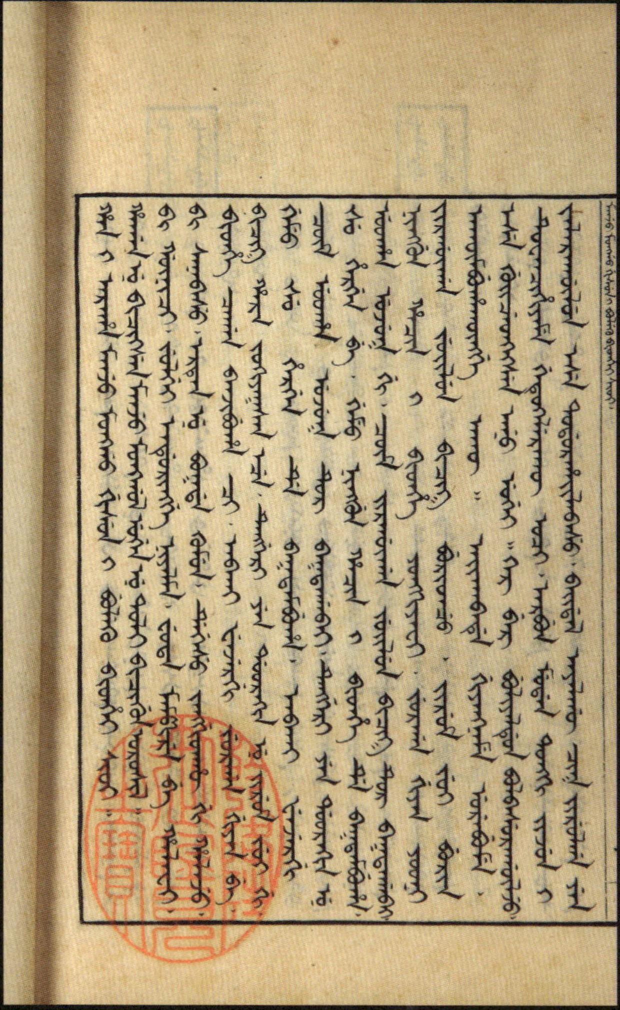

乾隆八年御製序
Preface by the Qianlong emperor in 1743

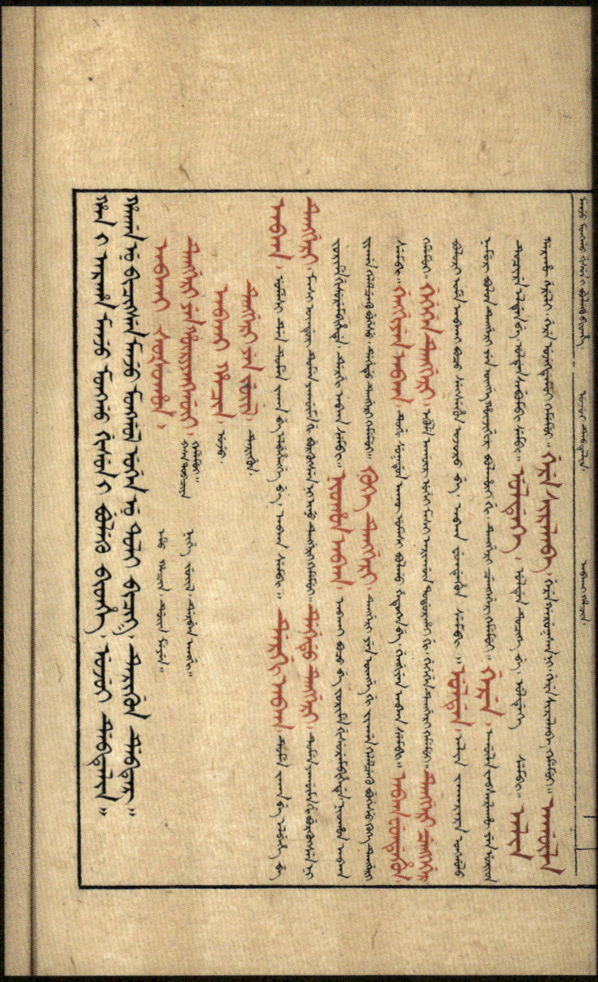

卷端
Beginning

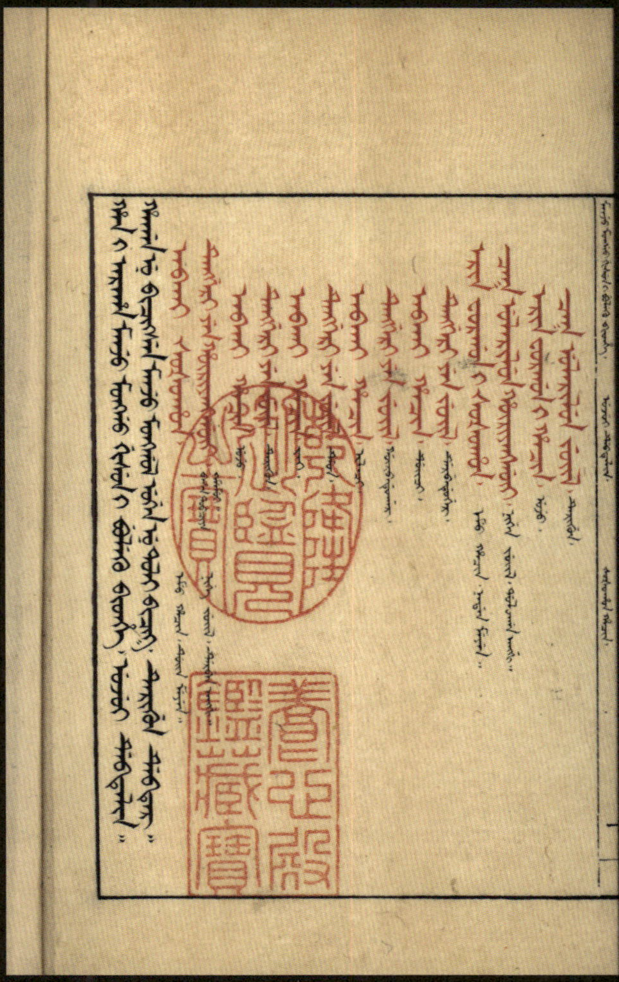

卷目
Contents

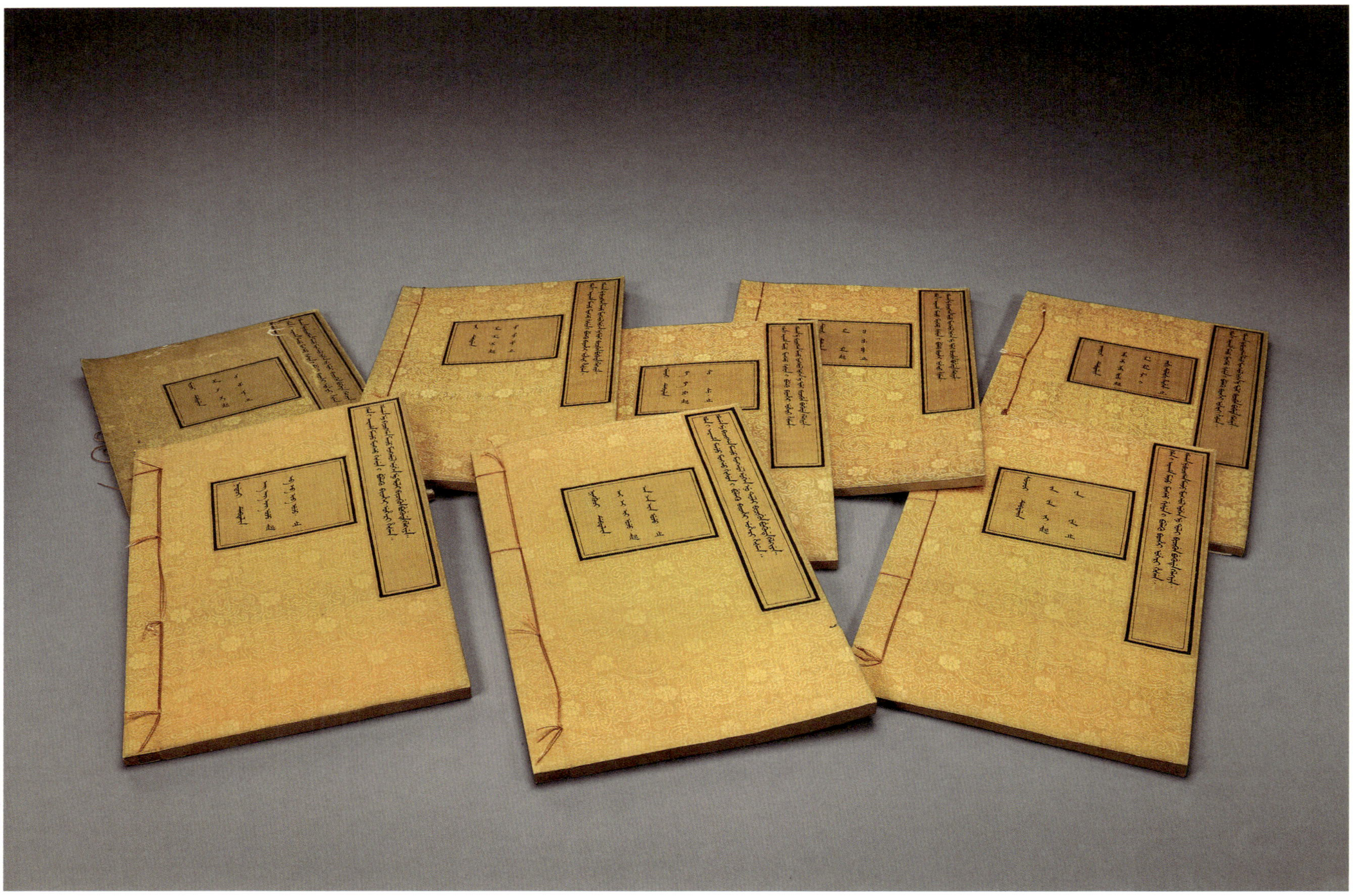

明黃色纏枝花紋暗花綾書面
Bright yellow twill-weave silk covers with veiled pattern of floral scrolls

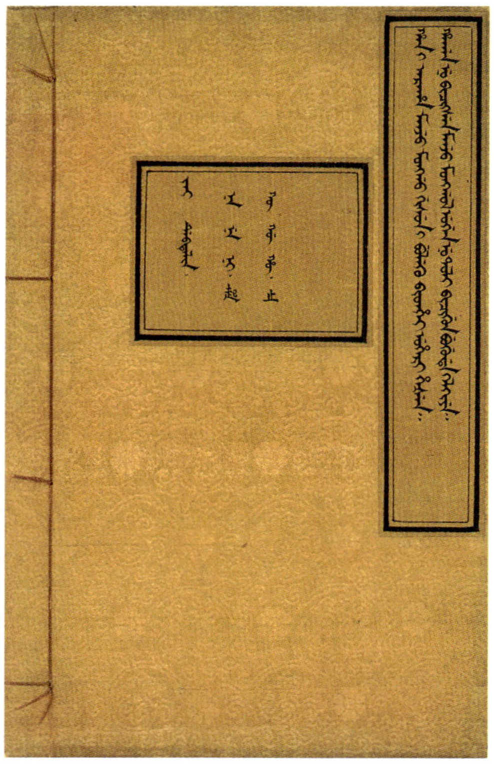

明黃色纏枝花紋暗花綾書面
Bright yellow twill-weave silk cover with veiled pattern of floral scrolls

書21875
《御製滿蒙文鑒總綱八卷》
清　高宗弘曆敕纂　永瑆等编
清乾隆四十一年（1776）武英殿刻滿蒙合璧本
開本　縱29.1厘米　横19厘米
版框　縱20.8厘米　横14.8厘米
八册　一函

18

Inventory number: Shu 21875
General Principles of the Manchu-Mongolian Dictionary
Eight chapters
Compiled in Manchu and Mongolian in 1776 at the order of the Qianlong emperor (r.1736-1795) by Yongji et. al.
Format: 29.1 × 19 cm
Frame: 20.8 × 14.8 cm
Eight volumes in one case

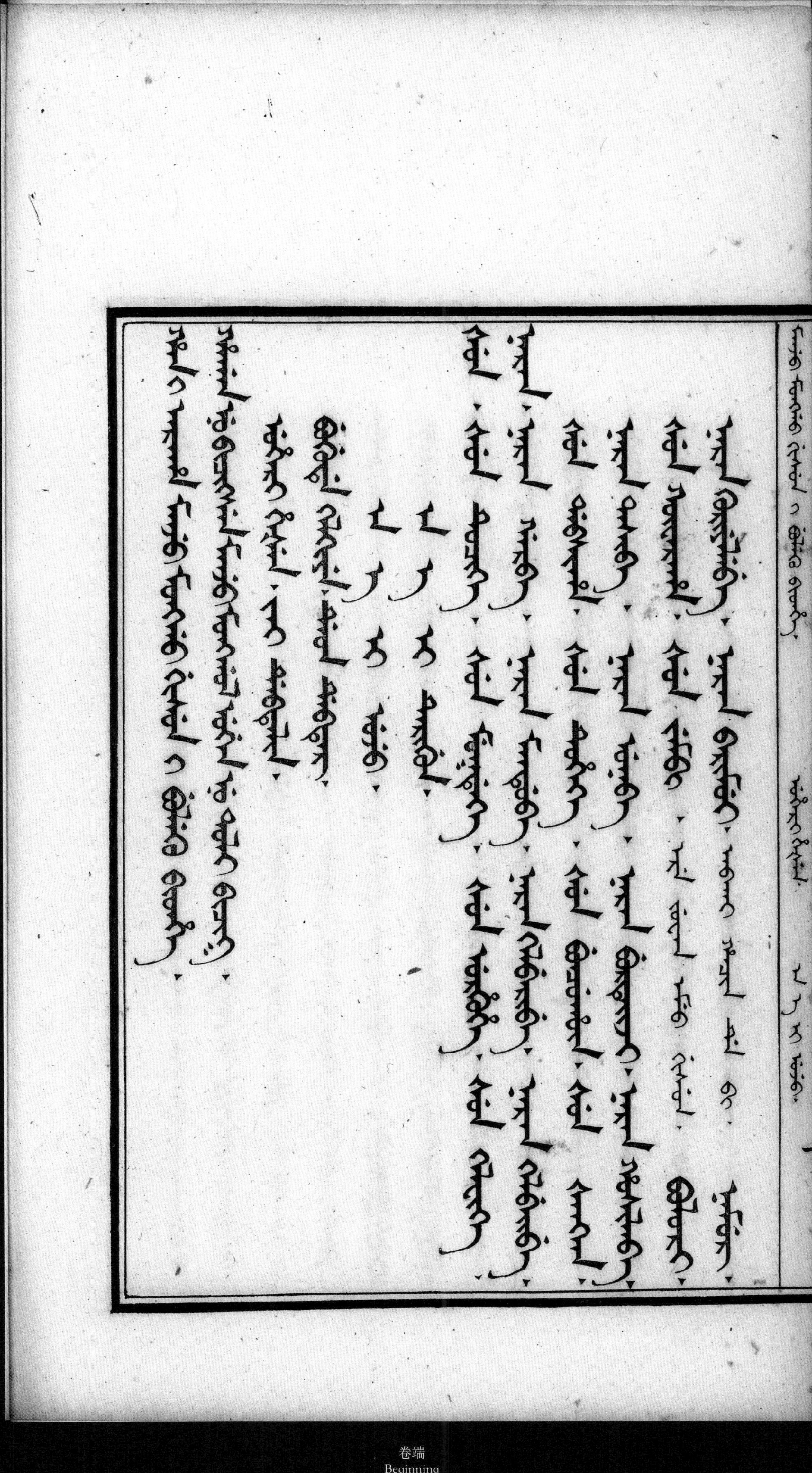

[illegible]

卷端
Beginning

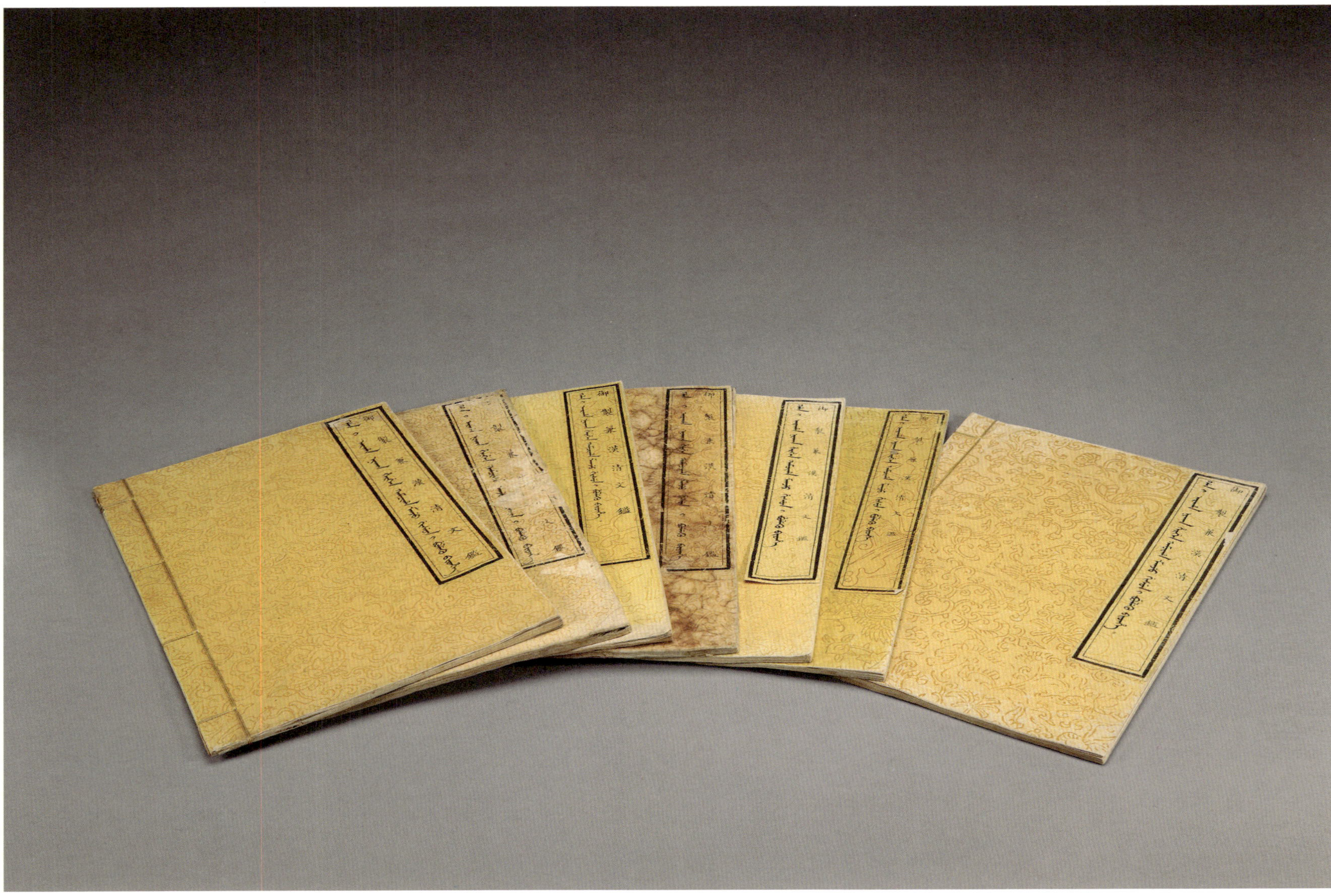

明黃色蝠連紋紙書面
Bright yellow paper covers with bat pattern

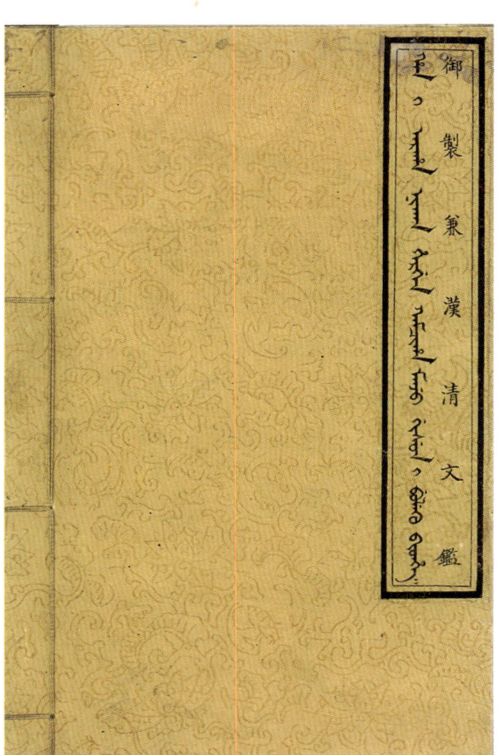

明黃色蝠連紋紙書面
Bright yellow paper cover with bat pattern

書21860
《御製兼漢清文鑒不分卷》
清　高宗弘曆敕撰
清乾隆年滿漢合璧修改稿本
開本　縱28.5厘米　橫18.5厘米
存十九册　一函

19

Inventory number: Shu 21860
Phonetically Transcribed Bilingual Dictionary of Chinese and the Official Language of the Qing
Compiled at the order of the Qianlong emperor (r.1736-1795)
Draft edition
Revised in Manchu and Chinese in the Qianlong period
Format: 28.5 × 18.5 cm
Nineteen volumes in one case extant today

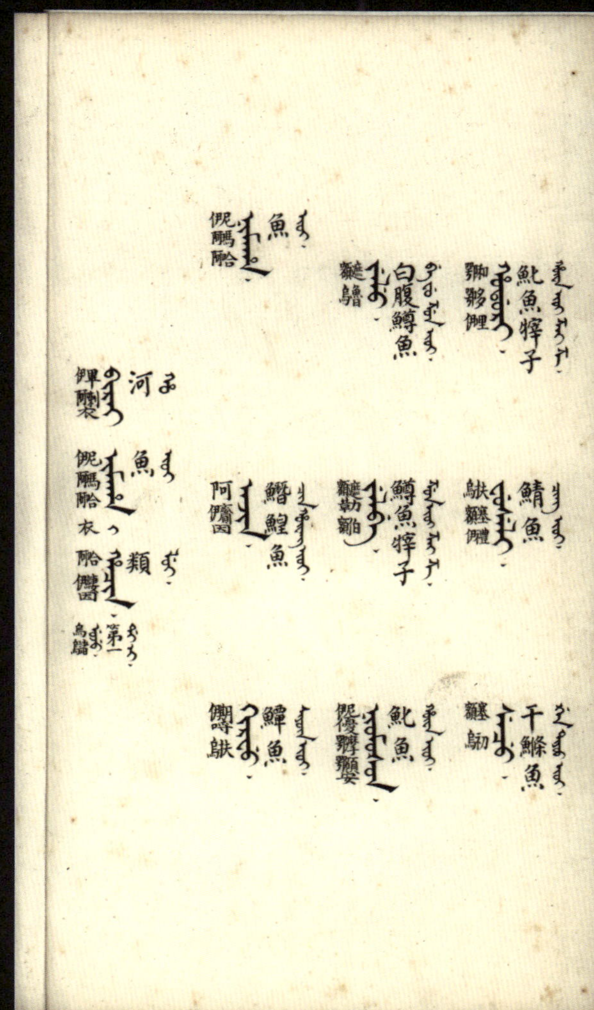

卷端
Beginning

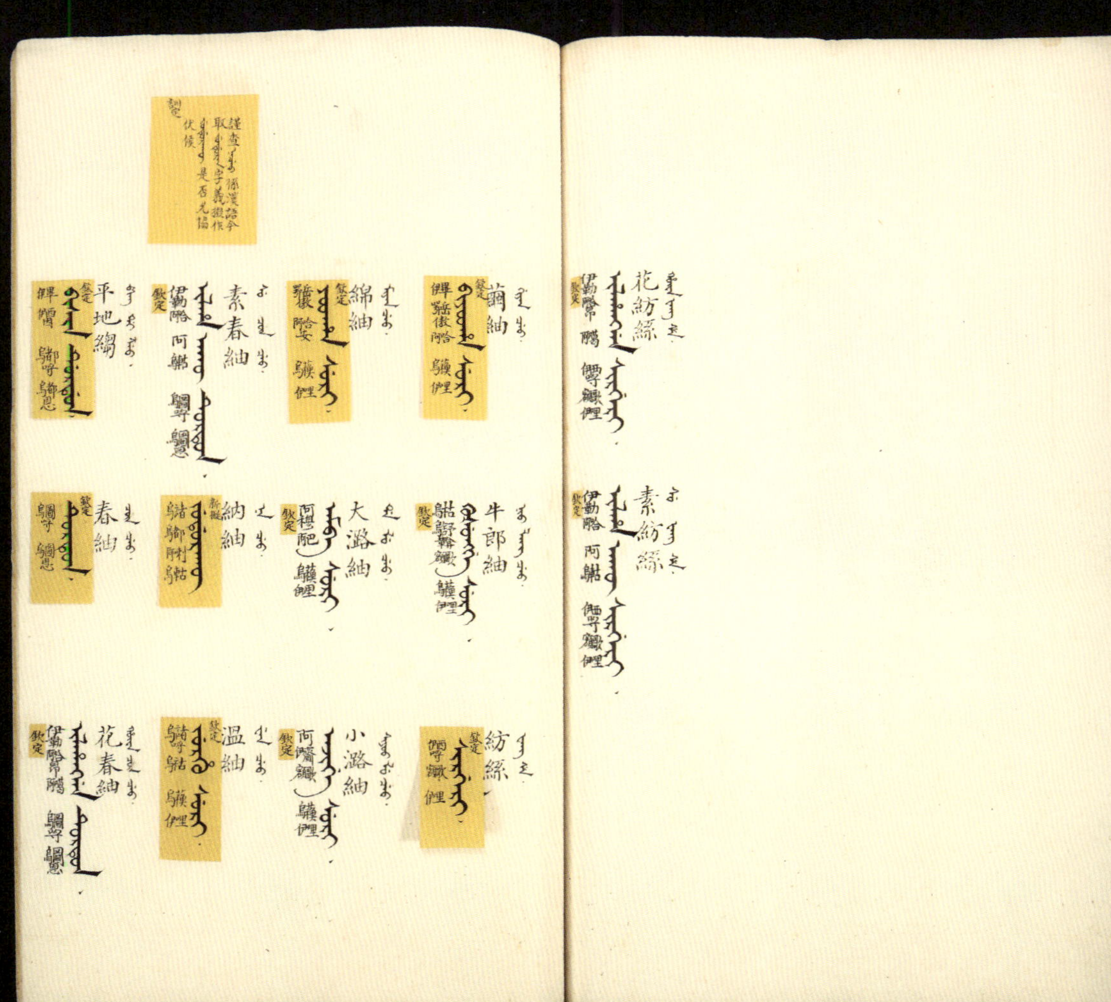

正文
Text

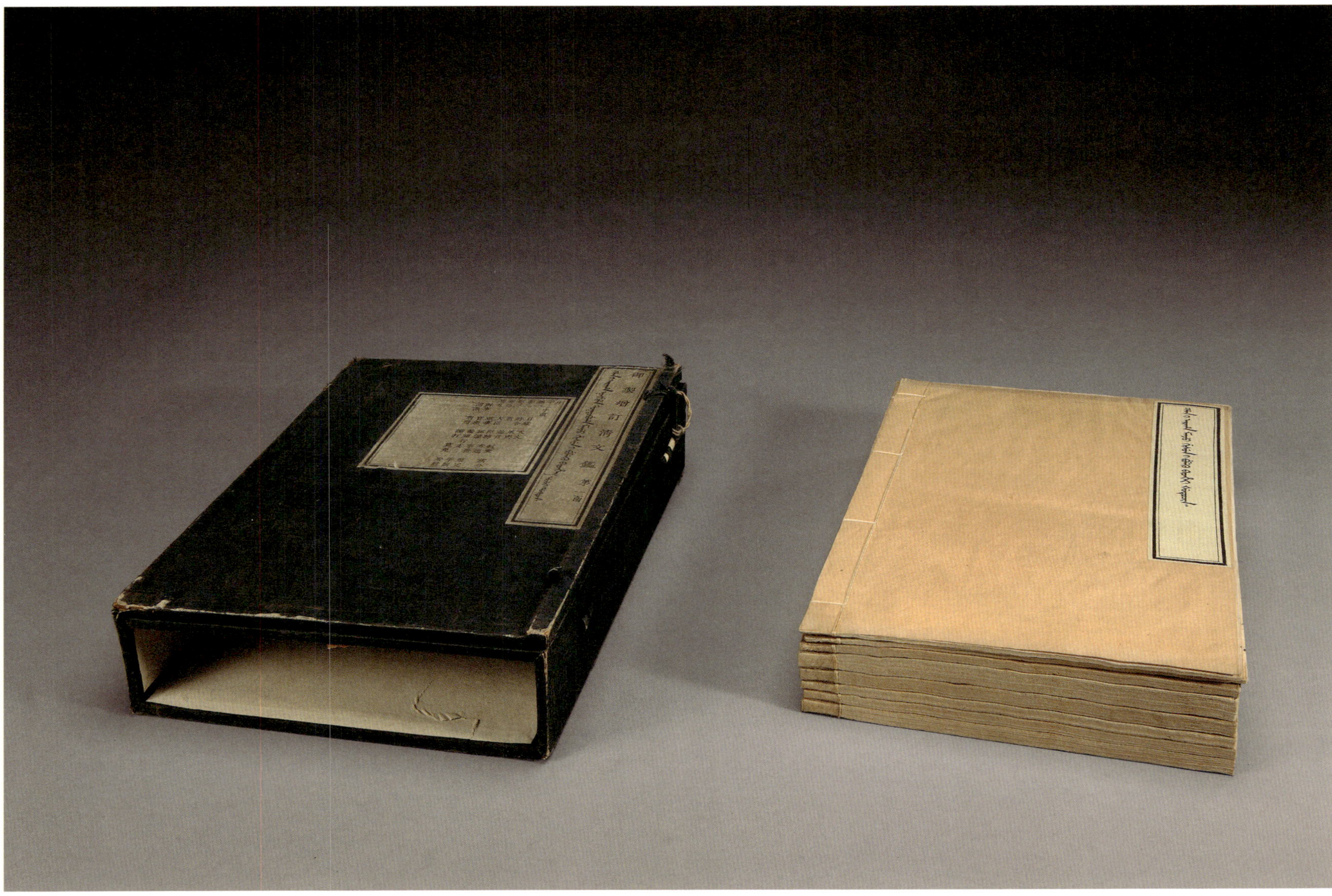

藍色素綢書函
Blue silk case

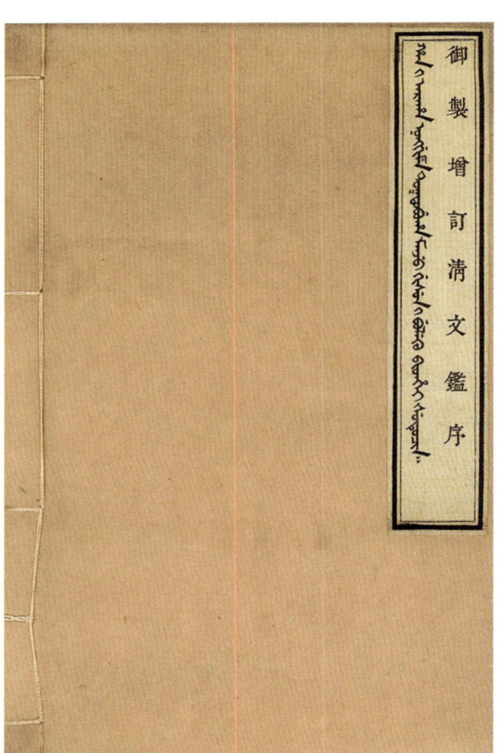

本色紙書面
Paper cover

20

書21850
《御製增訂清文鑒三十二卷首二卷總綱八卷補編四卷補編總綱一卷》
清　高宗弘曆敕撰　傅恒等纂
清乾隆三十六年（1771）武英殿刻滿漢合璧本
開本　縱31.5厘米　橫20.5厘米
版框　縱22.7厘米　橫18厘米
四十八册　八函

Inventory number: Shu 21850
Supplement to the Dictionary of the Qing Language
Thirty-two chapters as text, two chapters as preliminary remarks, eight chapters as general principles, four chapters as supplement to the text, one chapter as supplement to the general principle
Compiled at the order of the Qianlong emperor (r.1736-1795) by Fuheng et. al.
Printed in Manchu and Chinese in 1771 at the Hall of Martial Valour
Format: 31.5 × 20.5 cm
Frame: 22.7 × 18 cm
Forty-eight volumes in eight cases

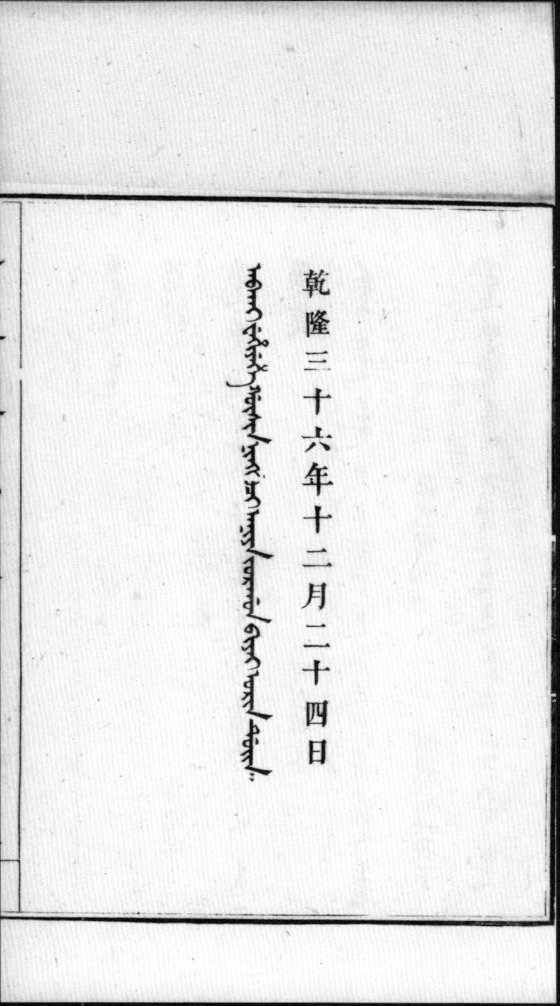

乾隆三十六年十二月二十四日

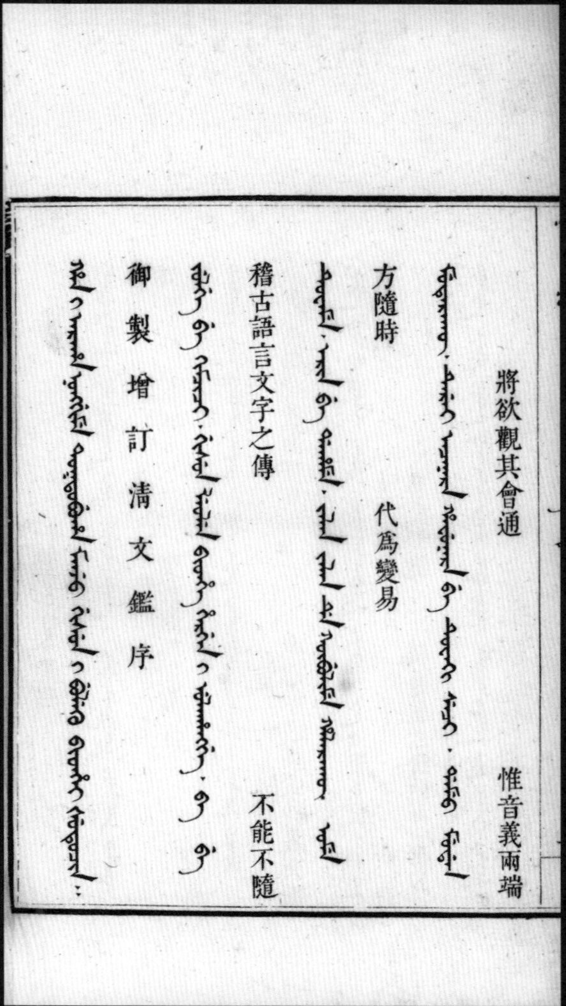

將欲觀其會通　惟音義兩端
方隨時　代爲變易
稽古語言文字之傳　不能不隨
御製增訂清文鑑序

乾隆三十六年御製序
Preface by the Qianlong emperor in 1771

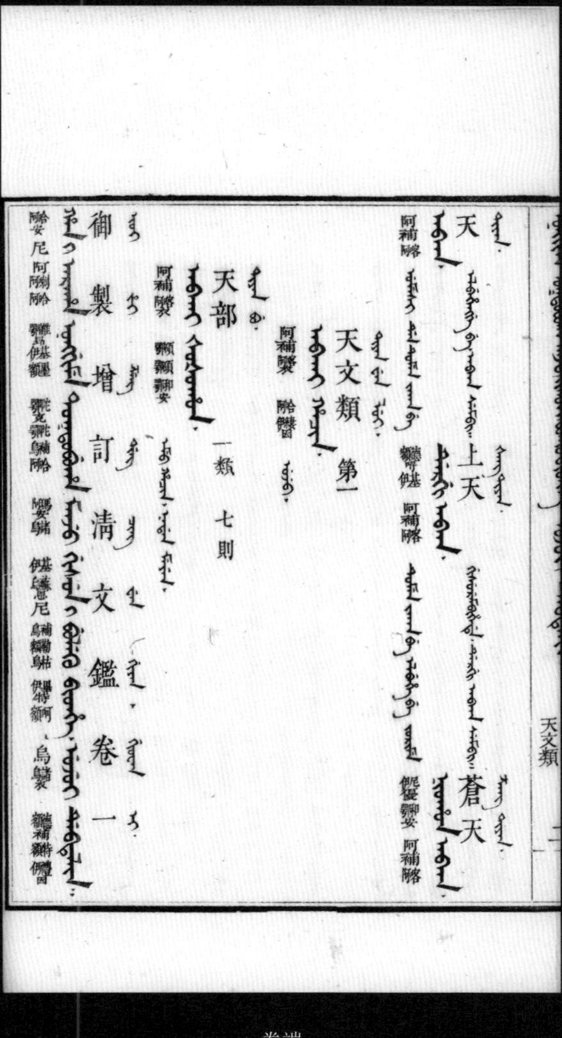

天　上天　蒼天
天文類　第一
天部　一類　七則
御製增訂清文鑑卷一

卷端
Beginning

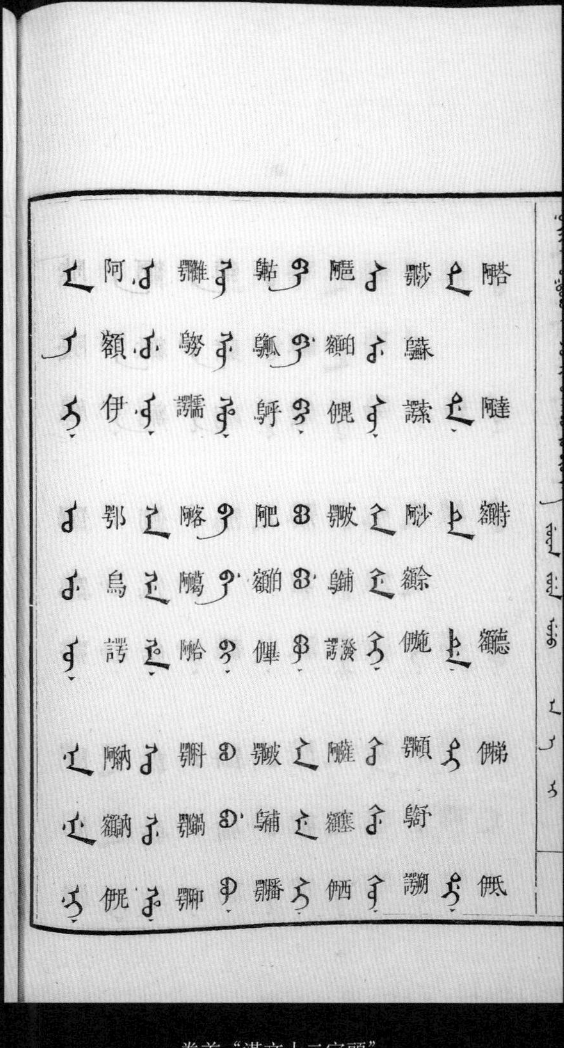

卷首“滿文十二字頭”
Preliminary remarks Twelve syllable groups of Manchu

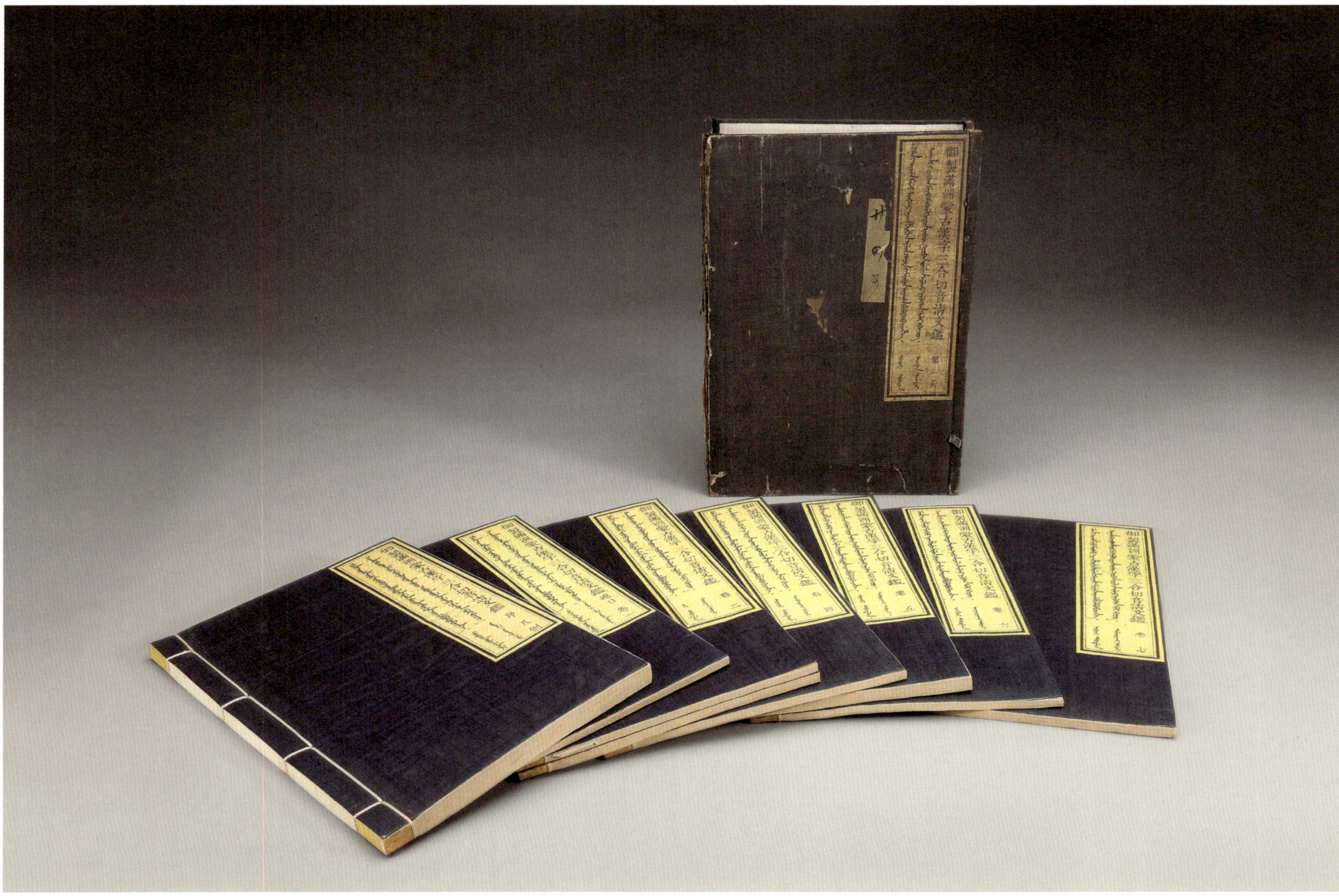

藍色素絹書函
Blue silk case

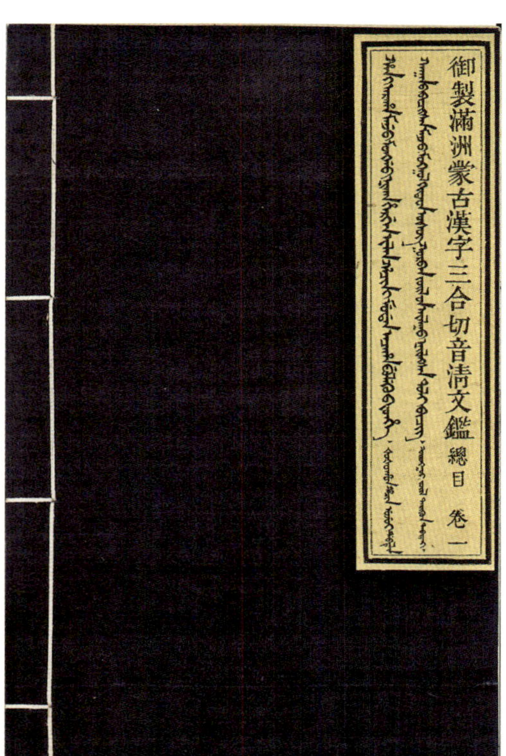

藍色素綢書面
Blue silk cover

書21863
《御製滿洲蒙古漢字三合切音清文鑑三十一卷首一卷》
清　高宗弘曆敕撰　阿桂等纂
清乾隆四十五年（1780）武英殿刻滿蒙漢合璧本
開本　縱30.8厘米　橫20厘米
版框　縱22.1厘米　橫17.1厘米
三十二册　四函

21

Inventory number: Shu 21863
Trilingual Dictionary of Manchu, Mongolian and Chinese Phonetically Transcribed, Adopting the Method of Qieyin
Thirty-one chapters as text, one chapter as preliminary remarks
Compiled at the order of the Qianlong emperor (r.1736-1795) by Agui et. al.
Printed in Manchu, Mongolian and Chinese in 1780
Format: 30.8 × 20 cm
Frame: 22.1 × 17.1 cm
Thirty-two volumes in four cases

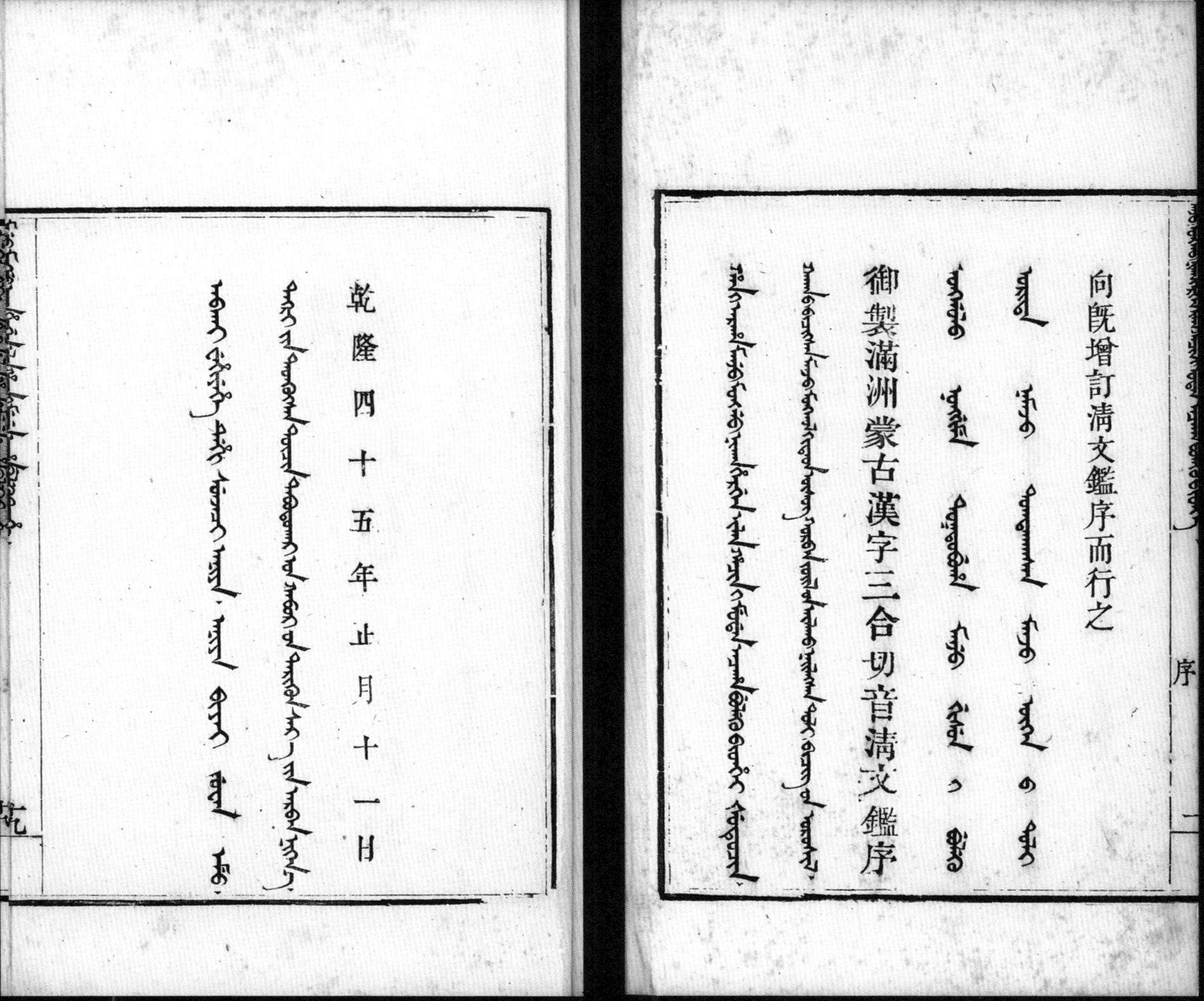

乾隆四十五年御製序
Preface by the Qianlong emperor in 1780

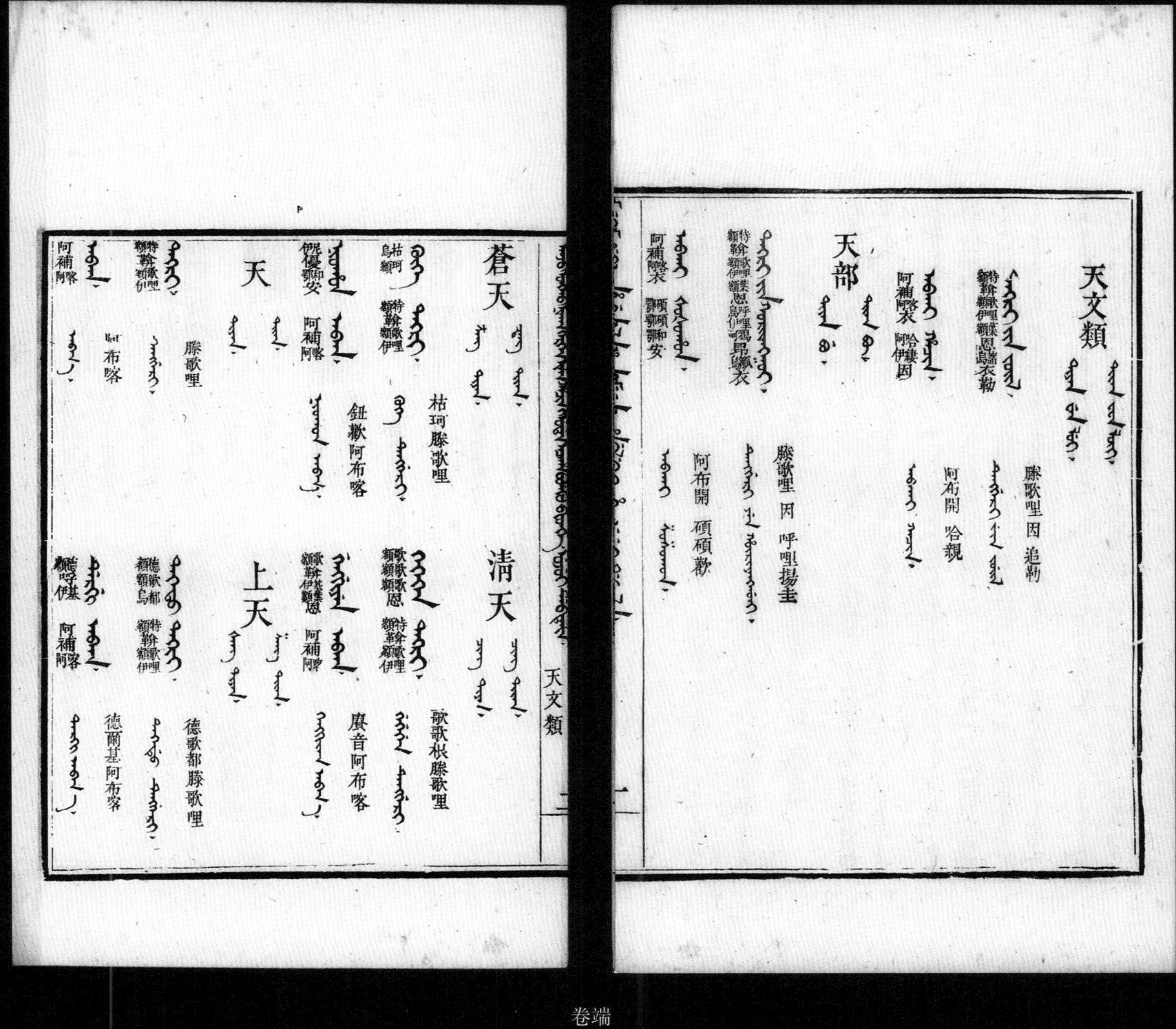

卷端
Beginning

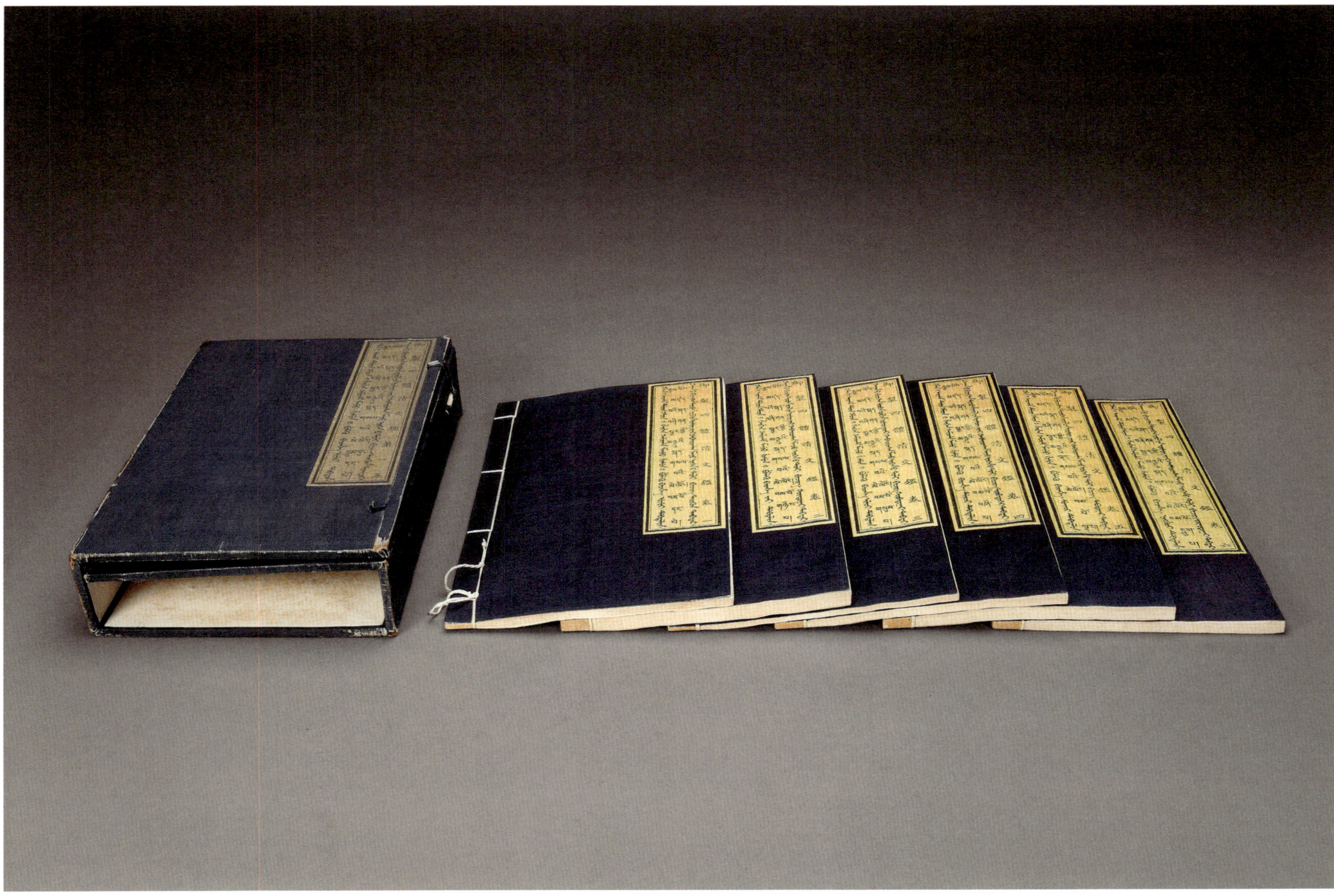

藍色素絹書面
Blue silk covers

書55
《御製四體清文鑒三十二卷補編四卷》
清　高宗弘曆敕撰
清乾隆五十九年（1794）武英殿刻滿藏蒙漢合璧本
開本　縱30.7厘米　橫18.8厘米
版框　縱21.7厘米　橫14.8厘米
三十六冊　六函

22

Inventory number: Shu 55
Dictionary of the Four Languages in the Qing Dynasty
Thirty-two chapters as text, four chapters as supplement
Compiled at the order of the Qianlong emperor (r.1736-1795)
Printed in Manchu, Tibetan, Mongolian and Chinese at the Hall of Martial Valour in 1794
Format: 30.7 × 18.8 cm
Frame: 21.7 × 14.8 cm
Thirty-six volumes in six cases

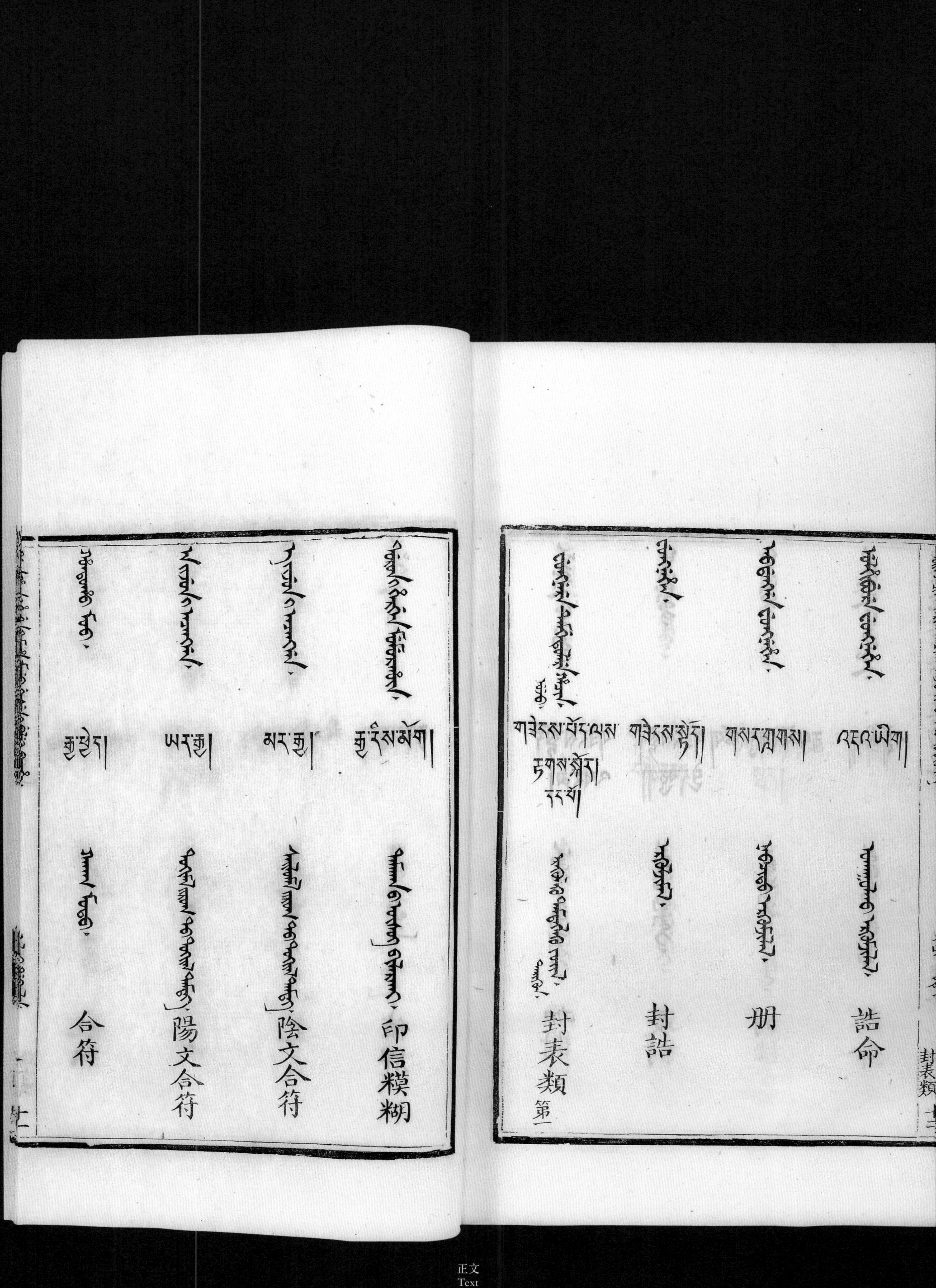

封表類第一

གཟེངས་བོད་ལས་ཧགས་སྐོར་དང་པོ། 封表類第一

འཇའ་ཡིག། 誥命

གསེར་གླེགས། 册

གཟེངས་སྤྲོད། 封誥

རྒྱ་རིས་མོག། 印信糢糊

མར་རྒྱ། 陰文合符

ཡར་རྒྱ། 陽文合符

རྒྱ་སྦྱེད། 合符

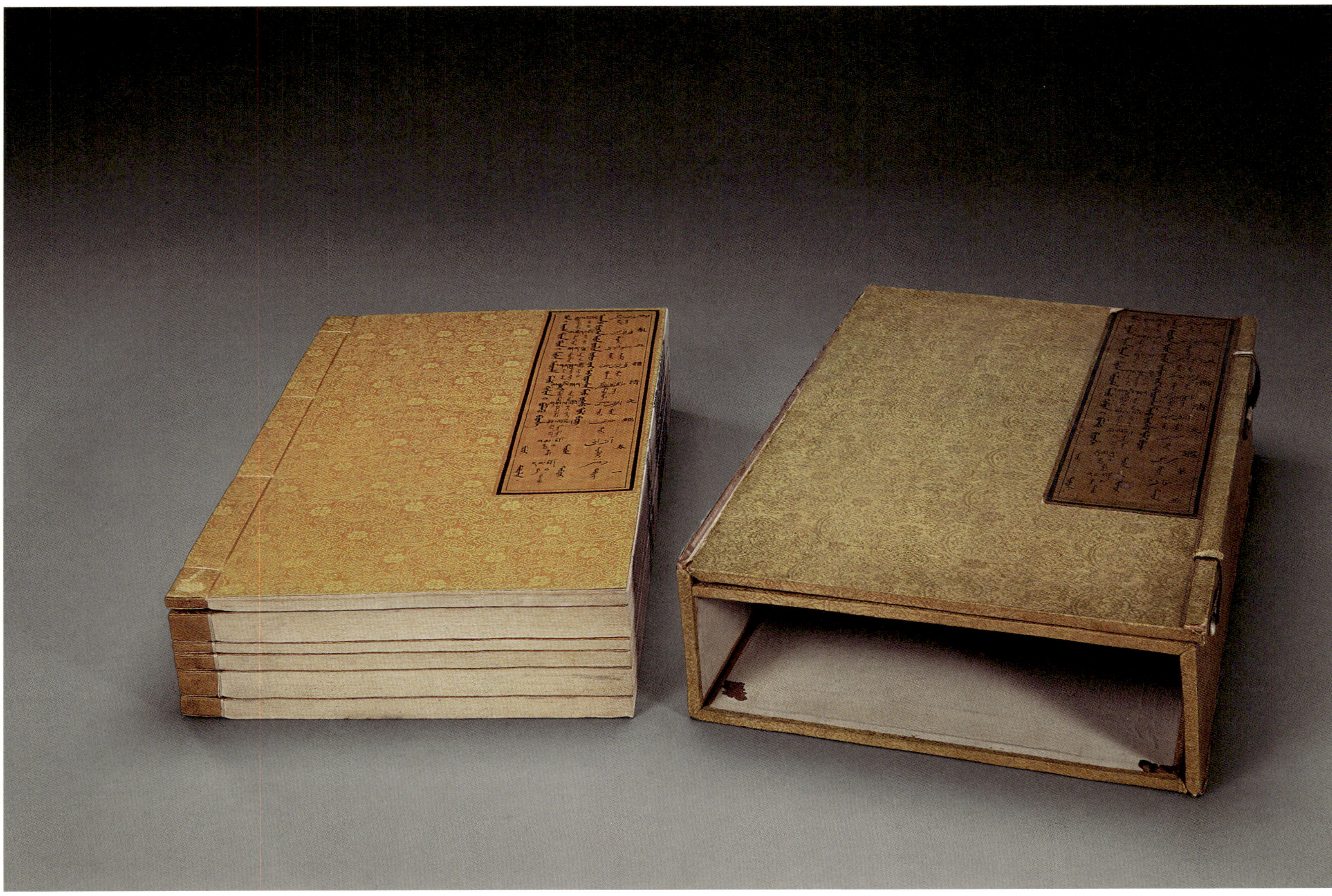

明黄色纏枝花紋暗花綾書函
Bright yellow twill-weave silk case with veiled pattern of floral scrolls

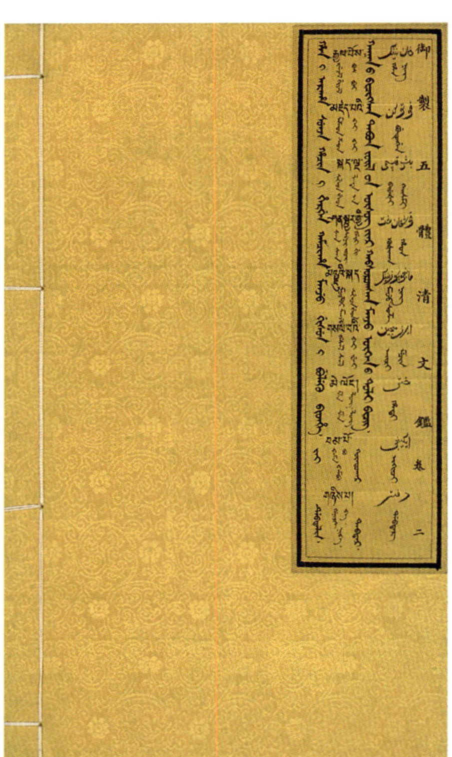

明黄色纏枝花紋暗花綾書面
Bright yellow twill-weave silk cover with veiled pattern of floral scrolls

書21840
《御製五體清文鑒三十二卷補編四卷》
清　清高宗弘曆敕撰
清乾隆五十九年（1794）内府精寫滿藏蒙維漢合璧本
開本　縱42厘米　橫24.5厘米
版框　縱34.2厘米　橫20.1厘米
三十六册　六函

23

Inventory number: Shu 21840
Dictionary of the Five Languages in the Qing Dynasty
Thirty-two chapters as text, four chapters as supplement
Written at the order of the Qianlong emperor (r.1736-1795)
Transcribed in Manchu, Tibetan, Mongolian, Uighur and Chinese by the Qing court in 1794
Format: 42 × 24.5 cm
Frame: 34.2 × 20.1 cm
Thirty-six volumes in six cases

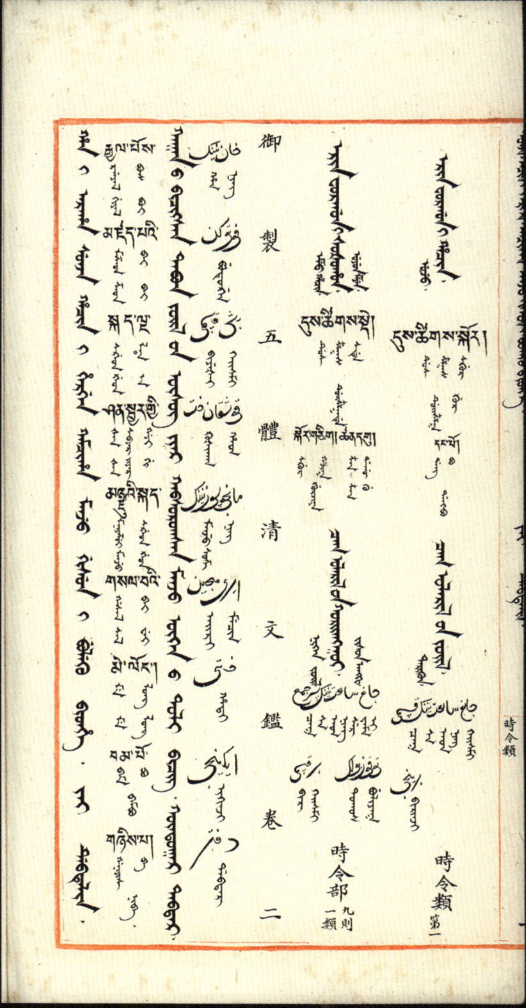

卷端
Beginning

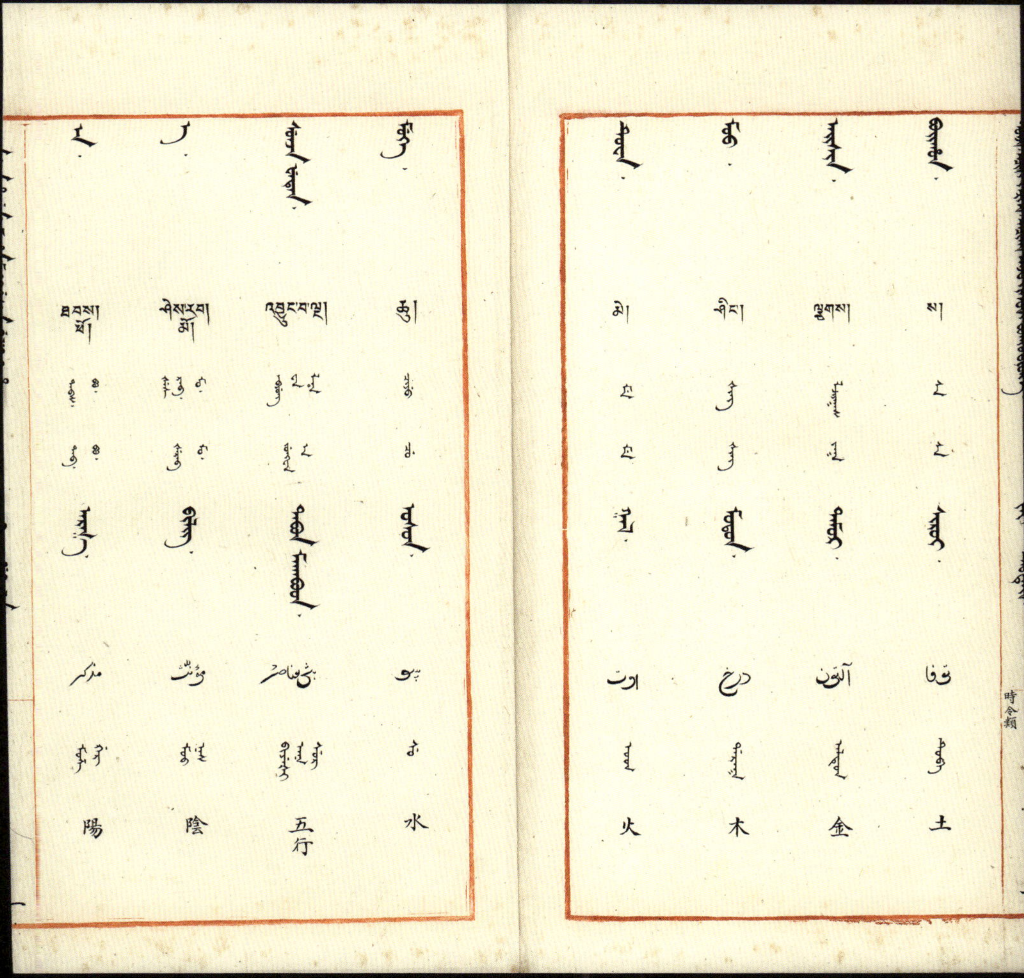

正文
Text

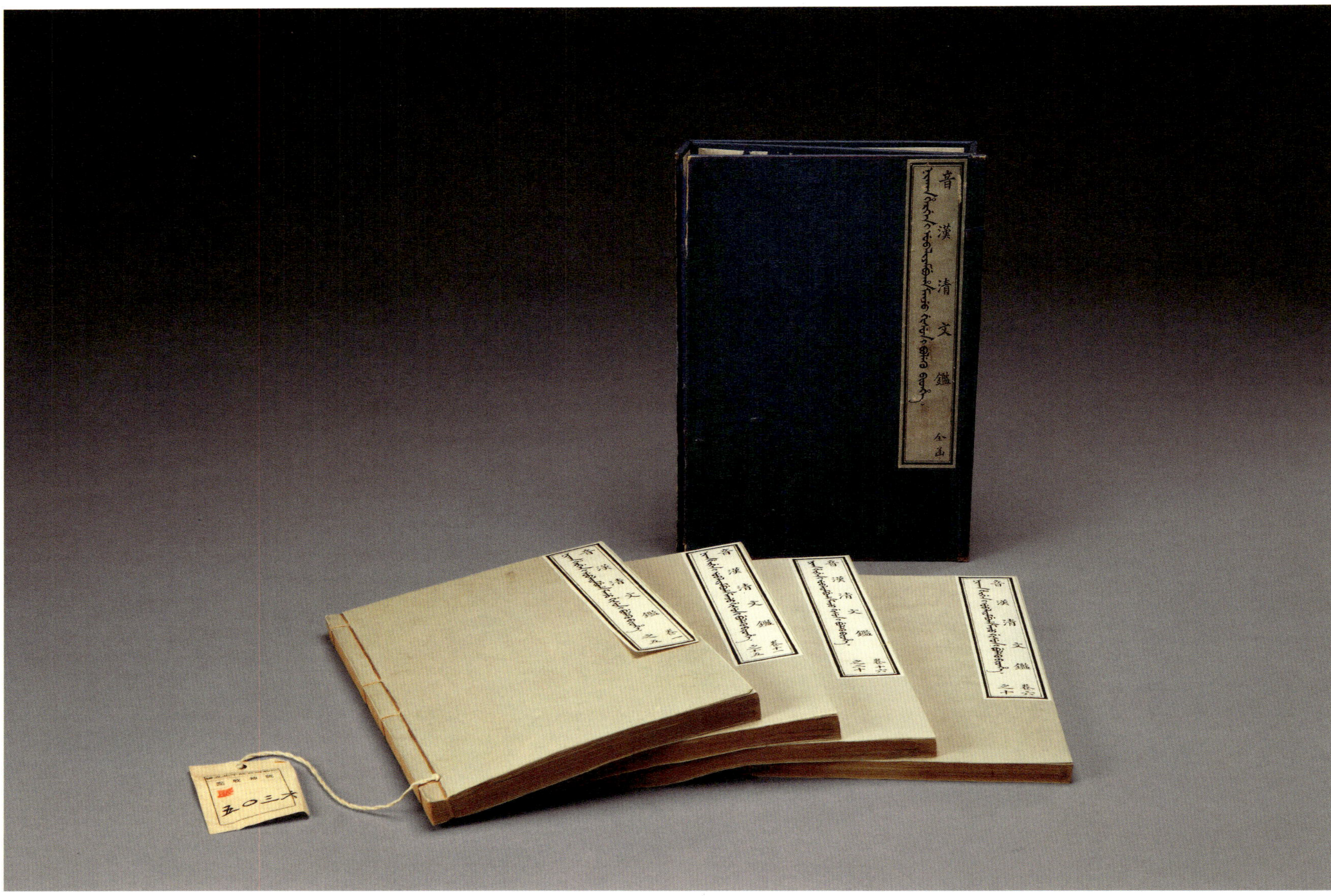

藍色素絹書函
Blue silk case

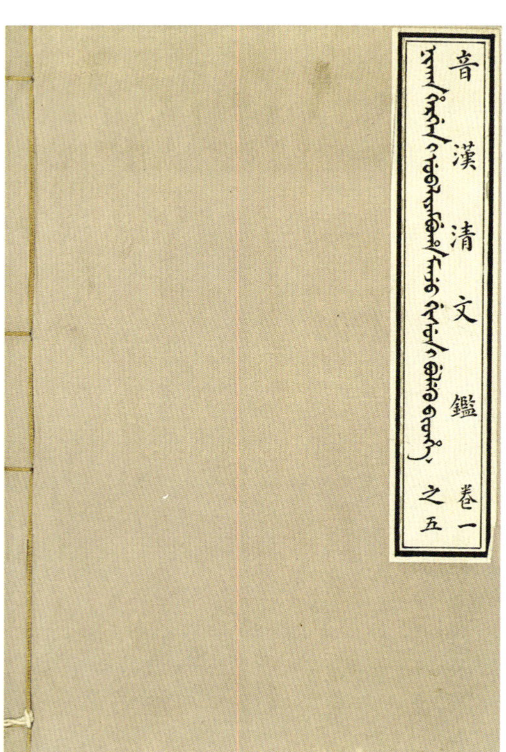

香色紙書面
Light brown paper cover

書21861

《音漢清文鑒二十卷》

清　董佳明鐸編

清雍正十三年（1735）刻滿漢合璧本

開本　縱23.7厘米　橫15.7厘米

版框　縱20.5厘米　橫14.6厘米

四冊　一函

24

Inventory number: Shu 21861

Manchu-Chinese Dictionary

Twenty chapters

Compiled by Dongjia Mingduo, Qing dynasty (1644-1911)

Printed in Manchu and Chinese in 1735

Format: 23.7 × 15.7 cm

Frame: 20.5 × 14.6 cm

Four volumes in one case

日月經天　江河行地

頒行敷教　內外遵循

義蘊宏深　註疏詳切

國語之大成　正萬世之永賴

清文鑑　集

欽惟

雍正十三年董佳明鐸序

Preface by Dongjia Mingduo in 1735

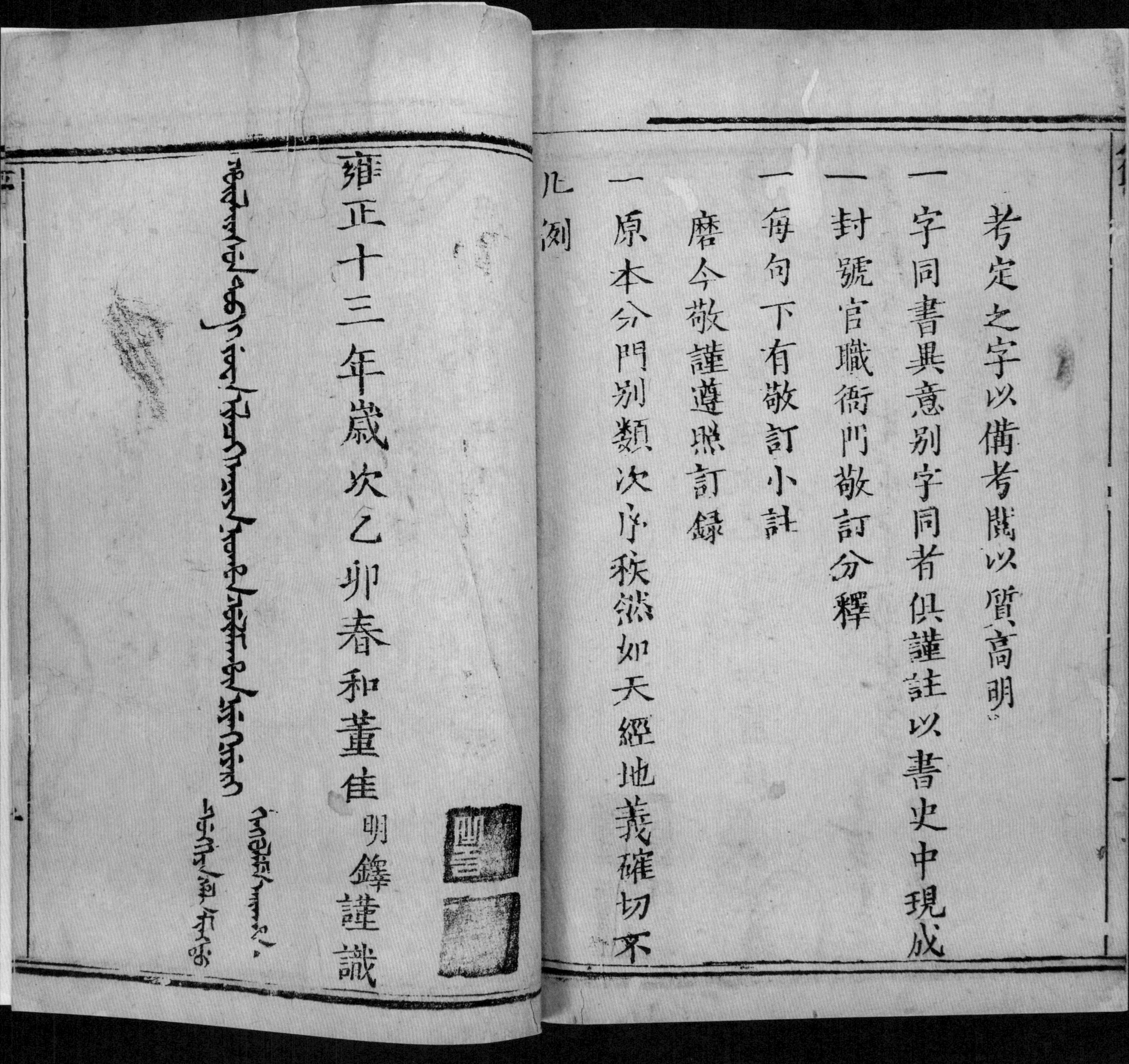
考定之字以備考閱以質高明
一字同書異意别字同者俱謹註以書史中現成
一封號官職衙門敬訂分釋
一每句下有敬訂小註
磨今敬謹遵照訂錄
一原本分門别類次序秩然如天經地義確切不
凡例
雍正十三年歲次乙卯春和董佳明鐸謹識

凡例
Notes on the use of the book

昧爽 黎明 天明了 大亮了

晨光 曙明之前 晨光現 東方明 天山曙明

蒼天 碧天 穹蒼 天肅 秋色慘淡

上天 指覆萬物者而言 清天

昊天

天 氣之輕清上浮至高無上覆萬物者爲天又包地轉旋于外化生萬物者又天無實形地之上空虛者皆天也又春爲蒼天夏爲昊天秋爲旻天冬爲上天又天有九野東方蒼天東南方陽天南方炎天西南方朱天西方顥天西北方幽天北方玄天東北方變天中央鈞天 又謂乾

天文類 一類 四段

音漢清文鑑 第一卷

卷端
Beginning

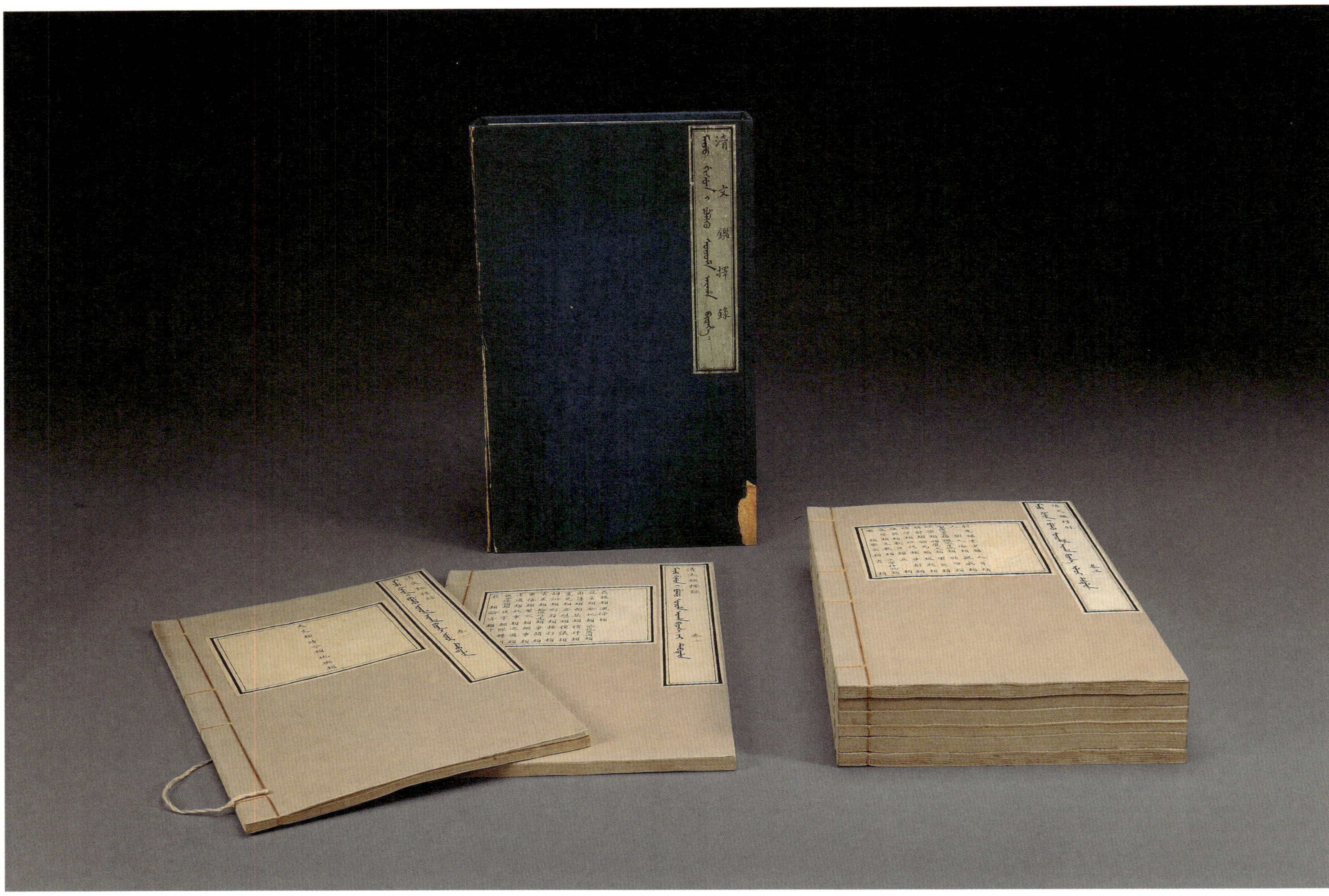

藍色素絹書函
Blue silk case

書21859
《清文鑑擇録八卷》
清　佚名輯
清内府精寫滿漢合璧本
開本　縱31.7厘米　橫19厘米
版框　縱22厘米　橫15.8厘米
八册　一函

25

Inventory number: Shu 21859
Selections from the Dictionary of the Qing Language
Eight chapters
Anonymous, Qing dynasty (1644-1911)
Transcribed in Manchu and Chinese by the Qing court
Format: 31.7 × 19 cm
Frame: 22 × 15.8 cm
Eight volumes in one case

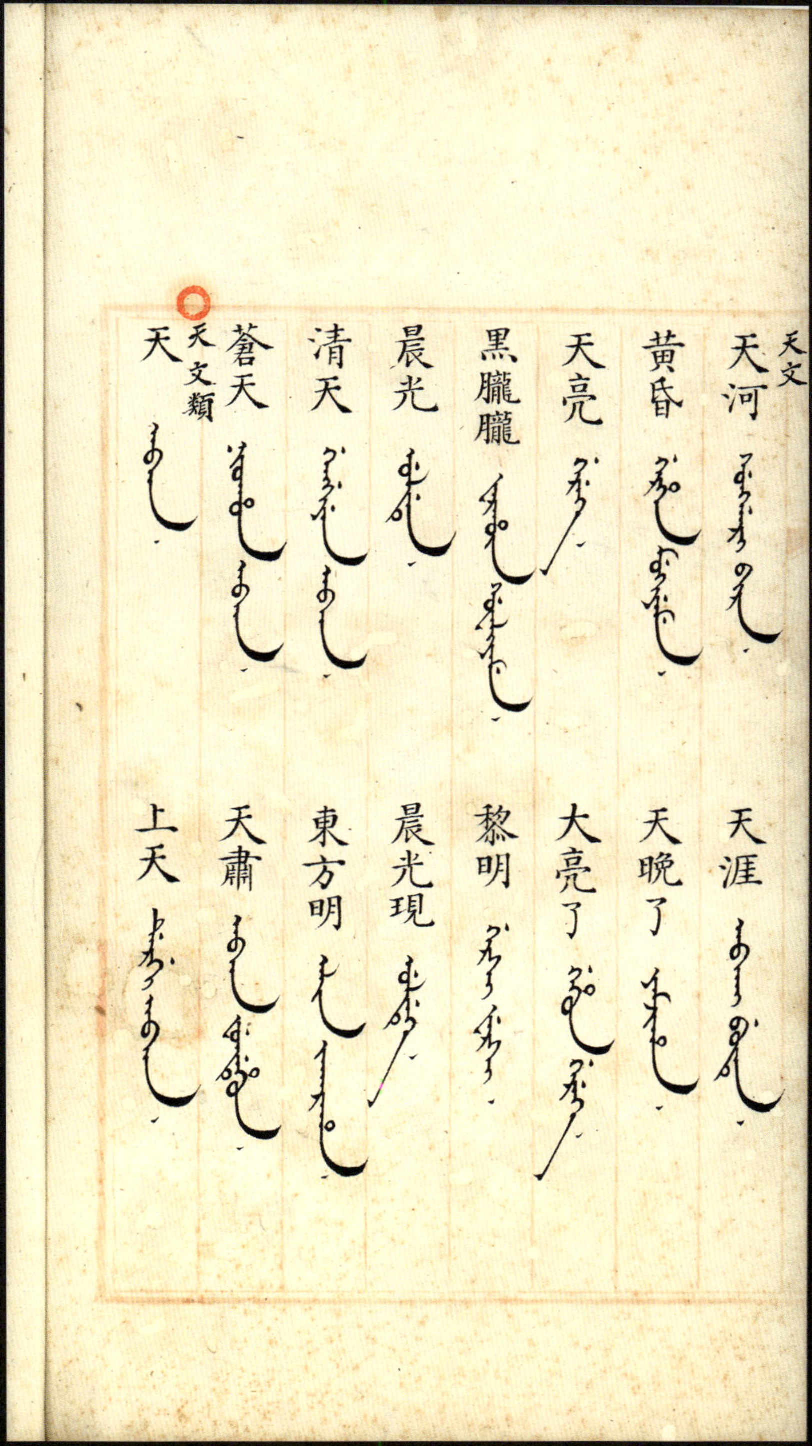

正文
Text

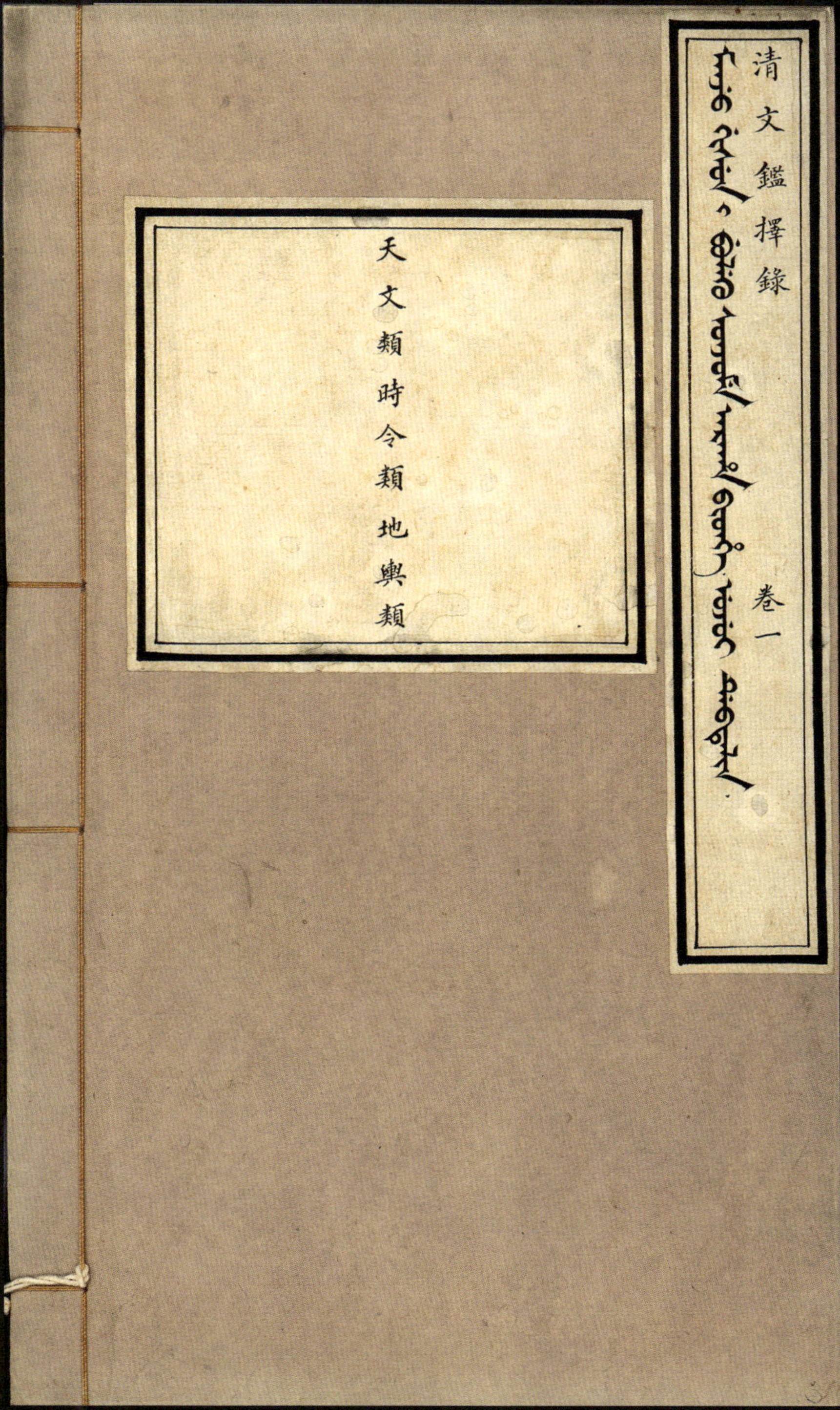

香色紙書面
Light brown paper cover

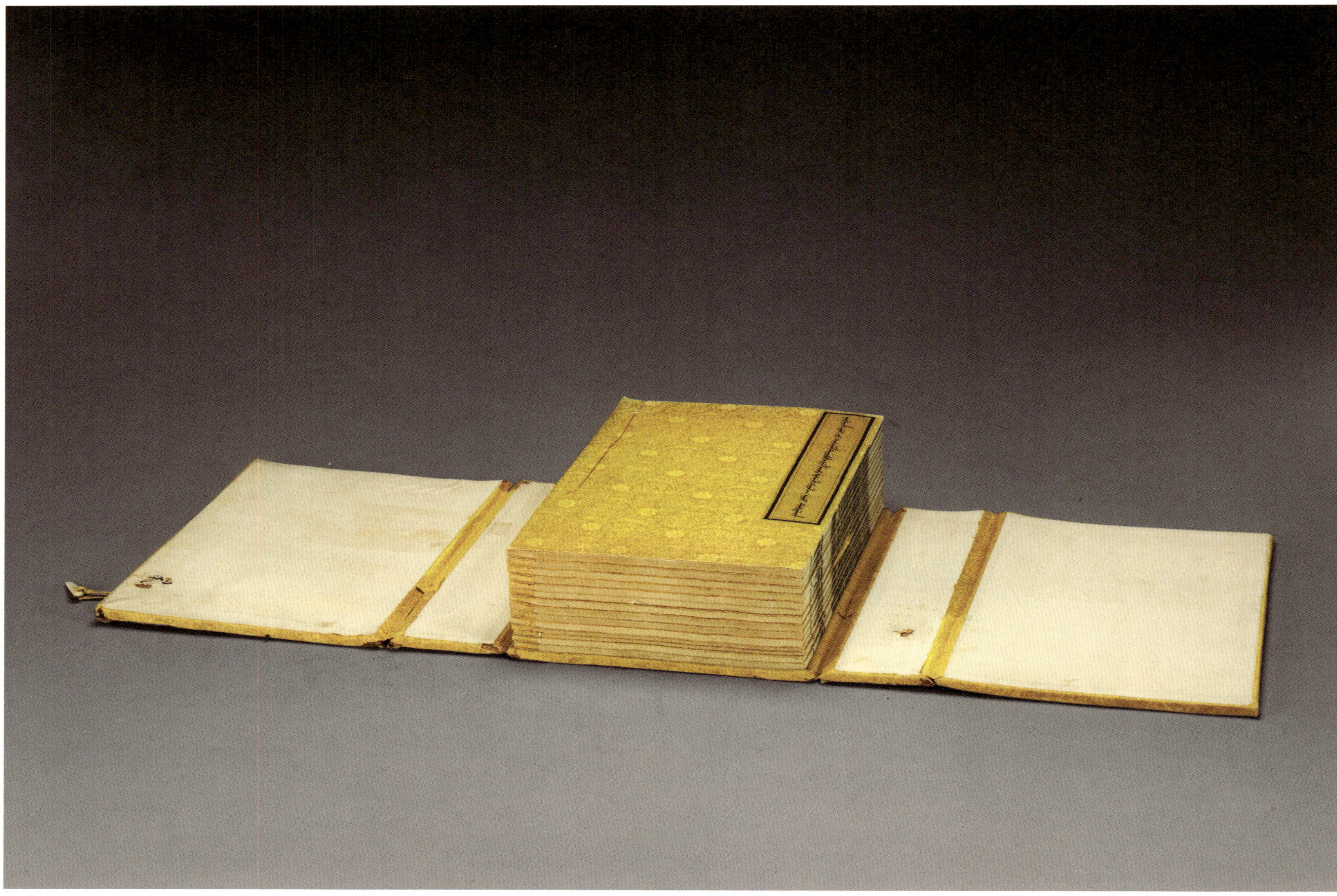

外觀
Exterior

書21790
《實録内摘出舊清語十四卷》
清　高宗弘曆敕撰
清乾隆年間内府刻滿文本
開本　縱28.4厘米　橫17.8厘米
版框　縱20.2厘米　橫14.6厘米
十四册　一函

26

Inventory number: Shu 21790
Old Qing Language Selected from Veritable Records
Fourteen chapters
Compiled at the order of the Qianlong emperor (r.1736-1795)
Printed in Manchu by the Qing court in the Qianlong period
Format: 28.4 × 17.8 cm
Frame: 20.2 × 14.6 cm
Fourteen volumes in one case

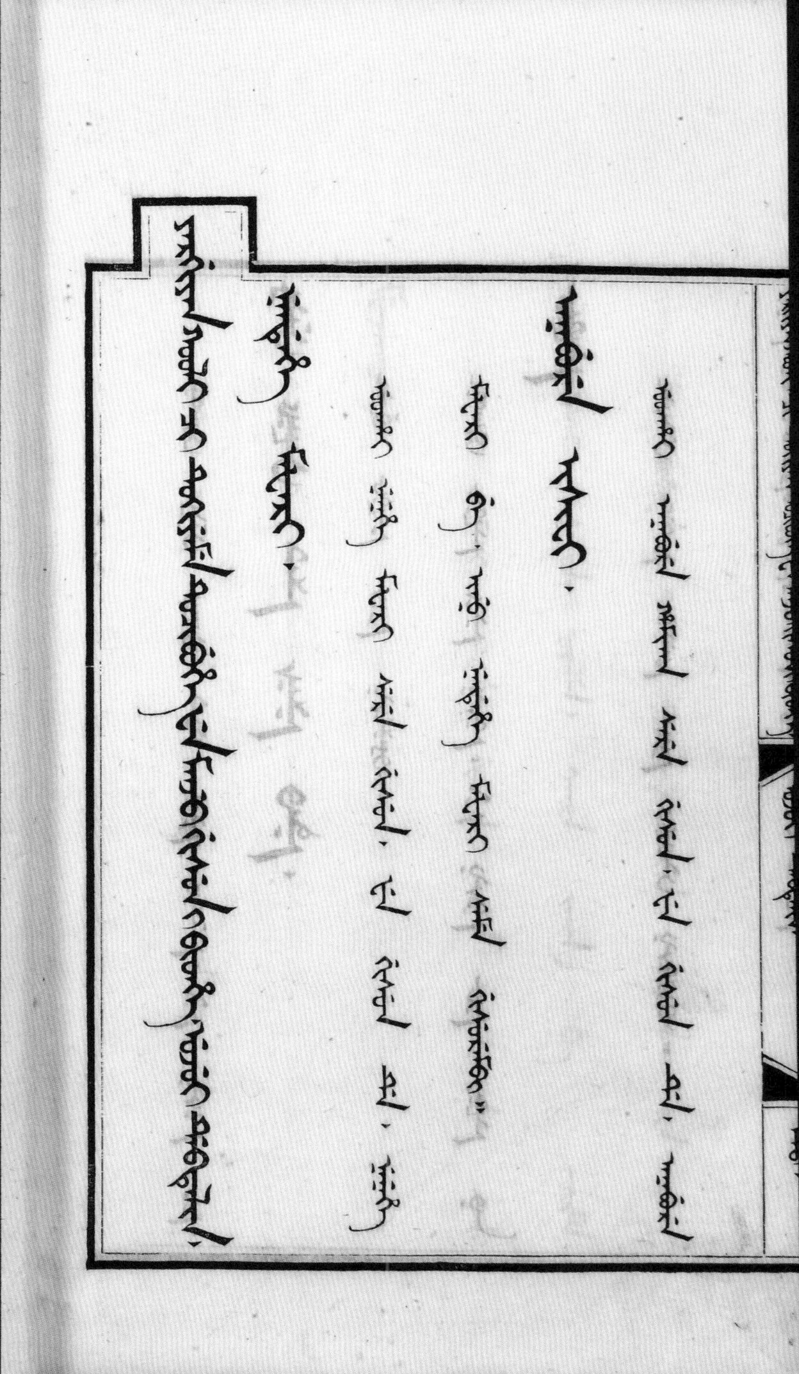

卷端
Beginning

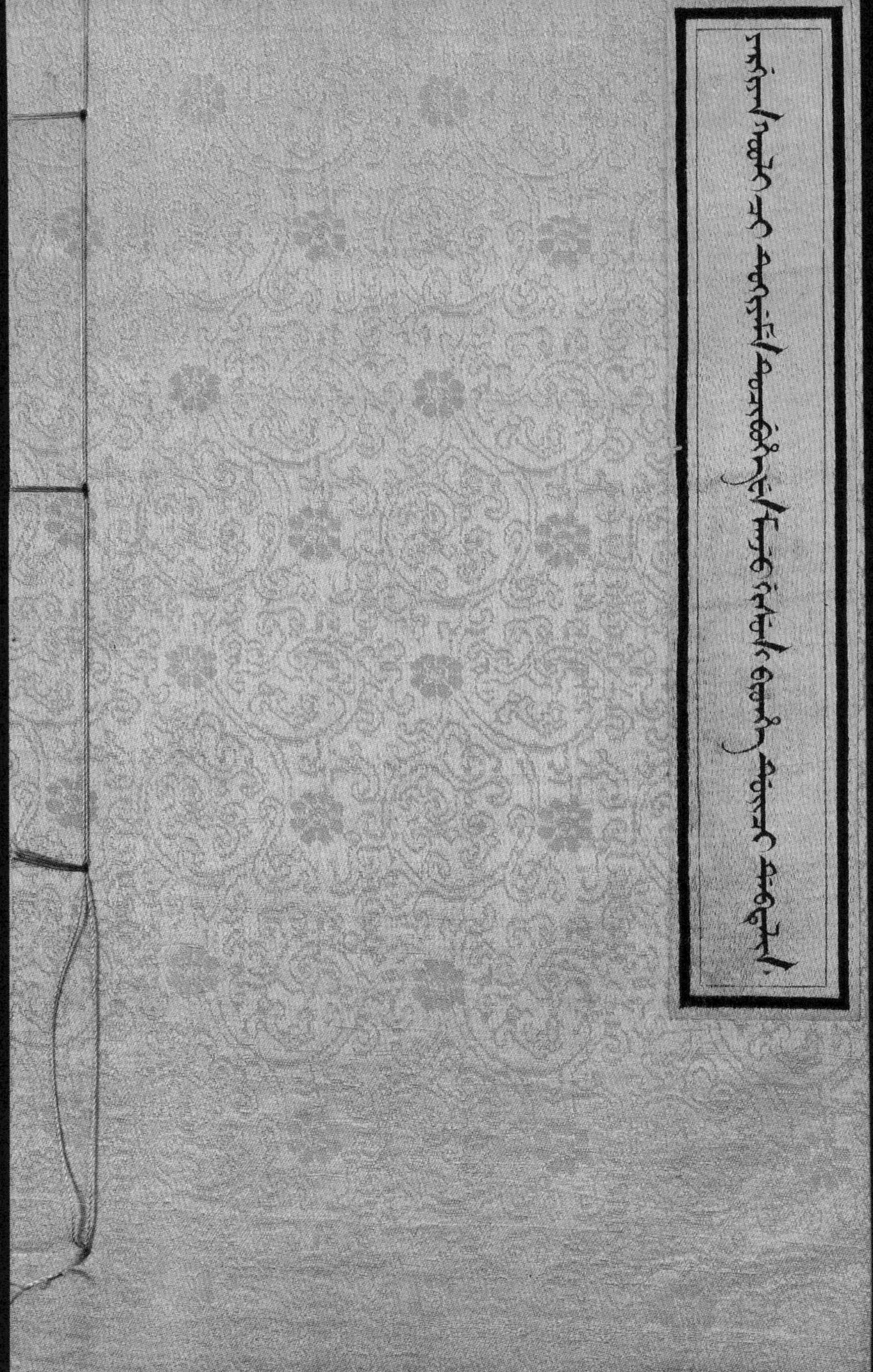

明黄色纏枝花紋暗花綾書面
Yellow twill-weave silk cover with veiled pattern of floral scrolls

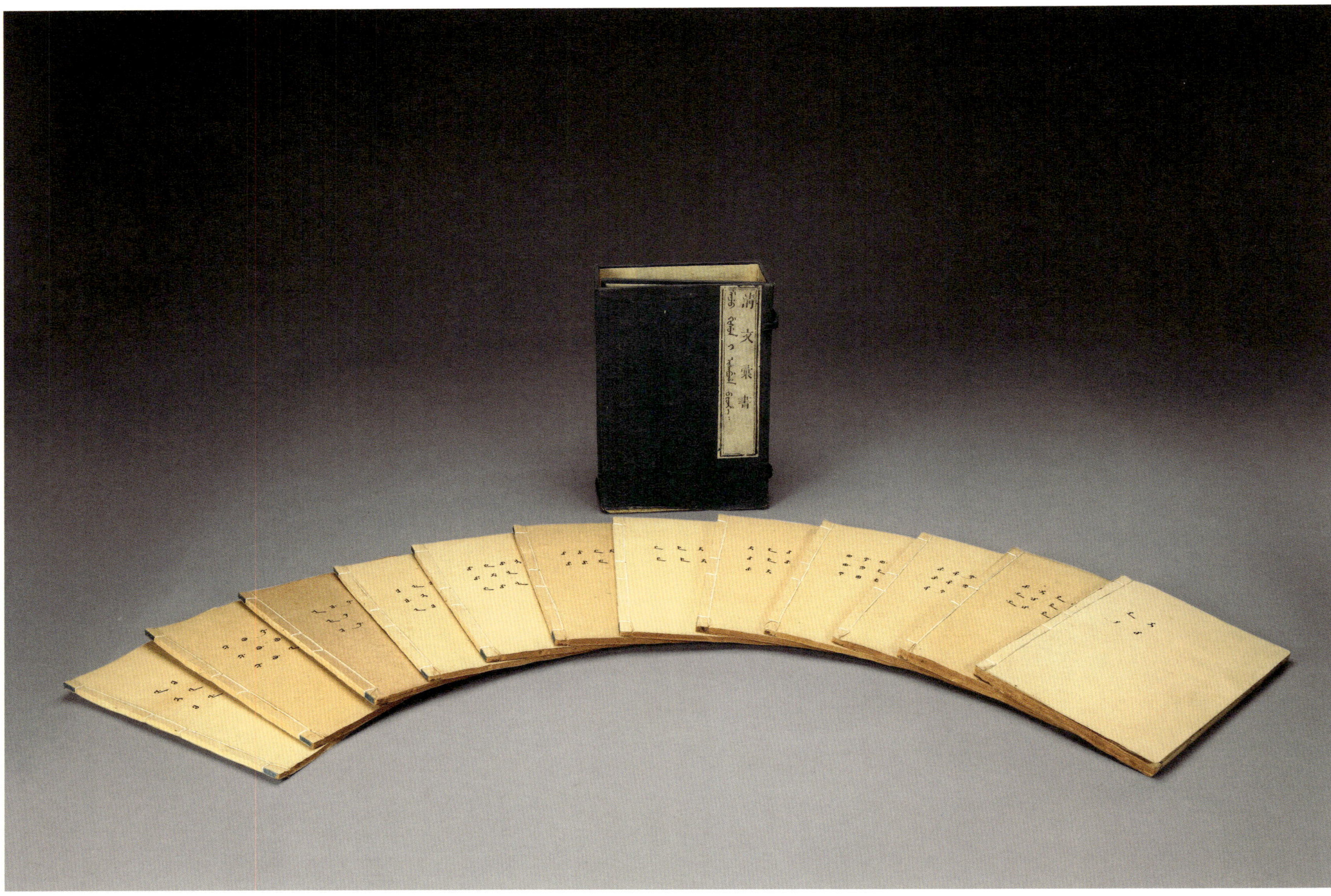

藍色布書函
Blue cloth case

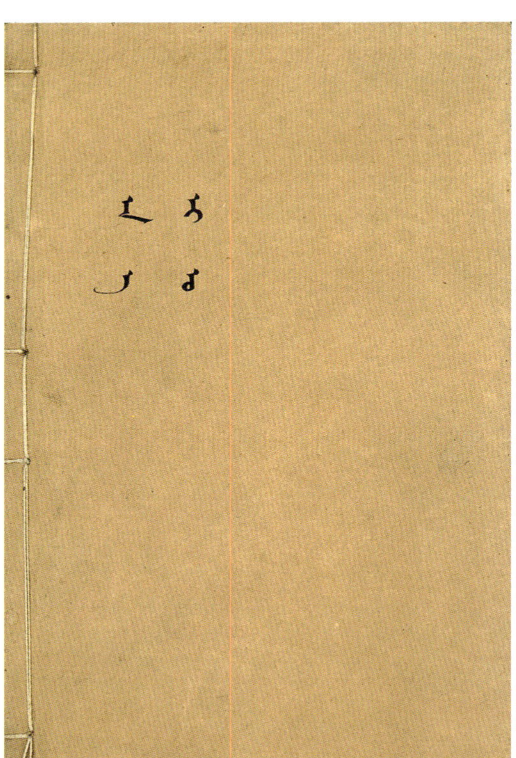

黃色紙書面
Yellow paper cover

27

書21820
《清文彙書十二卷》
清　李延基編
清乾隆十六年（1751）京都藜照閣藏版滿漢合璧本
開本　縱23.7厘米　橫16厘米
版框　縱20.9厘米　橫14.6厘米
十二册　一函

Inventory number: Shu 21820
Comprehensive Dictionary of the Qing Language
Twelve chapters
Li Yanji, Qing dynasty (1644-1911)
Printed in Manchu and Chinese in 1751 by the Lizhao Belvedere in Beijing
Format: 23.7 × 16 cm
Frame: 20.9 × 14.6 cm
Twelve volumes in one case

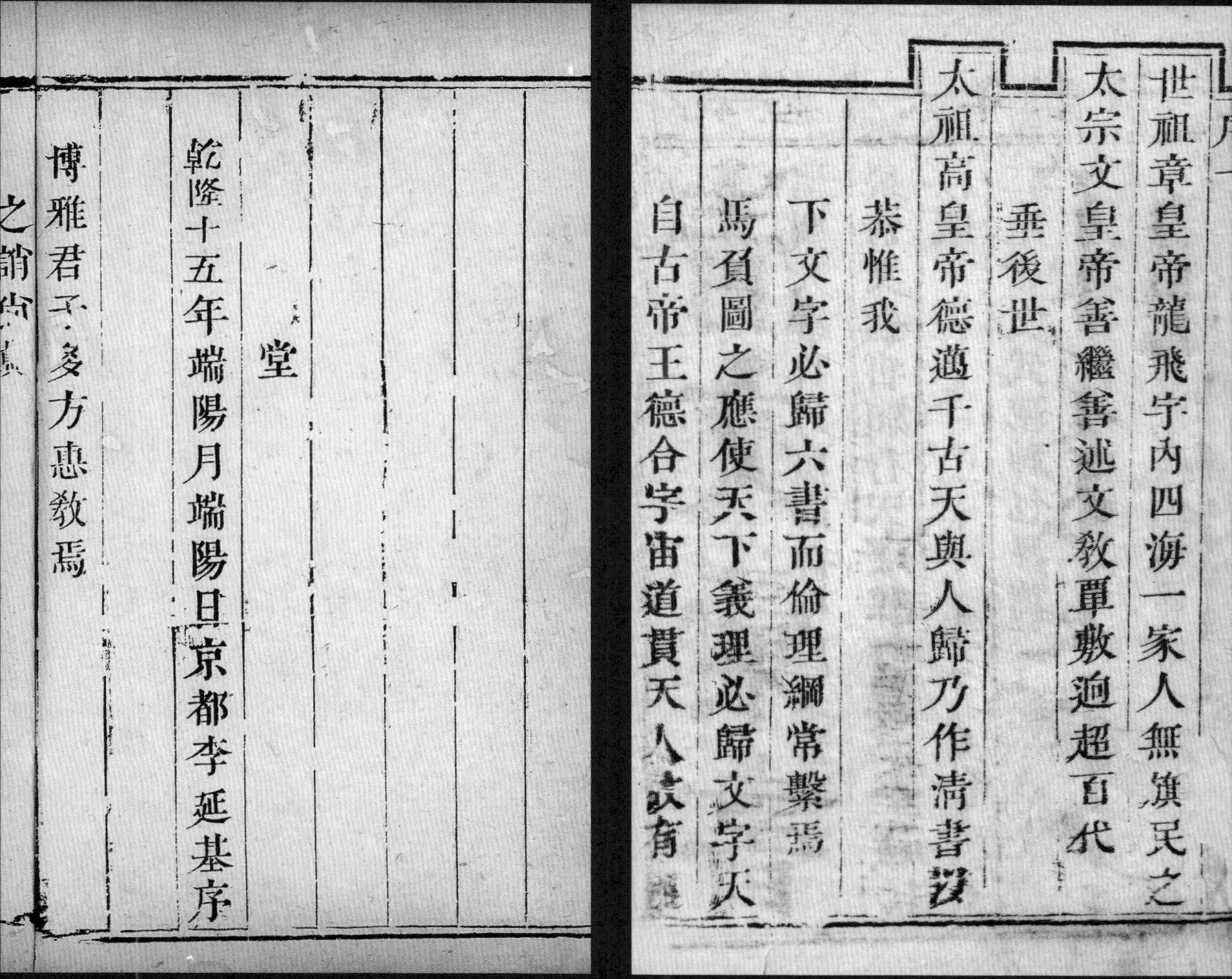

乾隆十五年李延基序
Preface by Li Yanji in 1750

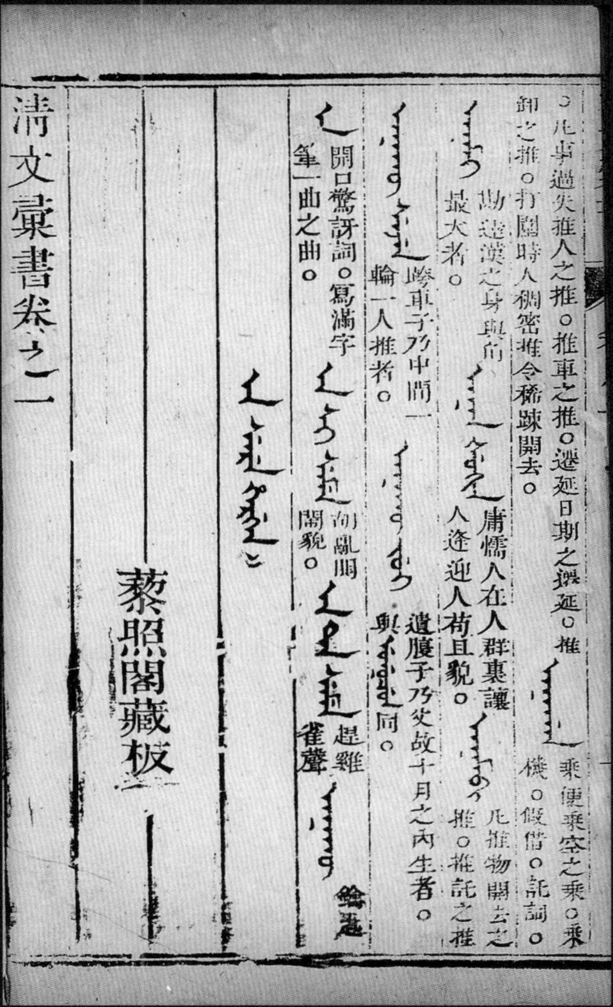

卷端
Beginning

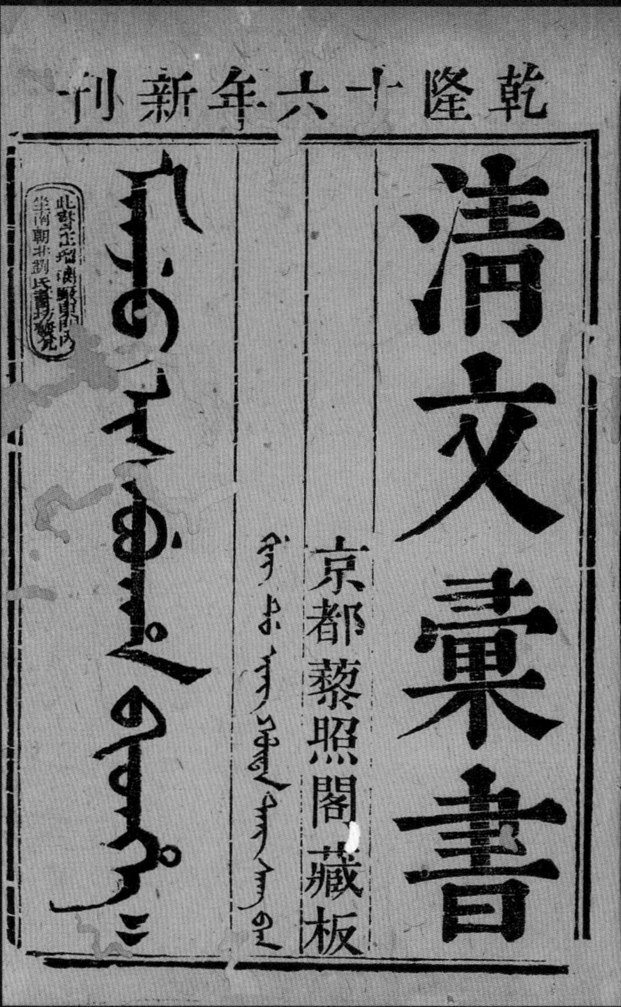

牌記
Copyright page

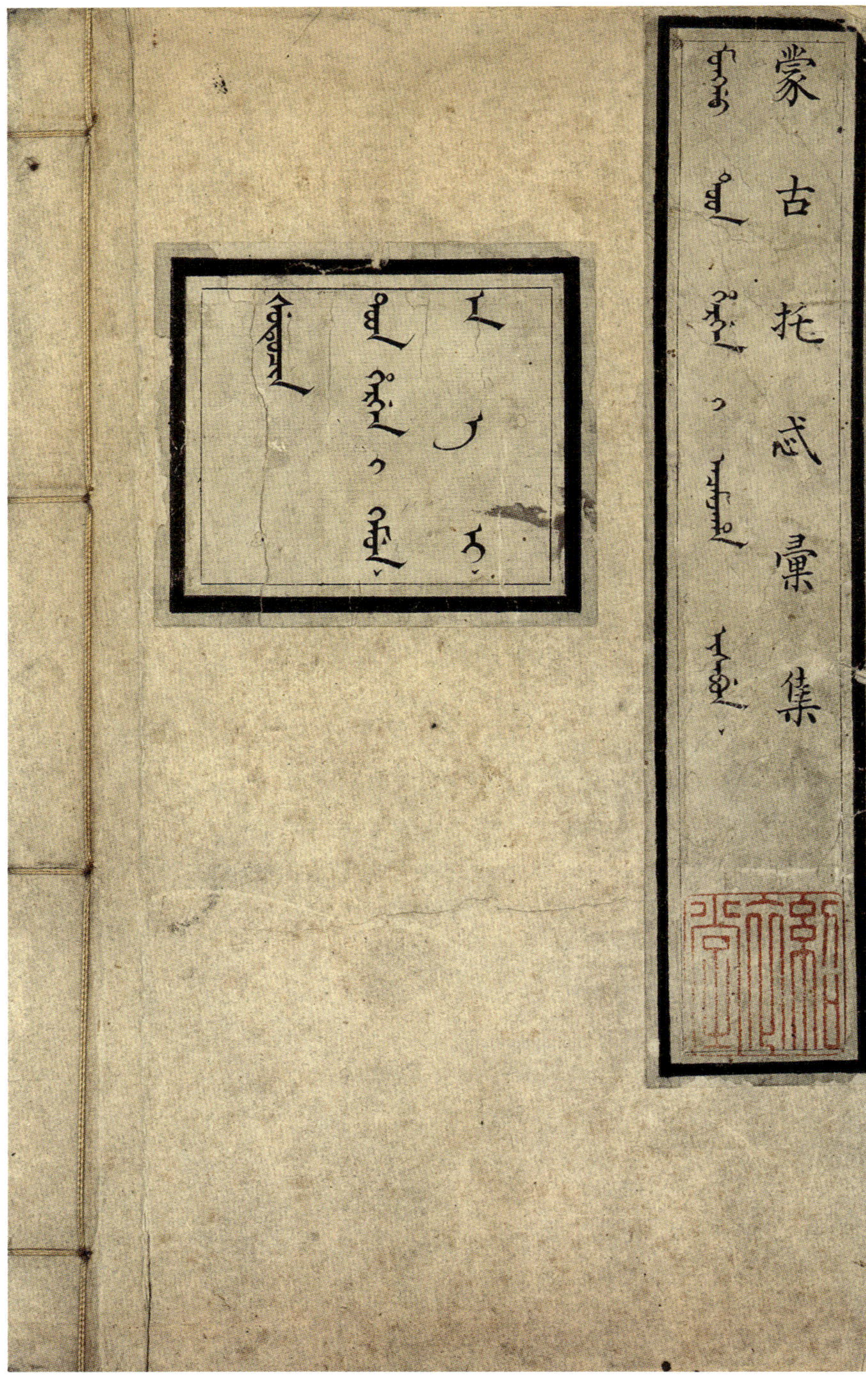

黄色紙書面
Yellow paper cover

28

書21832

《蒙古托忒彙集八卷》

清　富俊編

清嘉慶二年（1797）抄滿漢蒙合璧本

開本　縱28厘米　橫18.1厘米

版框　縱21厘米　橫15厘米

八冊　一函（其文種包括滿文、漢文、蒙文、托忒蒙古文四種）

Inventory number: Shu 21832

Tuote Mongolian Dictionary

Eight chapters

Compiled by Fujun, Qing dynasty (1644-1911)

Transcribed in Manchu, Chinese and Mongolian in 1797

Format: 28 × 18.1 cm

Frame: 21 × 15 cm

Eight volumes in one case

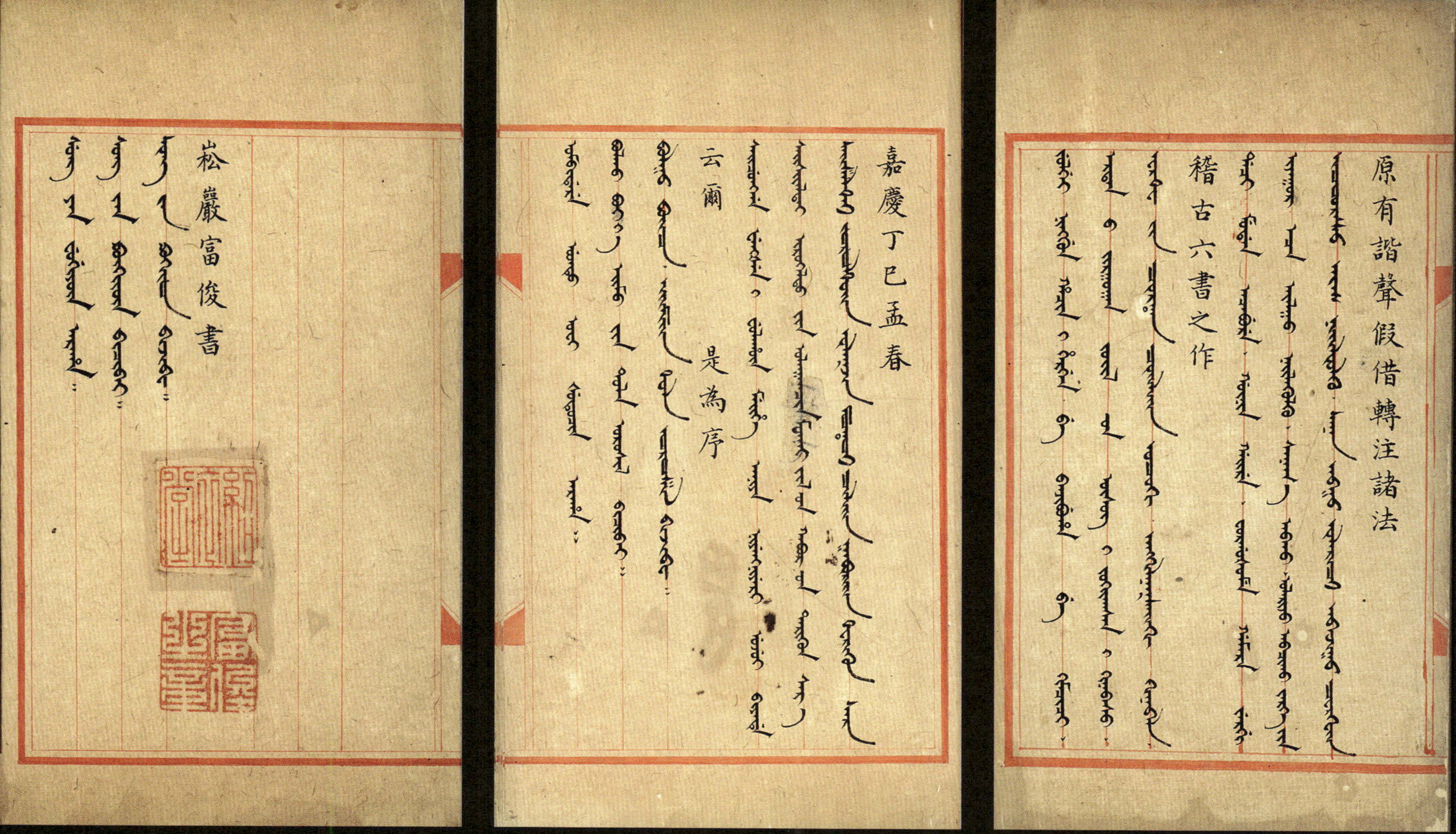

嘉慶二年富俊序
Preface by Fujun in 1797

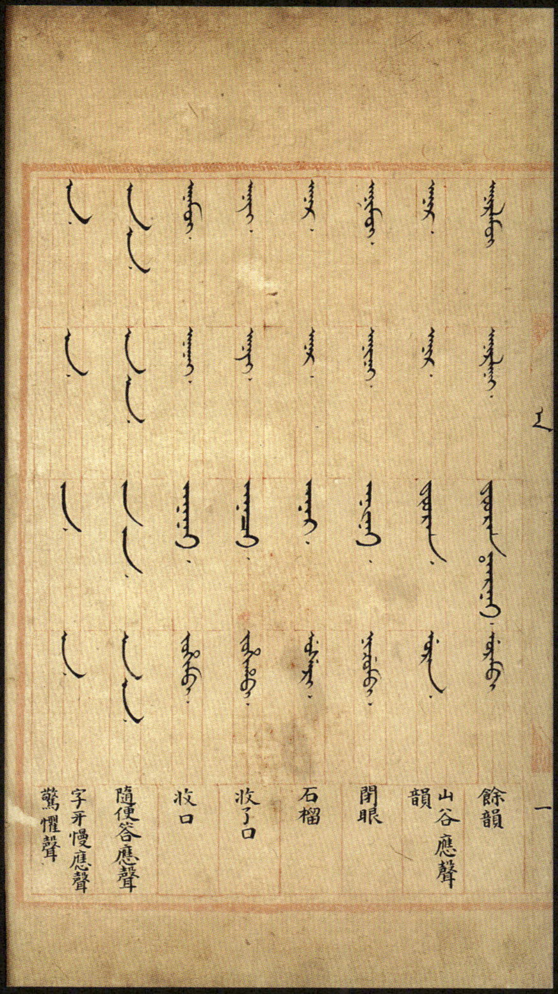

卷端
Beginning

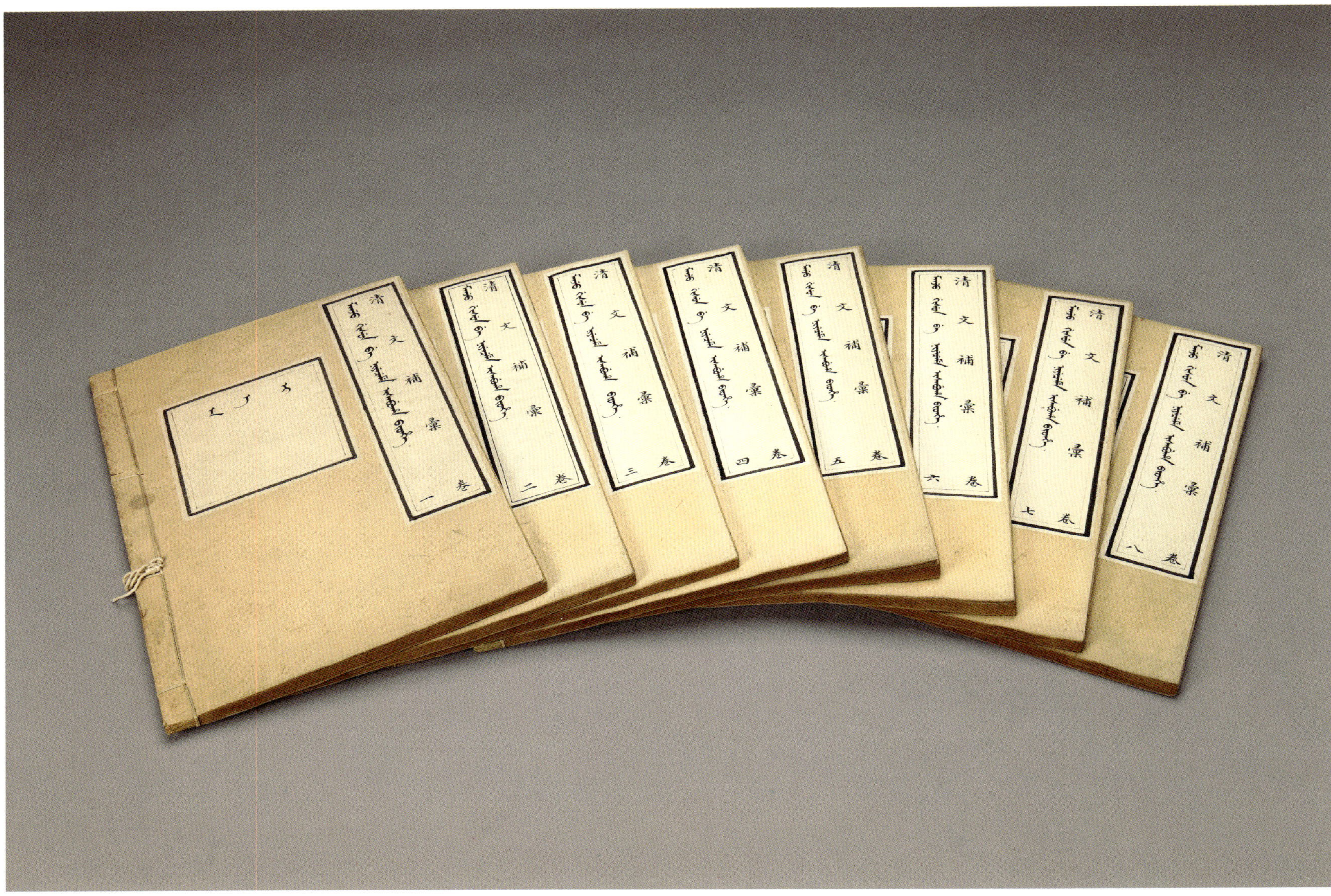

外觀
Exterior

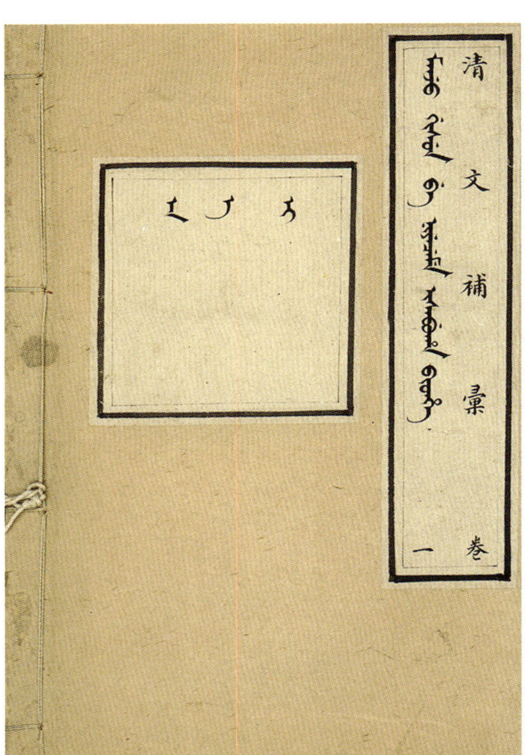

黄色紙書面
Yellow paper cover

書21829
《清文補彙八卷》
清　宜興撰
清乾隆五十一年（1786）刻滿漢合璧本
開本　縱24.6厘米　橫16.6厘米
版框　縱20.5厘米　橫15厘米
八册　一函

29

Inventory number: Shu 21829
Supplemental Dictionary of the Qing Language
Eight chapters
Written by Yixing, Qing dynasty (1644-1911)
Printed in Manchu and Chinese in 1786
Format: 24.6 × 16.6 cm
Frame: 20.5 × 15 cm
Eight volumes in one case

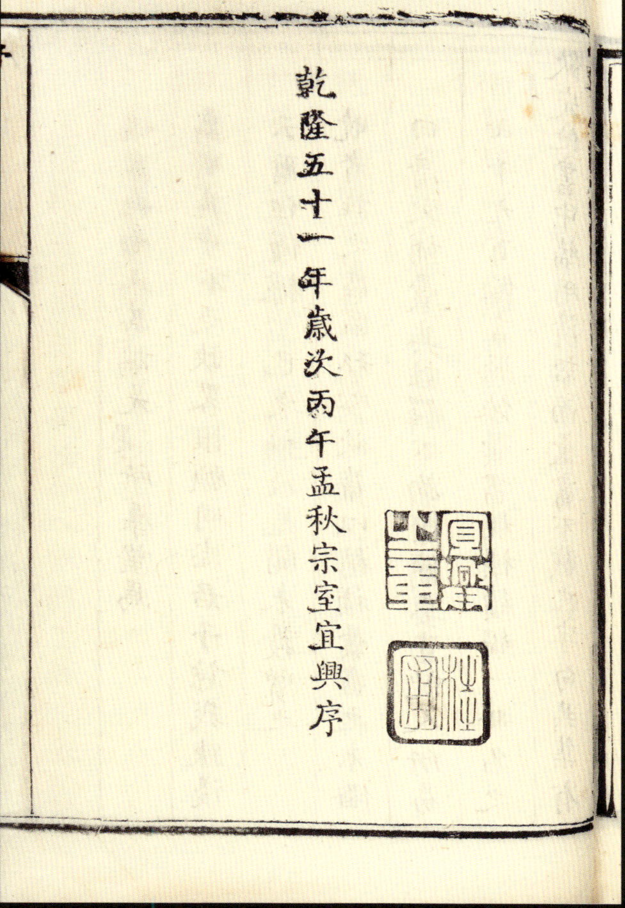

乾隆五十一年歲次丙午孟秋宗室宜興序

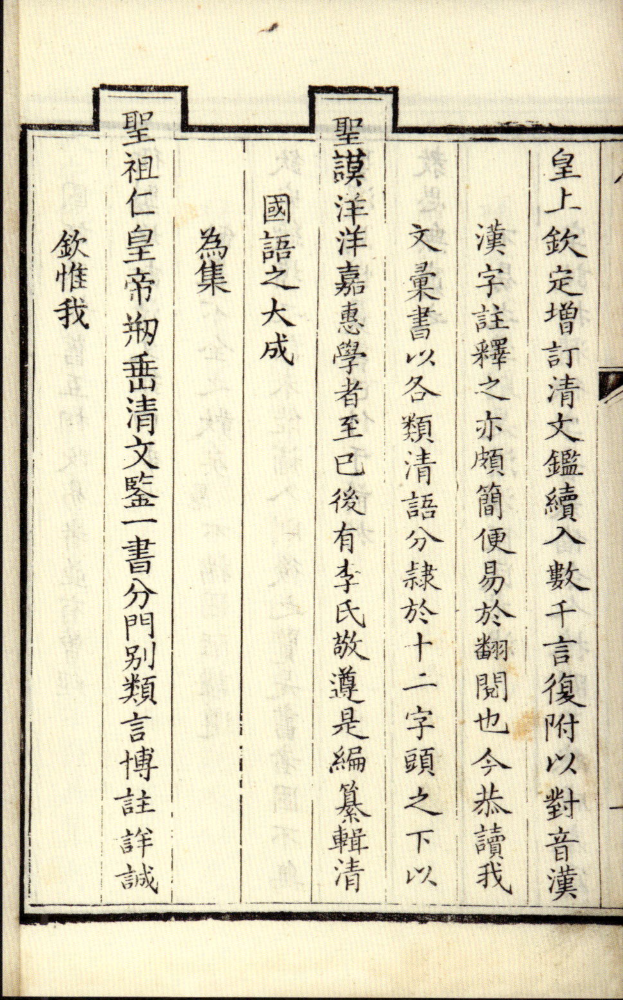

欽惟我
聖祖仁皇帝御製清文鑒一書分門別類言博註詳誠
為集
國語之大成
聖謨洋洋嘉惠學者至已後有李氏敬遵是編纂輯清
文彙書以各類清語分隸於十二字頭之下以
漢字註釋之亦頗簡便易於翻閱也今恭讀我
皇上欽定增訂清文鑑續入數千言復附以對音漢

嘉慶七年宗室宜興序
Preface by Yixing in 1802

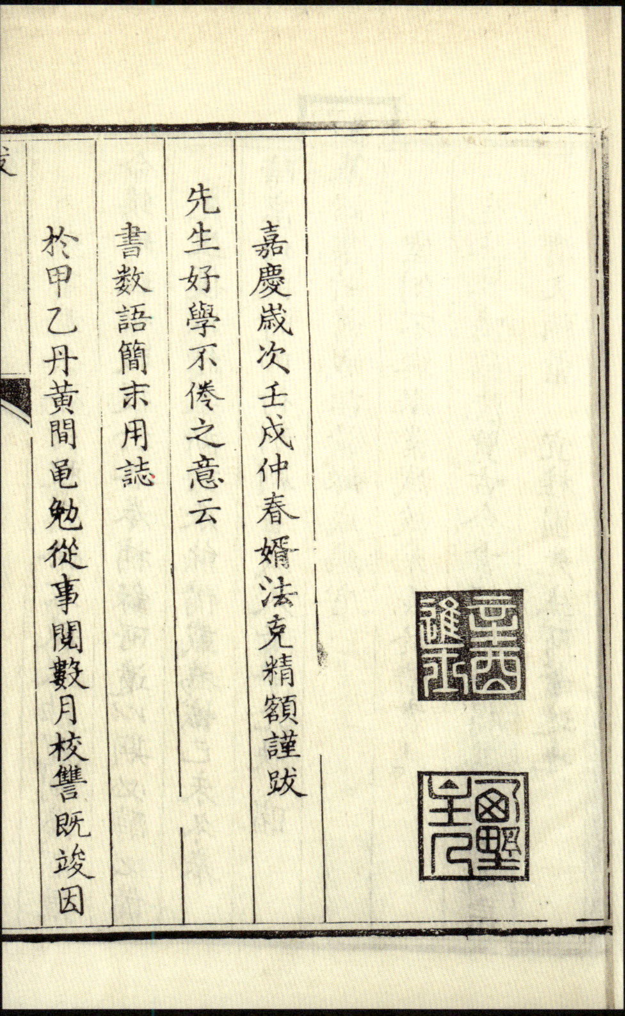

於甲乙丑黃間黽勉從事閱數月校讐既竣因
書數語簡末用誌
先生好學不倦之意云
嘉慶歲次壬戌仲春婿法克精額謹跋

婿法克精額跋
Postscript by Fakejing'e

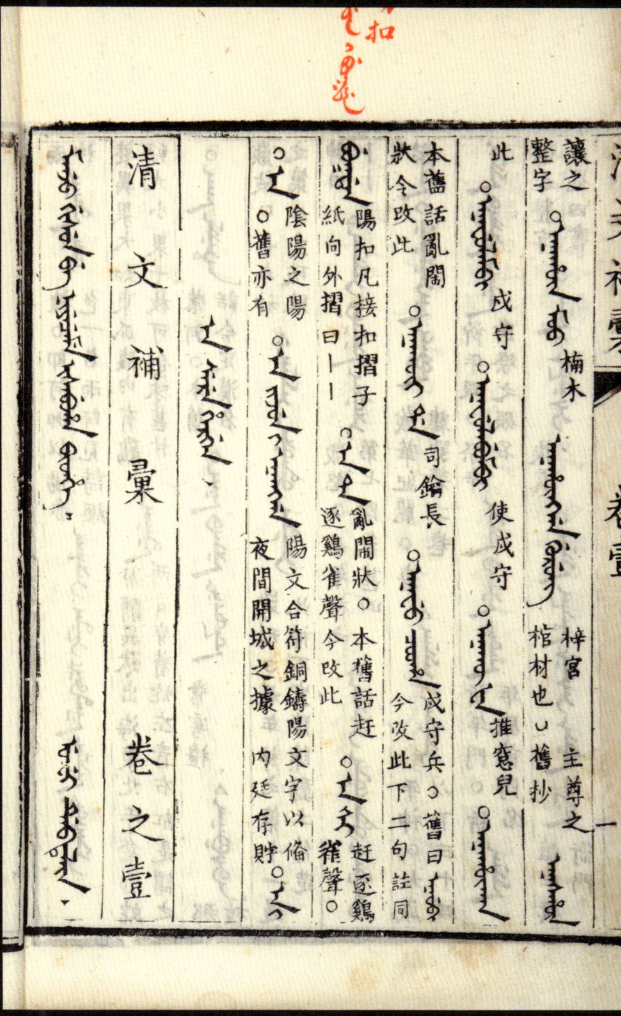

清文補彙卷之壹

卷端
Beginning

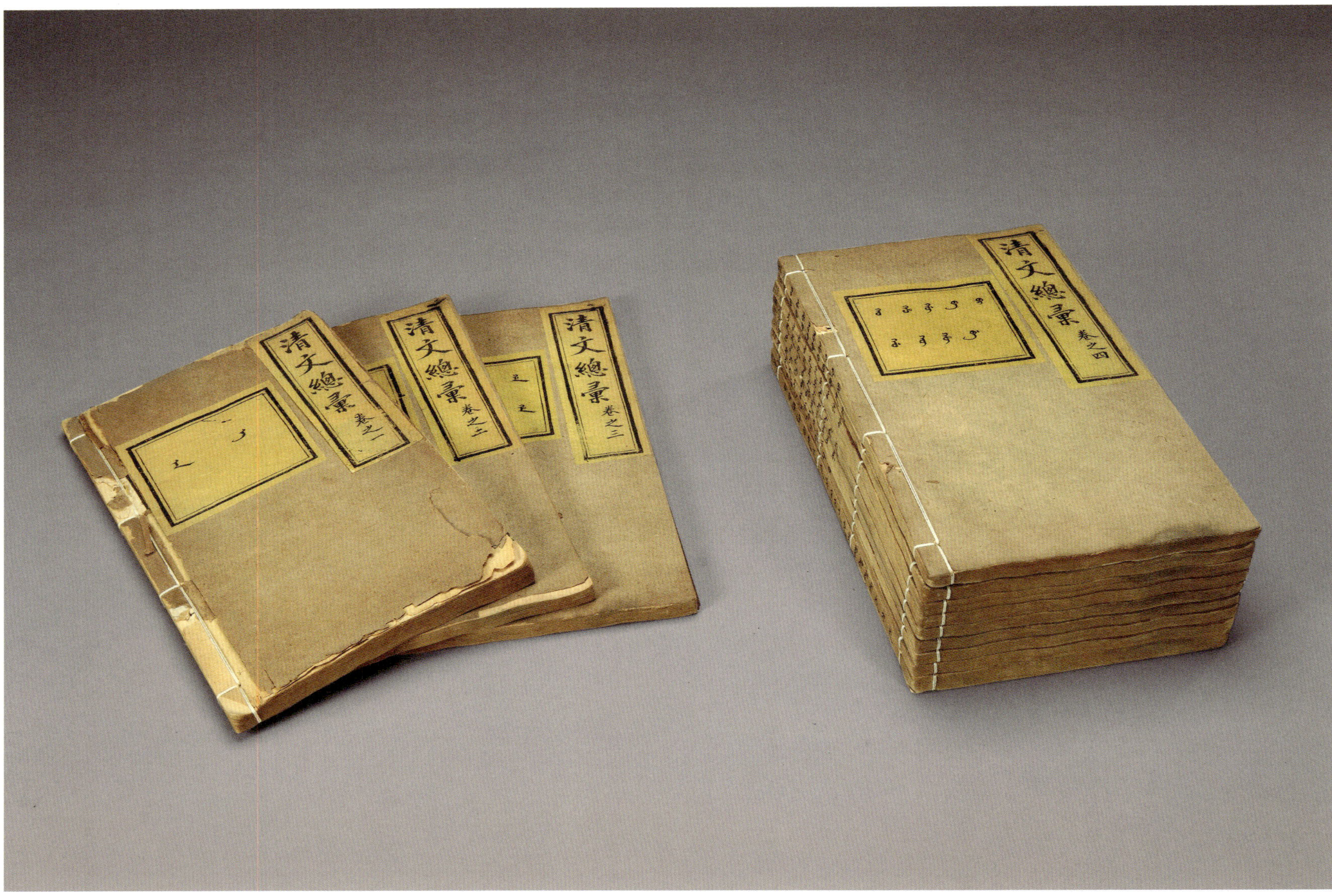

外觀
Exterior

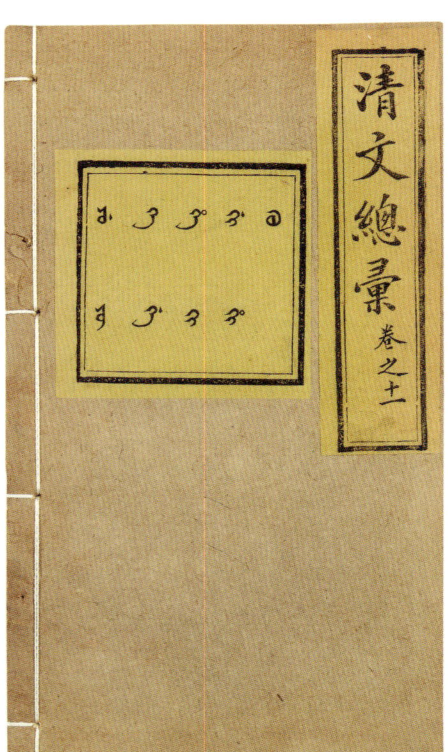

黄色紙書面
Yellow paper cover

30

書21818
《清文總彙十二卷》
清 志寬 培寬等編
清光緒二十三年（1897）荊州駐防翻譯總學刻滿漢合璧本
開本 縱26.9厘米 橫15.5厘米
版框 縱18.8厘米 橫14.1厘米
十二册 一函

Inventory number: Shu 21818
Complete Dictionary of the Qing Language
Twelve chapters
Compiled by Zhikuan, Peikuan et. al., Qing dynasty (1644-1911)
Printed in Manchu and Chinese in 1897 by Translation Institute of Jingzhou Garrison
Format: 26.9 × 15.5 cm
Frame: 18.8 × 14.1 cm
Twelve volumes in one case

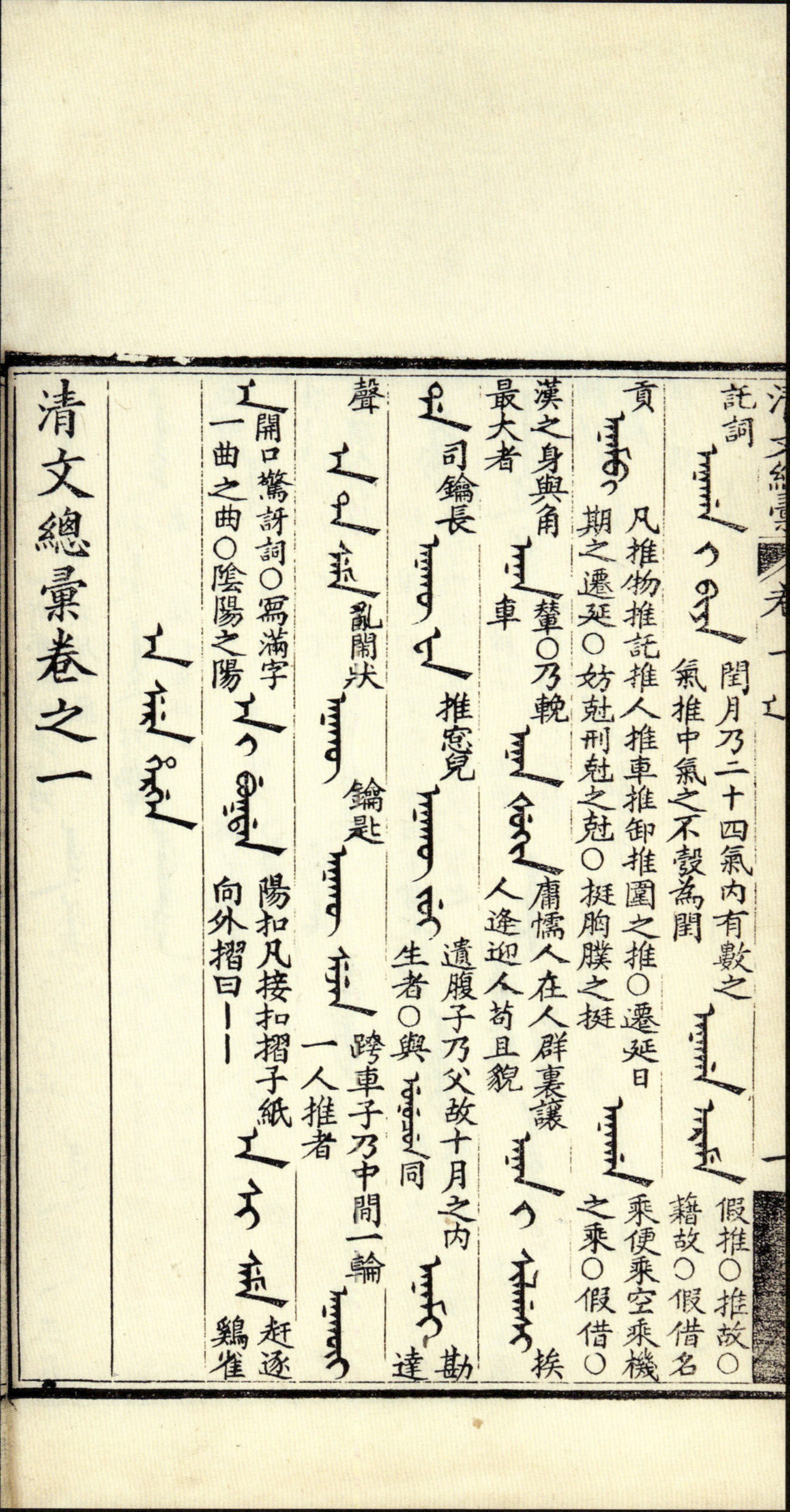

清文總彙 卷一 一

託詞 閏月乃二十四氣內有數之氣推中氣之不設為閏 假推○推故○藉故○假借名

貢 凡推物推託推人推車推御推圍之推○遷延日期之遷延○妨尅刑尅之尅○挺胸膛之挺 乘便乘空乘機之乘○假借○

漢之身與角最大者 輦○乃輓車 庸懦人在人群裏讓人逢迎人苟且貌 挨

司鑰長 推窗兒 遺腹子乃父故十月之內生者○與 同 勘達

聲 亂鬧狀 鑰匙 跨車子乃中間一輪一人推者

開口驚訝詞○寫滿字一曲之曲○陰陽之陽 陽扣凡接扣摺子紙向外摺曰ㄧㄧ 赶逐鵪鶉

清文總彙卷之一

卷端
Beginning

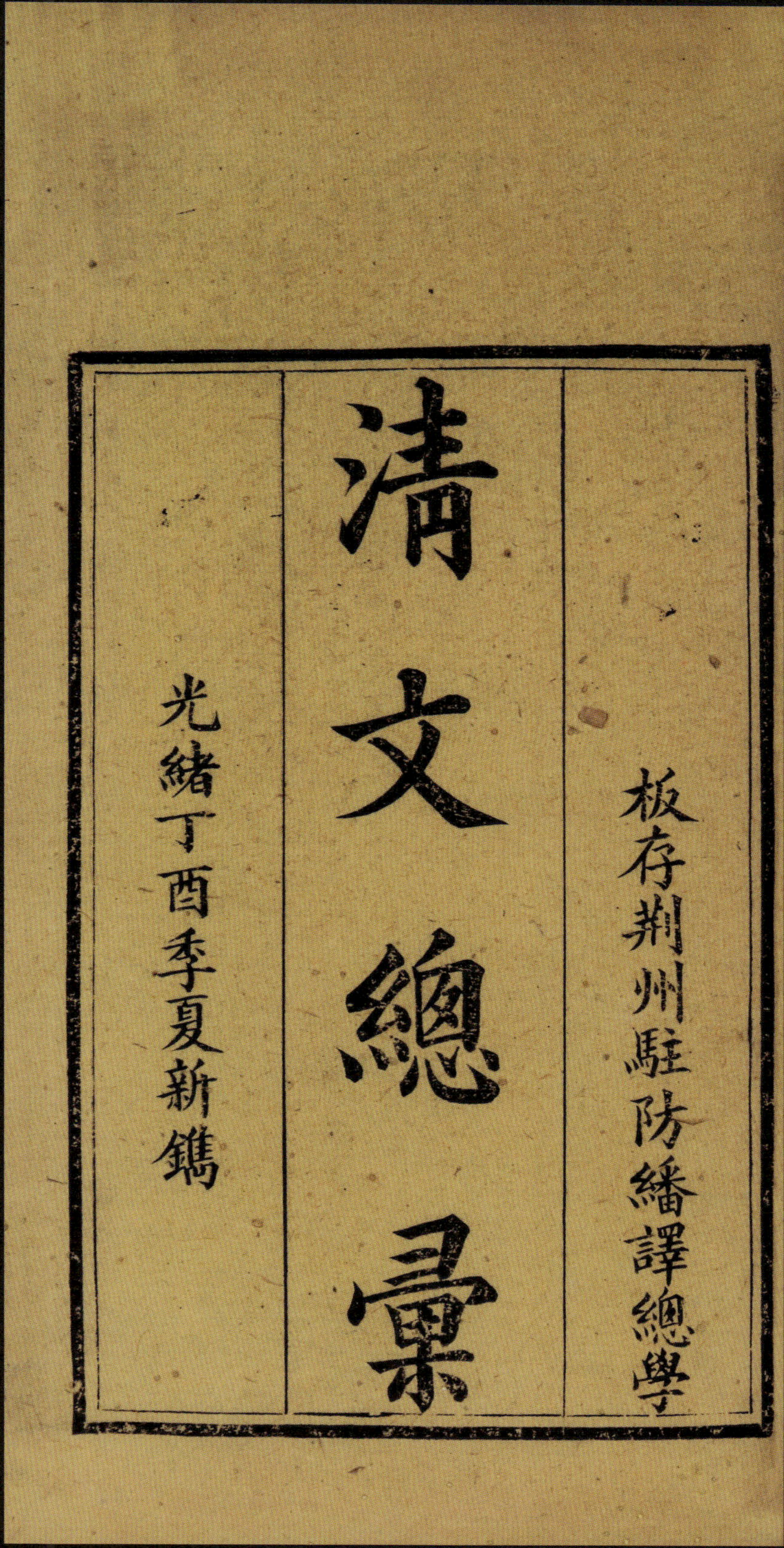

清文總彙

光緒丁酉季夏新鐫

板存荊州駐防繙譯總學

牌記
Copyright paper

八旗滿蒙臣僕尤沐
聖學淵深鉅細靡遺共遵為經國成憲要典凡屬
語氣之輕重無不剖析精微仰見
人政治下至草木昆蟲以及字義之虛實
欽定增訂清文鑑數千言附以對音漢字上之天
御製清文鑑一書又復
類繁賾音義奧衍經
國朝肇立文書四子經史次第繙譯嗣因事

云剖劂告成敬誌數語於左

光緒二十三年三月穀旦宗室祥亨識

光緒二十三年宗室祥亨序
Preface by Xiangheng in 1897

嗜學之士望洋興嘆寬等賦性庸愚茅
塞難開縱有修復之心恨無點金之術
惟將二書合鈔成帙以資考證茲幸我
軍憲祥公蒞任斯土講求
國語不厭精詳現將四書對音暨合璧書經
等書先後刊印成帙津逮來學寬等不
敏幸逢其時復奉
命督修斯役故敢重以是請蒙
公欣然許可因二部合鈔為一名曰清文
總彙俾後學易於考證則斯書之成其
裨益豈淺鮮哉謹於光緒丙申秋卜吉
鳩工繕正付梓寒暑一遷而鐫刻告竣
用是勉跋數語於簡末用述
宜李二公啟迪後世之苦心即以誌我
祥公樂育不倦之至意云

後學佐領志寬 舉人培寬等敬跋

培寬、志寬等跋
Postscript by Zhikuan, Peikuan et. al.

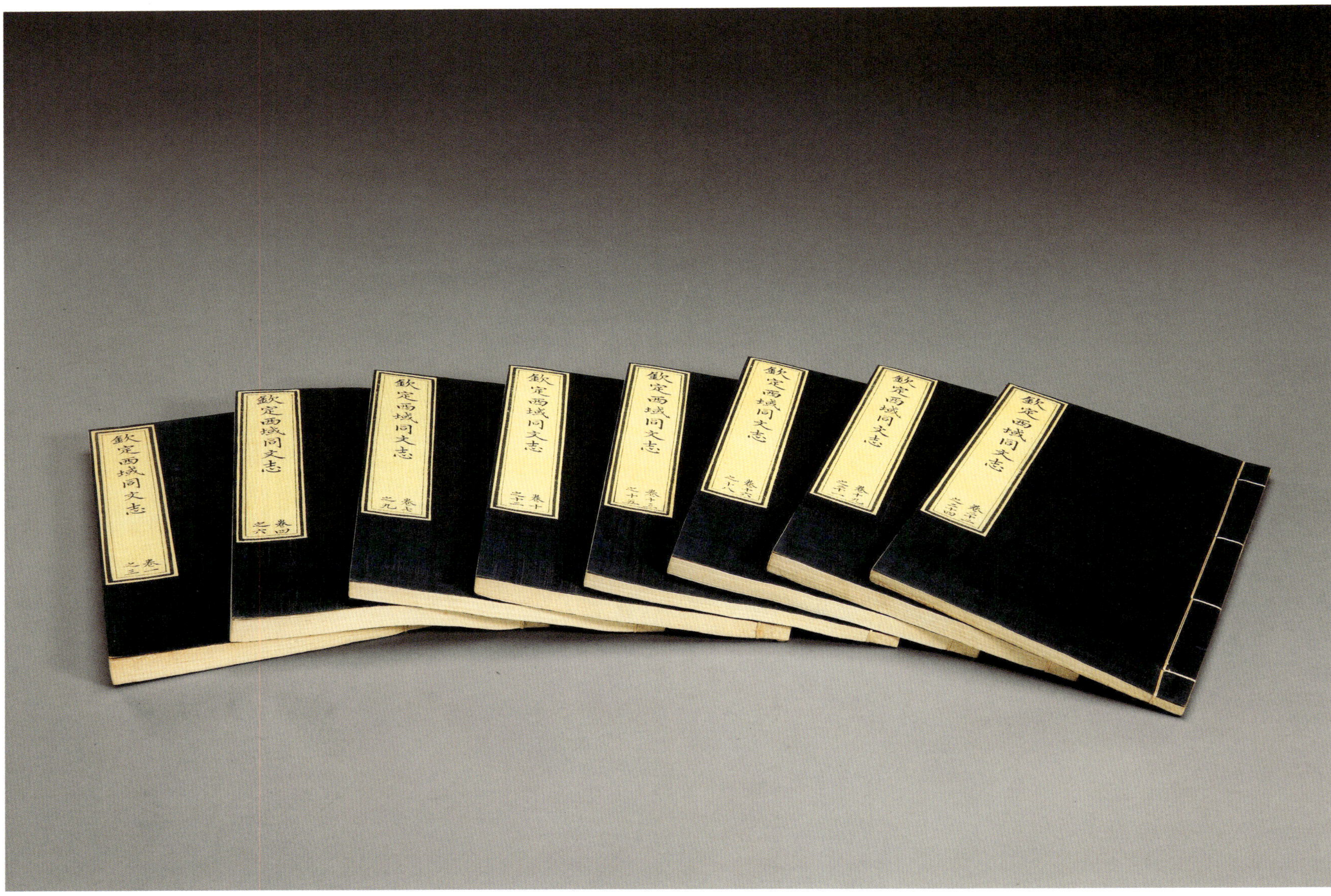

藍色素絹書面
Blue silk covers

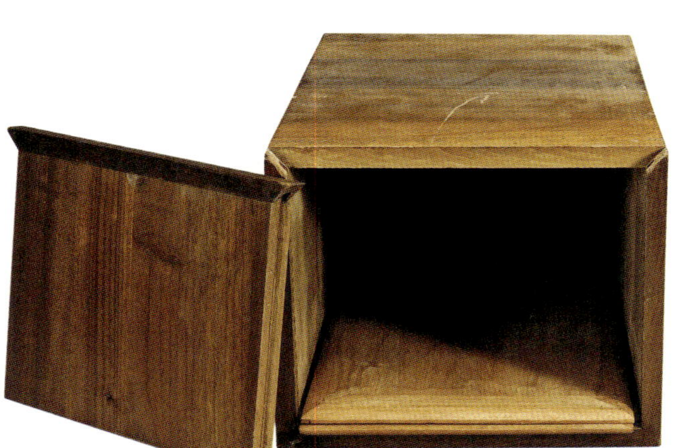

楠木書盒
Nanmu case

書59
《欽定西域同文志二十四卷》
清　傅恒等奉敕撰
清乾隆二十八年（1763）武英殿刻滿漢蒙藏維托忒六体合璧本
開本　縱27.7厘米　橫17.5厘米
版框　縱18.8厘米　橫14.1厘米
八册　一函（其文種包括滿文、漢文、蒙文、維吾爾、托忒蒙古文六種）

31 Inventory number: Shu 59
Geographical Dictionary of Places and Names in the Western Region
Twenty-four chapters
Written at the order of the Qianlong emperor (r.1736-1795) by Fuheng et. al.
Printed in Manchu, Chinese, Mongolian, Tibetan, Uighur and Tuote in 1763 at the Hall of Martial Valour
Format: 27.7 × 17.5 cm
Frame: 18.8 × 14.1 cm
Eight volumes in one case

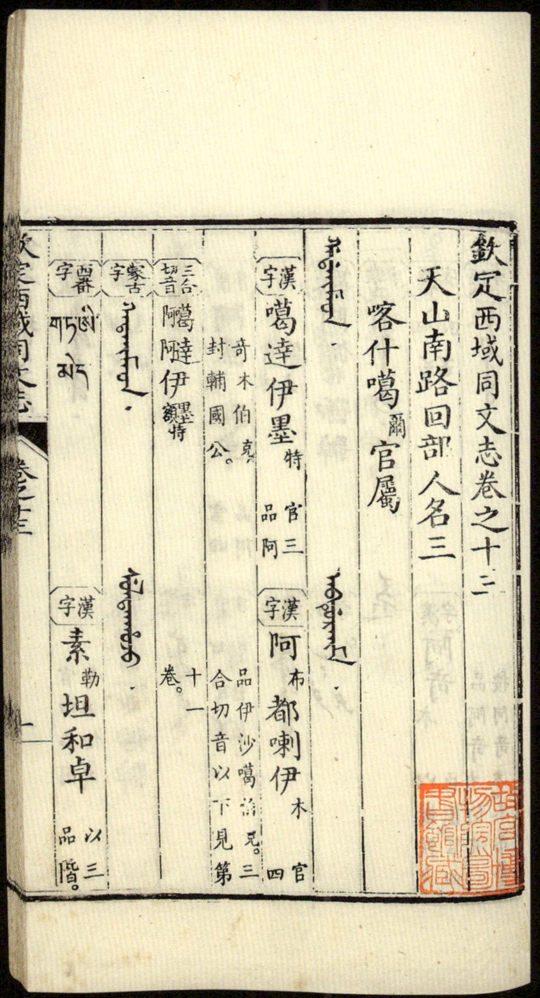

卷端
Beginning

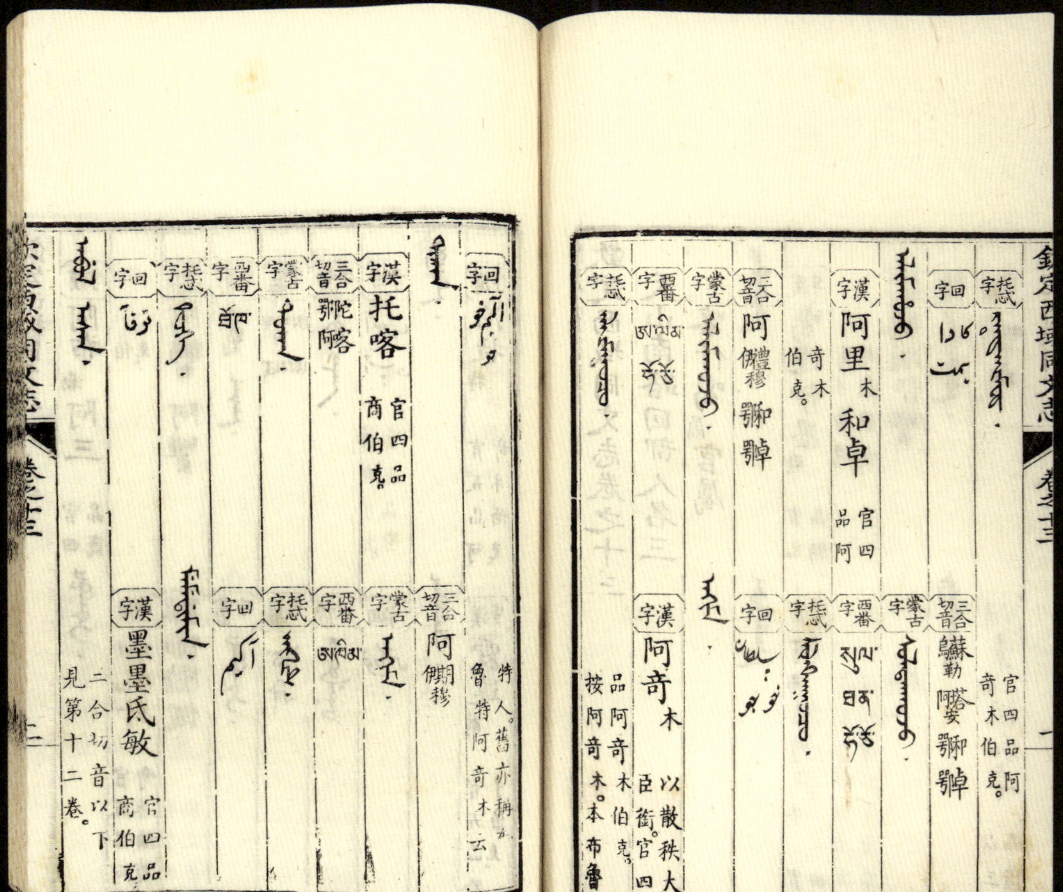

正文
Text

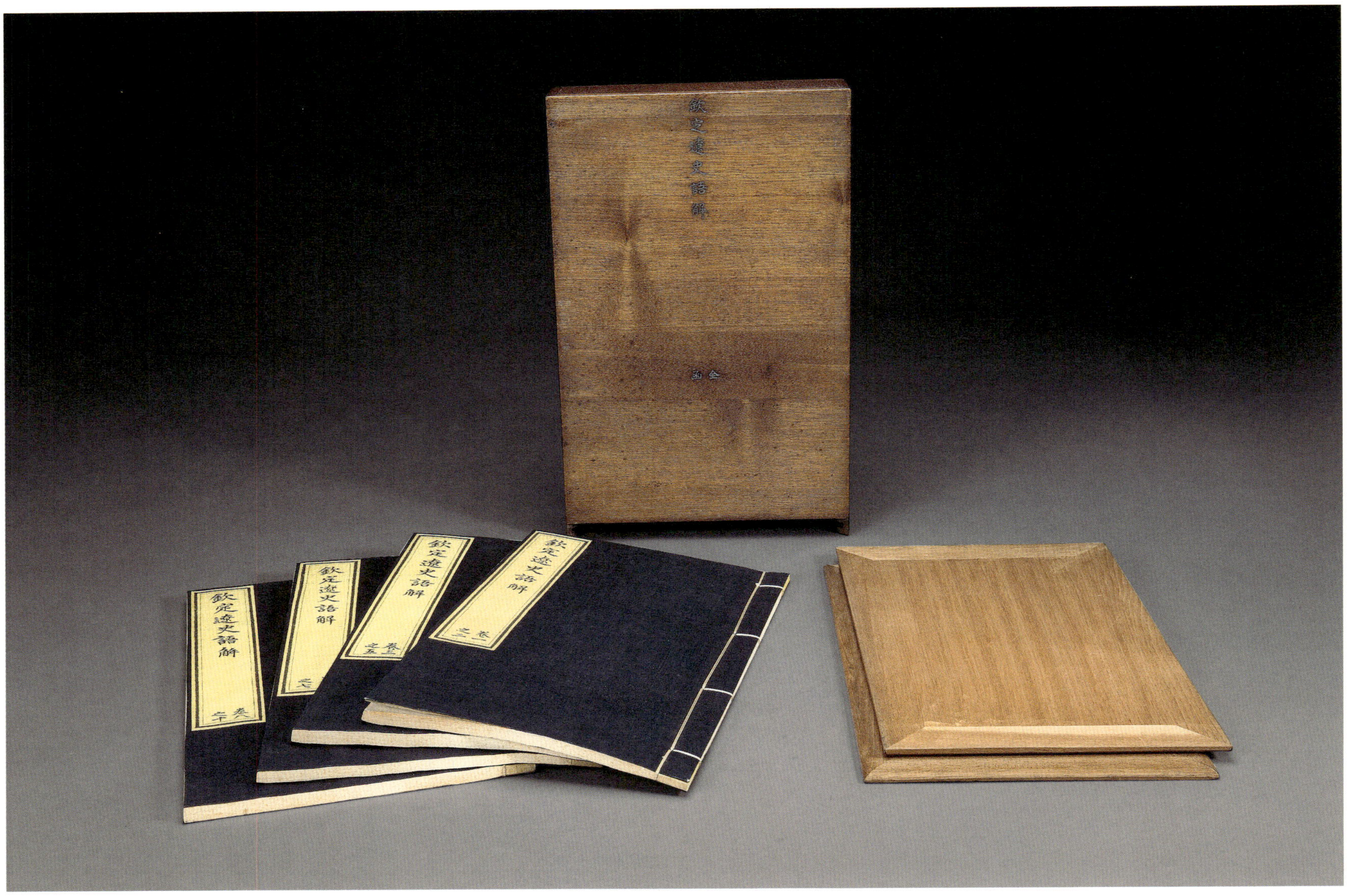

“欽定遼史語解”花梨木書盒
Rosewood case of *Dictionary for Terms in the History of Liao*

書74
《欽定遼金元三史語解四十六卷》
清　高宗弘曆敕譯
清乾隆四十六年（1781）武英殿刻滿漢合璧本
開本　縱30.7厘米　橫18.8厘米
版框　縱21.4厘米　橫15.4厘米
十八册　四木盒

32

Inventory number: Shu 74
Dictionary for Terms in the Histories of Liao, Jin and Yuan
Forty-six chapters
Translated at the order of the Qianlong emperor (r.1736-1795)
Printed in Manchu and Chinese in 1781 at the Hall of Martial Valour
Format: 30.7 × 18.8 cm
Frame: 21.4 × 15.4 cm
Eighteen volumes in four wood cases

欽定遼史語解卷一

按遼以索倫語爲本語解內但釋解義概不複注索倫語其中姓氏地名官名人名無解義者俱以今地名八旗姓氏通譜官名改字面訂之

君名

按遼世系編次其非太祖本支者列於後

后妃　皇子　公主附

ᠴᡳᠰᠠᠨ ᡥᠠᠨ

朔伊 沙阿婁 晗阿婁

奇善汗 滿洲語奇善鮮明也汗君長之稱卷一作奇首可汗遼始祖

ᡴᡝᡩᡠᠨ

珂額 鄂烏

克敦 蒙古語幾數之謂卷三十二作可敦遼遠祖

ᠪᠠᡨᡠ

巴圖 阿烏

巴圖 蒙古語結實也卷三十七作勃突遼五世祖

“欽定遼史語解”卷端

Beginning of *Dictionary for Terms in the History of Liao*

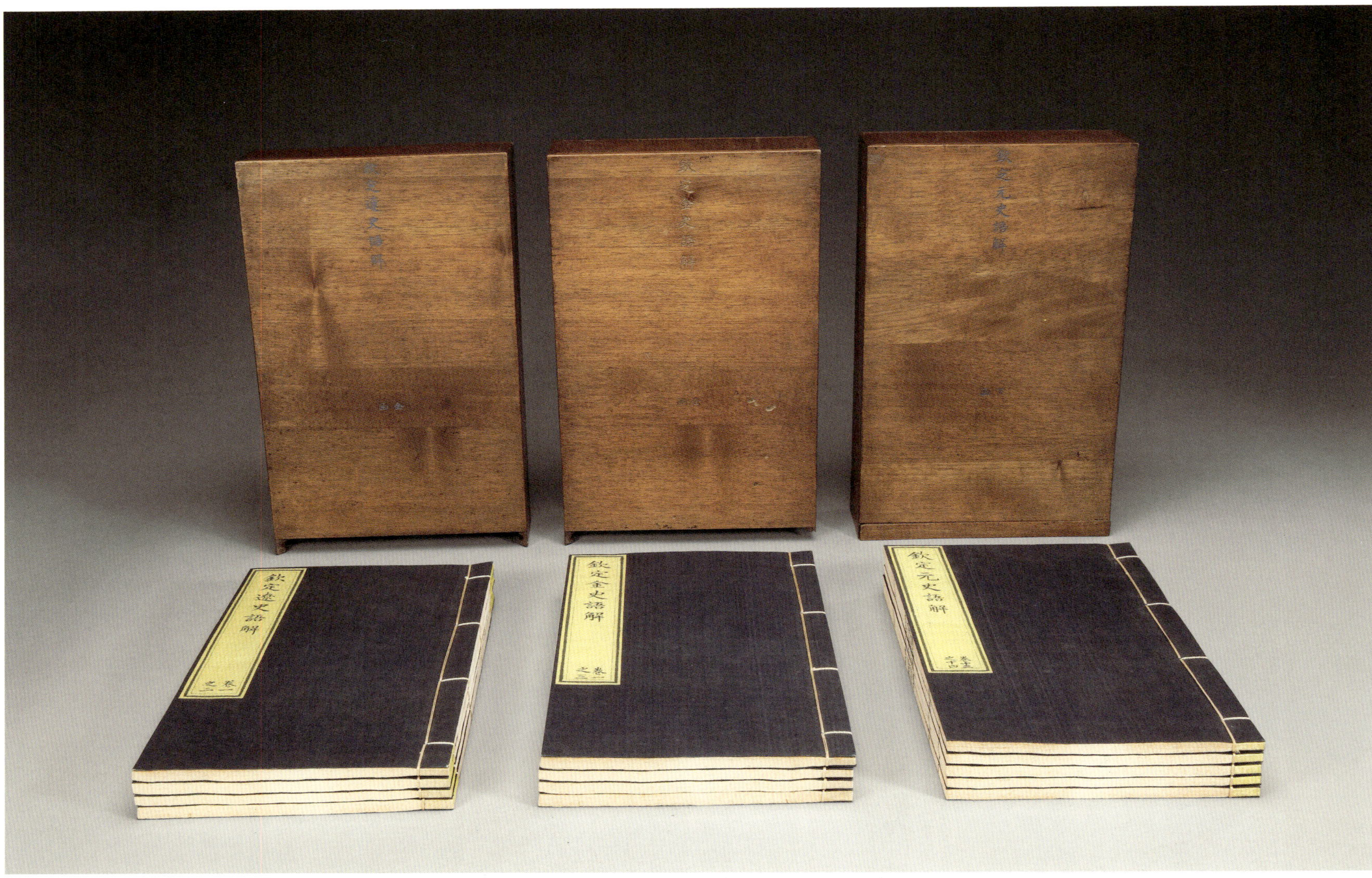

“欽定金史語解”花梨木書盒
Rosewood case of *Dictionary for Terms in the History of Jin*

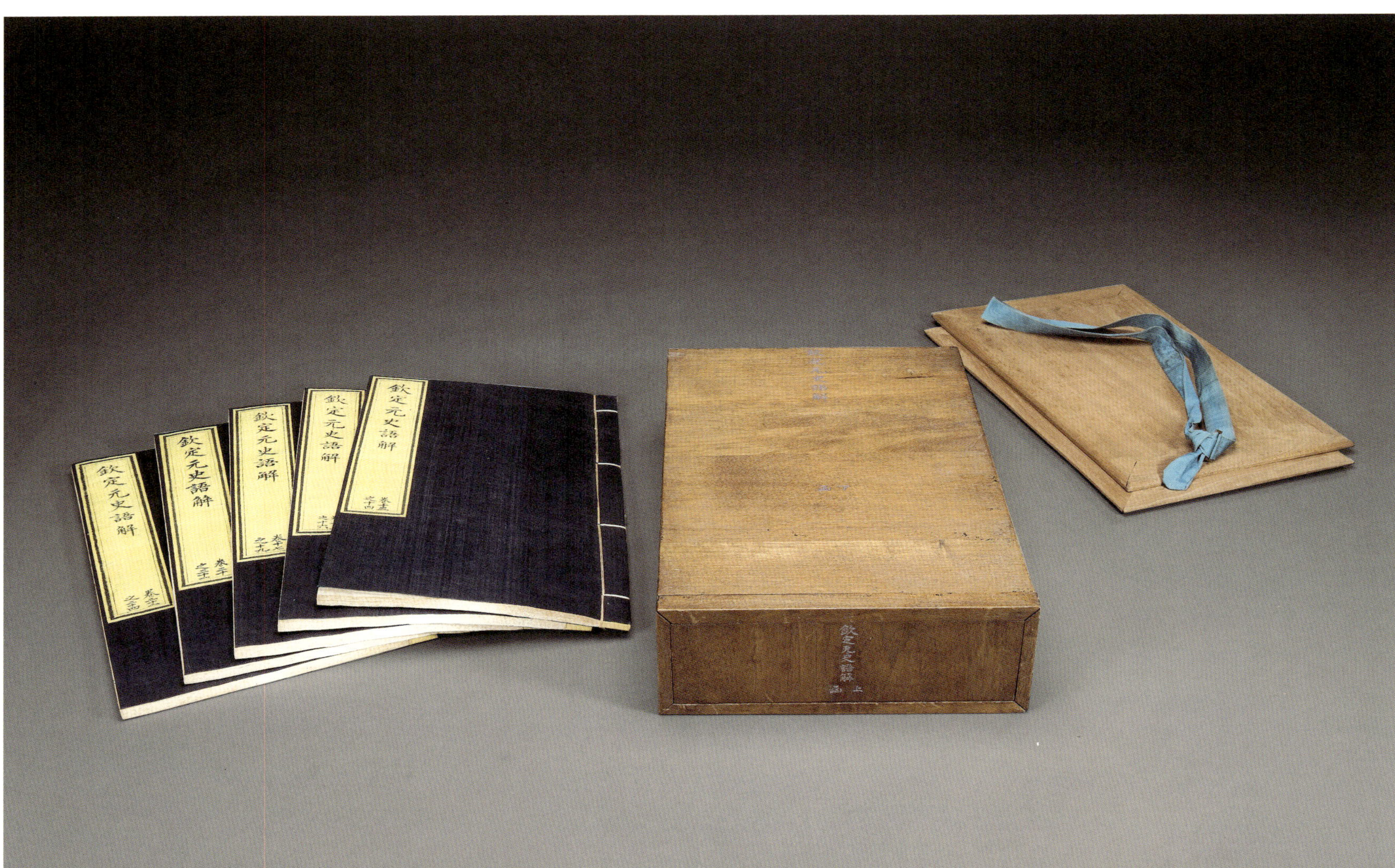

“欽定元史語解”花梨木書盒
Rosewood case of *Dictionary for Terms in the History of Yuan*

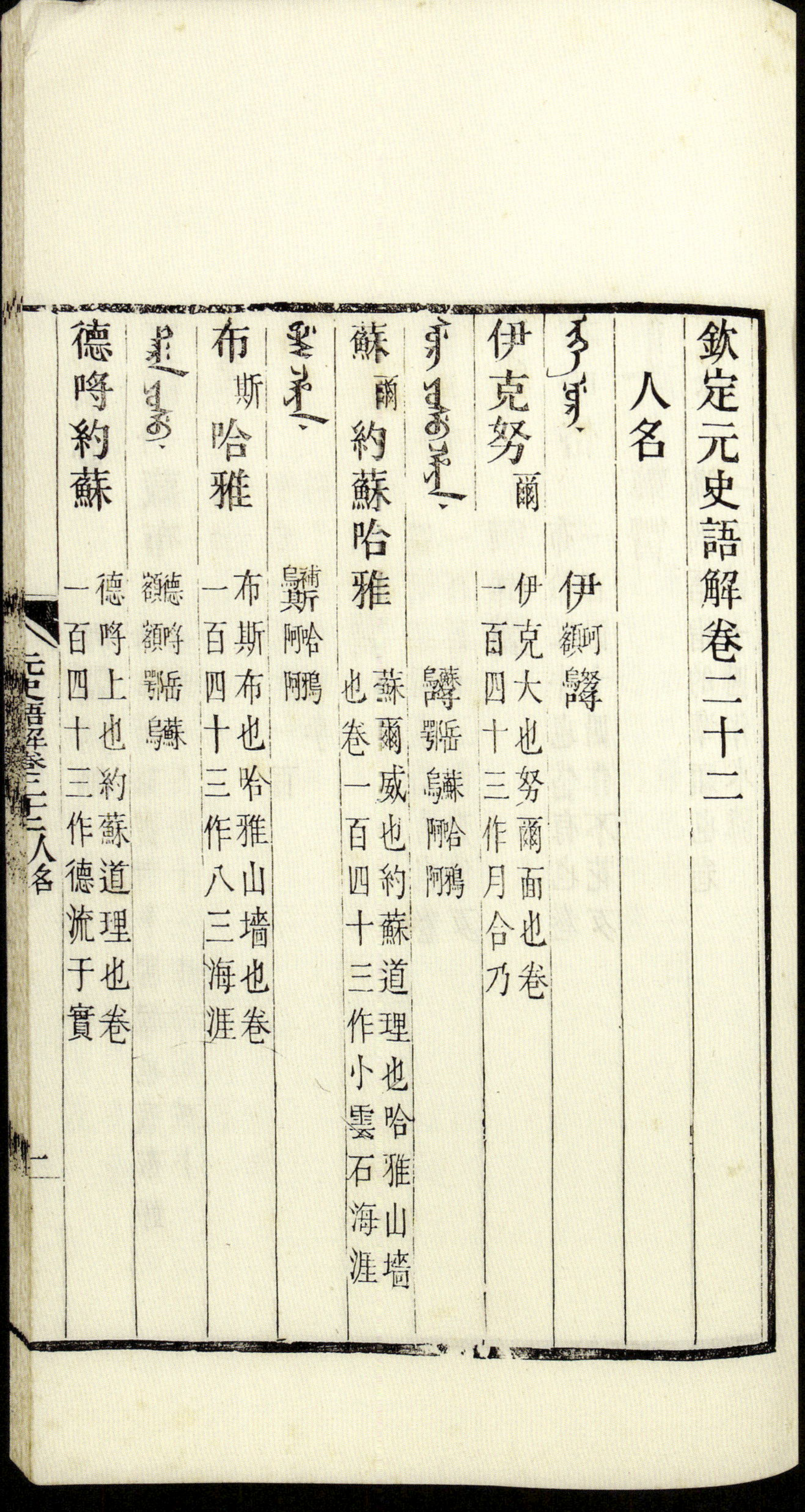

欽定元史語解卷二十二

人名

伊克努爾 伊克大也努爾面也卷一百四十三作月合乃

蘇爾約蘇哈雅 蘇爾威也約蘇道理也哈雅山墻也卷一百四十三作小雲石海涯

布斯哈雅 布斯布也哈雅山墻也卷一百四十三作八三海涯

德吗約蘇 德吗上也約蘇道理也卷一百四十三作德流于實

元史語解卷二十二 人名 二

"欽定元史語解"卷端

Beginning of *Dictionary for Terms in the History of Yuan*

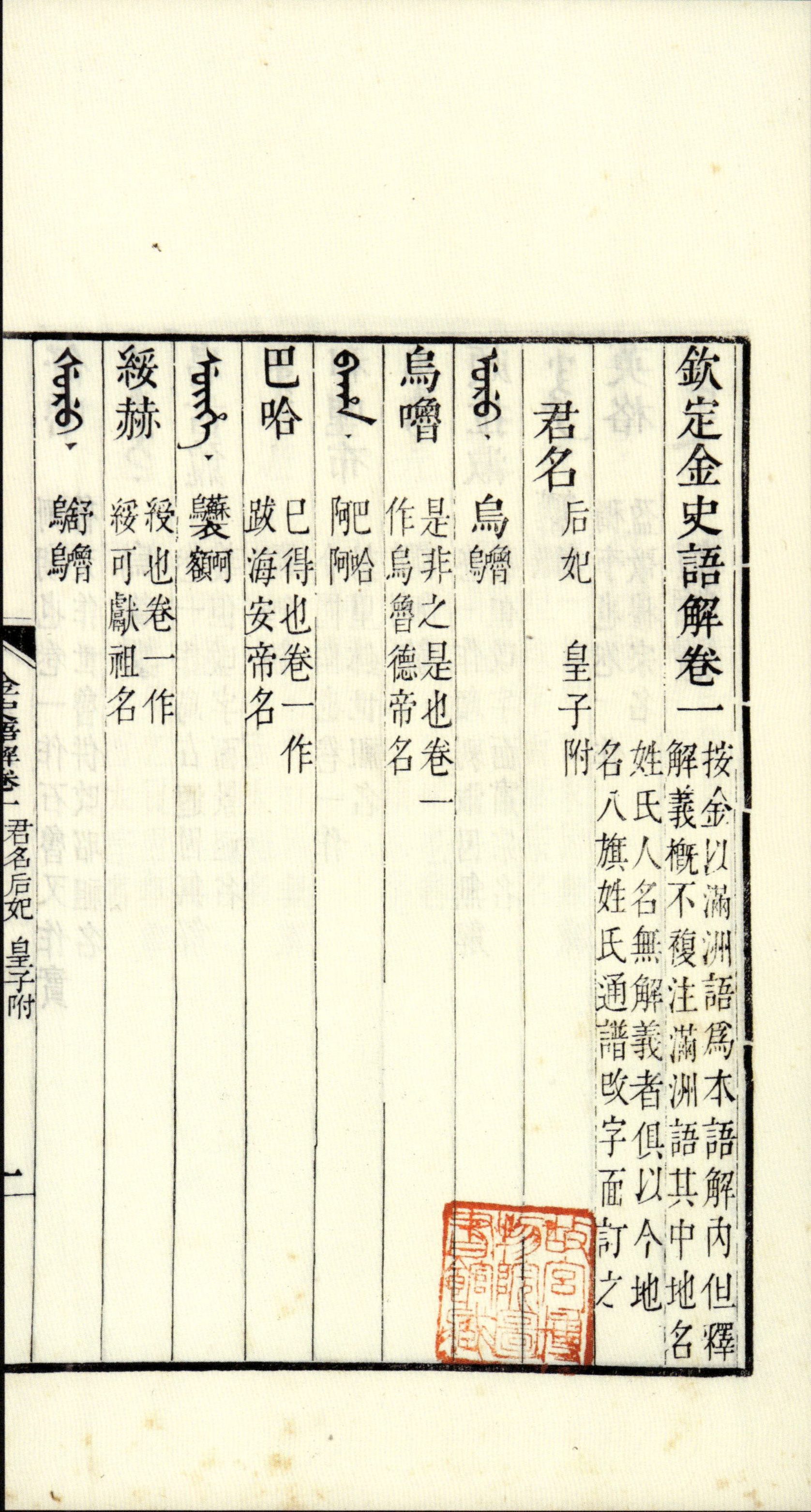

欽定金史語解卷一

按金以滿洲語為本語解內但釋解義概不復注滿洲語其中地名姓氏人名無解義者俱以今地名八旗姓氏通譜改字面訂之

君名 后妃 皇子附

烏嚕 是非之是也卷一作烏魯德帝名

巴哈 巳得也卷一作跋海安帝名

綏赫 綏也卷一作綏可獻祖名

金史語解卷一 君名后妃 皇子附 二

"欽定金史語解"卷端

Beginning of *Dictionary for Terms in the History of Jin*

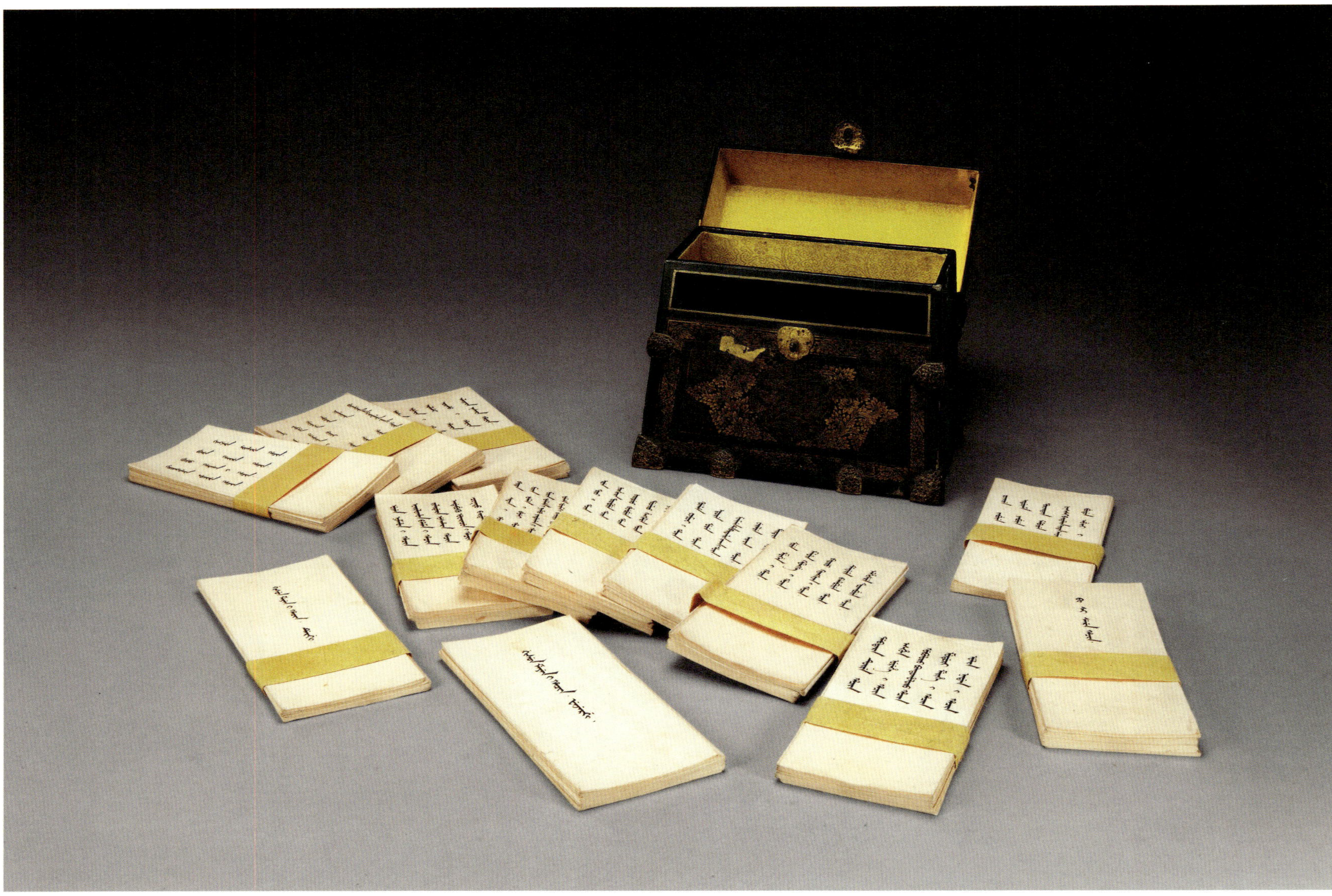

外觀
Exterior

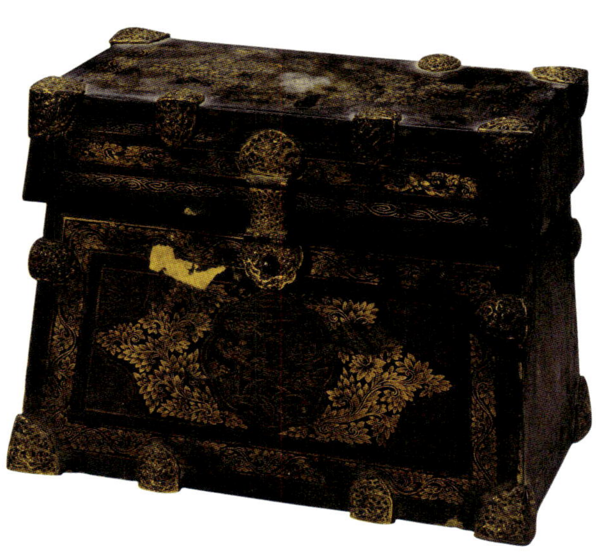

黑漆描金書箱
Bookcase covered with black lacquer in gold tracery

書21836
《滿蒙漢字書不分卷》
清　佚名輯
清內府精寫滿蒙漢合璧本
開本　縱19.9厘米　横9.1厘米
二十五册　二函（其蒙語部分由滿文字母轉寫而成）

33

Inventory number: Shu 21836
Manchu-Mongolian-Chinese Dictionary
Anonymous, Qing dynasty (1644-1911)
Transcribed in Manchu, Mongolian and Chinese by the Qing court
Format: 19.9 × 9.1 cm
Twenty-five volumes in two cases

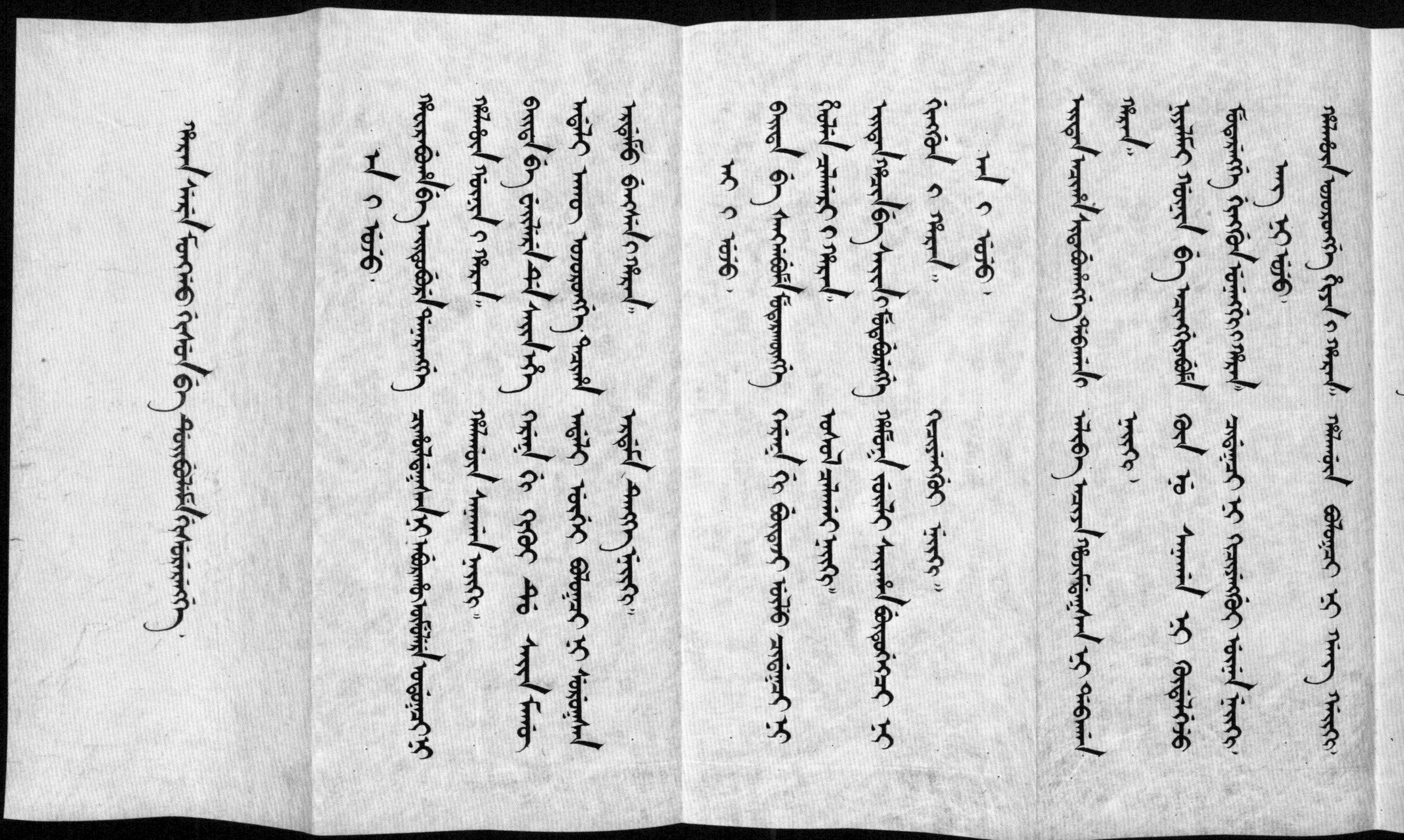

卷端
Beginning

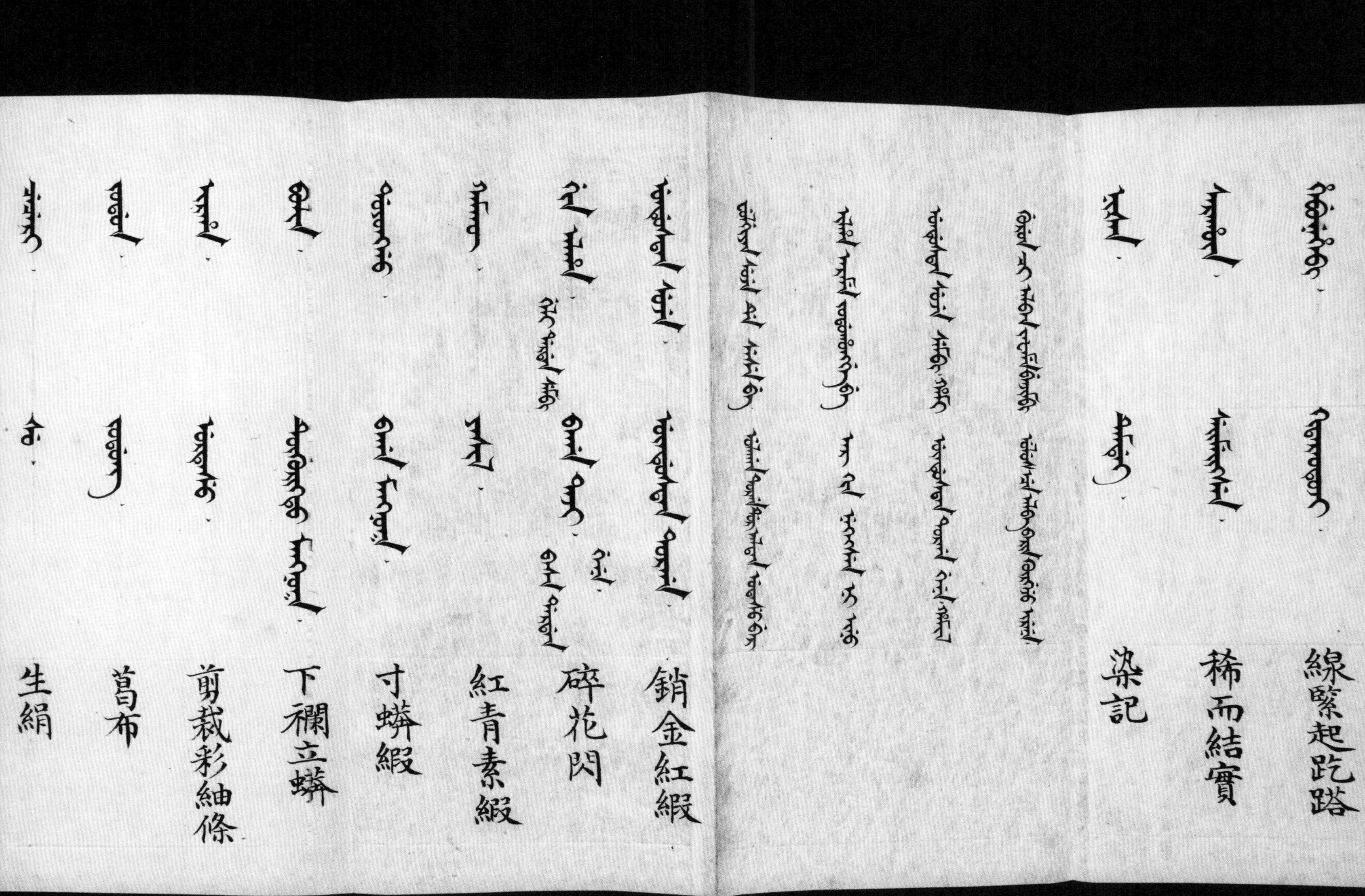

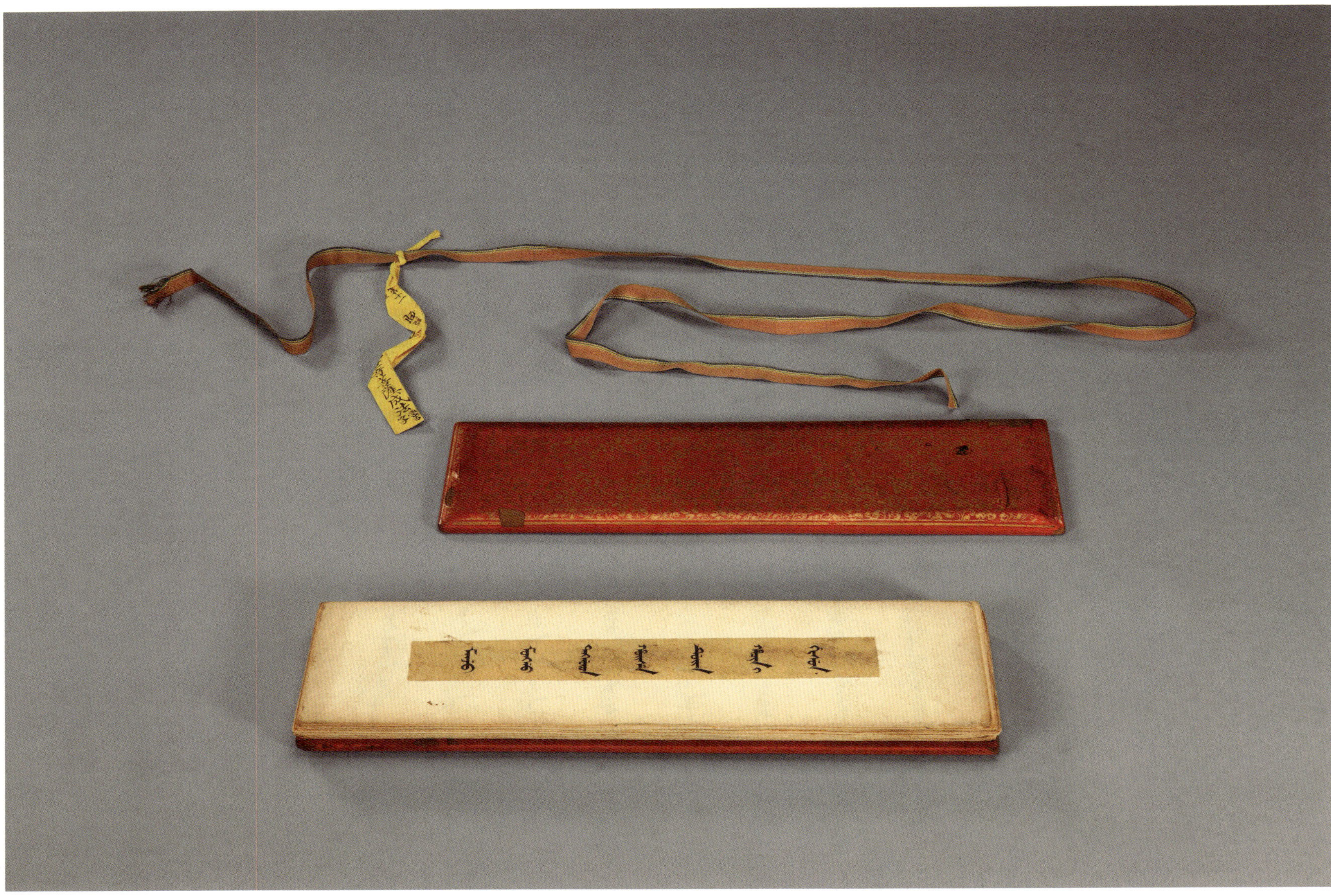

紅色描金纏枝蓮紋護經板
Red protective board traced with golden pattern of lotus scrolls

書27218
《滿蒙藏維四體字書一卷》
清　佚名輯
清內府精寫滿蒙藏維合璧本
開本　縱6.9厘米　橫27.7厘米
一冊　一夾（其蒙藏維語部分由滿文字母轉寫而成）

34

Inventory number: Shu 27218
Manchu-Mongolian-Tibetan-Uighur Dictionary
Anonymous, Qing dynasty (1644-1911)
Transcribed in Manchu, Mongolian, Tibetan and Uighur by the Qing court
Format: 6.9 × 27.7 cm
One volume protected with two boards

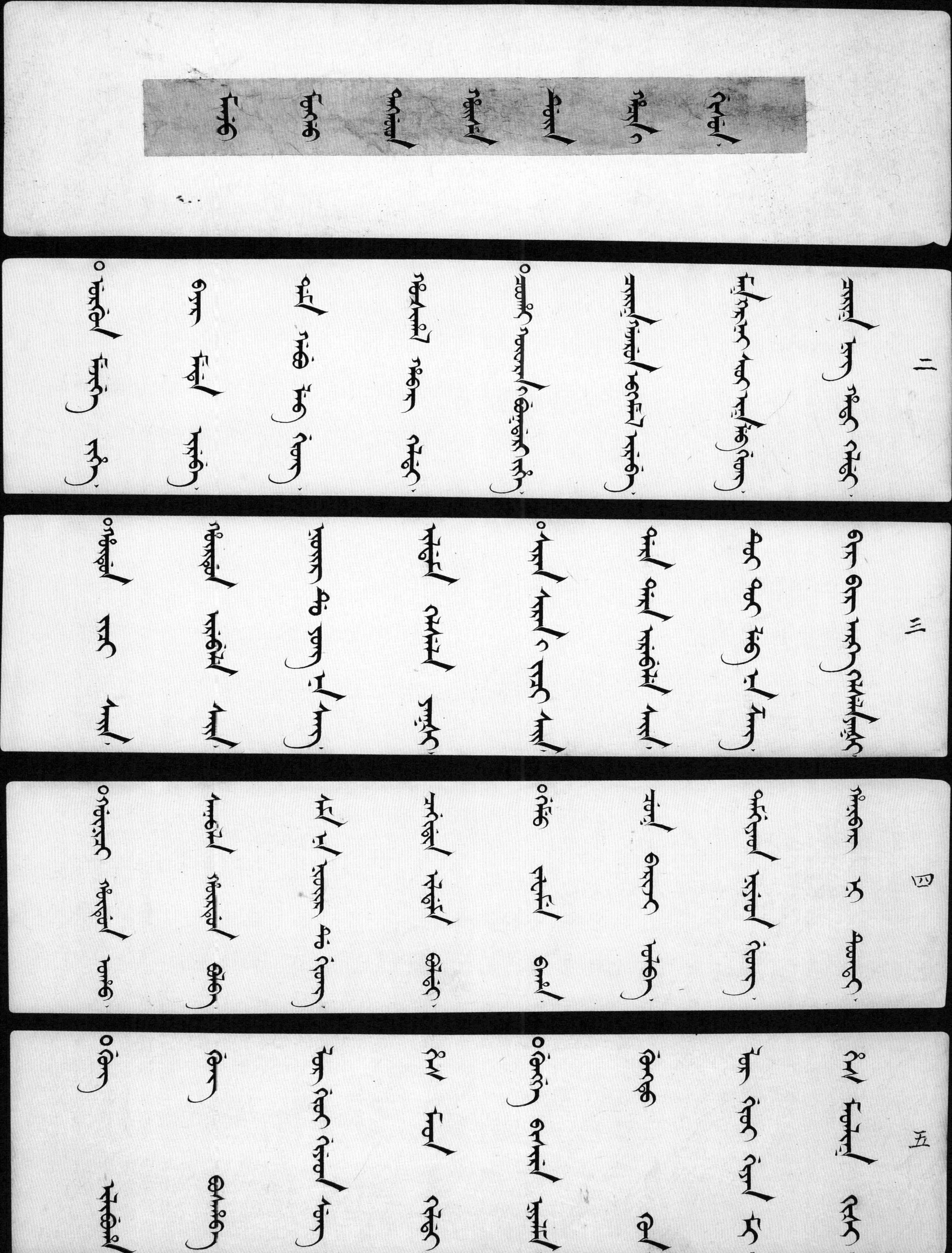

正文
Text

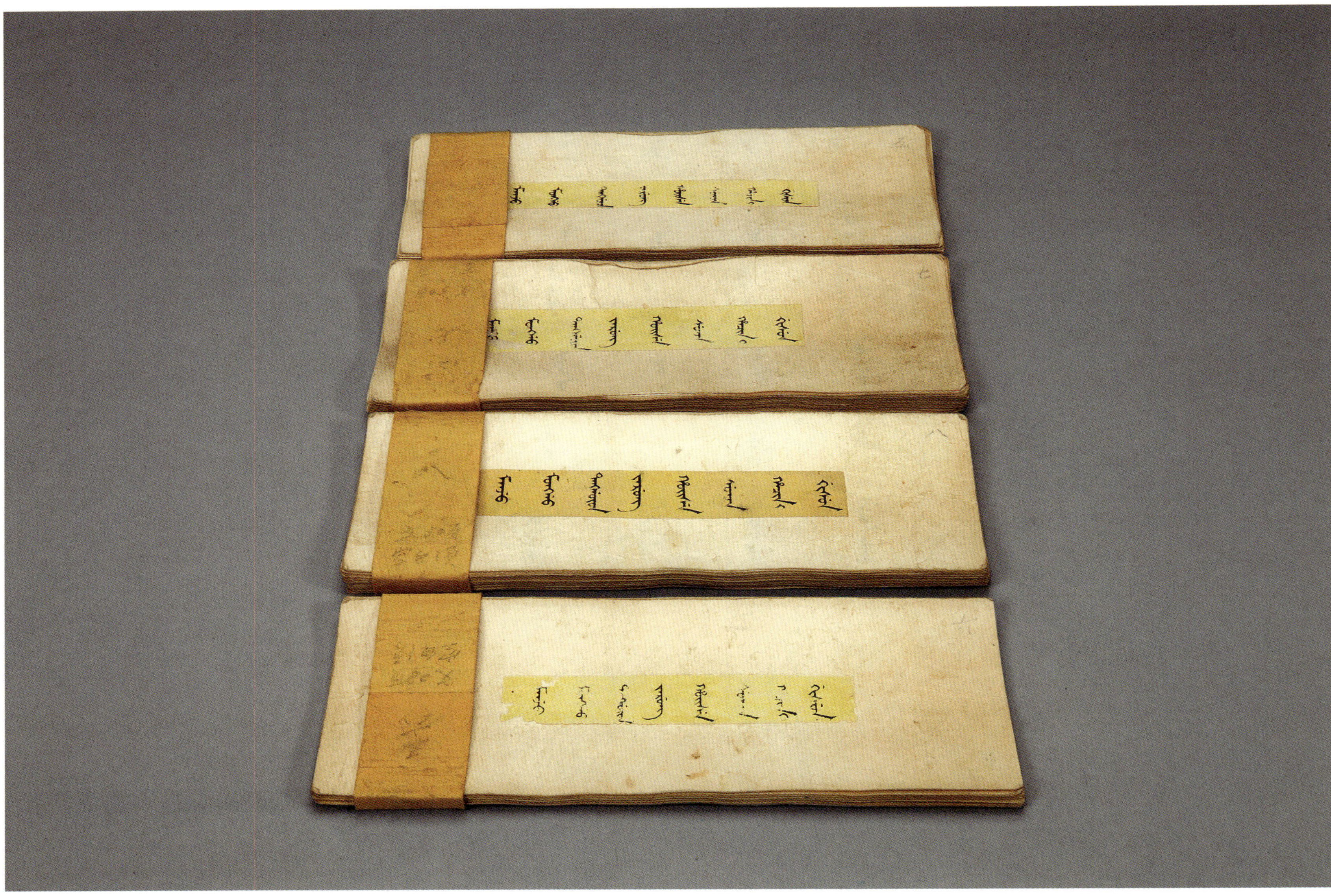

黄色紙書面
Yellow paper covers

書21841
《滿蒙藏嘉戎維語五體字書不分卷》
清　佚名輯
清乾隆年內府精寫滿蒙藏嘉戎維合璧本
開本　縱22.1厘米　橫7.5厘米
八帙　二匣（其蒙藏嘉戎維語部分由滿文字母轉寫而成）

35

Inventory number: Shu 21841
Manchu-Mongolian-Tibetan-Jiarong-Uighur Dictionary
Anonymous, Qing dynasty (1644-1911)
Transcribed in Manchu, Mongolian, Tibetan, Jiarong and Uighur by the Qing court in the Qianlong period (r.1736-1795)
Format: 22.1 × 7.5 cm
Eight volumes in two cases

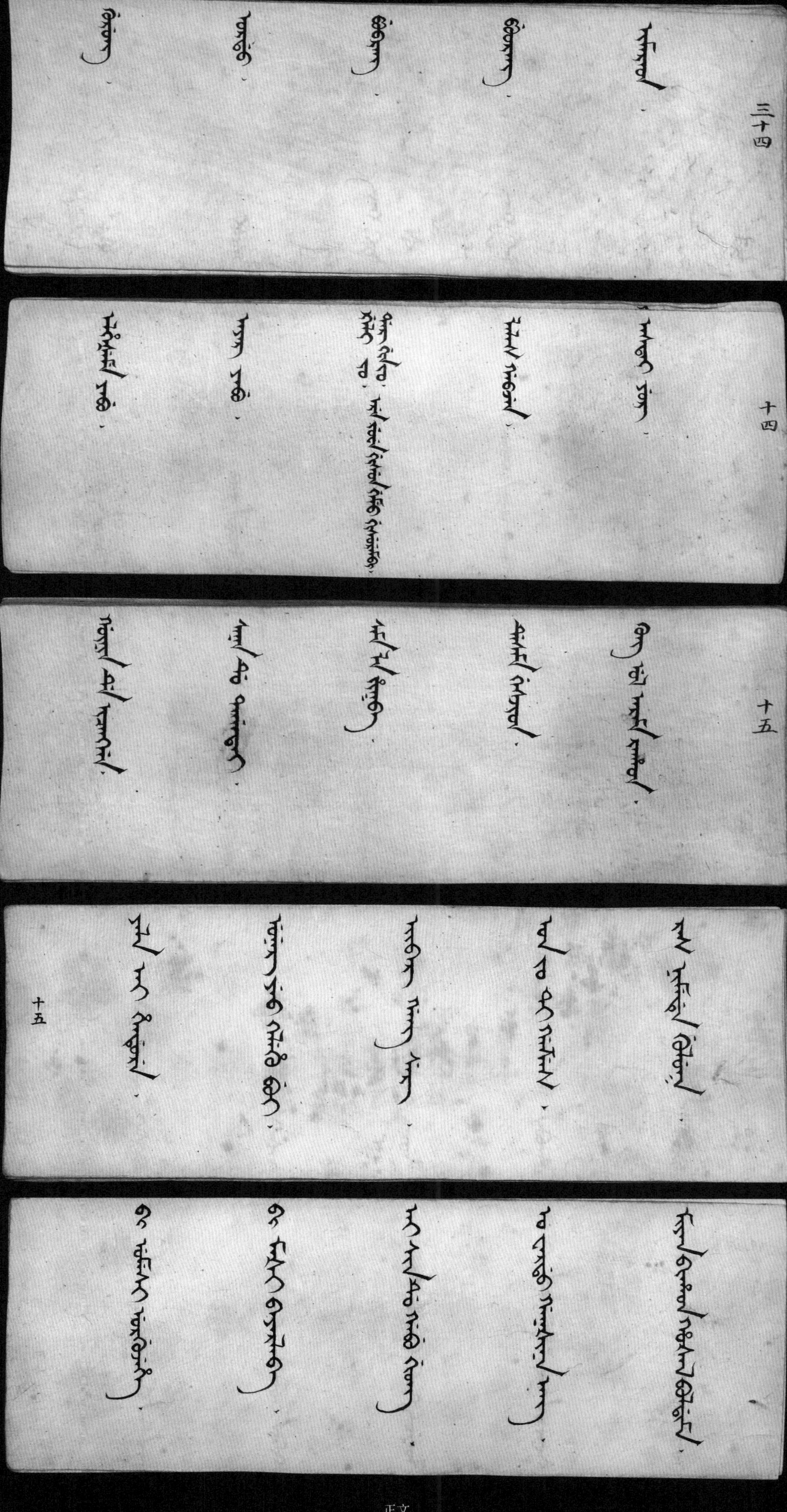
三十四
十四
十五
十五

正文
Text

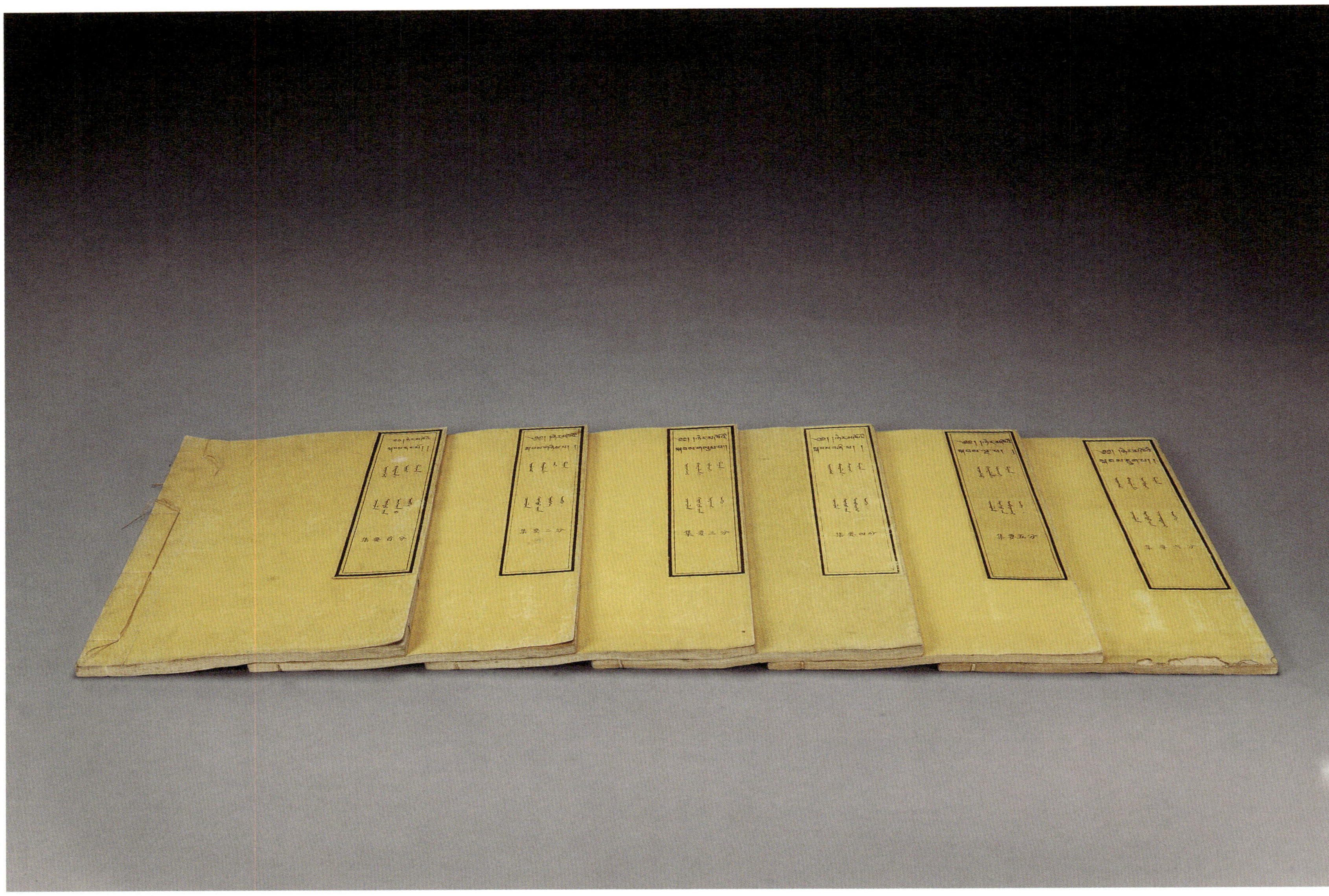

外觀
Exterior

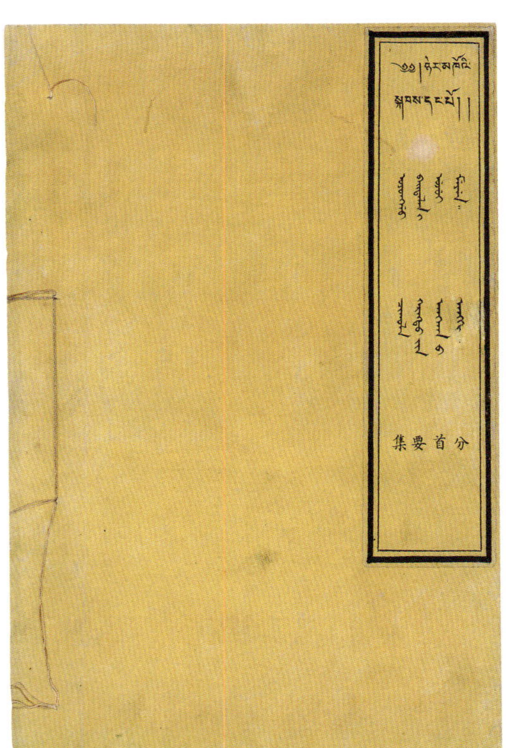

明黃色紙書面
Bright yellow paper cover

36

書21834

《集要二卷》

清　佚名輯

清乾隆年梵藏滿蒙漢合璧修改稿本

開本　縱30厘米　橫19.7厘米

版框　縱21.3厘米　橫16厘米

六冊　一函

Inventory number: Shu 21834

Condensed Buddhist Dictionary in Five Languages

Two chapters

Anonymous, Qing dynasty (1644-1911)

Draft edition

Revised in Sanskrit, Tibetan, Manchu, Mongolian and Chinese in the Qianlong period (r.1736-1795)

Format: 30 × 19.7 cm

Frame: 21.3 × 16 cm

Six volumes in one case

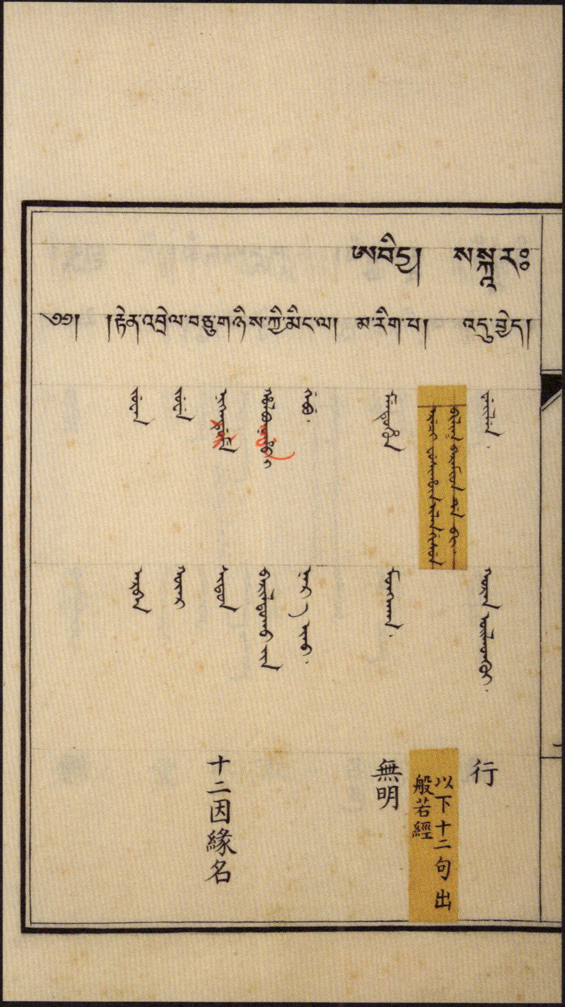
行
以下十二句出般若經
無明
十二因緣名

卷端
Beginning

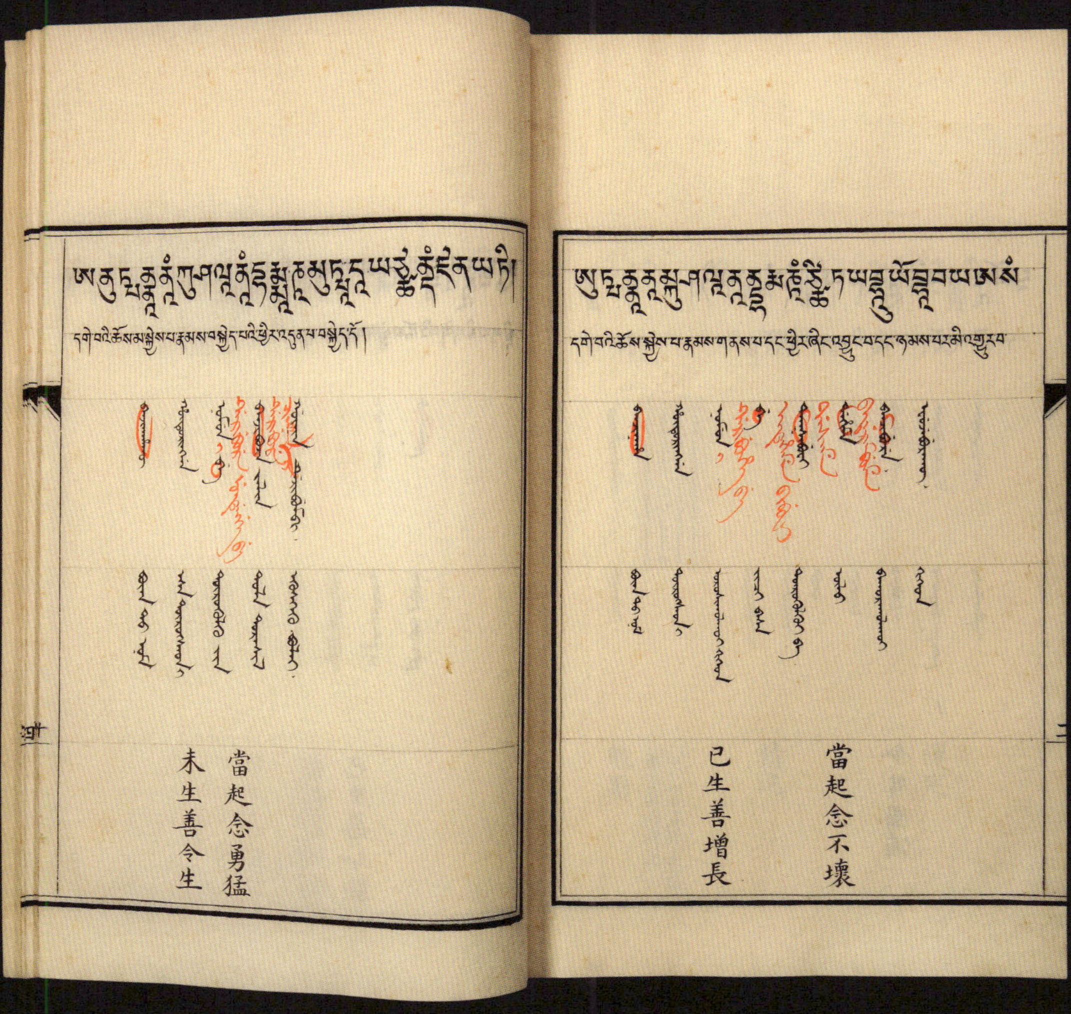
當起念不壞
已生善增長
當起念勇猛
未生善令生

正文
Text

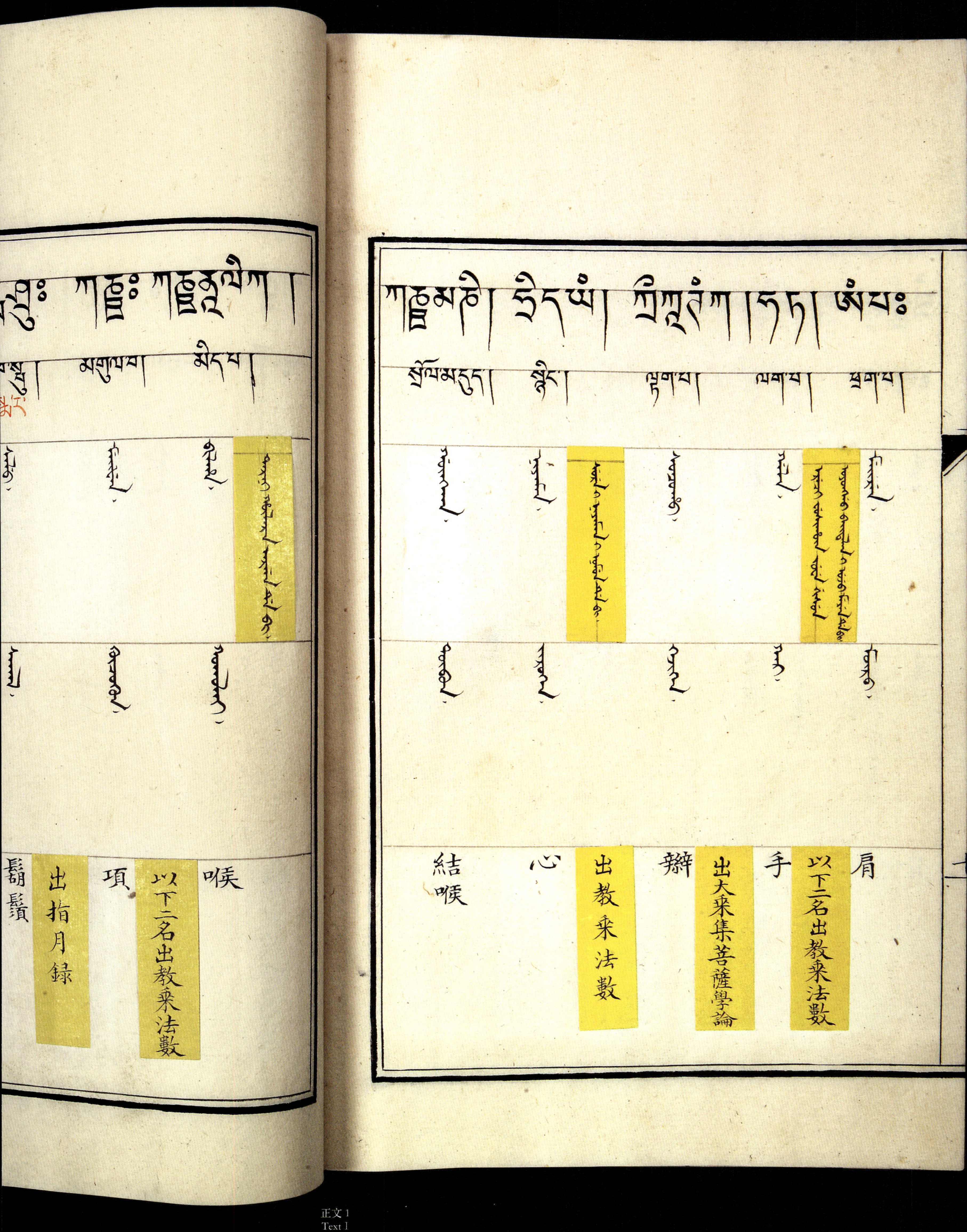

肩	手	辮	心	結喉
ཨཾ་སཿ	ཧསྟ།	ཀྲི་ཀཱ་ཎཀ།	ཧྲི་ད་ཡཾ།	ཀཎྛ་མ་ཎི།
ཕྲག་པ།	ལག་པ།	ལྡག་པ།	སྙིང་།	གྲོལ་མཛུད།
[illegible]	[illegible]	[illegible]	[illegible]	[illegible]
[illegible]	[illegible]	[illegible]	[illegible]	[illegible]
肩（以下二名出教乘法數）	手	辮（出大乘集菩薩學論）	心（出教乘法數）	結喉

喉	項	鬍鬚
ཀཎྛ་ལཱི་ཀ།	ཀཎྛཿ	…ཤྲུཿ
མིད་པ།	མགུལ་པ།	…སྨ་ར།
[illegible]	[illegible]	[illegible]
[illegible]	[illegible]	[illegible]
喉	項（以下二名出教乘法數）	鬍鬚（出指月錄）

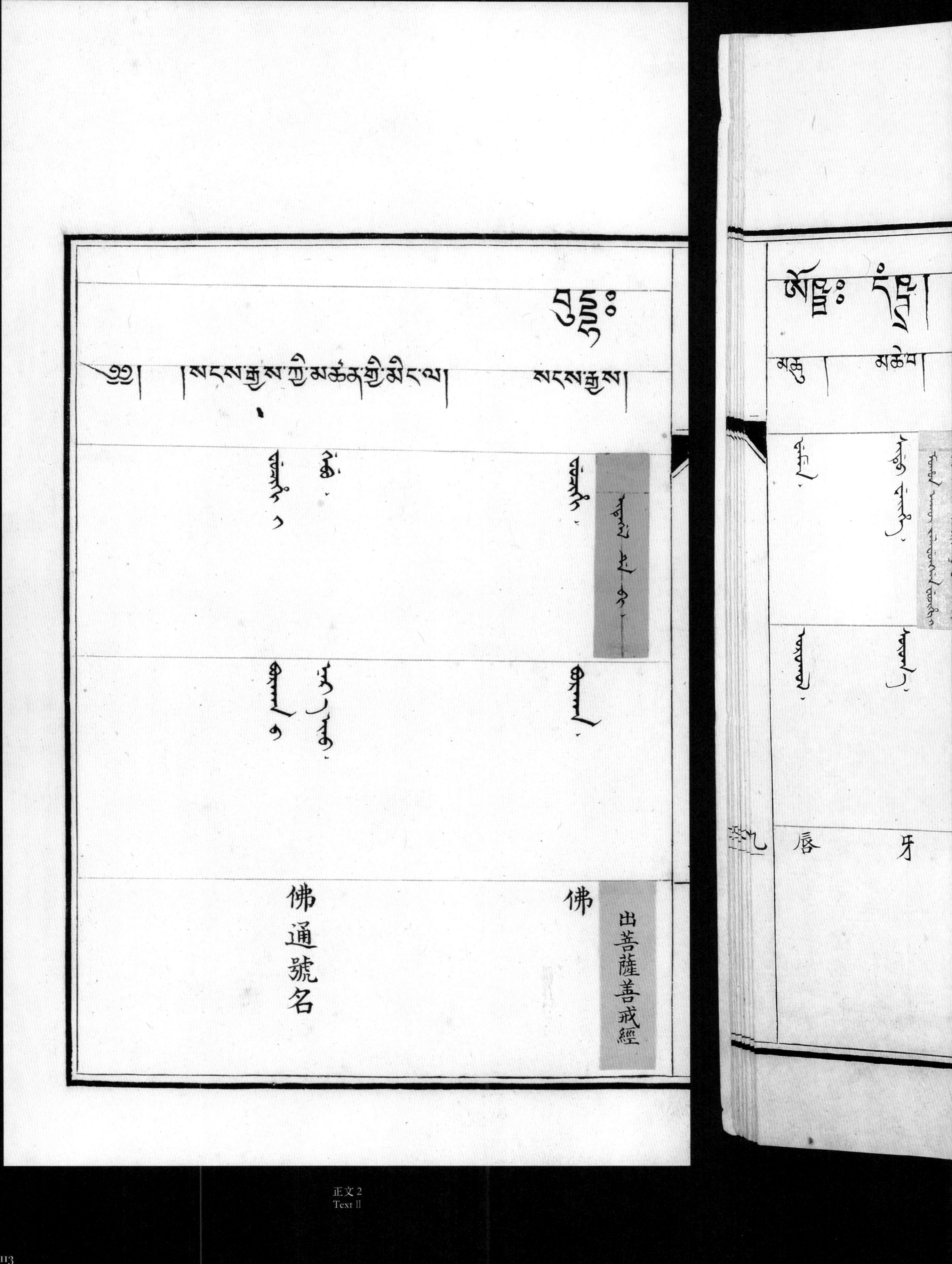

བུདྡྷཿ

སངས་རྒྱས།

佛

出菩薩善戒經

༡༢། །སངས་རྒྱས་ཀྱི་མཚན་གྱི་མིང་ལ།

佛通號名

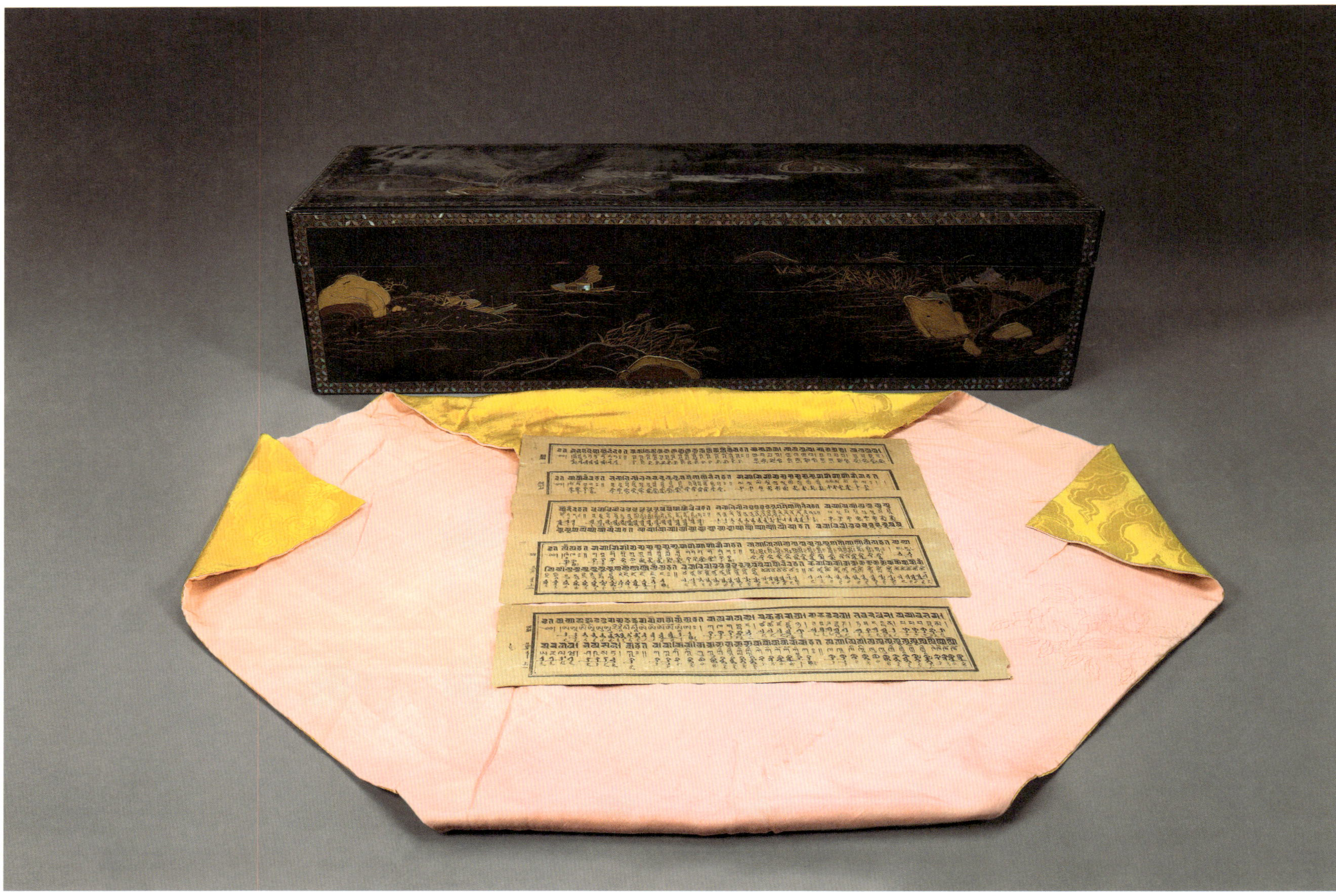

黑漆描金嵌螺鈿書盒及明黃色地暗花綾夾袱
Sutra case covered with black lacquer, traced in gold and inlaid with mother-of-pearls and bright yellow twill-weave silk bundle with veiled pattern

37

書27158
《四體阿禮嘎禮字一卷》
清　佚名輯
清康熙年刻梵藏蒙滿合璧本
開本　縱11.2厘米　橫40.8厘米
版框　縱9.1厘米　橫35.1厘米
一册　一包（其滿文係後人加寫而成）

Inventory number: Shu 27158
The Ali Gali Transliterations of the Four Languages
Anonymous, Qing dynasty (1644-1911)
Printed in Sanskrit, Tibetan, Mongolian and Manchu in the Kangxi period (r.1662-1722)
Format: 11.2 × 40.8 cm
Frame: 9.1 × 35.1 cm
One case in one bundle
The Manchu part supplemented later

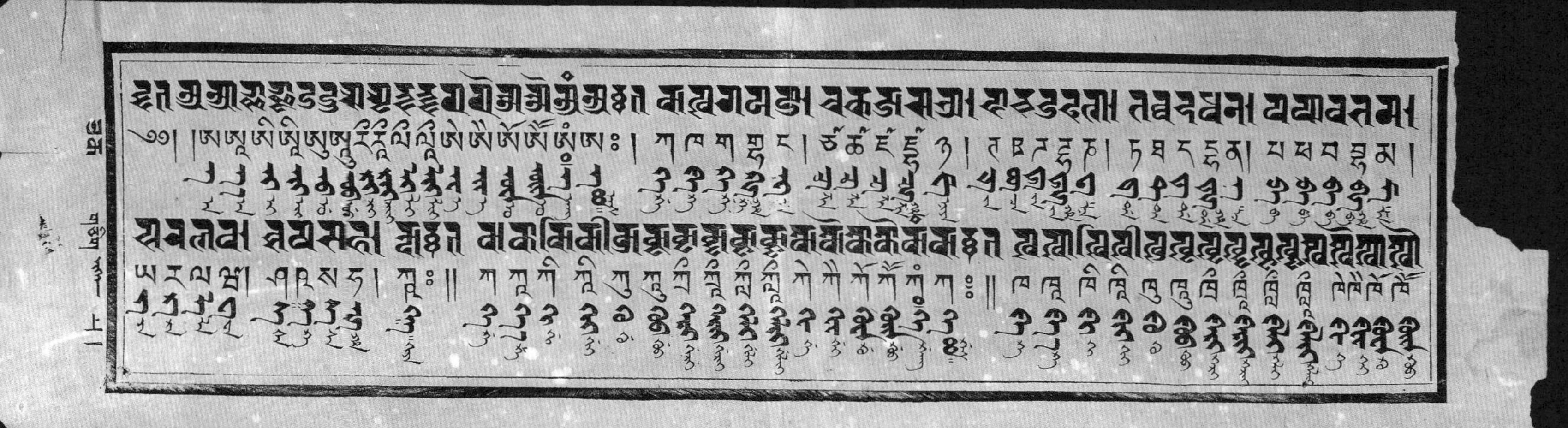

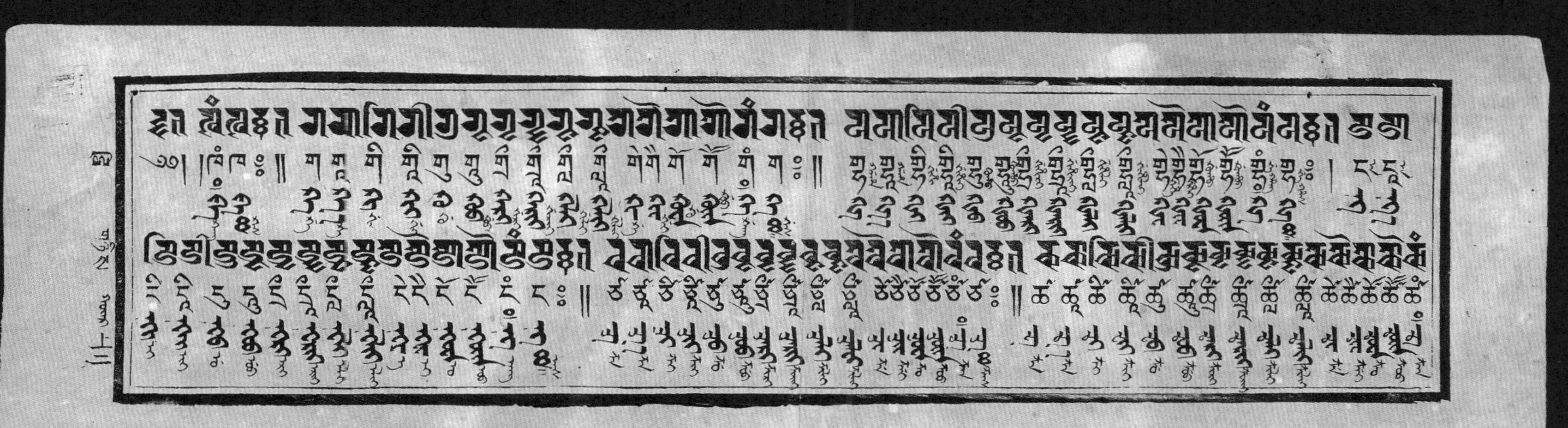

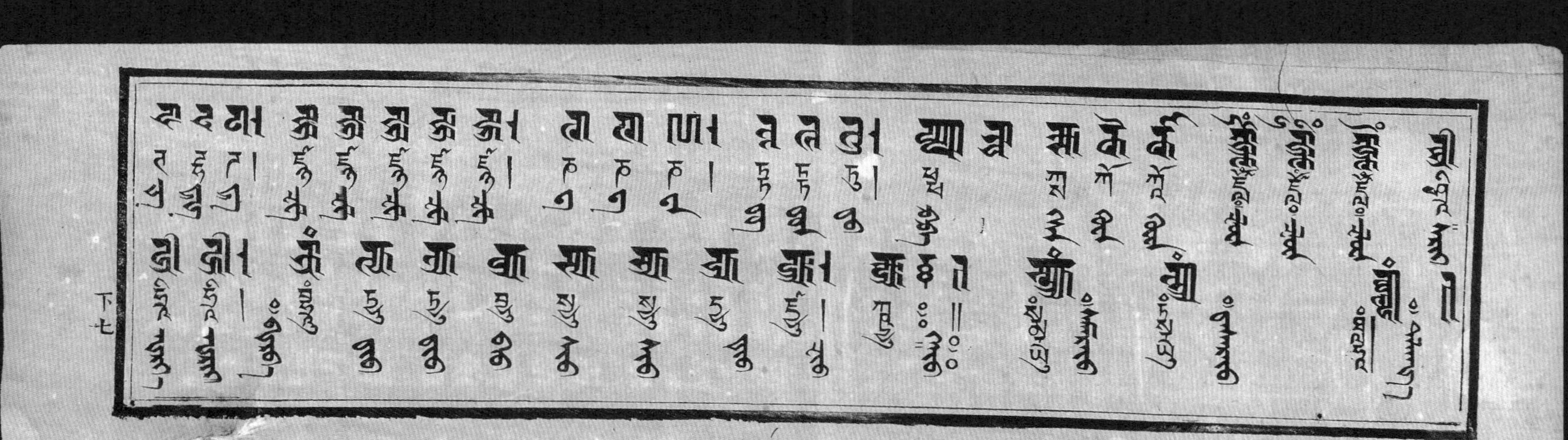

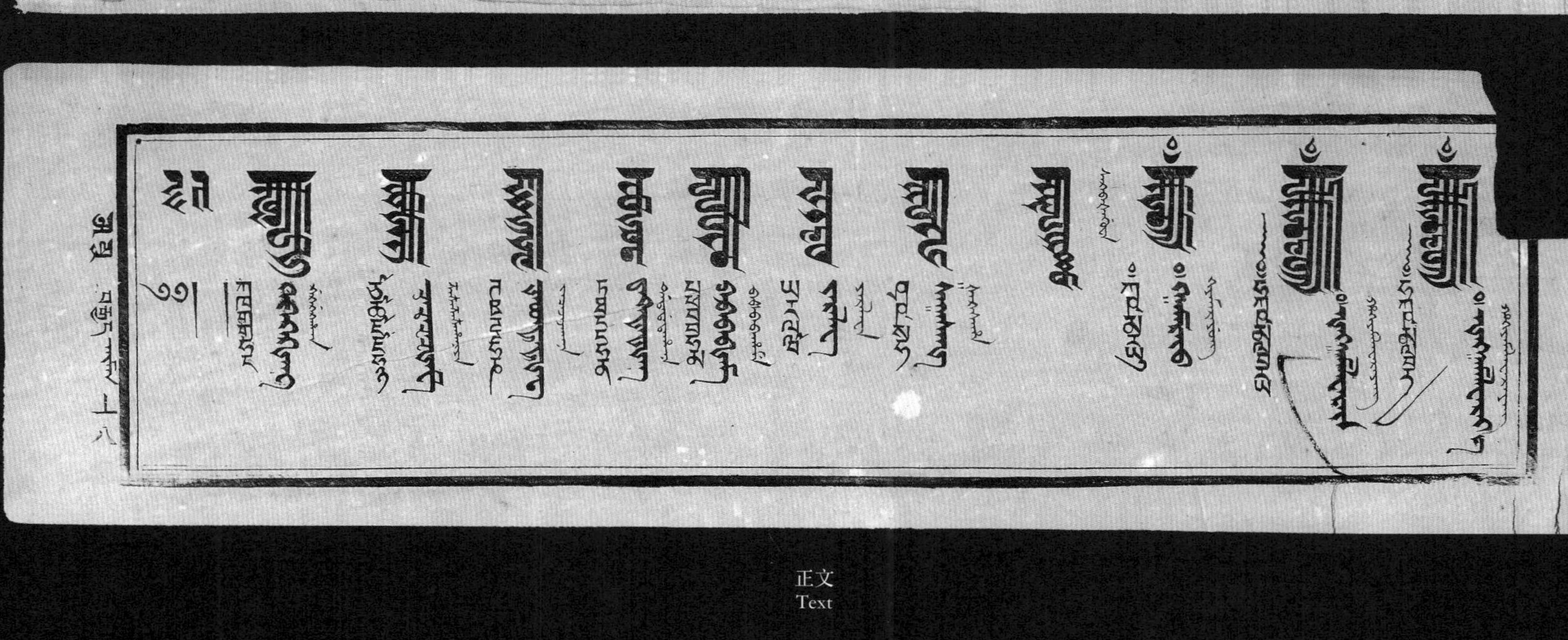

正文
Text

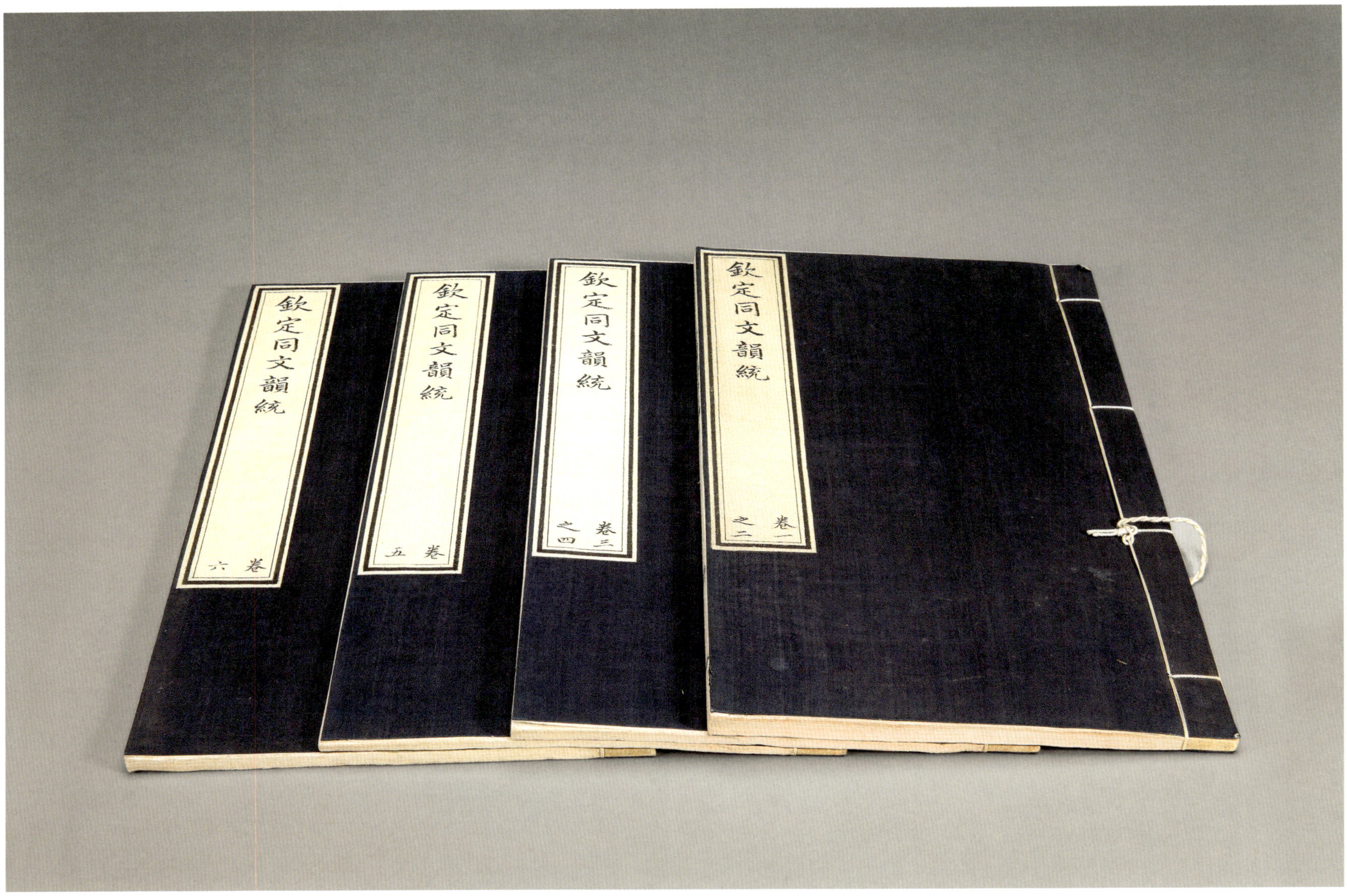

藍色素絹書面
Blue silk covers

書62
《欽定同文韻統六卷》
清　允祿等奉敕撰
清乾隆十五年(1750)武英殿刻套印漢滿梵藏合璧本
開本　縱30.8厘米　橫19.5厘米
版框　縱21.1厘米　橫14厘米
四冊　一函

38

Inventory number: Shu 62
Unified Syllables Imperially Commissioned
Six chapters
Compiled at the order of the Qianlong emperor (r.1736-1795) by Yunlu et. al.
Chromatographic edition
Printed in Chinese, Manchu, Sanskrit and Tibetan in 1750 at the Hall of Martial Valour
Format: 30.8 × 19.5 cm
Frame: 21.1 × 14 cm
Four volumes in one case

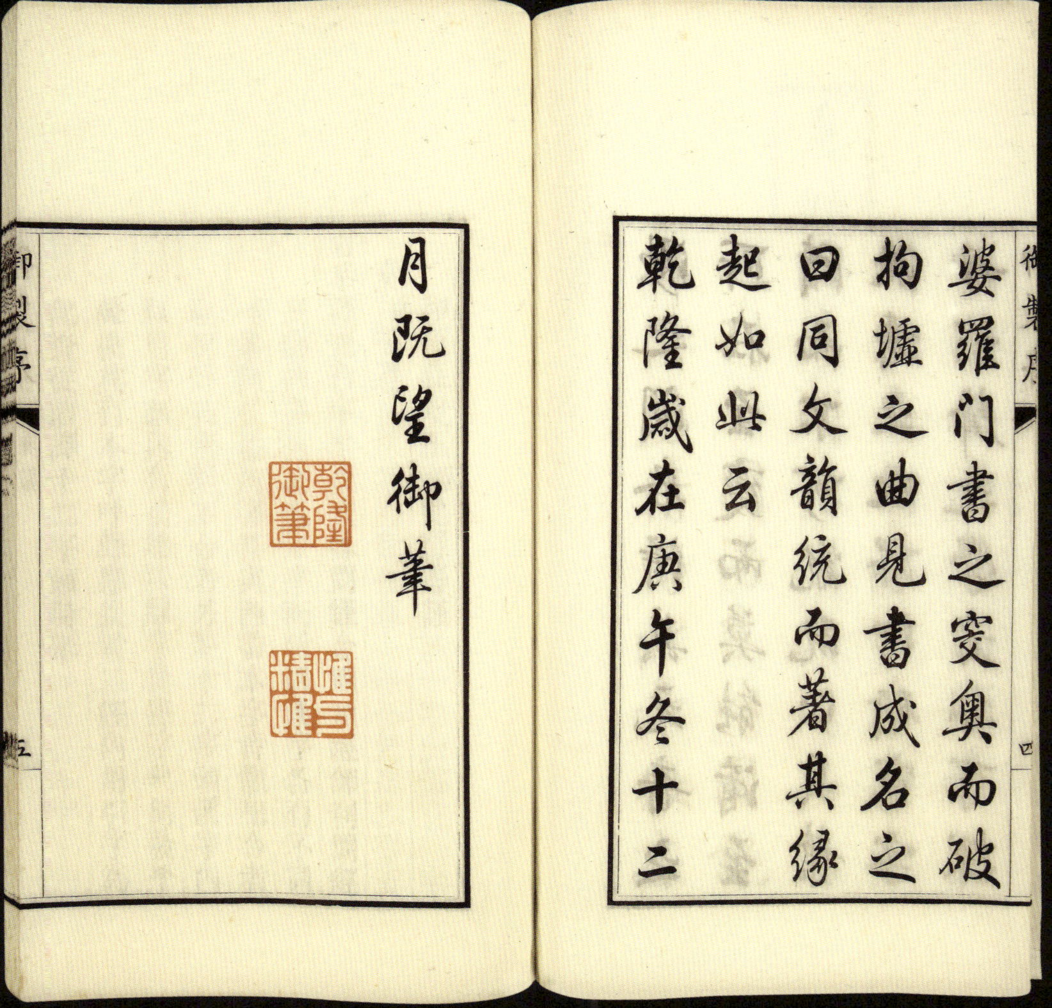

乾隆十五年御製序
Preface by the Qianlong emperor in 1747

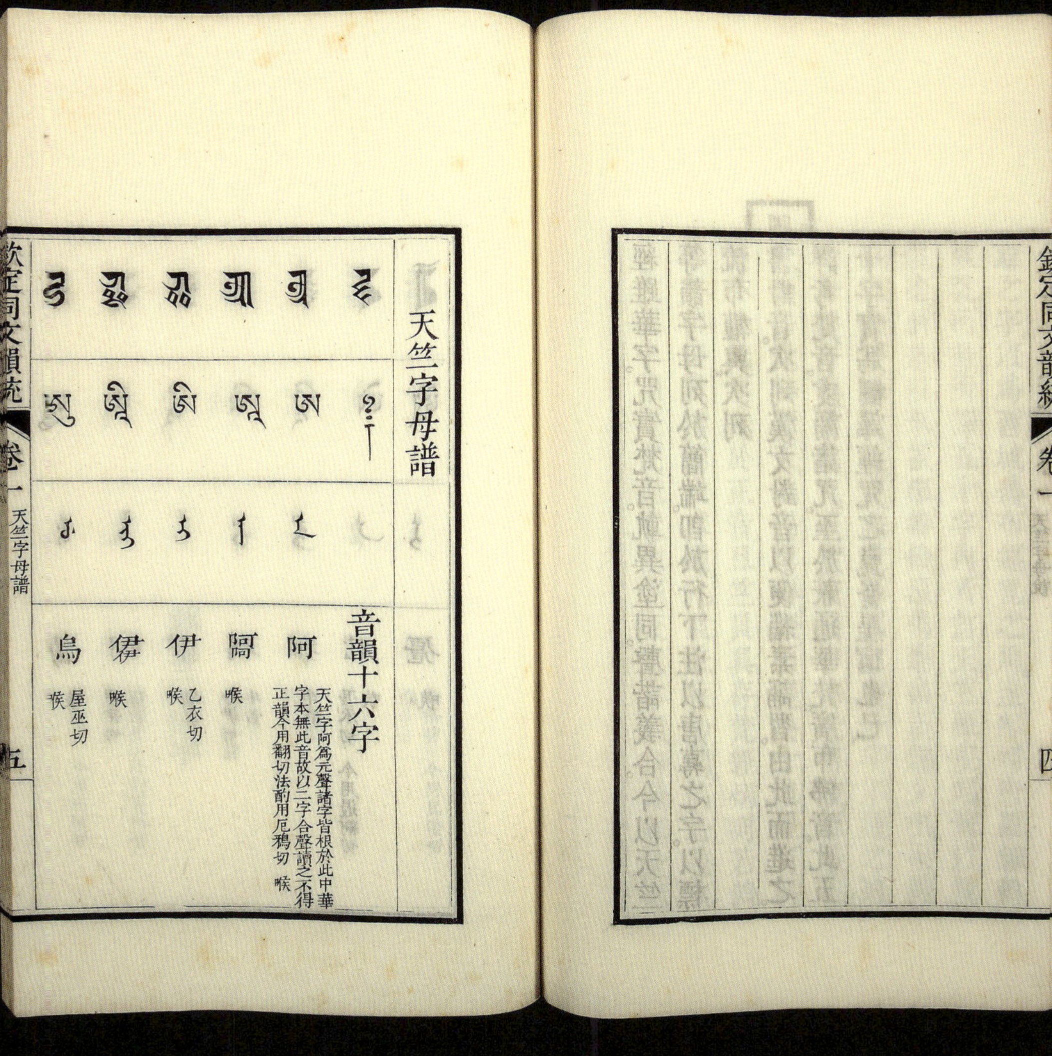

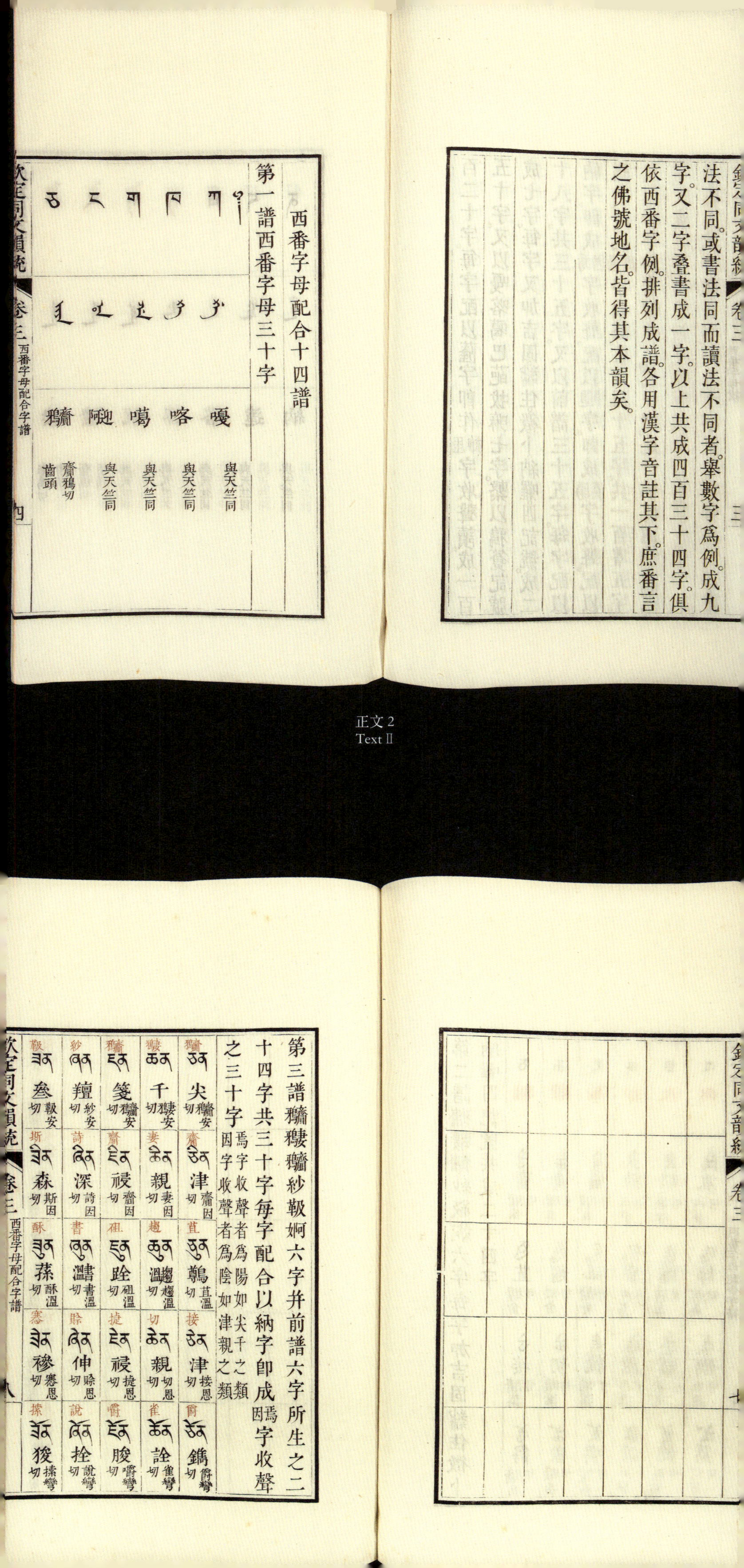

法不同。或書法同而讀法不同者。舉數字爲例。成九字。又二字疊書成一字。以上共成四百三十四字。俱依西番字例。排列成譜。各用漢字音註其下。庶番言之佛號地名。皆得其本韻矣。

西番字母配合十四譜

第一譜西番字母三十字

ཀ	ཁ	ག	ང	ཅ
嘎	喀	噶	⿰口迦	⿰鵶齋
與天竺同	與天竺同	與天竺同	與天竺同	齋鵶切 齒頭

正文 2

Text II

第三譜⿰鵶齋⿰齒婁⿰鵶齋紗靸婀六字并前譜六字所生之二十四字共三十字每字配合以納字即成焉因字收聲之三十字焉字收聲者爲陽如尖千之類因字收聲者爲陰如津親之類

⿰鵶齋 ཙན 尖 ⿰鵶齋安切	⿰齒婁 ཚན 千 ⿰齒婁安切	⿰鵶齋 ཛན 箋 ⿰鵶齋安切	紗 ཤན 羶 紗安切	靸 སན 叄 靸安切
齋 ཙིན 津 齋因切	妻 ཚིན 親 妻因切	齋 ཛིན 祲 齋因切	詩 ཤིན 深 詩因切	斯 སིན 森 斯因切
苴 ཙུན 鷷 苴溫切	趨 ཚུན ⿰溫趨 趨溫切	砠 ཛུན 跧 砠溫切	書 ཤུན ⿰溫書 書溫切	酥 སུན 孫 酥溫切
接 ཙེན 津 接恩切	切 ཚེན 親 切恩切	捷 ཛེན 祲 捷恩切	賖 ཤེན 伸 賖恩切	塞 སེན 穇 塞恩切
雋 ཙོན 鐫 雋彎切	雀 ཚོན 詮 雀彎切	⿰口雋 ཛོན 脧 ⿰口雋彎切	說 ཤོན 拴 說彎切	搎 སོན 狻 搎彎切

辨之甚明。且無虛圈影響。則誠歐陽氏修序韻總。所謂櫛之於髮。績之於絲。雖細且多而條理不亂者矣。雖然。梵即華也。蓋惟不知梵。故不知華之所自來。今旣知梵之可爲華。乃眞知華之不殊梵。諦思而冥契之。聲音之道。所爲一以貫之者。庶幾左右逢源而自得之矣。

華言三十六字母

舊傳神珙字母三十字。梁山僧守溫增六字。爲三十六字。

字母	清濁	音	五音
見	清	牙音	角
溪	次清	牙音	角
羣	濁	牙音	角
疑	半清半濁	牙音	角
端	清	舌頭音	徵
透	次清	舌頭音	徵
定	濁	舌頭音	徵
泥	半清半濁	舌頭音	徵

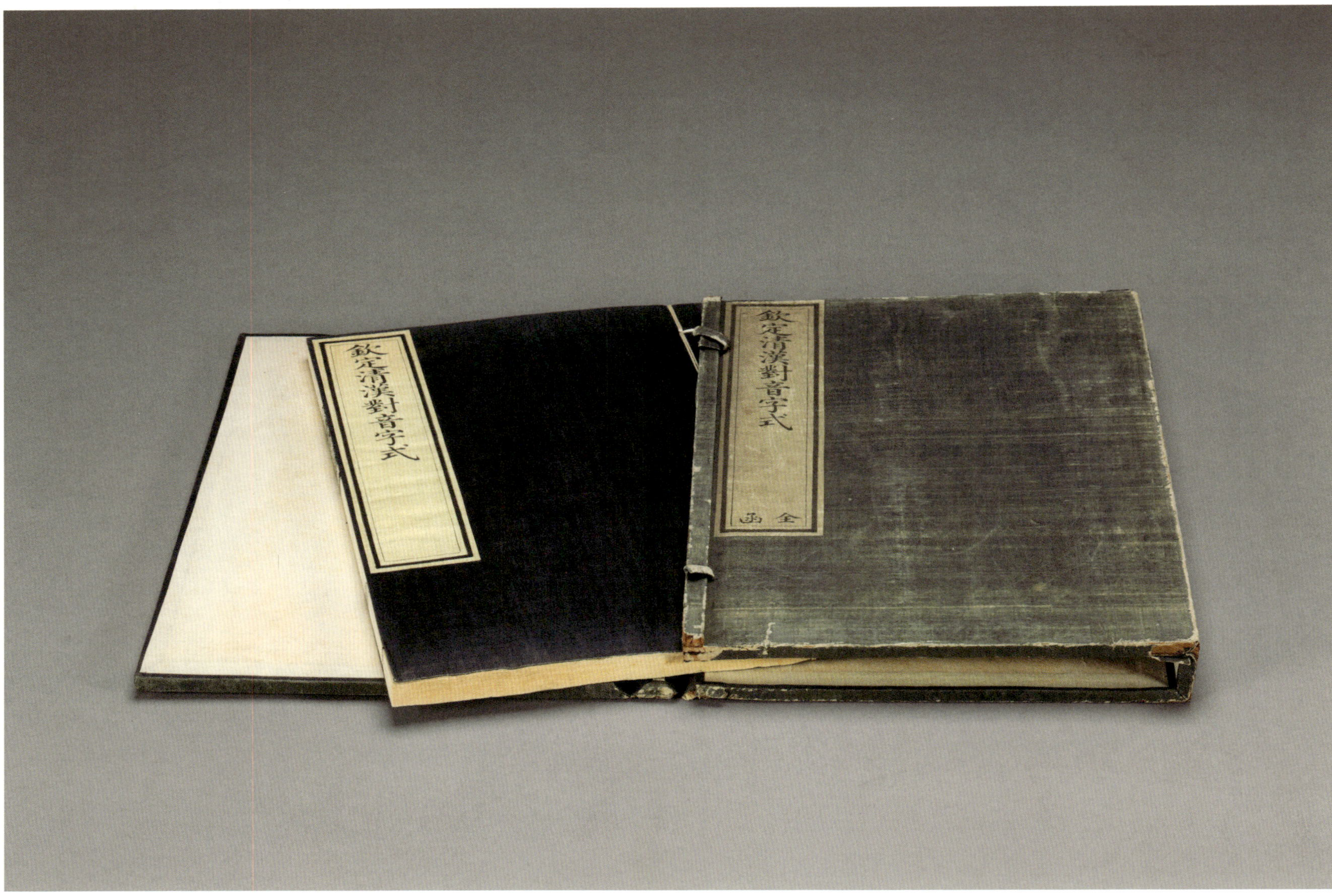

藍色素絹書函
Blue silk case

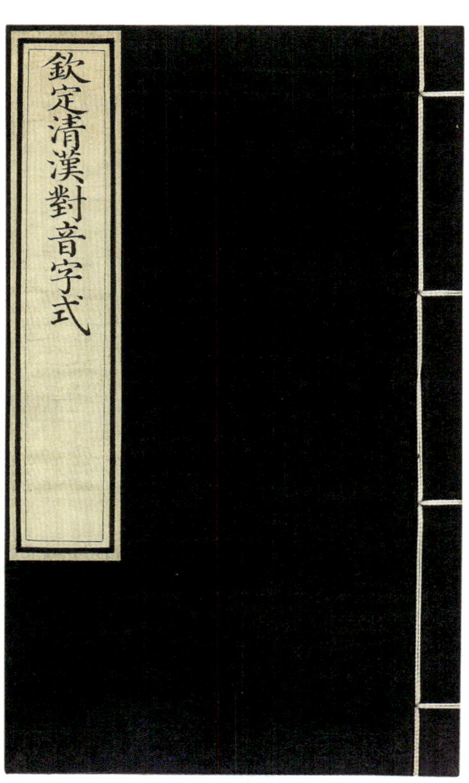

藍色素絹書面
Blue silk cover

書21796
《欽定清漢對音字式一卷》
清　高宗弘曆敕撰
清乾隆三十七年（1772）武英殿刻滿漢合璧本
開本　縱27.5厘米　橫17厘米
版框　縱19.4厘米　橫14.1厘米
一冊　一函

39

Inventory number: Shu 21796
Patterns of Manchu and Chinese Corresponding Phones
One chapter
Written at the order of the Qianlong emperor (r.1736-1795)
Printed in Manchu and Chinese in 1772 at the Hall of Martial Valour
Format: 27.5 × 17 cm
Frame: 19.4 × 14.1 cm
One volume in one case

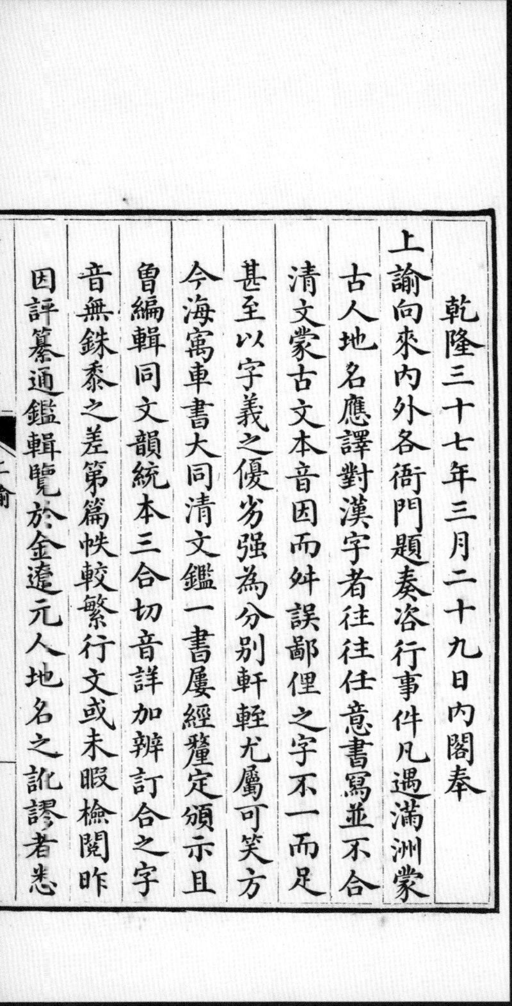
乾隆三十七年三月二十九日内閣奉
上諭向來内外各衙門題奏咨行事件凡遇滿洲蒙
古人地名應譯對漢字者往往任意書寫並不合
清文蒙古文本音因而舛誤鄙俚之字不一而足
甚至以字義之優劣強為分别軒輊尤屬可笑方
今海㝢車書大同清文鑑一書屢經釐定頒示且
曾編輯同文韻統本三合切音詳加辨訂合之字
音無銖黍之差第篇帙較繁行文或未暇檢閱昨
因評纂通鑑輯覽於金遼元人地名之訛謬者悉

乾隆三十七年上諭
Imperial edict in 1772

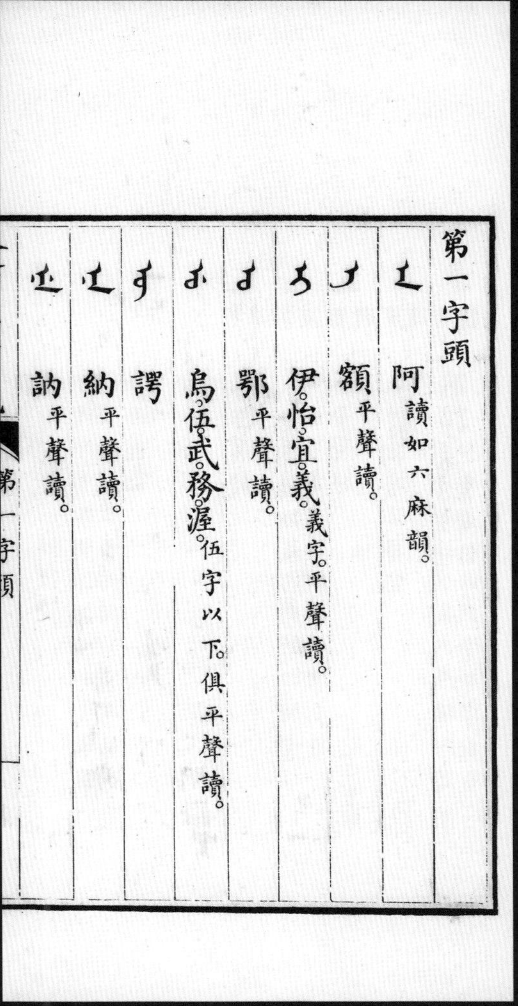
第一字頭
阿讀如六麻韻。
額平聲讀。
伊怡宜義。義字平聲讀。
鄂平聲讀。
烏伍武務渥。伍字以下俱平聲讀。
諤
納平聲讀。
訥平聲讀。

卷端
Beginning

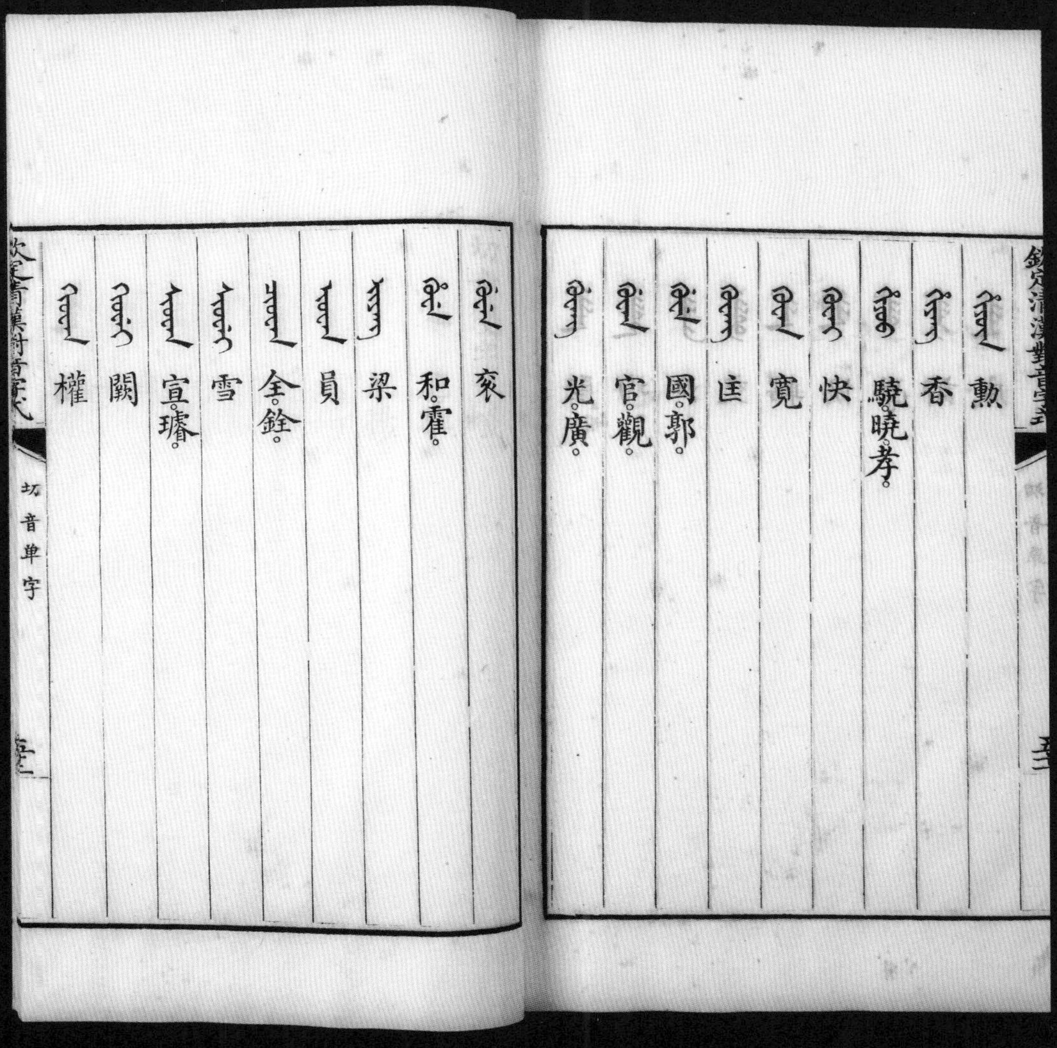
欽定清漢對音字式
勲
香
驍曉孝
快
寬
匡
國郭
官觀
光廣
三

欽定清漢對音字式　切音單字
衮
和霍
梁
員
全銓
雪
宣璿
闕
權

正文
Text

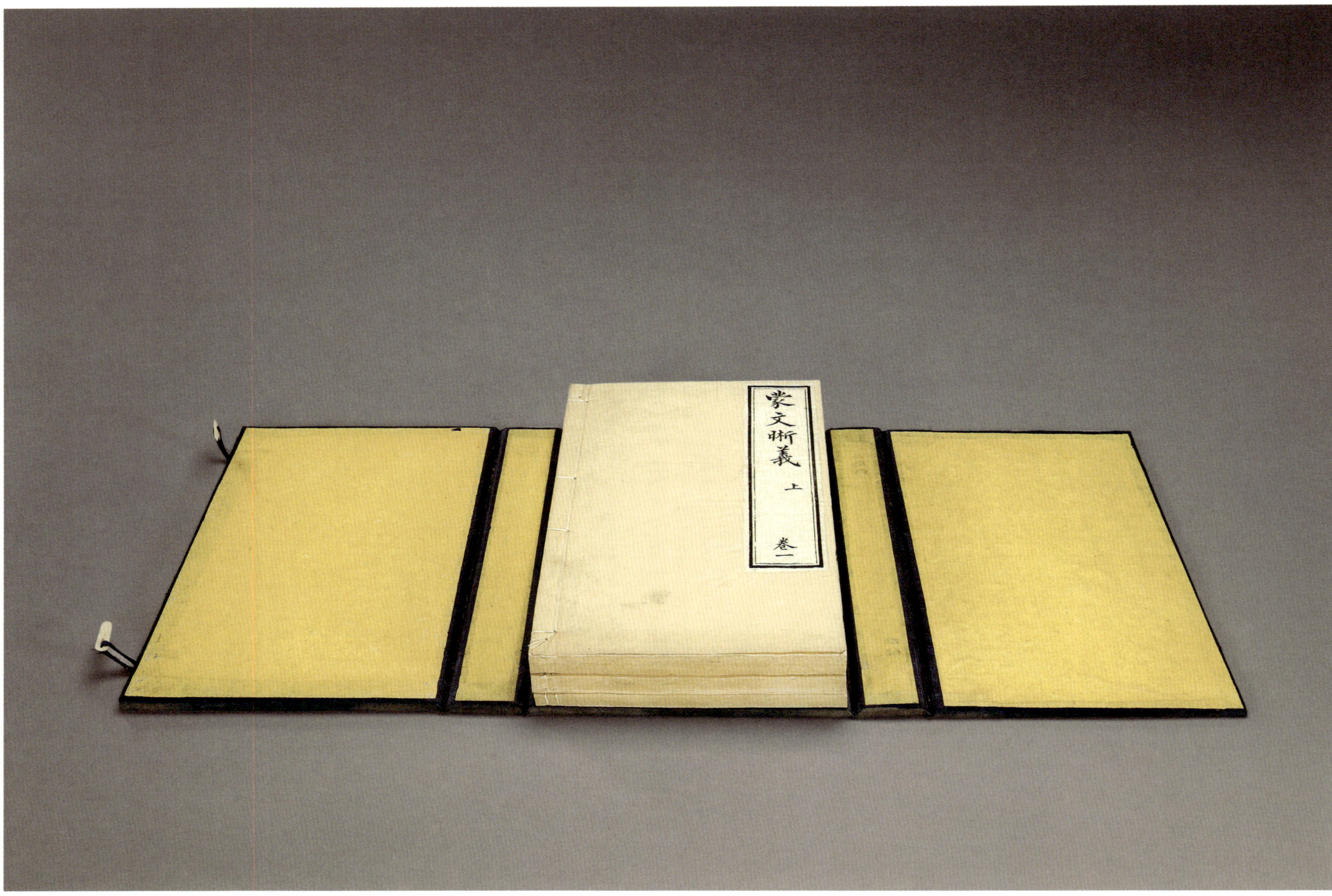

外觀
Exterior

40 書21813

《蒙文指要四卷》

清　景煇編　賽尚阿增補輯　春圃音德布校
清道光二十八年（1848）刻滿蒙漢合璧本
開本　縱29.3厘米　橫18厘米
版框　縱20.5厘米　橫15.6厘米
四冊　一函

Inventory number: Shu 21813

Essentials of Mongolian

Four chapters
Compiled by Jinghui, supplemented by Saisangga and proofread by Chunpuyindebu
Printed in Manchu, Mongolian and Chinese in 1848
Format: 29.3 × 18 cm
Frame: 20.5 × 15.6 cm
Four volumes in one case

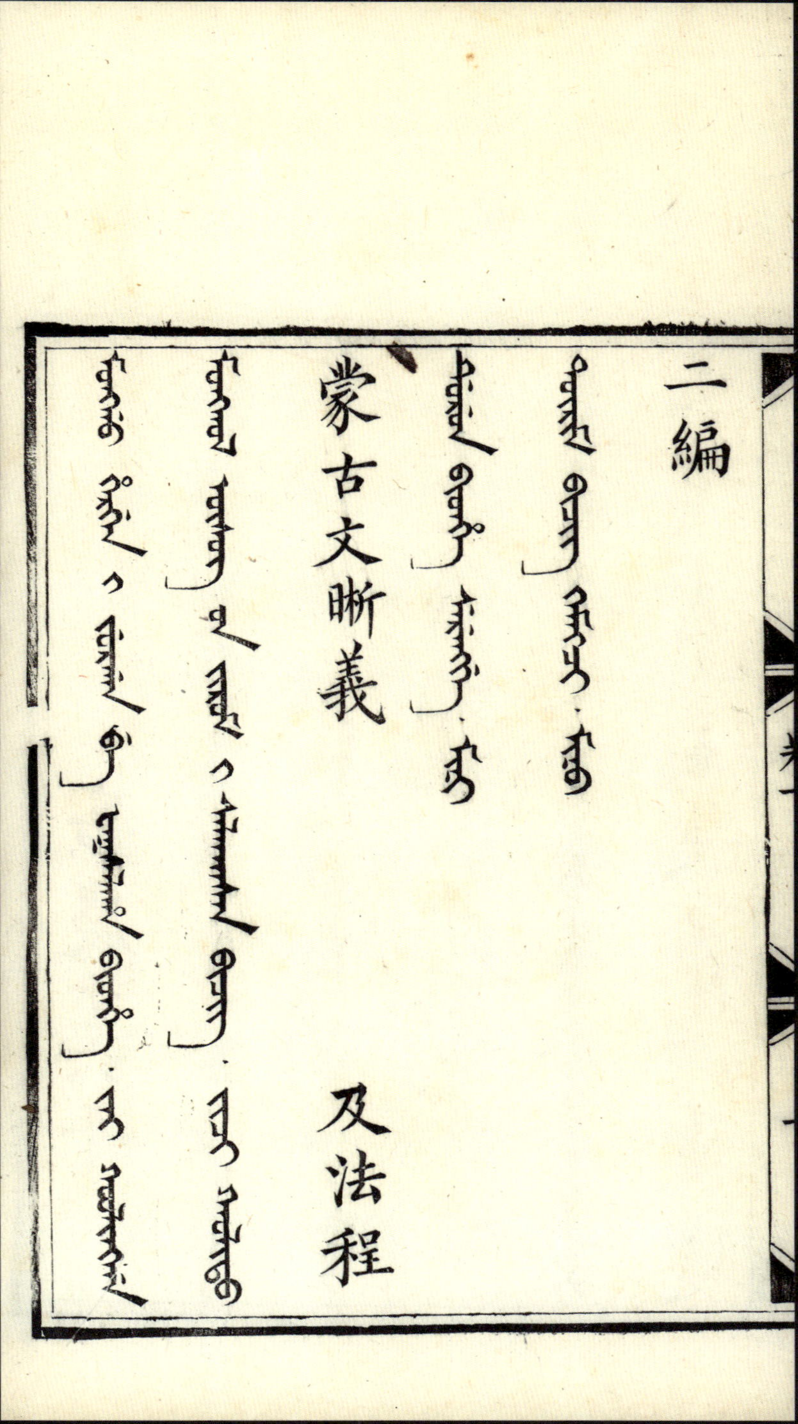

道光二十八年富俊序
Preface by Fujun in 1848

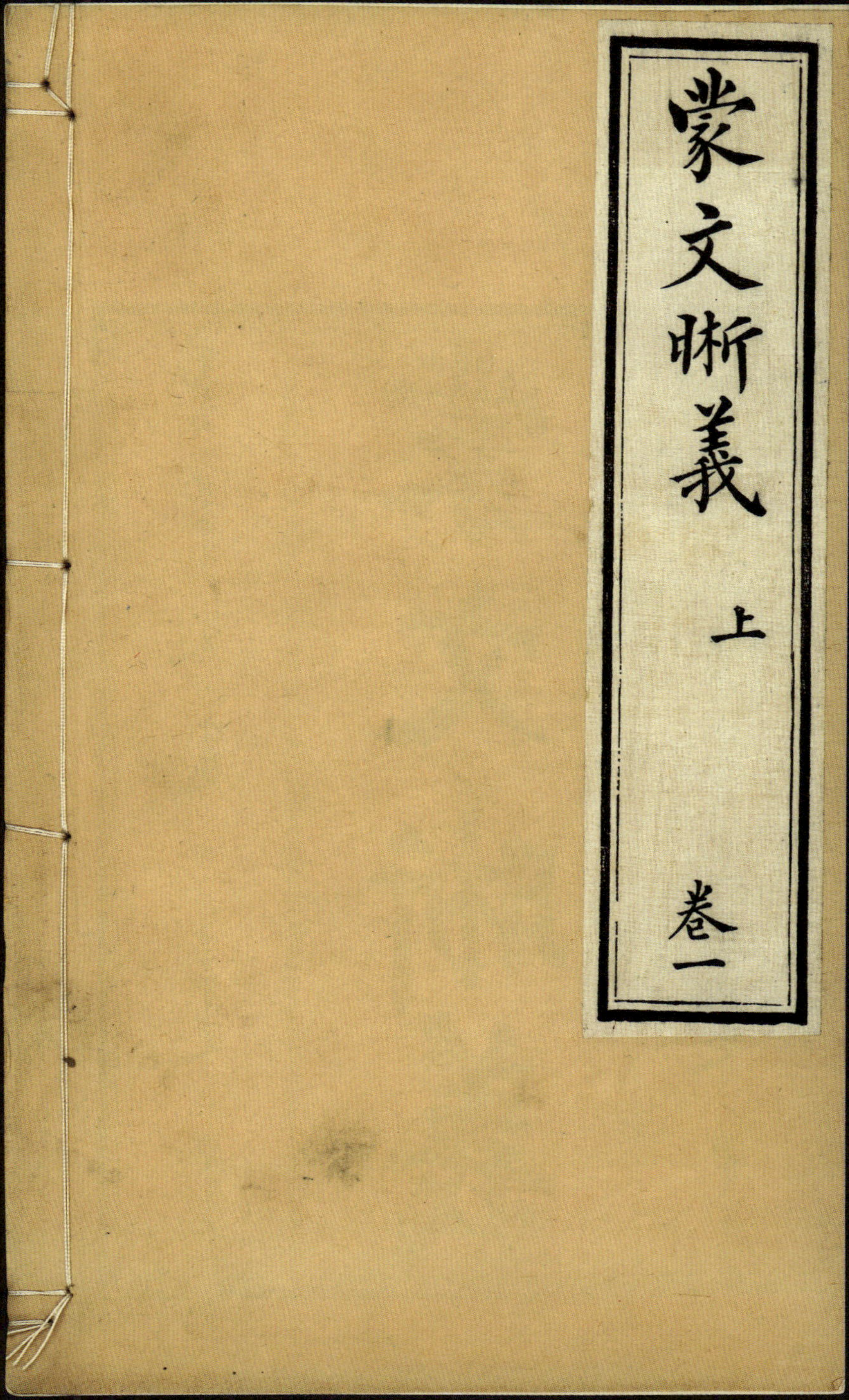

黃色紙書面
Yellow paper cover

蒙文晰義

因何

為何

怎麽的

怎麽

何必

下用

做什麽

下用

任憑寬

值什麽

值什麽

嘆聲

什麽

怪人聲

如

如

如

如

等字俱倣此

如

等字俱倣此

不變字

凡下雪下雹等字俱同

反目

常用鑑註

削樹枝

衰敗

鈌

安逸

攏髮

衣襟捲

染物

狠乏

結皮

誇晦了

大駝頭响聲

磨麩

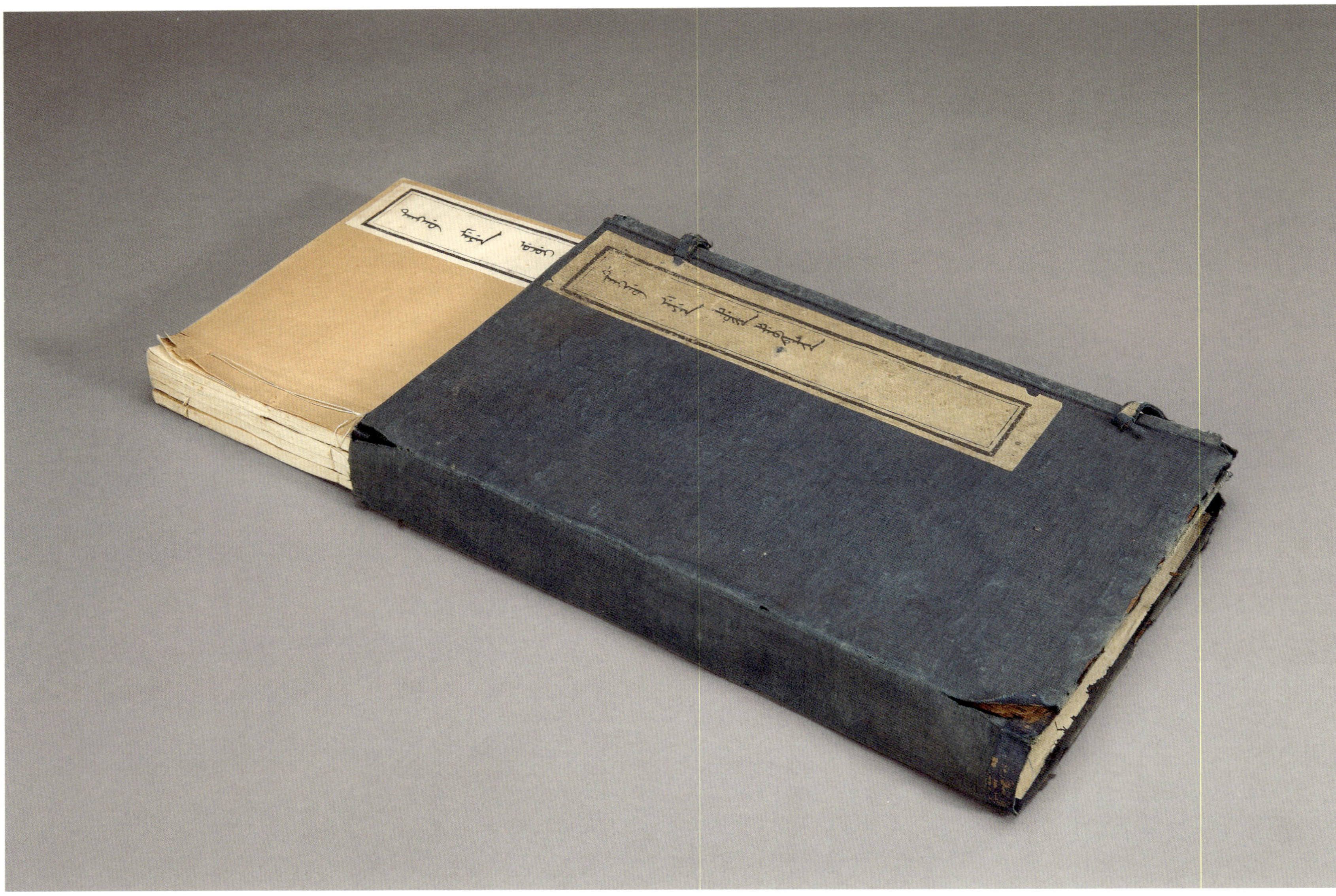

藍色素布書函
Blue cloth case

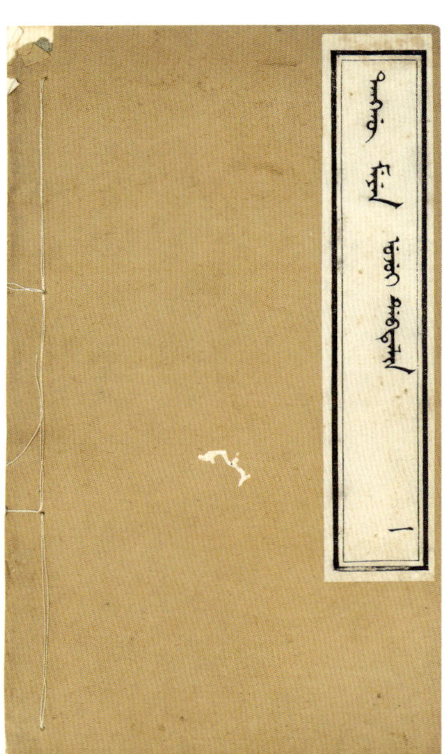

黄色紙書面
Yellow paper cover

書21881
《一百條四卷》
清　佚名輯
清刻滿漢合璧本
開本　縱25.4厘米　横15厘米
版框　縱18.5厘米　横12.4厘米
四册　一函

41

Inventory number: Shu 21881
One Hundred Conversational Terms
Four chapters
Anonymous, Qing dynasty (1644-1911)
Printed in Manchu and Chinese in the Qing dynasty
Format: 25.4 × 15 cm
Frame: 18.5 × 12.4 cm
Four volumes in one case

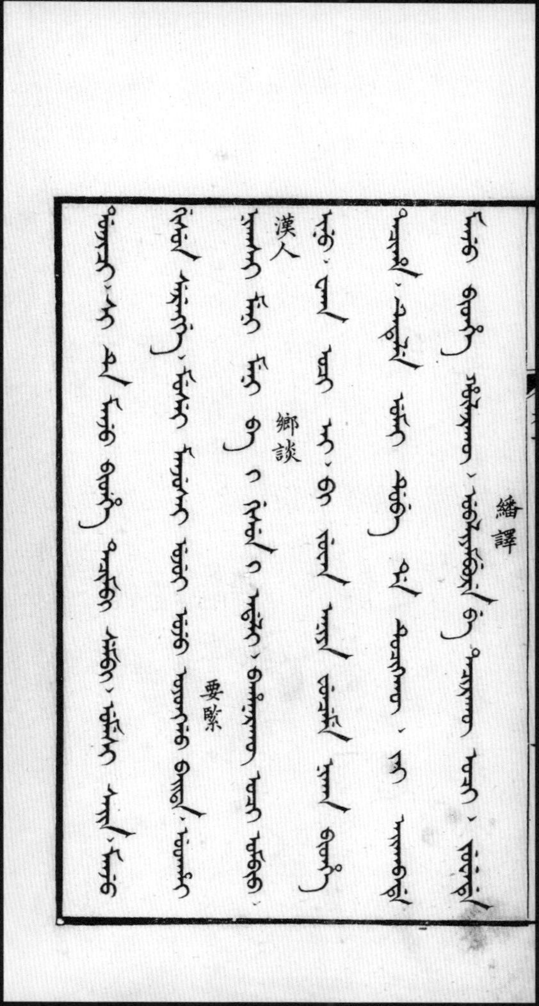

卷端
Beginning

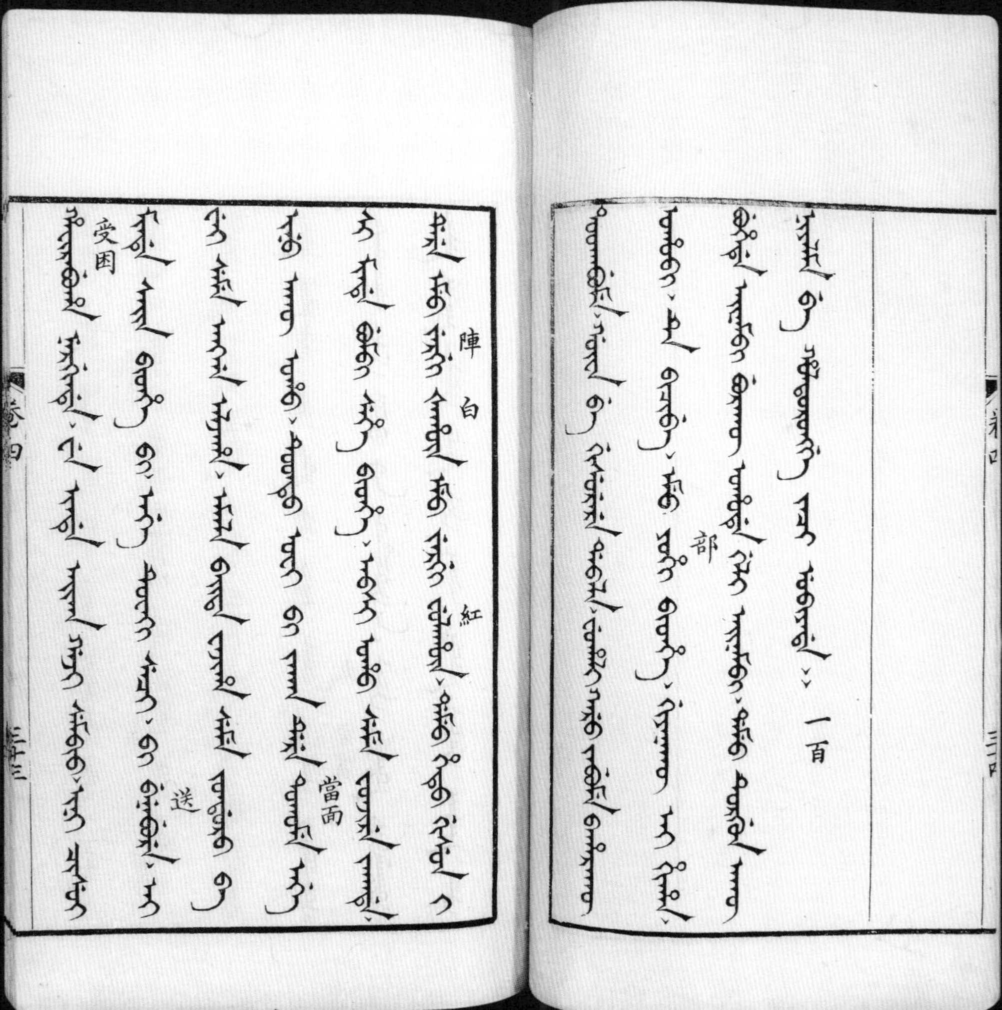

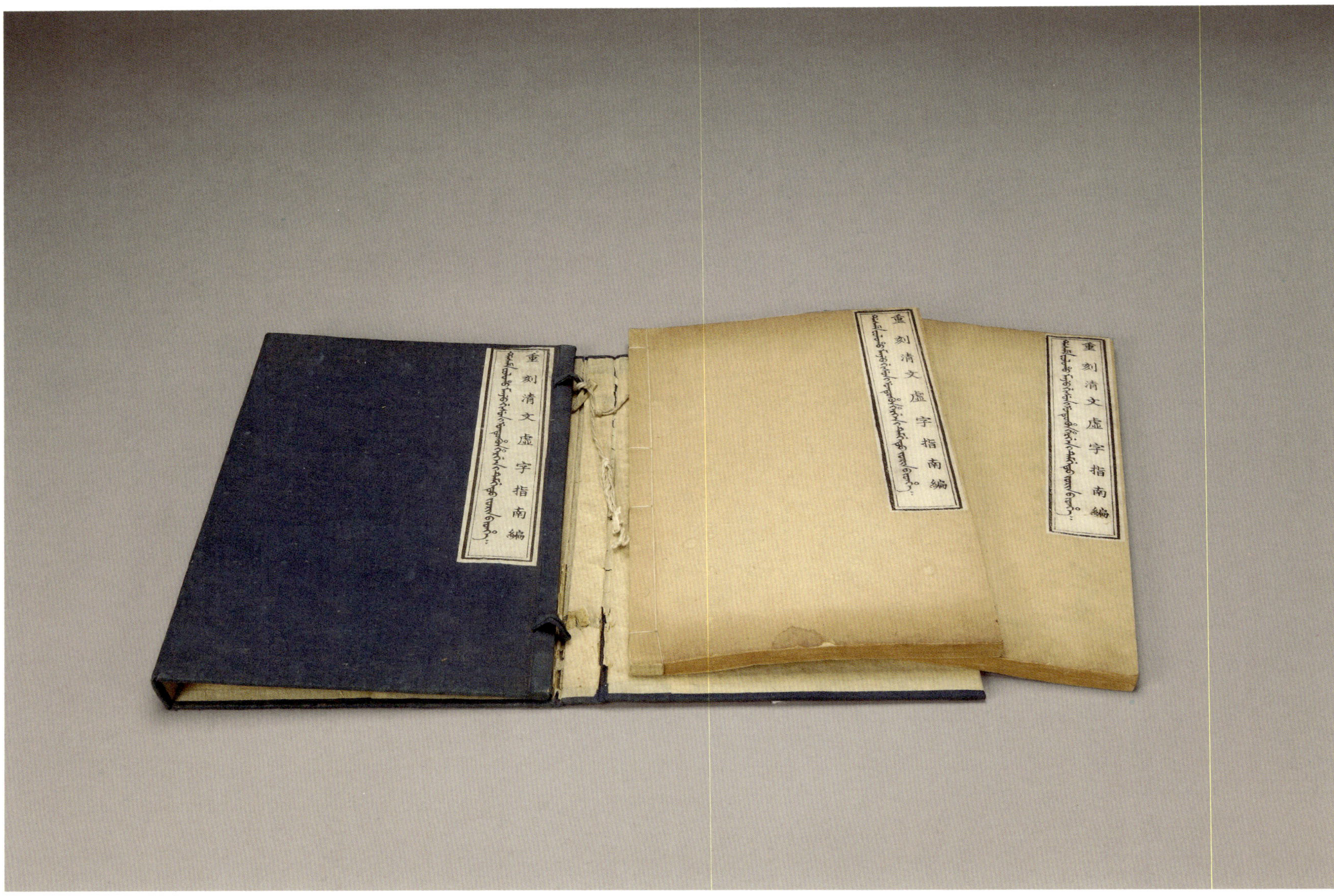

藍色素布書函
Blue cloth case

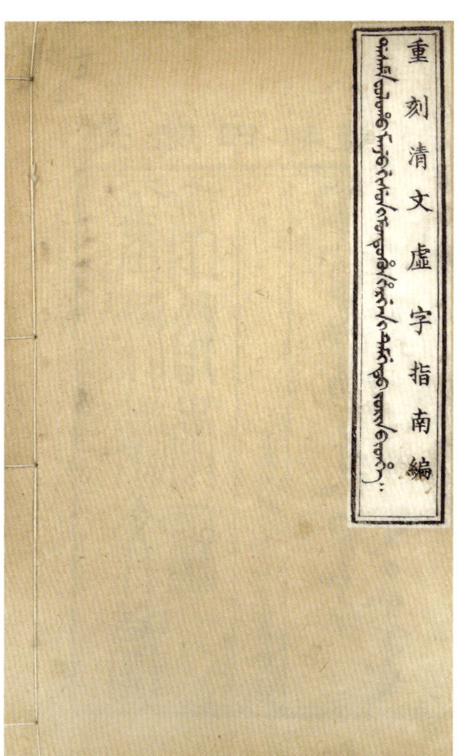

黃色紙書面
Yellow paper cover

42

書21833
《重刻清文虛字指南編二卷》
清　萬福撰　鳳山訂
清光緒二十年（1894）京都隆福寺聚珍堂刻滿漢合璧本
開本　縱27.3厘米　橫17厘米
版框　縱19.5厘米　橫14.9厘米
二册　一函

Inventory number: Shu 21833
Reprinted Version of the Guidebook of Manchu Function Words
Two chapters
Written by Wanfu and emended by Fengshan, Qing dynasty (1644-1911)
Printed in Manchu and Chinese in 1894 at the Juzhentang Bookstore, Longfu Temple, Beijing
Format: 27.3 × 17 cm
Frame: 19.5 × 14.9 cm
Two volumes in one case

光緒甲午年重刻

重刻清文虛字指南編

京都隆福寺聚珍堂書坊梓行

而文亦由辭而顯也 夫
是道以文明
言之無文 行之不遠
悉屬傳文之具 孔子曰
興 辭有古今
文無清漢 皆為載道之
清文虛字指南編序

牌記及萬福撰原序
Copyright page and preface by Wanfu

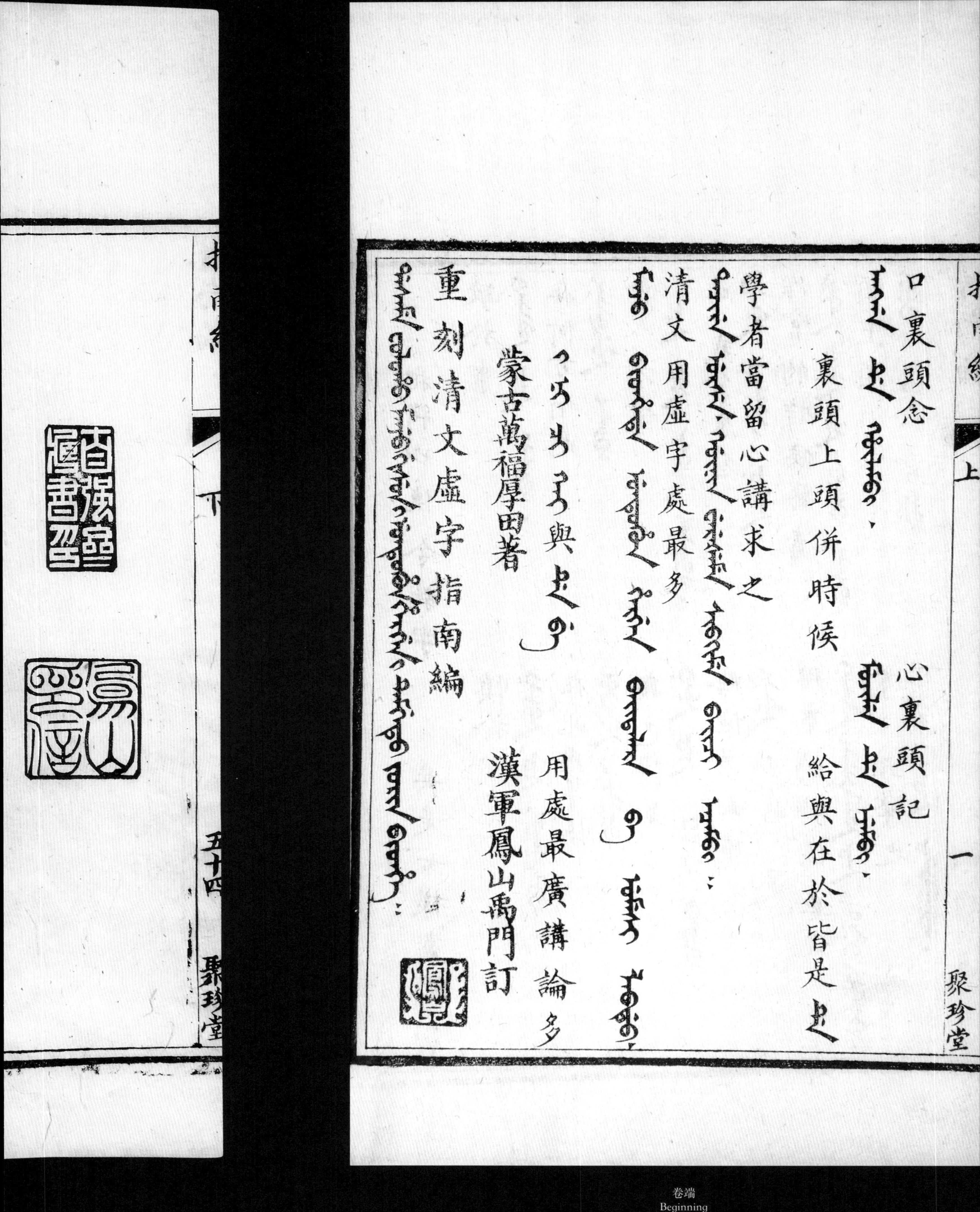

重刻清文虛字指南編

蒙古萬福厚田著　漢軍鳳山禹門訂

清文用虛字處最多　用處最廣講論多

學者當留心講求之

裏頭上頭併時候　給與在於皆是

口裏頭念　心裏頭記

與

卷端
Beginning

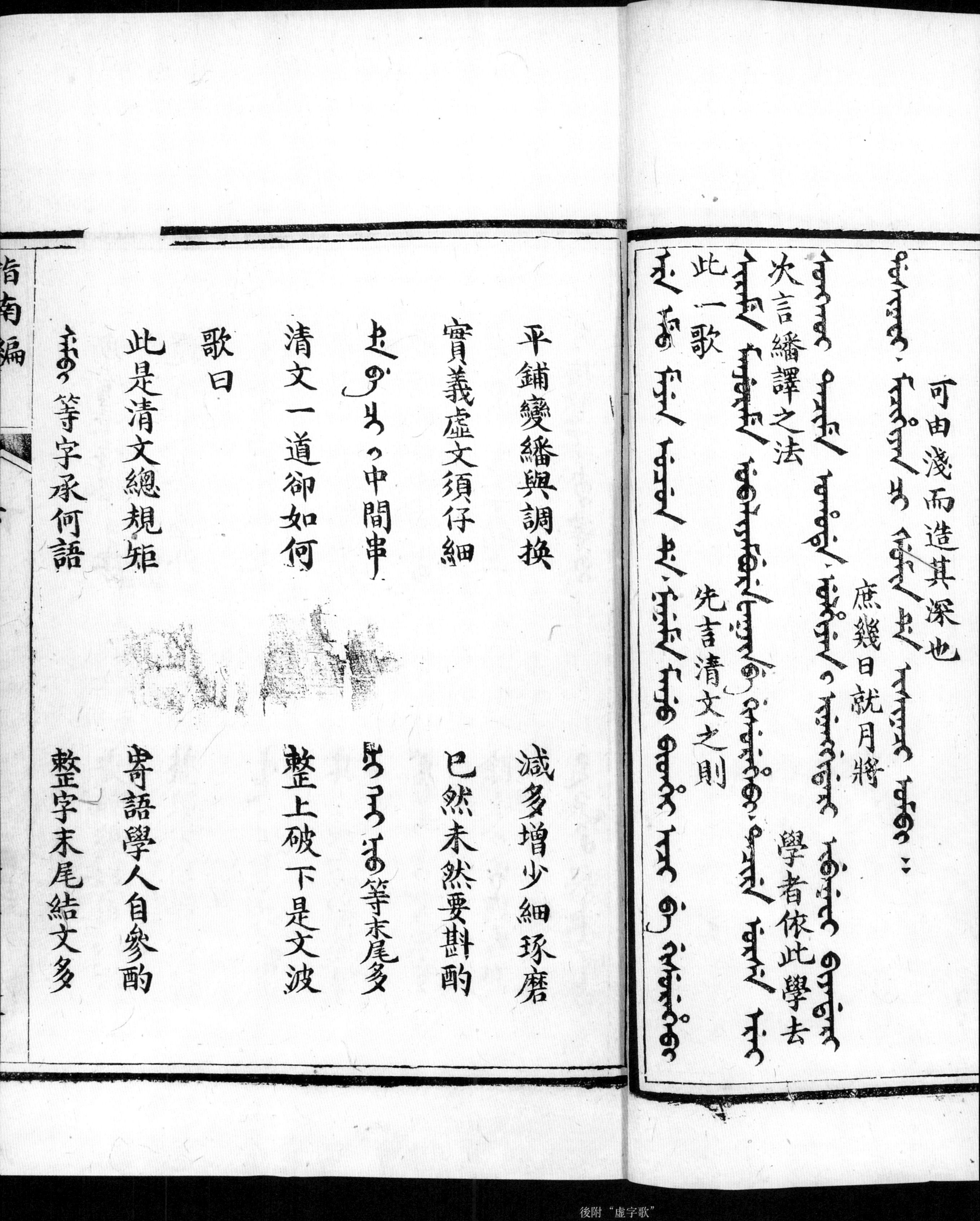

可由淺而造其深也

庶幾日就月將　學者依此學去

次言繙譯之法

此一歌　先言清文之則

平鋪變繙與調換　減多增少細琢磨

實義虛文須仔細　已然未然要斟酌

[Manchu]中間串　[Manchu]等末尾多

清文一道卻如何　整上破下是文波

歌曰

此是清文總規矩　寄語學人自參酌

[Manchu]等字承何語　整字末尾結文多

後附"虛字歌"

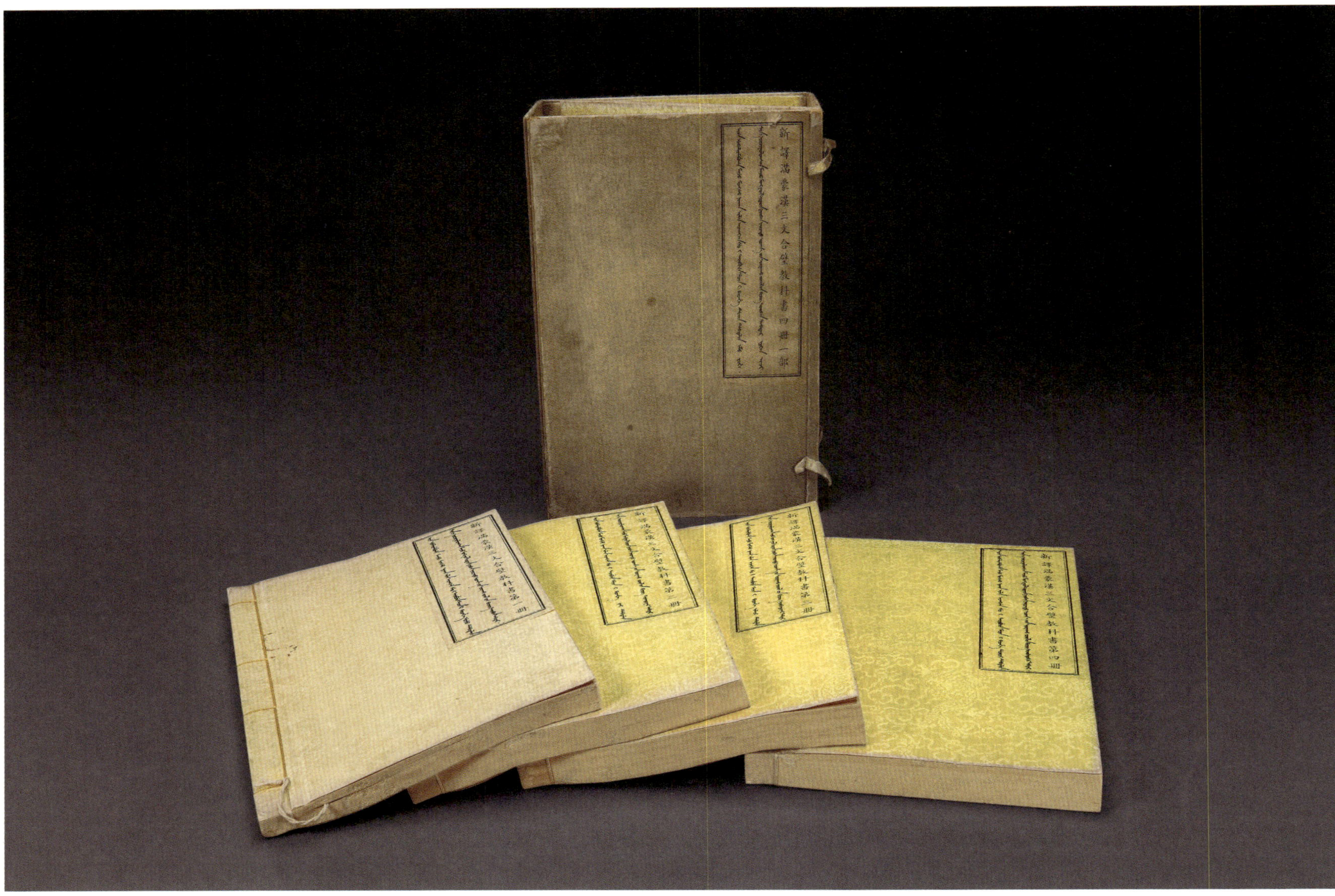

明黃色雲龍紋暗花綾書函
Bright yellow twill-weave silk cover with veiled pattern of dragons in clouds

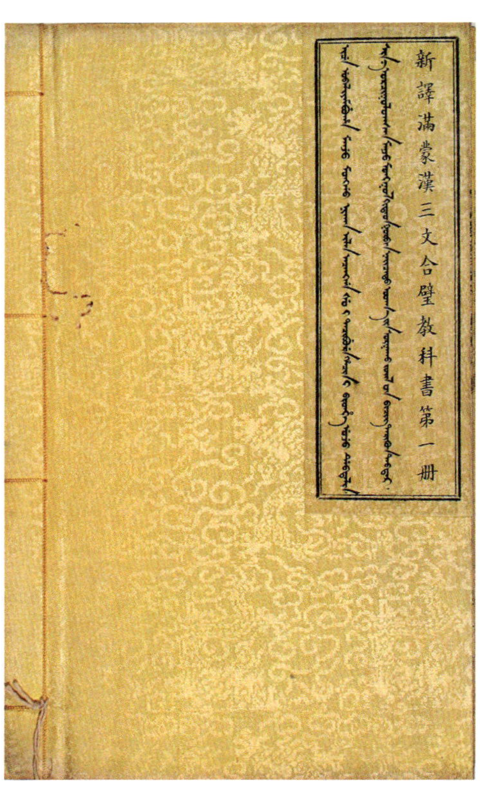

明黃色雲龍紋暗花綾書面
Bright yellow twill-weave silk cover with veiled pattern of dragons in clouds

書21784
《滿蒙漢三文合璧教科書八卷》
清　蔣維喬　莊俞編　榮德譯
清宣統二年（1910）內府精寫滿蒙漢合璧本
開本　縱34厘米　橫21厘米
版框　縱26.3厘米　橫16.9厘米
十册　二函

43

Inventory number: Shu 21784
Manchu-Mongolian-Chinese Textbook
Eight chapters
Compiled by Jiang Weiqiao and Zhuang Yu, translated by Rongde, Qing dynasty (1644-1911)
Transcribed in Manchu, Mongolian and Chinese in 1910 by the Qing court
Format: 34 × 21 cm
Frame: 26.3 × 16.9 cm
Ten volumes in two cases

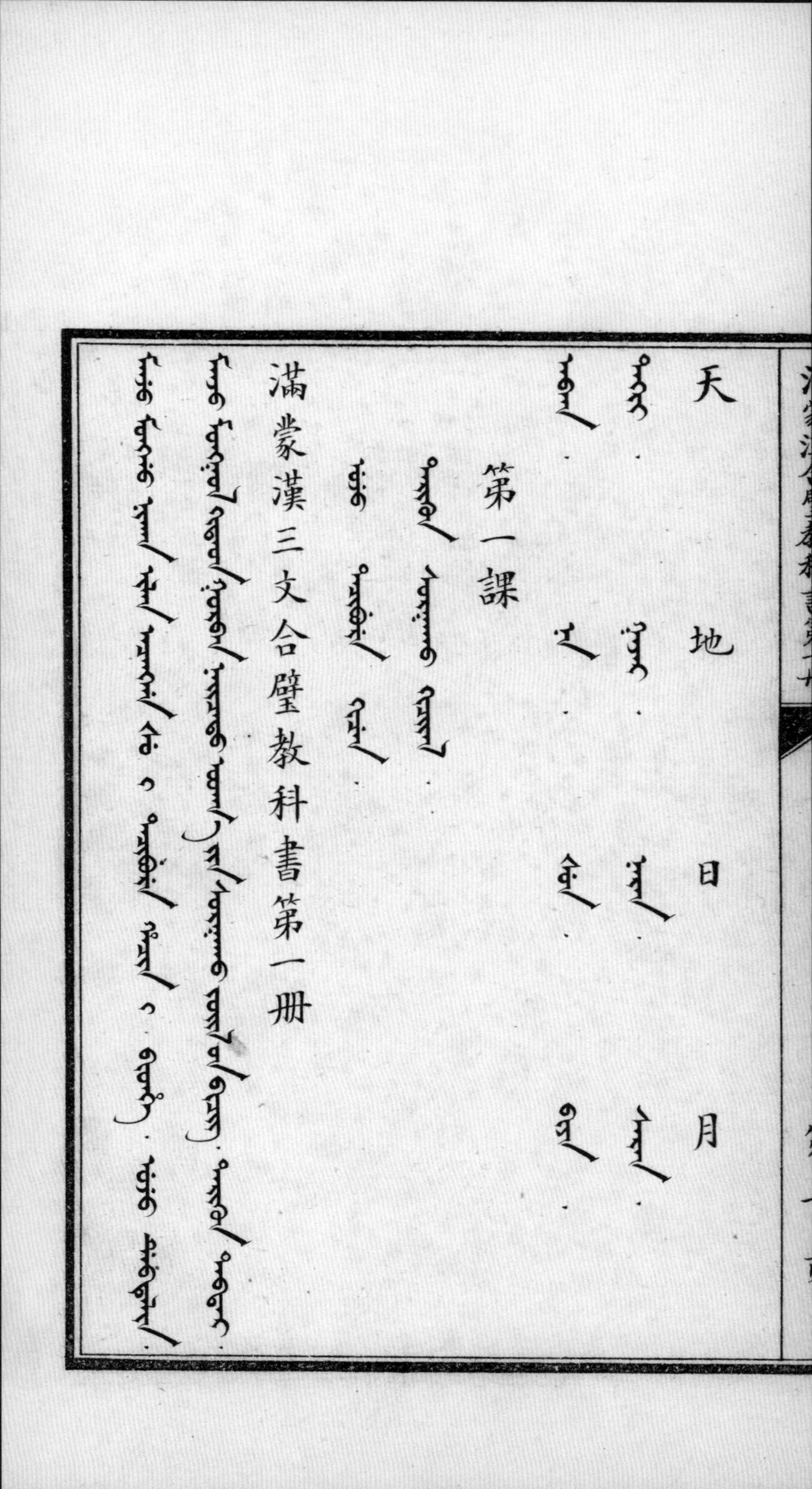

卷端
Beginning

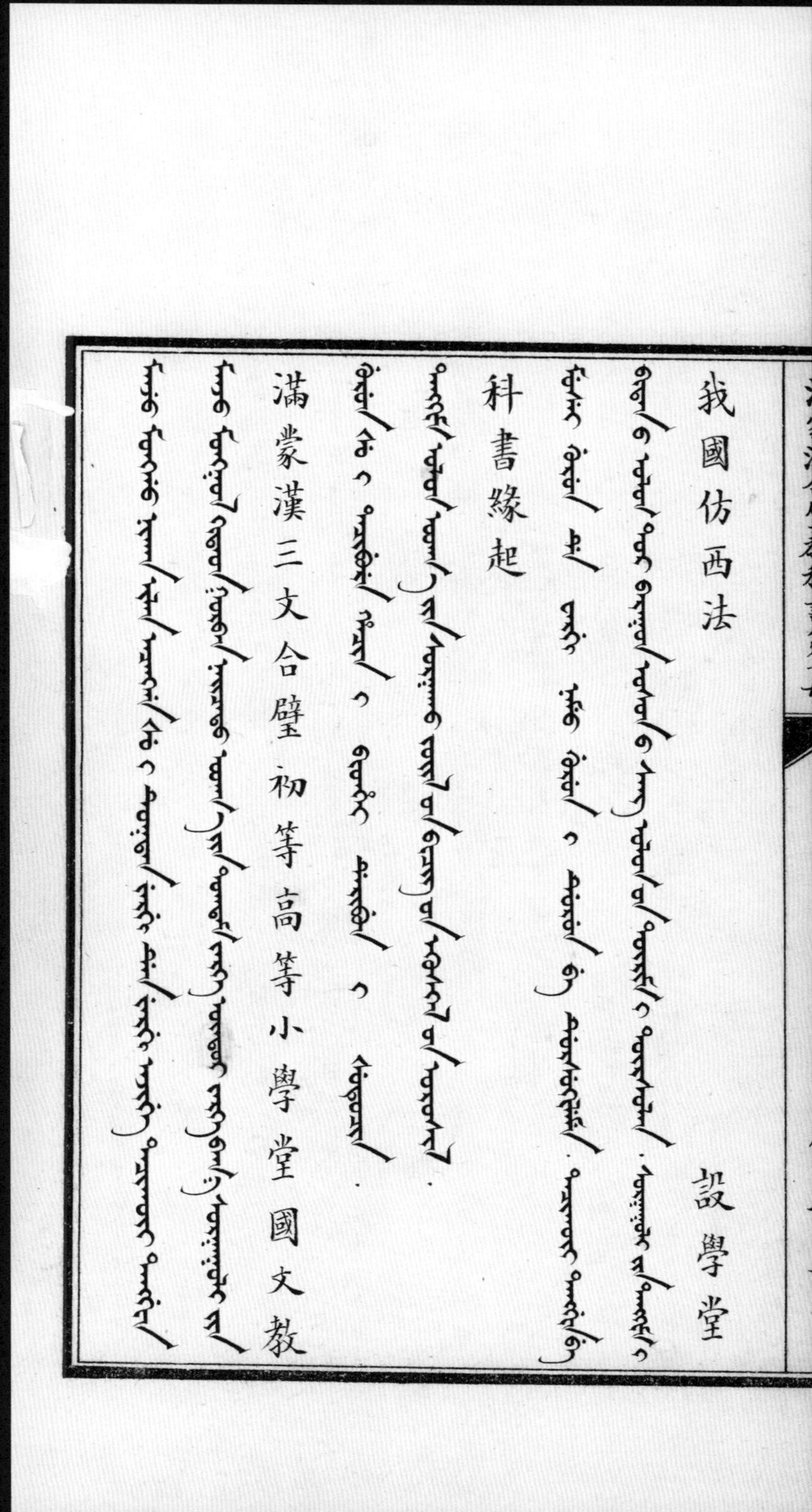

宣統元年序
Preface in 1909

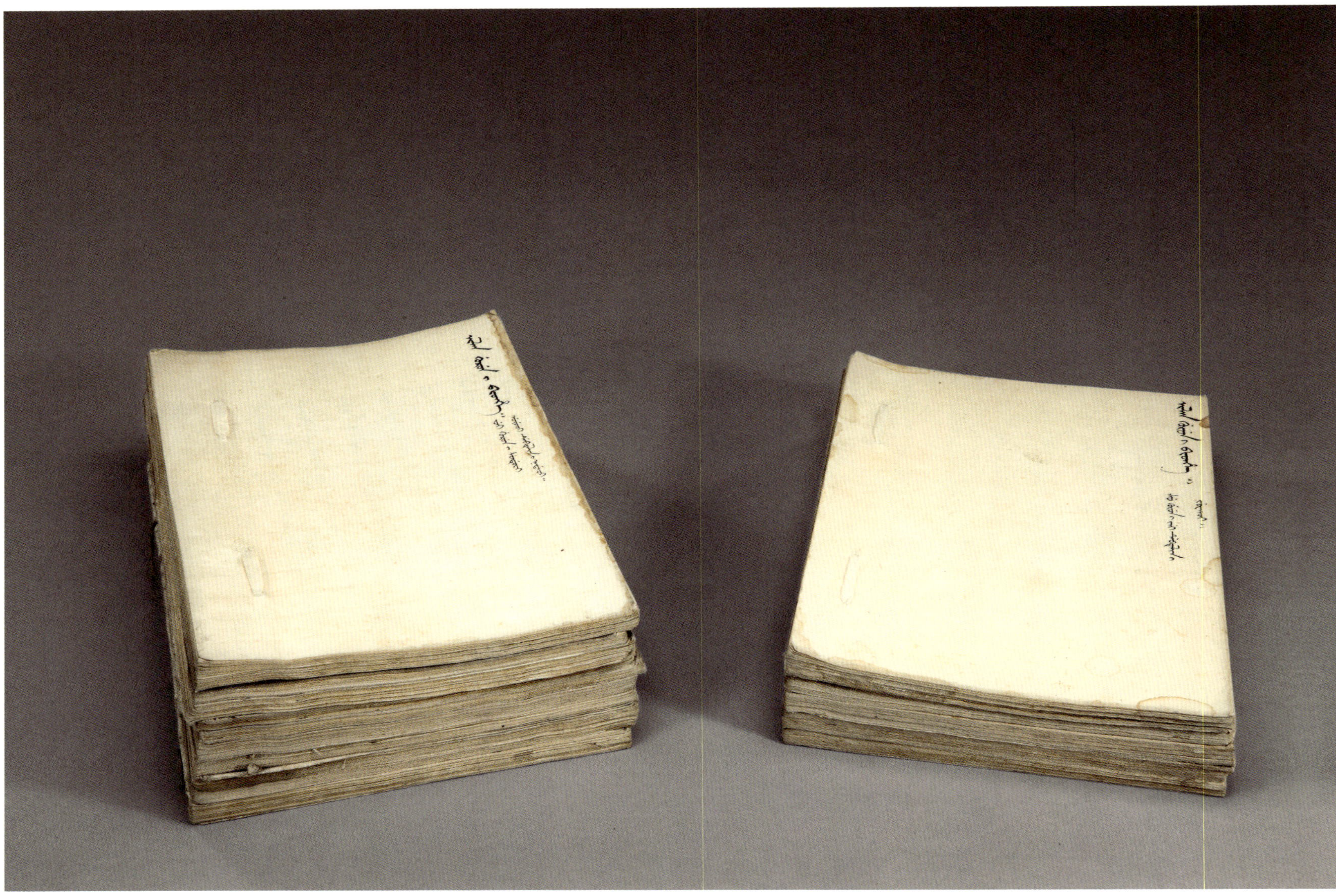

外觀
Exterior

黃色紙書面
Yellow paper cover

書21928
《三國志六十五卷》
晉　陳壽撰　清佚名譯
清鈔滿漢合璧本
開本　縱27厘米　橫18厘米
存十四冊　一函（人名、地名等專有名詞後注漢文）

44

Inventory number: Shu 21928
Records of the Three Kingdoms
Sixty-five chapters
Written by Chen Shou, Jin dynasty (265-420)
Translator unknown, Qing dynasty (1644-1911)
Transcribed in Manchu and Chinese in the Qing dynasty
Format: 27 × 18 cm
Fourteen volumes in one case extant today, with terms like names and places in Chinese

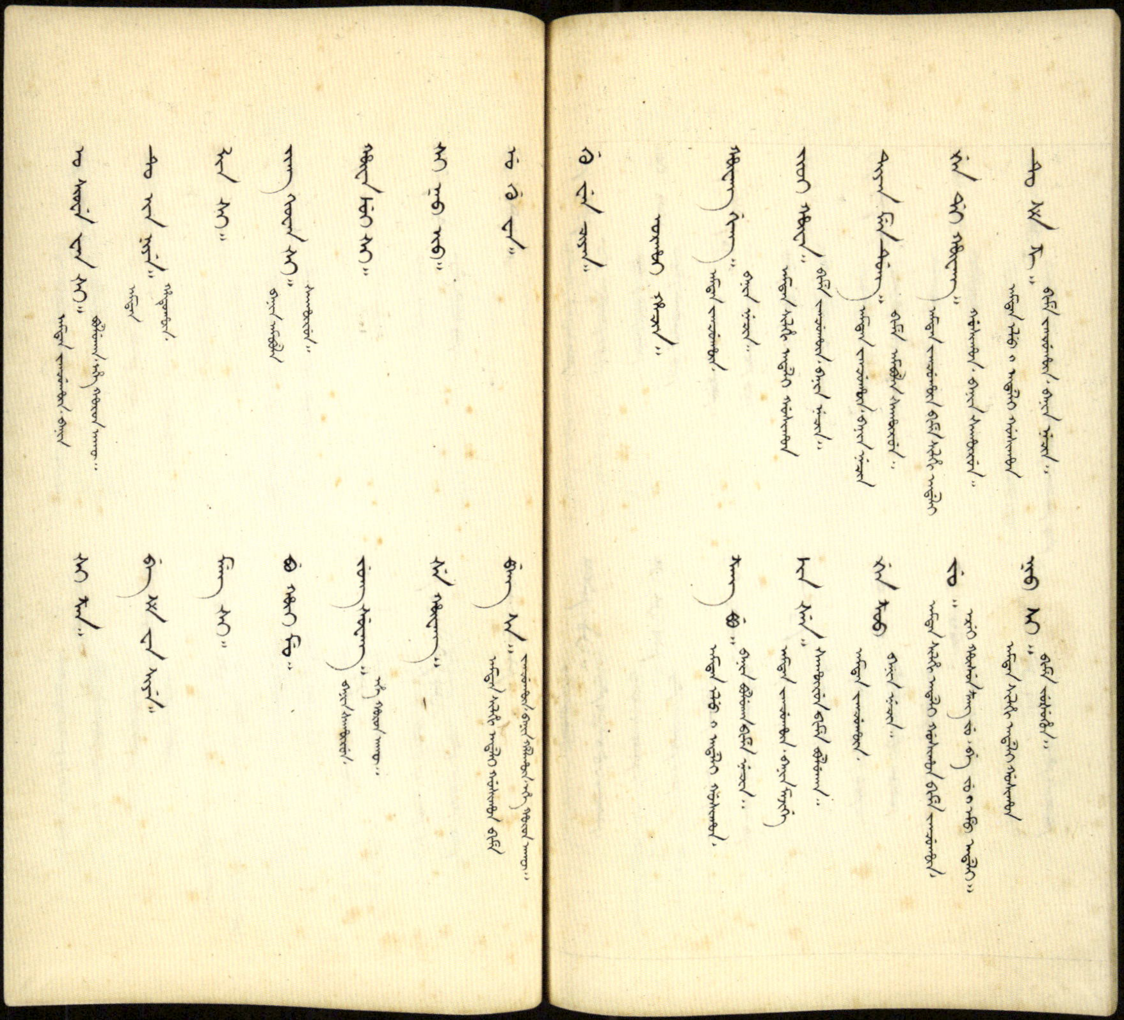

卷首人物簡介
Brief biographies of main figures

卷端
Beginning

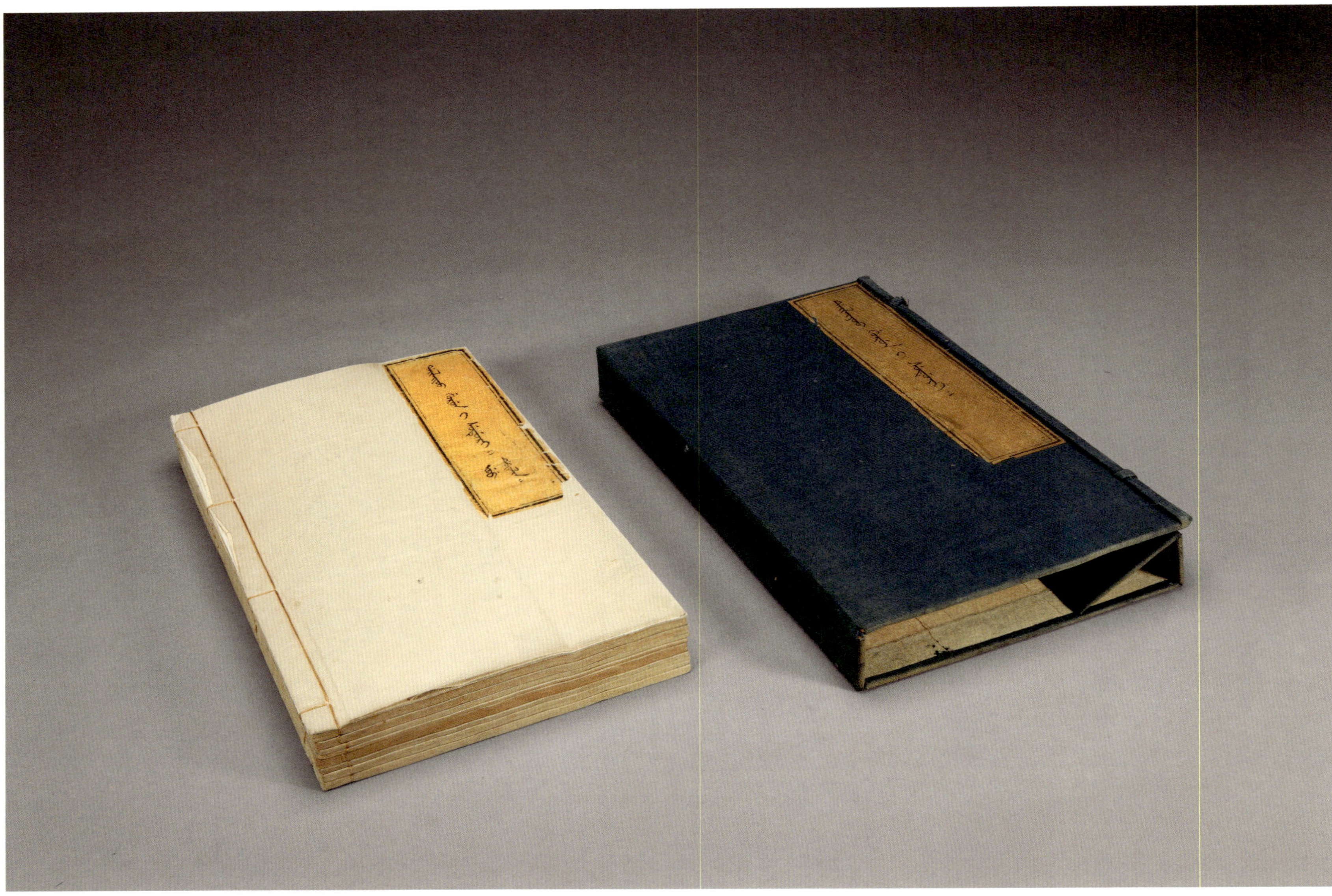

藍色素絹書函
Blue silk case

書21914
《遼史八卷》
元　脱脱等撰　清　希福等譯
清順治三年（1646）内府刻滿文本
開本　縱35.4厘米　横21.3厘米
版框　縱26.5厘米　横19.2厘米
八册　一函

45

Inventory number: Shu 21914
History of Liao
Eight chapters
Written by Tuotuo et. al., Yuan dynasty (1271-1368)
Translated by Xifu et. al., Qing dynasty (1644-1911)
Transcribed in Manchu in 1646 by the Qing court
Format: 35.4 × 21.3 cm
Frame: 26.5 × 19.2 cm
Eight volumes in one case

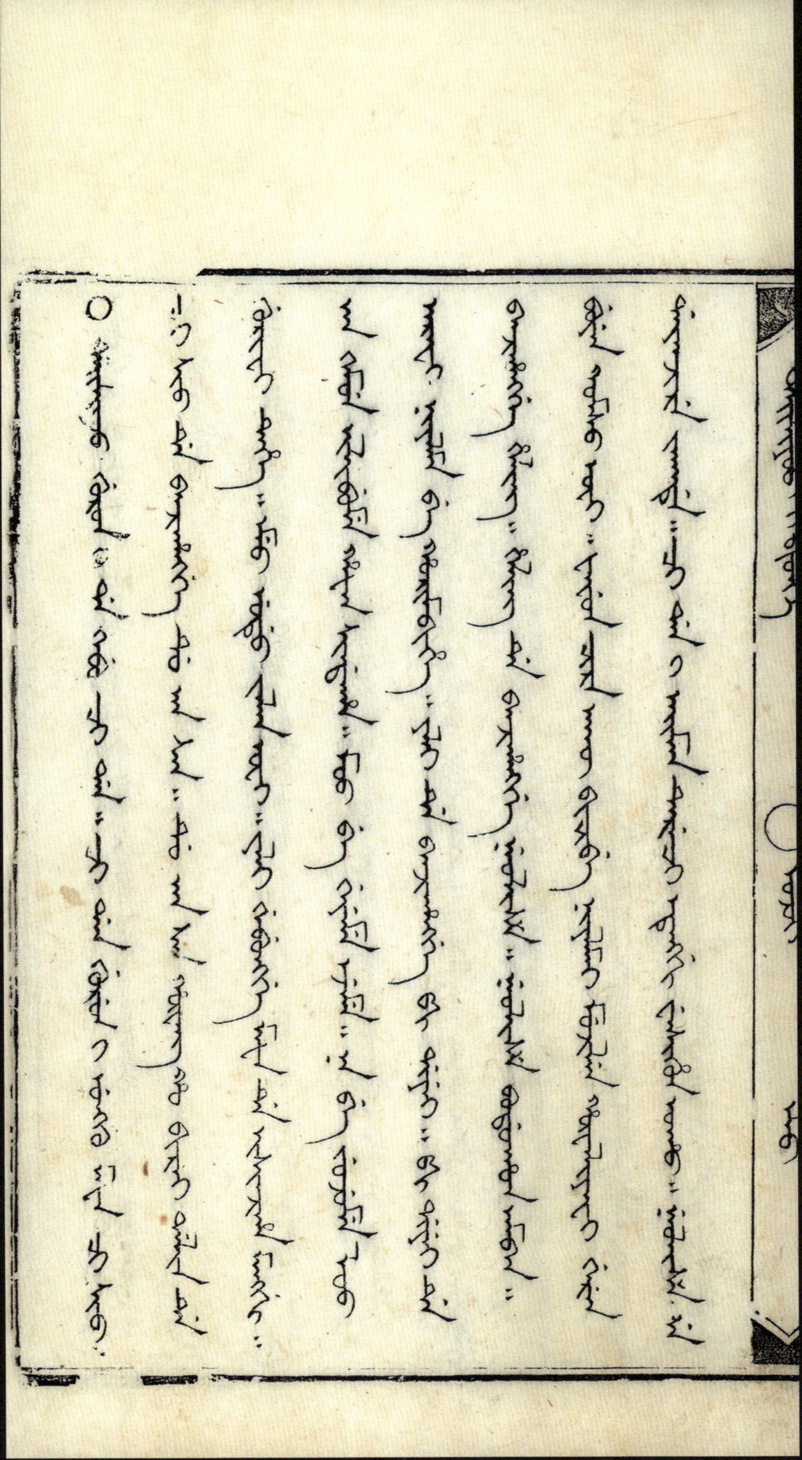

卷端
Beginning

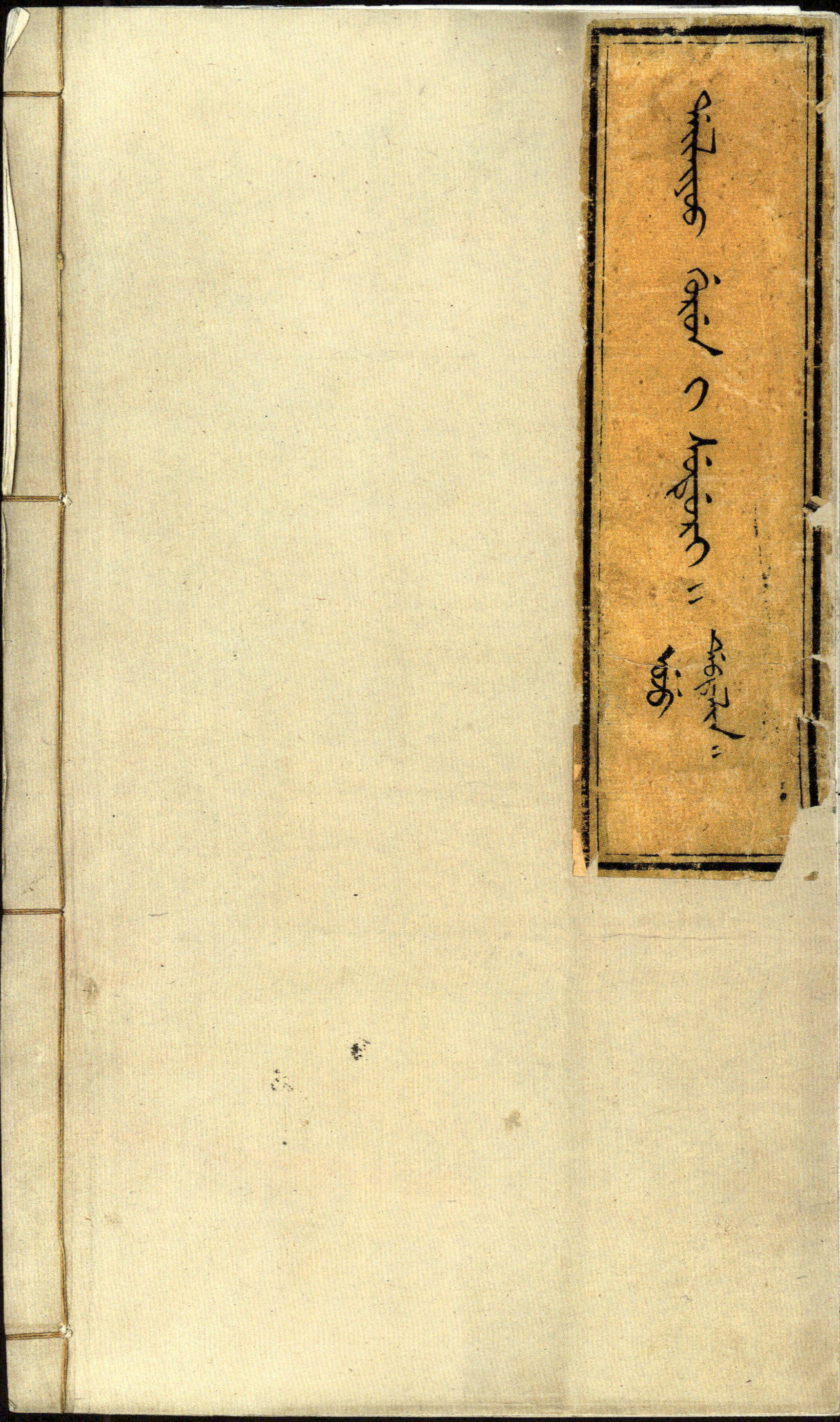

香色紙書面
Light brown paper cover

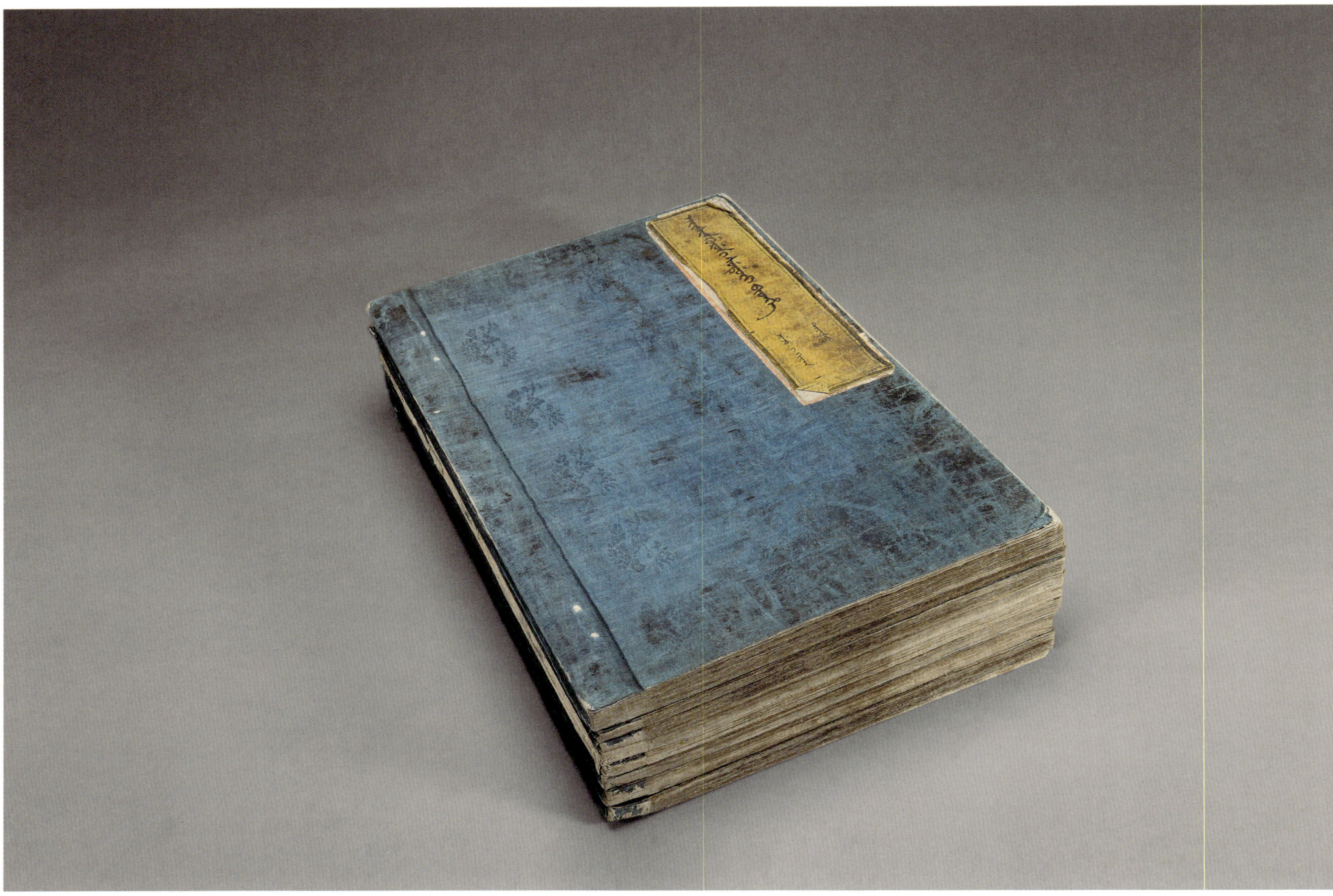

藍色折枝花紋暗花緞書面
Blue satin cover with veiled pattern of floral sprays

藍色折枝花紋暗花緞書面
Blue satin cover with veiled pattern of floral sprays

46

書21916
《金史八卷》
元　脱脱等撰　清　希福等譯
清順治元年（1644）內府精寫滿文本
開本　縱37.5厘米　橫24.7厘米
版框　縱32.1厘米　橫22厘米
八册　一函

Inventory number: Shu 21916
History of Jin
Eight chapters
Written by Tuotuo et. al., Yuan dynasty (1271-1368)
Translated by Xifu et. al., Qing dynasty (1644-1911)
Transcribed in Manchu in 1644 by the Qing court
Format: 37.5 × 24.7 cm
Frame: 32.1 × 22 cm
Eight volumes in one case

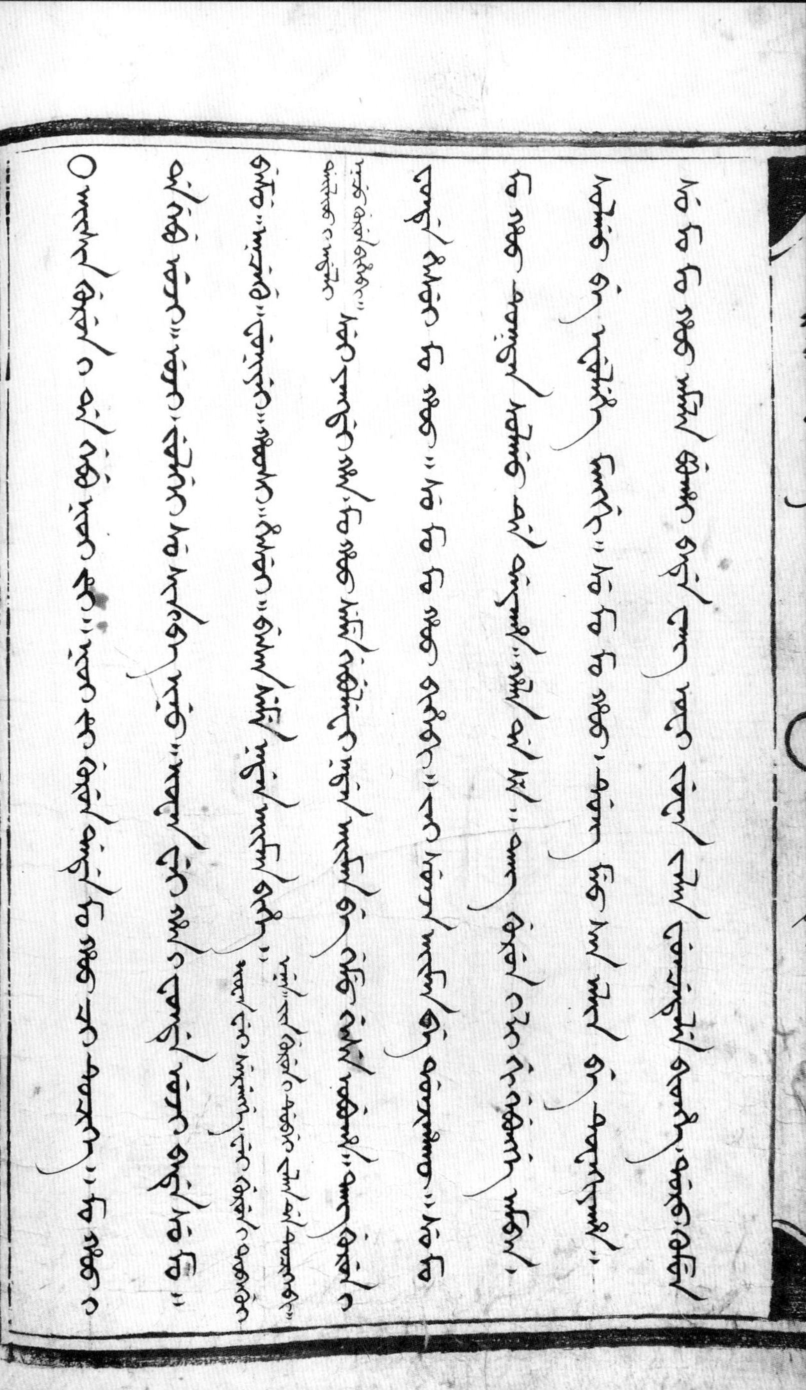

卷端
Beginning

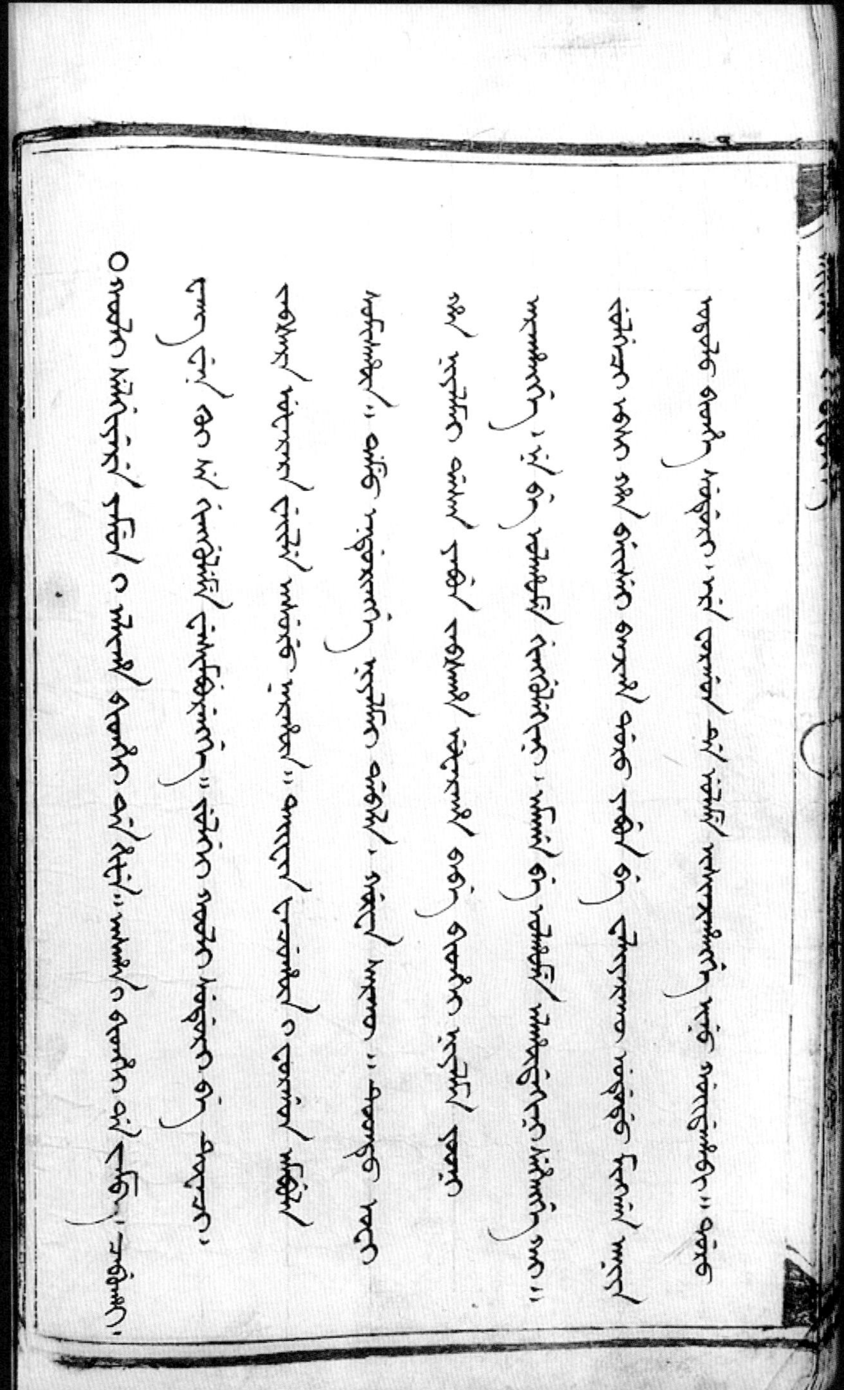

顺治元年序
Memorial in 1644

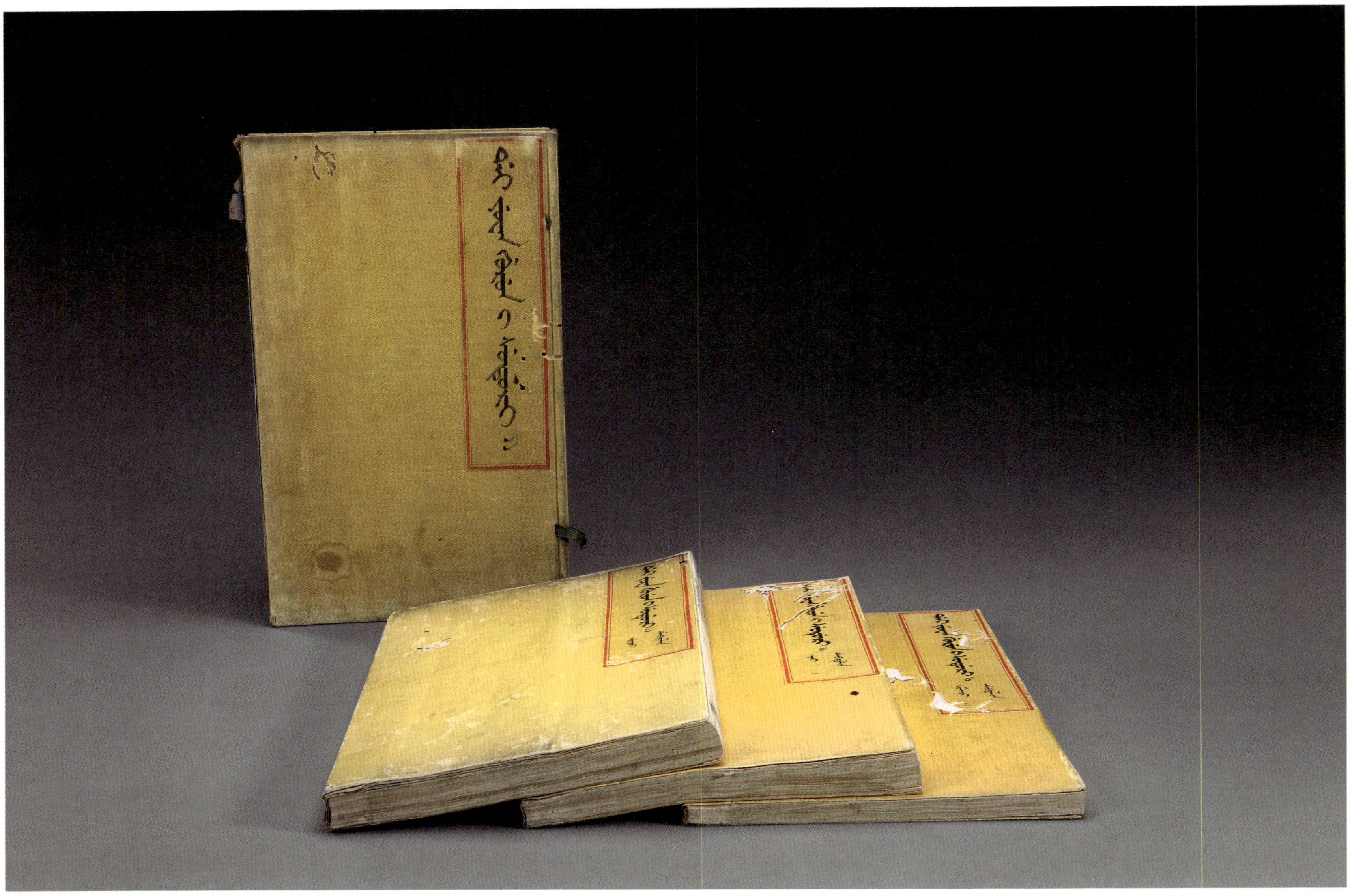

明黄色素緞書函
Bright yellow satin case

47

書21920

《元史十五卷》

明　宋濂等撰　清　希福等譯
清順治元年（1644）内府精寫滿文本
開本　縱36.6厘米　横22.2厘米
版框　縱27.5厘米　横19厘米
十五册　四函

Inventory number: Shu 21920

History of Yuan

Fifteen chapters
Written by Song Lian et. al., Ming dynasty (1368-1644)
Translated by Xifu et. al., Qing dynasty (1644-1911)
Transcribed in Manchu in 1644 by the Qing court
Format: 36.6 × 22.2 cm
Frame: 27.5 × 19 cm
Fifteen volumes in four cases

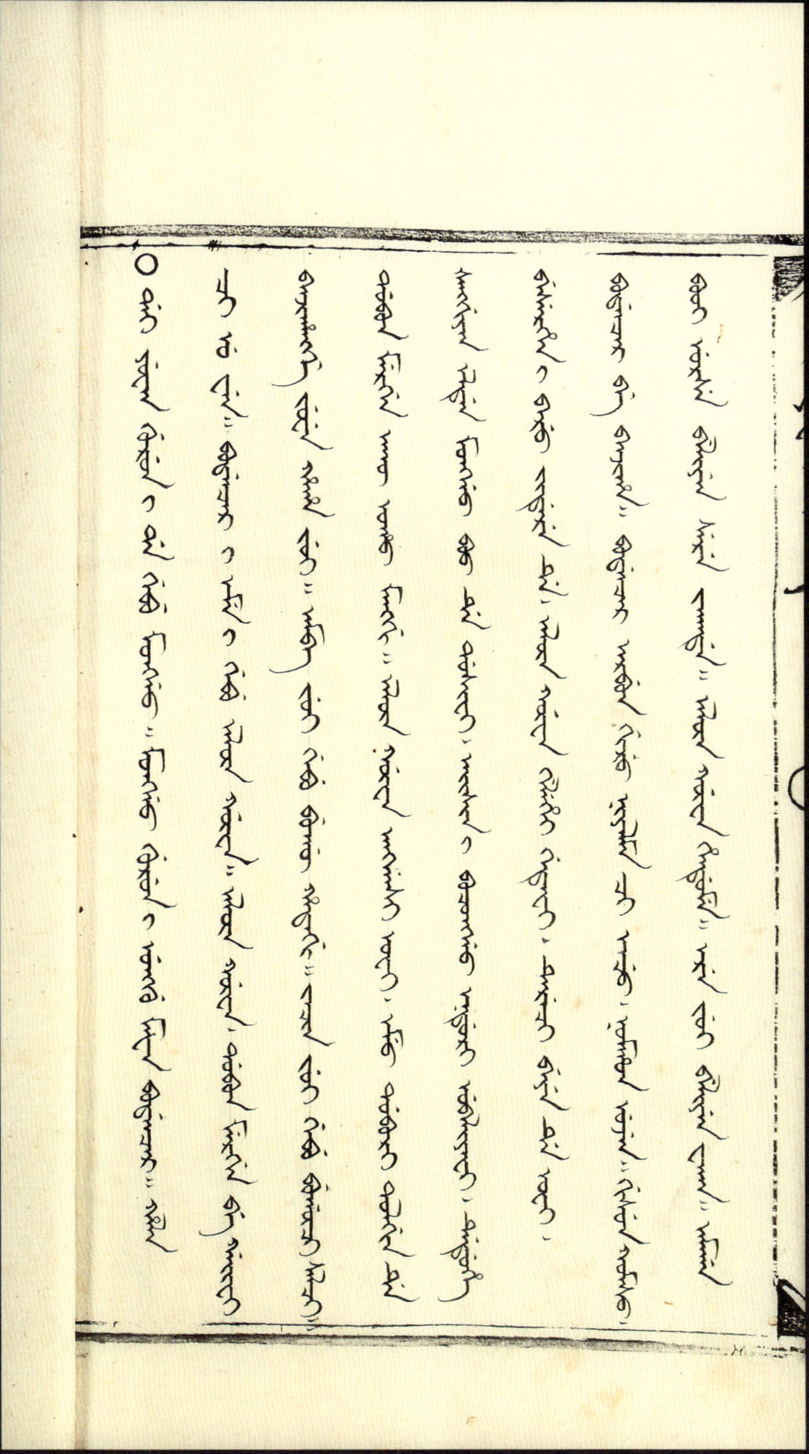

卷端
Beginning

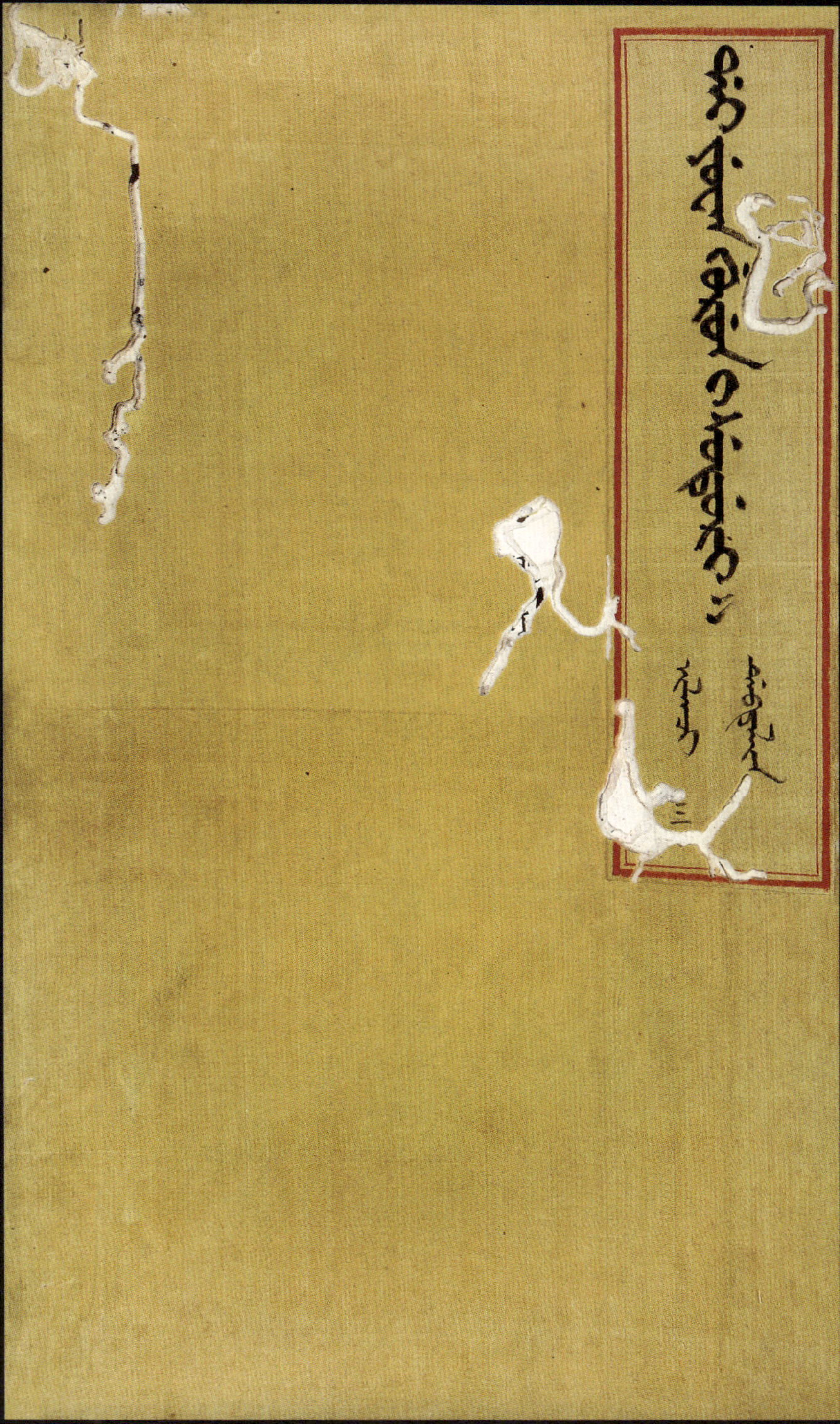

明黄色素缎書面
Bright yellow satin cover

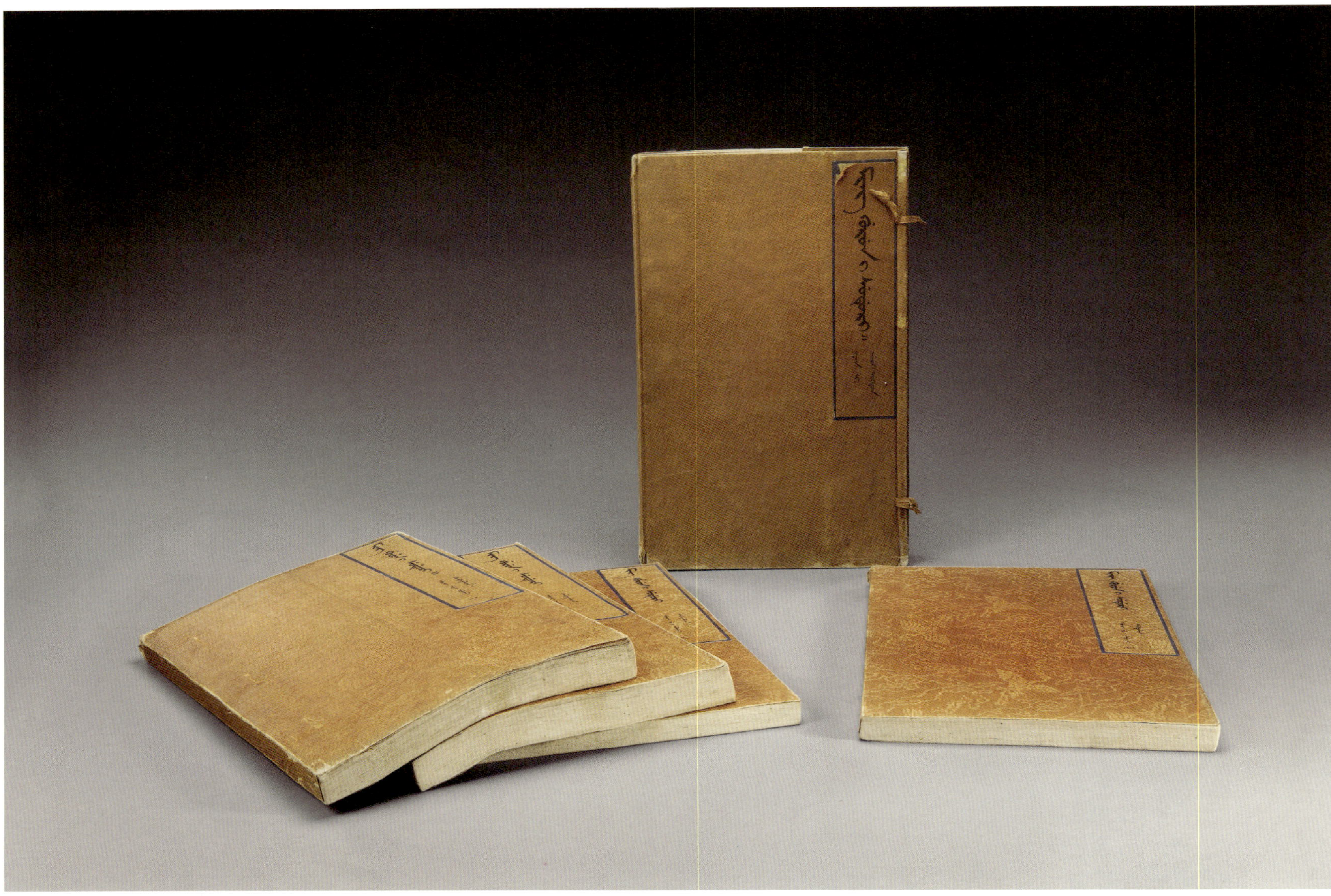

絳色雲鳳紋暗花綾書函
Brown twill-weave silk case with veiled phoenix and cloud pattern

48

書21924
《明史九十七卷》
清　張廷玉等撰　佚名譯
清康熙年內府精寫滿文本
開本　縱37.7厘米　橫23.3厘米
版框　縱26.5厘米　橫19.1厘米
九十七册　二十二函

Inventory Number: Shu 21924
History Of Ming
Ninety-Seven Chapters
Written By Zhang Tingyu et. al., Qing Dynasty (1644-1911)
Translator unknown, Qing Dynasty
Transcribed in Manchu by the Qing Court
Format: 37.7 × 23.3 Cm
Frame: 26.5 × 19.1 Cm
Ninety-seven volumes In twenty-two cases

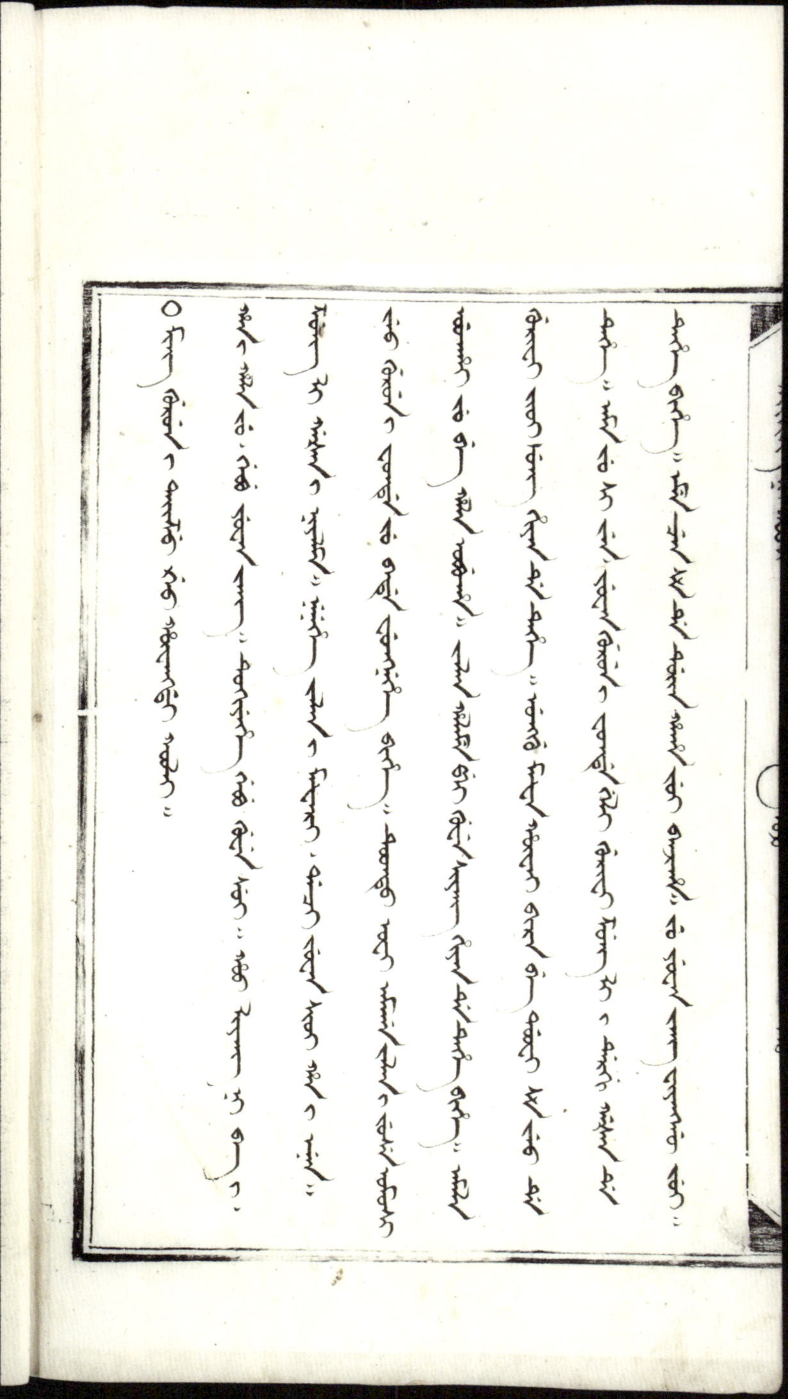

卷端
Beginning

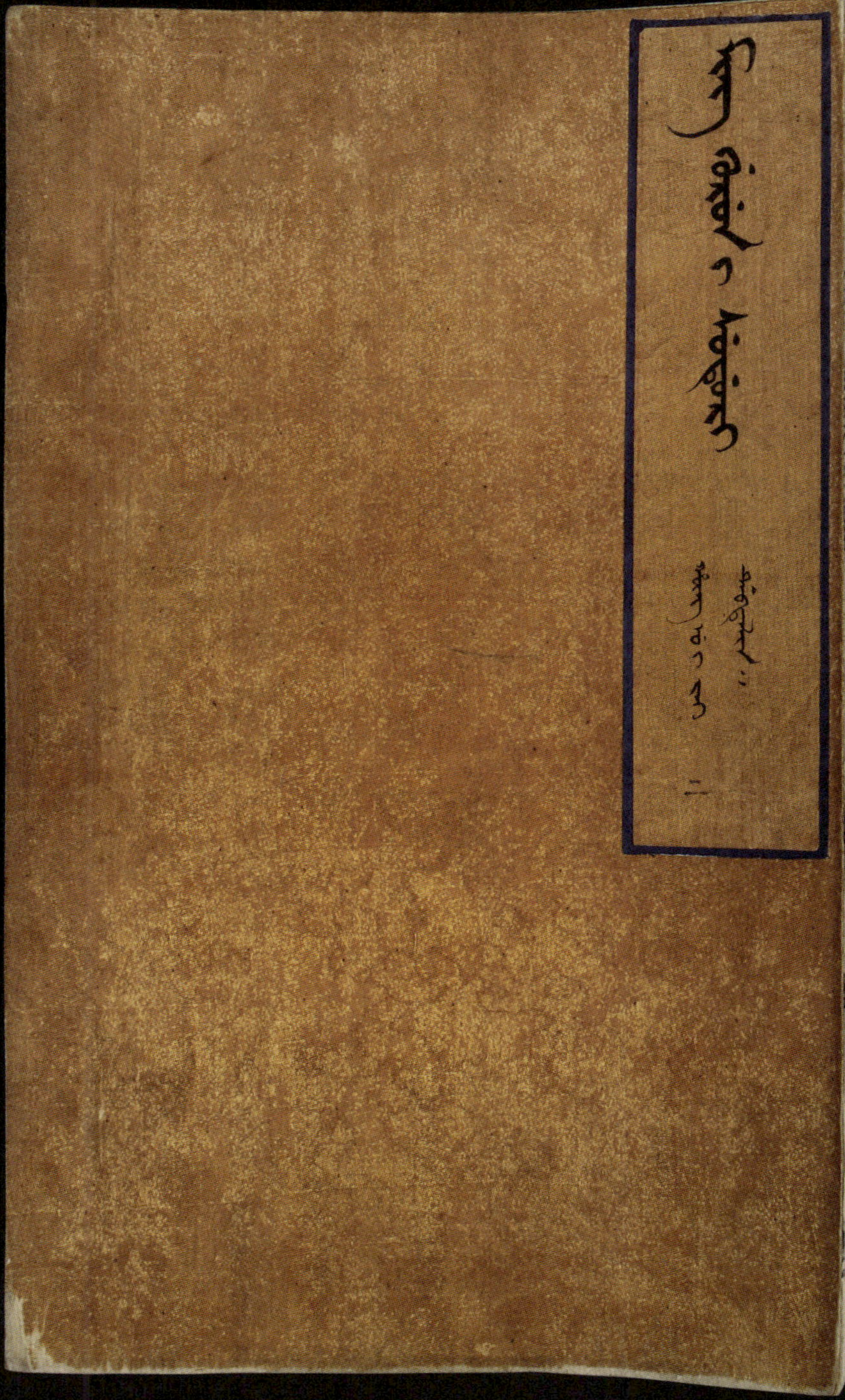

絳色雲鳳紋暗花綾書面
Brown twill-weave silk cover with veiled phoenix and cloud pattern

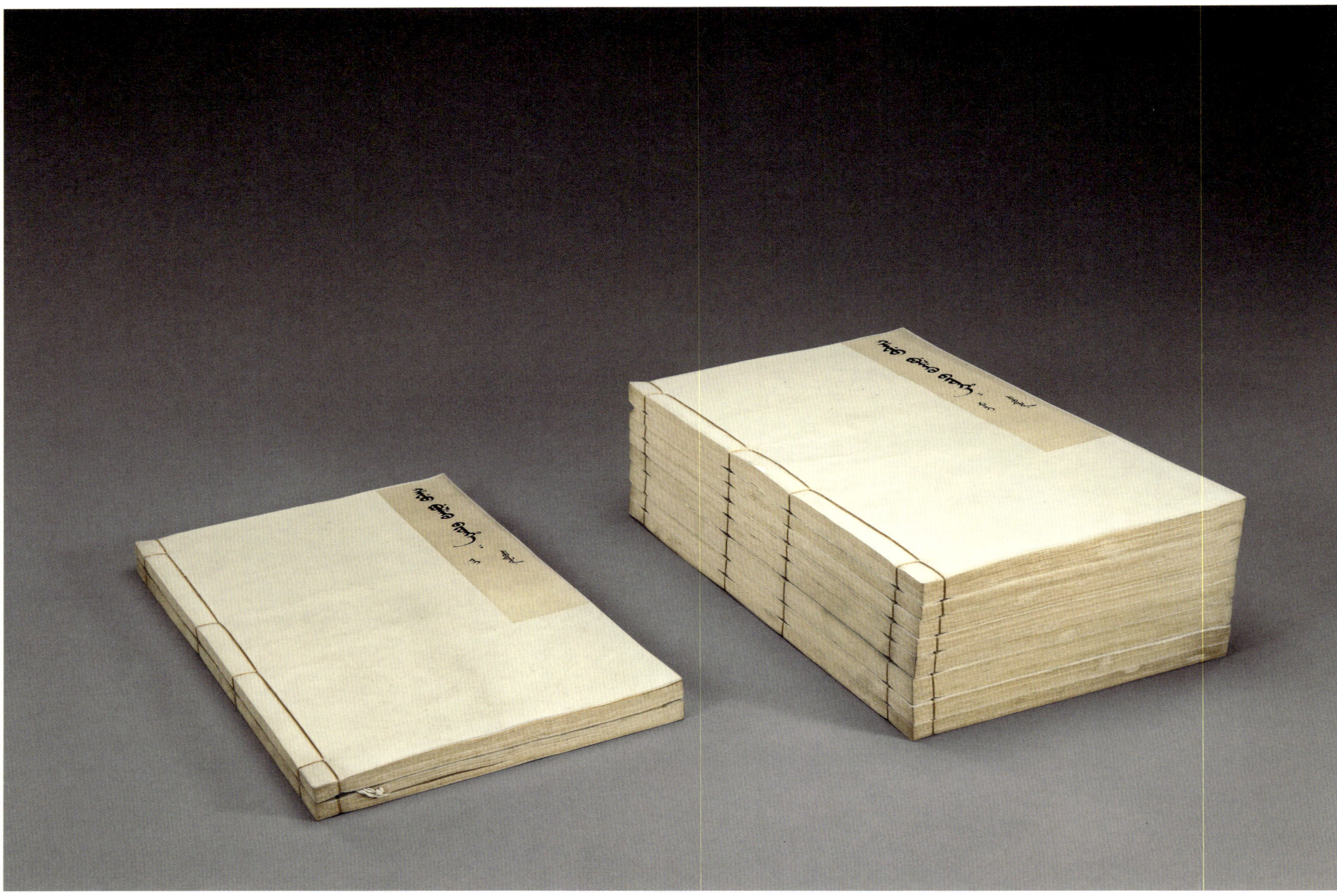

香色紙書面
Light brown paper covers

香色紙書面
Light brown paper cover

書21928

《通鑒彙纂八十卷》

明　王世貞編　清　達海譯
清康熙三年（1664）內府刻滿文本
開本　縱38.8厘米　橫22.7厘米
版框　縱28.2厘米　橫20.6厘米
八十册　八函

49

Inventory number: Shu 21928

Collection of Brief History

Eighty chapters
Compiled by Wang Shizhen, Ming dynasty (1368-1644)
Translated by Dahai, Qing dynasty (1644-1911)
Printed in Manchu in 1664 by the Qing court
Format: 38.8 × 22.7 cm
Frame: 28.2 × 20.6 cm
Eighty volumes in eight cases

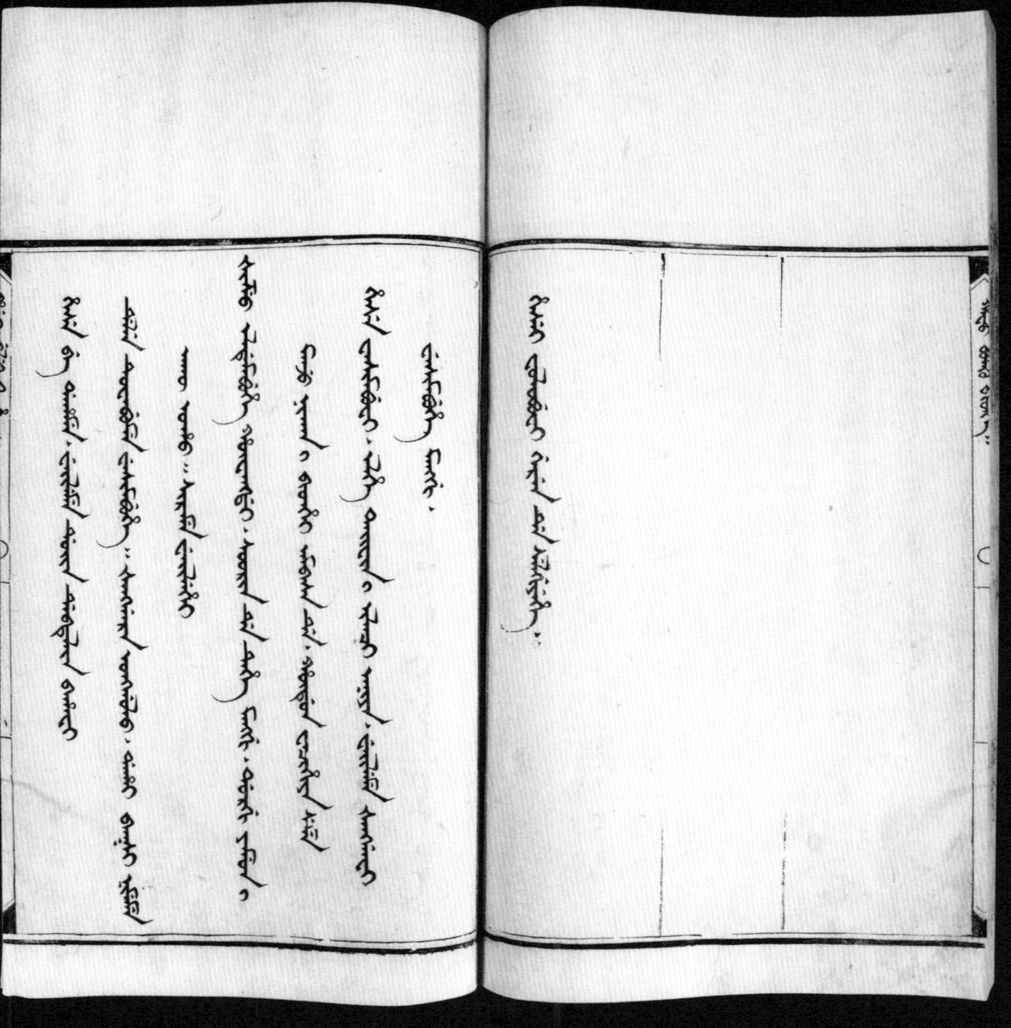

康熙三年序
Preface in 1664

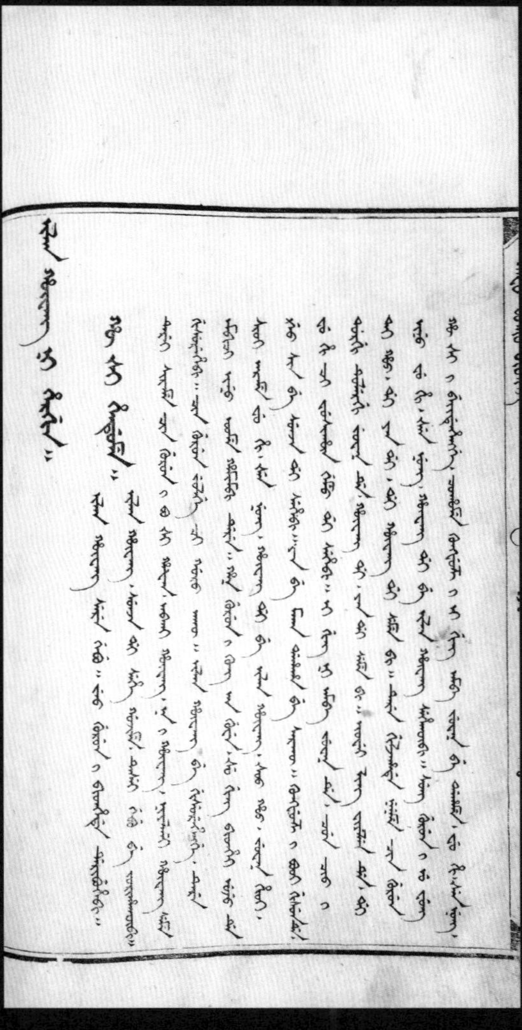

卷端
Beginning

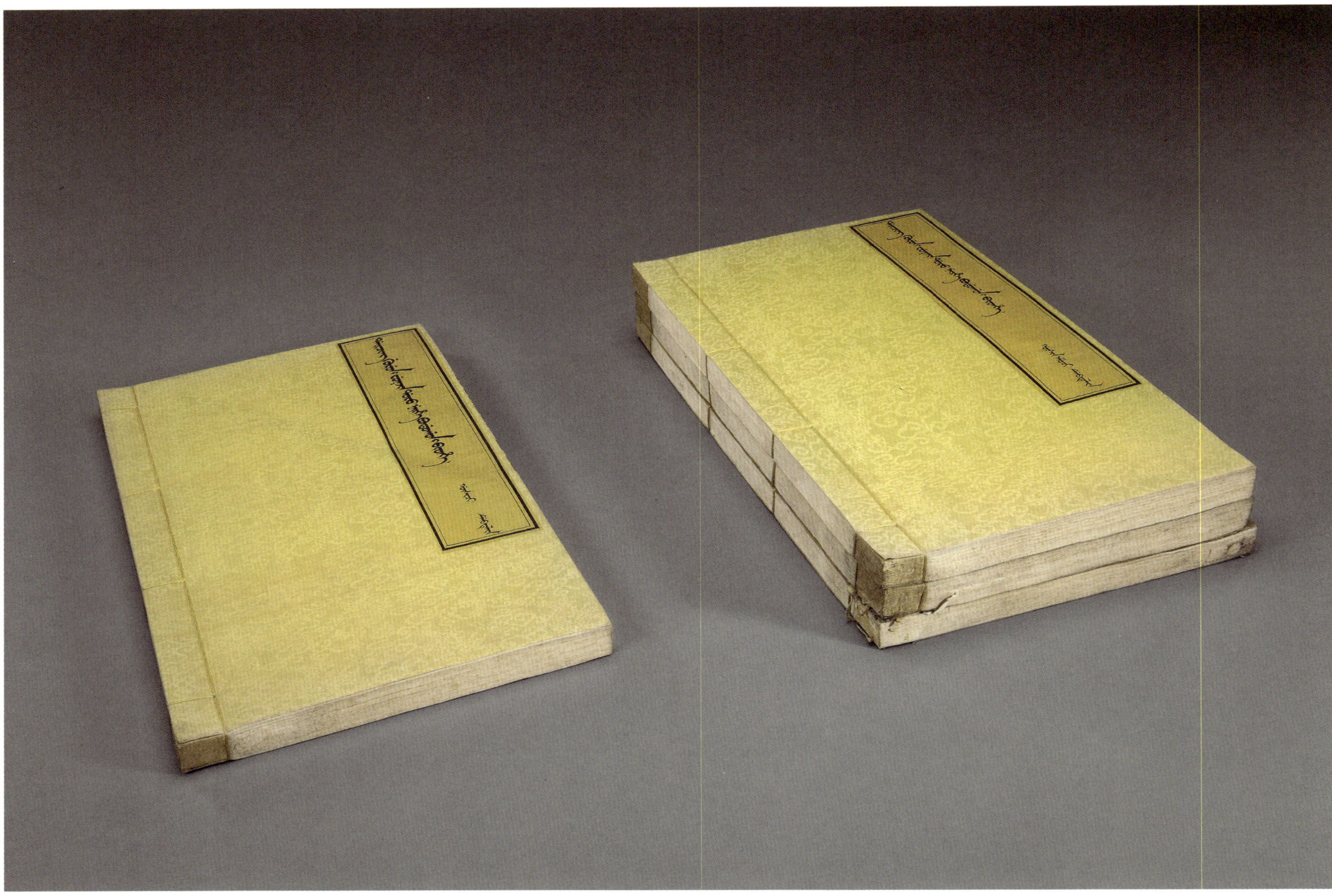

明黃色雲龍紋暗花綾書面
Bright yellow twill-weave silk covers with veiled dragon and cloud pattern

書21947
《大清開國方略三十二卷》
清　阿桂等奉敕撰
清乾隆年内府朱絲欄精寫滿文本
開本　縱40.4厘米　橫23.4厘米
版框　縱28.2厘米　橫18.3厘米
存八册　一函（存卷6、7、9、11、22、30－32）

50 Inventory number: Shu 21947
The Qing Strategies on Establishing the State
Thirty-two chapters
Compiled by imperial order by Agui et. al., Qing dynasty (1644-1911)
Transcribed in Manchu in red columns by the Qing court in the Qianlong period (r.1736-1795)
Format: 40.4 × 23.4 cm
Frame: 28.2 × 18.3 cm
Eight volumes in one case extant today, including the following chapters: 6, 7, 9, 11, 22, 30-32

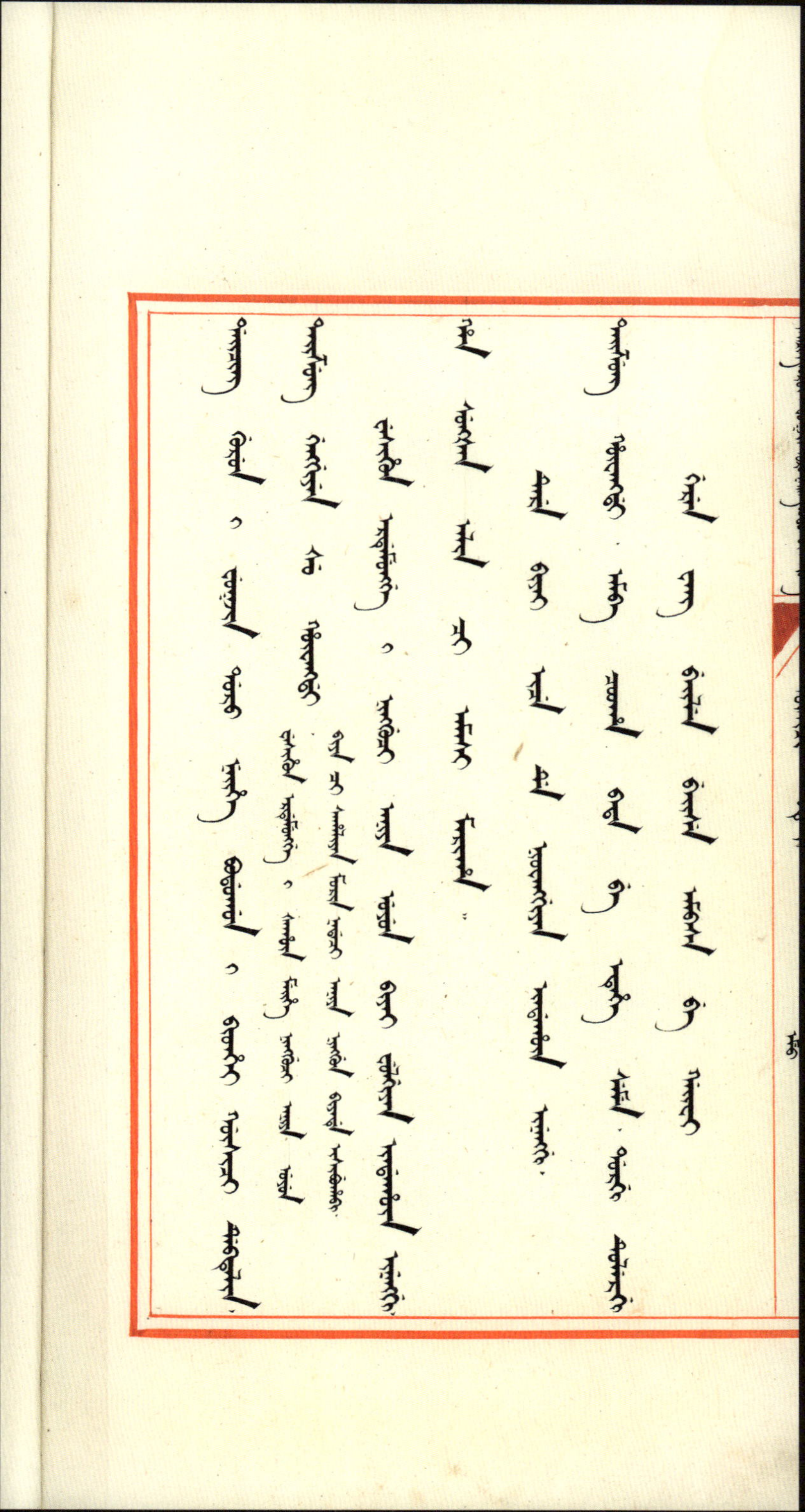

卷端
Beginning

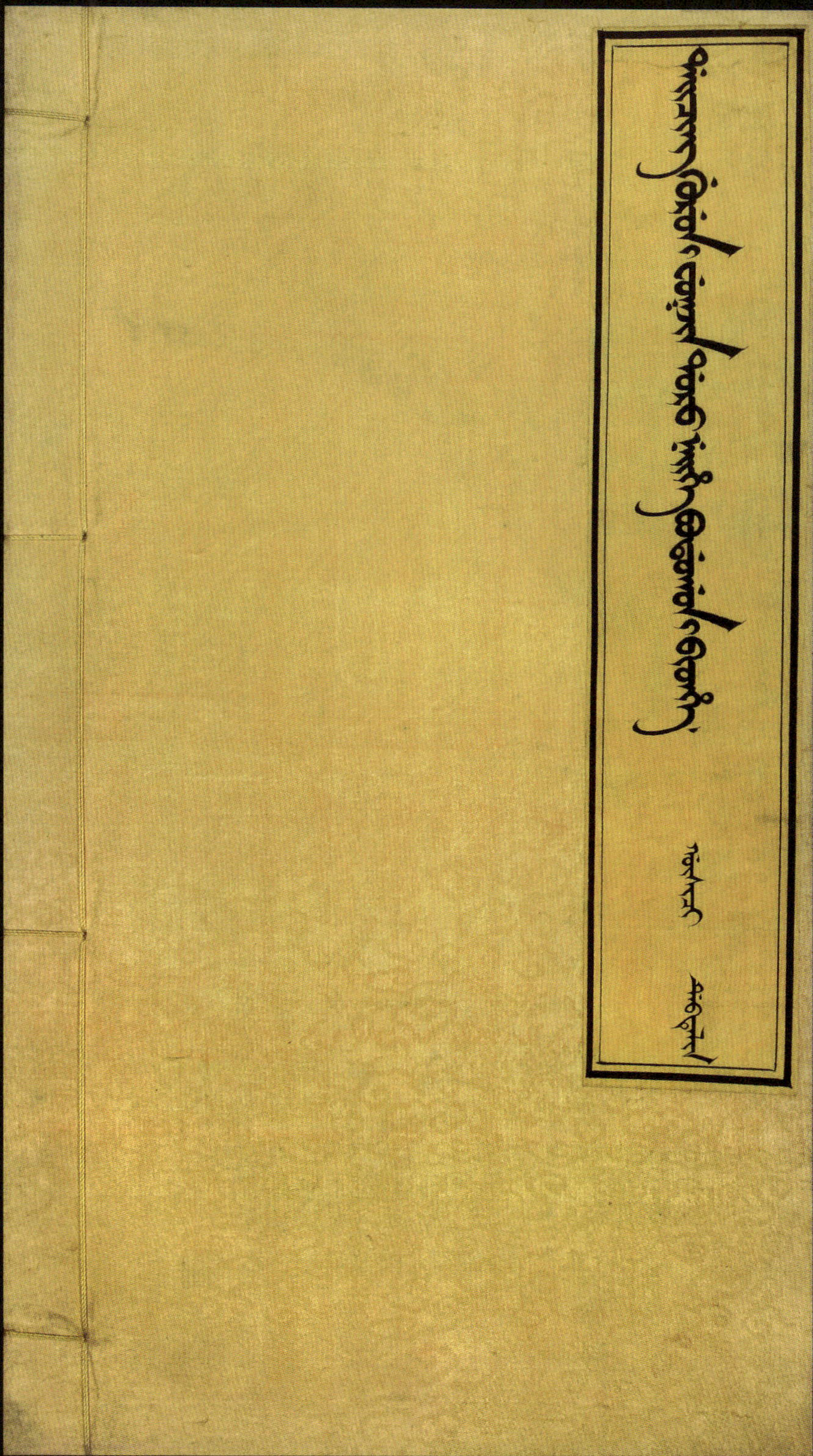

明黄色雲龍紋暗花綾書面
Bright yellow twill-weave silk cover with veiled dragon and cloud pattern

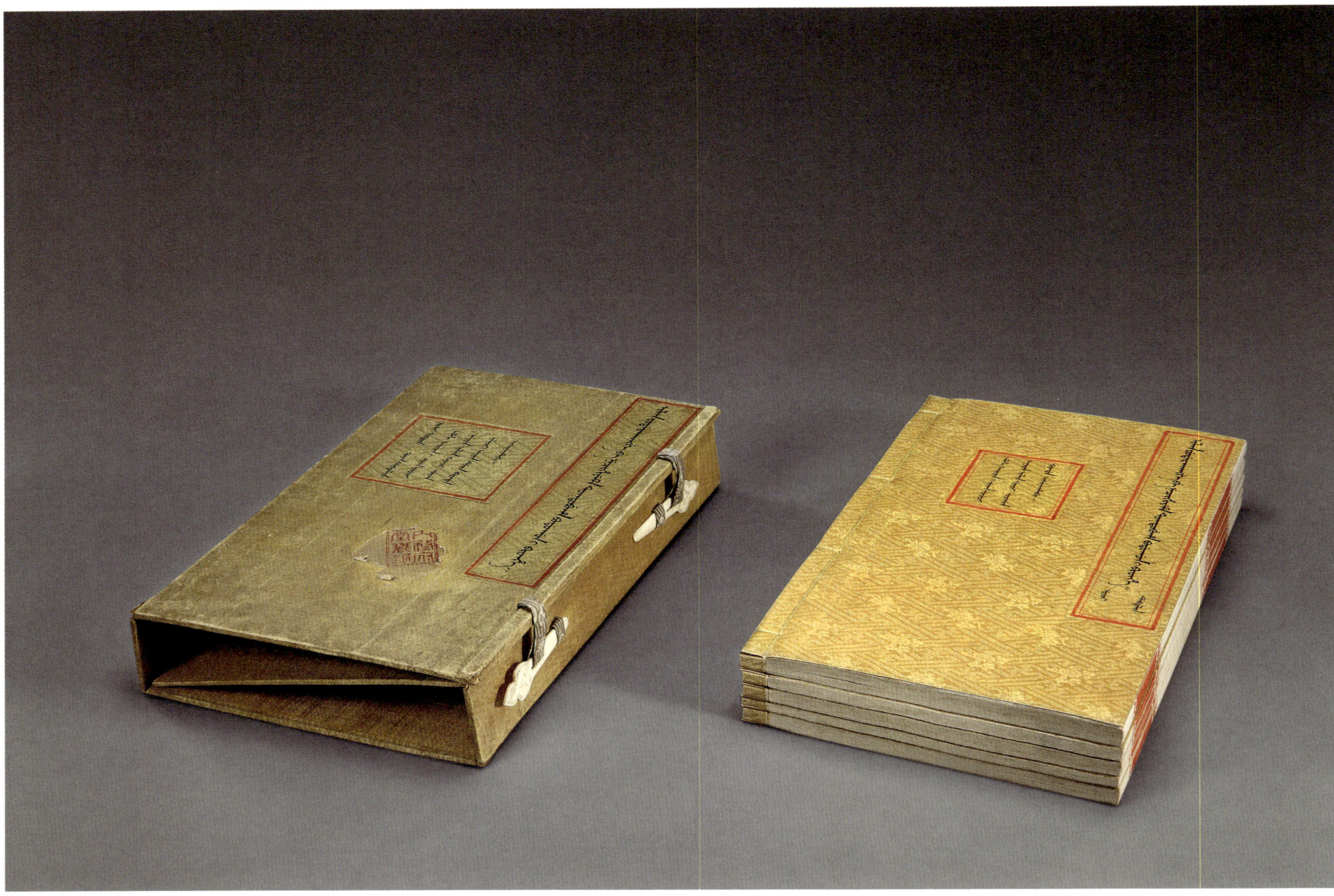

明黃色萬字曲水朵花紋暗花綾書函
Bright yellow twill-weave silk cover with veiled swastika and floral pattern

書21968
《平定三逆方略六十卷》
清　勒德洪等奉敕撰
清康熙二十五年（1686）内府朱絲欄精寫滿文本
開本　縱31.7厘米　橫19.2厘米
版框　縱25厘米　橫16.8厘米
51 存四十册　六函（存卷1－11、21－49）

Inventory number: Shu 21968
The Qing Strategies on Suppressing the Three Rebels
Sixty chapters
Written by imperial order by Ledehong et. al., Qing dynasty (1644-1911)
Transcribed in Manchu in red columns by the Qing court in 1686
Format: 31.7 × 19.2 cm
Frame: 25 × 16.8 cm
Forty volumes in six cases extant today, including the following chapters: 1-11, 21-49

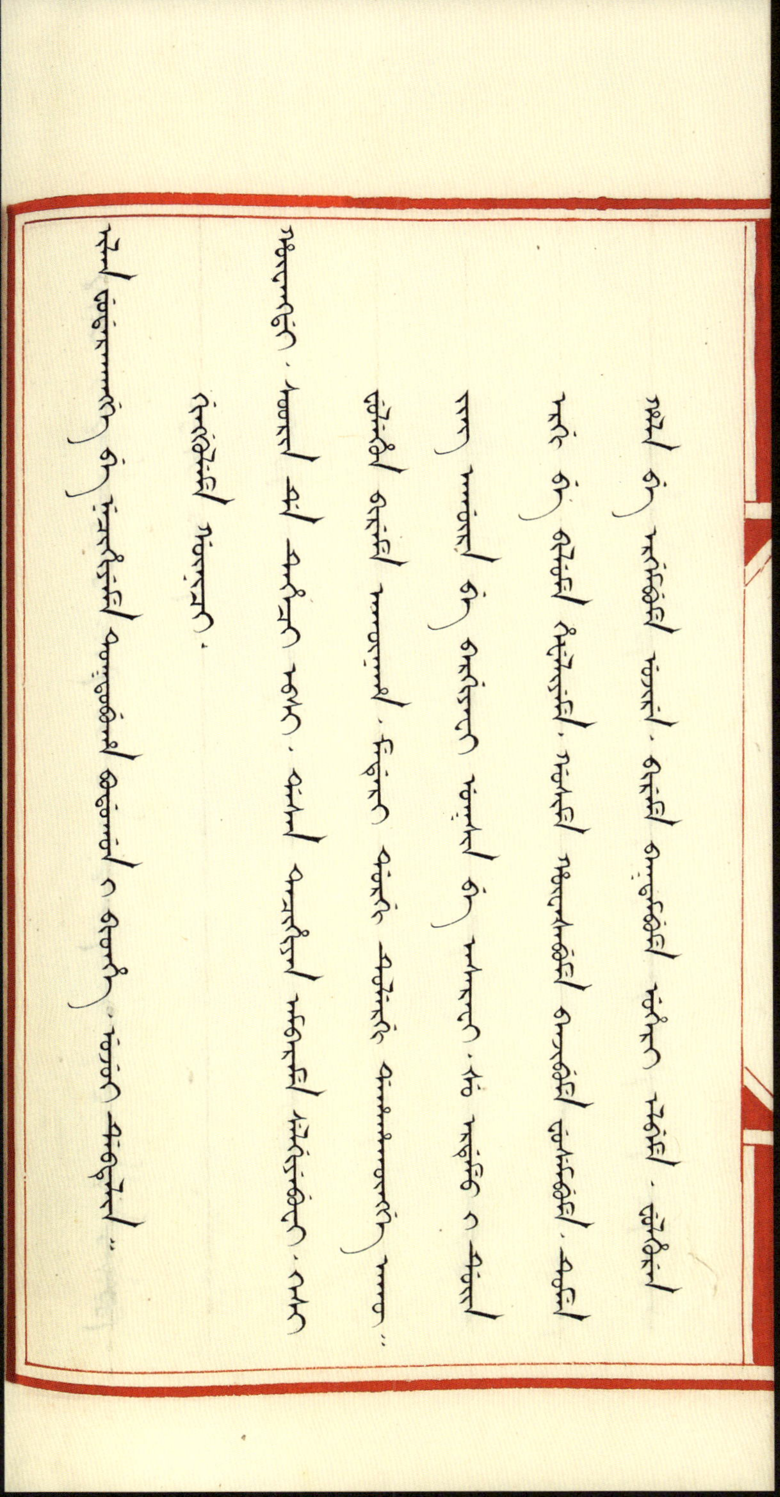

卷端
Beginning

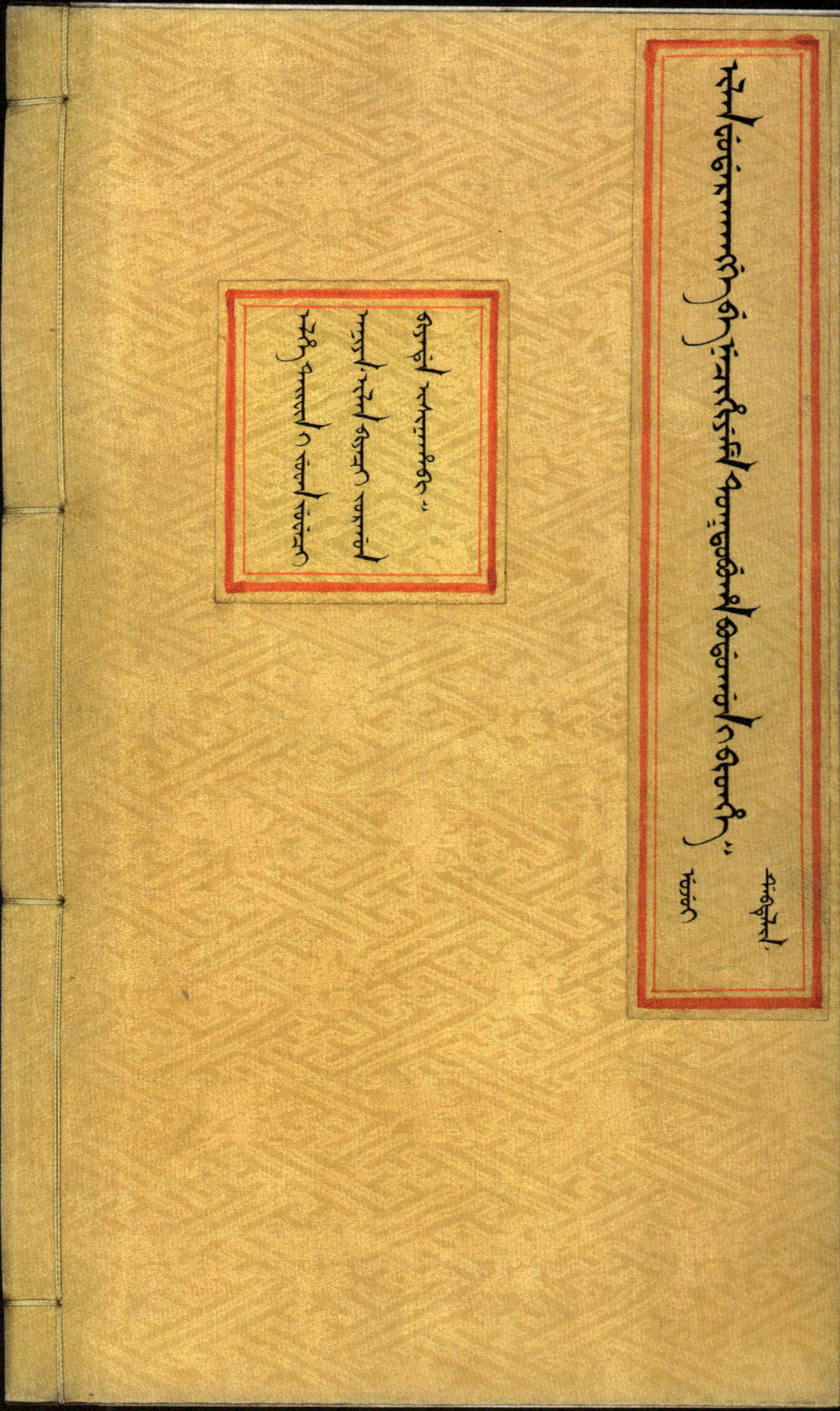

明黄色萬字曲水朵花紋暗花綾書面
Bright yellow twill-weave silk cover with veiled swastika and floral pattern

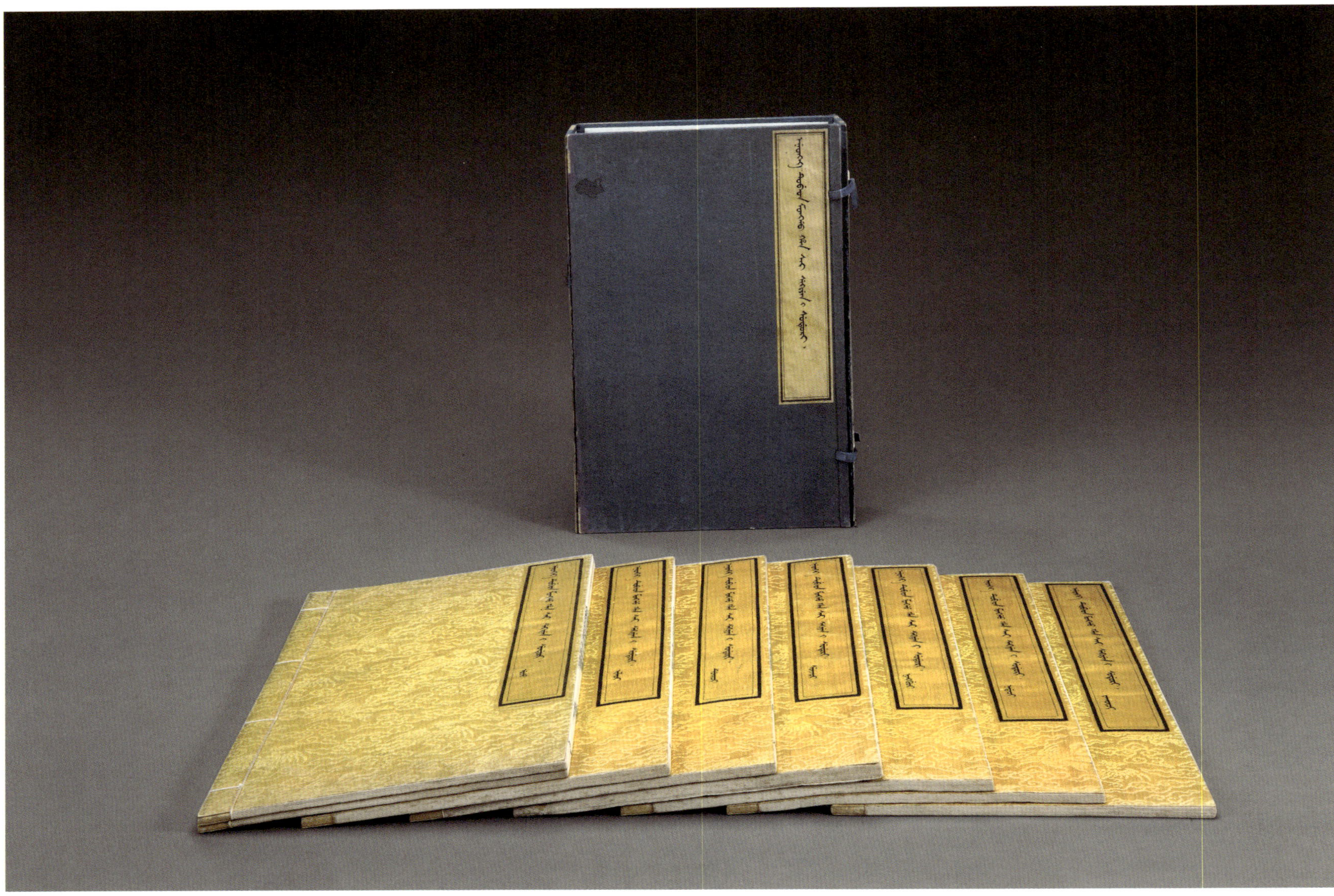

藍色素絹書函
Blue silk case

書21973
《蒙古源流八卷》
清　小徹辰薩囊臺吉撰
清乾隆三十八年（1773）武英殿刻滿文本
開本　縱30.2厘米　橫19.2厘米
版框　縱19厘米　橫14.2厘米
八冊　一函

52

Inventory number: Shu 21973
Origin and Development of Mongolia
Eight chapters
Written by Sagang Secen, Qing dynasty (1644-1911)
Printed in Manchu in 1773 at the Hall of Martial Valour
Format: 30.2 × 19.2 cm
Frame: 19 × 14.2 cm
Eight volumes in one case

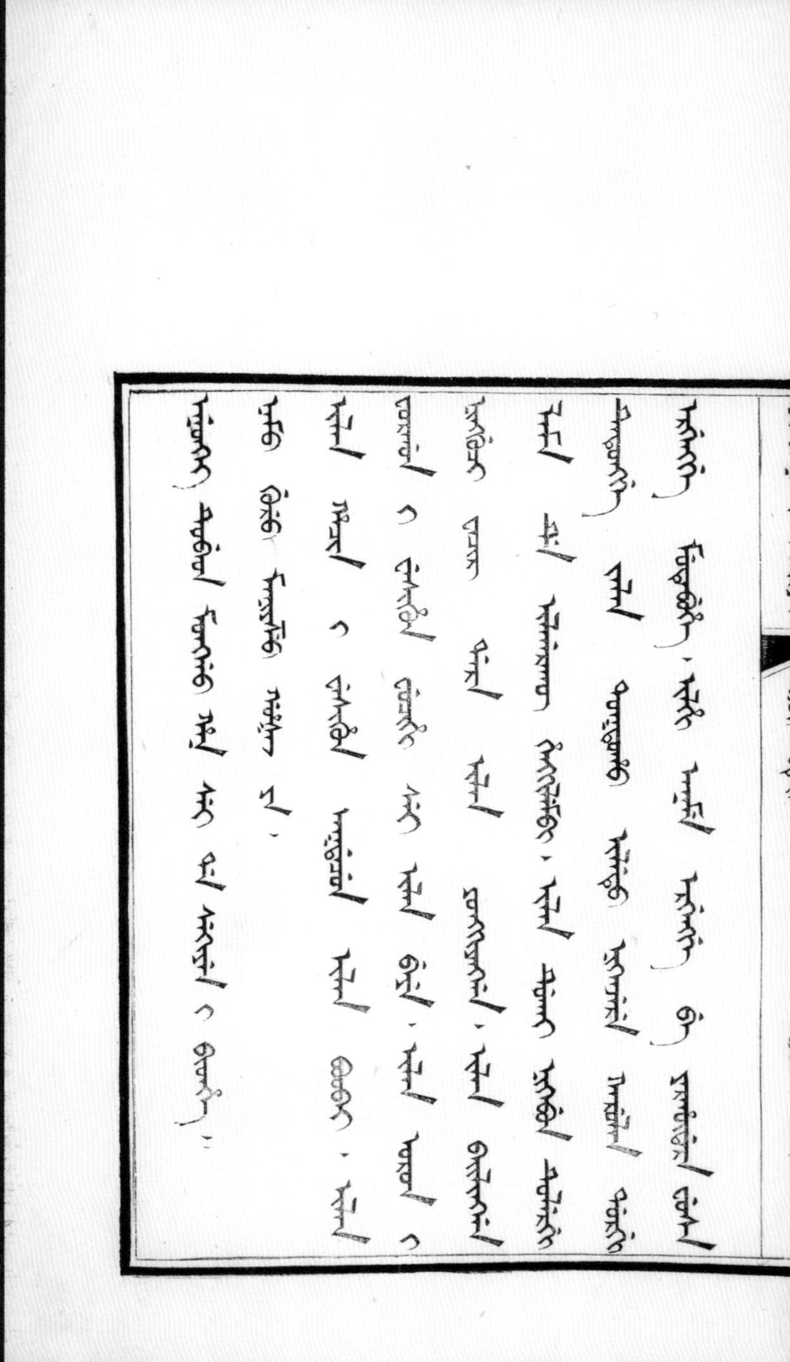

卷端
Beginning

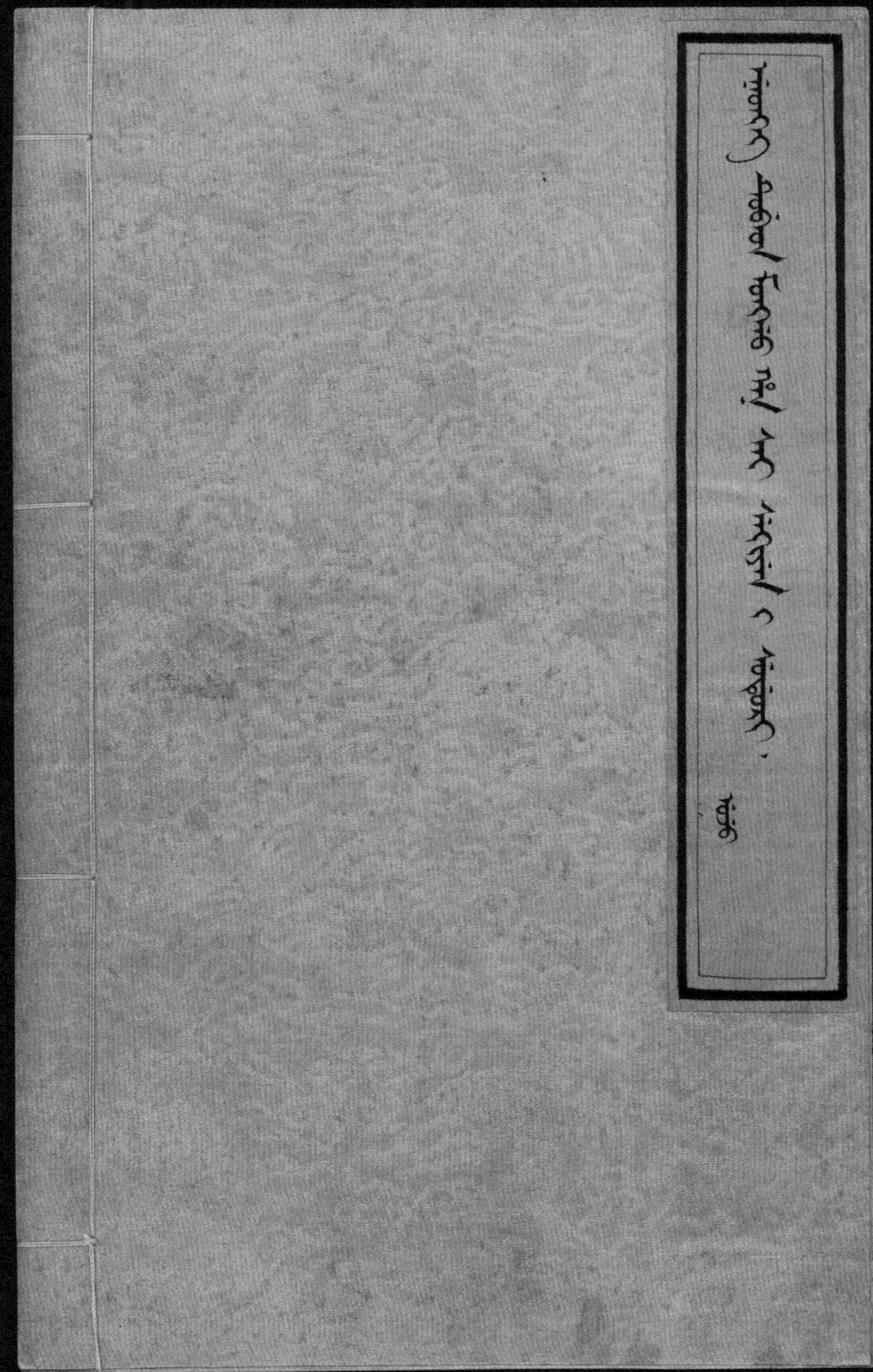

明黄色雲鳳紋暗花綾書面
Bright yellow twill-weave silk cover with veiled phoenix and cloud pattern

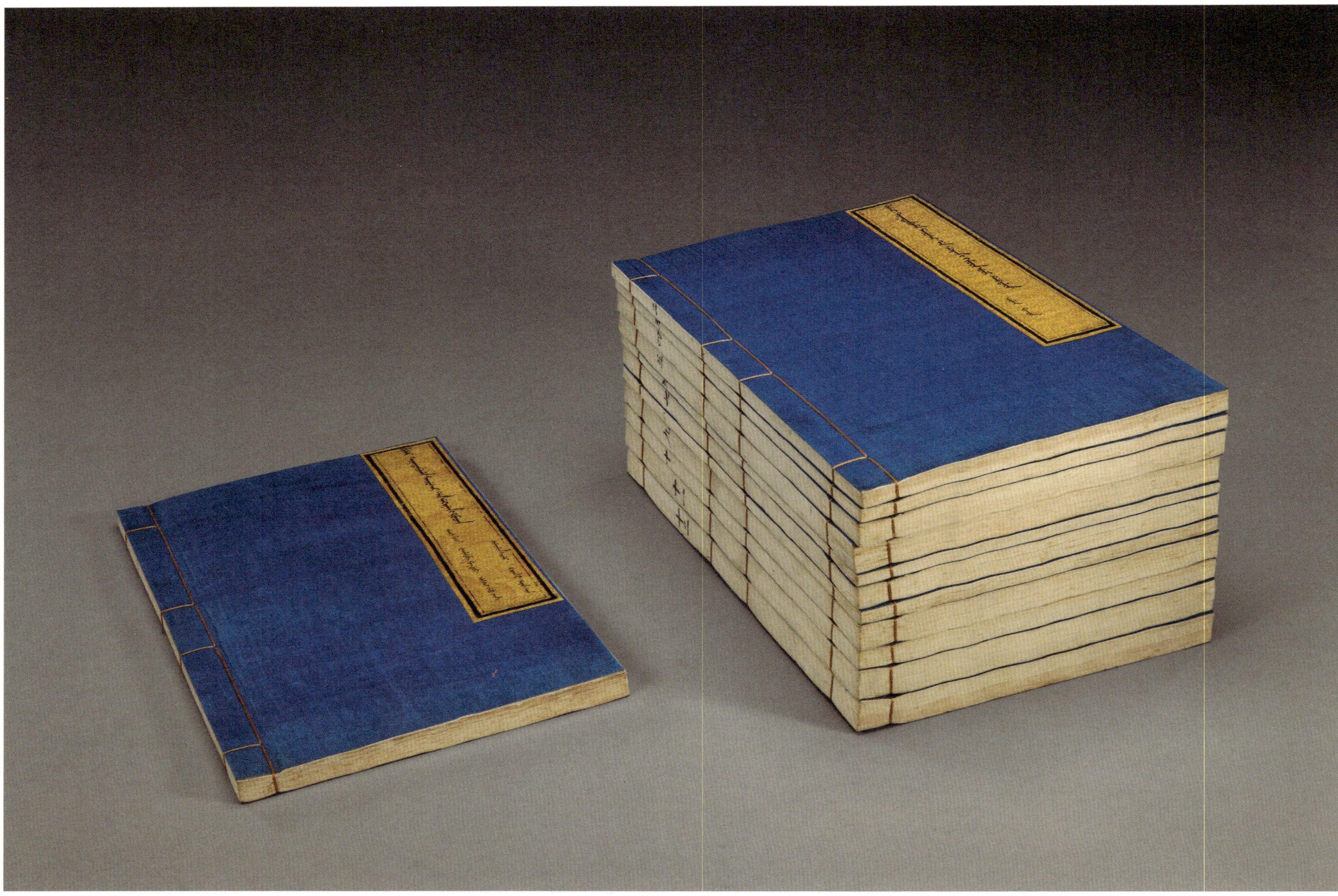

藍色素絹書面
Blue silk case

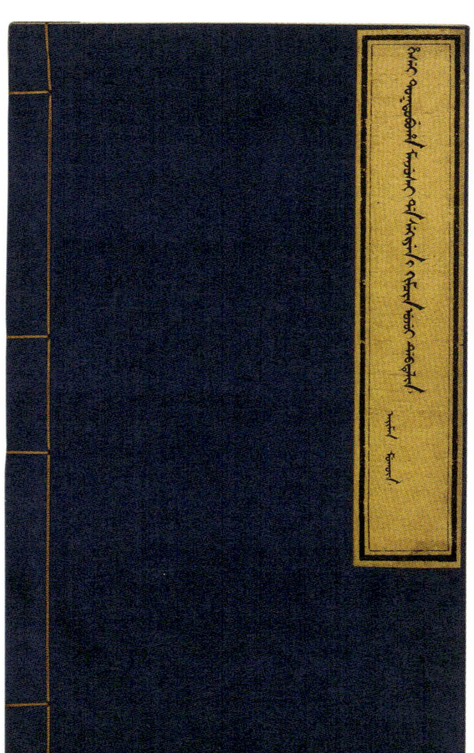

藍色素絹書面
Blue silk cover

53

書21980
《欽定滿州源流考二十卷首一卷》
清　阿桂等奉敕撰
清乾隆年內府朱絲欄精寫滿文本
開本　縱32.5厘米　橫20厘米
版框　縱23.5厘米　橫16.6厘米
二十一册　一函

Inventory number: Shu 21980
A Study of the Origin and Development of Manchuria
Twenty chapters as text, one chapter as preliminary remarks
Written by imperial order by Agui et. al., Qing dynasty (1644-1911)
Transcribed in Manchu in red columns by the Qing court in the Qianlong period (r.1736-1795)
Format: 32.5 × 20 cm
Frame: 23.5 × 16.6 cm
Twenty-one volumes in one case

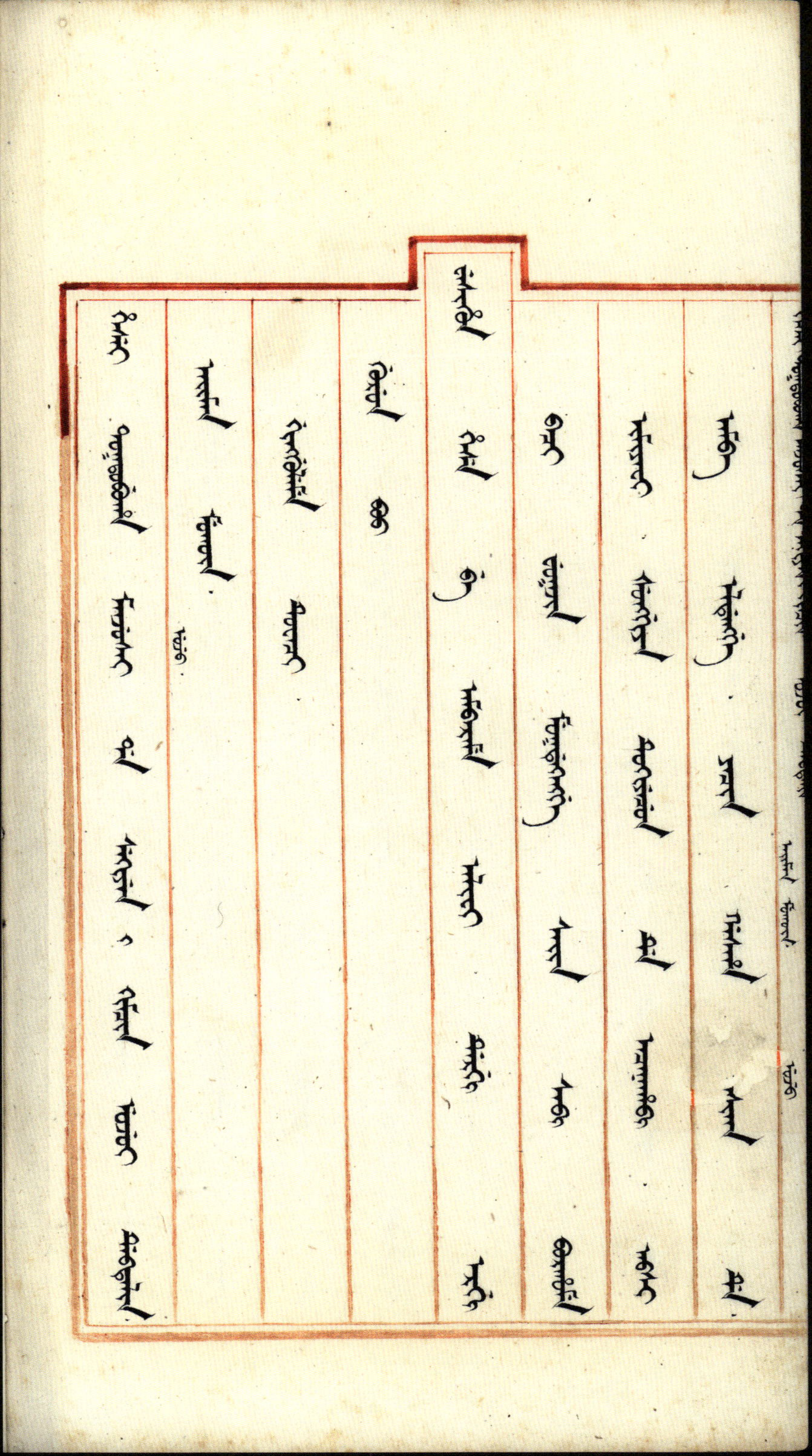

卷端
Beginning

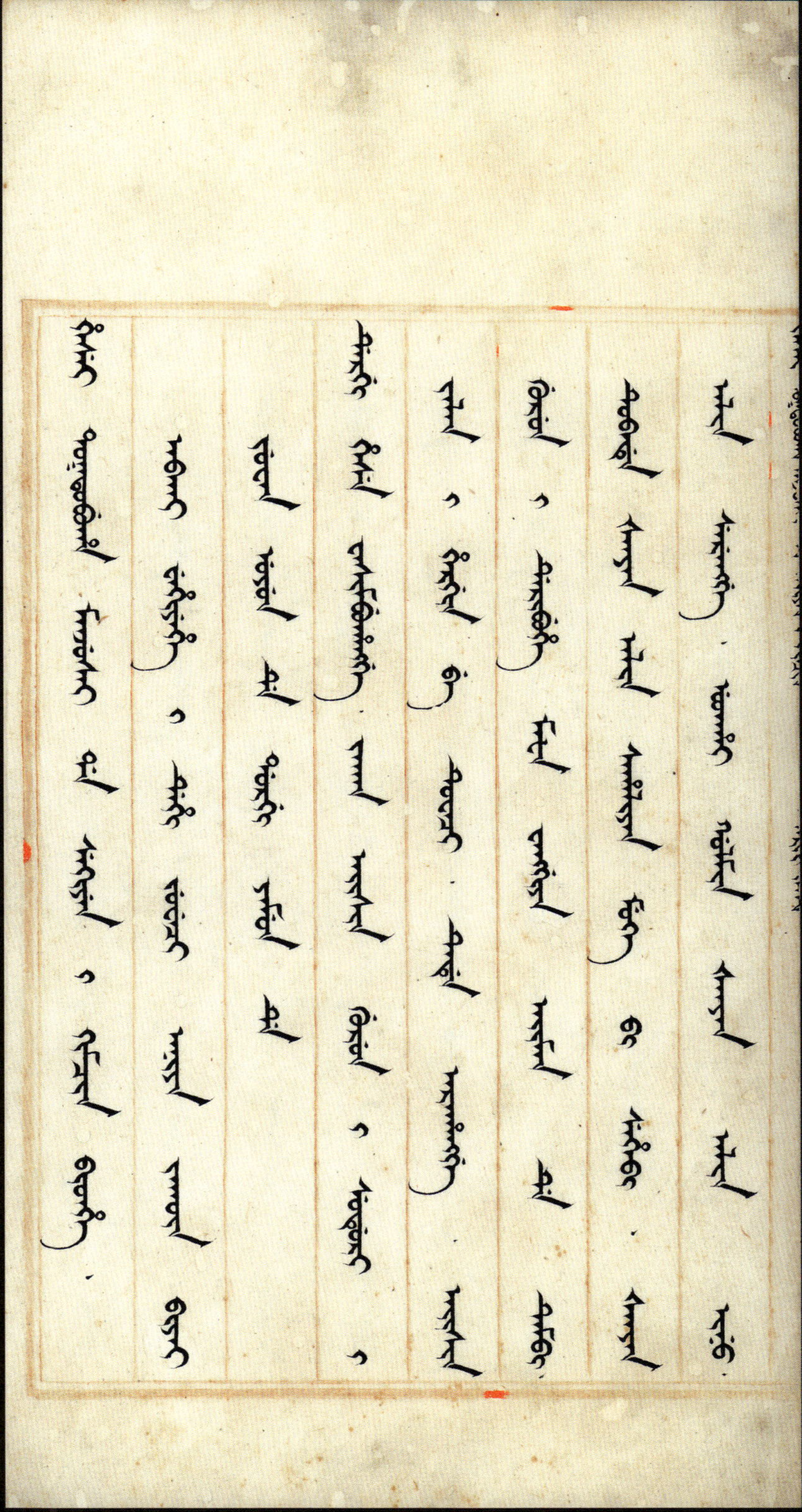

乾隆四十二年上諭
Imperial edict in 1777

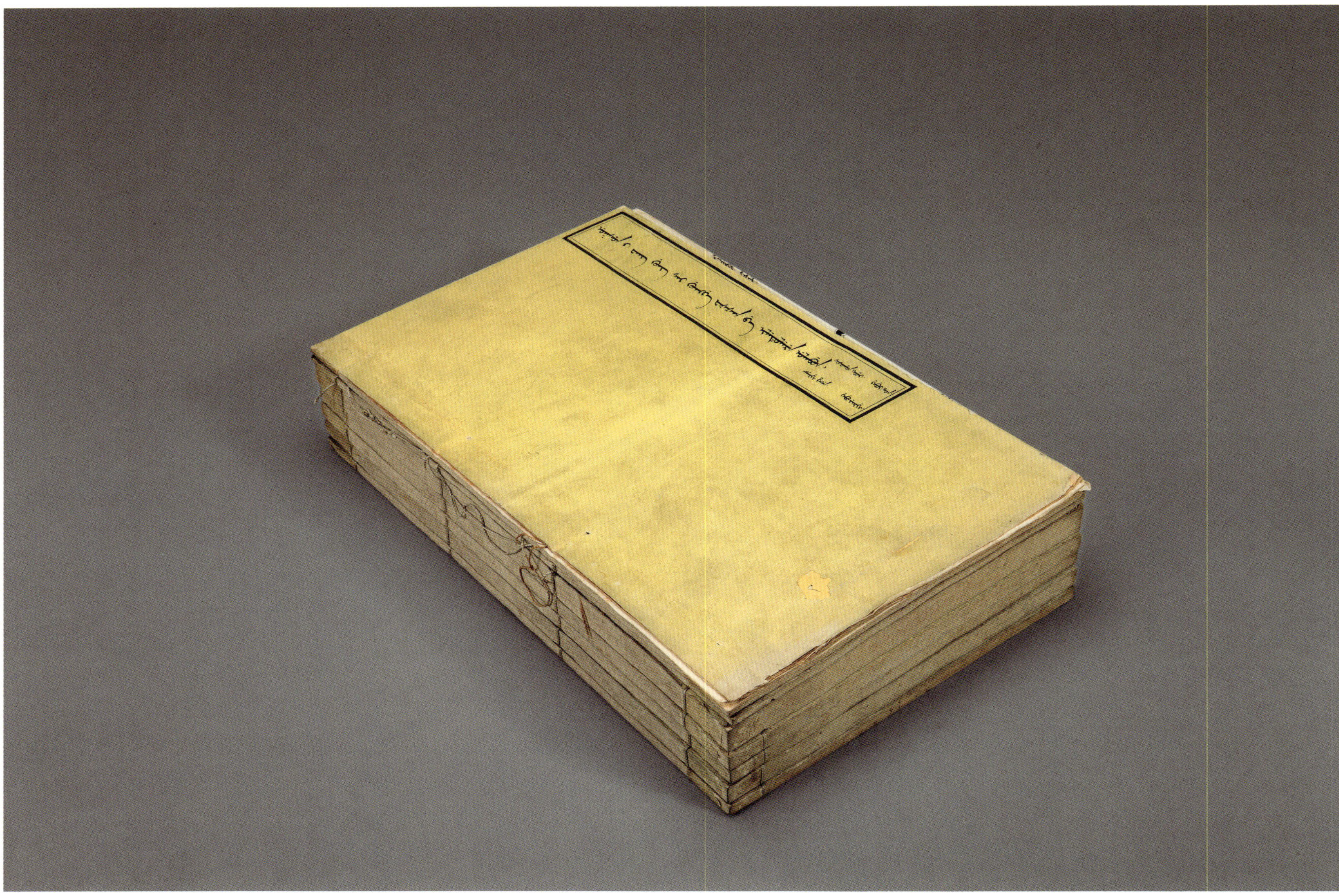

明黃色紙書面
Bright yellow paper cover

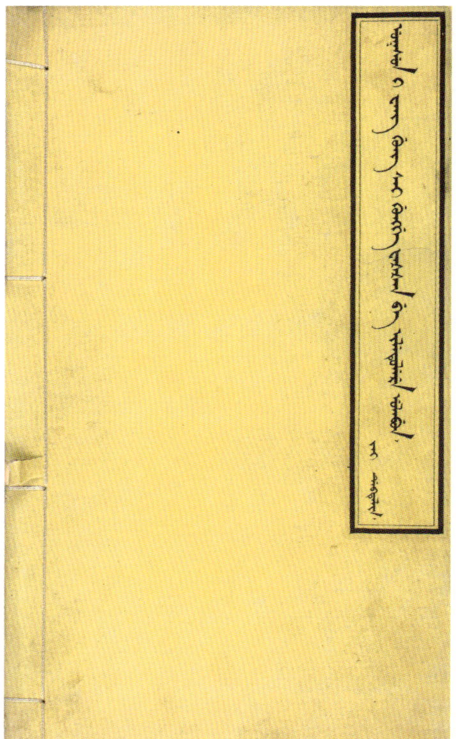

明黃色紙書面
Bright yellow paper cover

54

書22018
《宗室王公功績表傳五卷首二卷》
清　允祕等奉敕撰
清乾隆二十九年（1764）武英殿刻滿文本
開本　縱24.5厘米　橫20.5厘米
版框　縱23.5厘米　橫17厘米
七册　一函

Inventory number: Shu 22018
Tables and Biographies of the Nobility's Achievements
Written by imperial order by Yunmi et. al., Qing dynasty (1644-1911)
Printed in Manchu in 1764 at the Hall of Martial Valour
Format: 24.5 × 20.5 cm
Frame: 23.5 × 17 cm
Seven volumes in one case

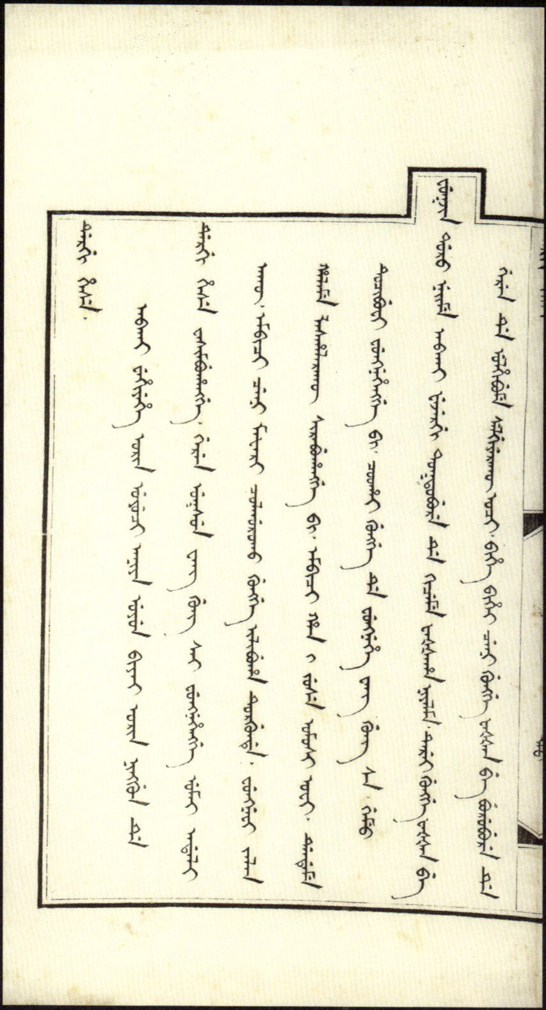

上諭
Imperial edict

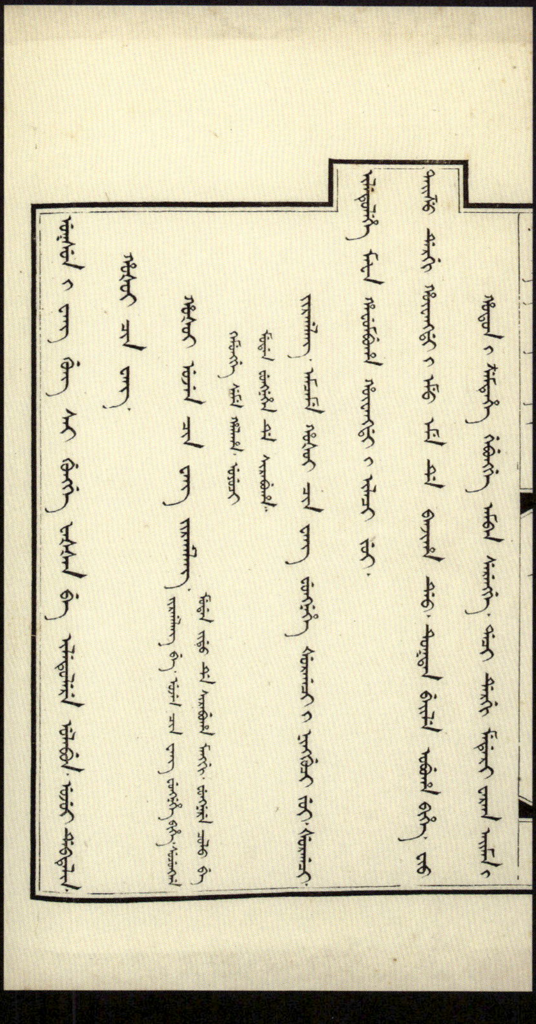

卷端
Beginning

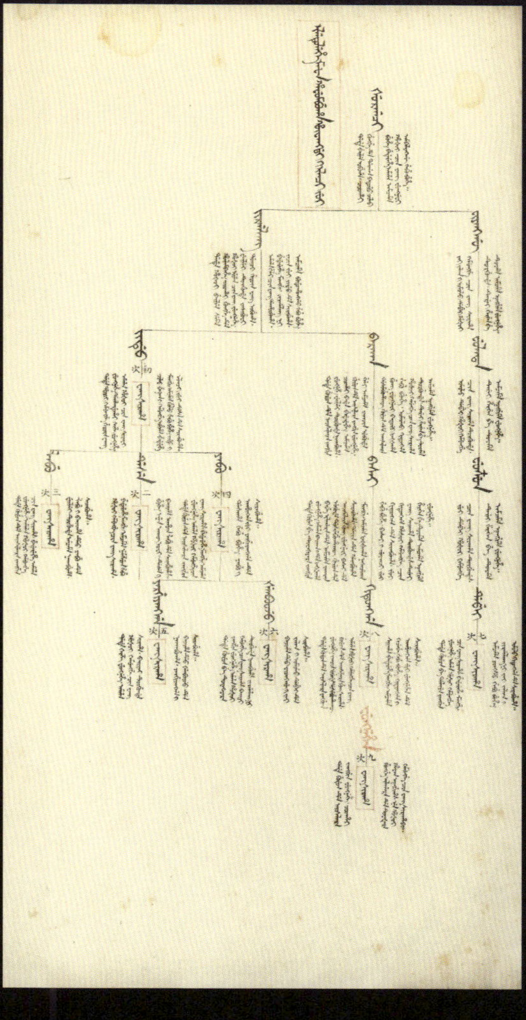

世襲表
Hereditary table

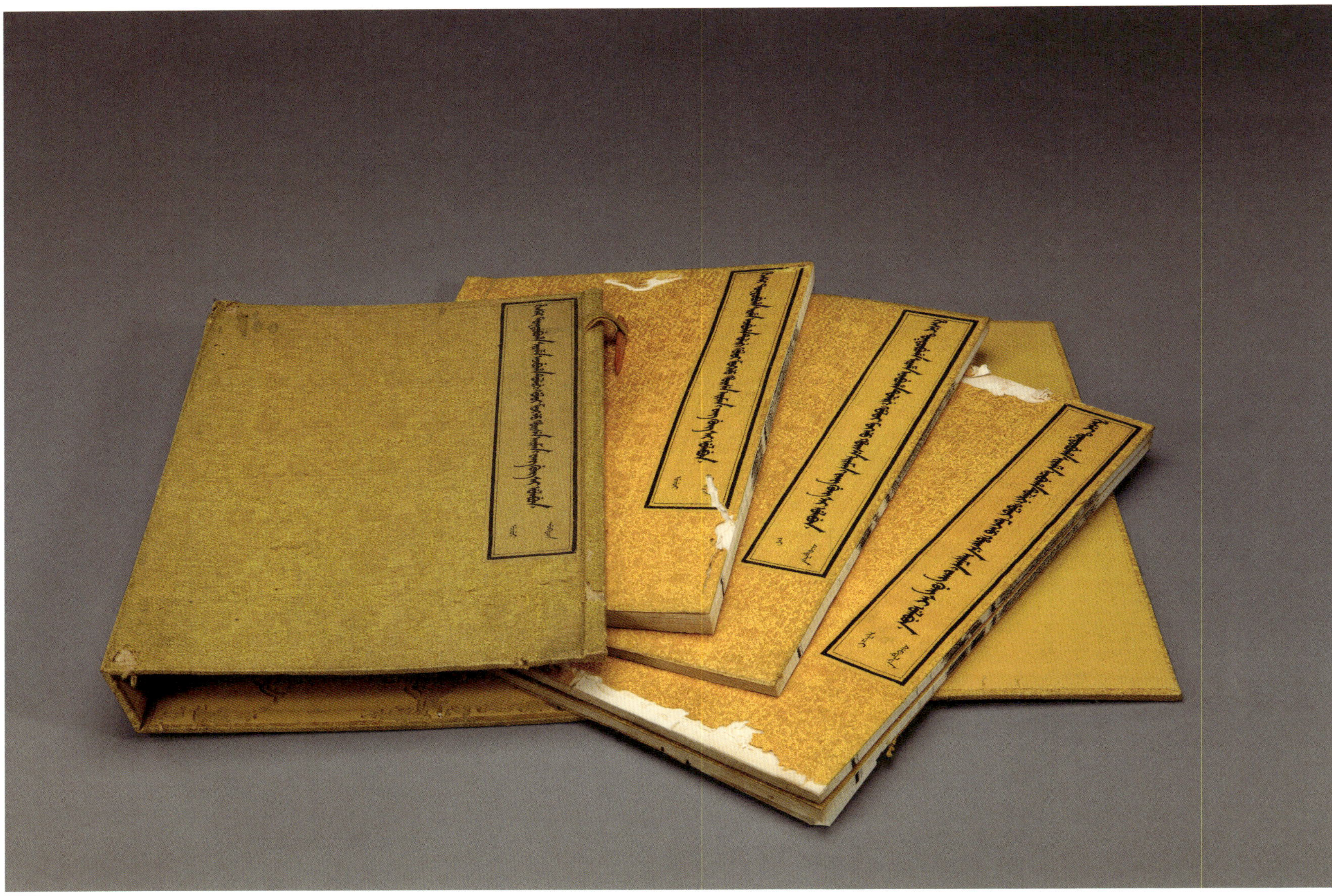

明黃色纏枝花紋暗花綾書函
Bright yellow twill-weave silk case with veiled pattern of floral scrolls

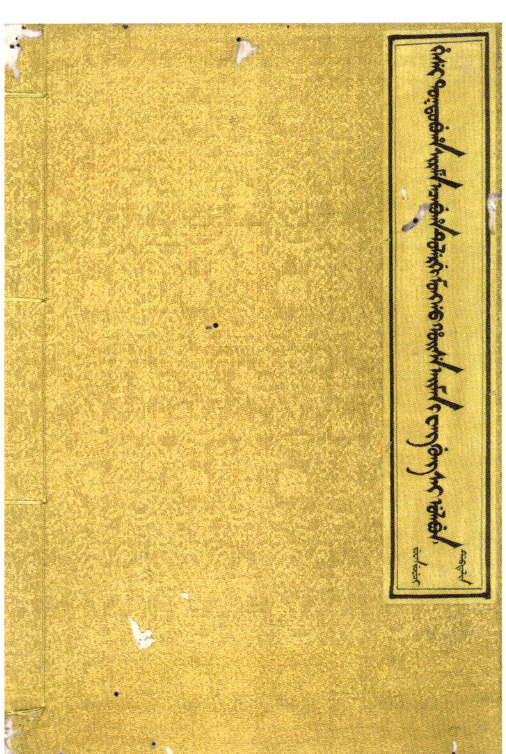

明黃色纏枝花紋暗花綾書面
Bright yellow twill-weave silk cover with veiled pattern of floral scrolls

55

書22038
《欽定續纂外藩蒙古回部王公傳十二卷》
清　穆彰阿等奉敕撰
清道光二十九年（1849）武英殿刻滿文本
開本　縱36.5厘米　橫24厘米
版框　縱26.5厘米　橫20.1厘米
十二册　三函

Inventory number: Shu 22038
Sequel to Biographies of Mongolian and Uigurian Princes
Written by imperial order by Mujangga et. al., Qing dynasty (1644-1911)
Printed in Manchu in 1849 at the Hall of Martial Valour
Format: 36.5 × 24 cm
Frame: 26.5 × 20.1 cm
Twelve volumes in three cases

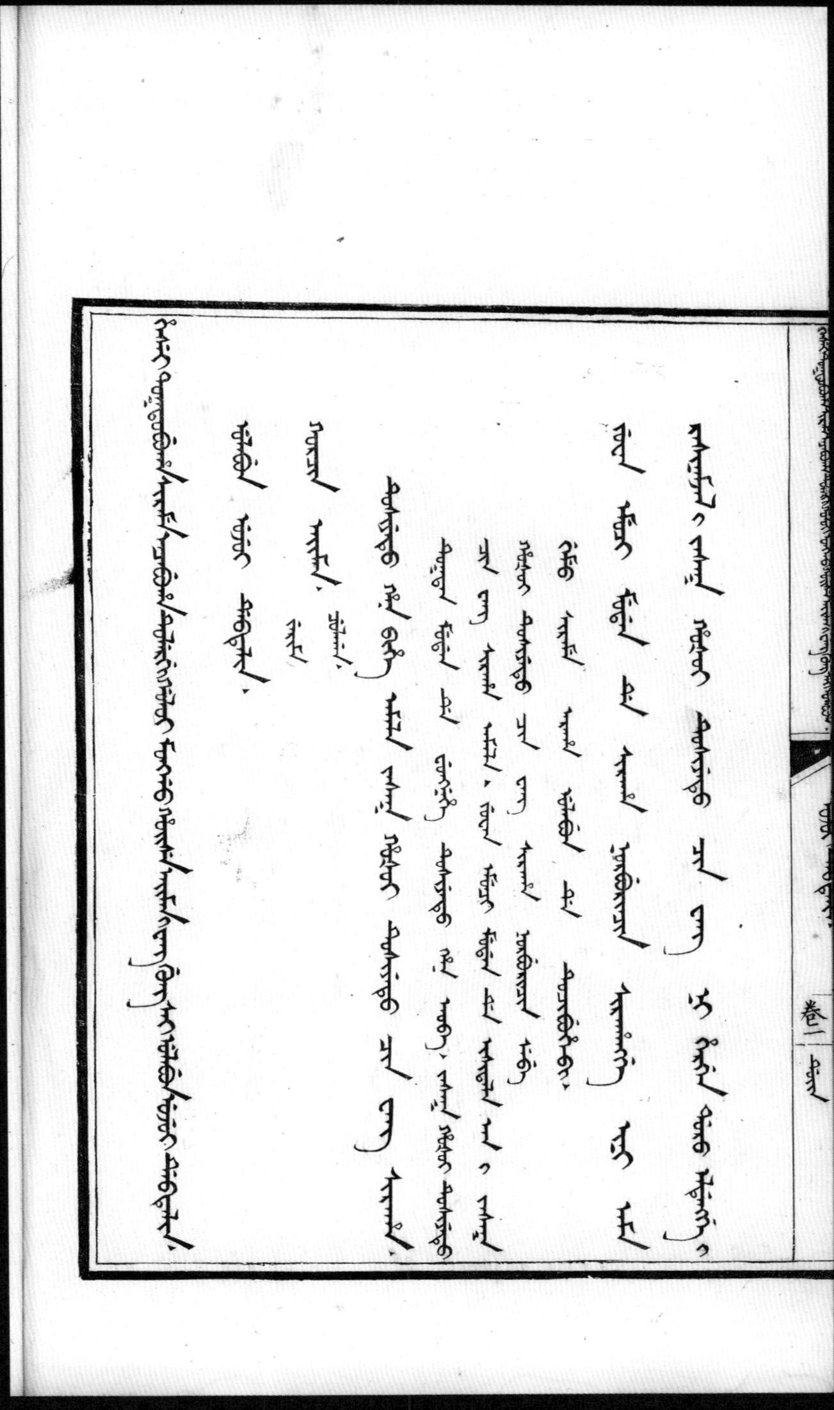

卷端
Beginning

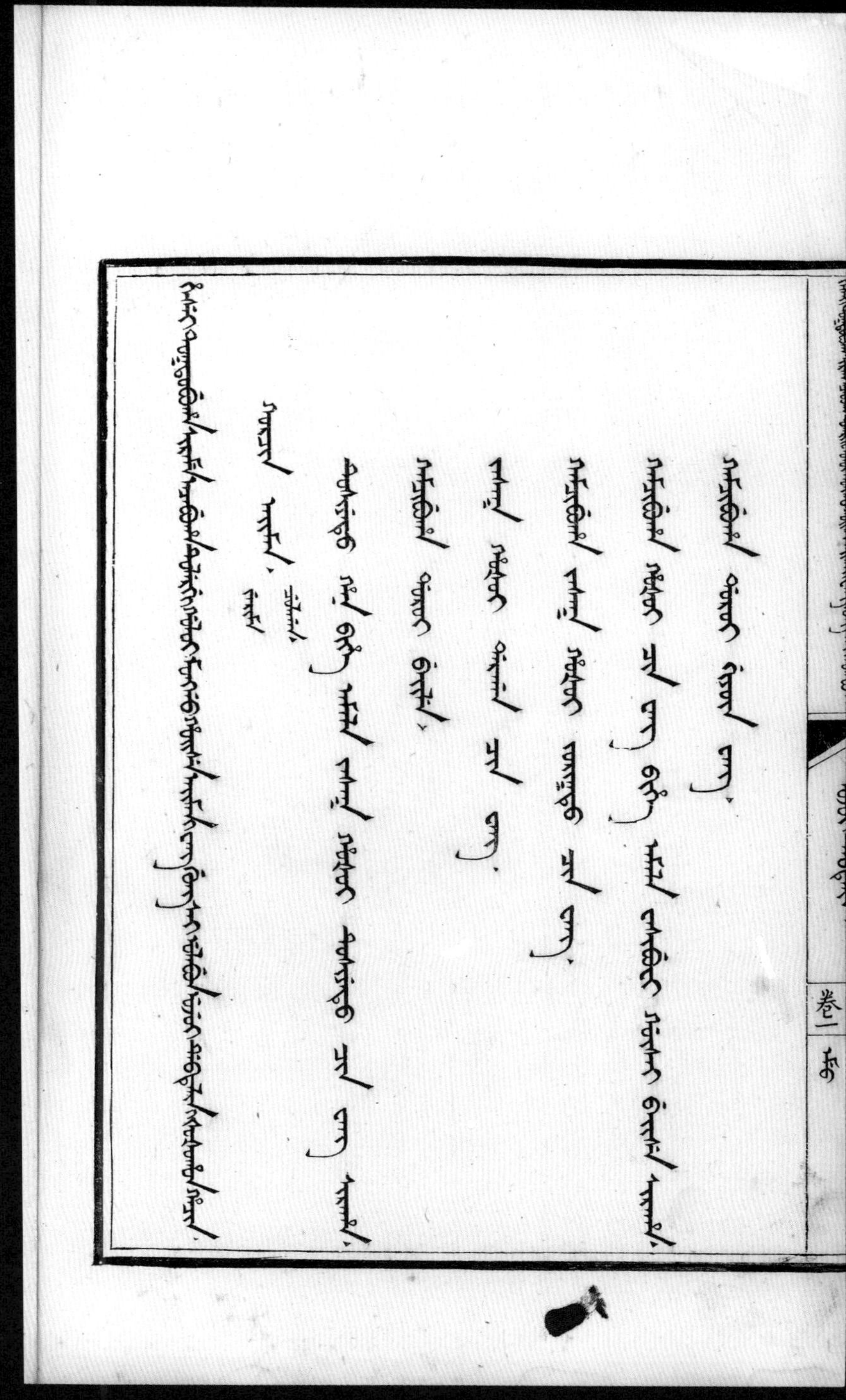

目録
Contents

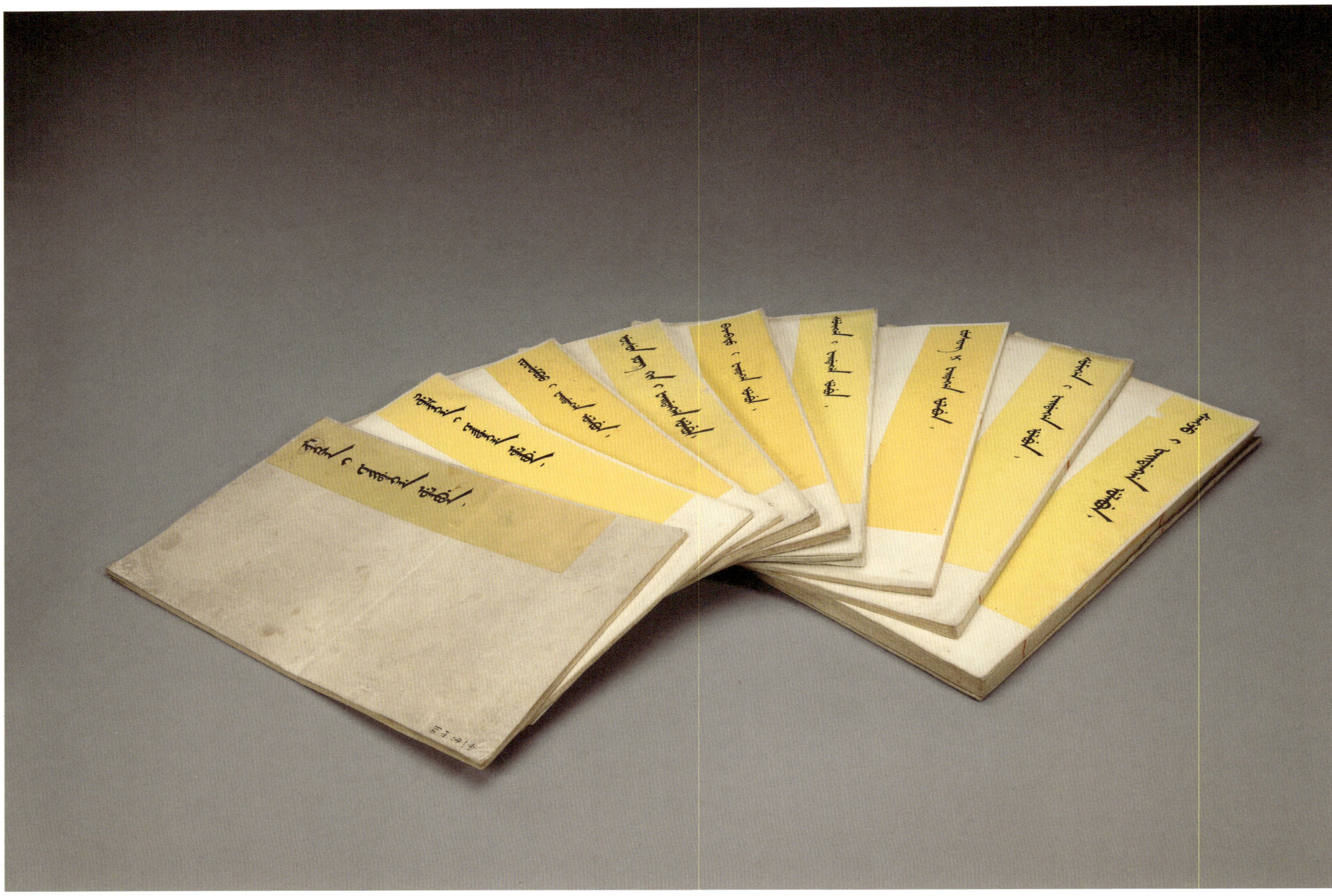

外觀
Exterior

書22049
《大清國史大臣列傳》（擬訂）
清　國史館編
清道光年内府朱絲欄滿文修改稿本
開本　縱40厘米　橫23.8厘米
版框　縱29.2厘米　橫18厘米
56 九百三十册　八十三函（上有修改黄色浮簽）

Inventory number: Shu 22049
Biographies of the Qing Ministers
Compiled by Institute of the National History, Qing dynasty (1644-1911)
Draft edition
Revised in Manchu in red columns by the Qing court in the Daoguang period (r.1821-1850)
Format: 40 × 23.8 cm
Frame: 29.2 × 18 cm
930 volumes in eighty-three cases, with yellow strips of paper indicating revisions

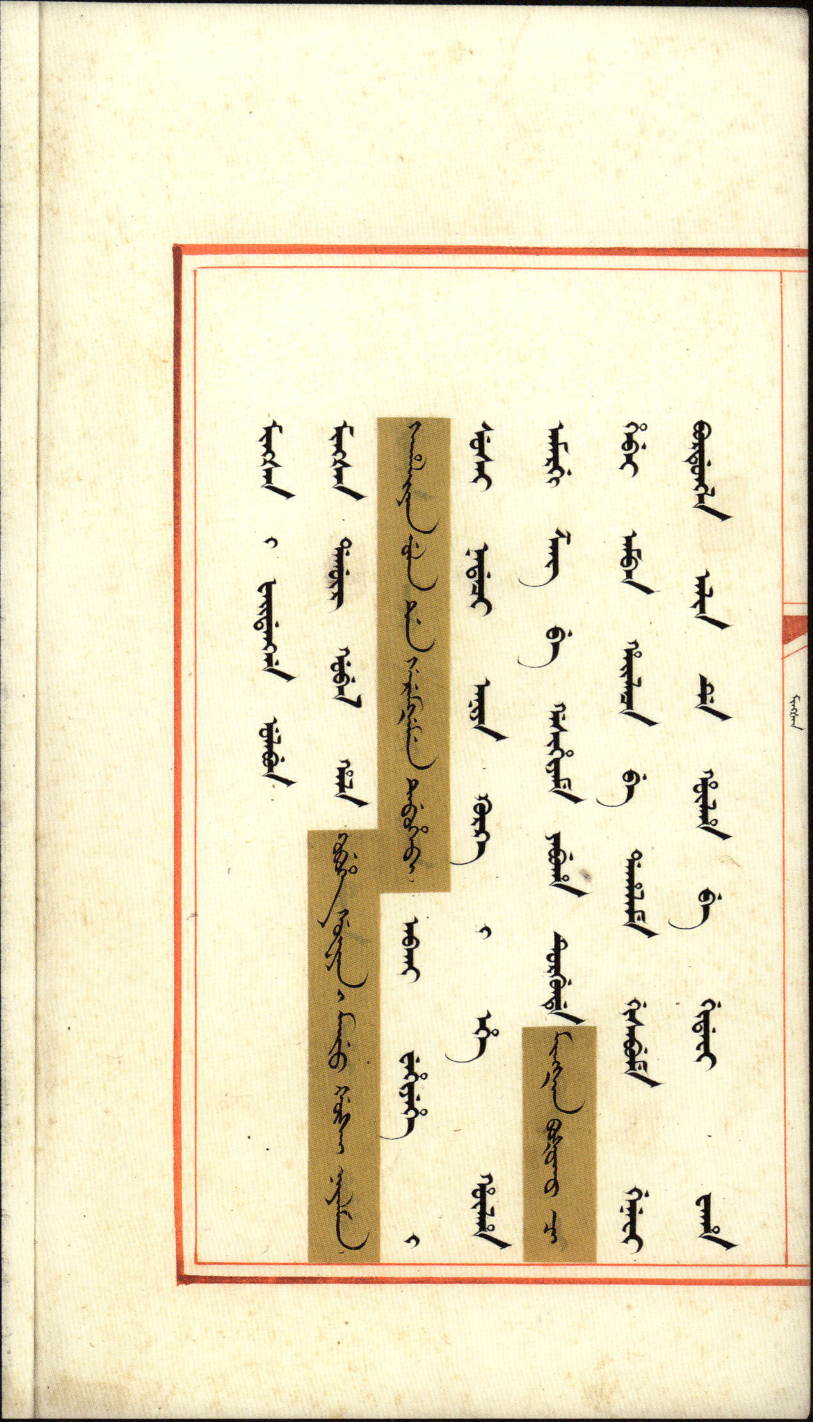

卷端
Beginning

黄色紙書面
Yellow paper cover

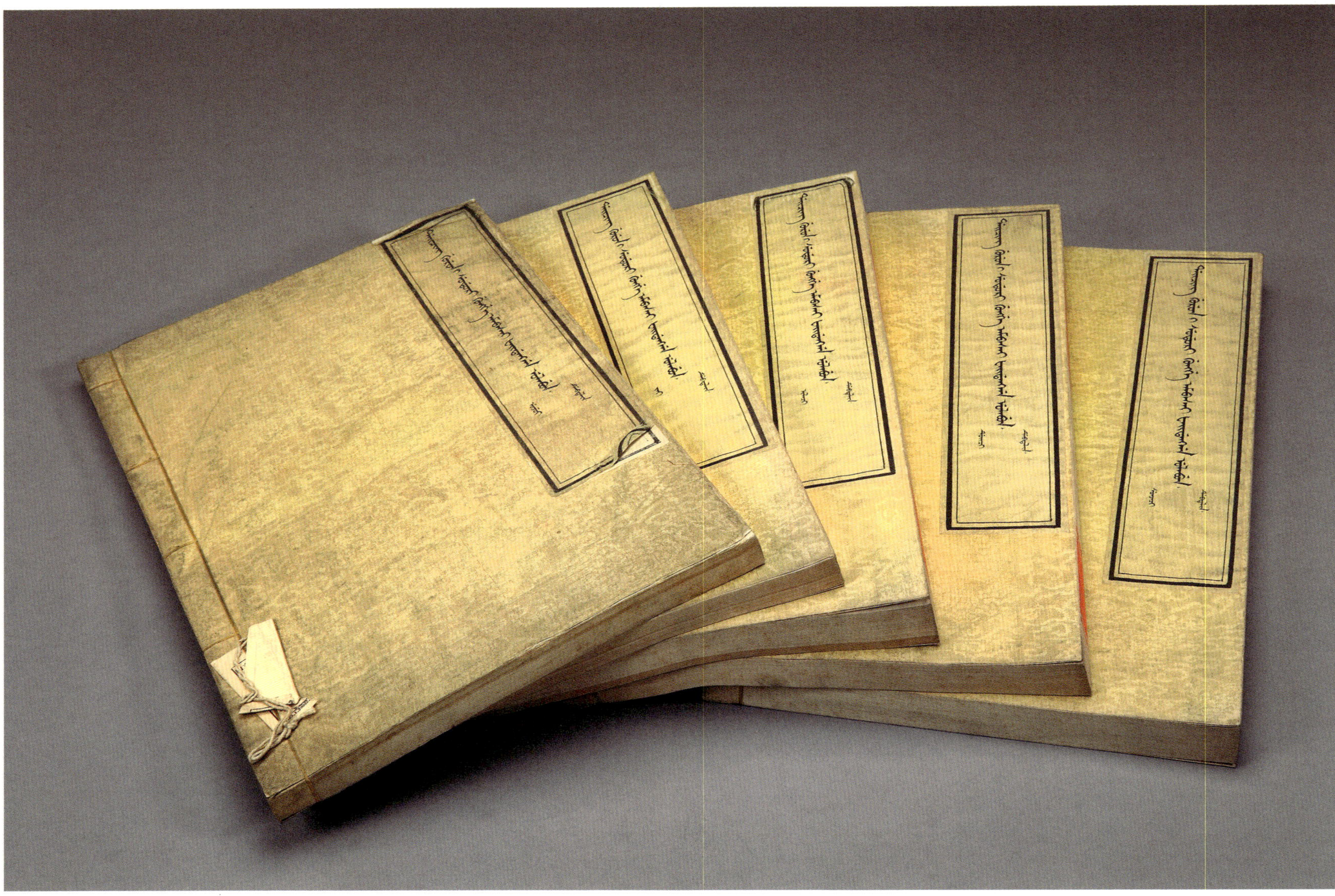

外觀
Exterior

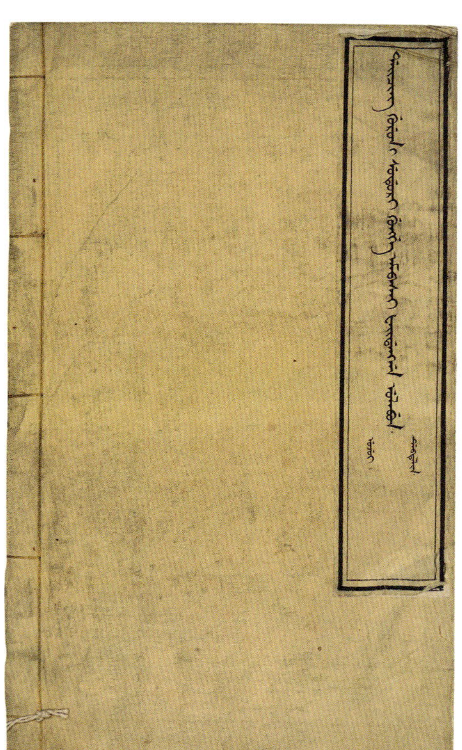

明黄色雲龍紋暗花綾書面
Bright yellow twill-weave silk cover with veiled dragon and cloud pattern

57

書22058
《大清國史功臣列傳》
清　國史館编
清内府朱絲欄精寫滿文本
開本　縱37.5厘米　横22.5厘米
版框　縱28.5厘米　横18.6厘米
存二十一册　四函

Inventory number: Shu 22058
Biographies of the Meritorious Officials in the Qing History
Compiled by Institute of the National History, Qing dynasty (1644-1911)
Transcribed in Manchu in red columns by the Qing court
Format: 37.5 × 22.5 cm
Frame: 28.5 × 18.6 cm
Twenty-one volumes in four cases extant today

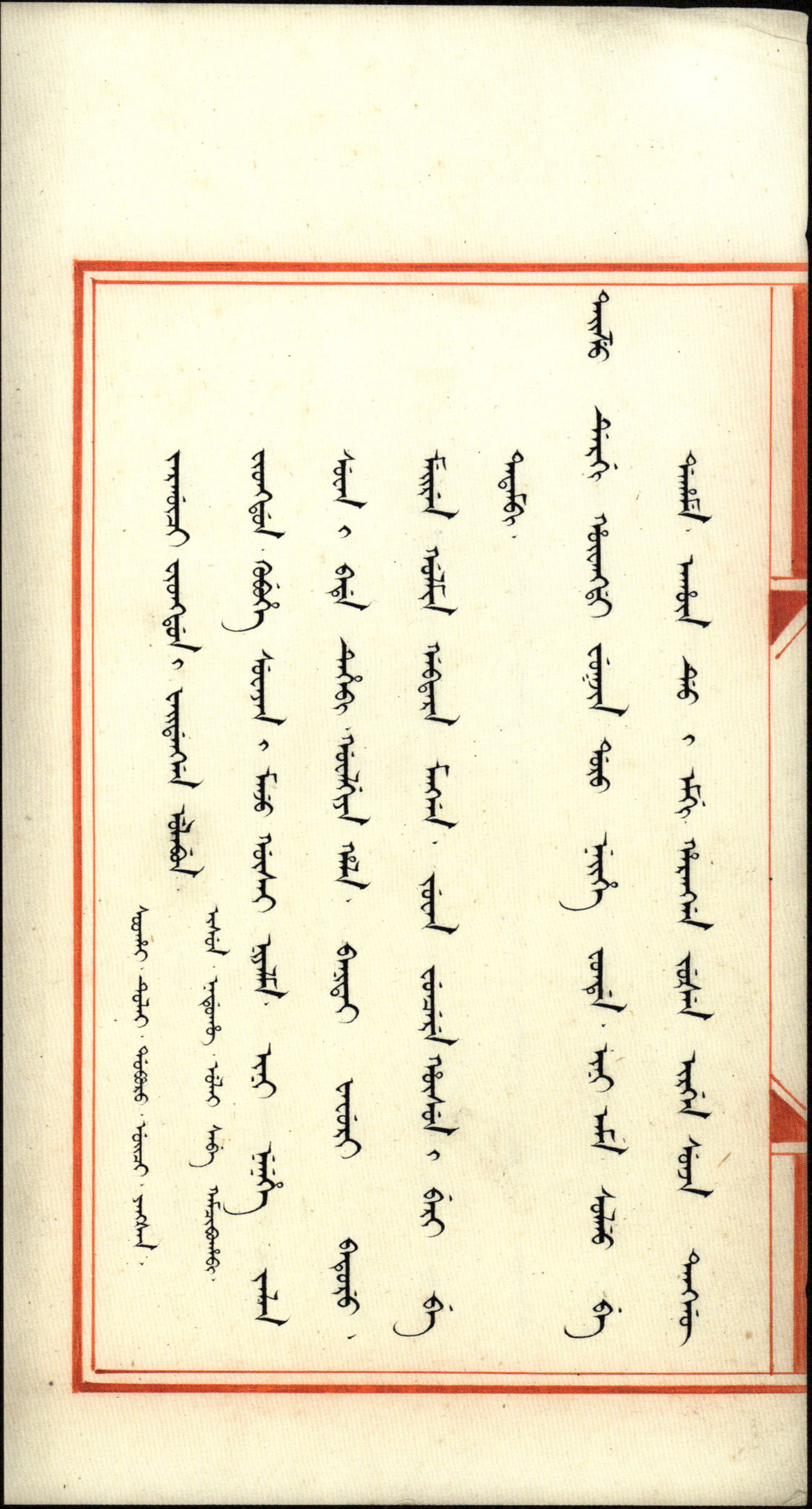

卷端
Beginning

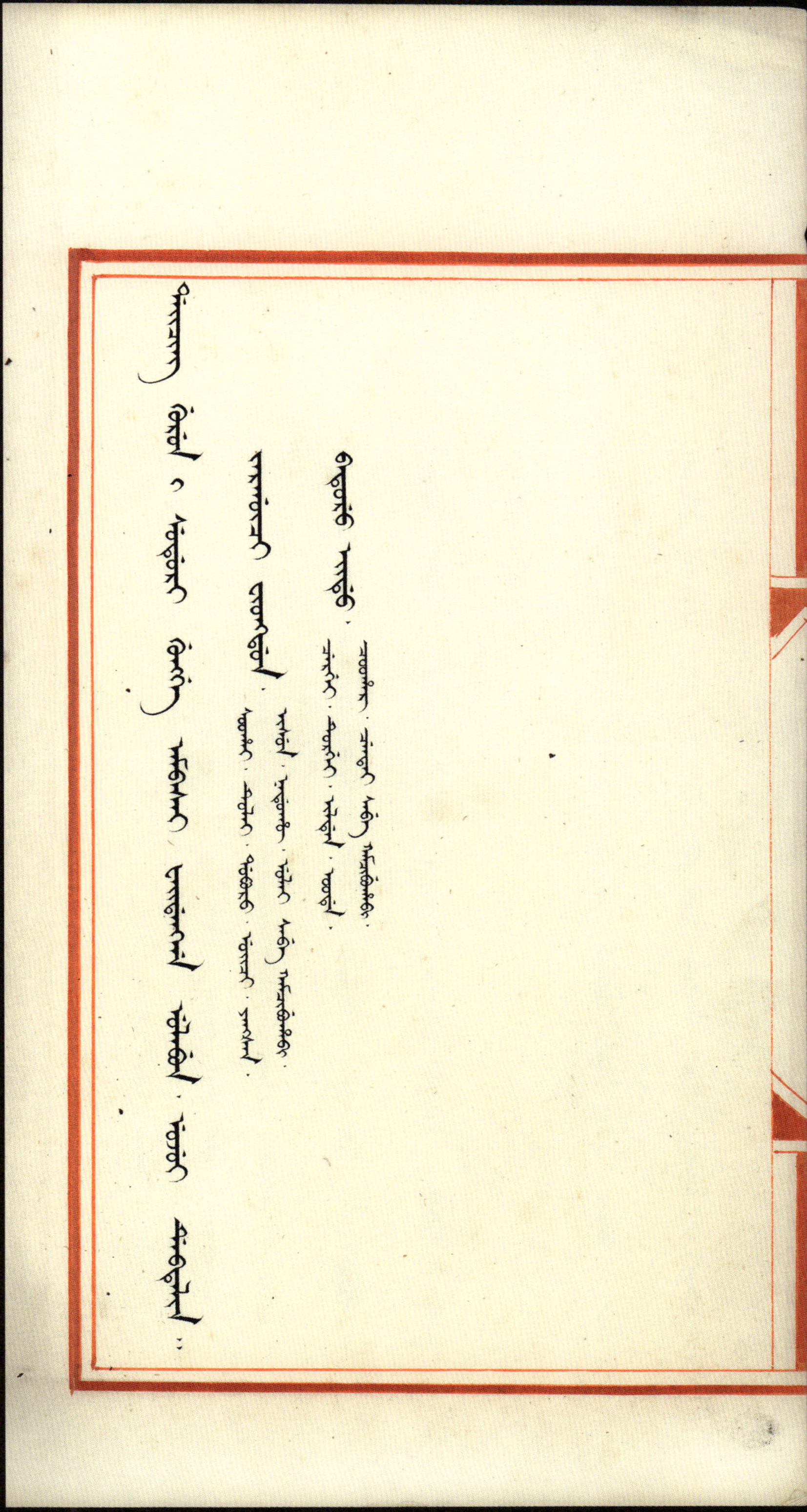

卷目
Contents

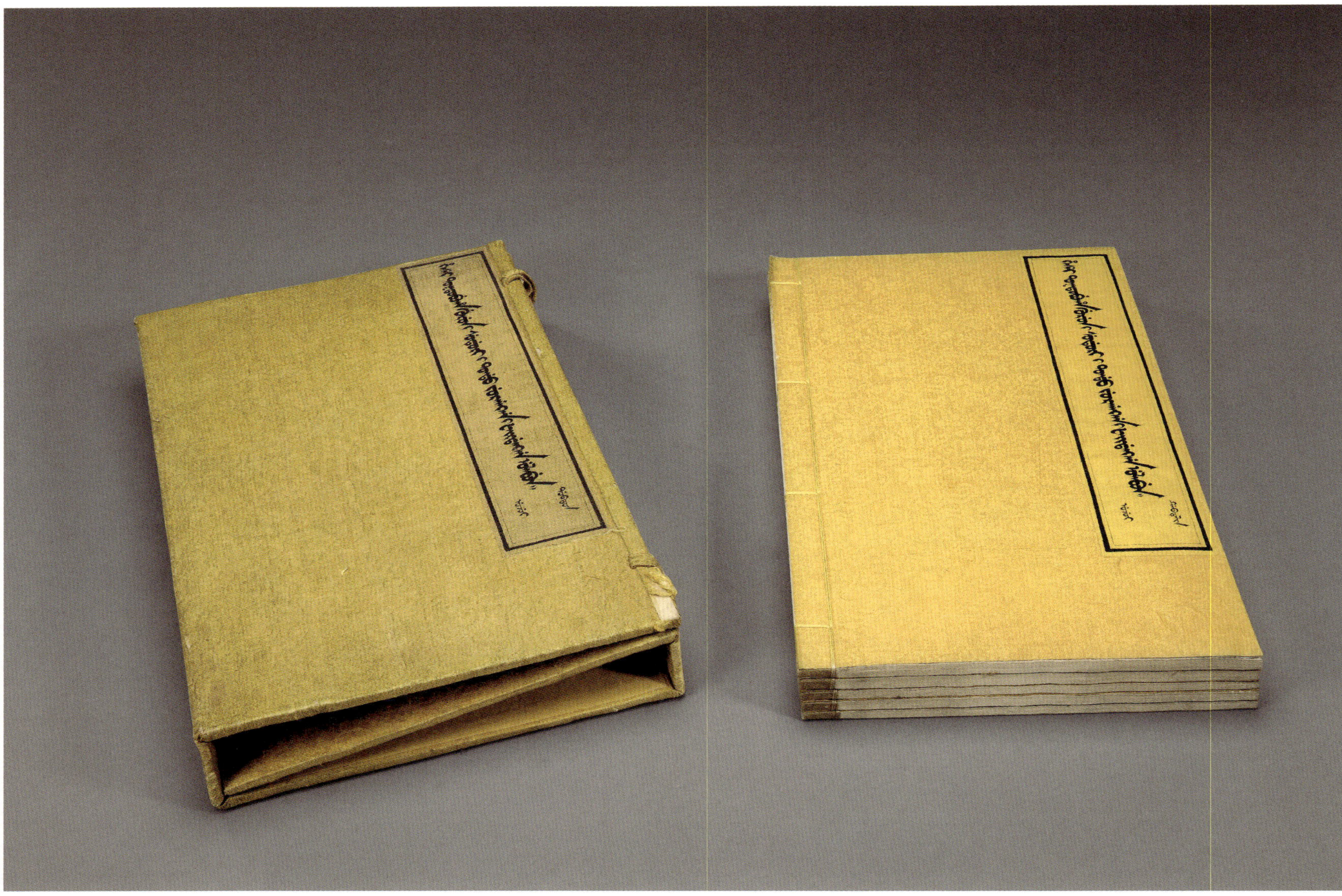

明黄色纏枝花紋暗花綾書面
Bright yellow twill-weave silk cover with veiled pattern of floral scrolls

書22067
《欽定國史忠義列傳十九卷》
清　國史館編
清内府朱絲欄精寫滿文本
開本　縱39.8厘米　横23.6厘米
版框　縱29厘米　横17.8厘米
十九册　四函

58

Inventory number: Shu 22067
Biographies of the Loyal and Righteous Subjects in the Qing History, Made by Imperial Order
Nineteen chapters
Compiled by Institute of the National History, Qing dynasty (1644-1911)
Transcribed in Manchu in red columns by the Qing court
Format: 39.8 × 23.6 cm
Frame: 29 × 17.8 cm
Nineteen volumes in four cases

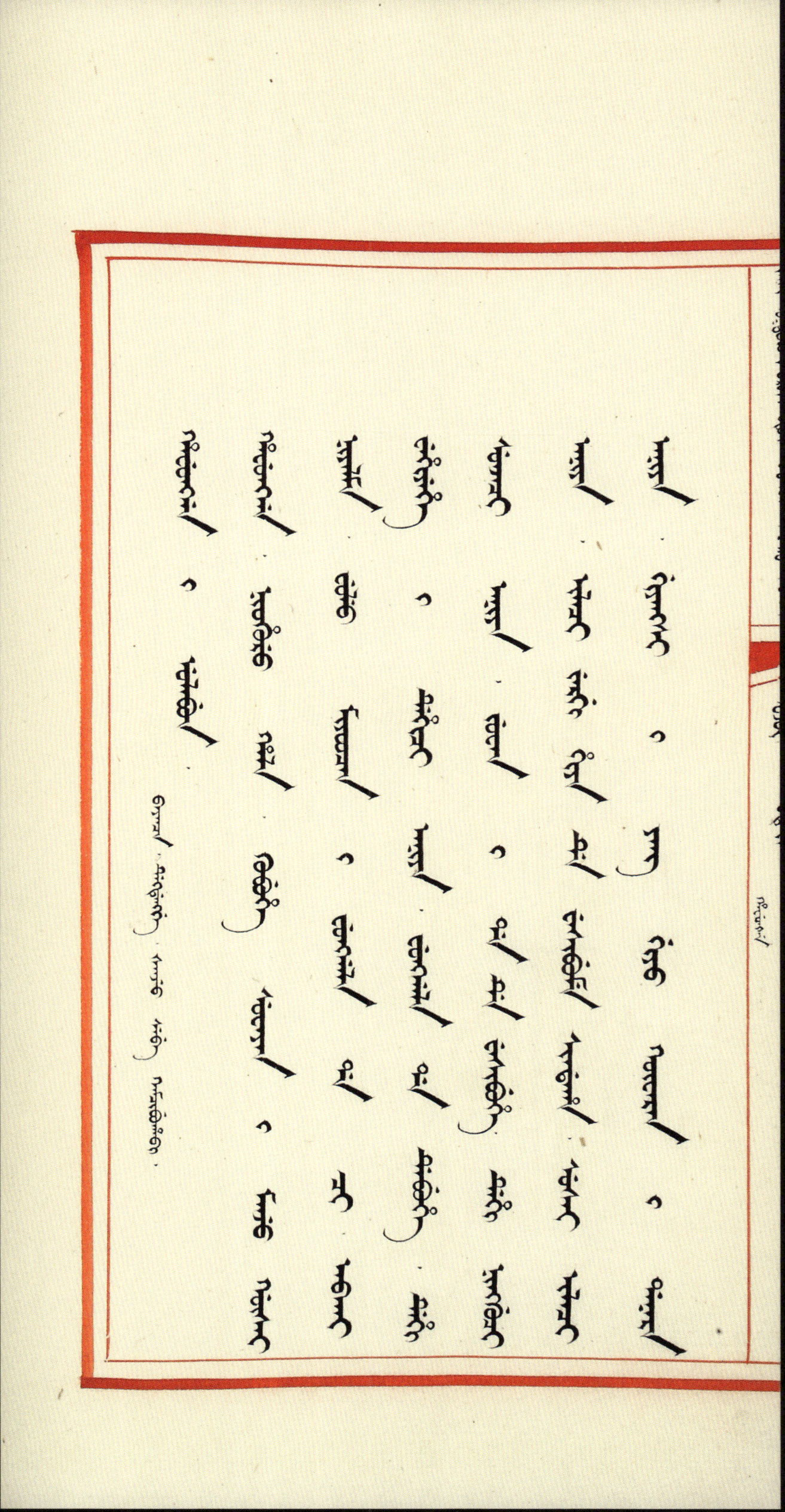

卷端
Beginning

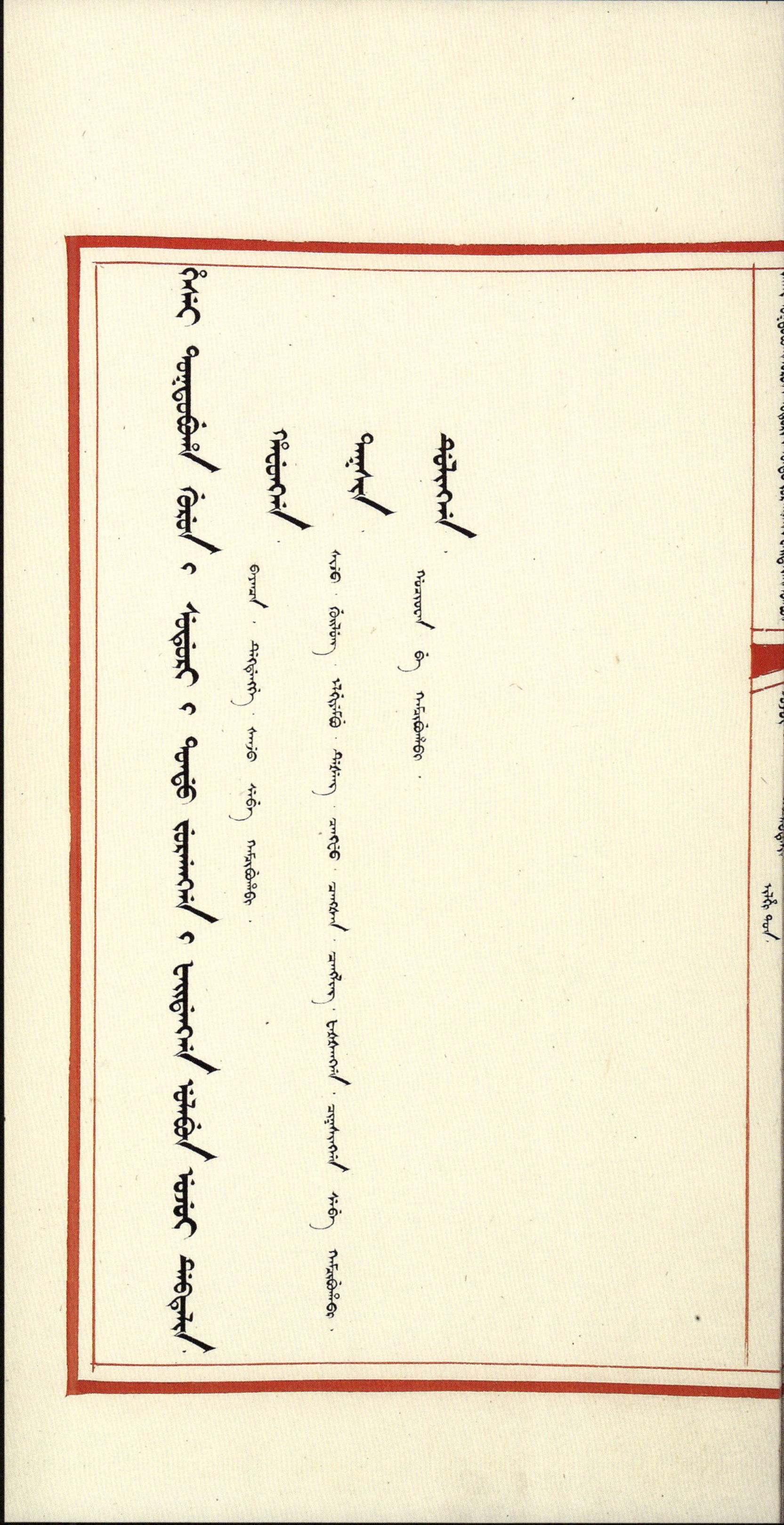

卷目
Contents

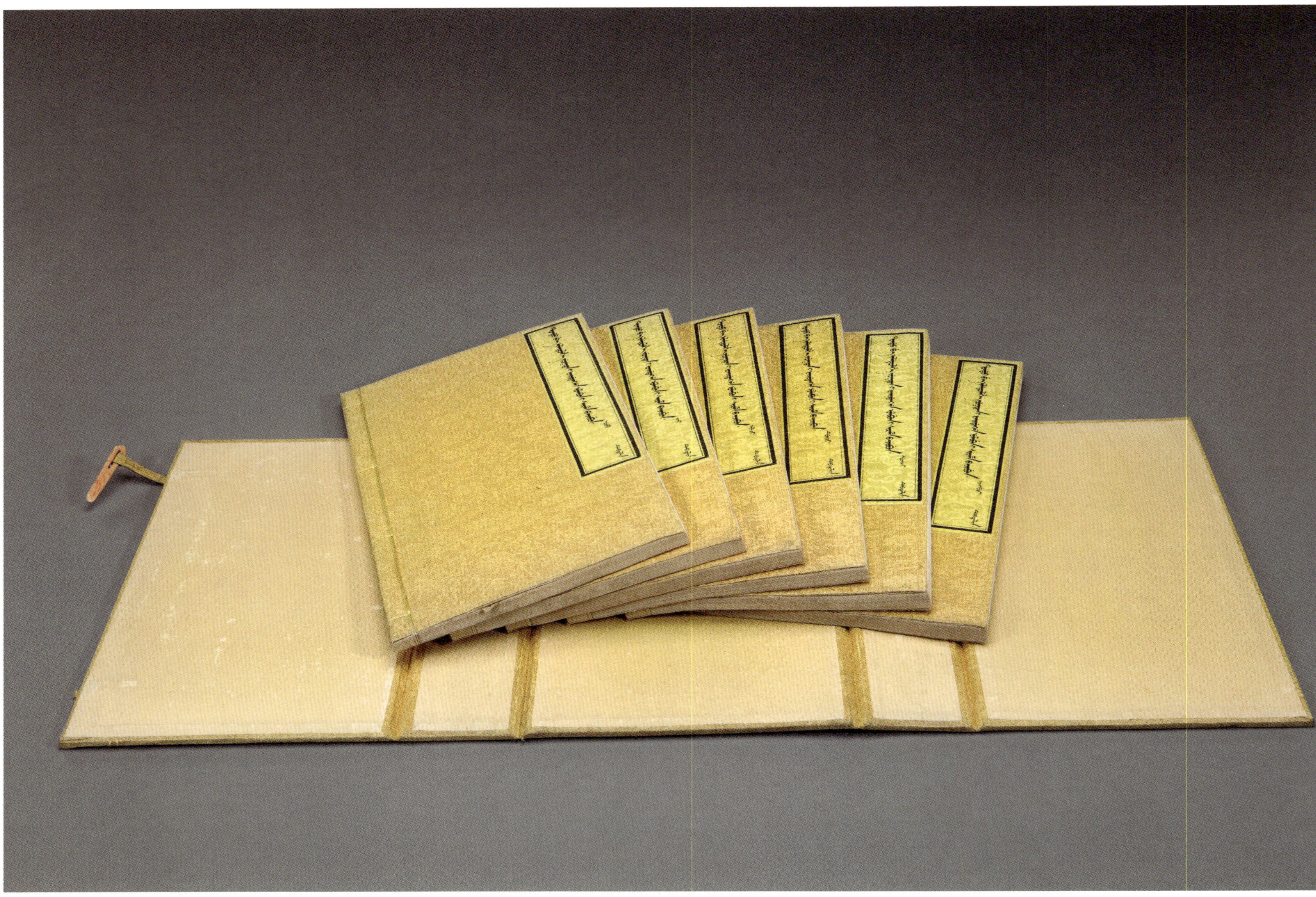

外觀
Exterior

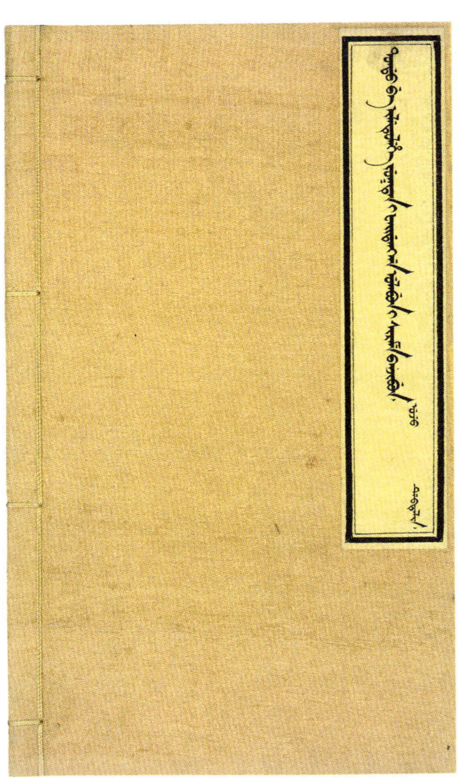

明黃色暗花綾書面
Bright yellow twill-weave silk cover with veiled pattern

書22077
《昭忠祠列傳續編一百二十卷》
清　長萃總纂
清內府朱絲欄精寫滿文本
開本　縱29厘米　橫17.5厘米
版框　縱19厘米　橫14.6厘米
一百二十册　二十函

59

Inventory number: Shu 22077
Biographies of the Martyrs in the Shrine of Manifest Loyalty
120 chapters
Compiled by Changcui et. al., Qing dynasty (1644-1911)
Transcribed in Manchu in red columns by the Qing court
Format: 29× 17.5 cm
Frame: 19 ×14.6 cm
120 volumes in twenty cases

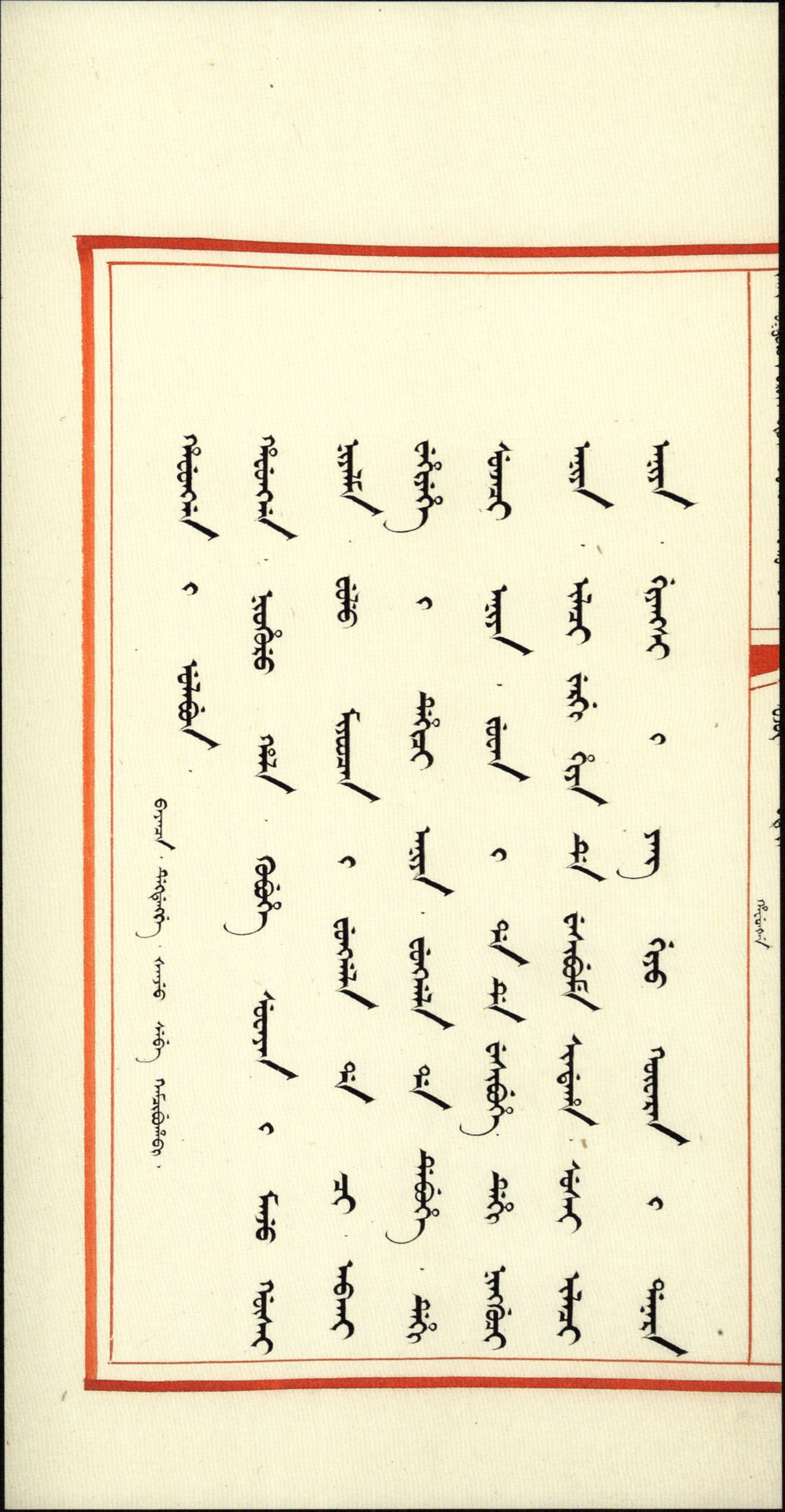

卷端
Beginning

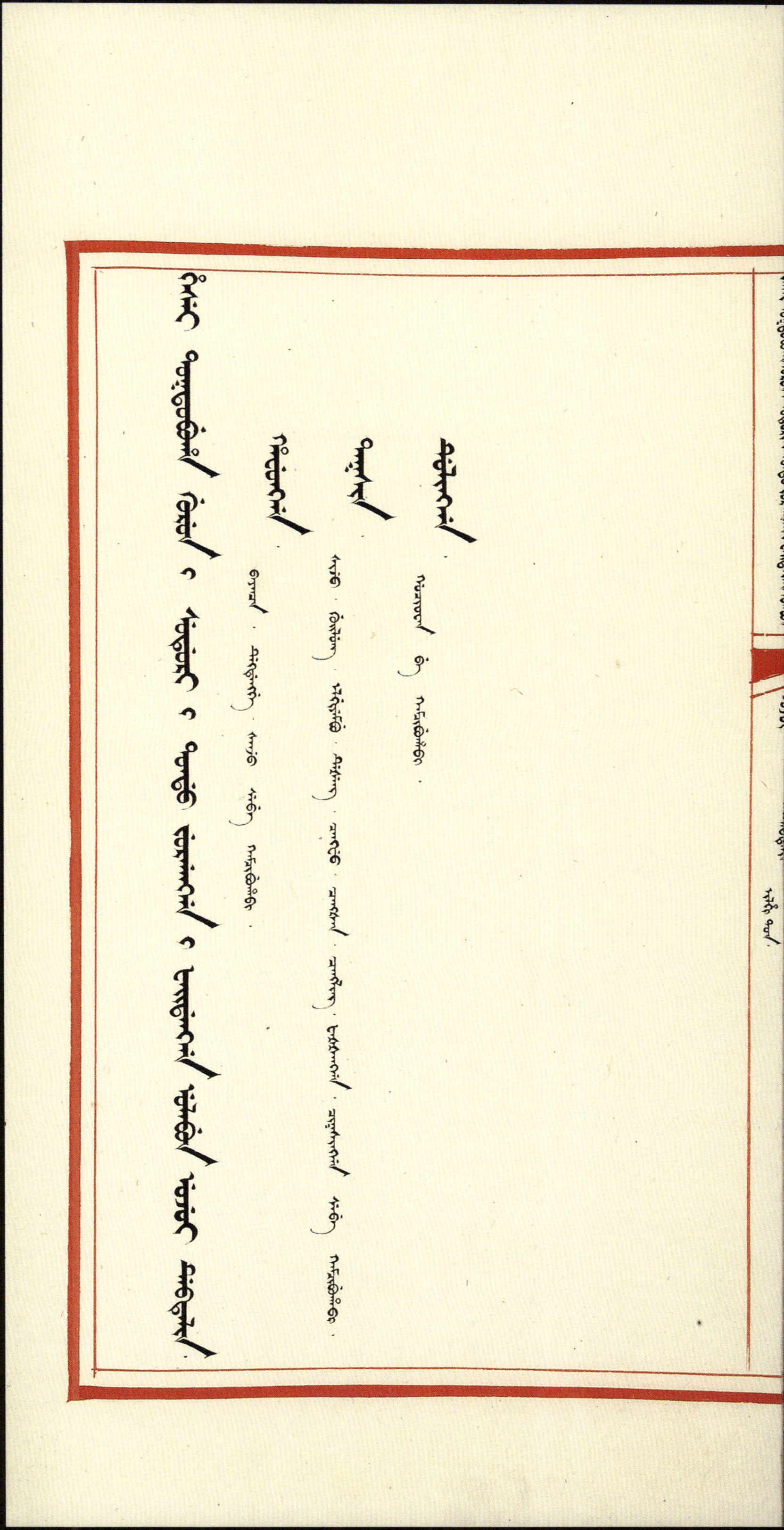

卷目
Contents

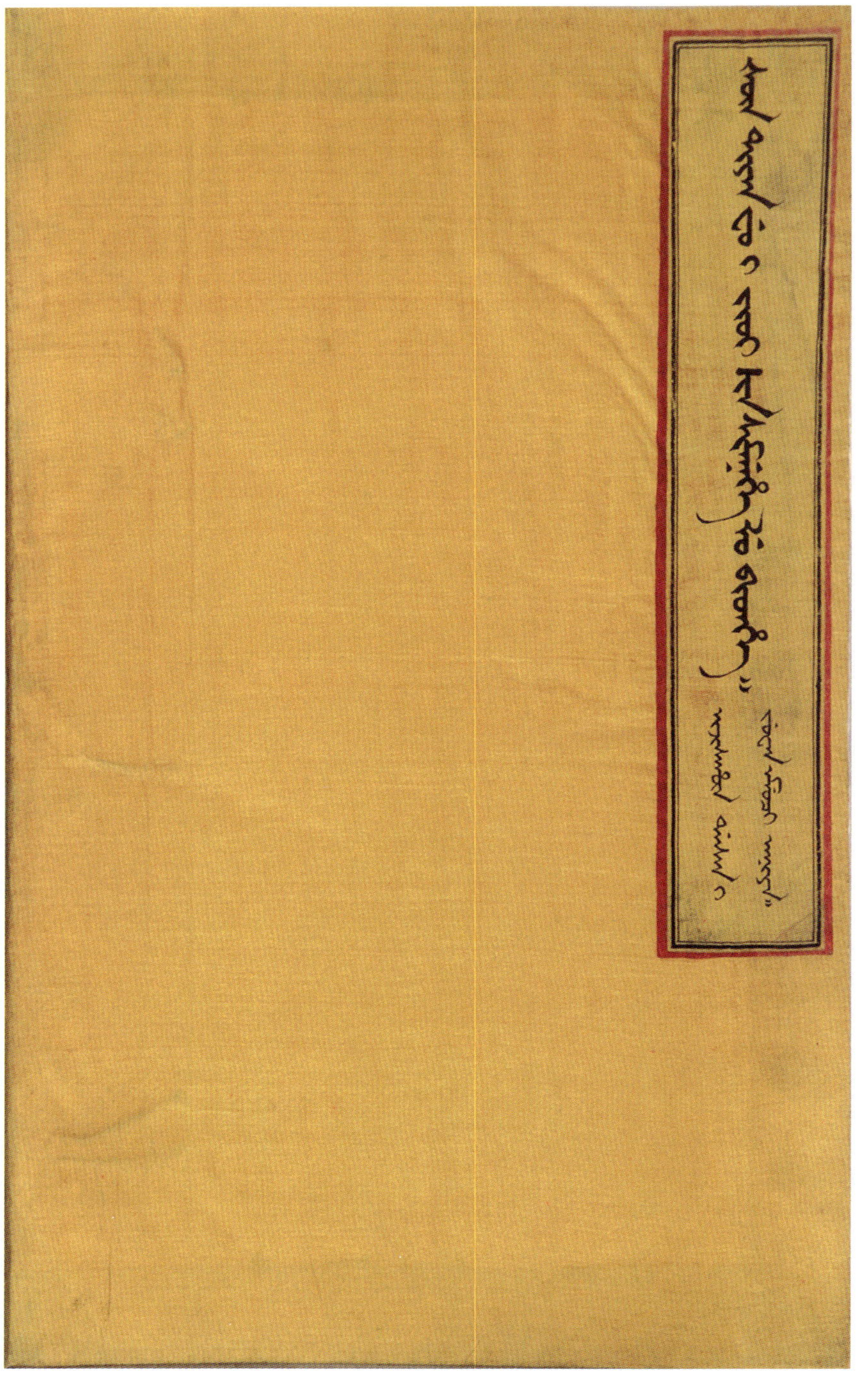

明黄色素絹書面
Bright yellow silk cover

書22086

《順天鄉試題名一卷》

清　佚名輯

清順治十一年（1654）内府刻滿蒙漢合璧本

開本　縱41.5厘米　橫24.8厘米

版框　縱22.4厘米　橫14.6厘米

一册　一函

60

Inventory number: Shu 22086

Names of Juren (Successful Candidates at the Provincial-level Imperial Examination of Shuntian)

One chapter

Anonymous, Qing dynasty (1644-1911)

Printed in Manchu, Mongolian and Chinese in 1654 by the Qing court

Format: 41.5 × 24.8 cm

Frame: 22.4 × 14.6 cm

One volume in one case

第七名 胡實圡 正黄旗鄂貌克兎牛录

第六名 戴名阿 鑲藍旗社兒代牛录

第五名 武大禪 正黄旗哈其藍牛录

第四名 庫勒内 鑲藍旗胡什卜牛录

第三名 舒書 鑲白旗索紅牛录

第二名 卓樂 正紅旗格把庫牛录

第一名 趙山 正紅旗卜兒孫牛录

中式舉人滿洲六十名

第七名 古盧格 鑲紅旗恩刻牛录

第六名 胡把 正黄旗額依圖牛录

第五名 奇他特 鑲黄旗三他牛录

第四名 拜達兒 鑲紅旗色内格牛录

第三名 多爾機 鑲黄旗席喇拜牙喇牛录

第二名 把拜 鑲黄旗多多何牛录

第一名 博羅奇 正黄旗額依圖牛录

中式舉人蒙古二十五名

中試舉人名録
Names of *Juren*

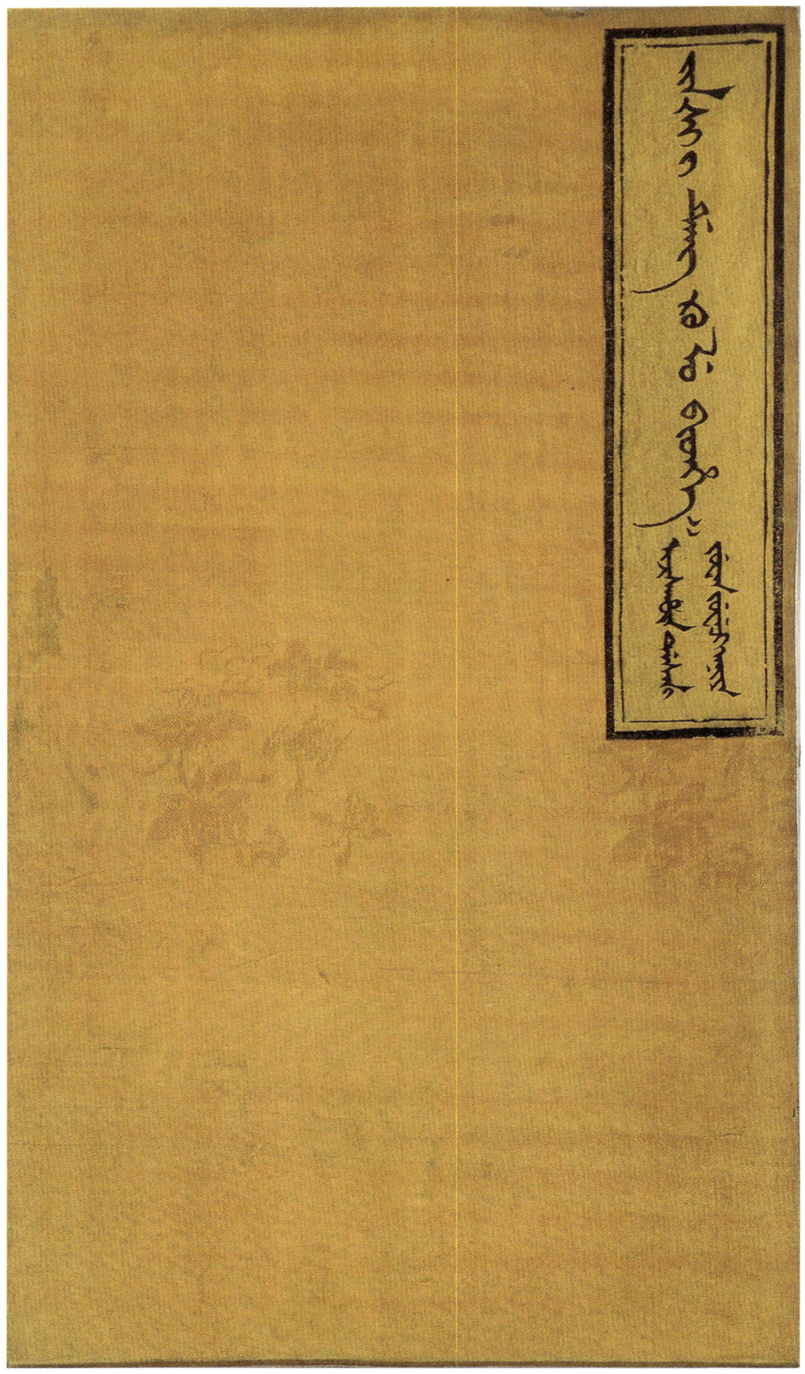

明黄色花蝶紋暗花綢書面
Bright yellow silk cover with veiled floral and butterfly pattern

書22083
《進士登科録一卷》
清　佚名輯
清順治十二年（1655）内府刻滿蒙合璧本
開本　縱38.7厘米　横22.5厘米
版框　縱22.1厘米　横14.3厘米
一冊　一函

61

Inventory number: Shu 22083
Records on Jinshi (Successful Candidates of the Highest-level Imperial Examination)
One chapter
Anonymous, Qing dynasty (1644-1911)
Printed in Manchu and Mongolian in 1655 by the Qing court
Format: 38.7 × 22.5 cm
Frame: 22.1 × 14.3 cm
One volume in one case

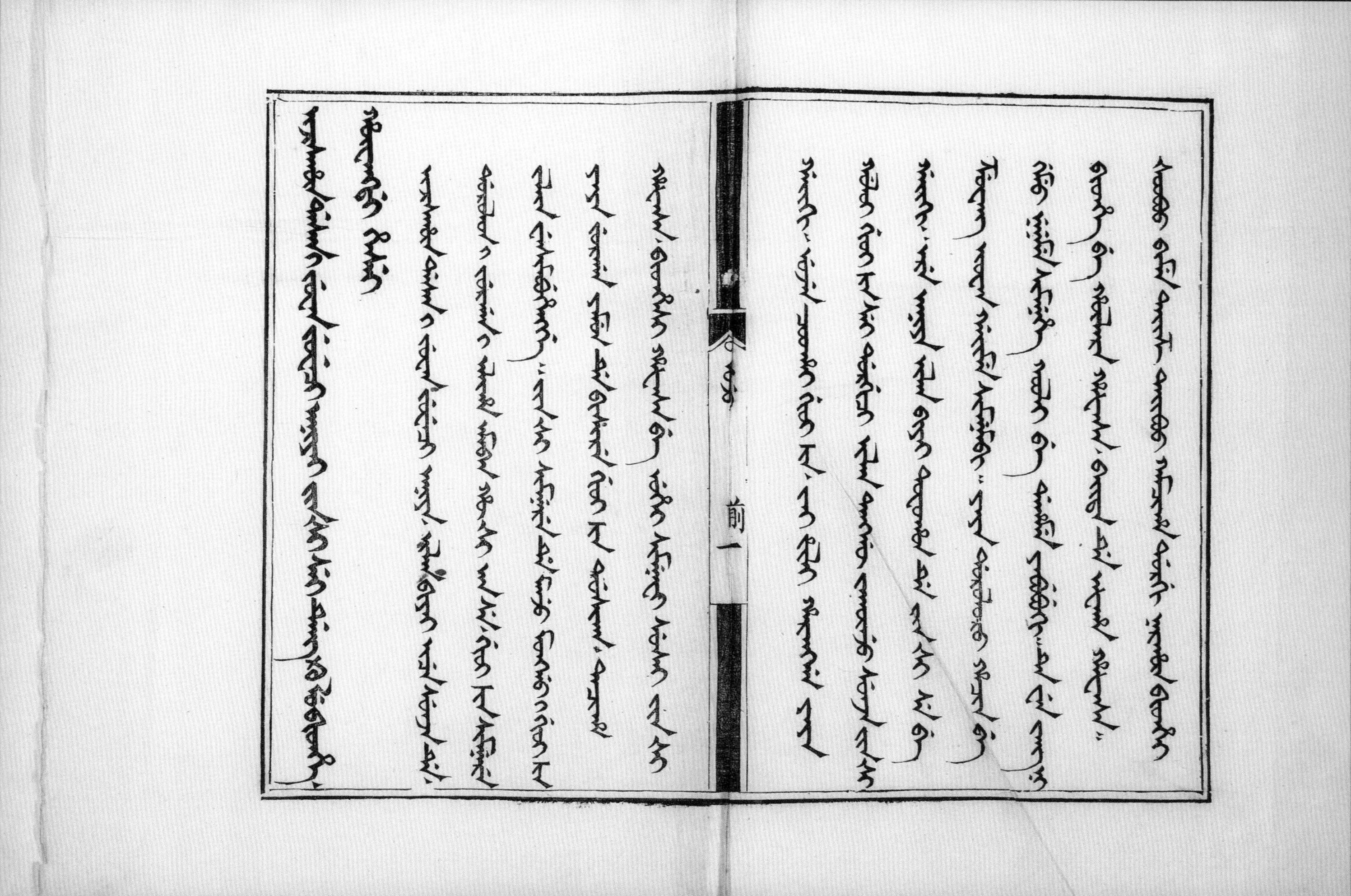

順治十二年上諭
Imperil edict in 1655

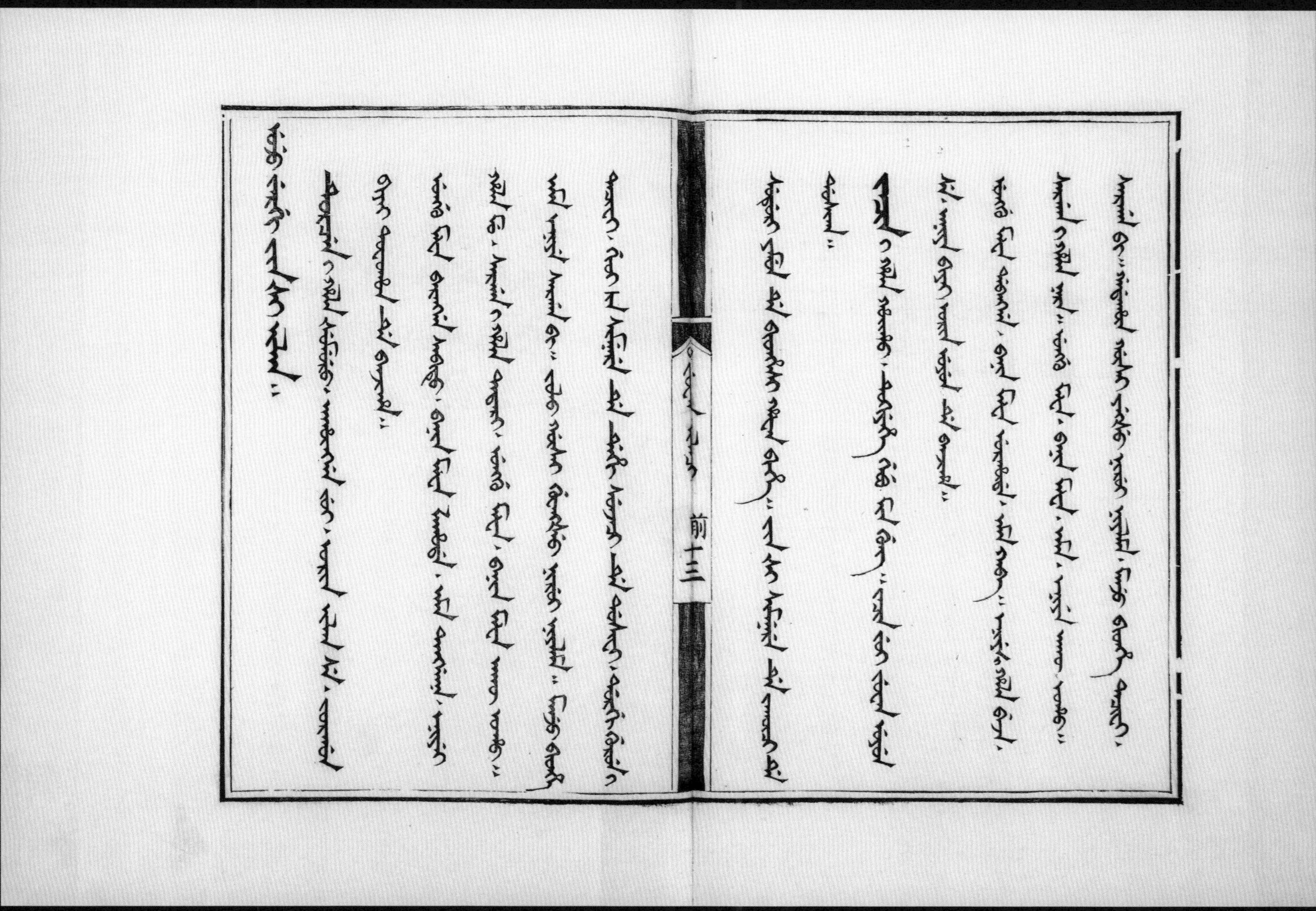

進士小傳
Brief biographies of the *Jinshi*

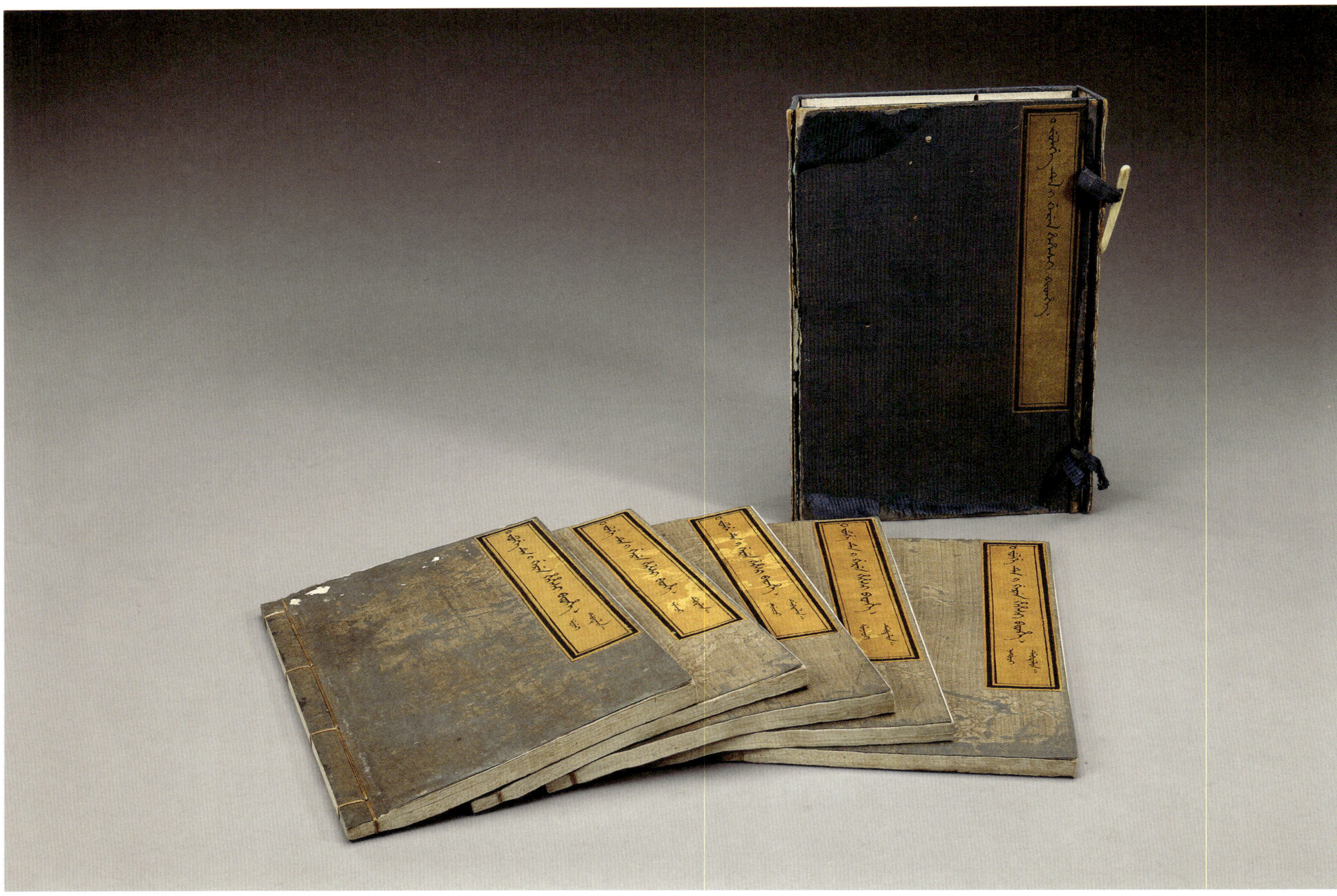

藍色朵梅紋暗花羅書函
Blue silk gauze case with veil pattern of plum blossoms

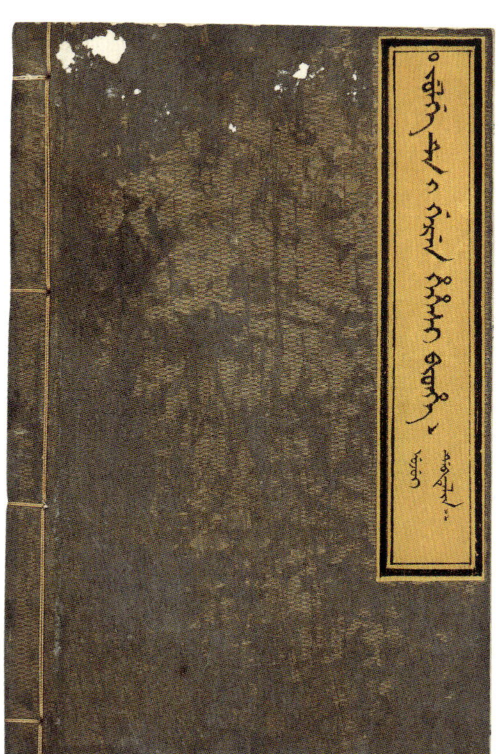

香色折枝梅花牡丹紋芝麻紗書面
Brown sesame-gauze cover decorated with sprays of plum blossoms and peonies

62

書22075
《古今列女傳六卷》
明　解縉等撰
清内府精寫滿文本
開本　縱26.1厘米　橫17.1厘米
版框　縱21.1厘米　橫14.9厘米
存五册　一函（缺卷2）

Inventory number: Shu 22075
Biographies of Exemplary Women of Past and Present
Six chapters
Written by Xie Jin et. al., Ming dynasty (1368-1644)
Transcribed in Manchu by the Qing court
Format: 26.1 × 17.1 cm
Frame: 21.1 × 14.9 cm
Five volumes in one case extant today, with the second chapter missing

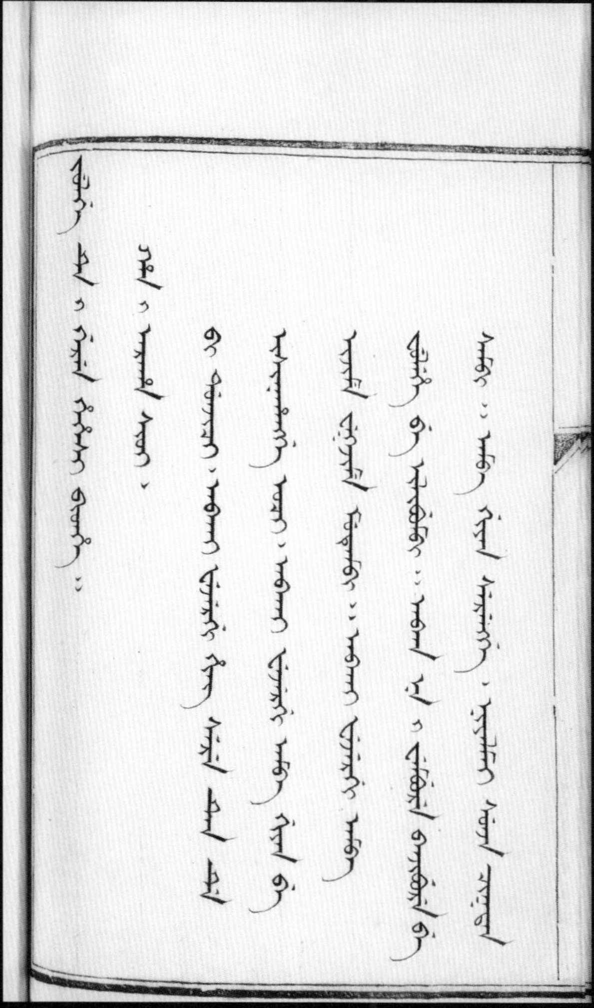

明永樂元年原序
Preface in 1403

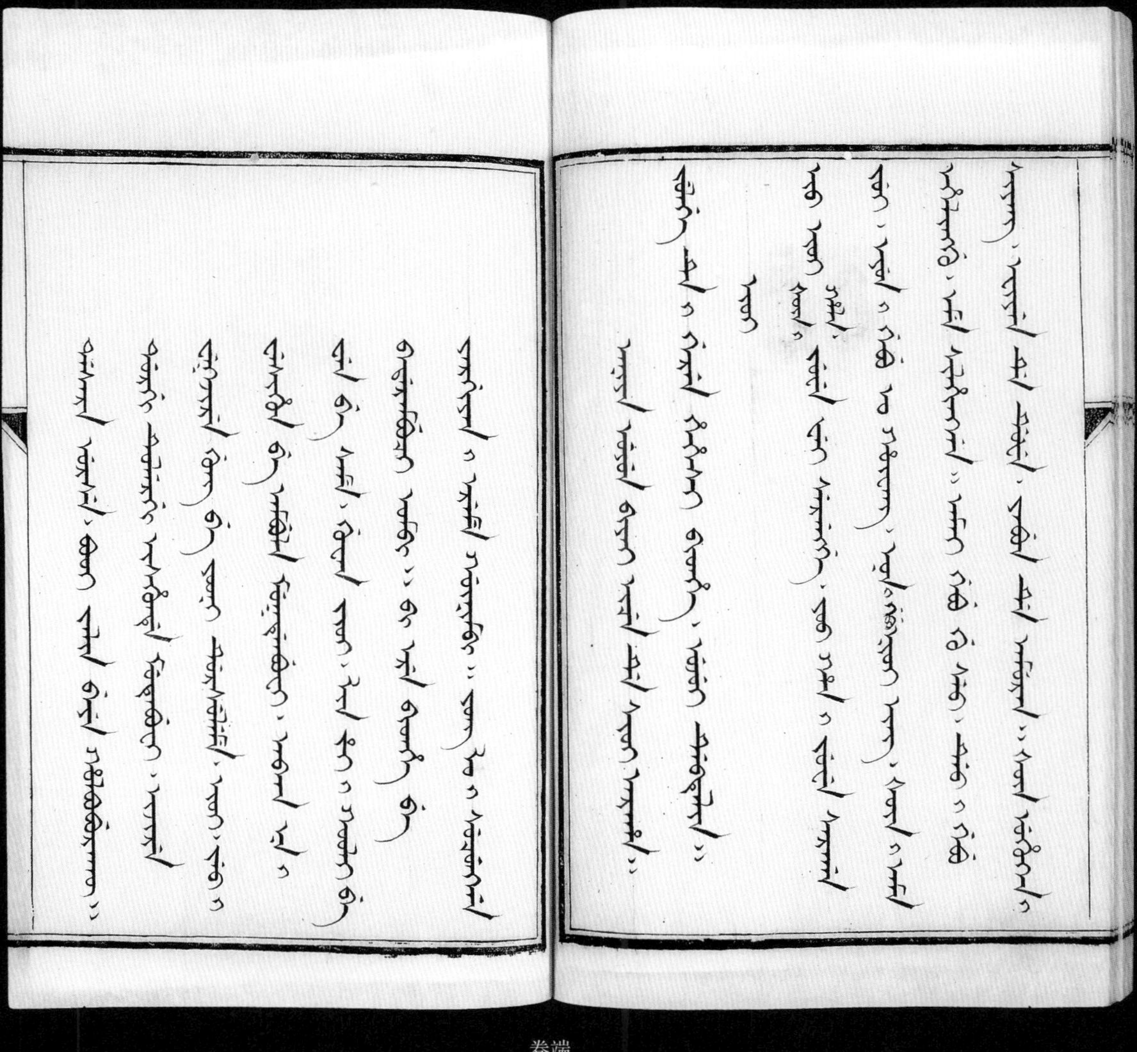

卷端
Beginning

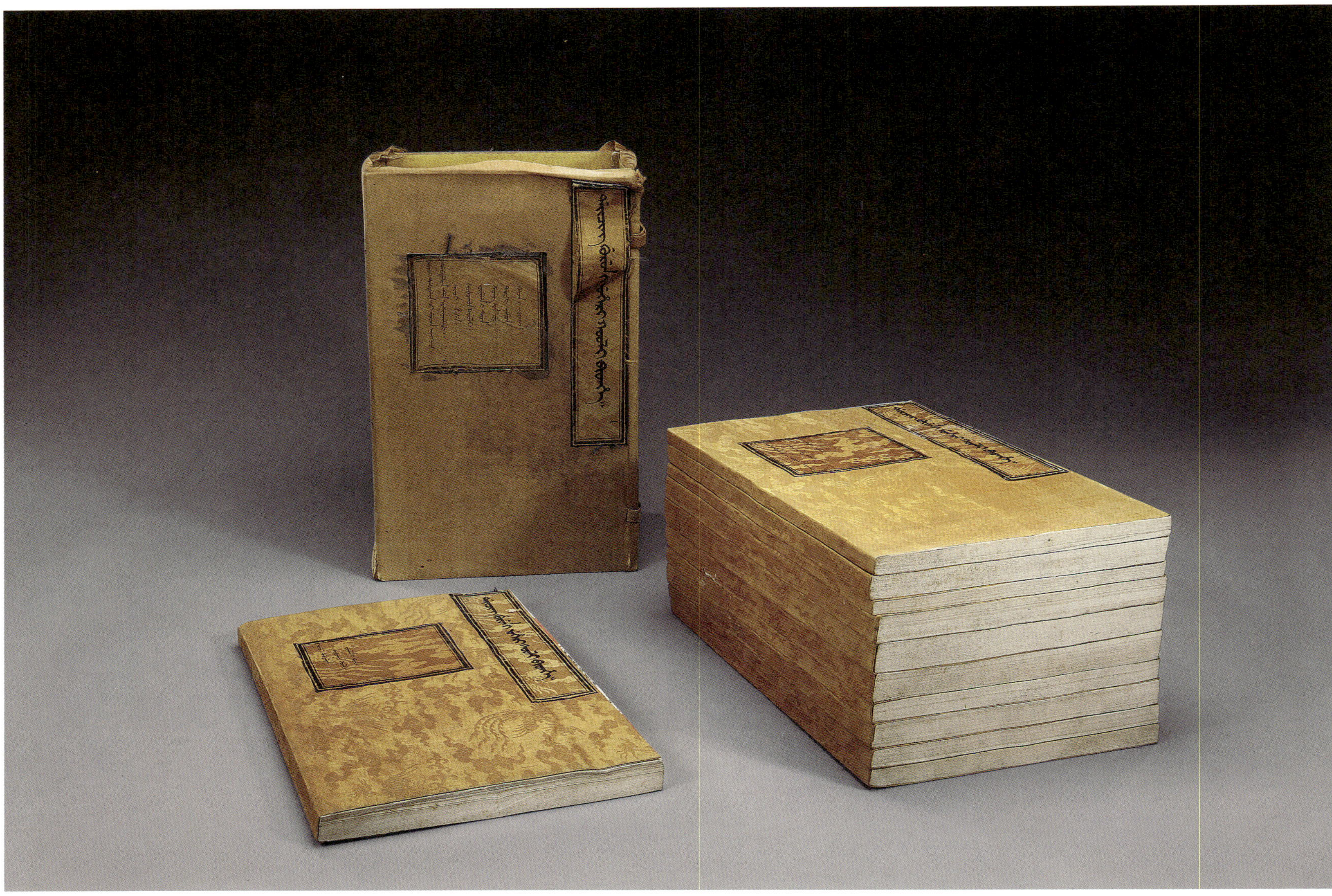

香色雲鳳紋暗花緞書函
Light brown twill-weave silk case with veiled phoenix and cloud pattern

63

書22099
《大清會典一百六二卷首一卷》
清　伊桑阿等奉敕撰
清康熙二十九年（1690）內府精寫滿文本
開本　縱35.5厘米　橫22.1厘米
版框　縱25.7厘米　橫18.1厘米
一百四十一册　十二函

Inventory number: Shu 22099
The Qing Institution
162 chapters as text, one chapter as preliminary remarks
Written by imperial order by Yisangga et al., Qing dynasty (1644-1911)
Transcribed in 1690 by the Qing court
Frame: 35.5 × 22.1 cm
Format: 25.7 × 18.1 cm
141 volumes in twelve cases

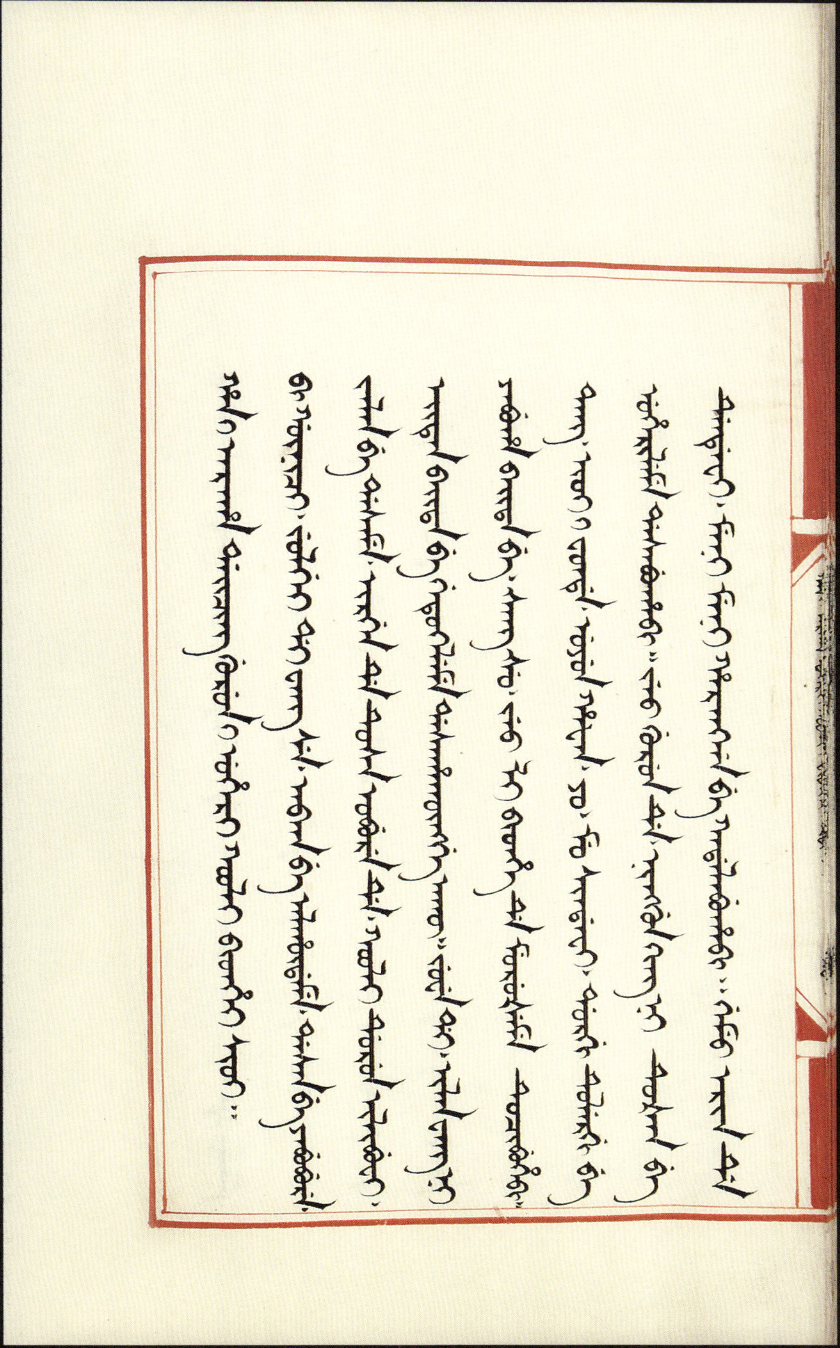

康熙二十九年御製序
Preface by the Kangxi emperor in 1690

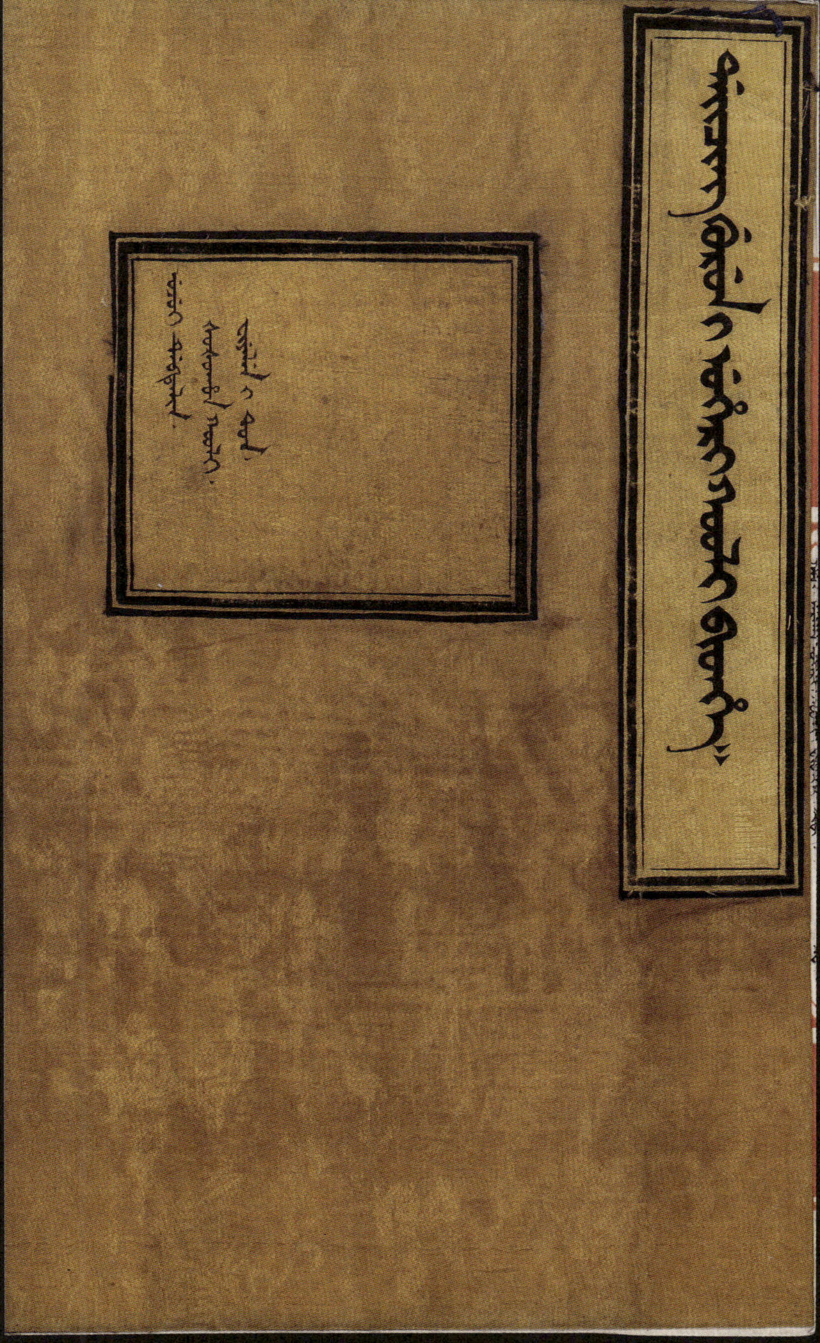

香色雲鳳紋暗花緞書面
Light brown twill-weave silk case with veiled phoenix and cloud pattern

[illegible]

[illegible]

[illegible]

[illegible]

[illegible]

[illegible]

[illegible]

[illegible]

[illegible]

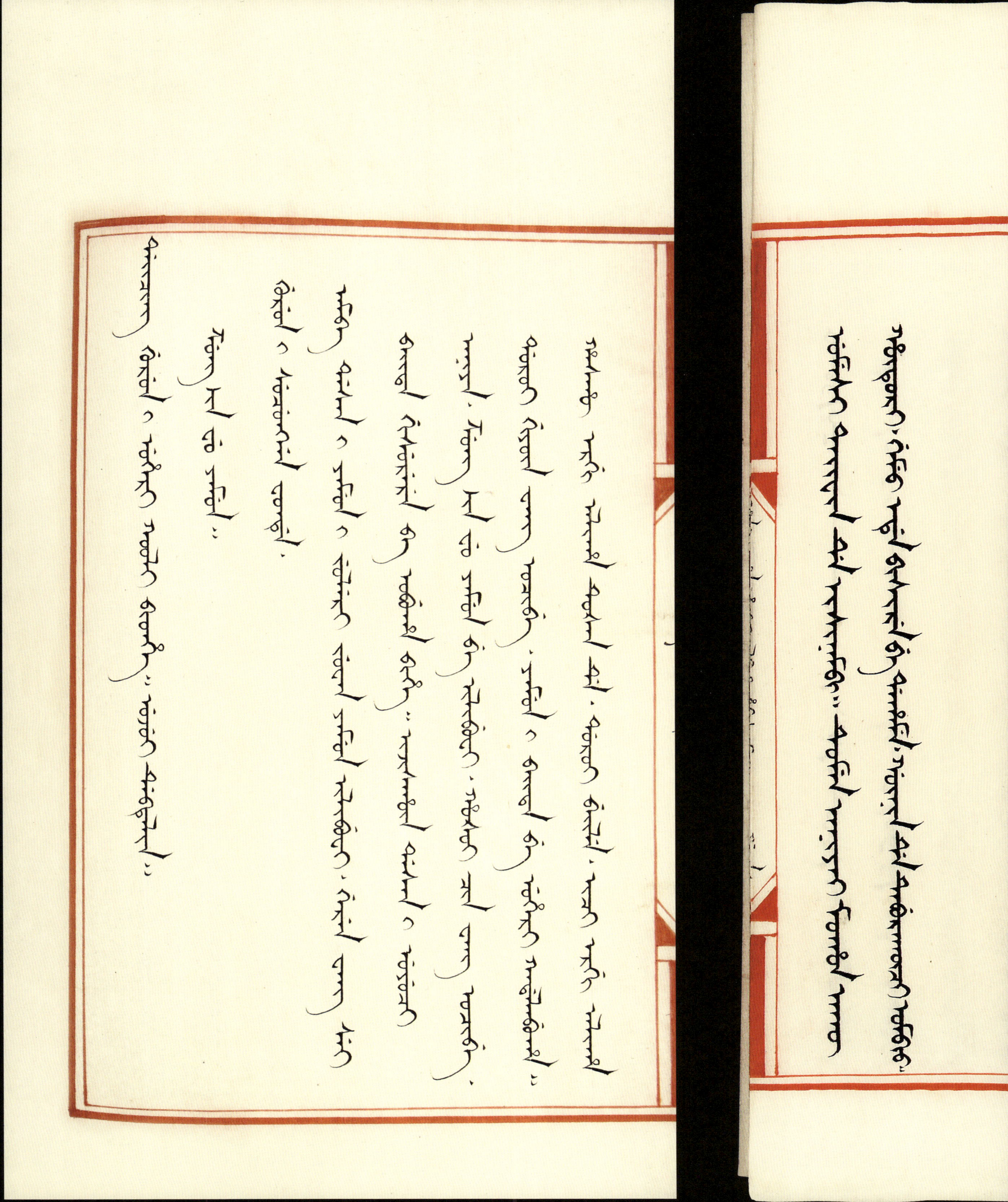

卷端
Beginning

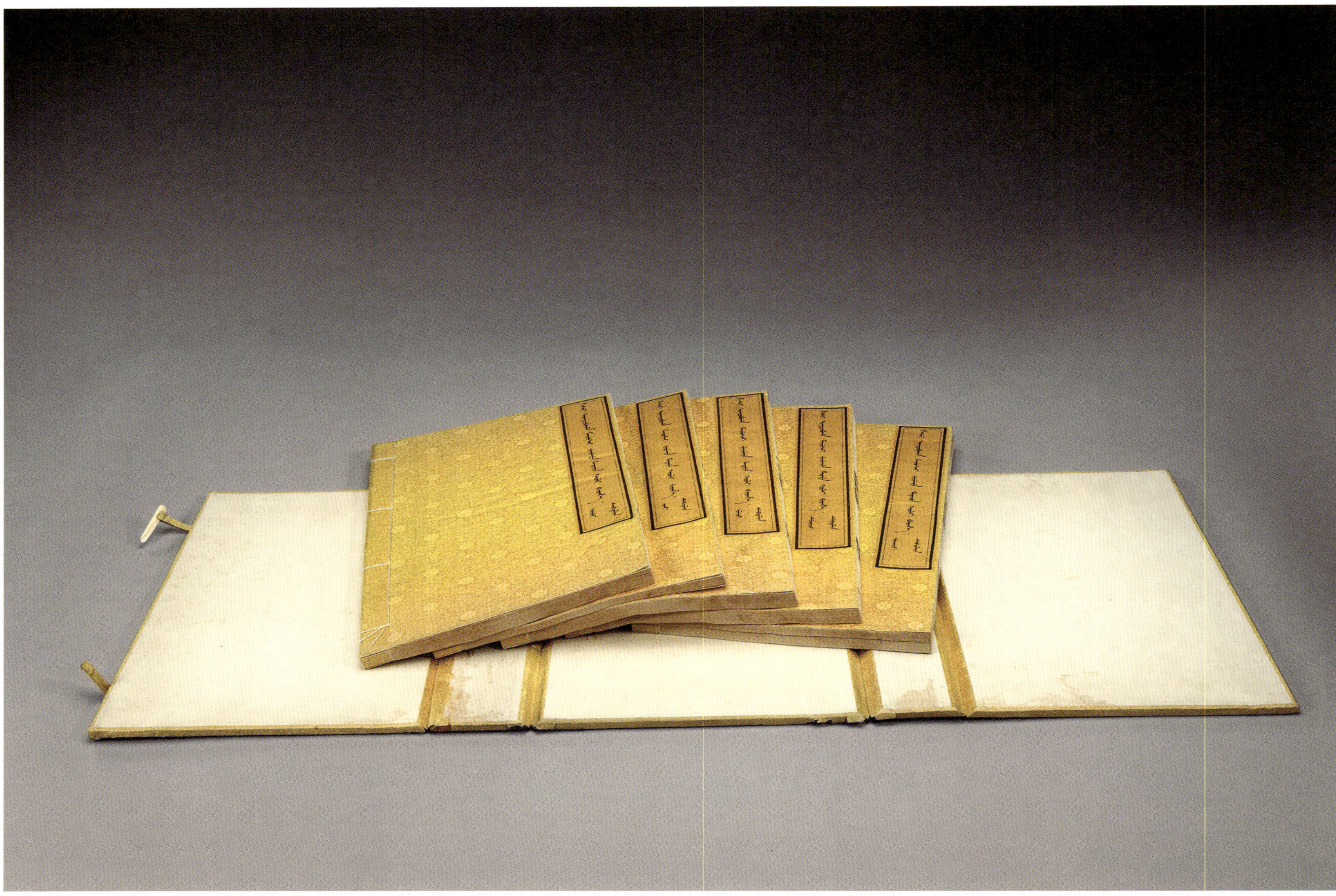

外觀
Exterior

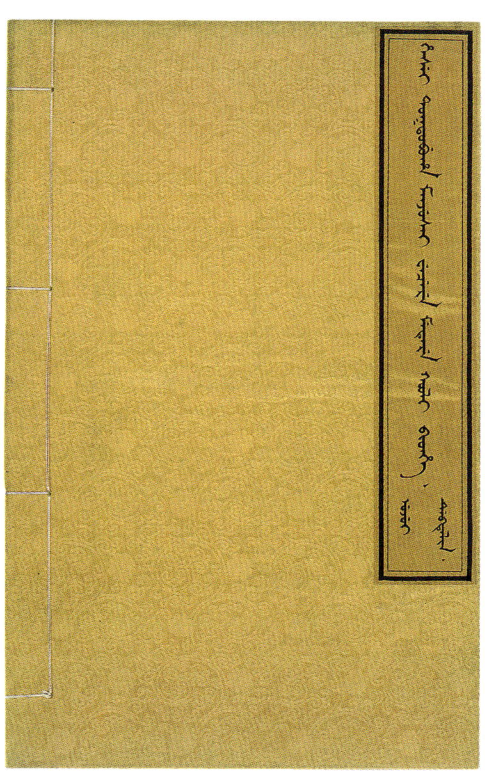

明黃色纏枝花紋暗花綾書面
Bright yellow twill-weave silk cover with veiled pattern of floral scrolls

64

書22098
《欽定滿洲祭神祭天典禮六卷》
清　允祿等奉敕撰
清乾隆十二年（1747）武英殿刻滿文本
開本　縱34.2厘米　橫22厘米
版框　縱23.5厘米　橫17.5厘米
六册　一函

Inventory number: Shu 22098
Manchu Sacrificial Rites to Worship Heaven and Deities
Six chapters
Written by imperial order by Yunlu et. al., Qing dynasty (1644-1911)
Printed in Manchu in 1747 at the Hall of Martial Valour
Format: 34.2 × 22 cm
Frame: 23.5 × 17.5 cm
Six volumes in one case

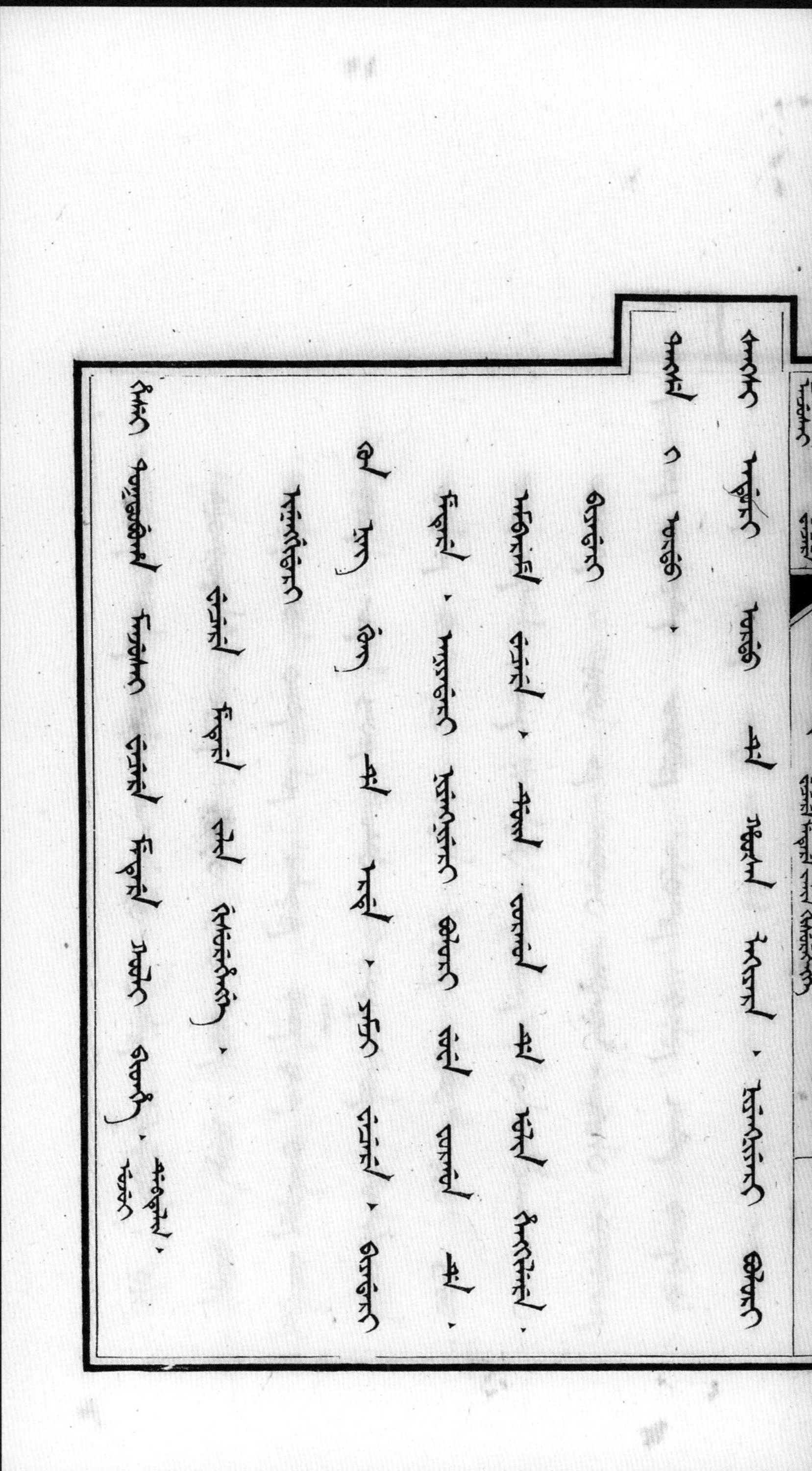

卷端
Beginning

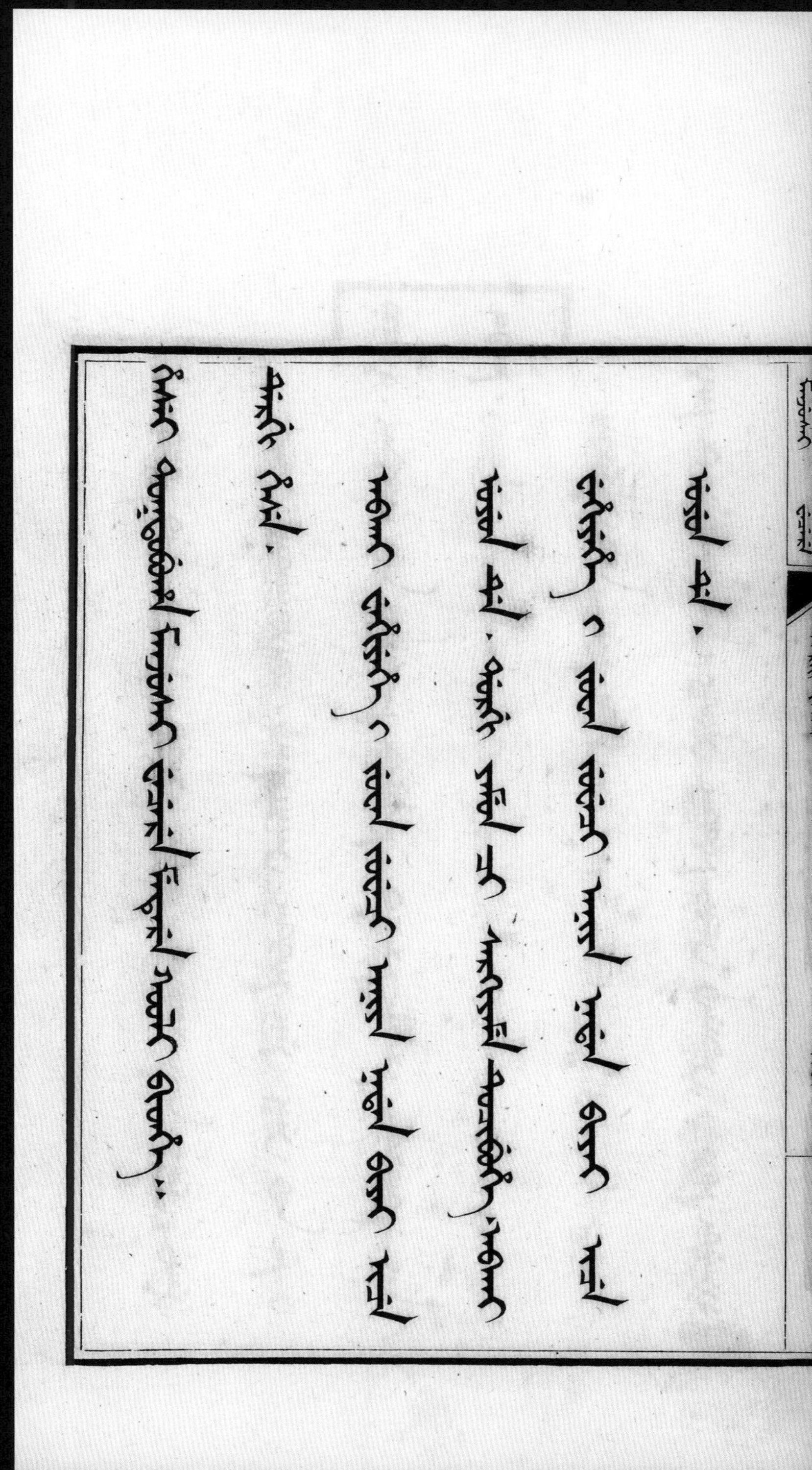

乾隆十二年上諭
Imperial edict in 1747

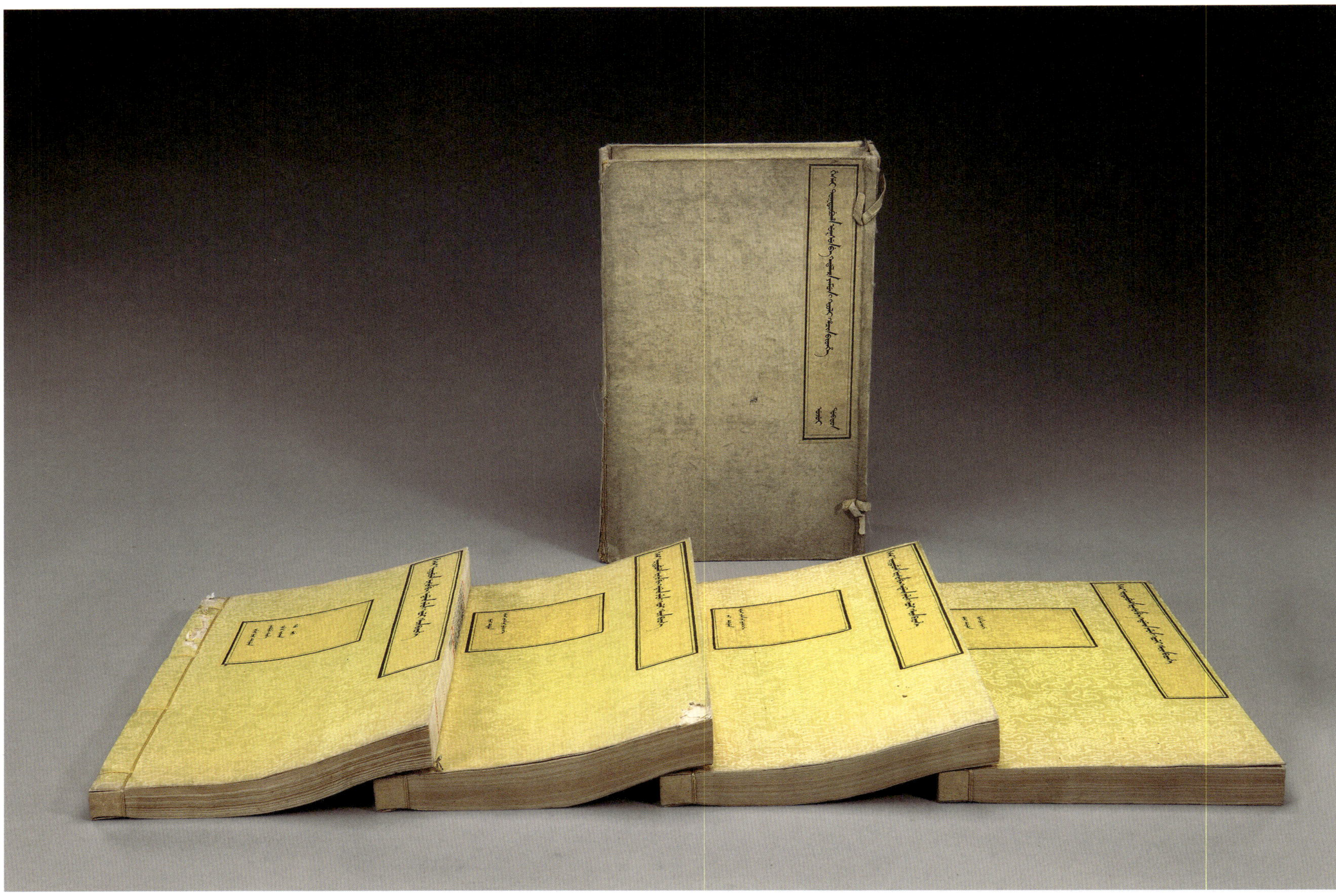

明黄色雲龍紋暗花綾書函
Bright yellow twill-weave silk case with veiled dragon and cloud pattern

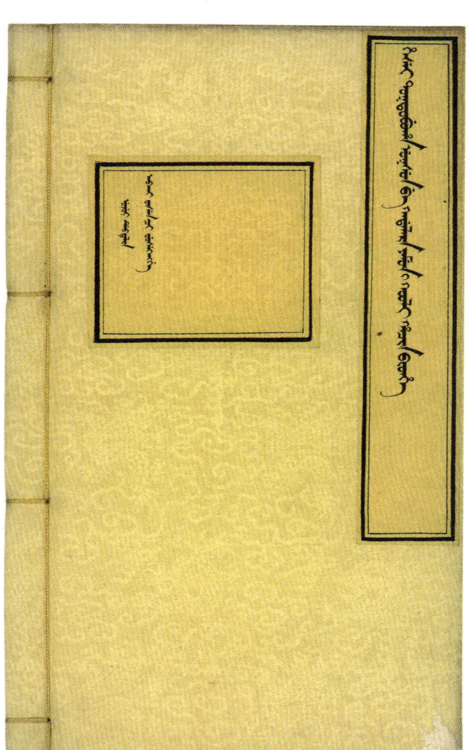

明黄色雲龍紋暗花綾書面
Bright yellow twill-weave silk cover with veiled dragon and cloud pattern

書22110
《欽定宗人府則例三十一卷首一卷》
清　載銓等奉敕撰
清道光二十九年（1849）朱絲欄精寫滿文本
開本　縱33厘米　橫20.2厘米
版框　縱21.9厘米　橫15.6厘米
三十二册　八函

65

Inventory number: Shu 22110
Rules and Regulations on Imperial Clan Court
Thirty-one chapters as text, one chapter as preliminary remarks
Compiled by imperial order by Zaiquan et. al., Qing dynasty (1644-1911)
Transcribed in Manchu in red columns in 1849
Frame: 33 × 20.2 cm
Format: 21.9 × 15.6 cm
Thirty-two volumes in eight cases

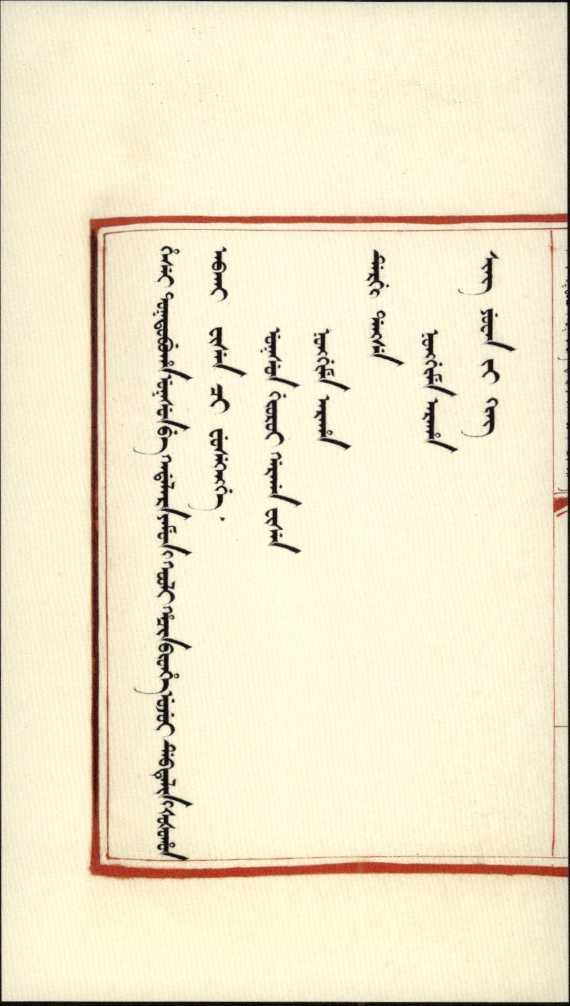

卷目
Contents

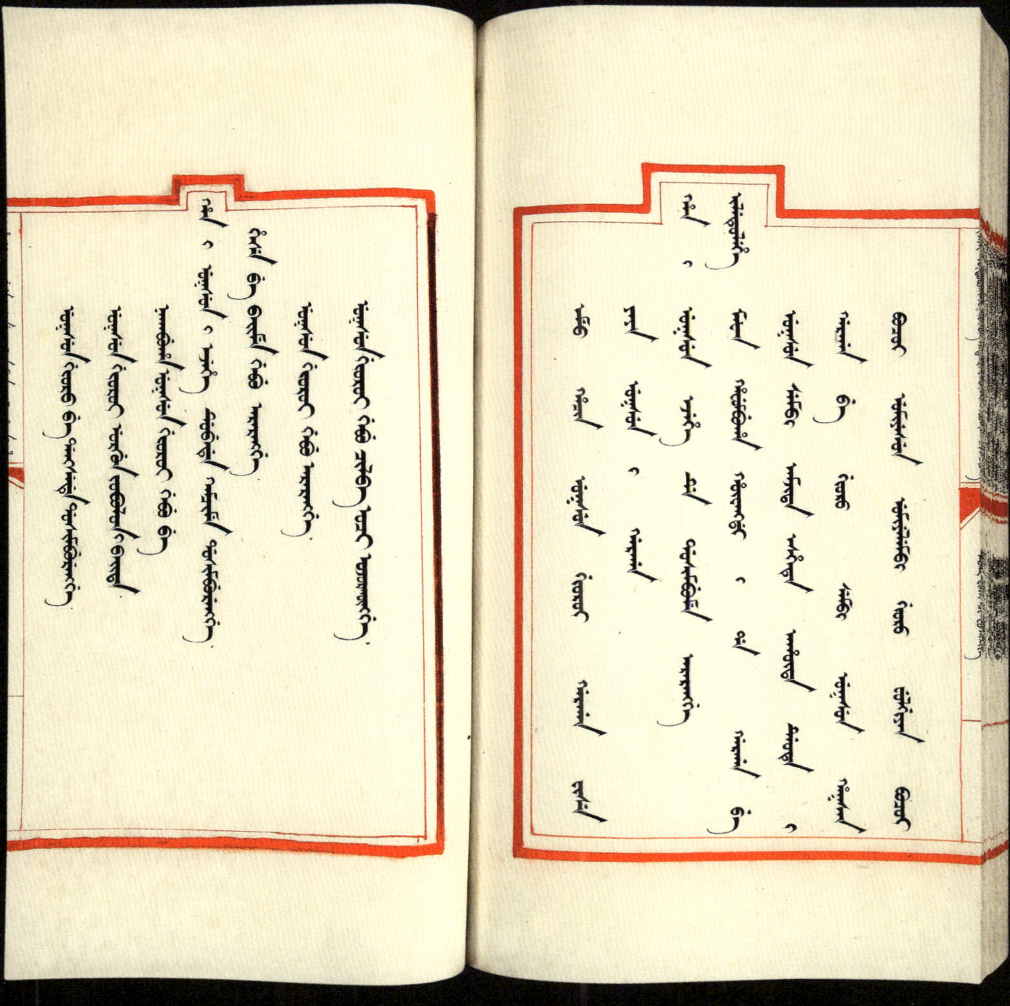

卷端
Beginning

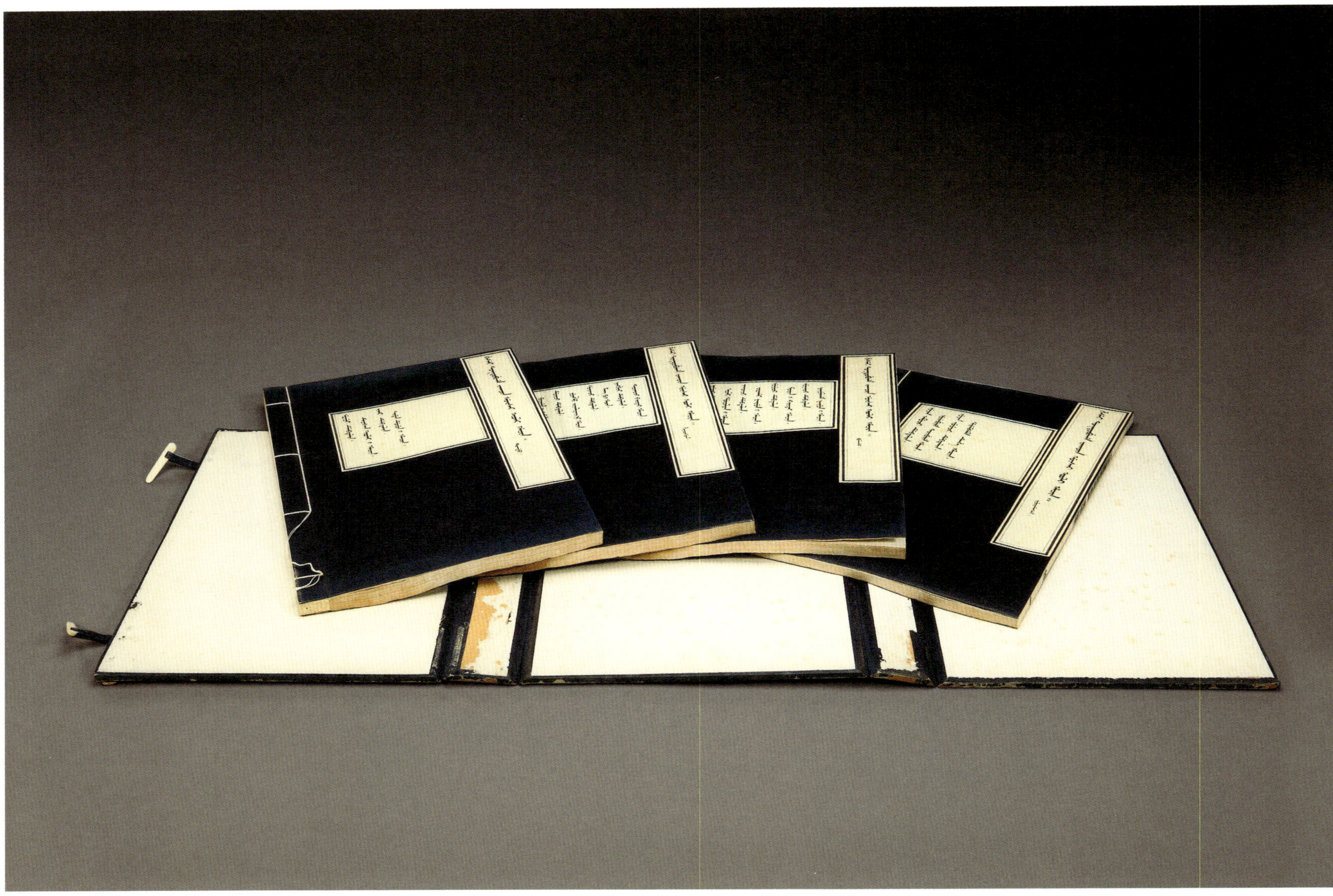

藍色素綢書函
Blue silk case

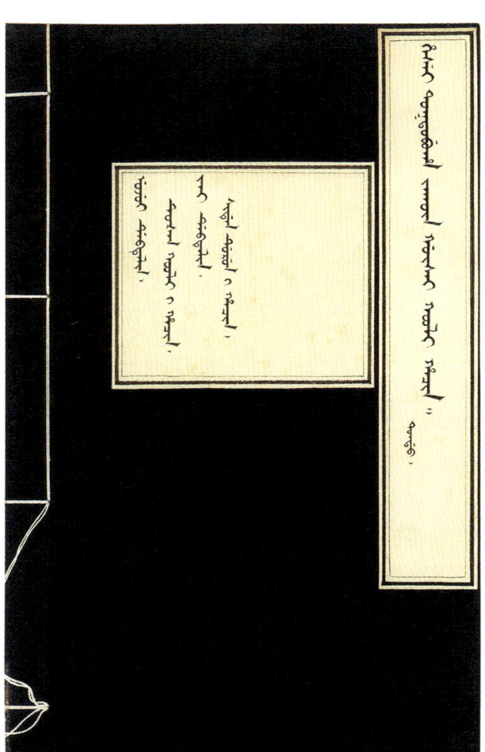

藍色素綢書面
Blue silk cover

書22131
《欽定八旗則例十二卷》
清　鄂爾泰等奉敕撰
清乾隆七年（1742）武英殿刻滿文本
開本　縱34.1厘米　橫21.6厘米
版框　縱23.5厘米　橫17厘米
四冊　一函

66

Inventory number: Shu 22131
Rules and Regulations on Eight Banners
Twelve chapters
Compiled by imperial order by Ortai et. al., Qing dynasty (1644-1911)
Printed in Manchu in 1742 at the Hall of Martial Valour
Frame: 34.1 × 21.6 cm
Format: 23.5 × 17 cm
Four volumes in one case

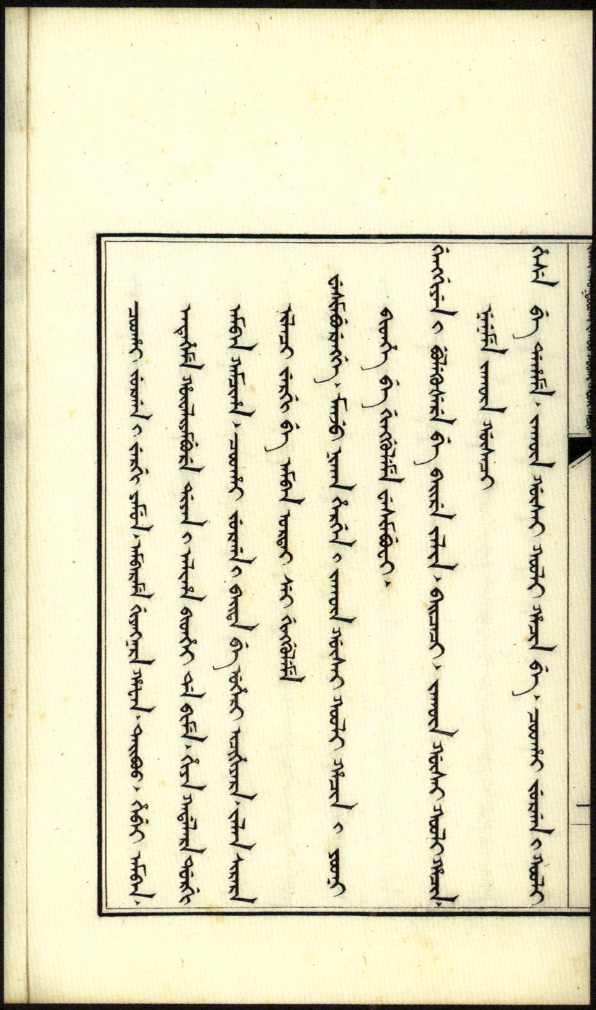

鄂爾泰奏摺
Memorial from Ortai

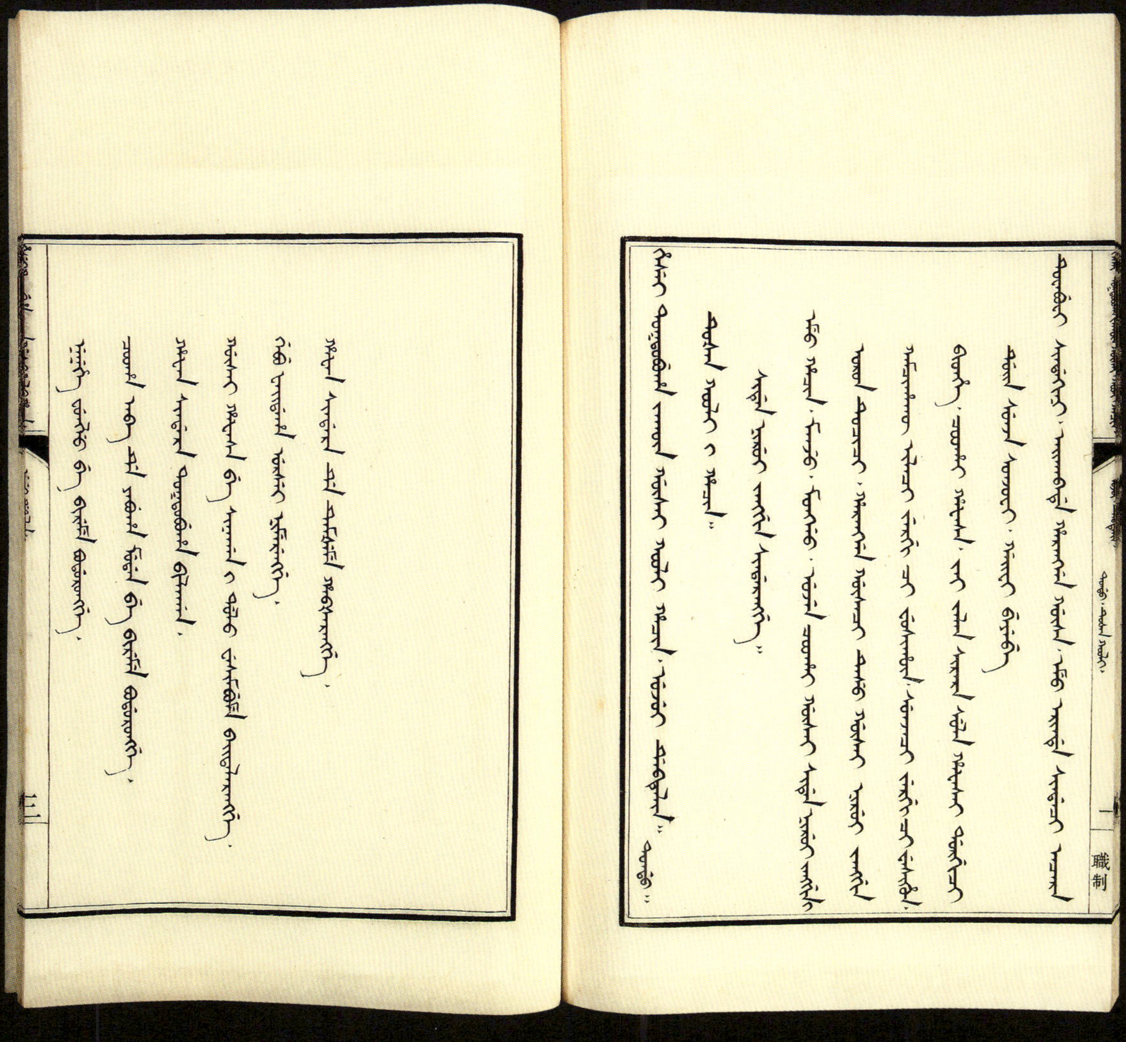

目錄及卷端
Contents and Beginning

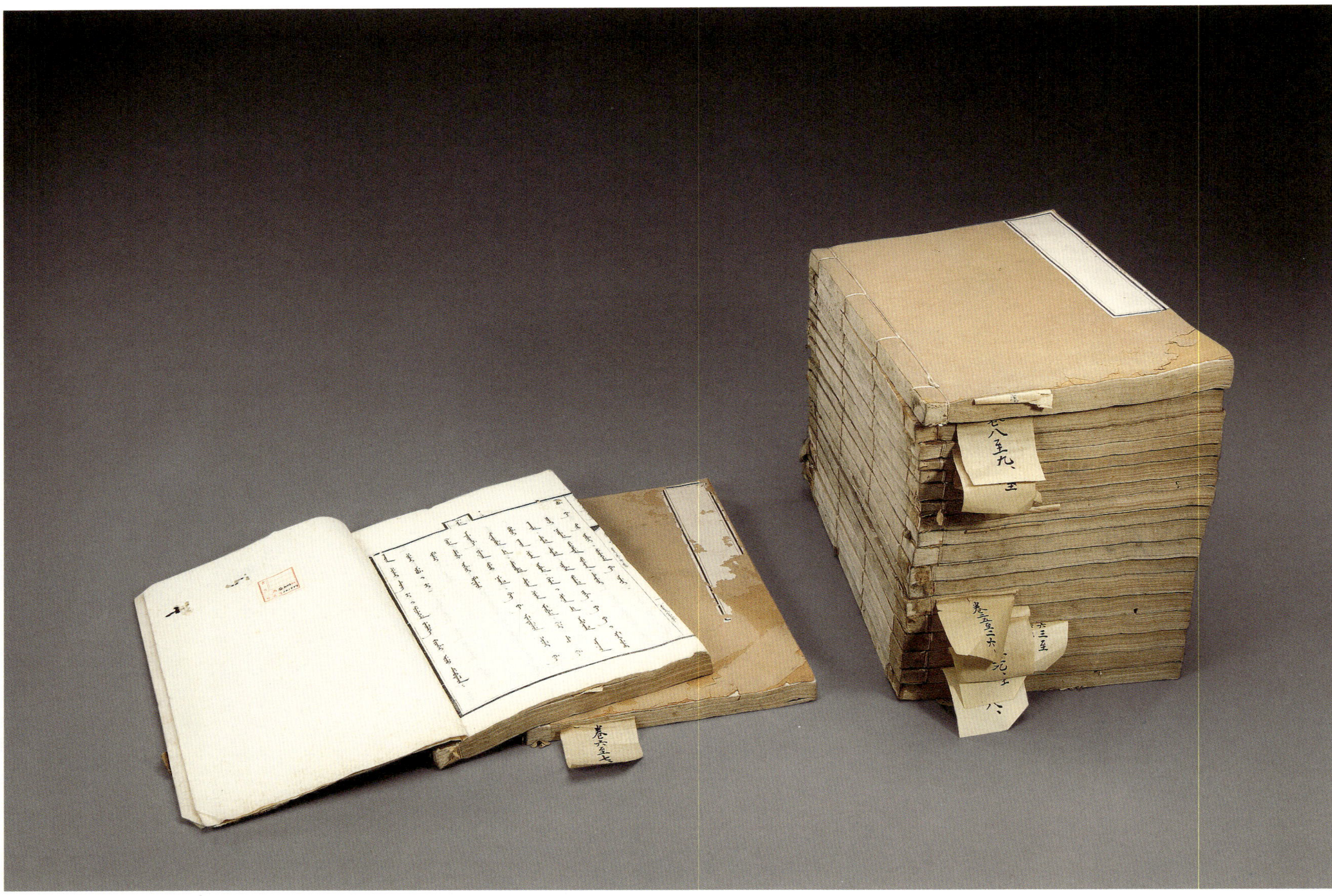

黄色紙書面
Yellow paper covers

書22127
《八旗通志初集二百五十卷目録二卷》
清　鄂爾泰等奉敕撰
清乾隆四年（1739）武英殿刻滿文本
開本　縱30.3厘米　橫19.8厘米
版框　縱23.6厘米　橫17.3厘米
存一百九册（存卷1－32、63－90、107－120、123－124、127－130、137－139、142－164、167－169、172－173、175－177、182－225、232－242、244－250）

67

Inventory number: Shu 22127
Comprehensive Records on the Eight Banners, First Compilation
250 chapters as text, two chapters as contents
Compiled by imperial order by Ortai et al., Qing dynasty (1644-1911)
Printed in Manchu in 1739 at the Hall of Martial Valour
Frame: 30.3 × 19.8 cm
Format: 23.6 × 17.3 cm
109 volumes extant today, including the following chapters: 1-32, 63-90, 107-120, 123-124, 127-130, 137-139, 142-164, 167-169, 172-173, 175-177, 182-225, 232-242, 244-250

卷端
Beginning

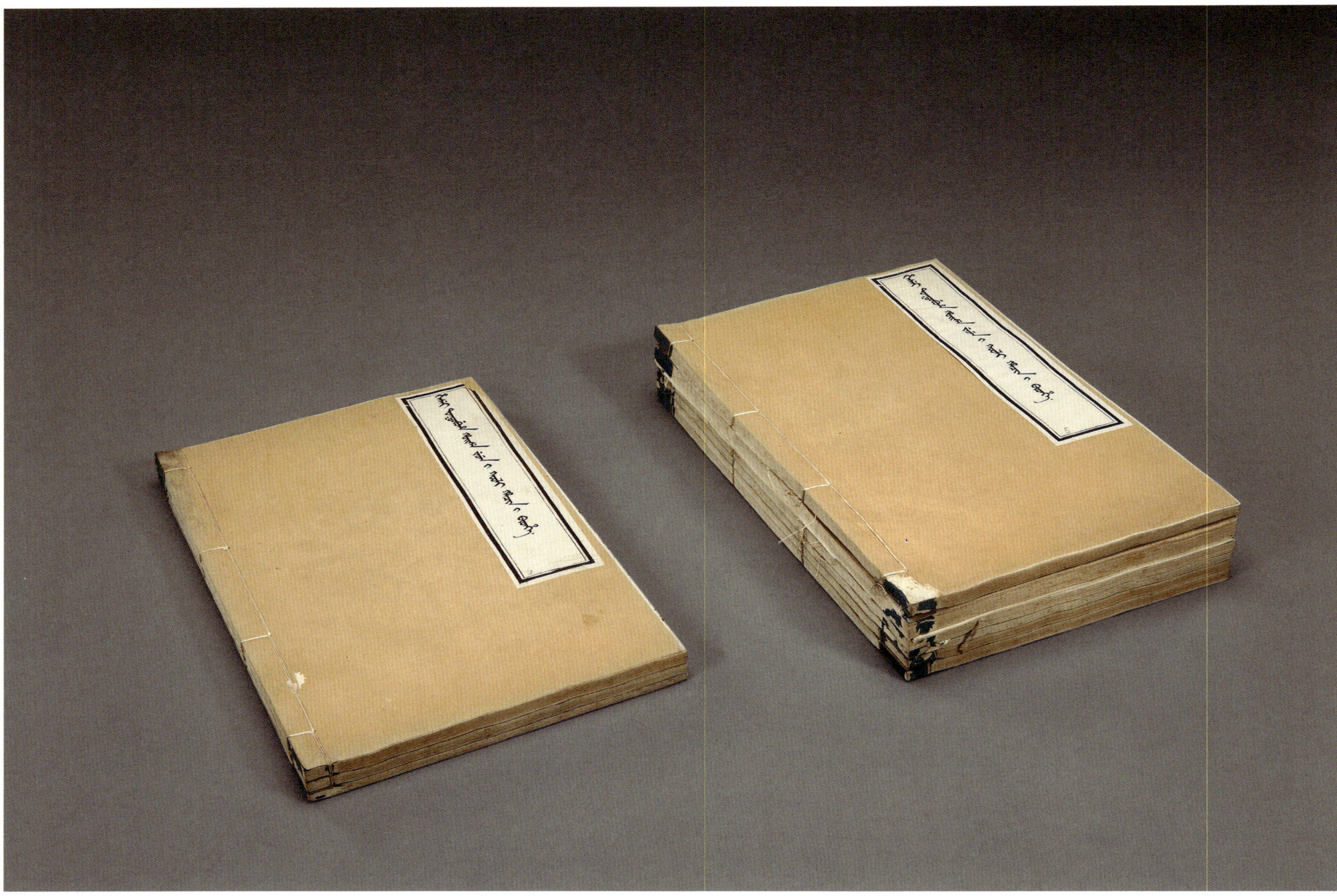

黄色紙書面
Yellow paper cover

黄色紙書面
Yellow paper cover

書22150
《欽定回疆則例八卷首一卷》
清　賽尚阿等奉敕撰
清道光二十二年（1842）武英殿刻滿文本
開本　縱29厘米　橫18.5厘米
版框　縱21.1厘米　橫16厘米
九册　一函

68

Inventory number: Shu 22150
Rules and Regulations on the Frontier of Uighur
Eight chapters as text, one chapter as preliminary remarks
Written by imperial order by Saisangga et. al., Qing dynasty (1644-1911)
Printed in Manchu in 1842 at the Hall of Martial Valour
Format: 29 × 18.5 cm
Frame: 21.1 × 16 cm
Nine volumes in one case

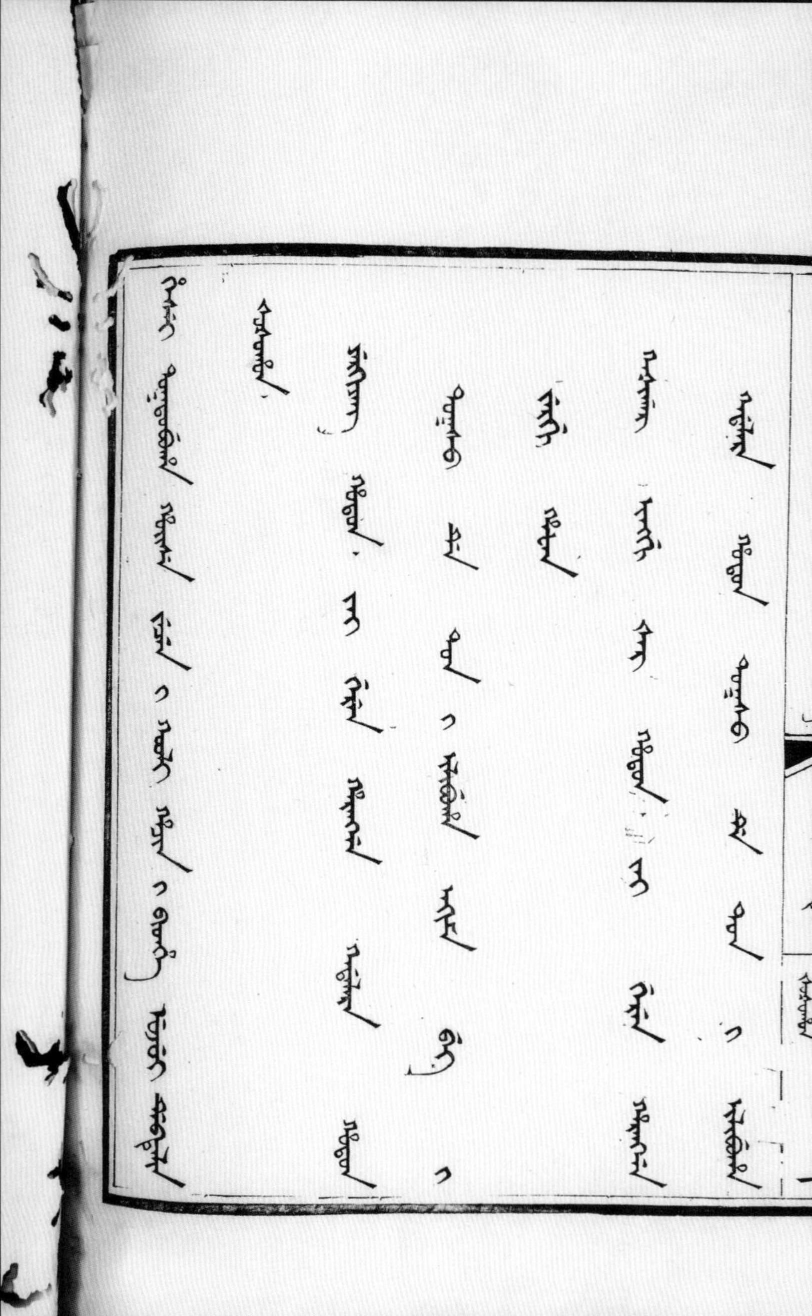

卷端
Beginning

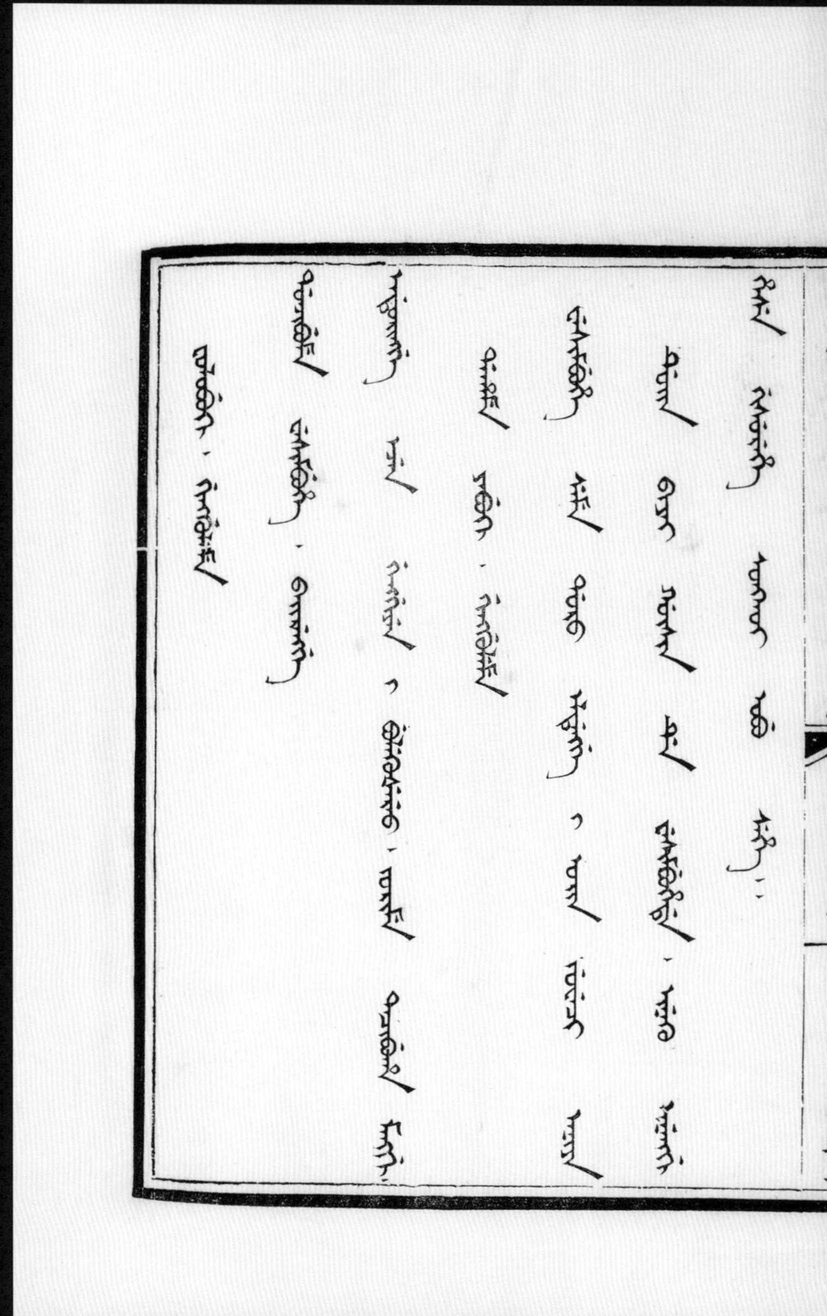

道光二十二年奏摺
Memorial in 1842

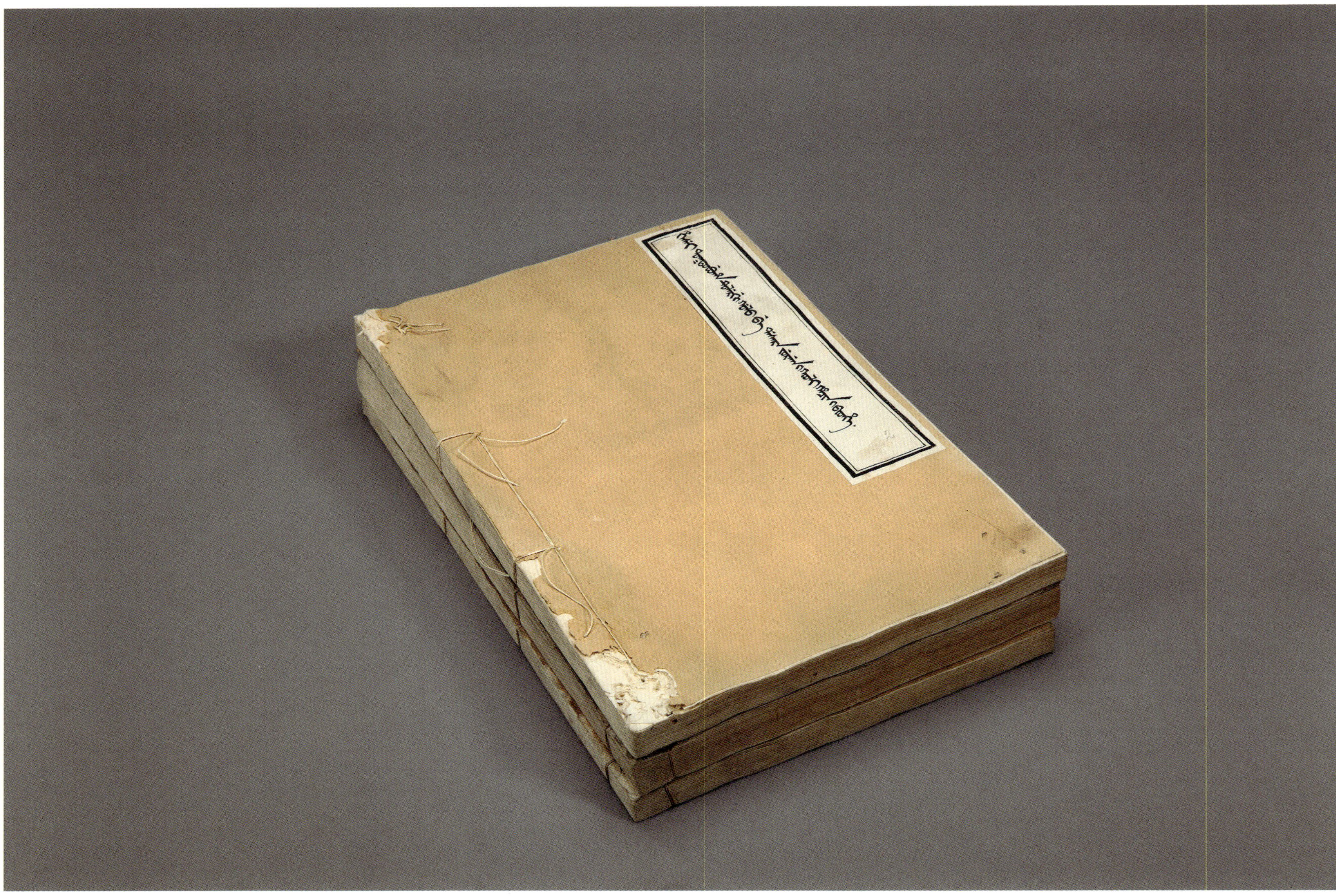

黄色紙書面
Yellow paper cover

書22149、書23060
《欽定理藩院則例六十三卷首三卷》
清　賽尚阿等撰
清道光二十二年（1842）武英殿刻滿文本
開本　縱28.7厘米　橫18.3厘米
版框　縱21.1厘米　橫16厘米
存三十九册（存首3卷、卷2－5、12、13、15、17－56、58－59、62－63）

69

Inventory number: Shu 22149, Shu 23060
Rules and Regulations on the Board for National Minority Affairs, Made by Imperial Order
Sixty-three chapters as text, three chapters as preliminary remarks
Written by Saisangga et. al., Qing dynasty (1644-1911)
Printed in Manchu in 1849 at the Hall of Martial Valour
Format: 28.7 × 18.3 cm
Frame: 21.1 × 16 cm
Thirty-nine volumes extant today, including preliminary remarks and the following chapters of the text: 2-5, 12, 13, 15, 17-56, 58-59, 62-63

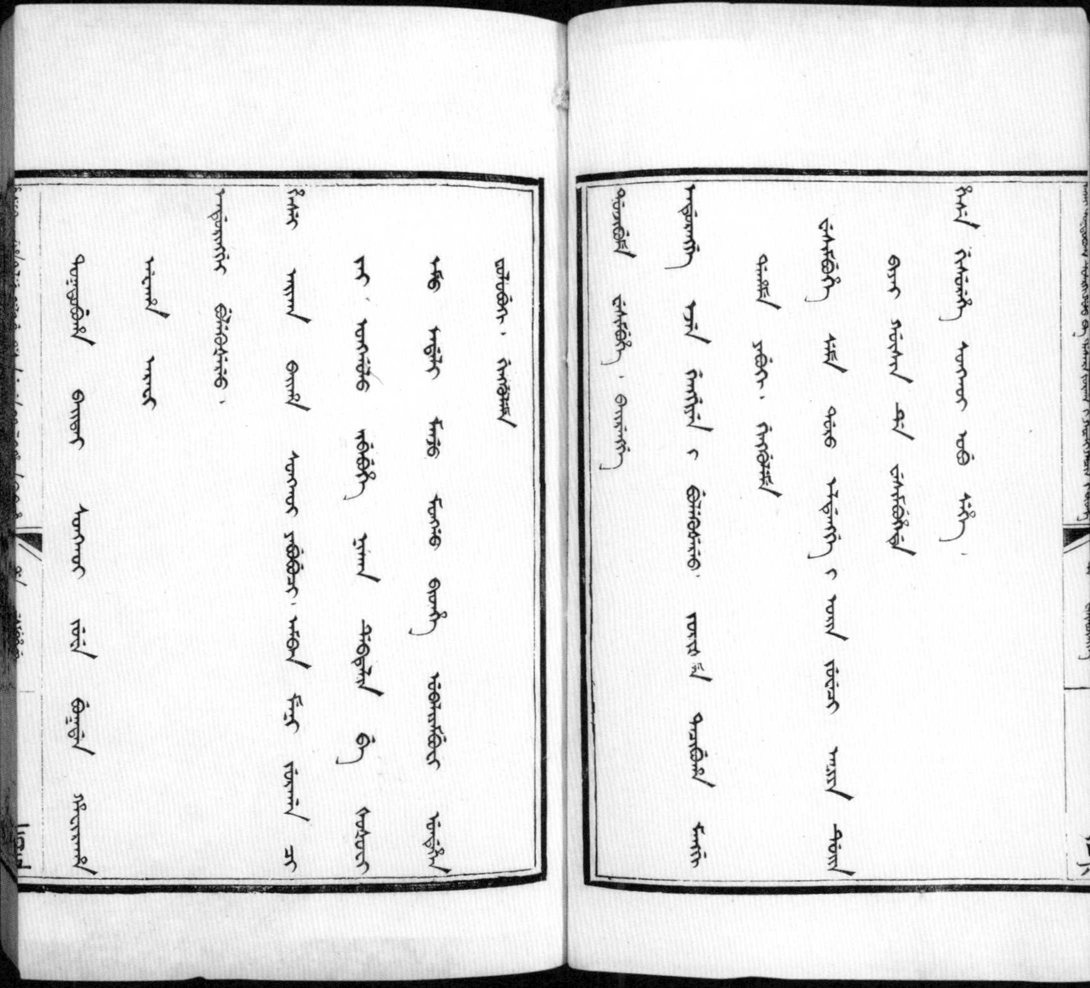

道光二十二年奏摺
Memorial in 1842

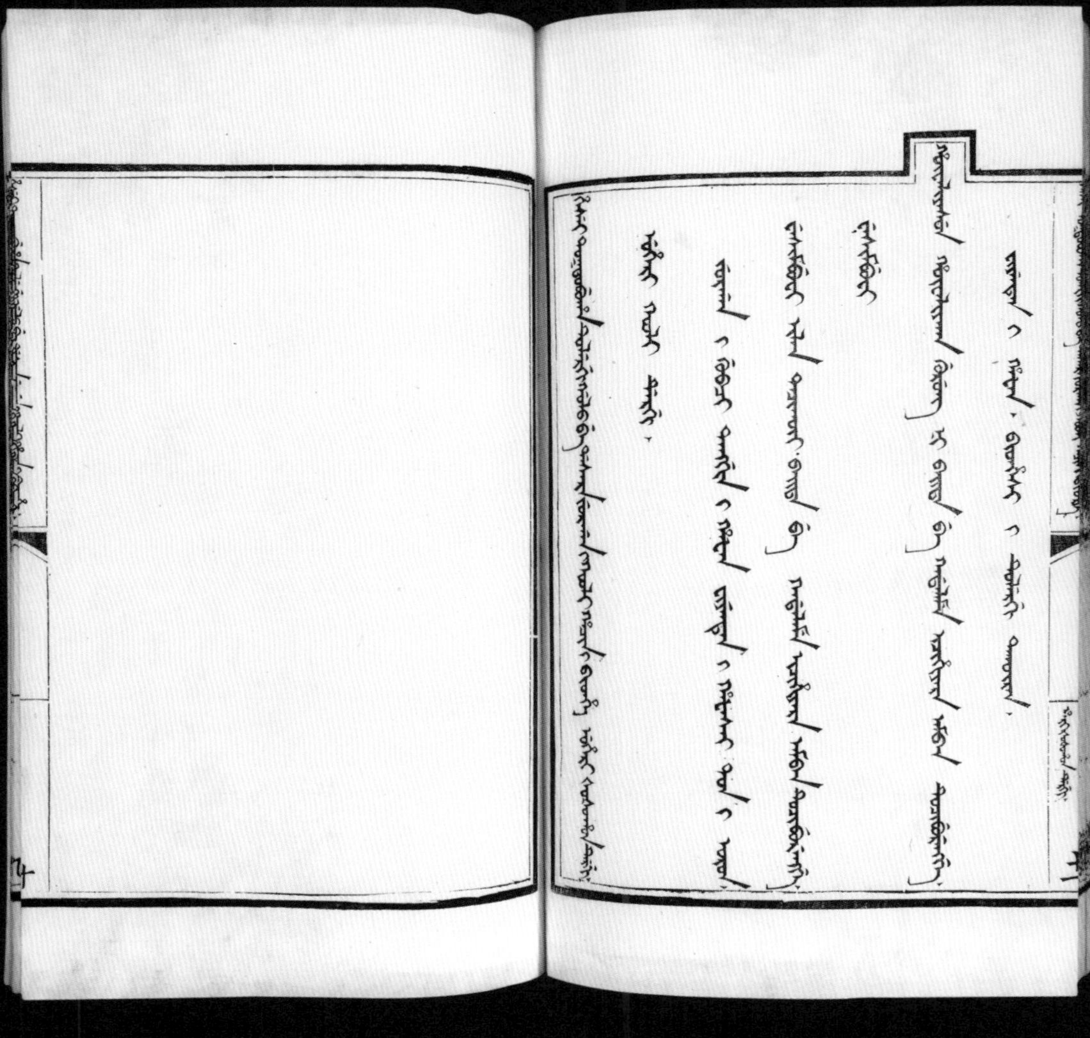

卷端

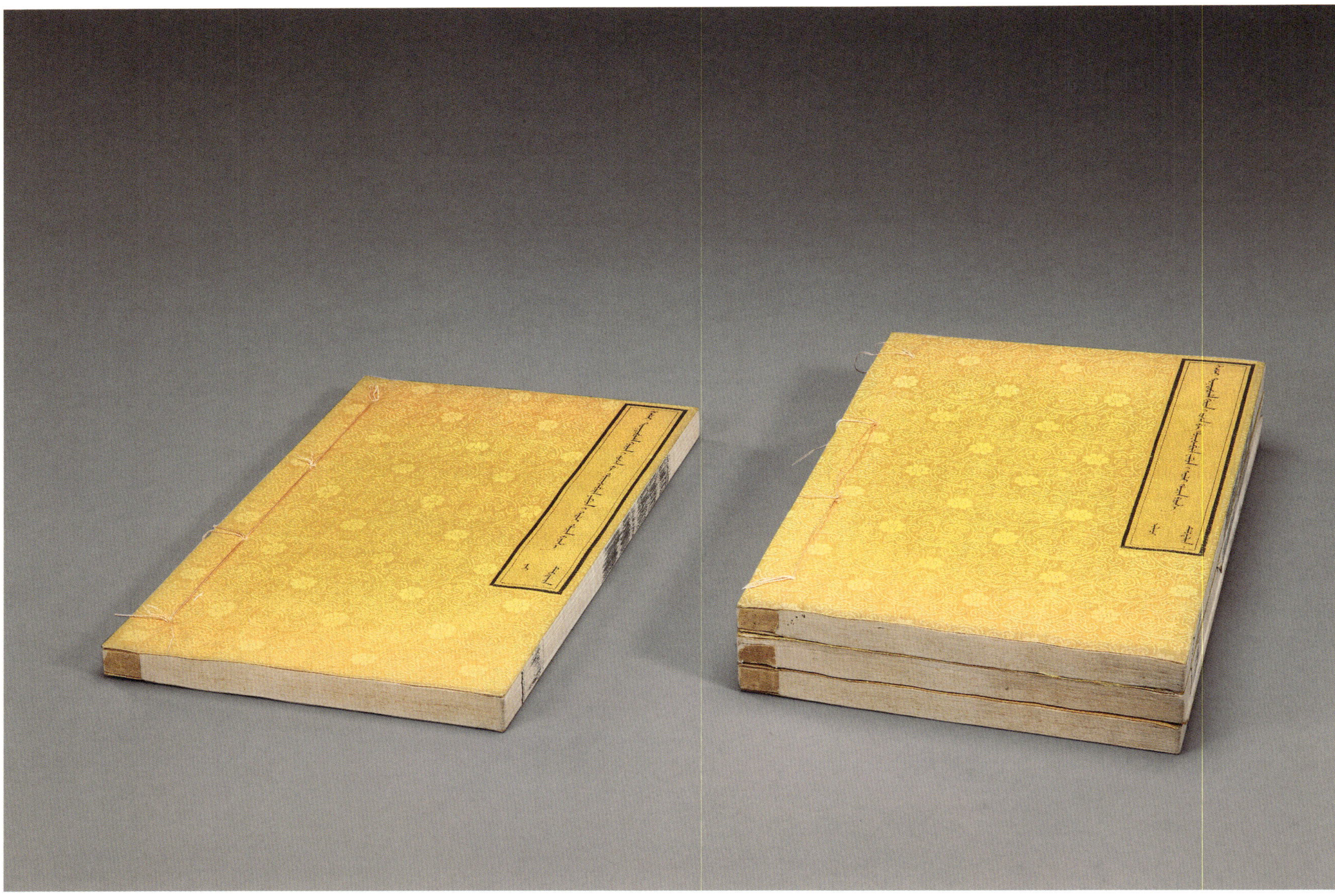

明黃色纏枝花紋暗花綾書面
Bright yellow twill-weave silk covers with veiled pattern of floral scrolls

明黃色纏枝花紋暗花綾書面
Bright yellow twill-weave silk cover with veiled pattern of floral scrolls

書22152
《欽定國子監則例三十卷首二卷》
清　蔡新等奉敕撰
清乾隆三十七年（1772）武英殿刻滿文本
開本　縱29.9厘米　橫19.7厘米
版框　縱22厘米　橫16厘米
四冊　一函

70

Inventory number: Shu 22152
Rules and Regulations on the Imperial Academy
Thirty chapters as text, two chapters as preliminary remarks
Written by imperial order by Cai Xin et. al., Qing dynasty (1644-1911)
Printed in Manchu in 1772 at the Hall of Martial Valour
Format: 29.9 × 19.7 cm
Frame: 22 × 16 cm
Four volumes in one case

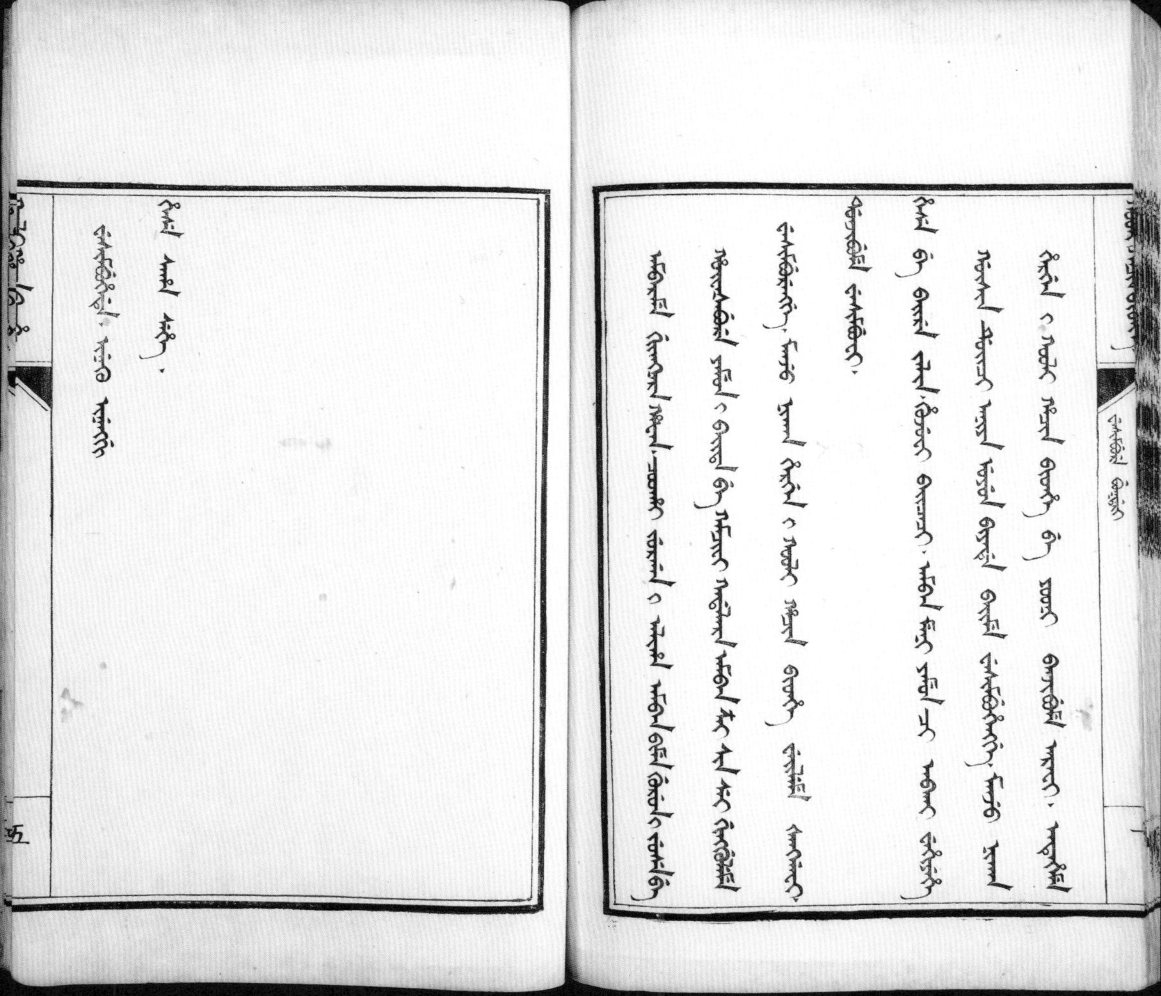

蔡新等奏疏
Memorial from Cai Xin et. al.

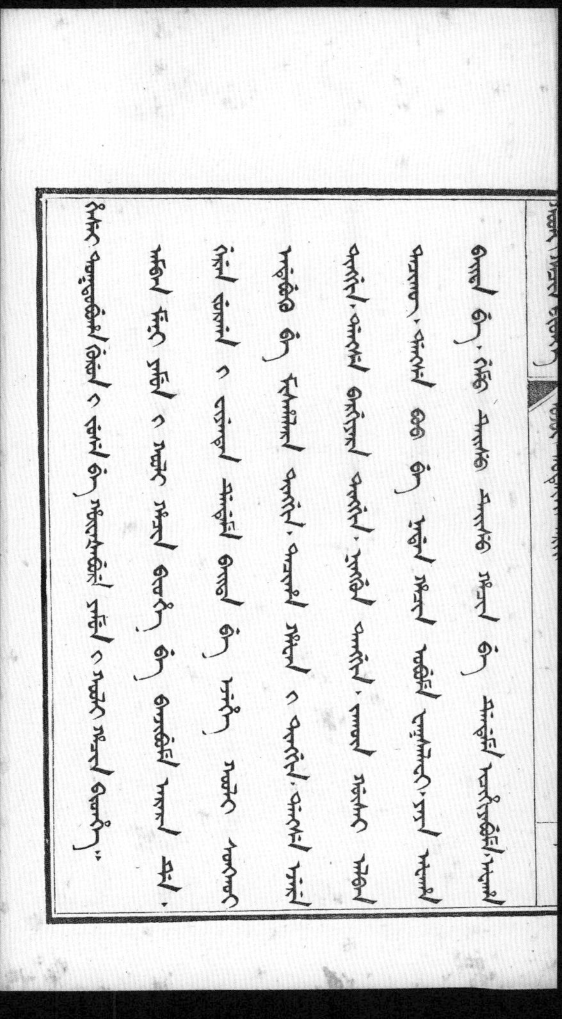

卷端
Beginning

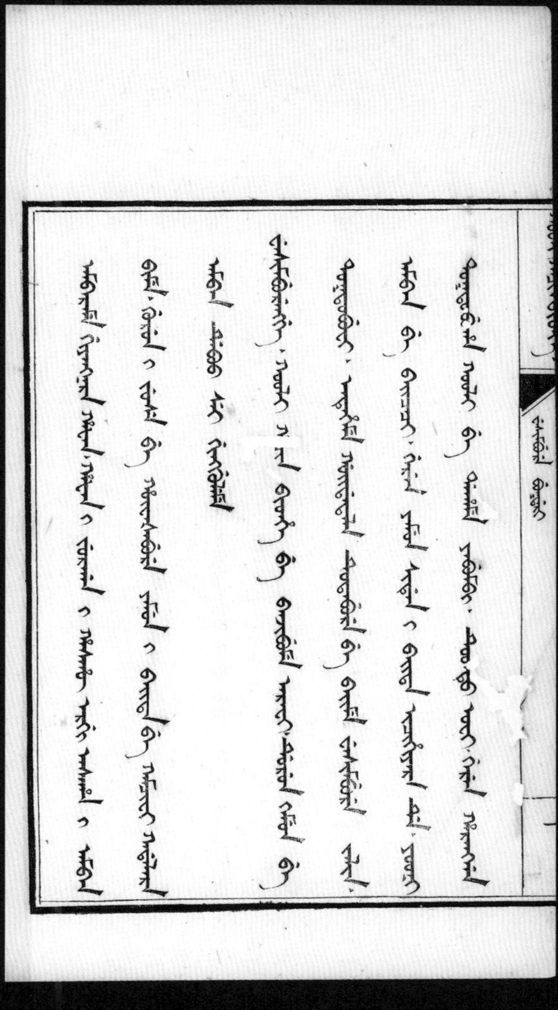

德保等奏疏
Memorial from Debao et. al.

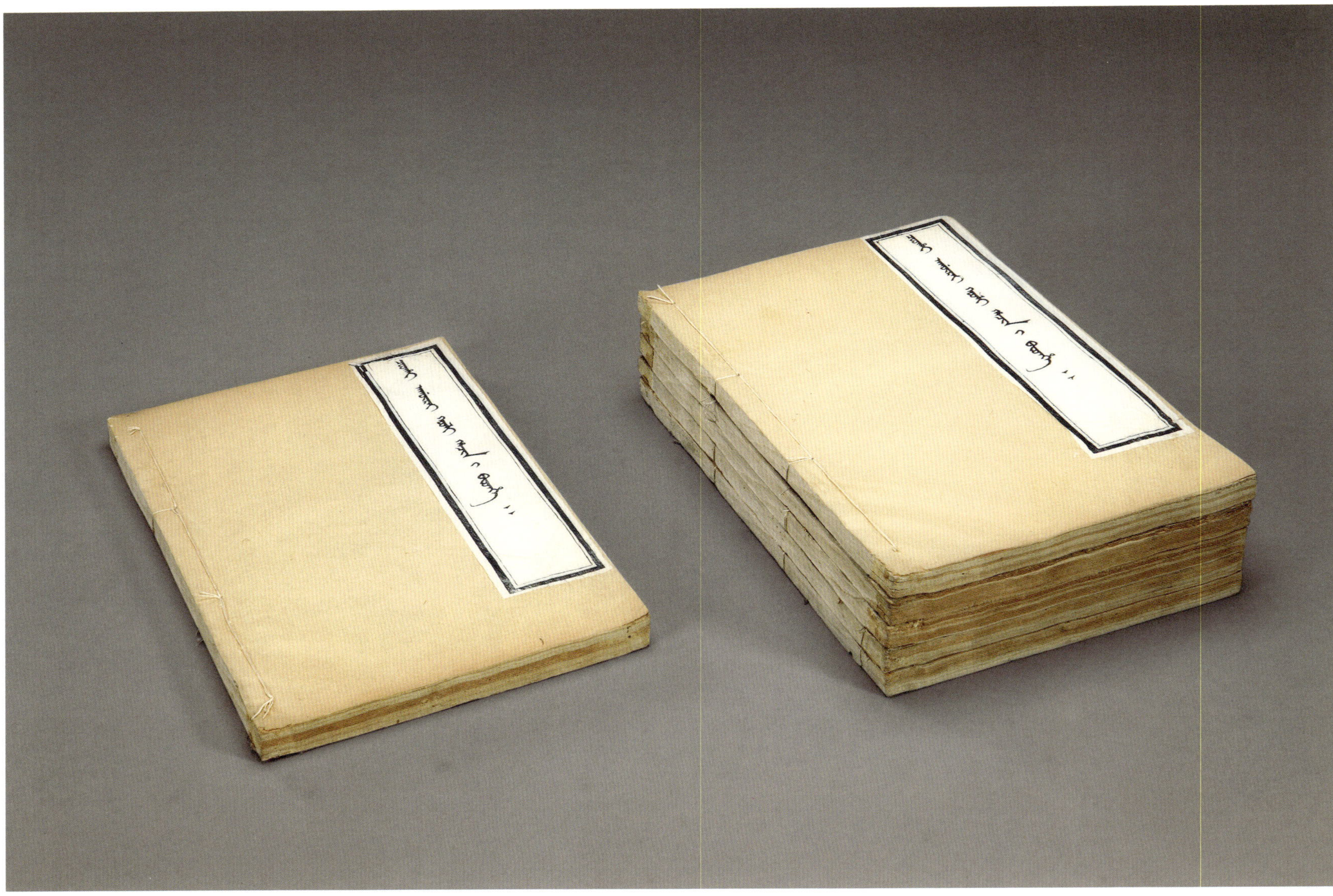

黄色紙書面
Yellow paper covers

書22239
《欽定軍器則例十二卷》
清　董誥等撰
清嘉慶九年（1804）武英殿刻滿文本
開本　縱26.7厘米　橫17.4厘米
版框　縱20.7厘米　橫16.1厘米
六冊　一函

71

Inventory number: Shu 22239
Rules and Regulations on Military Arms
Twelve chapters
Written by imperial order by Dong Gao et. al., Qing dynasty (1644-1911)
Printed in Manchu in 1804 at the Hall of Martial Valour
Format: 26.7 × 17.4 cm
Frame: 20.7 × 16.1 cm
Six volumes in one case

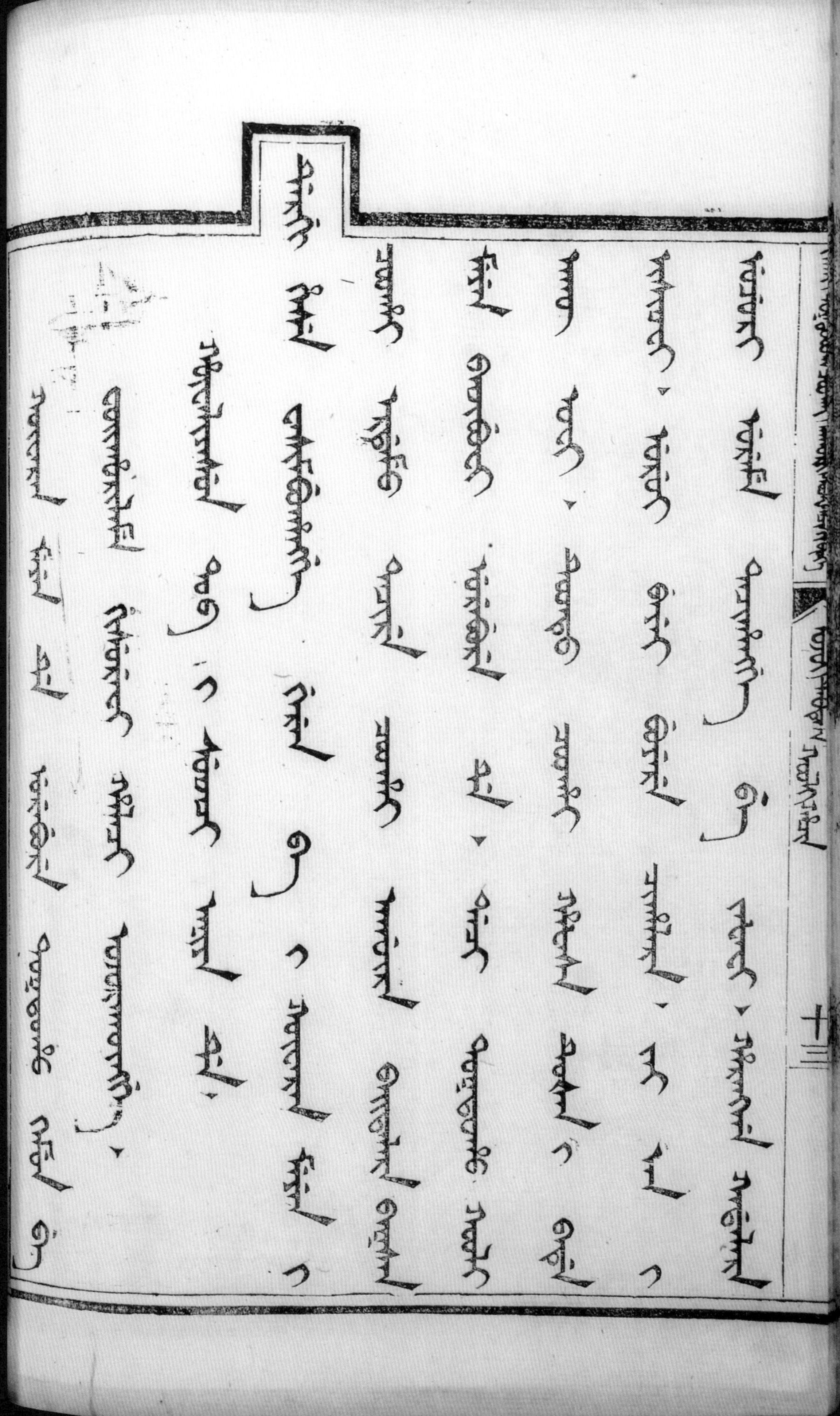

則例
Rules and regulations

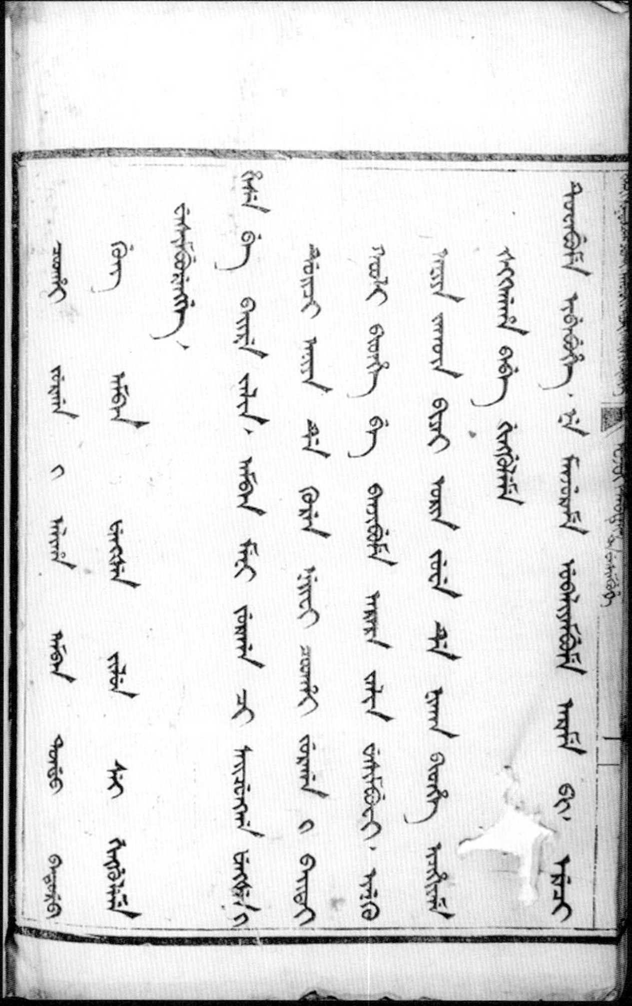

嘉慶九年奏摺1
Memorial in 1804 Ⅰ

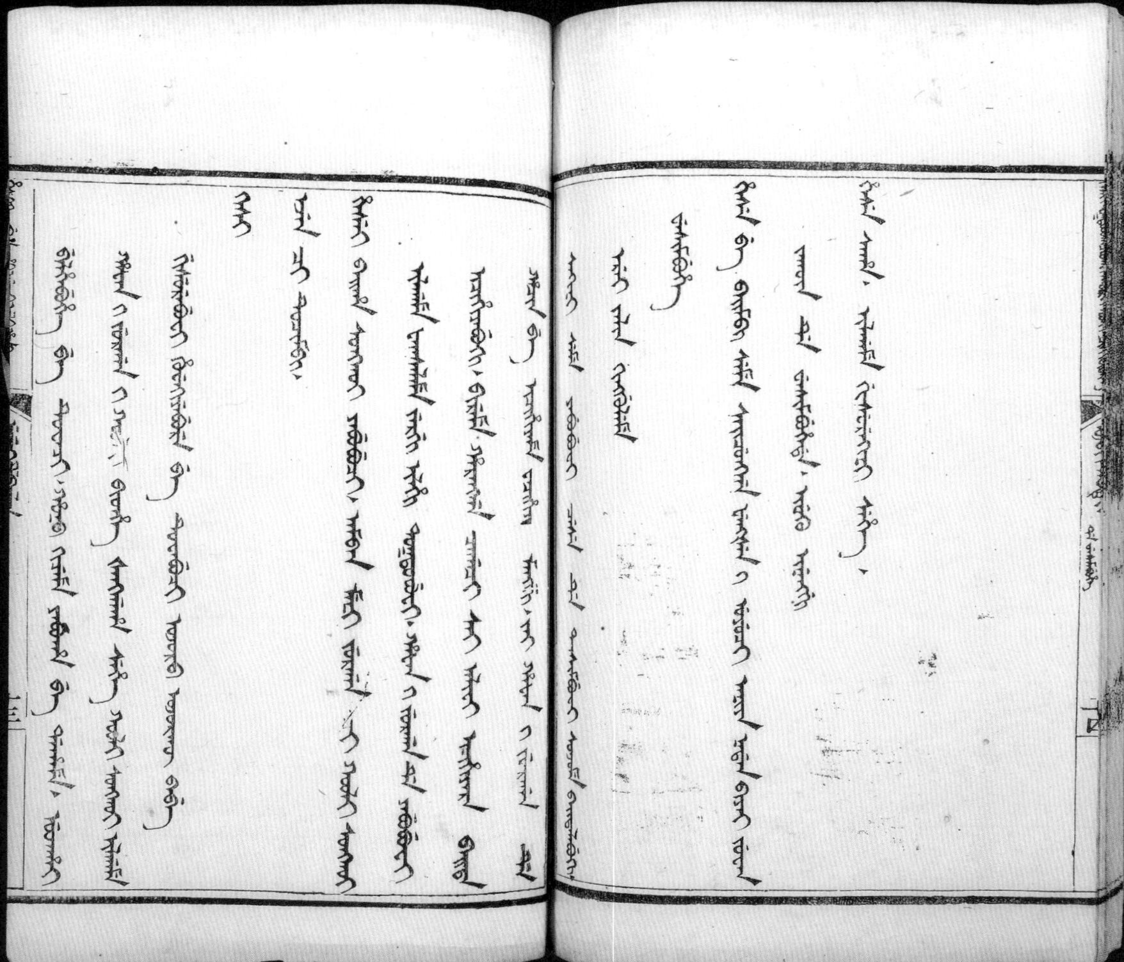

嘉慶九年奏摺2
Memorial in 1804 Ⅱ

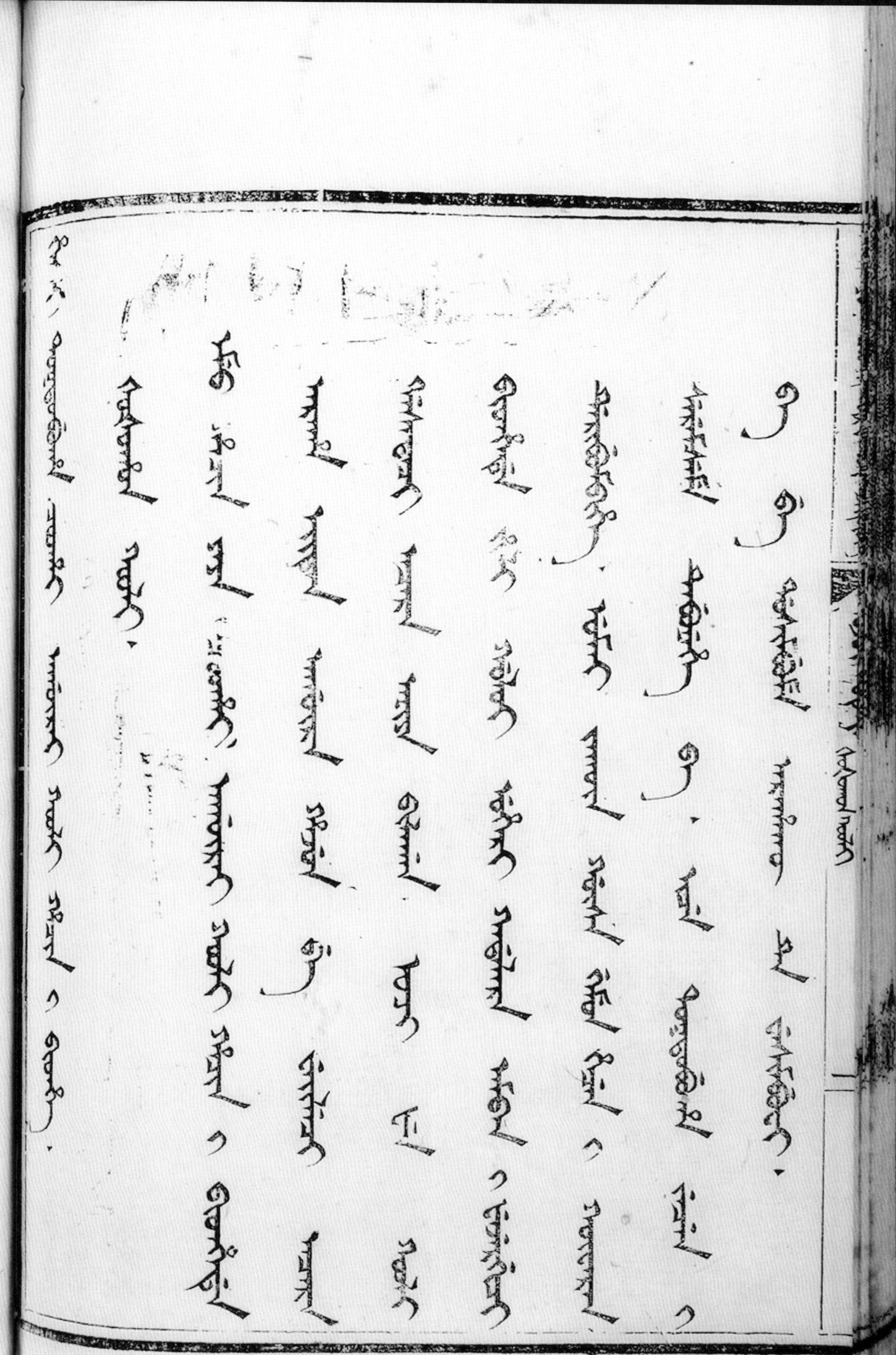

卷端
Beginning

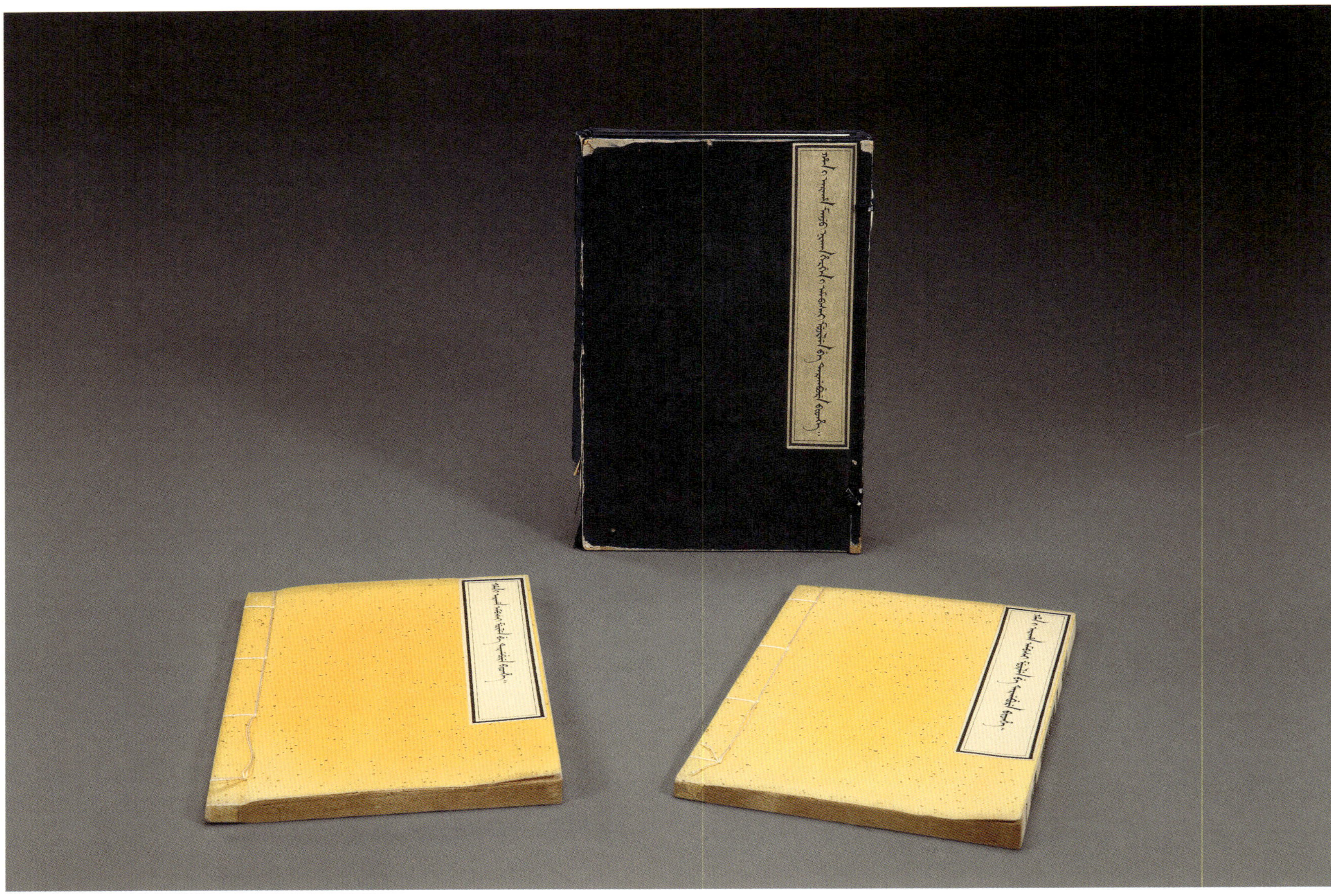

藍色素絹書函
Blue silk case

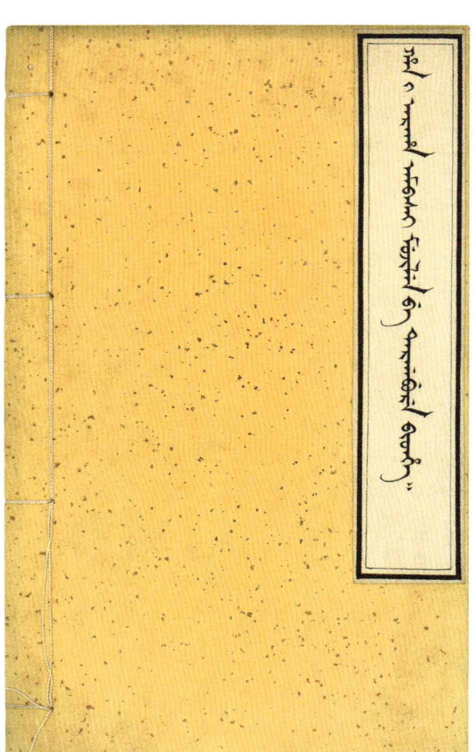

明黃色紙撒金書面
Bright yellow cover made of gold-sprinkled paper

72

書22185
《御製人臣敬心録一卷》
清　世祖福臨撰
清順治十二年（1655）內府刻滿文本
開本　縱23.5厘米　橫14.6厘米
版框　縱16.8厘米　橫11.5厘米
一册　一函（與另一部《御製人臣敬心録一卷》合函）

Inventory number: Shu 22185
Collection of Political Essays on Mental Cultivation of Officials
One chapter
Written by the Shunzhi emperor (r.1644-1661)
Printed in Manchu in 1655 by the Qing court
Format: 23.5 × 14.6 cm
Frame: 16.8 × 11.5 cm
One volume in one case, sharing the same case with another work with the same title

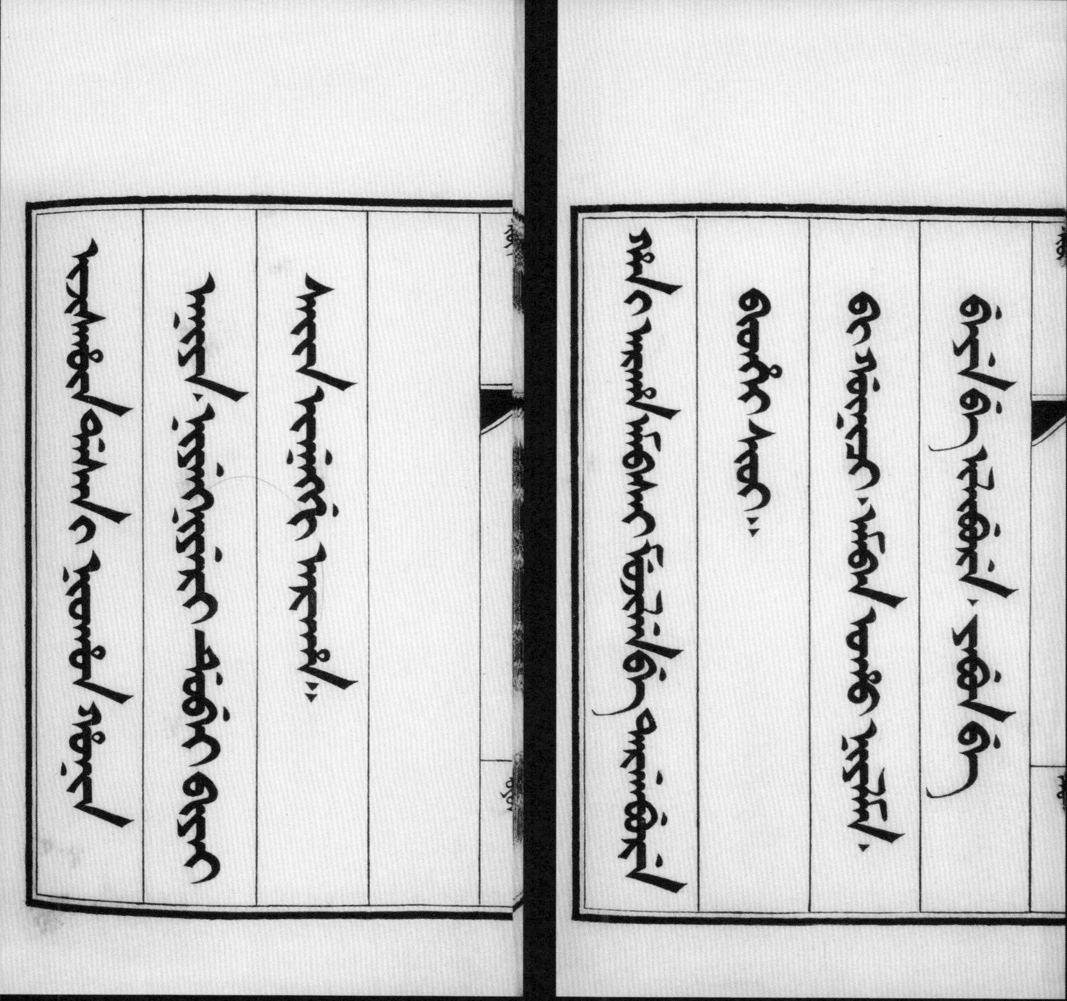

顺治十二年御製序
Imperial Preface in 1655

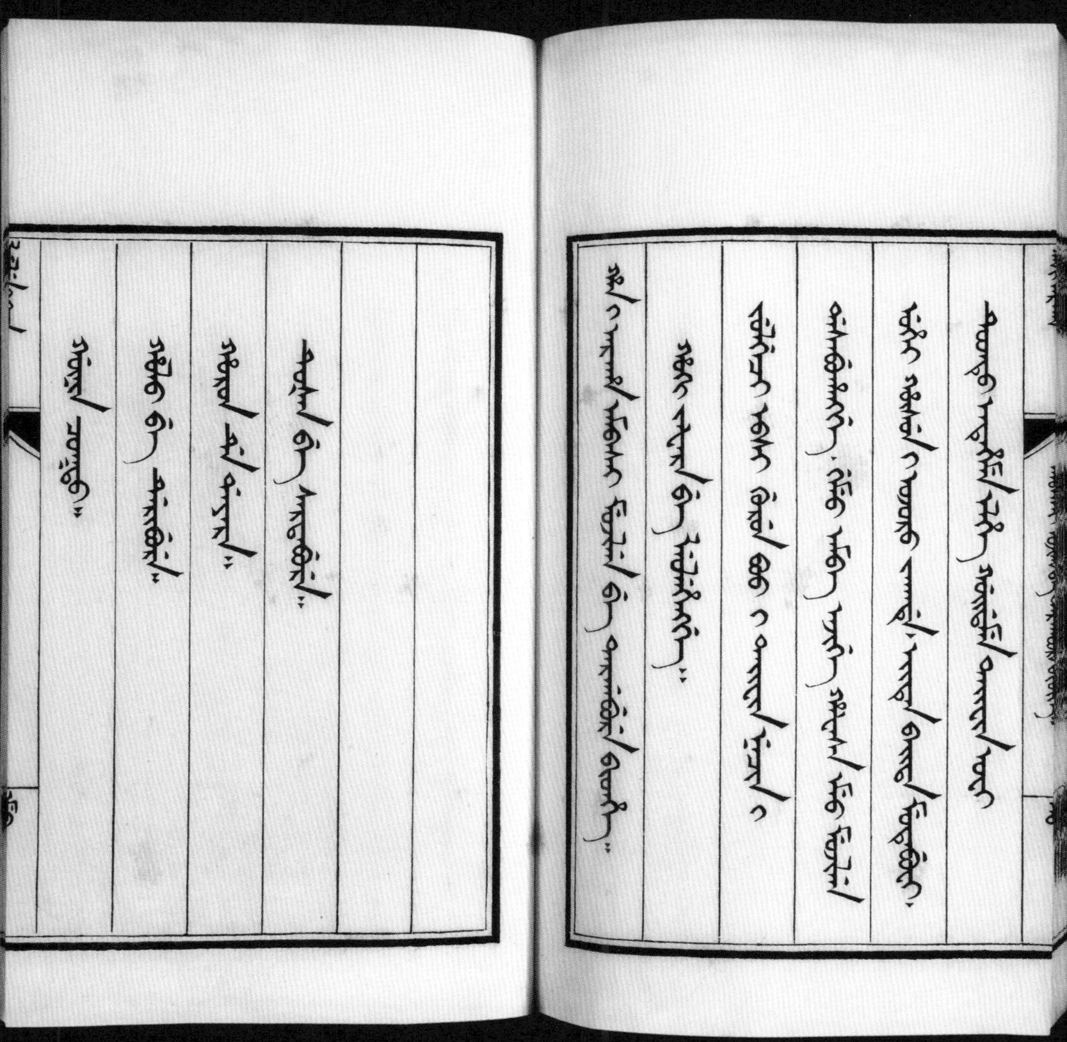

卷端

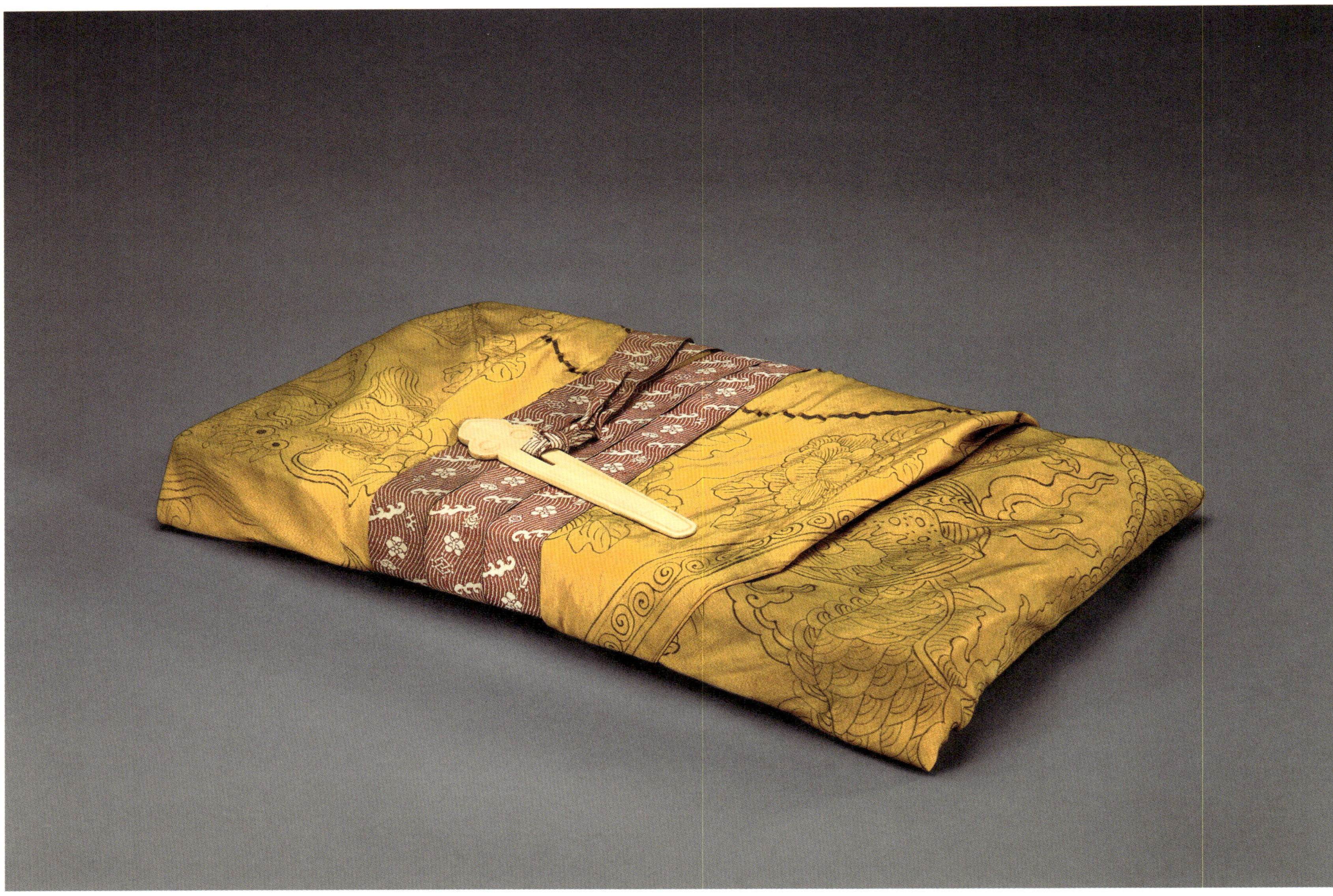

外觀
Exterior

書21982
《大清太祖高皇帝聖訓四卷》
清　太祖努爾哈赤撰
清乾隆四年（1739）内府朱絲欄精寫滿文小紅綾本
開本　縱37.5厘米　橫23厘米
版框　縱24.7厘米　橫17.6厘米
四册　二函

73

Inventory number: Shu 21982
Holy Teachings of the Taizu Emperor of the Qing
Four chapters
Compiled at the order of the Kangxi emperor (r.1662-1722)
Transcribed in Manchu in red columns on twill-weave silk in 1739 by the Qing court
Format: 37.5 × 23 cm
Frame: 24.7 × 17.6 cm
Four volumes in two cases

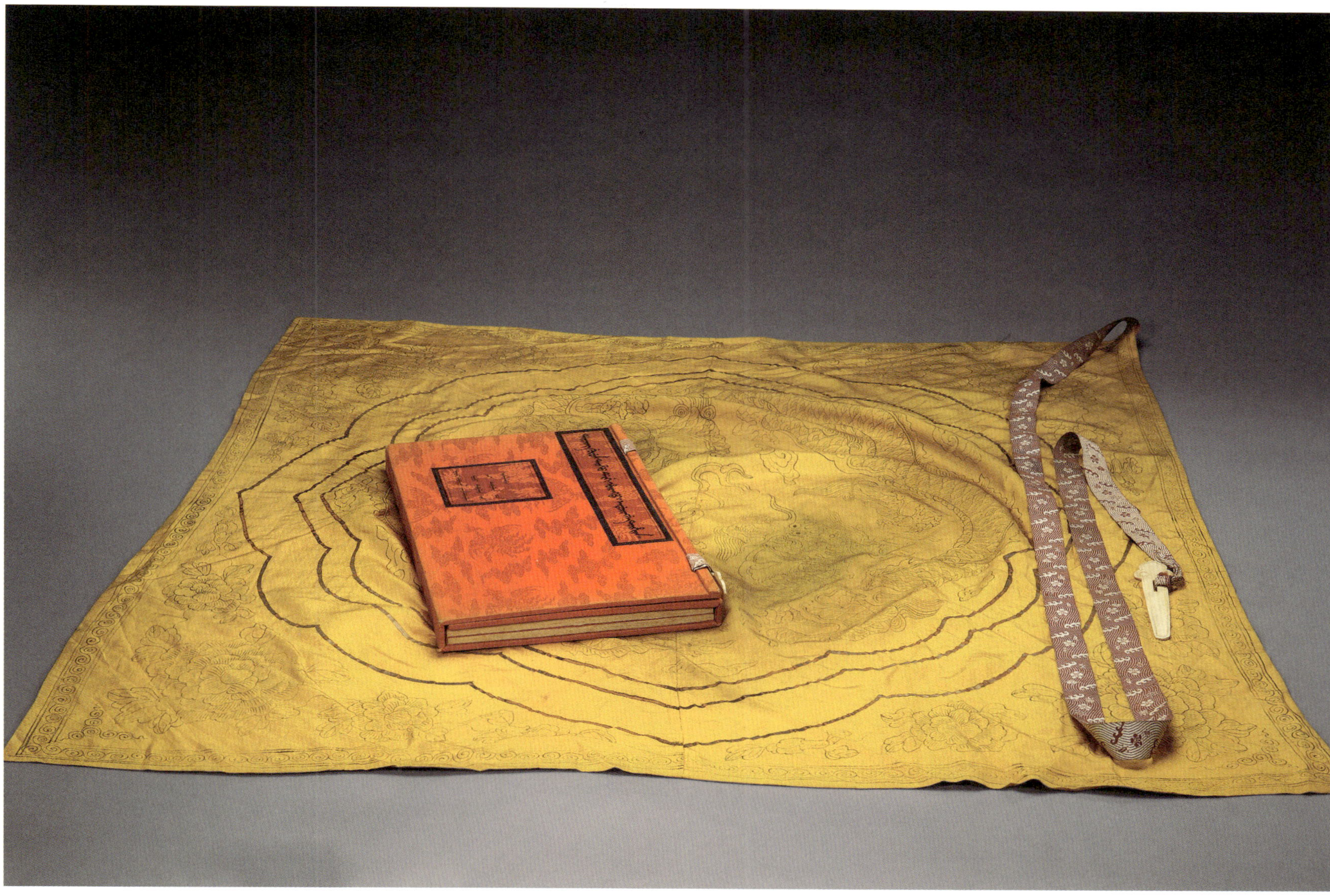

明黄色描雲龍紋夾袱
Bright yellow wrapping with dragon and cloud pattern

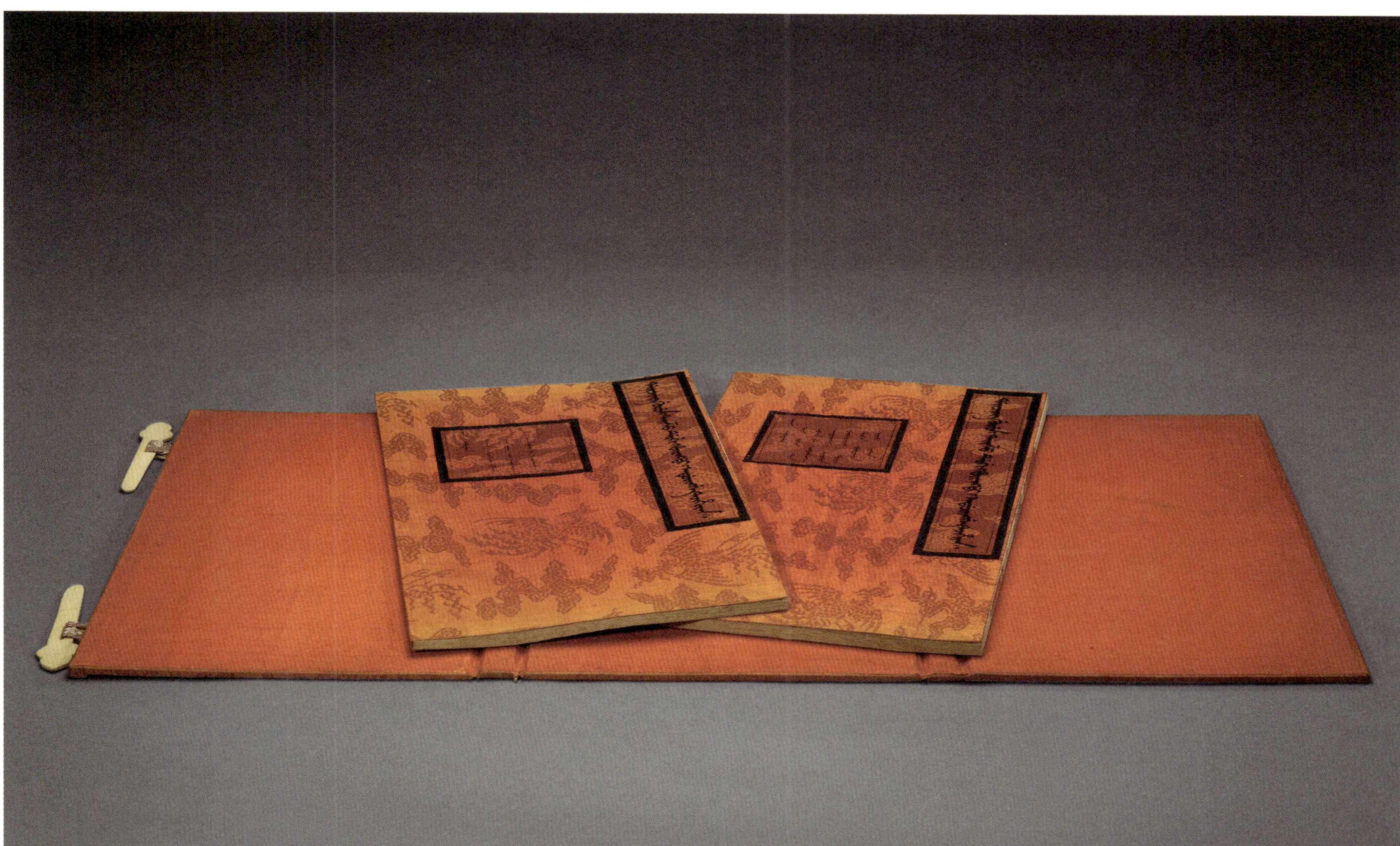

暗紅色雲鳳紋暗花綾書函
Dark red twill-weave silk case with veiled phoenix and cloud pattern

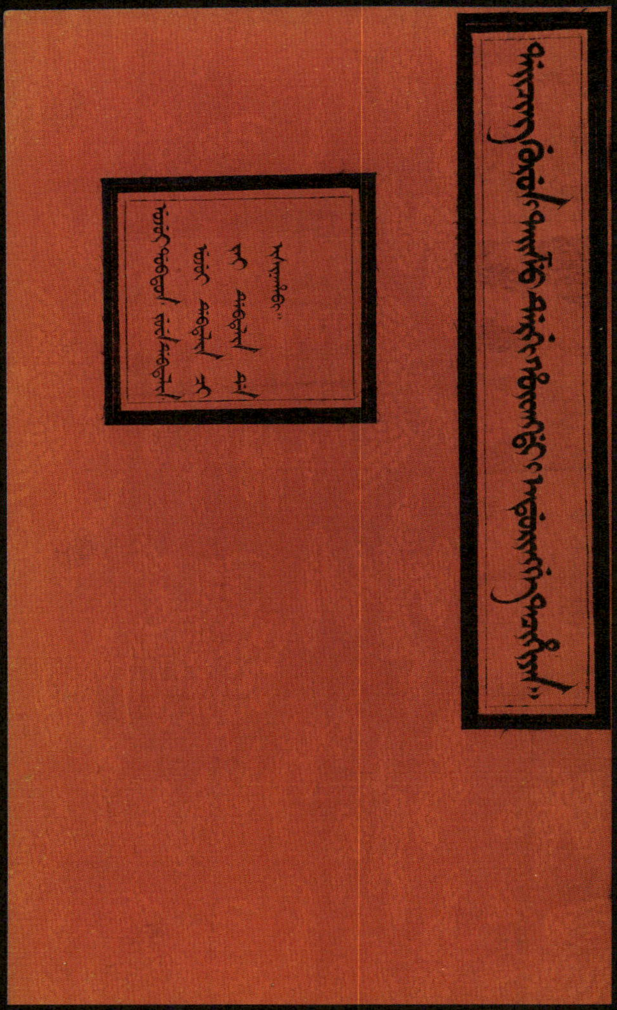

暗紅色雲鳳紋暗花綾書面
Dark red twill-weave silk cover with veiled phoenix and cloud pattern

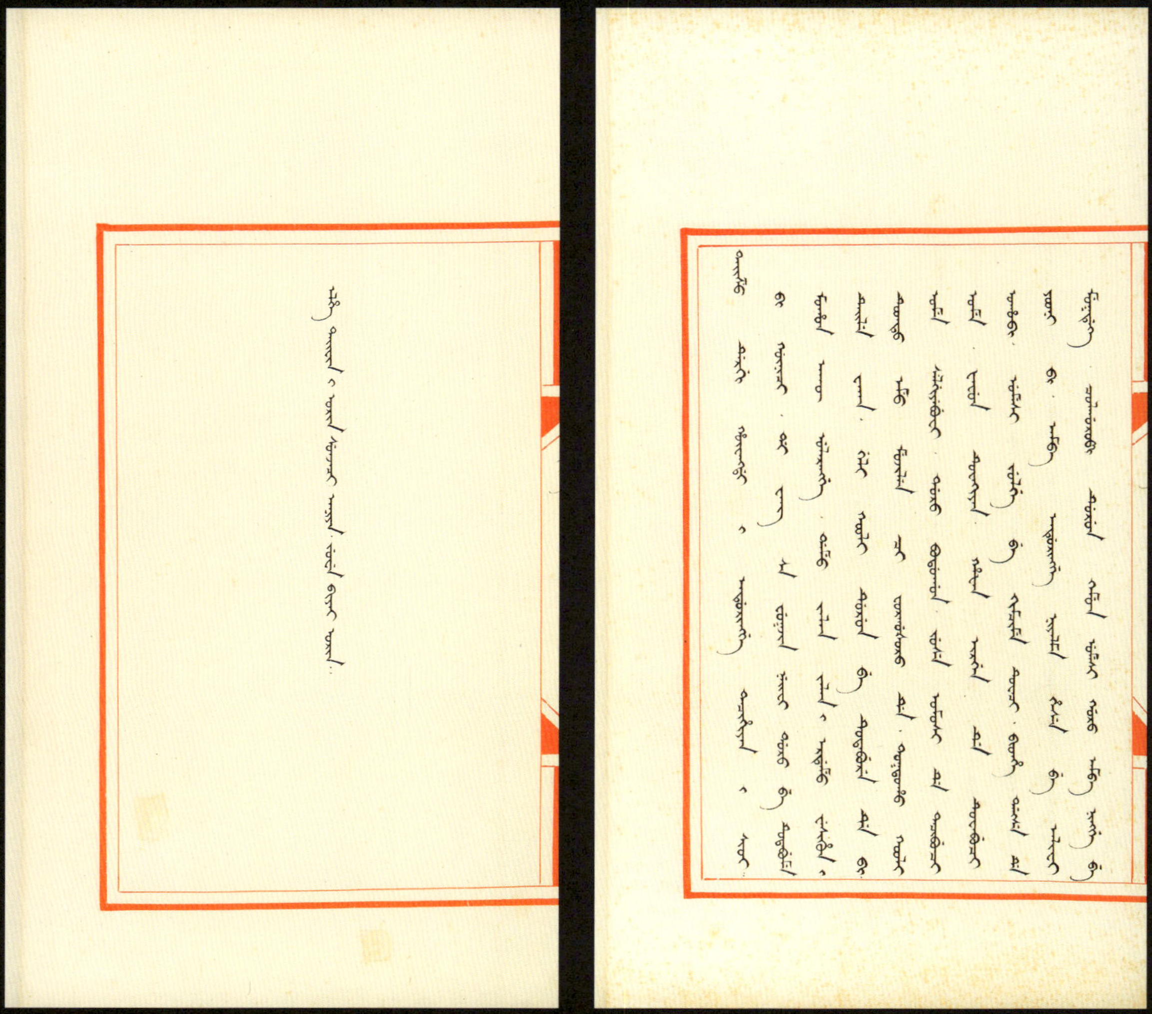

康熙二十五年御製序
Preface by the Kangxi emperor in 1686

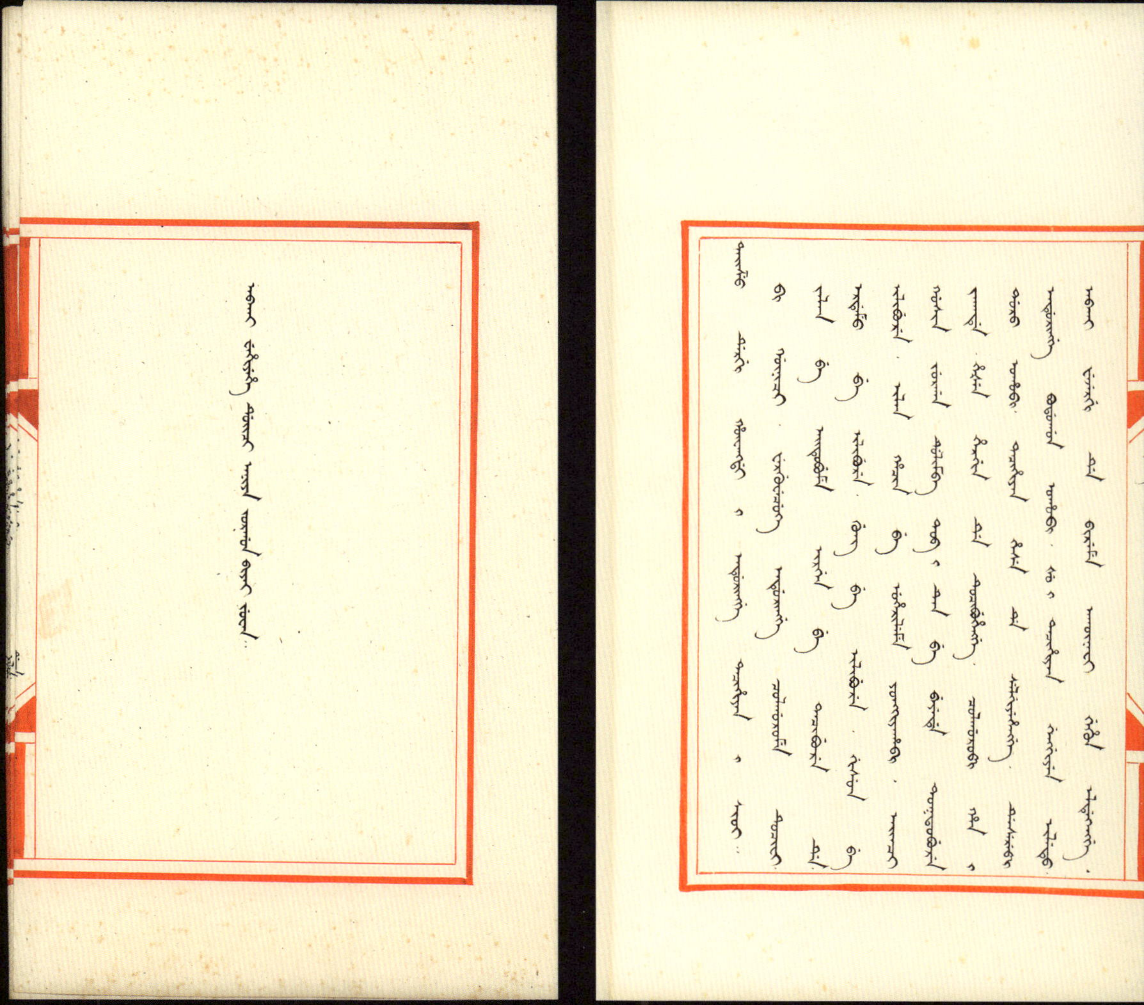

乾隆四年御製序
Preface by the Qianlong emperor in 1739

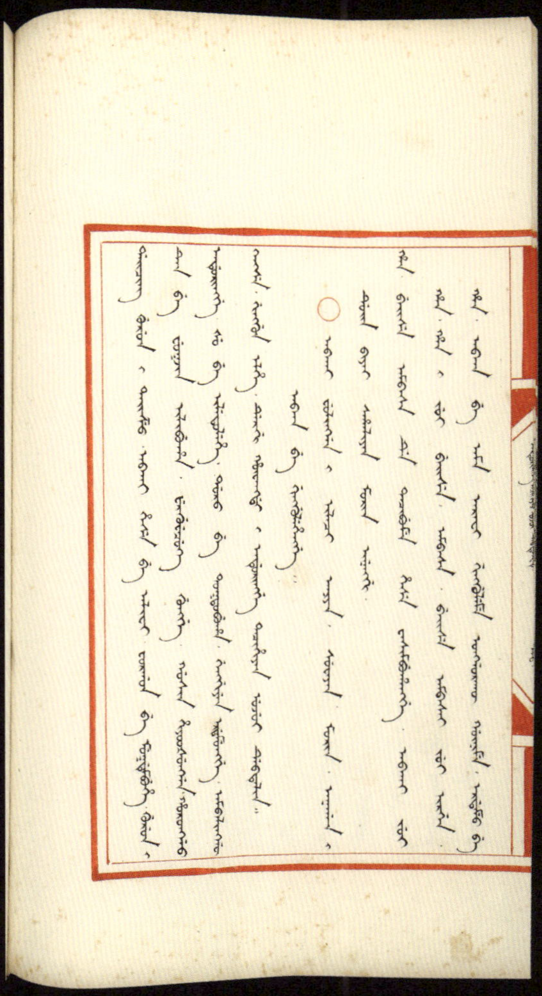

卷端
Beginning

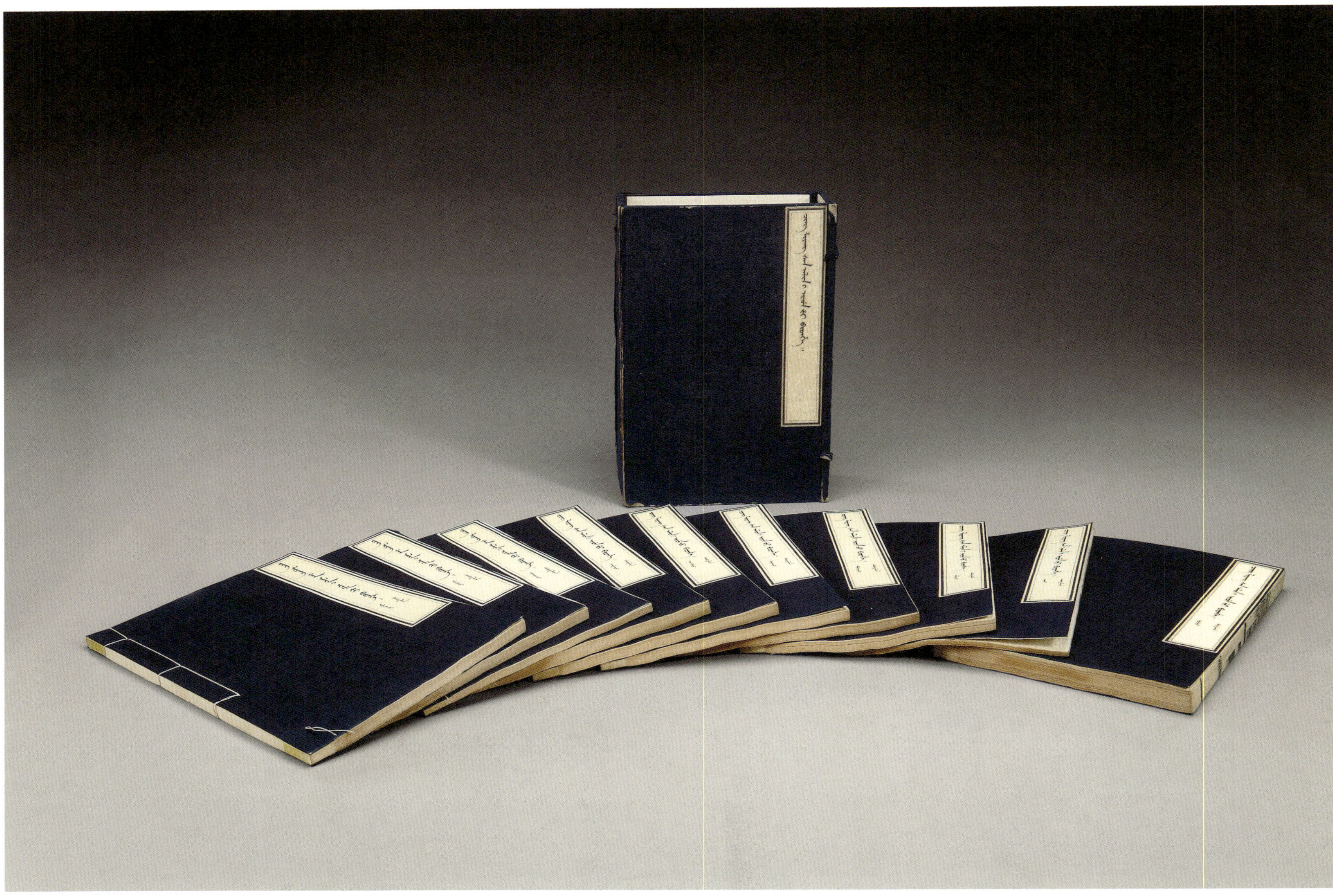

石青色素絹書函
Dark blue silk case

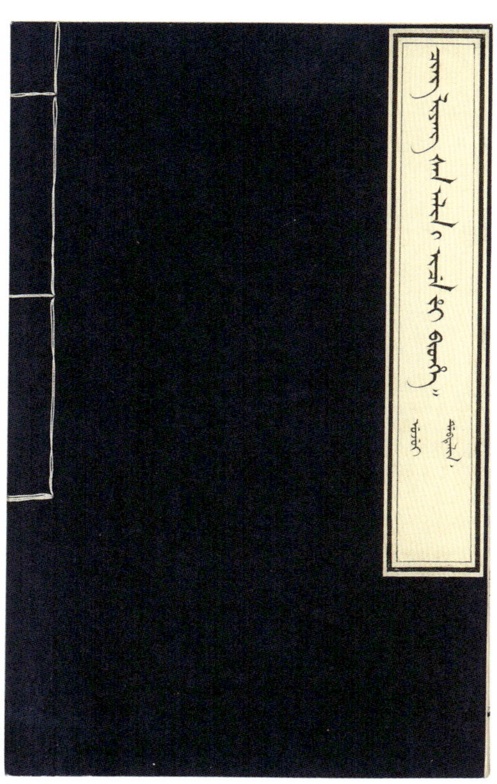

石青色素絹書面
Dark blue silk cover

74

書22090

《清凉山志十卷》

清　喇嘛羅卜藏丹巴撰
清康熙四十二年（1703）武英殿刻滿文本
開本　縱27.2厘米　橫17.7厘米
版框　縱20厘米　橫14.1厘米
十册　一函

Inventory number: Shu 22090

Records on Mount Wutai

Ten chapters
Written by Lama Blo-bzang-bstan-pa, Qing dynasty (1644-1911)
Printed in Manchu in 1703 at the Hall of Martial Valour
Format: 27.2 × 17.7 cm
Frame: 20 × 14.1 cm
Ten volumes in one case

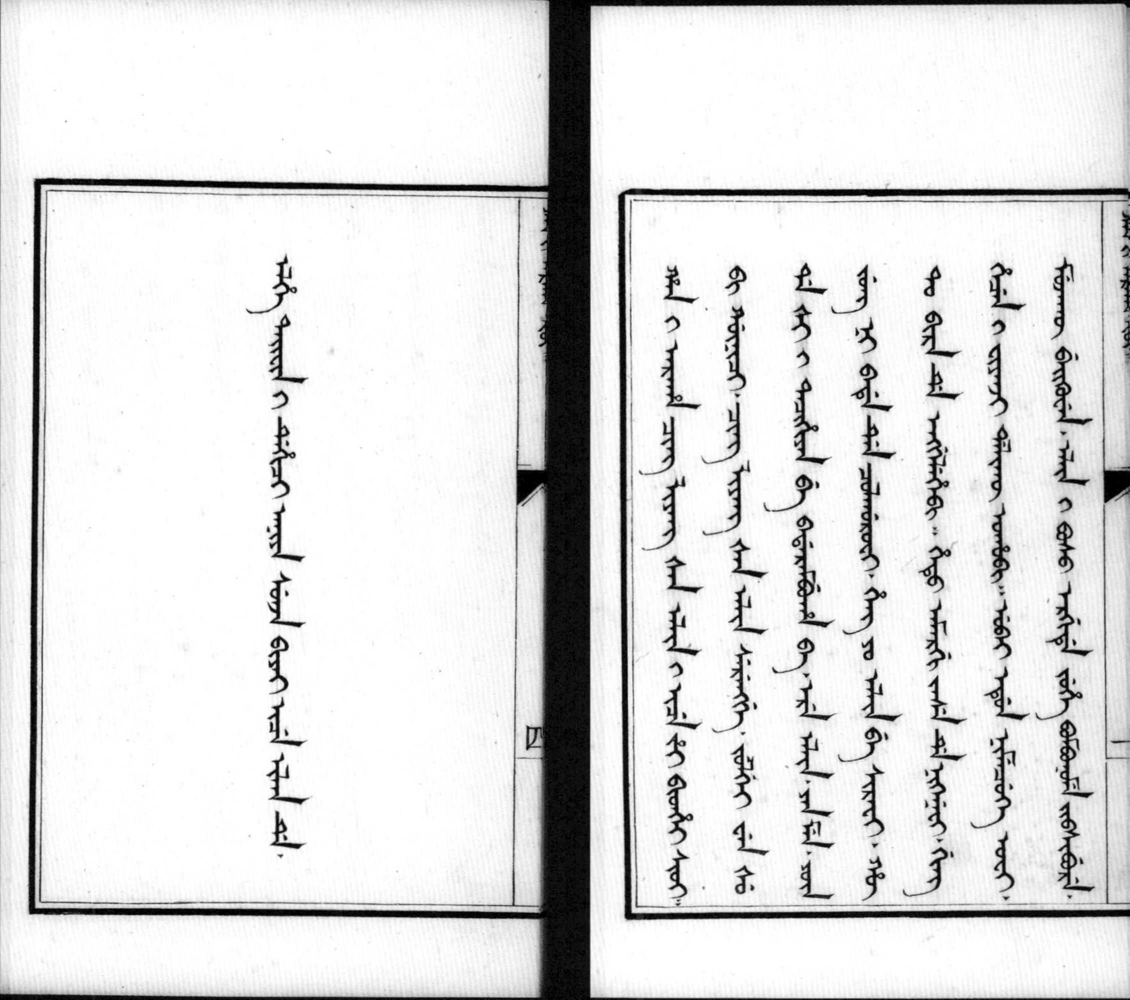

康熙四十年御製序
Preface by the Kangxi emperor in 1701

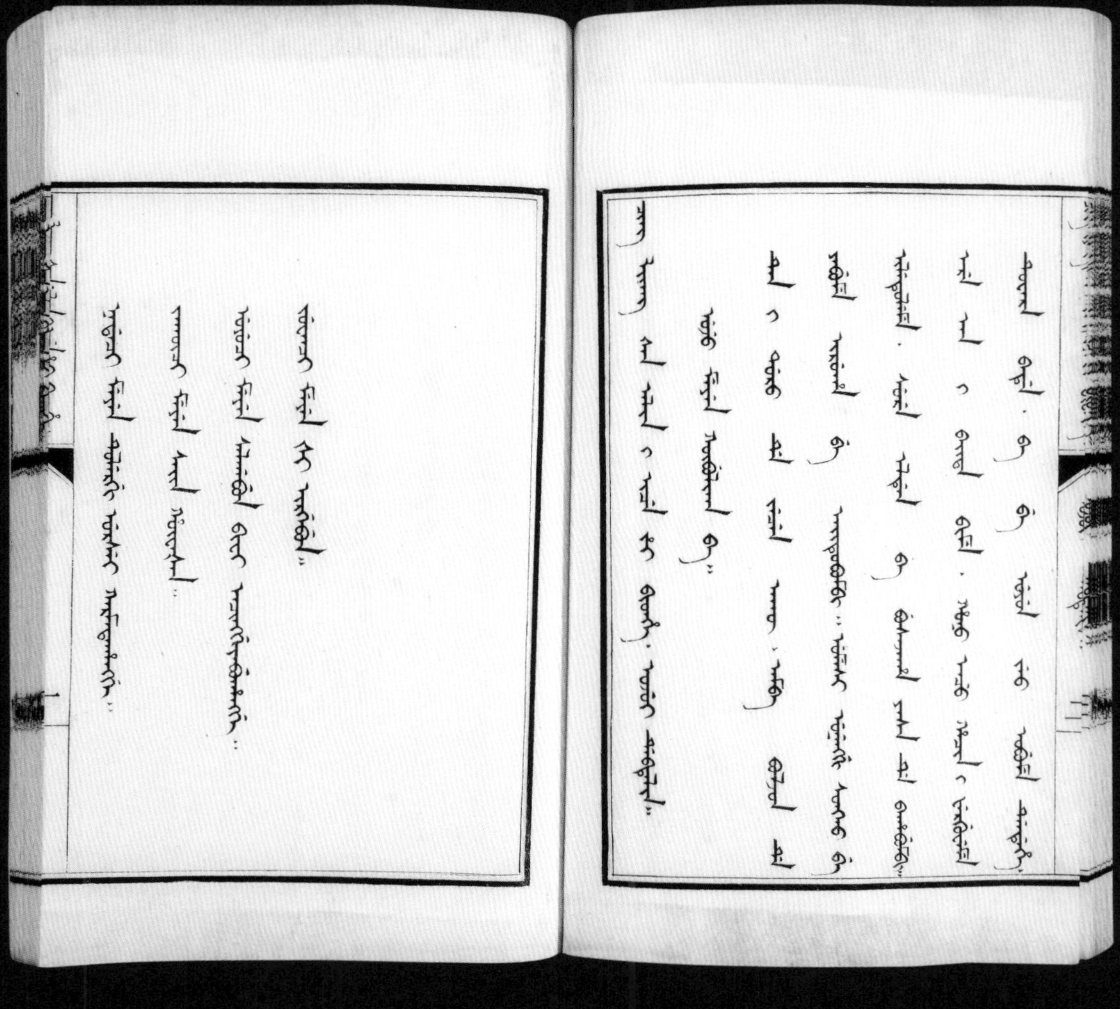

卷目及卷端

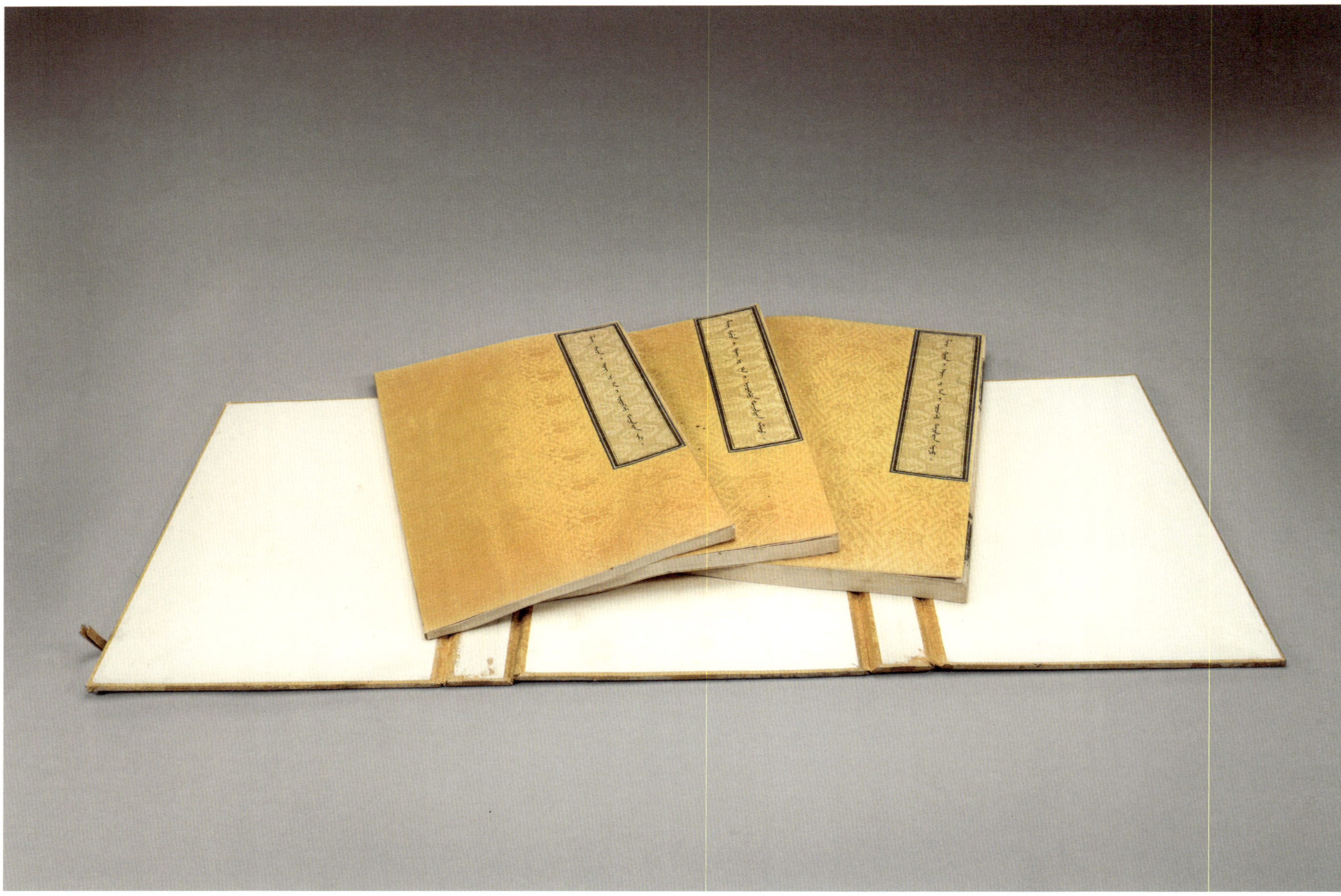

明黃色萬字曲水朵花紋暗花綾書函
Bright yellow twill-weave silk case with veiled swastika and floral pattern

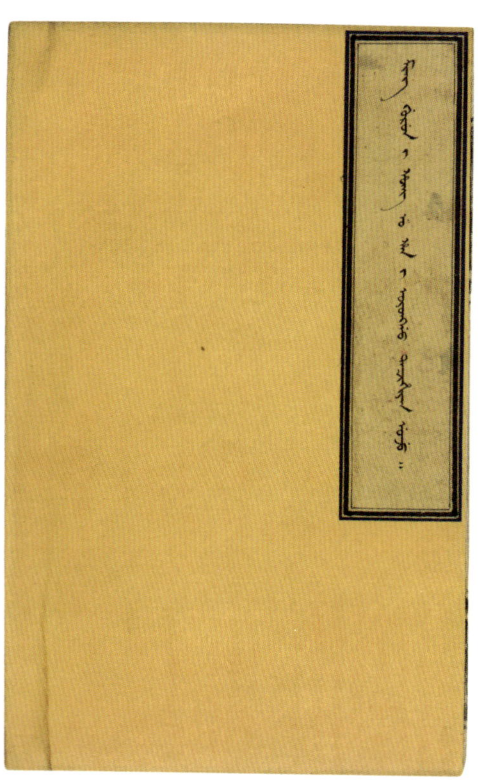

明黃色萬字曲水朵花紋暗花綾書面
Bright yellow twill-weave silk cover with veiled swastika and floral pattern

75

書22183
《明洪武寶訓六卷》
清　剛林等譯校
清順治三年（1646）內府精寫滿文本
開本　縱39厘米　橫24.2厘米
版框　縱31.6厘米　橫20.3厘米
六册　二函

Inventory number: Shu 22183
Valuable Teachings of the Hongwu Emperor
Six chapters
Translated and proofread by Ganglin et. al., Qing dynasty (1644-1911)
Transcribed in Manchu in 1646 by the Qing court
Format: 39 × 24.2 cm
Frame: 31.6 × 20.3 cm
Six volumes in two cases

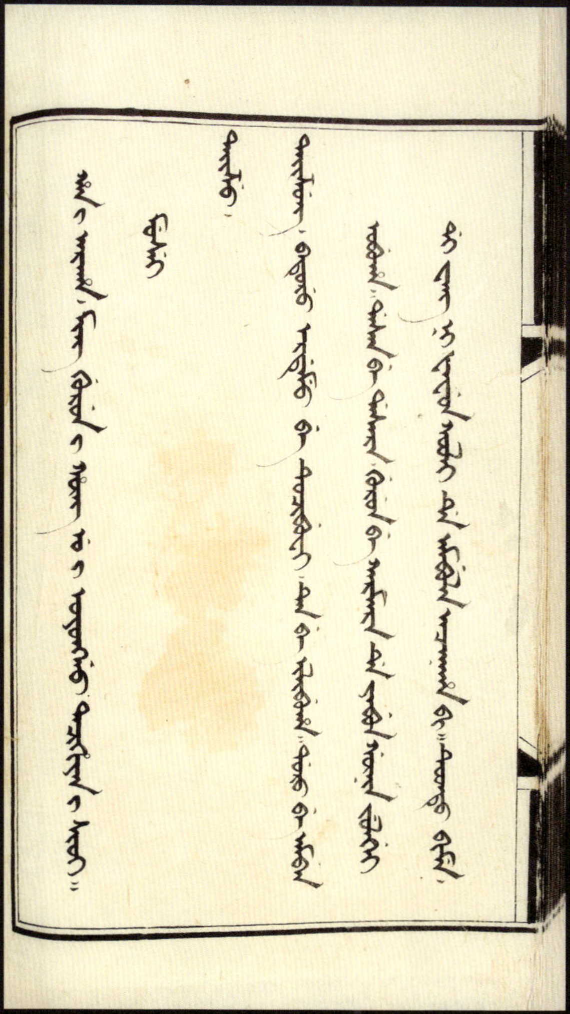

“御製明洪武寶訓”序
Imperial preface

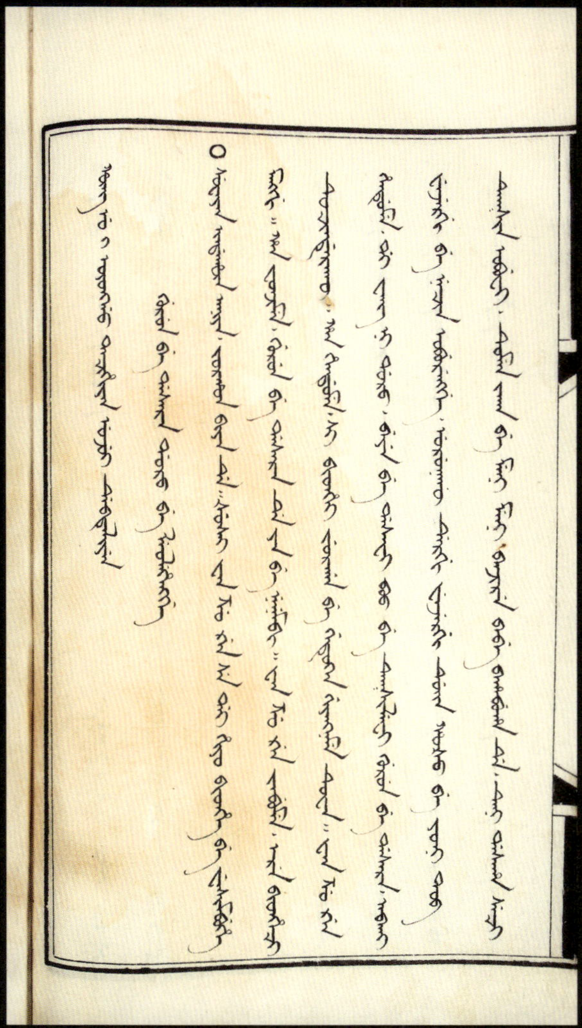

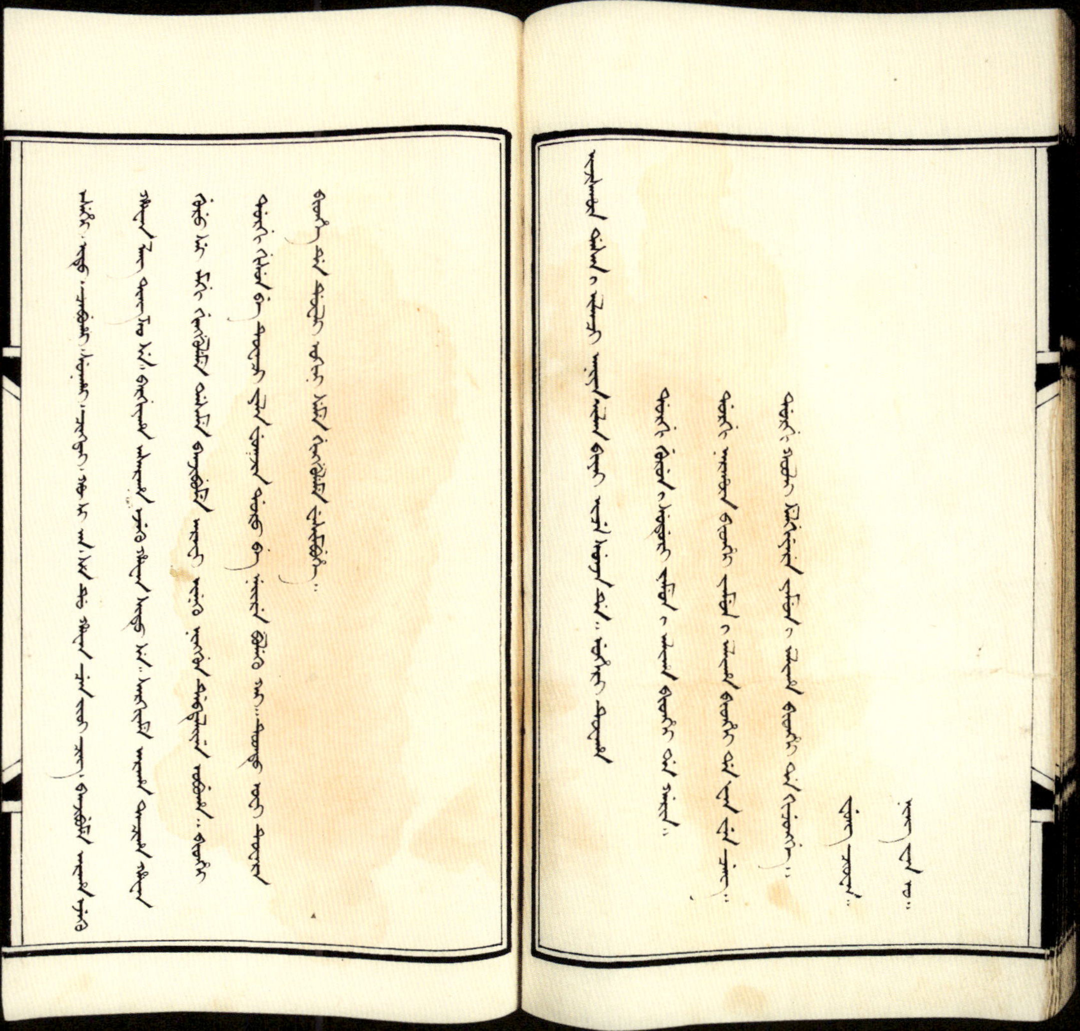

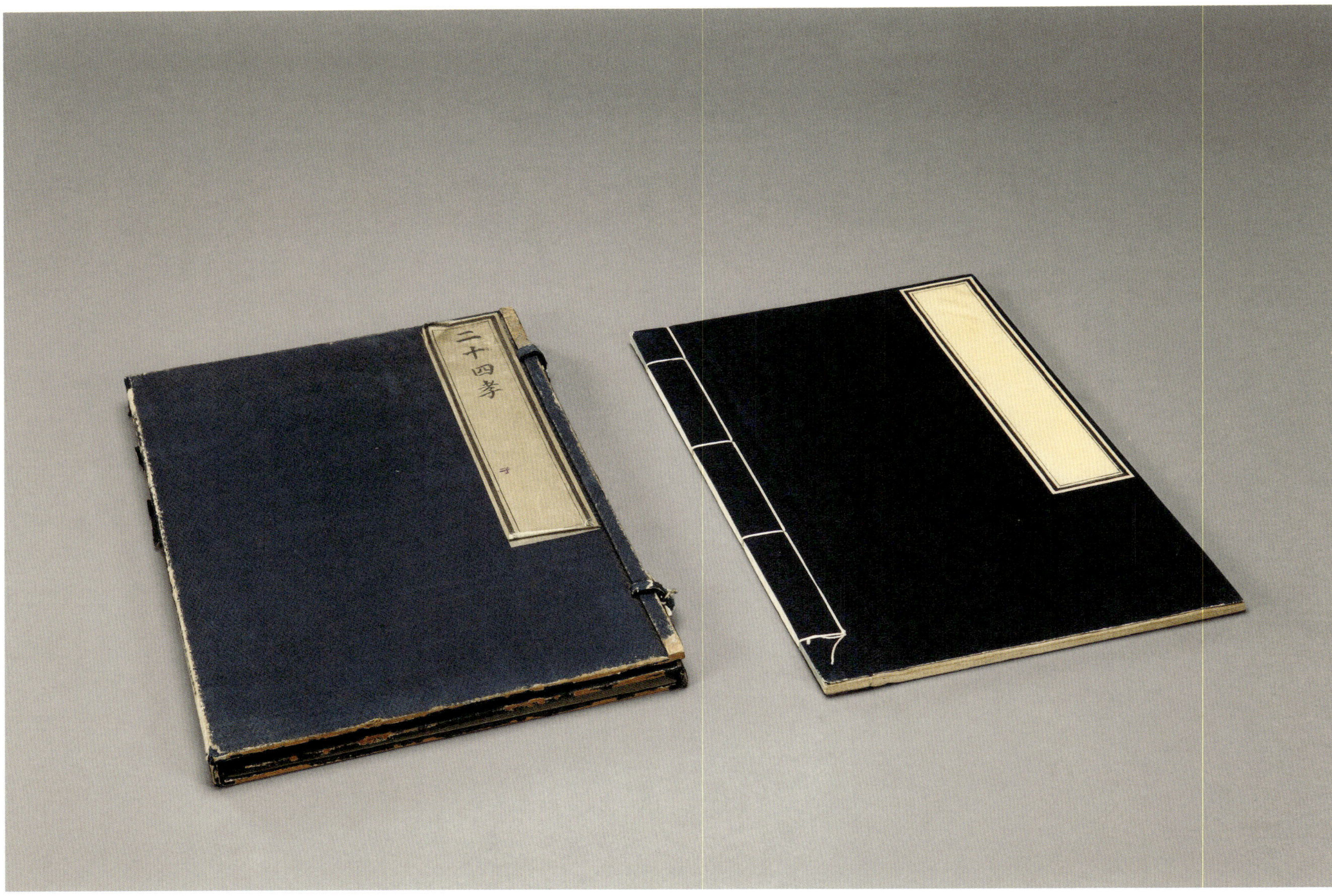

藍色萬字曲水紋暗花綾書面
Blue twill-weave silk cover with veiled swastika pattern

76

書22234
《二十四孝圖説不分卷》
清　佚名輯
清精寫墨繪滿文本
開本　縱33厘米　橫21.1厘米
版框　縱24.4厘米　橫17.1厘米
一册　一函

Inventory number: Shu 22234
Twenty-four Filial Exemplars Illustrated
Anonymous, Qing dynasty (1644-1911)
Transcribed in Manchu and painted in ink in the Qing dynasty
Format: 33 × 21.1 cm
Frame: 24.4 × 17.1 cm
One volume in one case

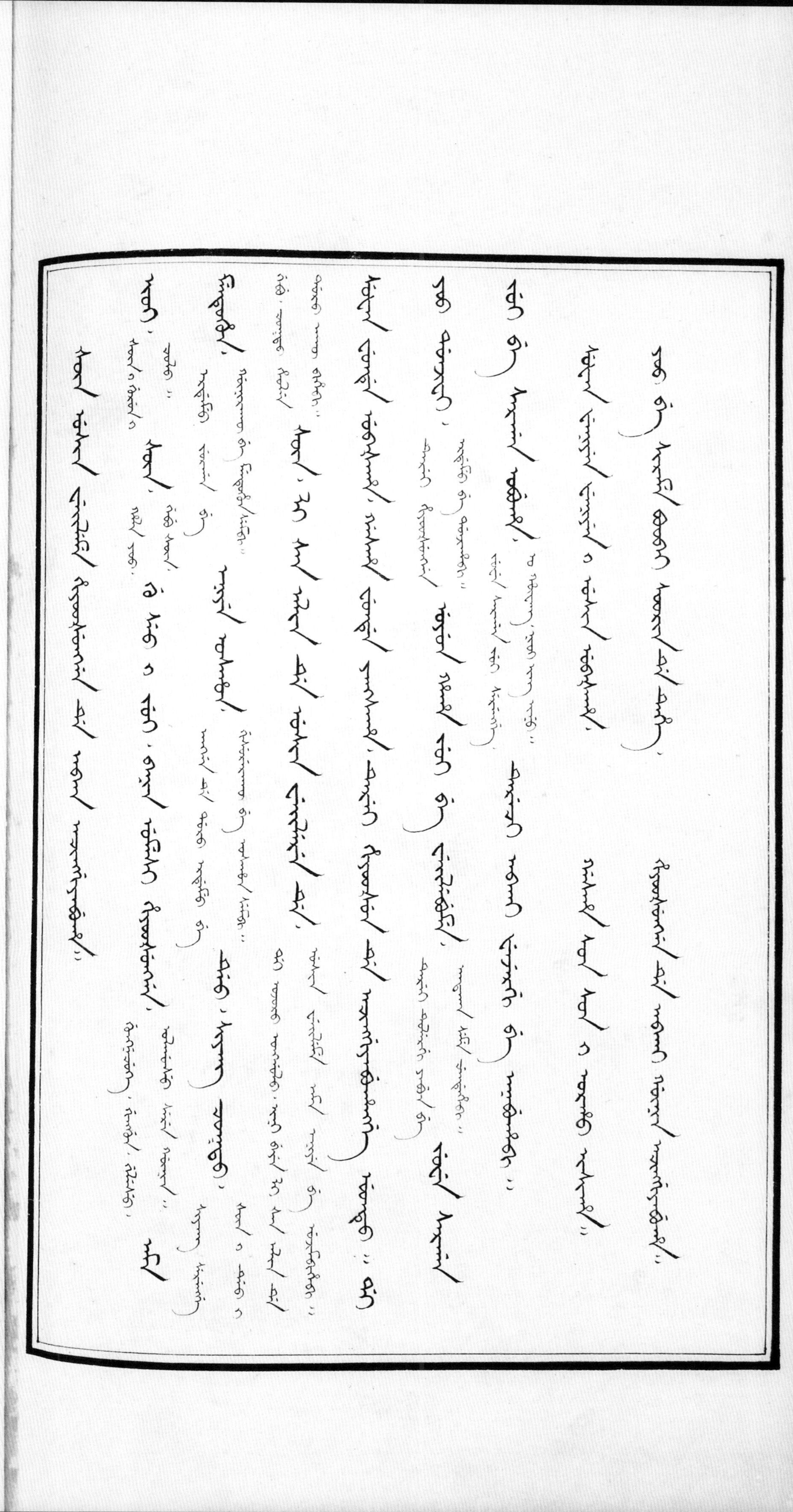

卷端
Beginning

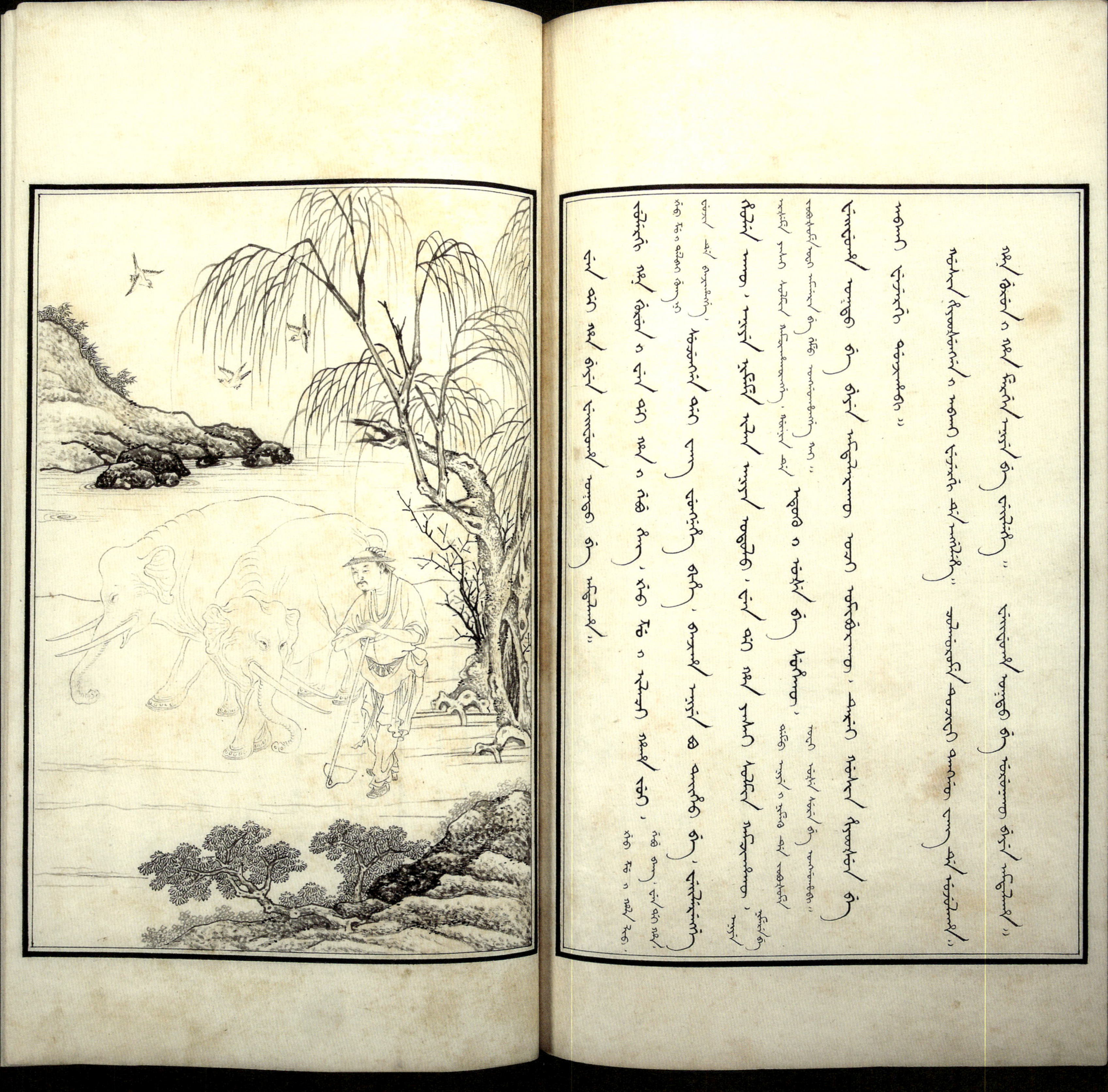

圖解 1
Illustrated explanation I

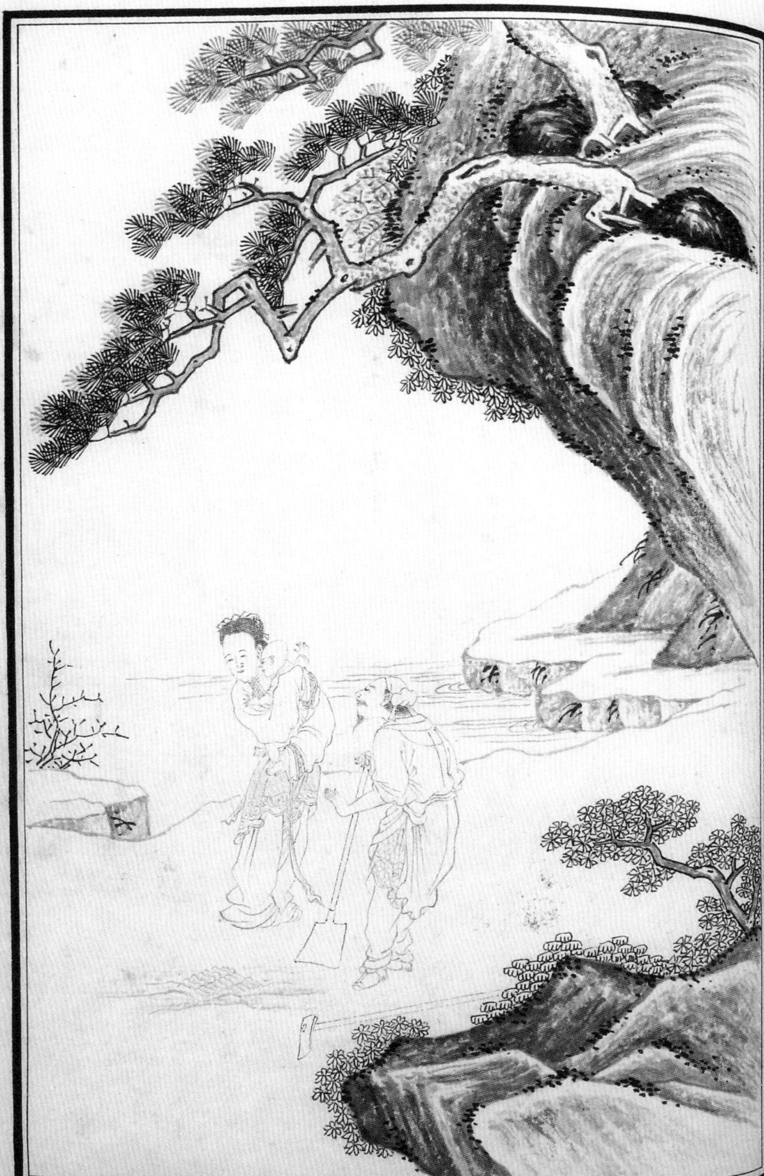

圖解 2

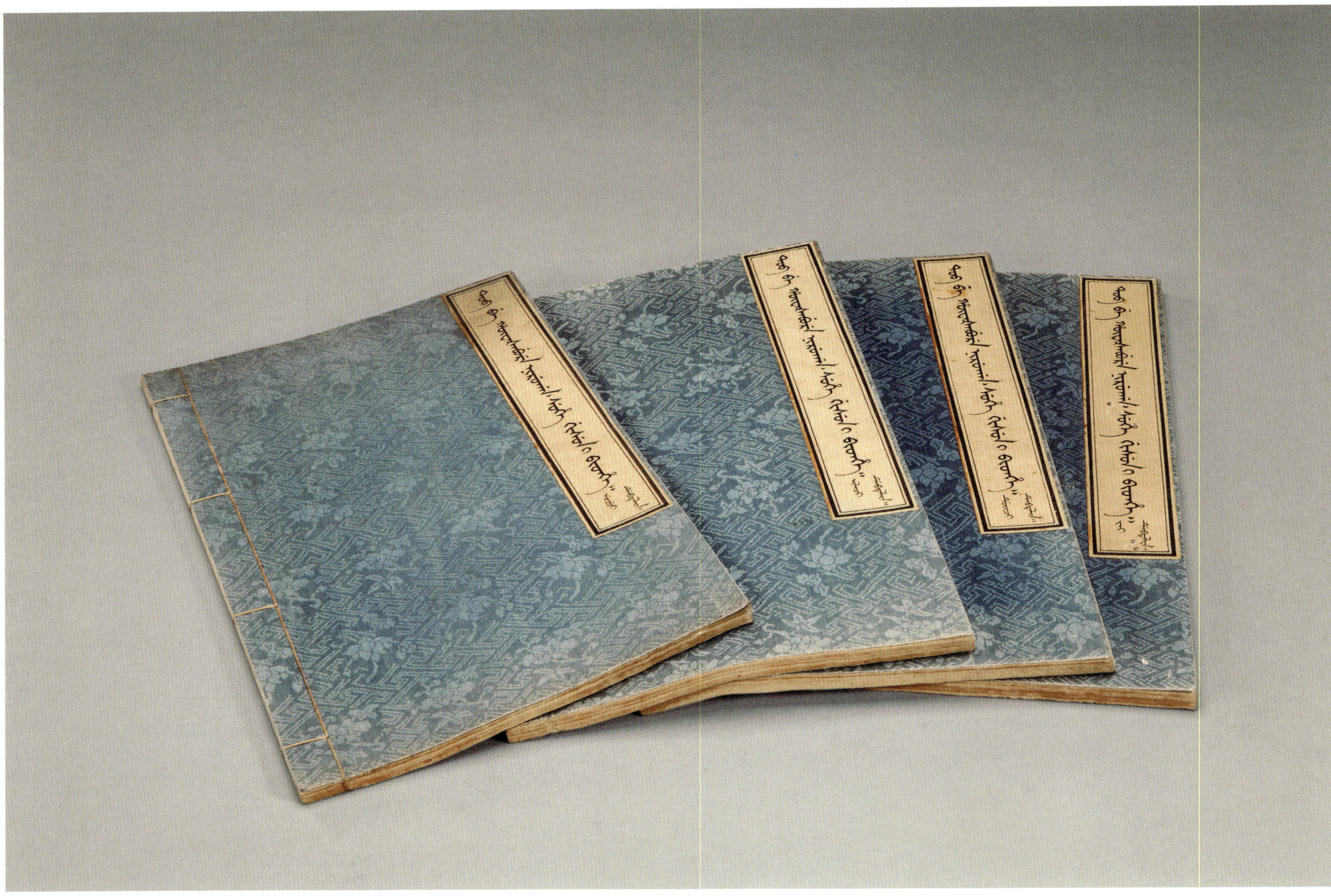

湖色曲水朵花紋暗花綾書面
Lake blue twill-weave silk covers with veiled swastika and floral pattern

77

書22211

《養正圖解四卷》

明　焦竑撰

清精寫彩繪滿文本

開本　縱35.7厘米　橫21.5厘米

版框　縱24.8厘米　橫17.9厘米

四册　一函

Inventory number: Shu 22211

Illustrated Explanation on Cultivating Propriety

Four chapters

Written by Jiao Hong, Ming dynasty (1368-1644)

Transcribed in Manchu and painted in colors in the Qing dynasty (1644-1911)

Format: 35.7 × 21.5 cm

Frame: 24.8 × 17.9 cm

Four volumes in one case

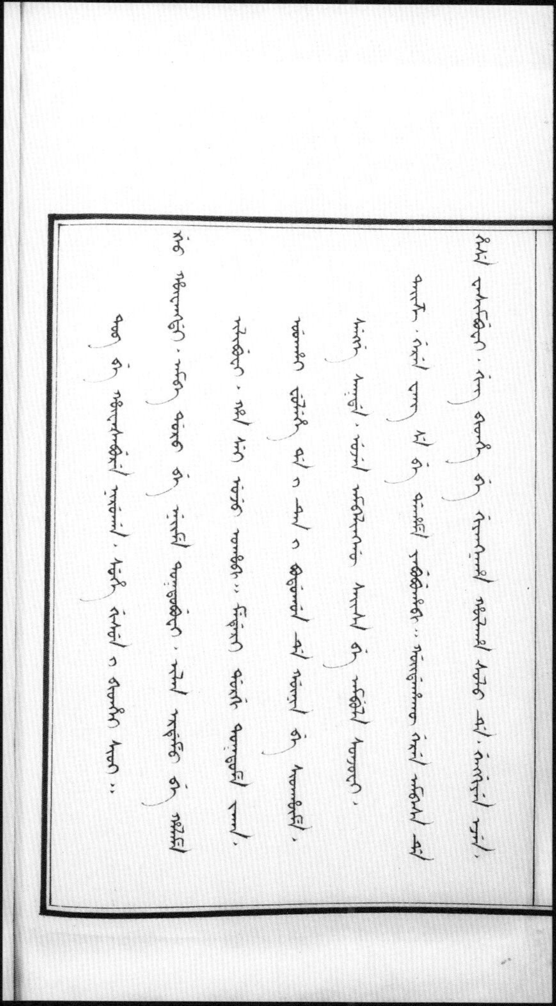

明萬曆二十五年序
Preface in 1597

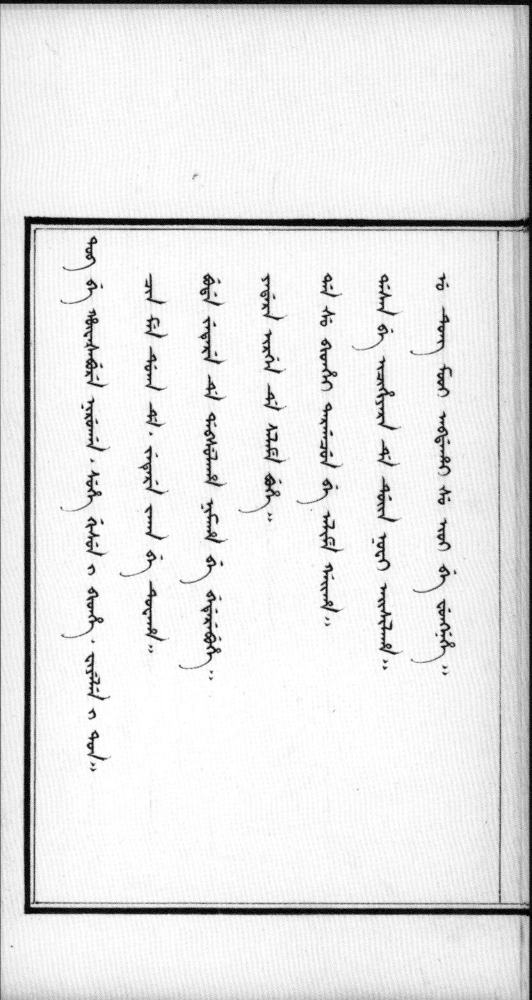

總目
Contents

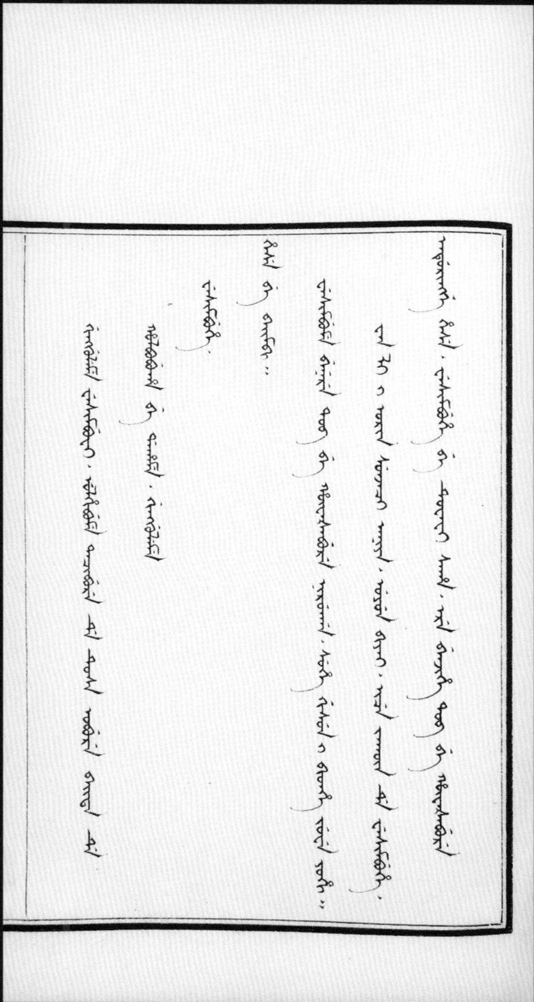

明萬曆二十五年奏
Memorial in 1597

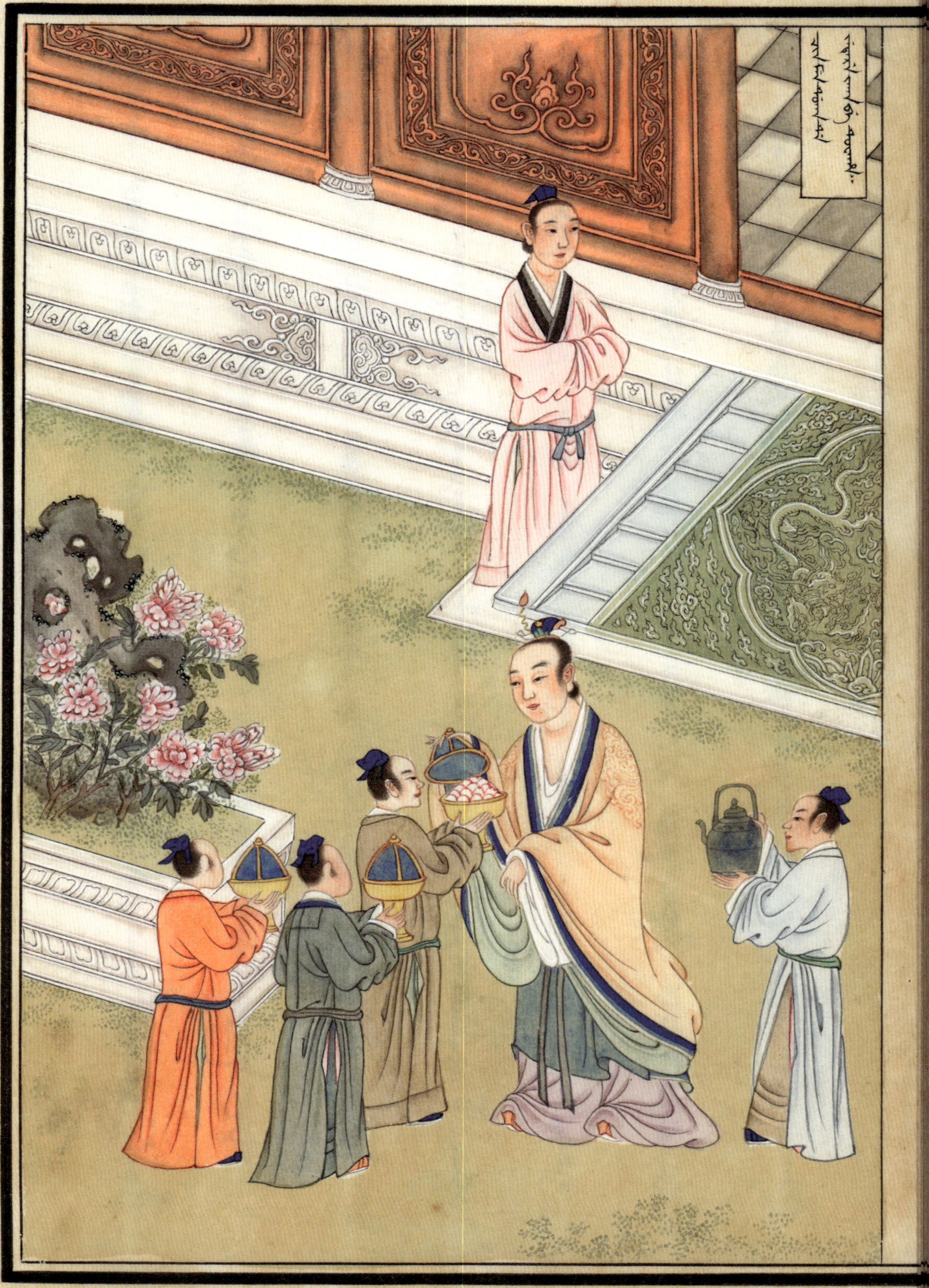

插圖
Illustration

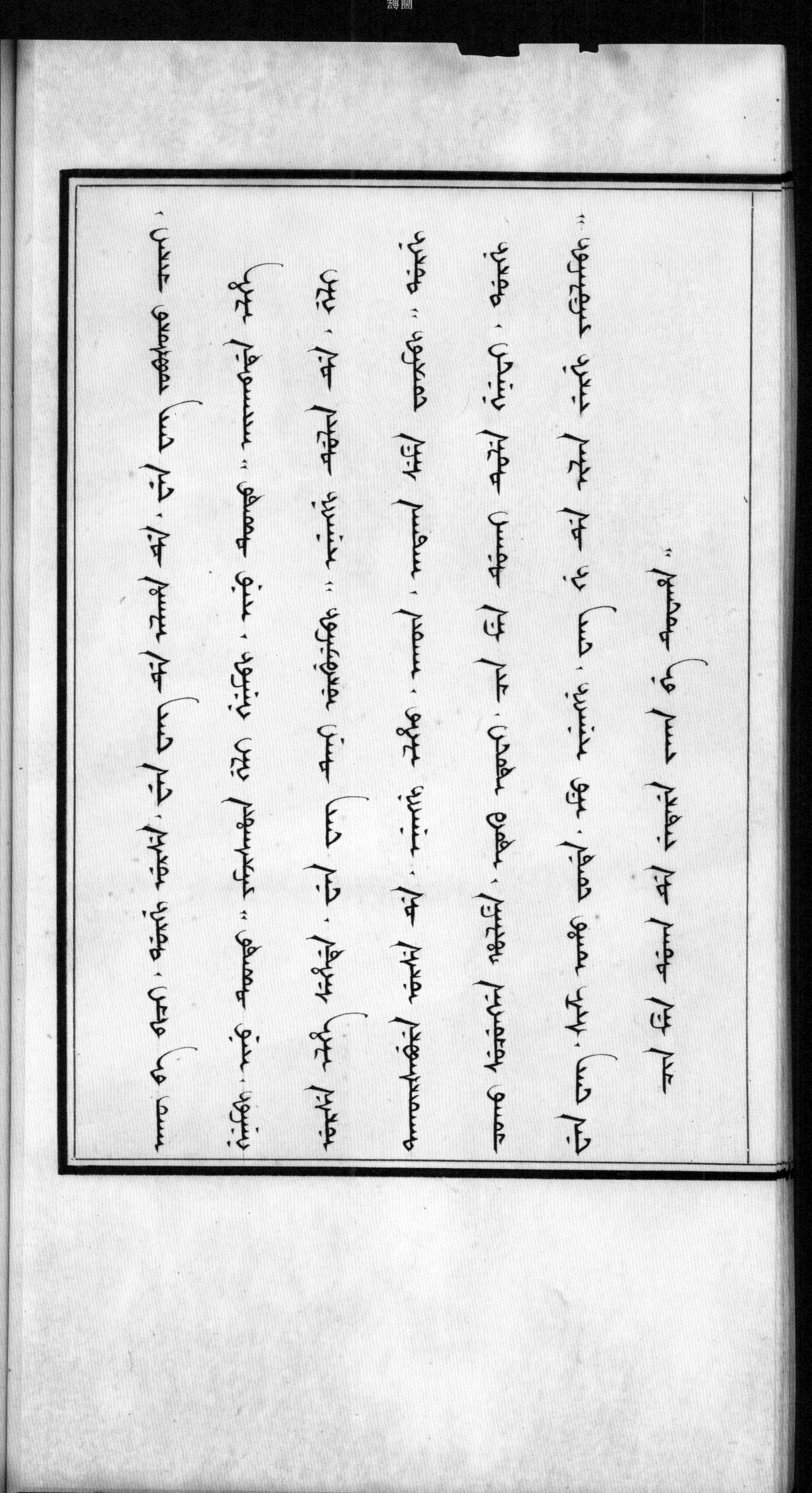

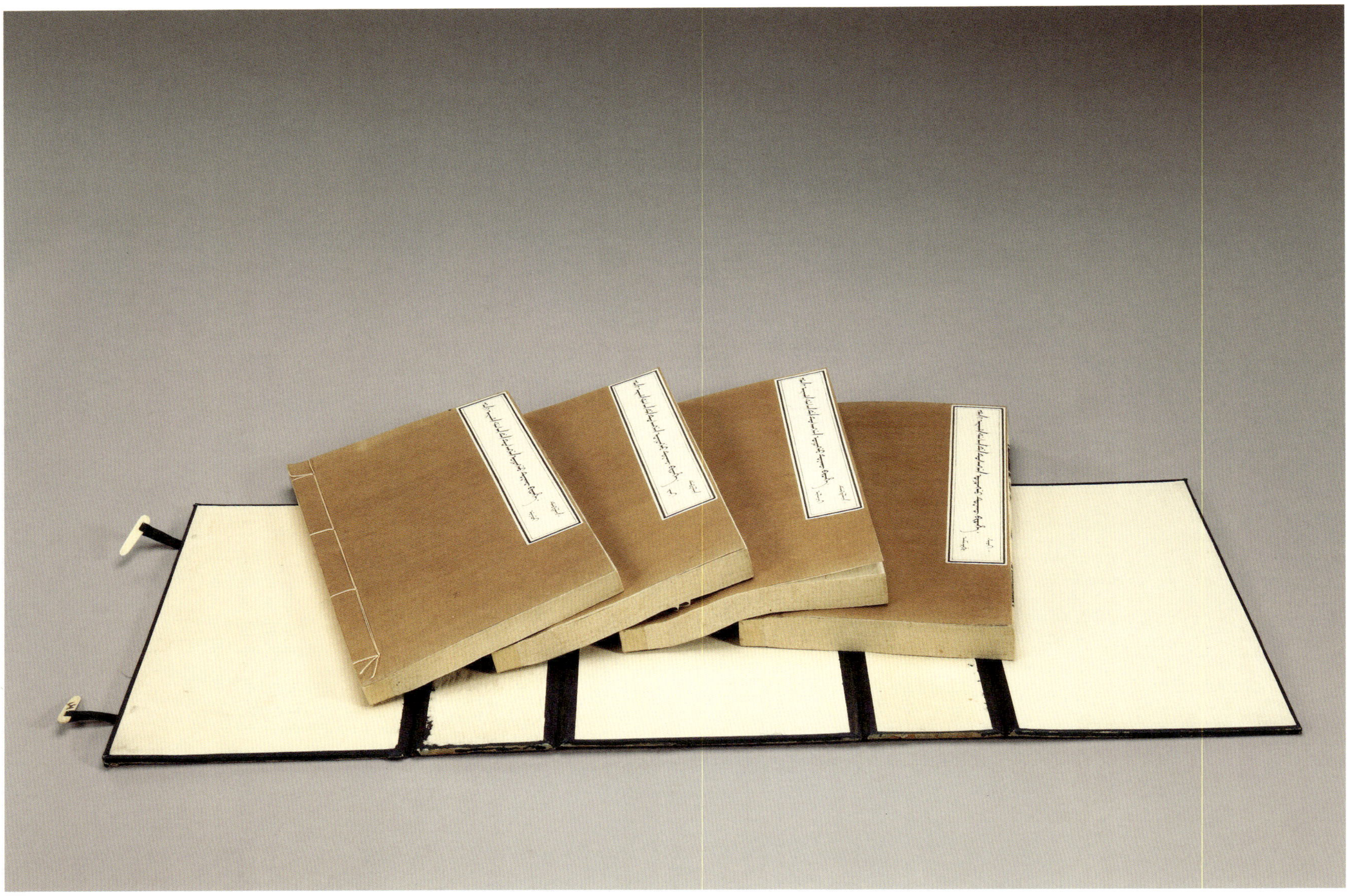

外觀
Exterior

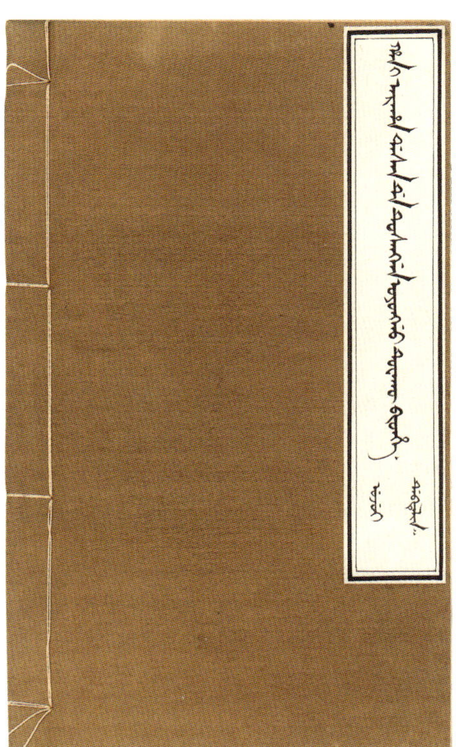

絳色紙書面
Brown paper cover

書22219
《御製資政要覽三卷後序一卷》
清　世祖福臨撰
清順治十二年（1655）內府刻滿文本
開本　縱24.5厘米　橫14.6厘米
版框　縱17.6厘米　橫12.2厘米
四冊　一函

78

Inventory number: Shu 22219
Essential Principles to Aid in Politics
Three chapters as text, one chapter as postscript
Written by the Shunzhi emperor (r.1644-1661)
Printed in Manchu in 1655 by the Qing court
Format: 24.5 × 14.6 cm
Frame: 17.6 × 12.2 cm
Four volumes in one case

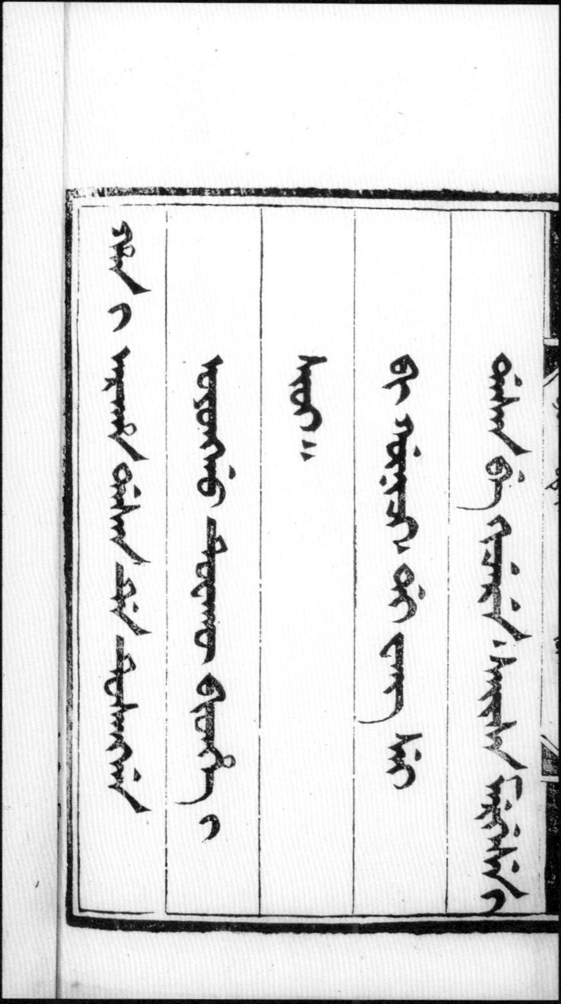

順治十二年御製序
Preface by the Shunzhi emperor in 1655

序及卷端
Preface and Beginning

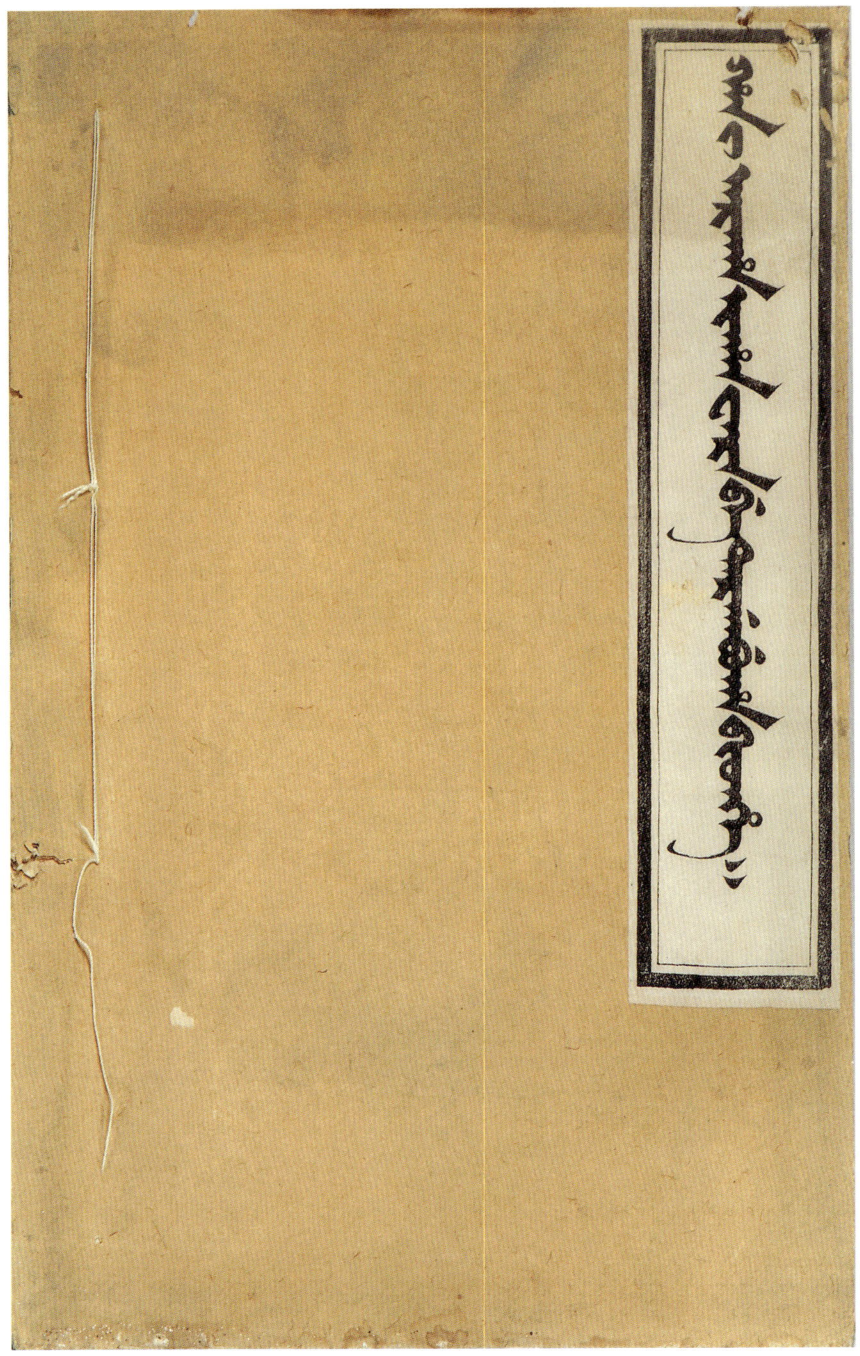

絳色紙書面
Brown paper cover

書22225
《御製牛戒一卷》
清　世祖福臨撰
清順治十三年（1656）內府刻滿文本
開本　縱33.6厘米　橫21.2厘米
版框　縱24厘米　橫16.8厘米
一册　一函

79

Inventory number: Shu 22225
Ox Commandment
One chapter
Written by the Shunzhi emperor (r.1644-1661)
Printed in Manchu in 1656 by the Qing court
Format: 33.6 × 21.2 cm
Frame: 24 × 16.8 cm
One volume in one case

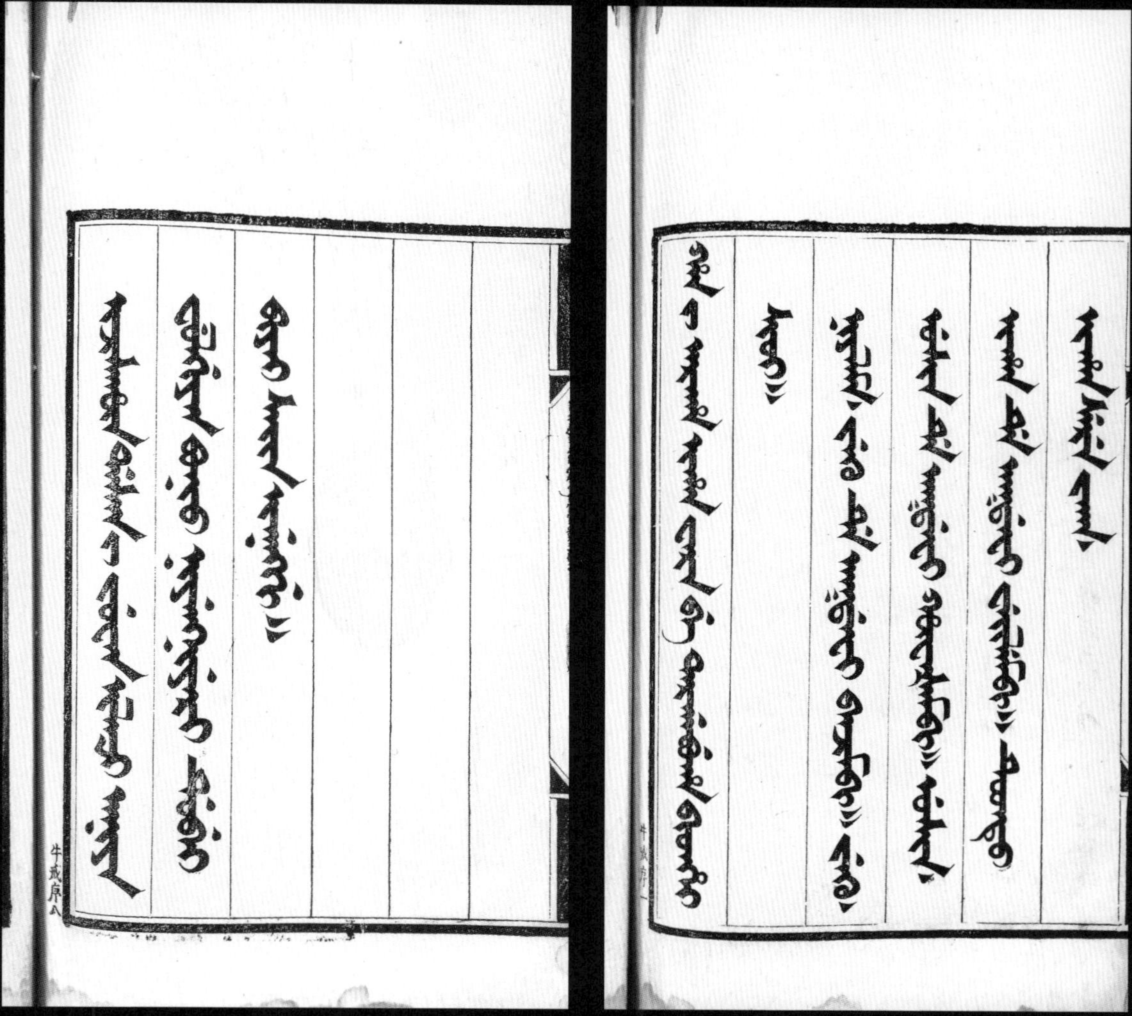

順治十三年御製序
Preface by the Shunzhi emperor in 1656

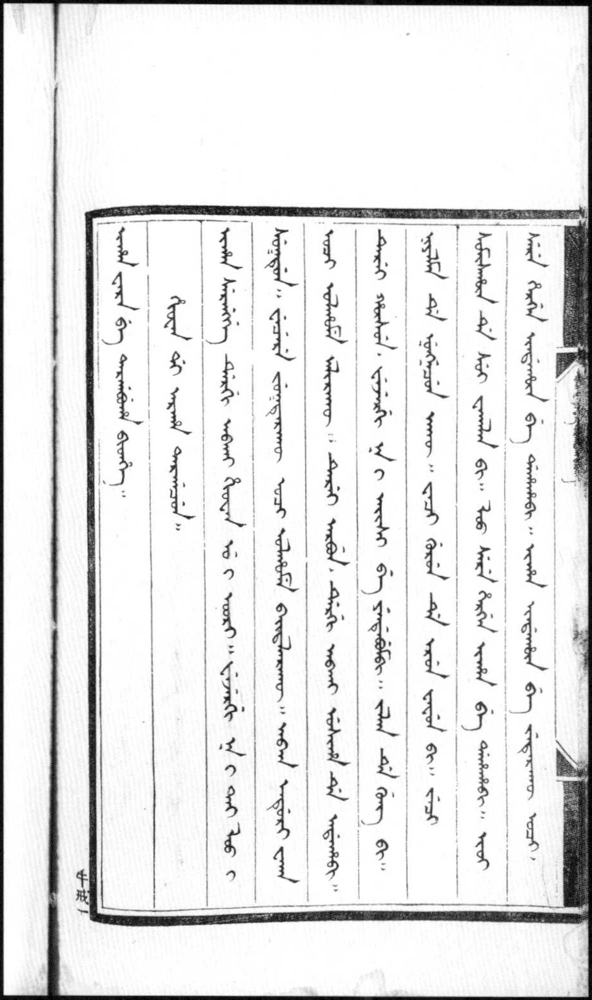

卷端
Beginning

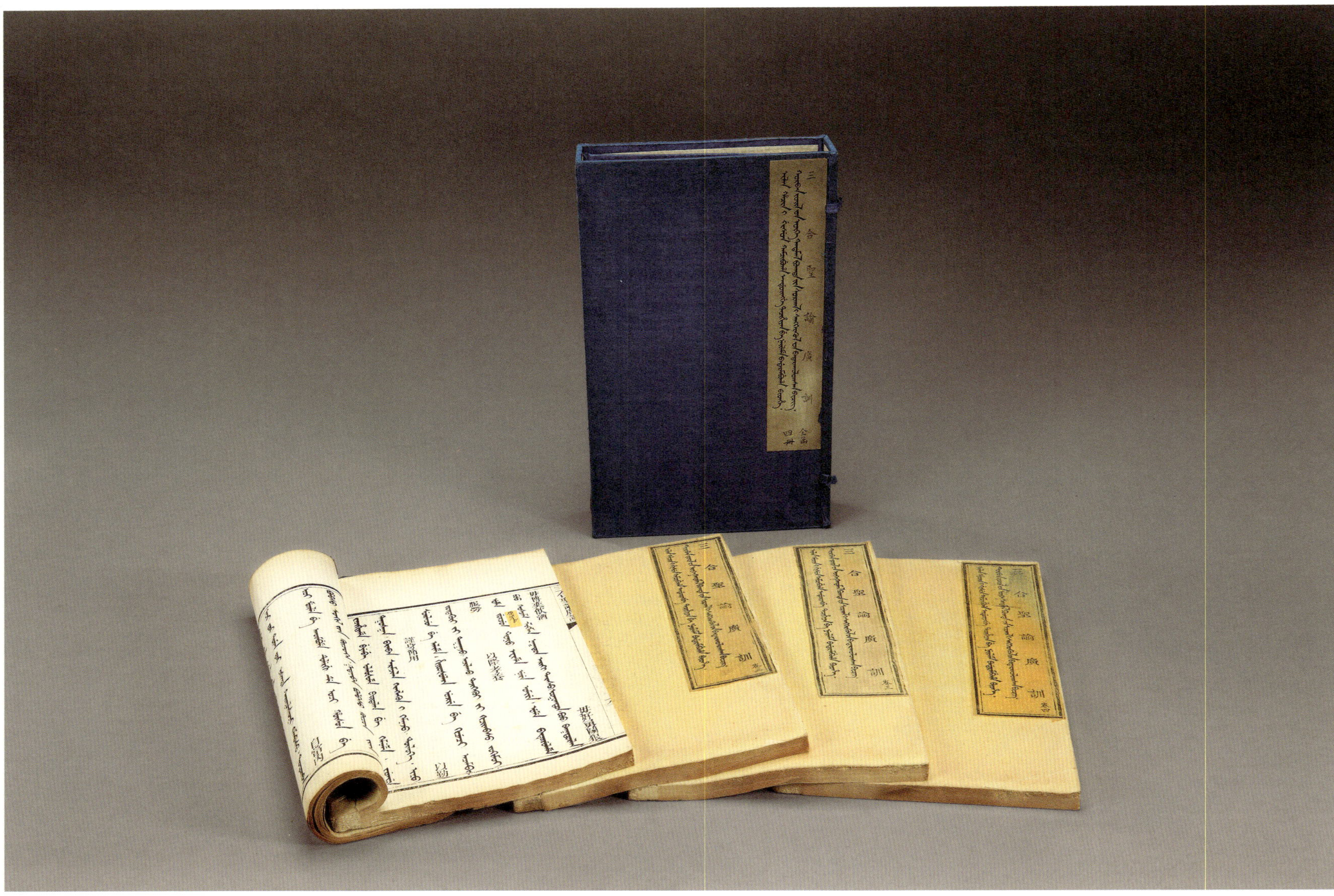

明黃色紙書面
Bright yellow paper covers

書22201
《三合聖諭廣訓四卷》
清　聖祖玄燁撰　世宗胤禛輯
清武英殿刻滿蒙漢合璧本
開本　縱30厘米　橫18.1厘米
版框　縱22.3厘米　橫15.5厘米
四冊　一函

80

Inventory number: Shu 22201
Amplified Instructions on the Sacred Edicts in Three Languages
Four chapters
Written by the Kangxi emperor (r.1662-1722), compiled by the Yongzheng emperor (r.1723-1735)
Printed in Manchu, Mongolian and Chinese at the Hall of Martial Valour
Format: 30 × 18.1 cm
Frame: 22.3 × 15.5 cm
Two volumes in one case

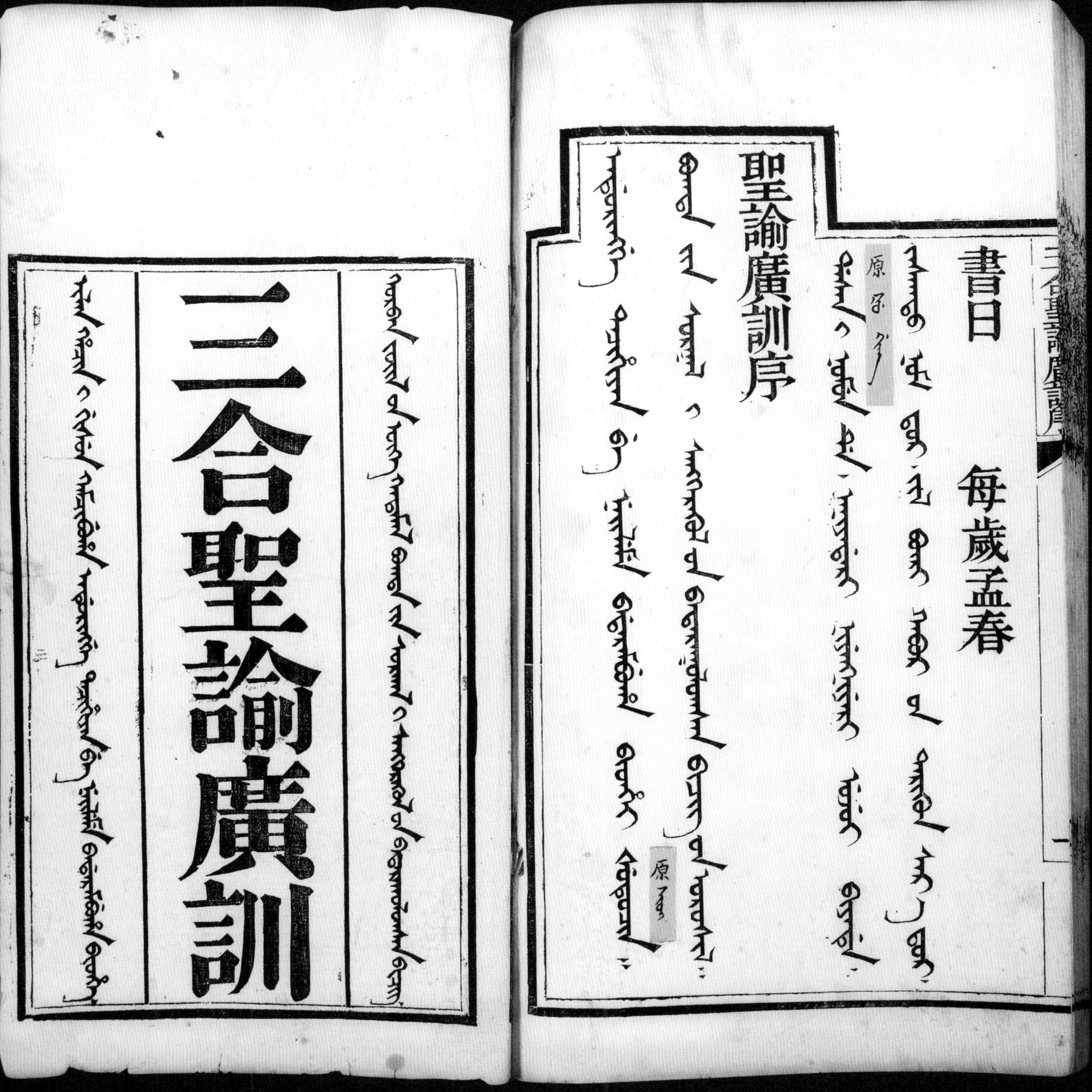

三合聖諭廣訓

聖諭廣訓序

書曰 每歲孟春

三合聖諭廣訓序

一

書名頁及雍正五年御製序
Title page and preface by the Yongzheng emperor in 1727

聖祖仁皇帝　臨御六十一年　法

我

敦孝弟以重人倫

明七教　以興民德

卷端

Beginning

首頁後篇二行末三字原 遵清語改

原

以節民性

記曰 司徒修六禮

原

原 今遵禮記新語改

遒人以木鐸徇於路

原 今遵書經新語改

原

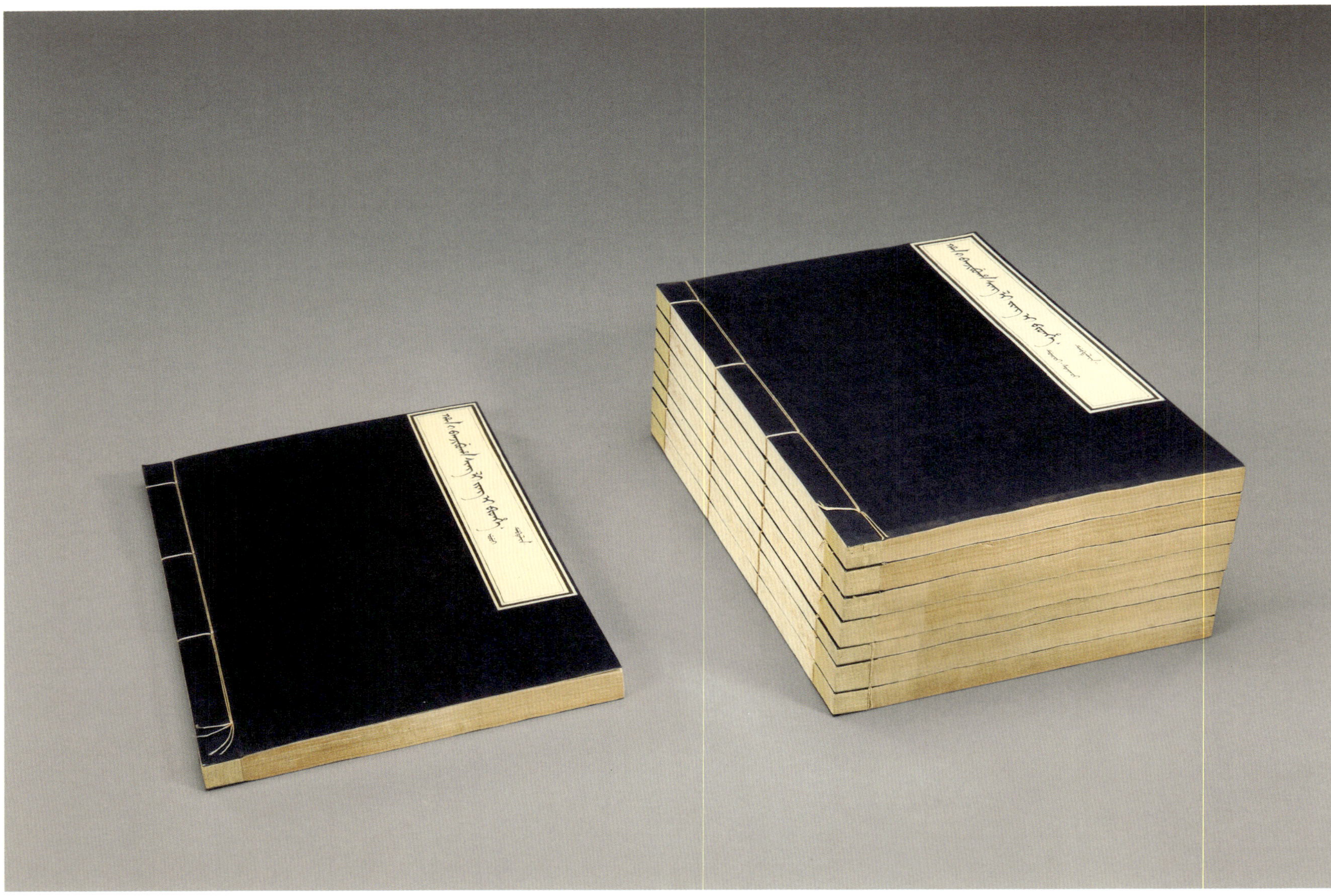

藍色素綢書面
Blue silk covers

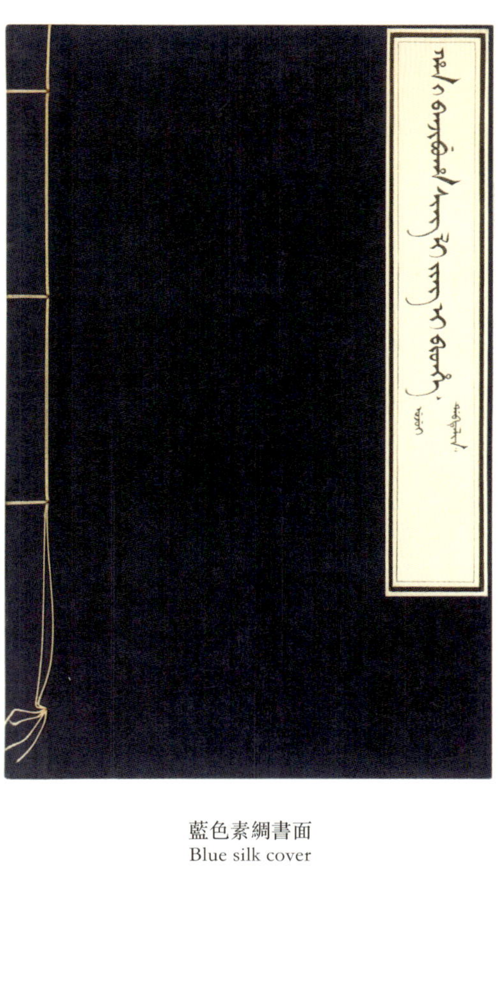

藍色素綢書面
Blue silk cover

書13448
《御纂性理精義十二卷》
清　李光地等奉敕纂
清康熙五十六年（1717）武英殿刻滿文本
開本　縱30.3厘米　橫19.8厘米
版框　縱21.4厘米　橫16.6厘米
八冊　一函

81

Inventory number: Shu 13448
Essence of Nature and Rationality
Twelve chapters
Compiled by imperial order by Li Guangdi et. al., Qing dynasty (1644-1911)
Printed in Manchu in 1717 at the Hall of Martial Valour
Format: 30.3 × 19.8 cm
Frame: 21.4 × 16.6 cm
Eight volumes in one case

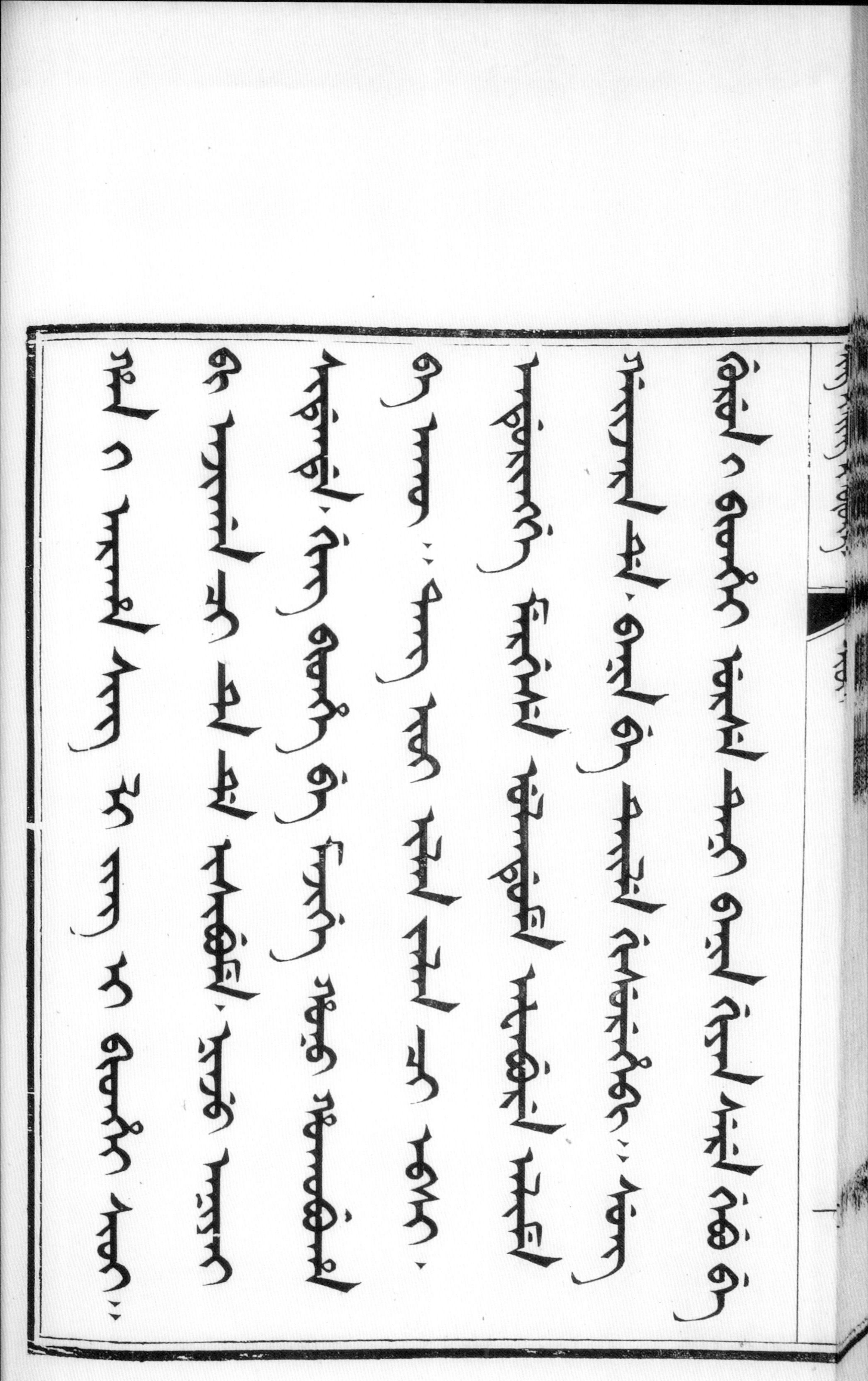

康熙五十六年御製序
Preface by the Kangxi emperor in 1717

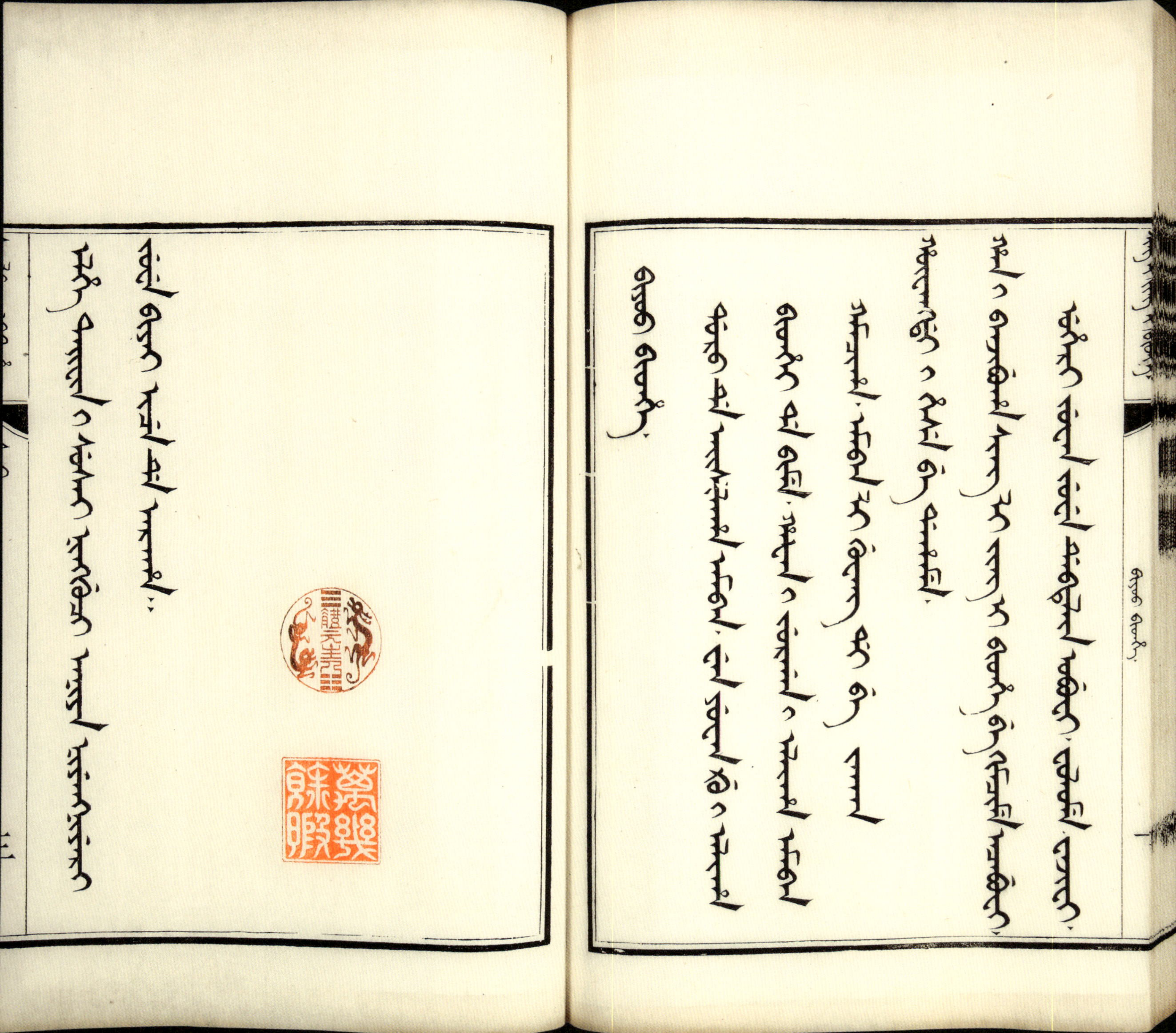

康熙五十六年序及李光地表
Preface in 1717 and Memorial by Li Guangdi

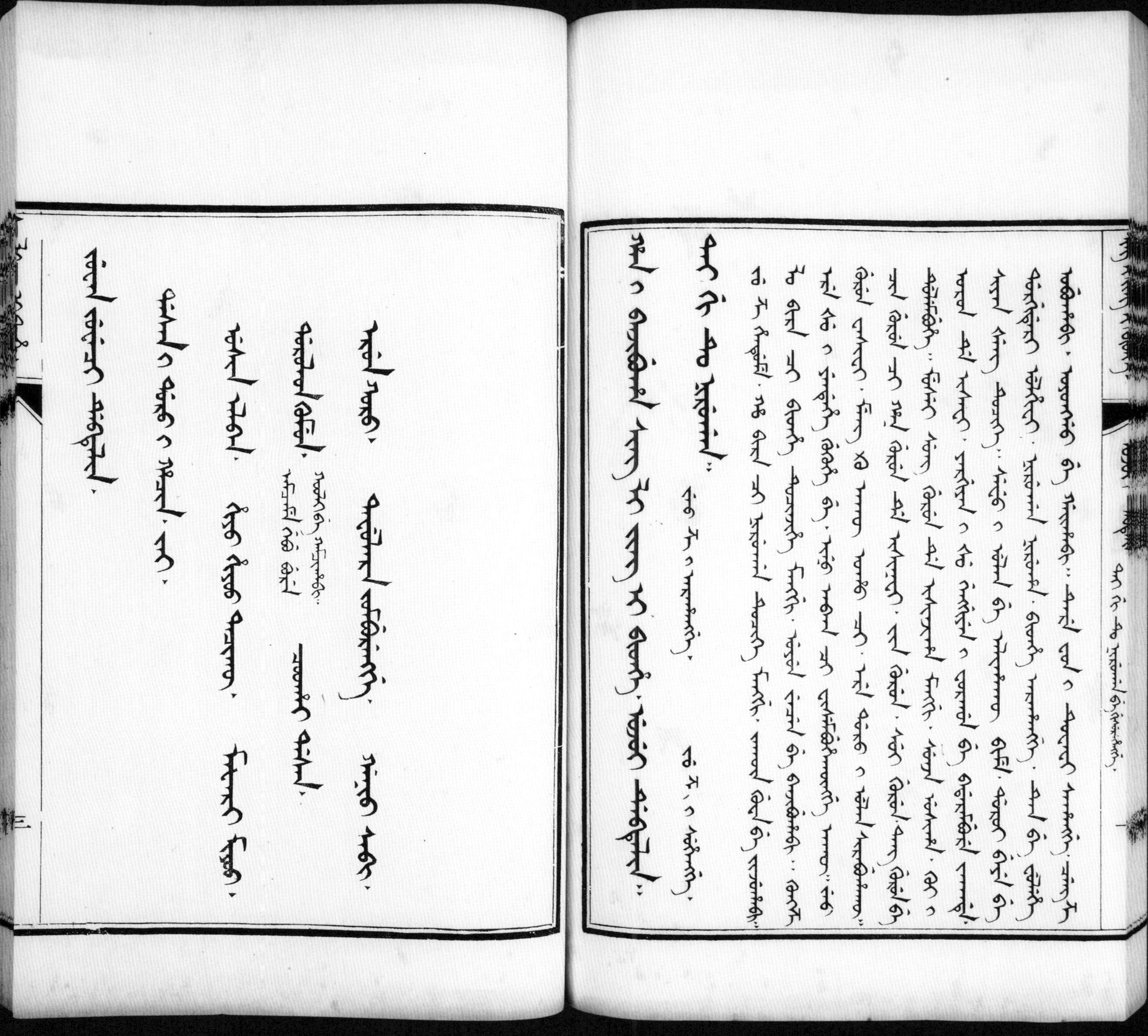

目録及卷端
Contents and Beginning

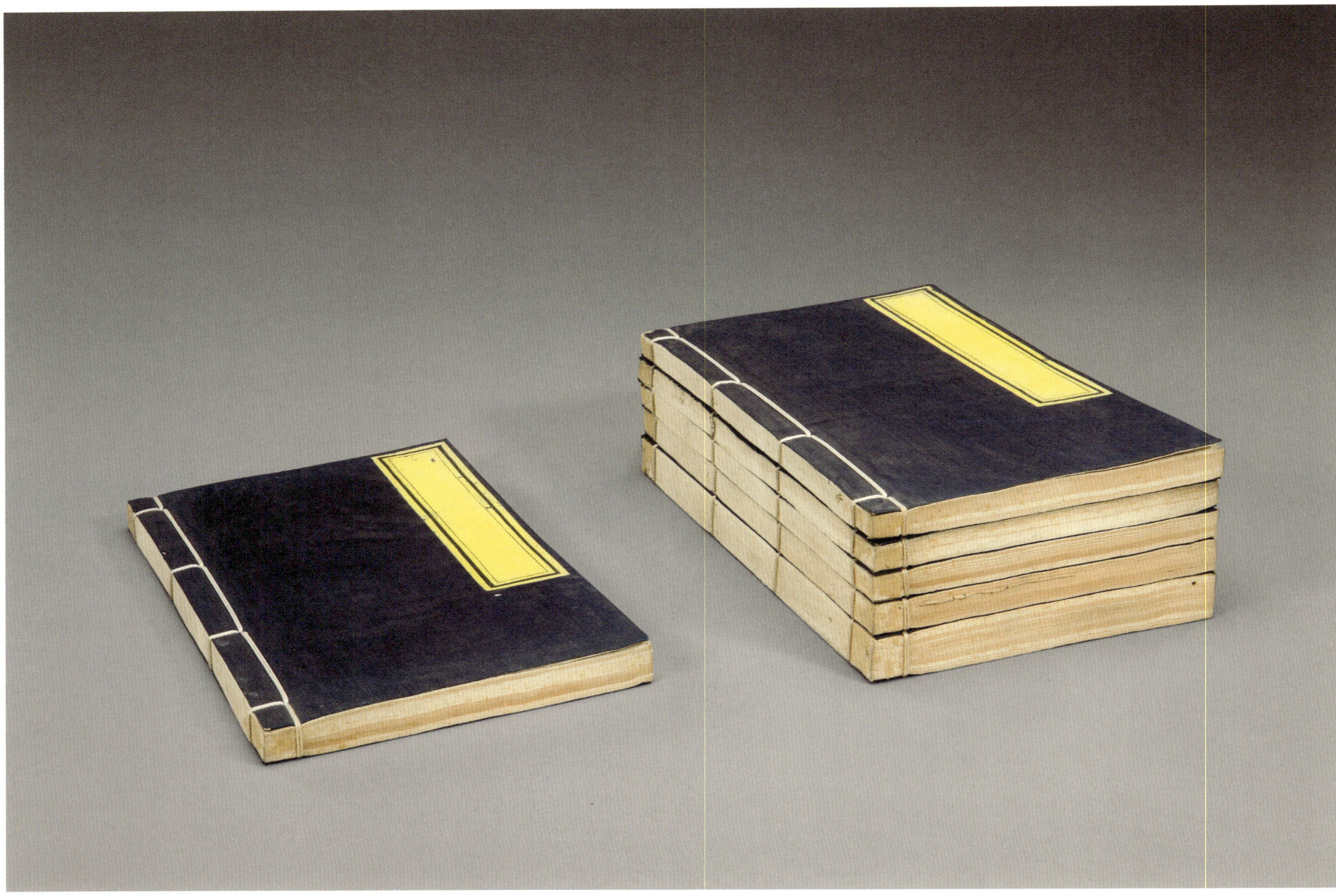

藍色素絹書面
Blue silk covers

書22173
《翻譯大學衍義四十三卷首一卷》
宋　真德秀撰　清　孟保等譯
清咸豐六年（1856）武英殿刻滿漢合璧本
開本　縱26.2厘米　橫15.6厘米
版框　縱19.2厘米　橫14.2厘米
五十一册　十函

82

Inventory number: Shu 22173
Exposition of the Great Learning
Forty-three chapters as text, one chapter as preliminary remarks
Written by Zhen Dexiu, Song dynasty (960-1279)
Translated by Mengbao et. al., Qing dynasty (1644-1911)
Printed in Manchu and Chinese in 1856 at the Hall of Martial Valour
Format: 26.2 × 15.6 cm
Frame: 19.2 × 14.2 cm
Fifty-one volumes in ten cases

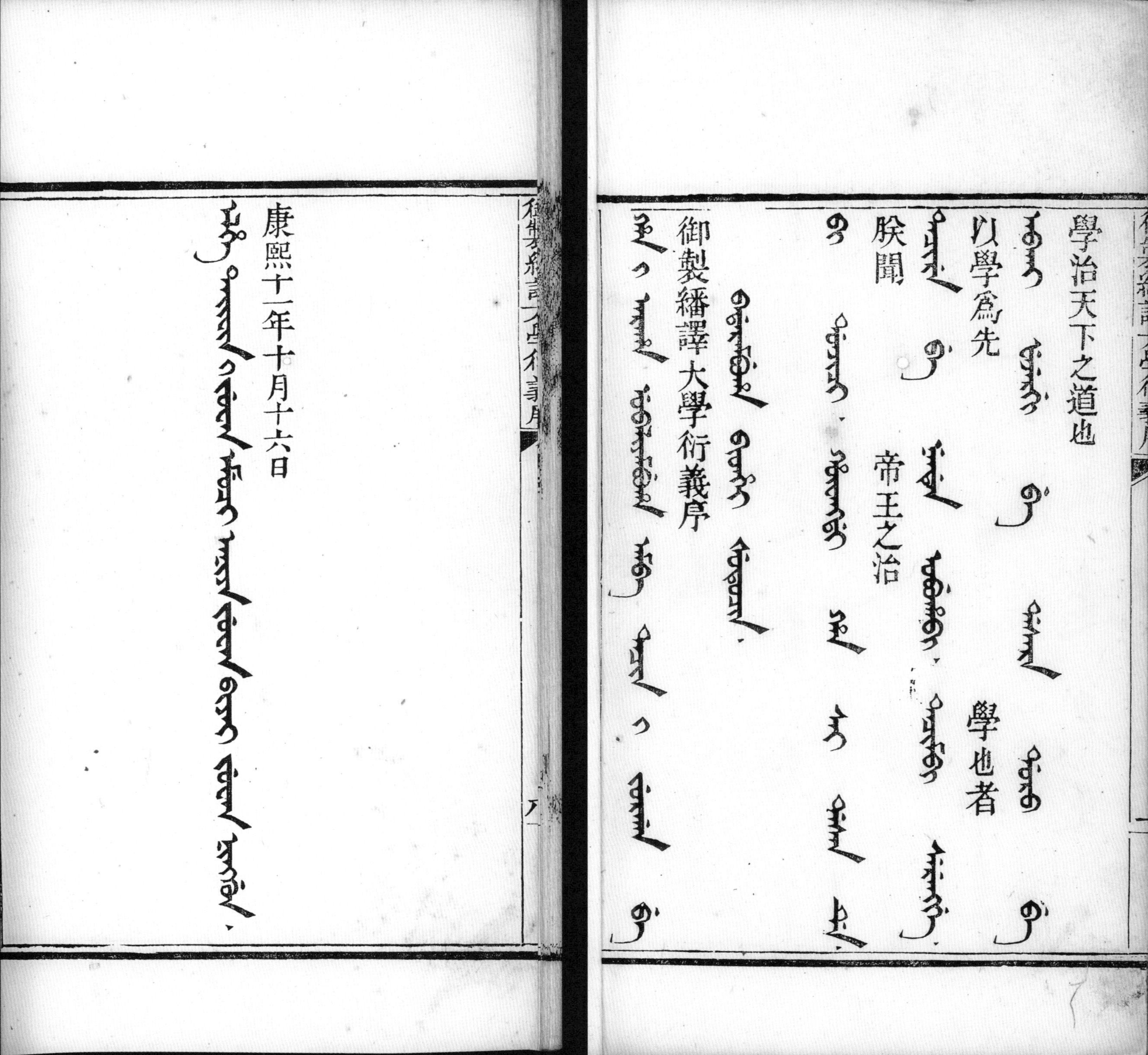

御製繙譯大學衍義序

康熙十一年十月十六日

御製繙譯大學衍義序

朕聞帝王之治

以學爲先　學也者

學治天下之道也

康熙十一年御製序

Preface by the Kangxi emperor in 1672

咸豐六年九月二十三日內閣奉

上諭

前據大學士文慶等

進呈前任巴里坤領隊大臣三等侍衛孟保繙

譯大學衍義一書

咸豐六年上諭

Imperial edict in 1856

大學衍義卷之一

帝王爲治之序

堯典 虞書篇名

典者常也

曰若稽古帝堯曰放勳

欽明文思安安允恭

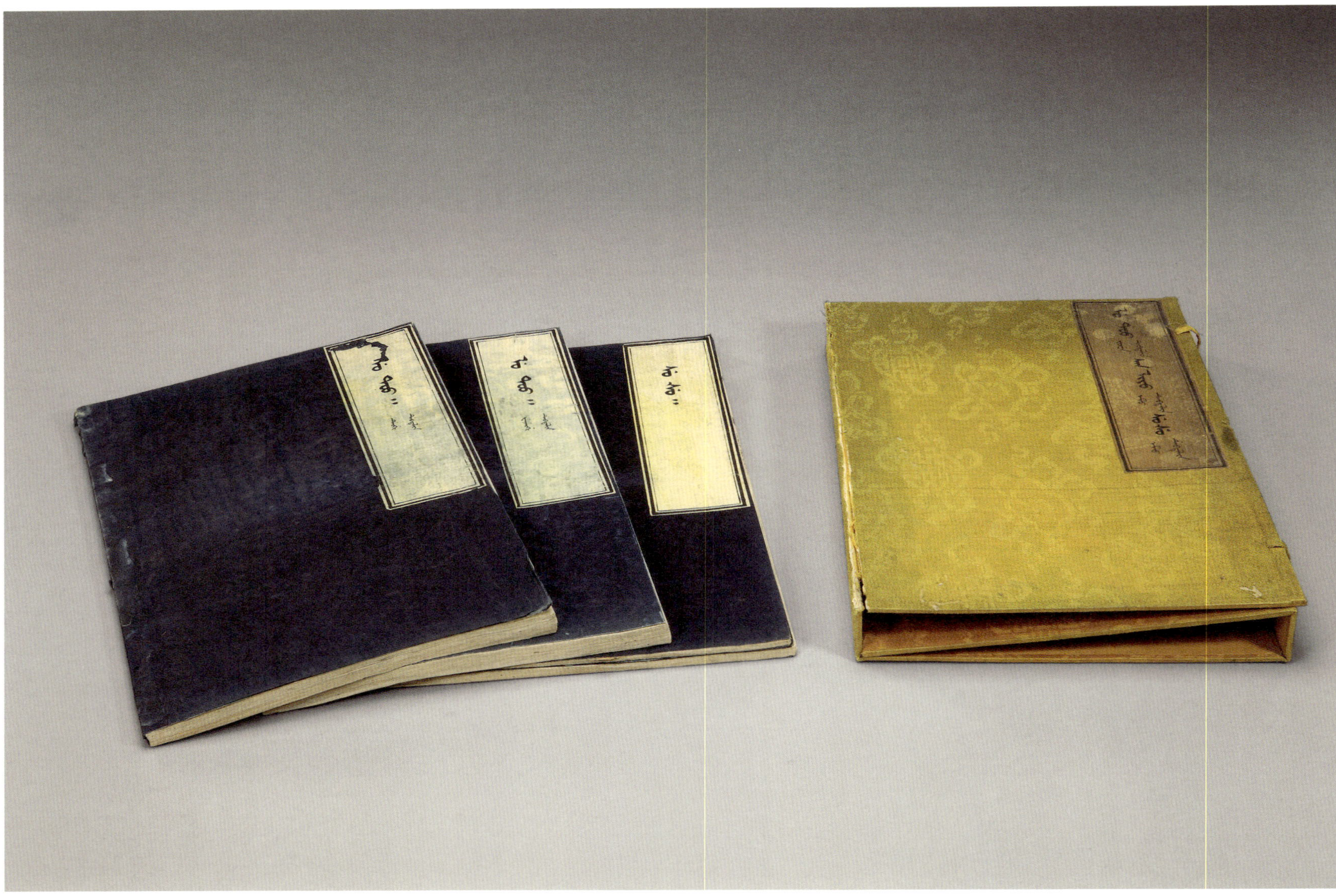

外觀
Exterior

藍色素纸書面
Blue paper cover

83

書22153

《素書一卷》

舊題秦　黄石公撰　宋　張商英注　清　達海等譯
清初精寫滿文本
開本　縱37.7厘米　橫23.8厘米
版框　縱30.5厘米　橫21.5厘米
一册（與《三略》、《六韜》合函）

Inventory number: Shu 22153

Pure Book

One chapter
Attributed to Huangshigong, Qin dynasty (221 BCE-206 BCE)
Annotated by Zhang Shangying, Song dynasty (960-1279)
Translated by Dahai et. al., Qing dynasty (1644-1911)
Transcribed in Manchu in the early Qing dynasty
Format: 37.7 × 23.8 cm
Frame: 30.5 × 21.5 cm
One volume, sharing the same case with *Three Military Strategies* and *Six Military Principles*

ᠨᡳᡴᠠᠨ ᡳ [illegible] ᠉ [illegible] [illegible] ᠉ [illegible] [illegible] ᠨᡳᡴᠠᠨ ᡳ [illegible]

[illegible] [illegible] ᠉ [illegible] [illegible] ᠉ [illegible] ᠉ [illegible] [illegible] [illegible] ᠪᡝ [illegible]

[illegible] ᠉ [illegible] [illegible] ᠨᡳᡴᠠᠨ [illegible] [illegible] ᠉ [illegible] [illegible] [illegible]

ᠨᡳᡴᠠᠨ ᡳ [illegible] [illegible] [illegible] [illegible] [illegible] [illegible] ᠉ [illegible] [illegible] [illegible]

[illegible] [illegible] ᠉ [illegible] ᠪᡝ [illegible] [illegible] [illegible] ᠪᡝ [illegible] ᠉ [illegible] [illegible] ᠈

ᠨᡳᡴᠠᠨ ᡳ [illegible] ᠈ [illegible] [illegible] ᠉ [illegible] ᠪᡝ [illegible] ᠪᡝ [illegible] ᠉ [illegible]

ᠨᡳᡴᠠᠨ ᡳ [illegible] ᠈ [illegible] ᠉ [illegible] [illegible] [illegible] [illegible] [illegible] [illegible] [illegible]

[illegible] ᠪᡝ [illegible] [illegible] ᠉

藍色紙書面
Blue paper cover

書22154
《三略一卷》
秦　黃石公撰　清　達海等譯
清初精寫滿文本
開本　縱37.7厘米　橫23.5厘米
版框　縱30.5厘米　橫21.5厘米
一冊（與《素書》、《六韜》合函）

84

Inventory number: Shu 22154
Three Military Strategies
One chapter
Written by Huangshigong, Qin dynasty (221 BCE-206 BCE)
Translated by Dahai et. al., Qing dynasty (1644-1911)
Transcribed in Manchu in the early Qing dynasty
Format: 37.7 × 23.5 cm
Frame: 30.5 × 21.5 cm
One volume, sharing the same case with *Pure Book* and *Six Military Principles*

ᠪᠣᡳᡥᠣᠨ ᡤᡳᠰᡠᡵᡝᡵᡝ ᠰᠠᡳᠨ ᠪᠣᡳᡥᠣᠨ᠉ ᠮᡝᠩᡤᡝ ᡳᠯᡳᡥᠠ ᡨᡠᡴᡳᠶᡝᡥᡝ ᡳ ᡩᡝᡵᡤᡳᠯᡝᠮᠪᡳ᠉

ᠨᡳᠩᡤᡠᠨ ᠪᠣᡳᡥᠣᠨ

ᠨᠣᠨᡤᡳᡥᠠ ᡳ ᠪᡳᠶᠠ ᡳ ᡝᡳᡥᡝᡨᡝᡴᡝ ᠪᡝᡳᡥᡝᡨᡝᡴᡝ ᡝᡵᡤᡳ ᡩᡝ ᠪᡳᠶᠠ ᡩᡝ ᠪᡳᡥᡝ᠉

ᠪᠣᡴᠣᠰᠣ ᠮᡠᡩᡝᠨ ᡳᠰᡳᠨᠠᡵᠠ ᠪᠠᡳᠮᡝ ᡳ ᡳᠴᡝᡥᡝᠩᡤᡝ

ᠨᠣᠨᡤᡳᡥᠠ ᡳ ᠪᡳᠶᠠ ᡳ ᡠᠵᡠ ᡳᠨᡝᠩᡤᡳ᠉

ᠰᡠᡵᡝᡥᡝ ᠪᠣᡳᡥᠣᠨ

ᡨᡝᡵᡝ ᡨᡠᠸᠠᡴᡳᠶᠠᡵᡳ ᡳ ᠪᡝᡳᡥᡝ ᡳᠴᡝᡥᡝᠩᡤᡝ᠉ ᡳᠴᡝᡨᡠᠸᠠ ᠪᠣᡥᠣᠨ ᡤᡝᡵᡝᠨ ᡨᡠᠸᠠᡵᠠ ᡩᡝ ᡳᠴᡝᠮᠪᡳ᠉ ᡨᡝᡵᡝ

ᡳᠴᡝᡥᡝᠩᡤᡝ ᡩᡝ ᡤᡡᠸᠠᠯᡳᠶᠠ ᡴᠣᡳᠮᠪᡠᡥᡝ᠉ ᡨᡝᡵᡝ ᡩᡝ ᡨᡝᡵᡝ ᡩᡝ ᡳᠴᡝᡨᡠᠸᠠᠮᠪᡳ᠉ ᠪᠣᡴᠣᠰᠣ ᡨᡝᡵᡝ ᡳ ᠪᡳᠶᠠ ᠪᡝᡥᡝ ᡩᡝ

ᠨᡳᠯᡝ ᠮᡠᡩᡝᠨ ᡤᡝᠮᡠᡥᡝᠨᠪᡳ ᠠᡴᡡ᠉ ᡨᡝᡵᡝ ᡳ ᠪᡳᠶᠠ ᡳᠴᡝᡥᡝᠩᡤᡝ ᡩᡝ ᠨᡳᠯᡝ ᠮᡠᡩᡝᠨ ᡥᡝᡵᡤᡝᠨᡳᠩᡤᡝ ᠠᡴᡡ᠉

ᡨᡝ ᠵᠠᠯᡳ ᠵᠠᠯᡳ

ᡝᠯᡝᡥᡝ ᡳ ᠪᠣᠣ᠉

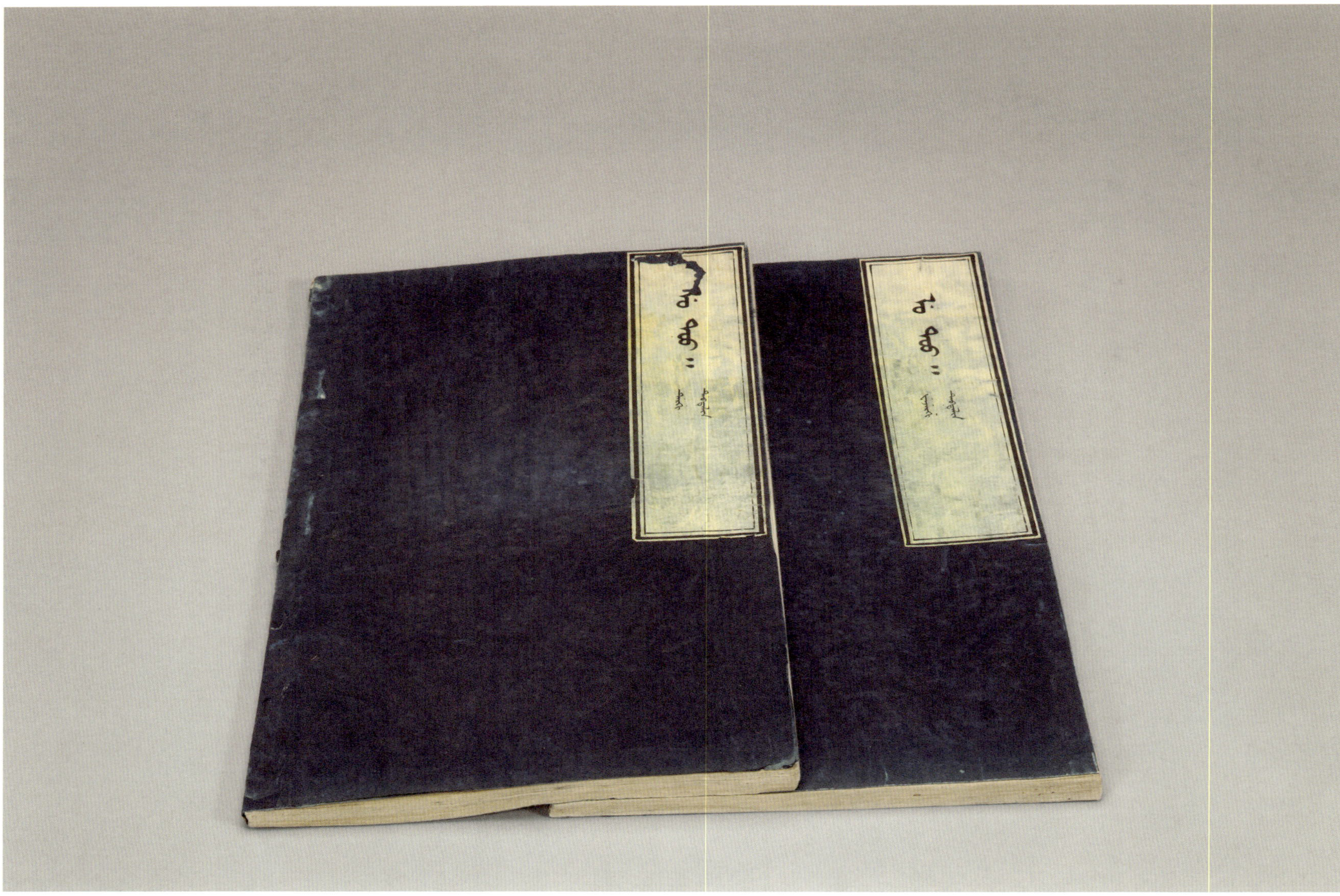

藍色紙書面
Blue paper covers

藍色紙書面
Blue paper cover

85

書22155

《六韜二卷》

周　吕望撰　清　達海等譯
清初精寫滿文本
開本　縱37.5厘米　橫23.5厘米
版框　縱30.5厘米　橫21.5厘米
二册（与《素書》、《三略》合函）

Inventory number: Shu 22155

Six Military Principles

Two chapters
Written by Lü Wang, Zhou dynasty (1046BEC-256BEC)
Translated by Dahai et. al., Qing dynasty (1644-1911)
Transcribed in Manchu in the early Qing dynasty
Format: 37.5 × 23.5 cm
Frame: 30.5 × 21.5 cm
Two volumes, sharing the same case with *Pure Book* and *Three Military Strategies*

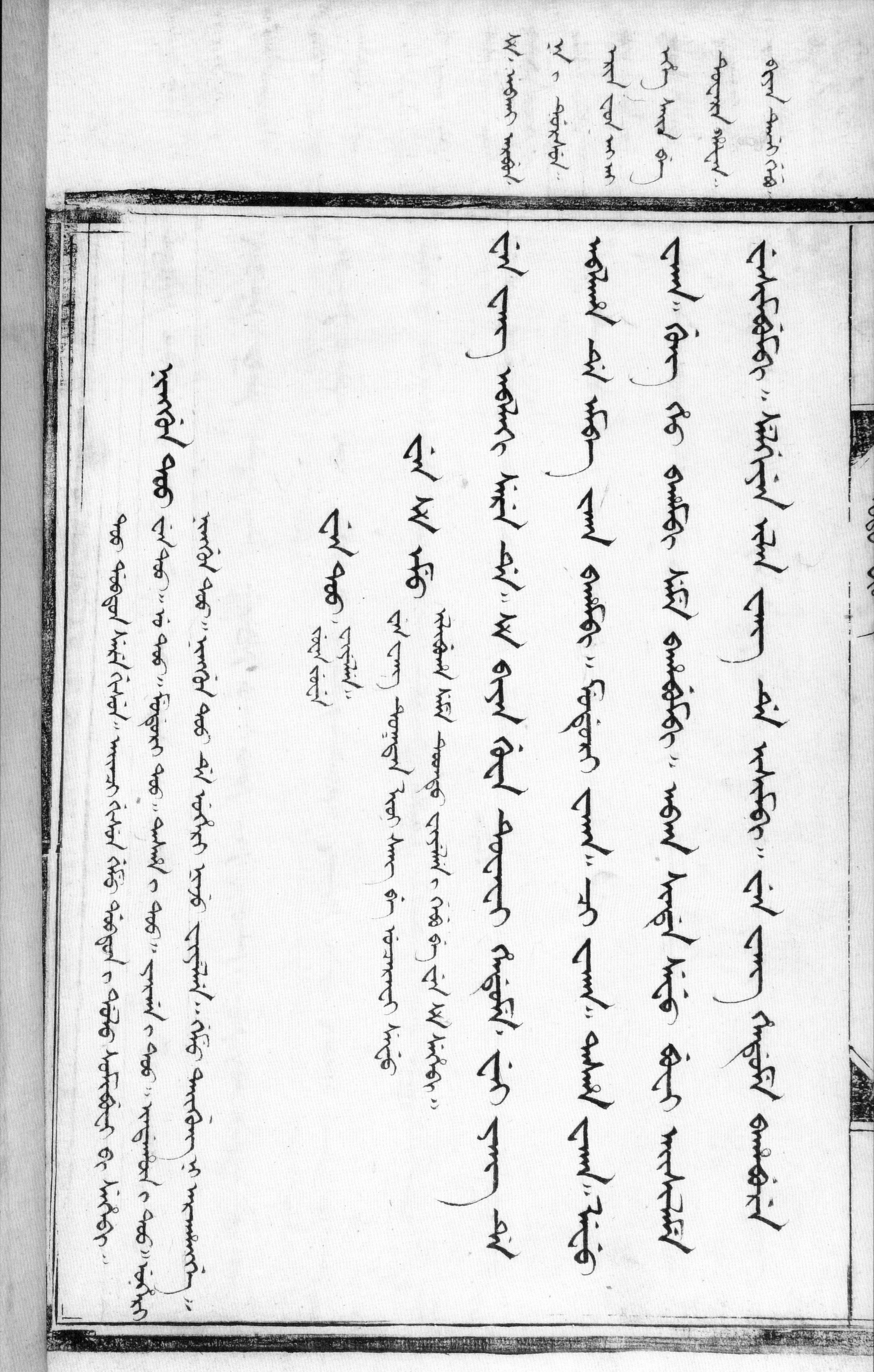

卷端
Beginning

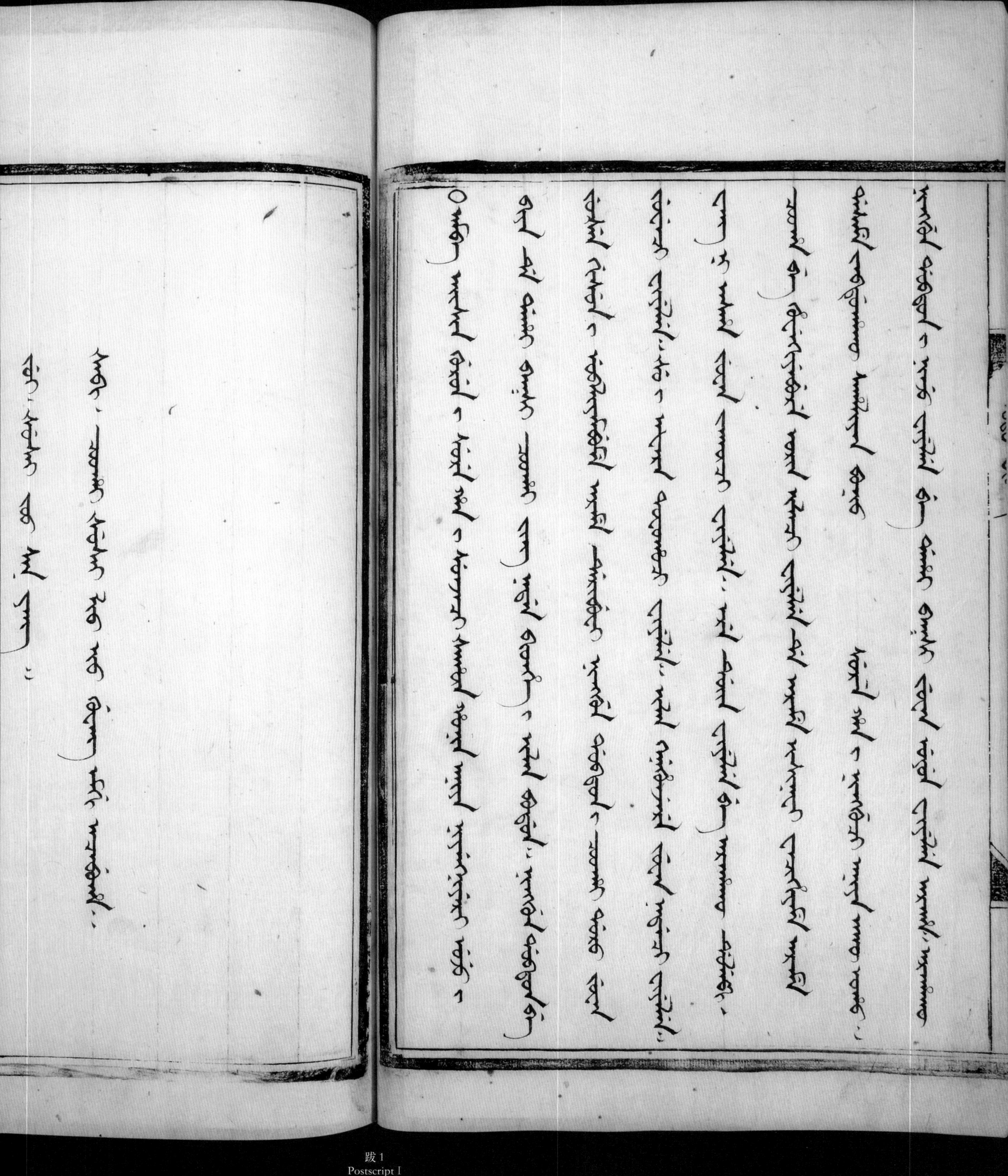

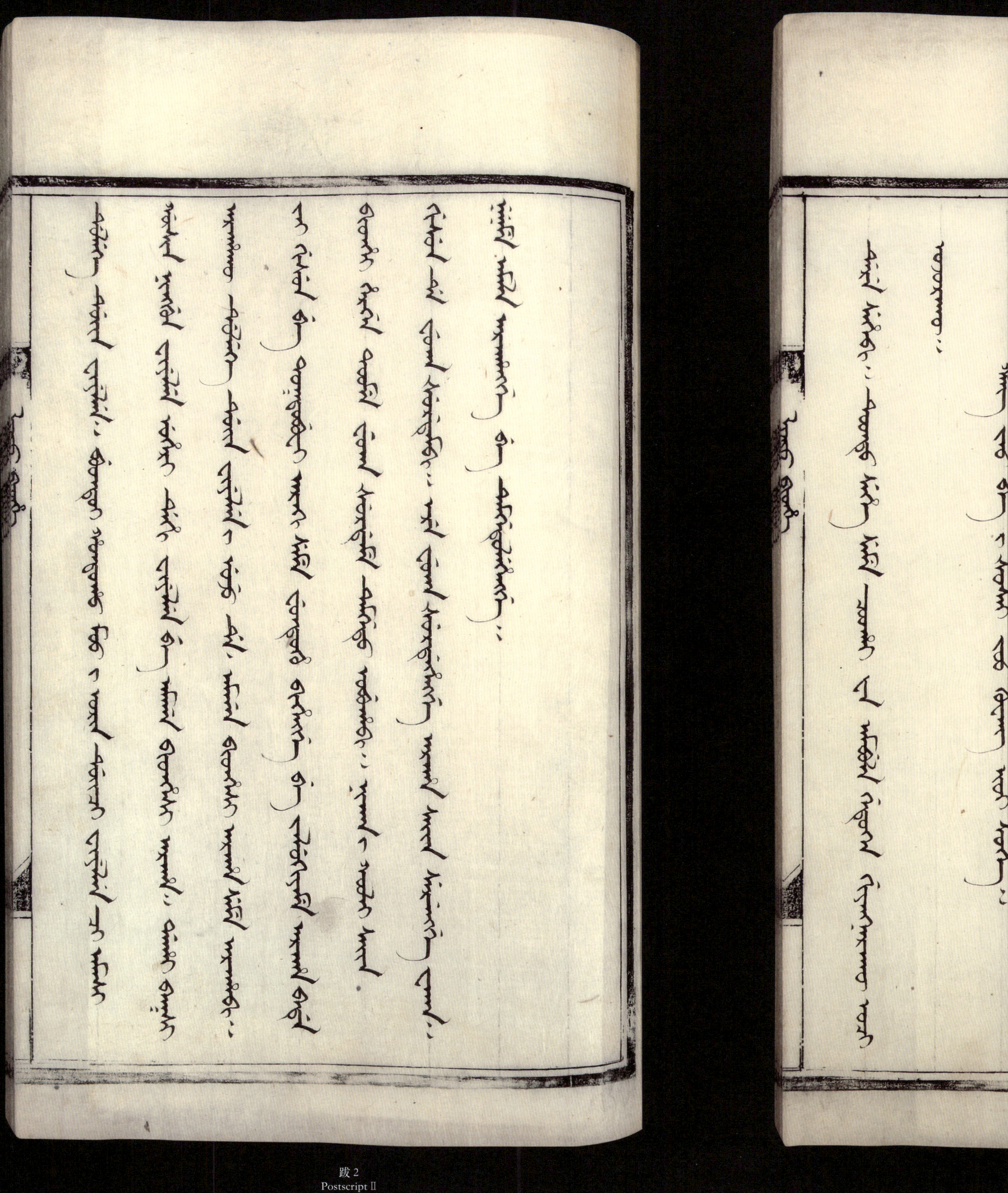

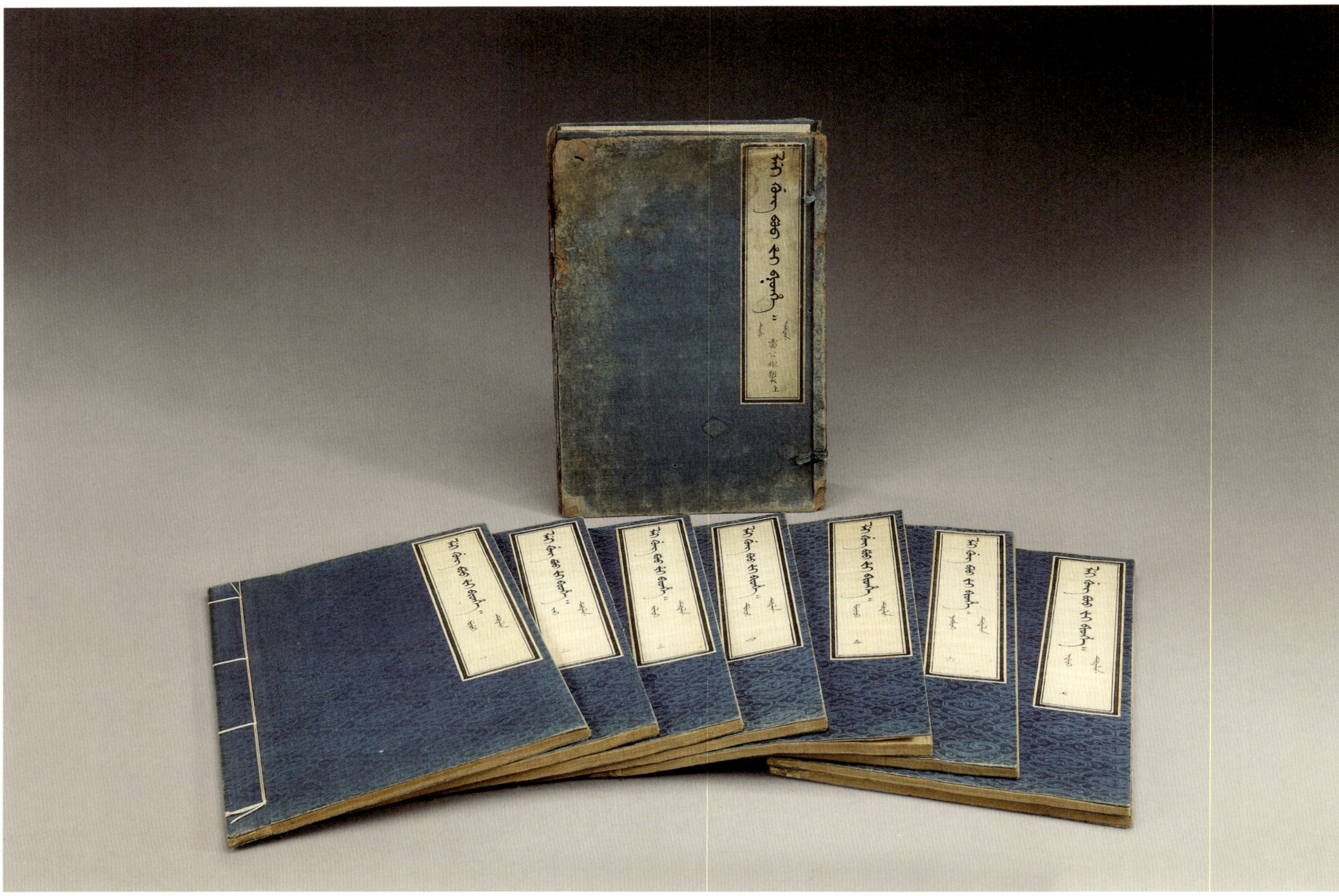

藍色如意雲紋暗花綾書函
Blue twill-weave silk case with veiled pattern ruyi-shaped clouds

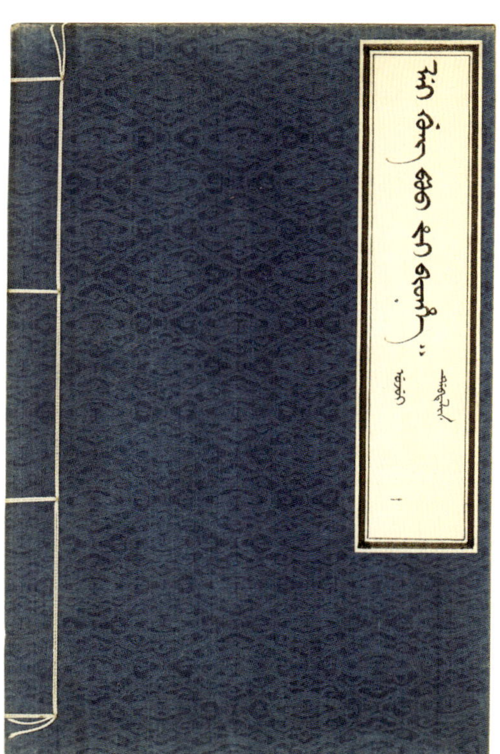

書22242

《雷公炮製書十六卷》

清　佚名輯

清康熙年鈔滿文本

開本　縱31厘米　橫20.1厘米

86 十六冊　二函

Inventory number: Shu 22242

Master Lei's Process of Preparing Chinese Medicine

Sixteen chapters

Anonymous, Qing dynasty (1644-1911)

Transcribed in Manchu in the Kangxi period (r.1662-1722)

Format: 31 × 20.1 cm

Sixteen volumes in two cases

藍色如意雲紋暗花綾書面
Blue twill-weave silk cover with veiled pattern ruyi-shaped clouds

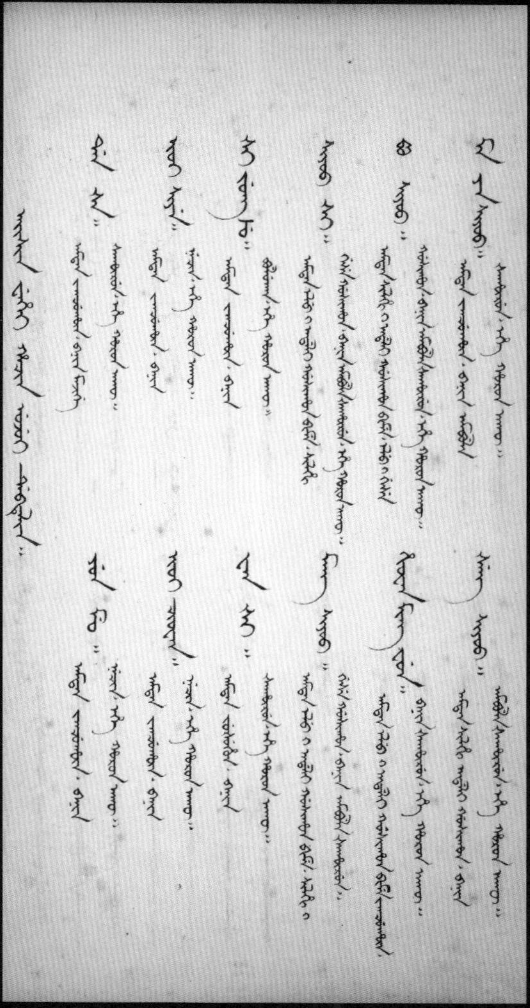

卷端
Beginning

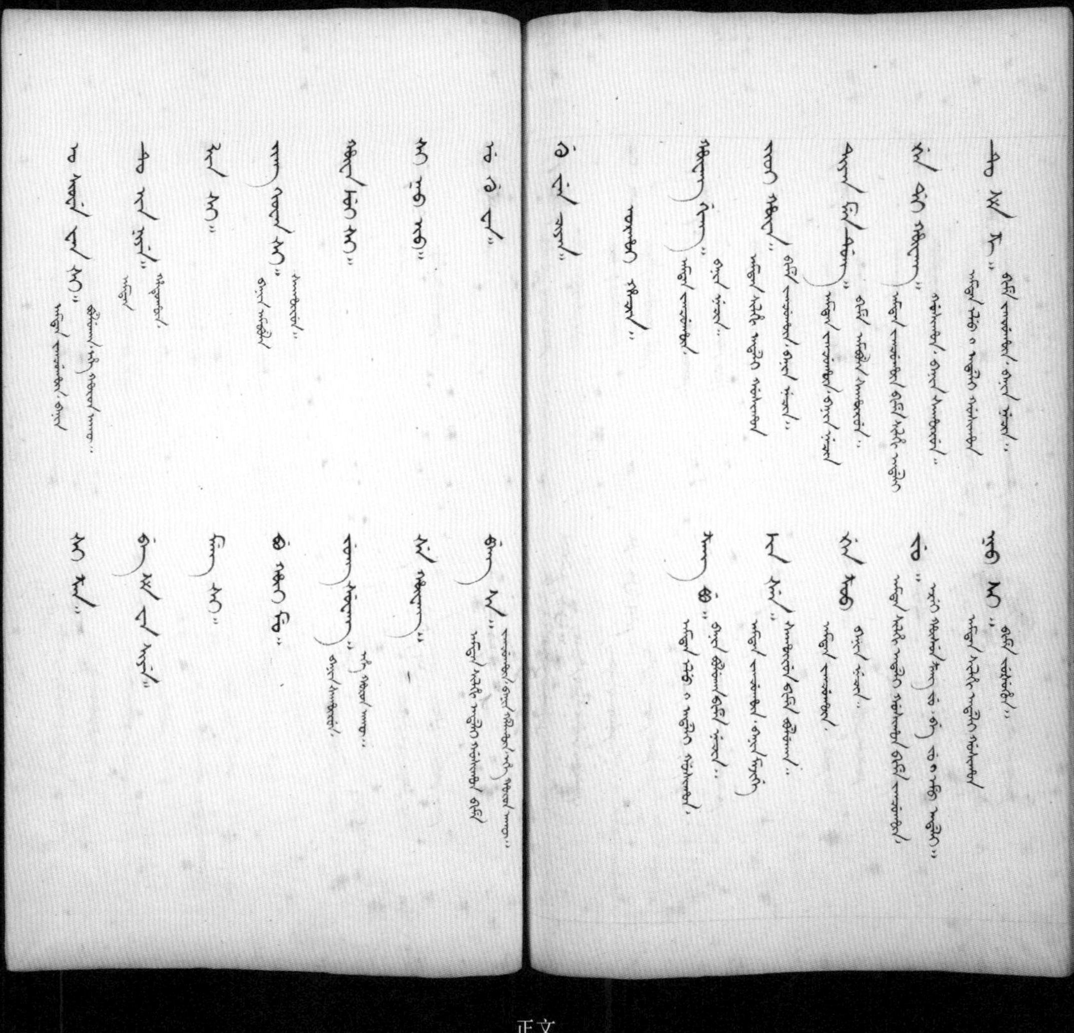

正文
Text

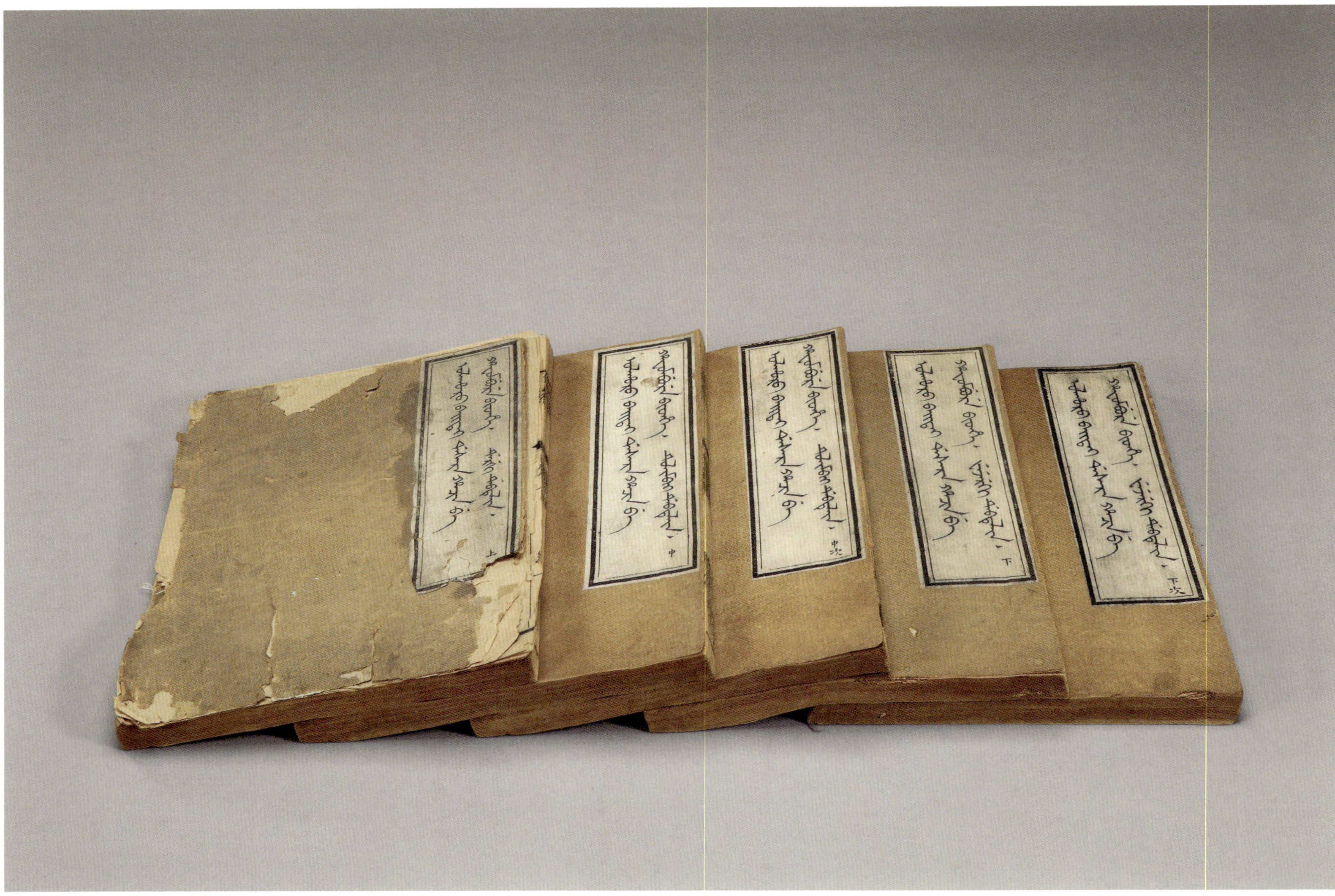

絳色紙書面
Brown paper covers

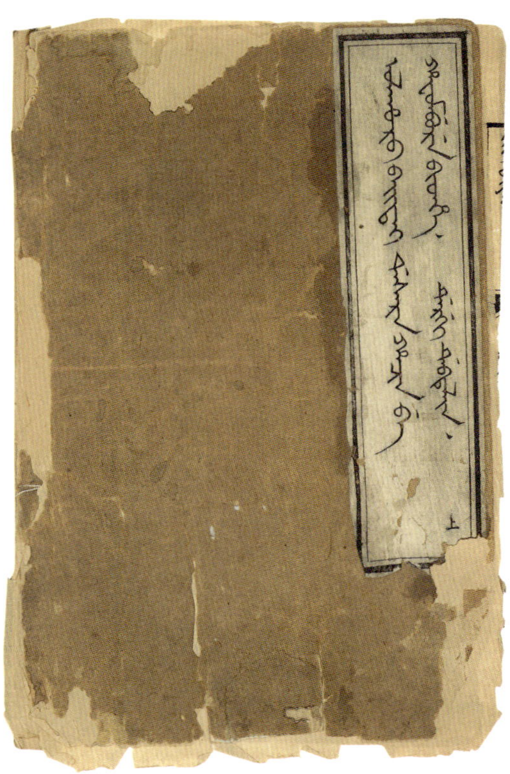

絳色紙書面
Brown paper cover

書22240
《醫藥治症通書三卷》
清　佚名輯
清康熙年刻滿文本
開本　縱24.2厘米　橫16.7厘米
版框　縱20厘米　橫14.8厘米
五冊　一函

87

Inventory number: Shu 22240
General Book on Therapeutics of Chinese Medicine
Three chapters
Anonymous, Qing dynasty (1644-1911)
Transcribed in Manchu in the Kangxi period (r.1662-1722)
Format: 24.2 × 16.7 cm
Frame: 20 × 14.8 cm
Five volumes in one case

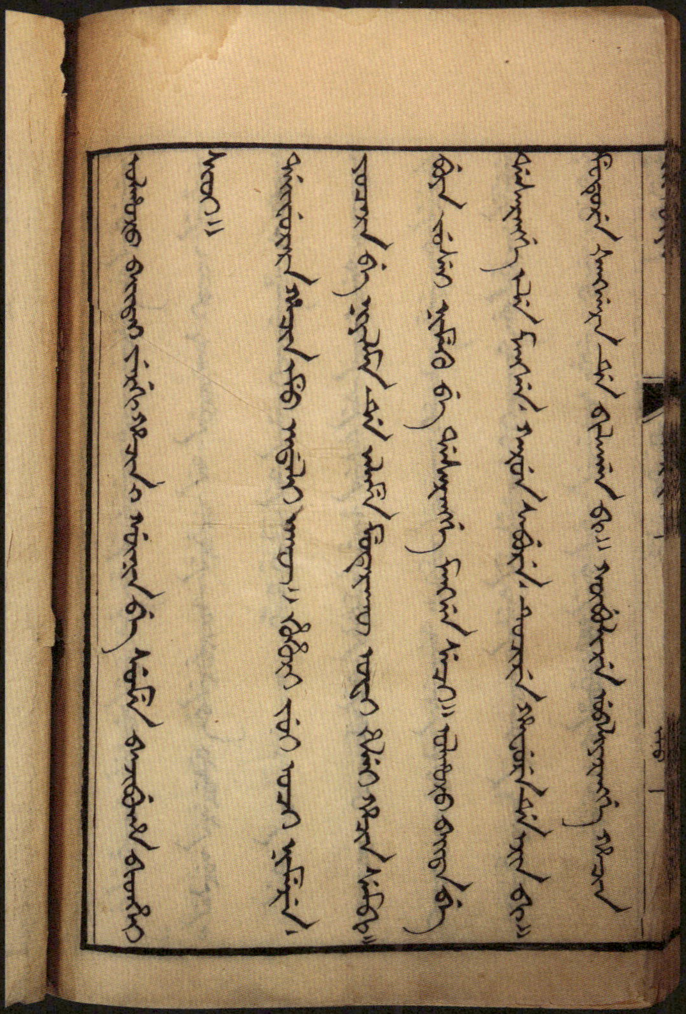

序
Preface

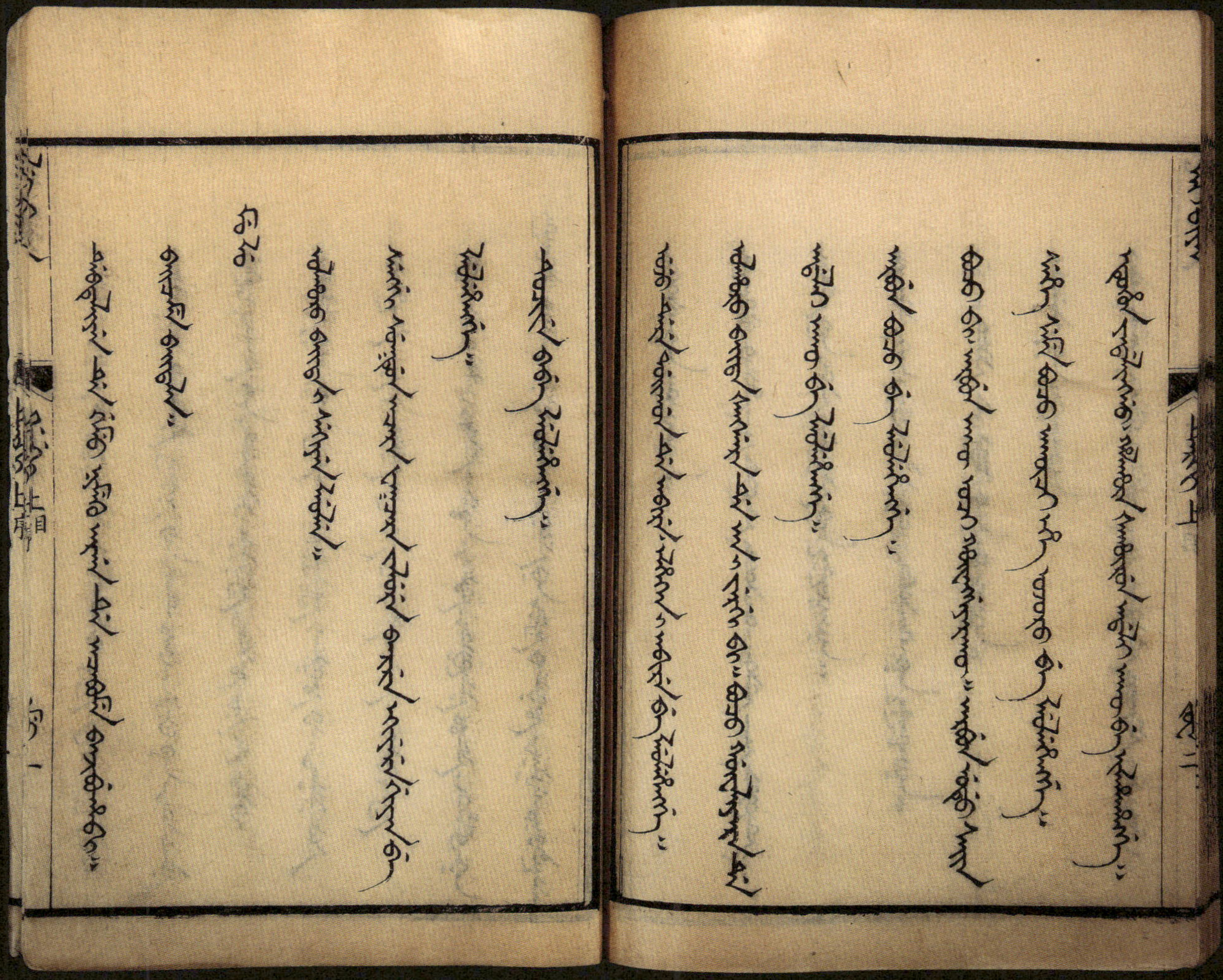

目録
Contents

ᠮᡠᡥᡝᠯᡝᠩᡤᡝ ᠪᡝᡳᡩᡝᠮᡝ ᡤᡝᠮᡠ ᡳ ᠮᡠᡥᡝᠯᡝᠩᡤᡝ᠉

ᠮᡠᡥᡝᠯᡝᠩᡤᡝ ᠪᡝᡵᡝᠨ ᠵᡠᠸᡝ ᡳ ᡤᡡᠨᡳᠨ ᠪᠣᠣ ᡝᠯᡝ ᠰᡝᡥᡝ᠈ ᡥᠠᡵᡤᠠᡧᠠᠮᡝ᠈
ᡩᠣᠣ ᠰᡝᠮᠪᡳ᠈ ᠪᡳᠰᡳᠨ ᠰᡝᠮᠪᡳ ᡩᠣᠣ ᠰᡝᠮᠪᡳ᠈ ᠰᡳᠨᡩᡝ ᠪᡳᠰᡳᠨ ᡩᠣᠣ
ᠰᡝᠮᠪᡳ᠈ ᠪᡳᠰᡳᡵᡝᠩᡤᡝ ᡥᠠᡵᡤᠠᡧᠠᠮᡝ ᠪᡳ᠈ ᡥᠠᡵᡤᠠᠰᠠᠨ ᠪᠣᠣᠯᠠᠮᡝ ᡳᡵᡤᡝᠨ
ᠮᡝᠨᡳᠩᡤᡝ ᡩᠣᠣ ᠰᡝᠮᠪᡳ᠈ ᠨᡳᠶᠠᠯᠮᠠ ᡳ ᠮᡝᠨᡳᠩᡤᡝ ᠰᡝᠮᠪᡳ
ᡥᡝᠨᡩᡠ ᠪᠣᠯᠣᡵᡳ ᡩᠣᠣ ᠪᠠᡳᡨᠠᠨ ᠰᡝᠮᠪᡳ ᡩᠣᠣ ᠰᡝᠮᠪᡳ᠈ ᠮᡠᡥᡝᠯᡝᠩᡤᡝ
ᠨᡳᡵᡠ ᠵᠠᠩᡤᡳᠨ ᠪᠣᡳᡤᠣᠨ ᠪᡝ᠈ ᠰᠠᡵᡤᠠᠨ ᡩᠣᠣ ᠰᡝᠮᠪᡳ᠈ ᠮᡠᡥᡝᠯᡝᠩᡤᡝ

ᠪᡠᠴᡝᡥᡝ ᠪᡝ ᡤᡳᠰᡠᡵᡝᠮᠪᡳ᠉

ᠵᠠᡴᠠ ᡨᡠᠸᠠᡵᠠ ᡨᠣᡵᡤᡳᠨ ᡨᠣᠰᠣᠮᠪᡳ ᠪᡝ ᡤᡳᠰᡠᡵᡝᠮᠪᡳ᠉

ᠪᡠᡥᡝᠮᠪᡳ ᠪᠣᡩᠣᠮᠪᡳ ᡨᡝᡵᡝ ᡨᡠᠸᠠᡵᠠ ᠮᡠᡩᠠᠨ᠈ ᠨᡳᡴᠠᠨ ᠪᡝ ᠪᠠᡥᠠᠨᡳ ᠪᡝ

ᡤᡳᠰᡠᡵᡝᠮᠪᡳ᠉

ᠰᡳᠨᡳ ᠰᡝᠪᡝ ᠪᡳ ᡳ ᡩᠣᠨᠵᡳᡥᡝ ᠪᡠᡥᡝᠮᠪᡳᡥᡝ ᡤᡳᠰᡠᡵᡝᠮᠪᡳ᠉

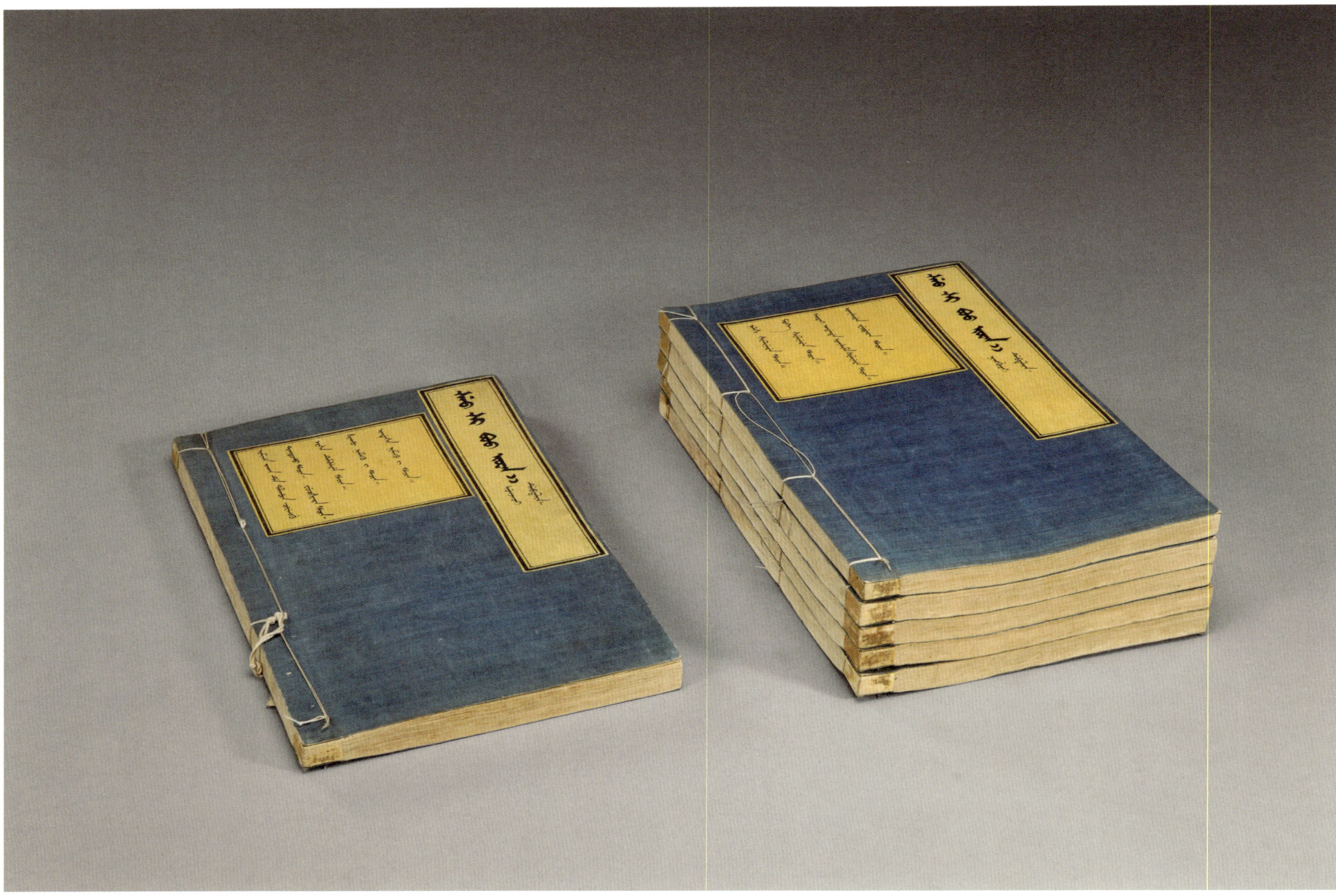

淺藍色素絹書面
Light blue silk covers

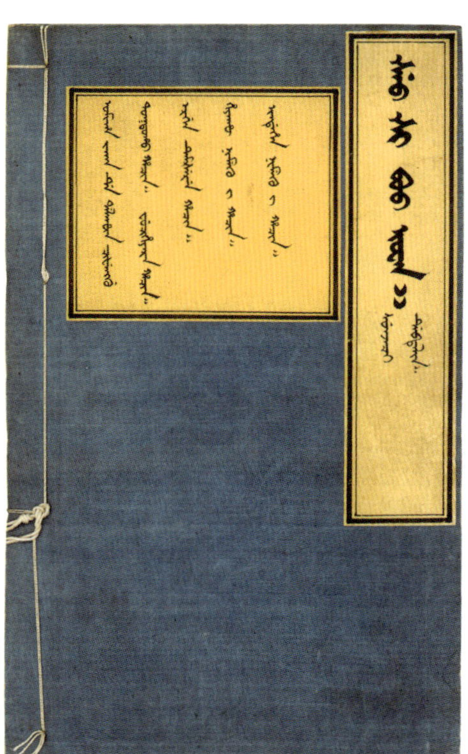

淺藍色素絹書面
Light blue silk cover

書22241
《壽世保元二十二卷》
明　龔廷賢撰
清滿文鈔本
開本　縱29.3厘米　橫18厘米
版框　縱22.2厘米
88 存二十二册　三函（存卷5－7、13－15、18、20－32；卷數不明二册）

Inventory number: Shu 22241
Longevity and Vitality Preservation
Twenty-two chapters
Gong Tingxian, Ming dynasty (1368-1644)
Transcribed in Manchu in the Qing dynasty (1644-1911)
Format: 29.3 × 18 cm
Frame: 22.2 cm
Twenty-two volumes in three cases extant today, including the following chapters: 5-7, 13-15, 18, 20-32, and two volumes of unknown chapters

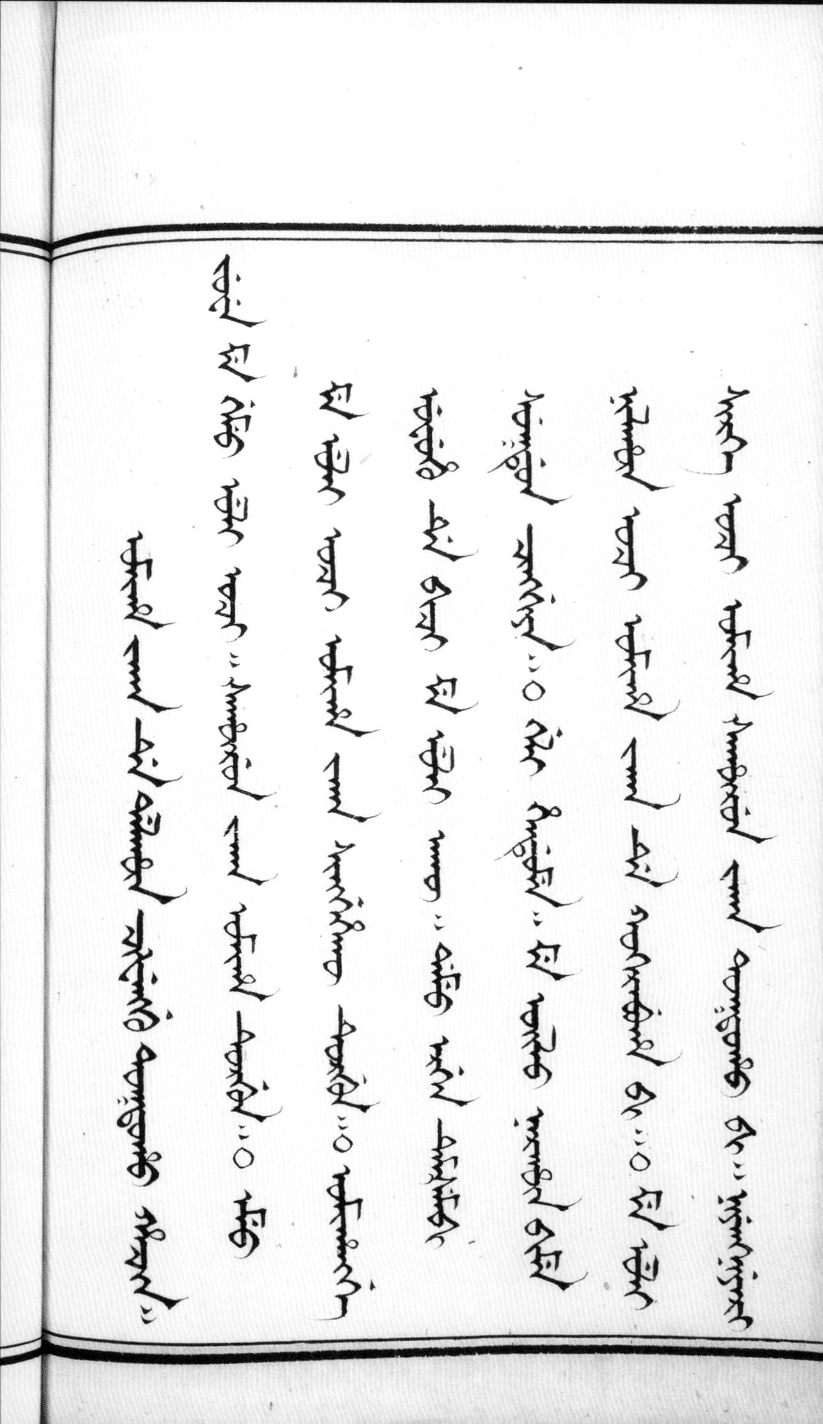

卷端
Beginning

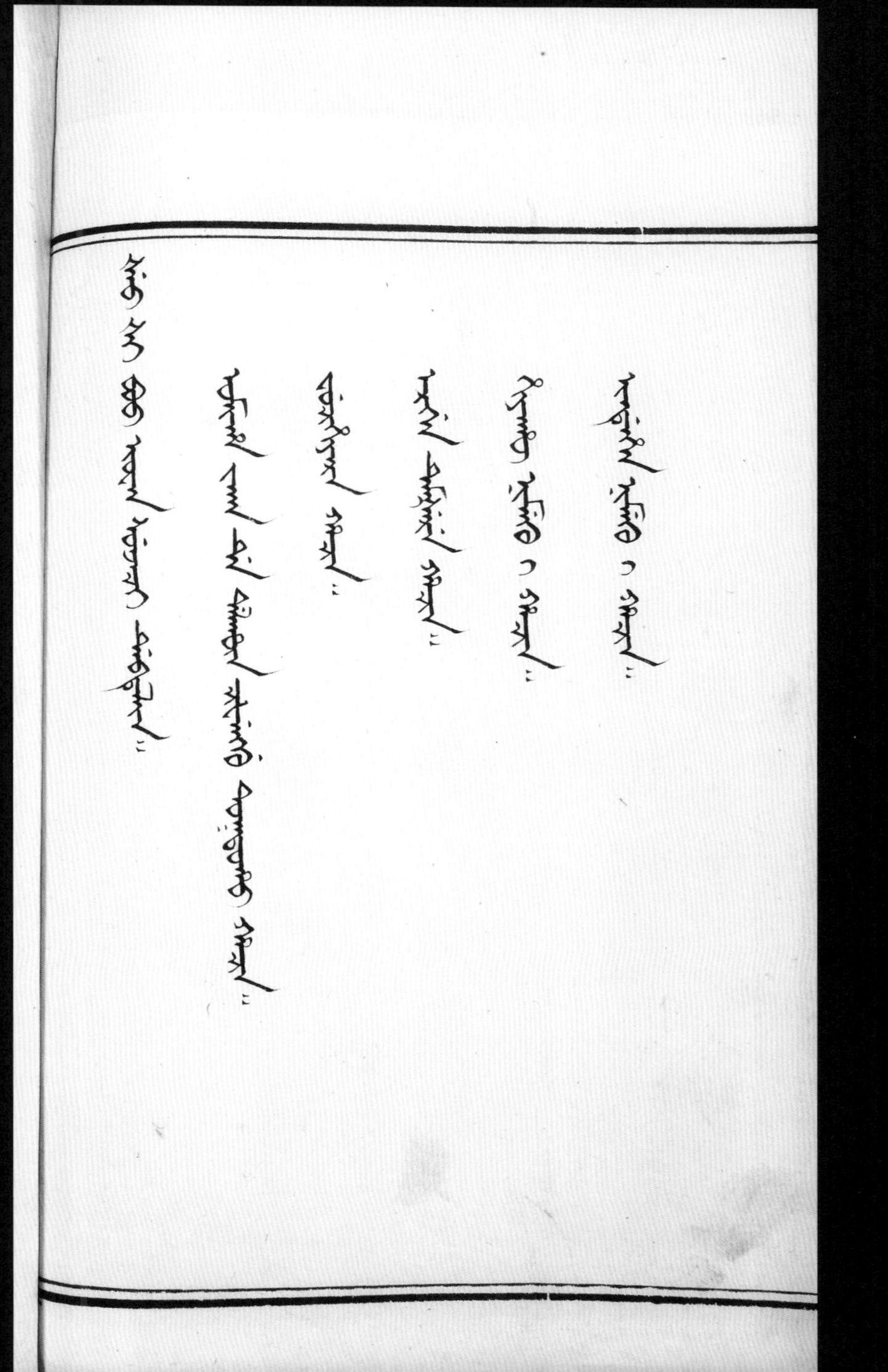

卷目
Contents

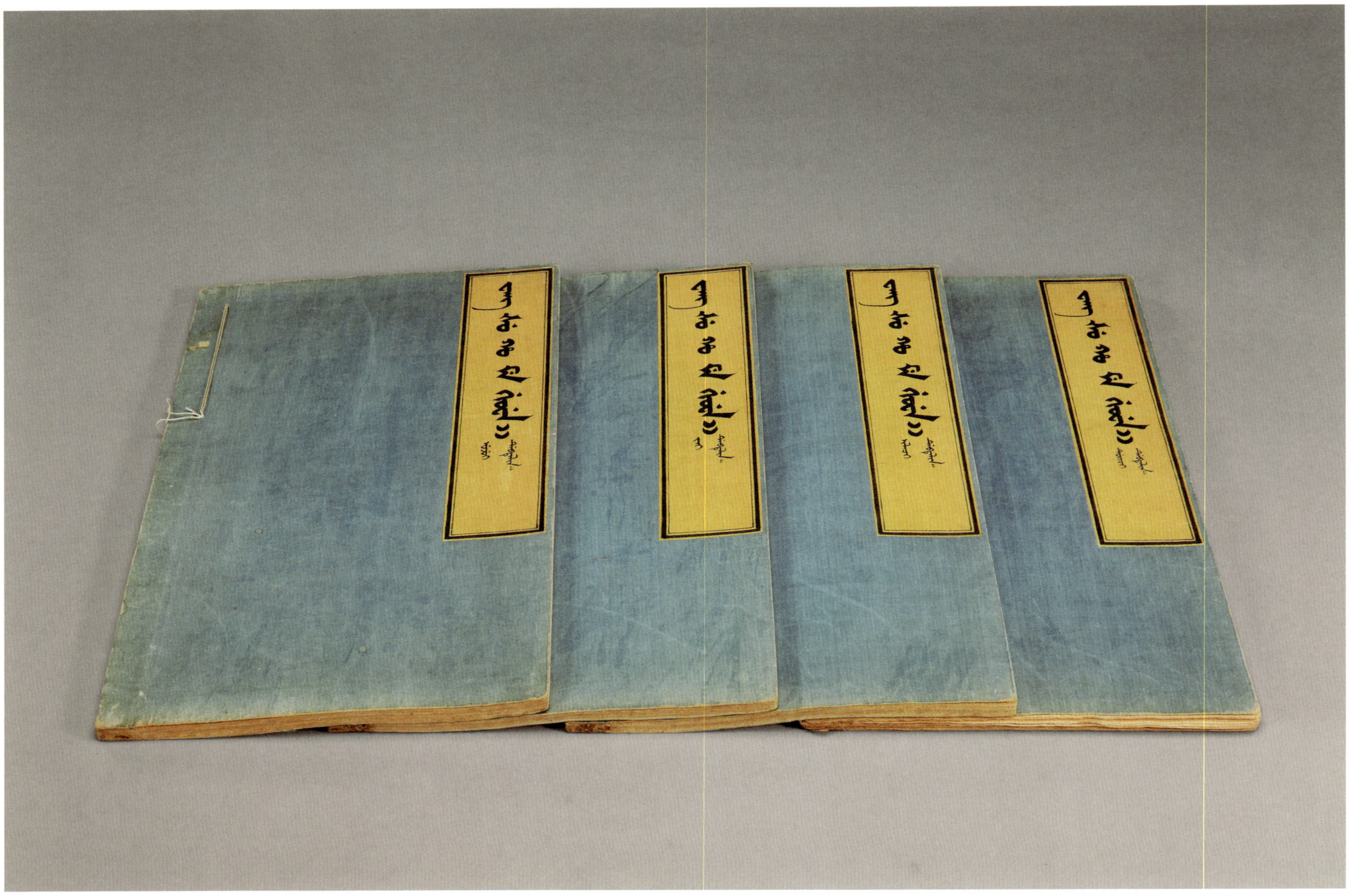

藍色素絹書面
Light blue silk covers

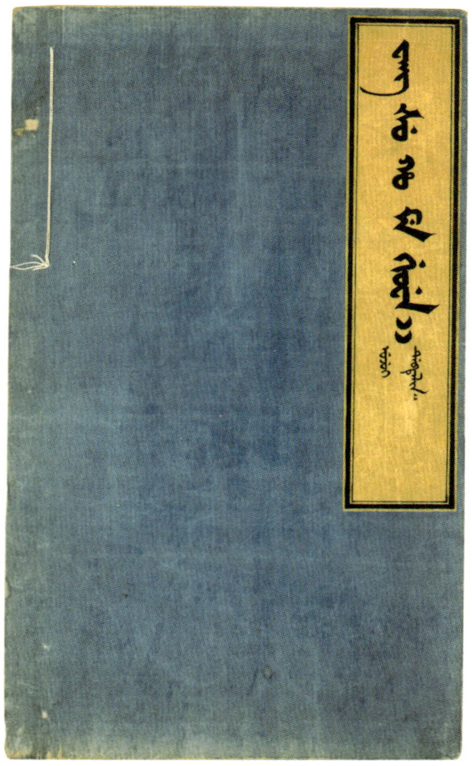

藍色素絹書面
Light blue silk cover

書22244
《王叔和脉訣四卷》
清　佚名輯
清康熙年鈔滿文本
開本　縱29.2厘米　橫18厘米
四冊　一函

89

Inventory number: Shu 22244
Wang Shuhe's Pulse Classic
Four chapters
Compiler unknown, Qing dynasty (1644-1911)
Transcribed in Manchu in the Kangxi period (r.1662-1722)
Format: 29.2 × 18 cm
Four volumes in one case

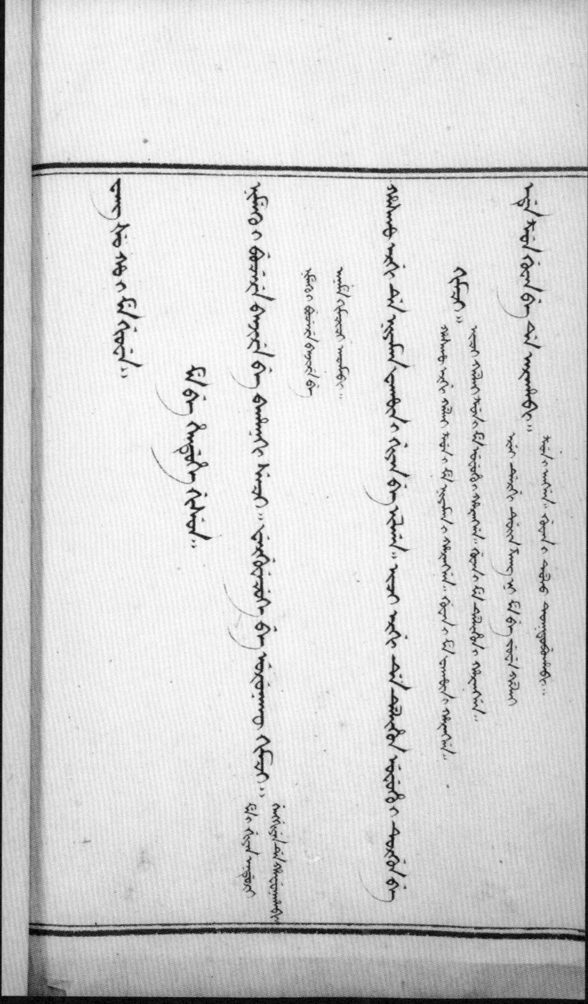

卷端
Beginning

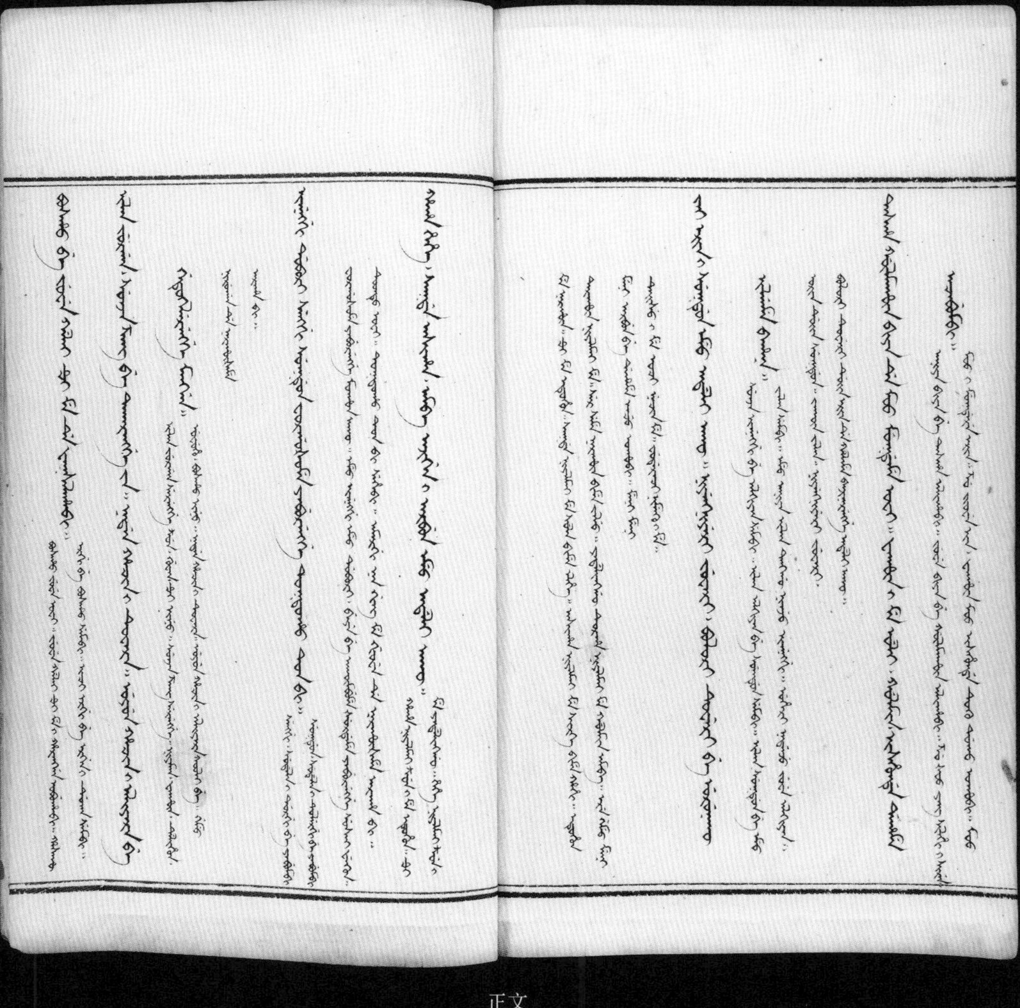

正文
Text

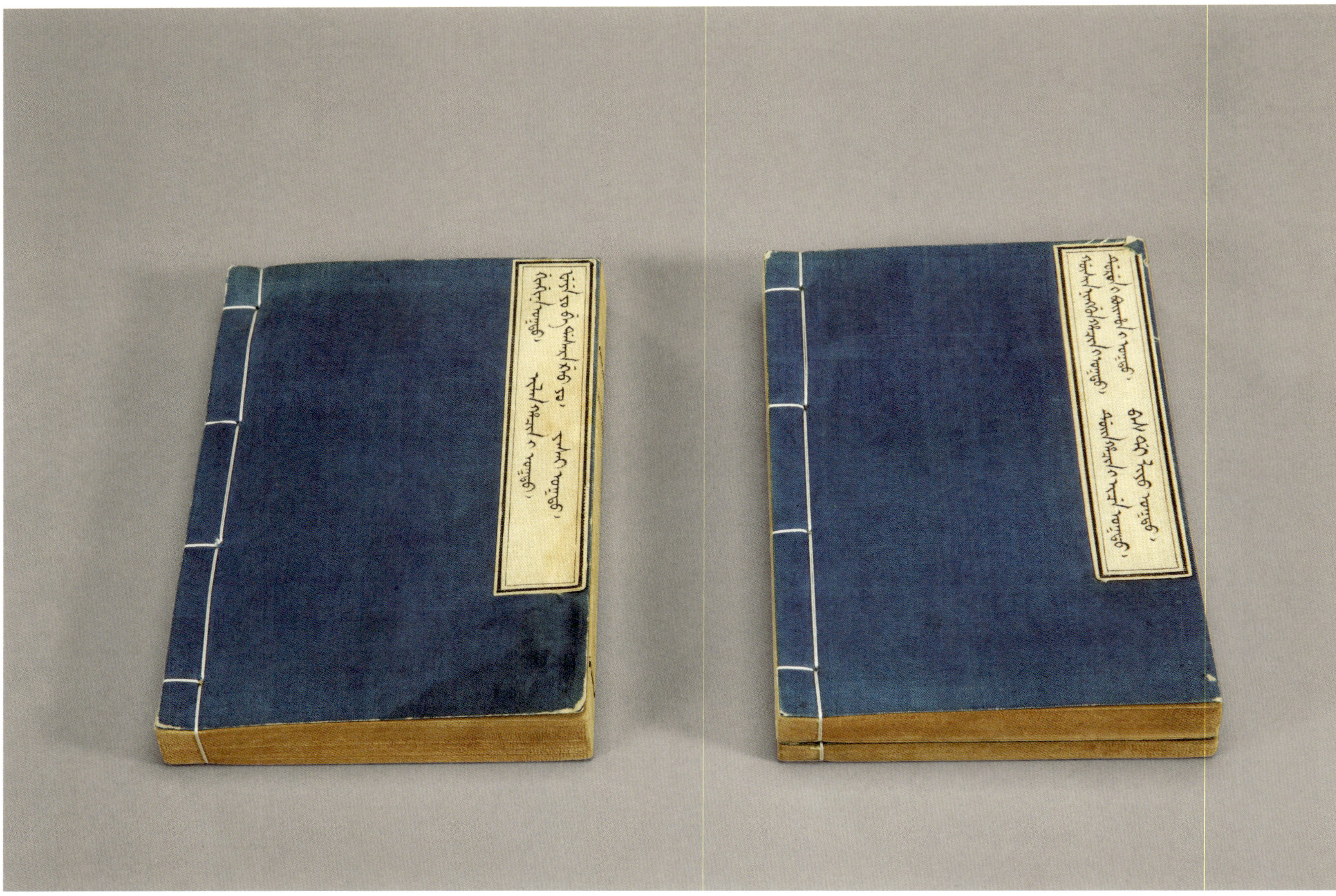

藍色素絹書面
Blue silk covers

書22243
《西洋藥書不分卷》
清　佚名輯
清康熙年內府精寫滿文袖珍本
開本　縱14.2厘米　橫9.5厘米
版框　縱9.9厘米　橫8厘米
三冊　一函

90

Inventory number: Shu 22243
Western Medicine
Anonymous, Qing dynasty (1644-1911)
Miniature edition
Transcribed in Manchu by the Qing court in the Kangxi period (r.1662-1722)
Format: 14.2 × 9.5 cm
Frame: 9.9 × 8 cm
Three volumes in one case

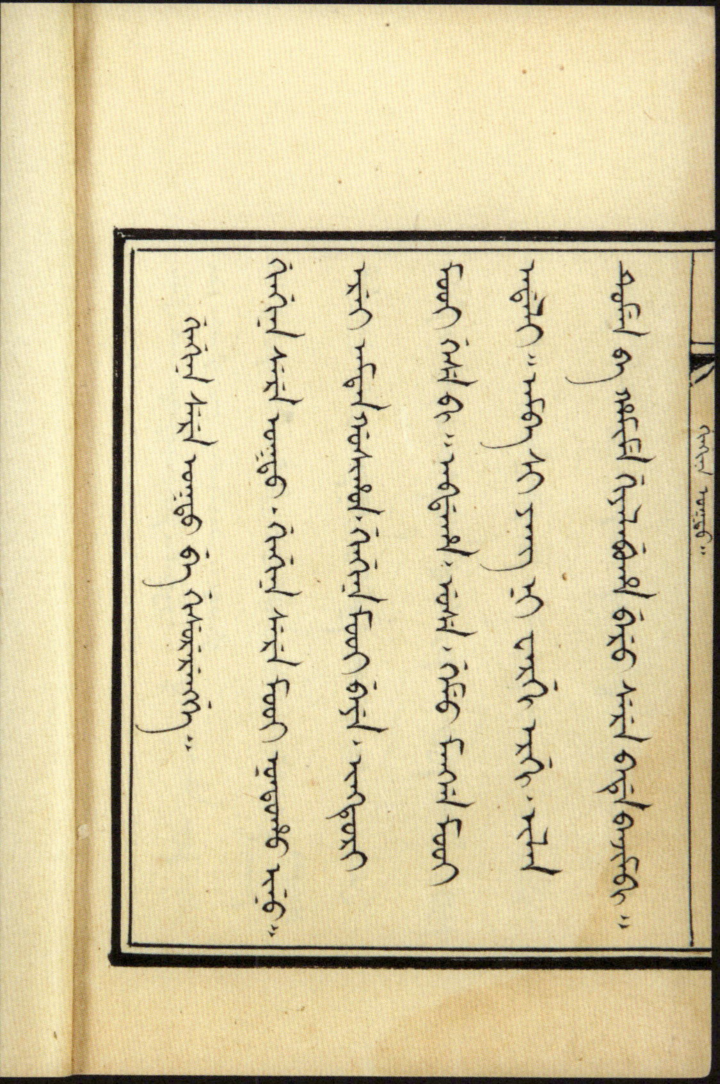

卷端
Beginning

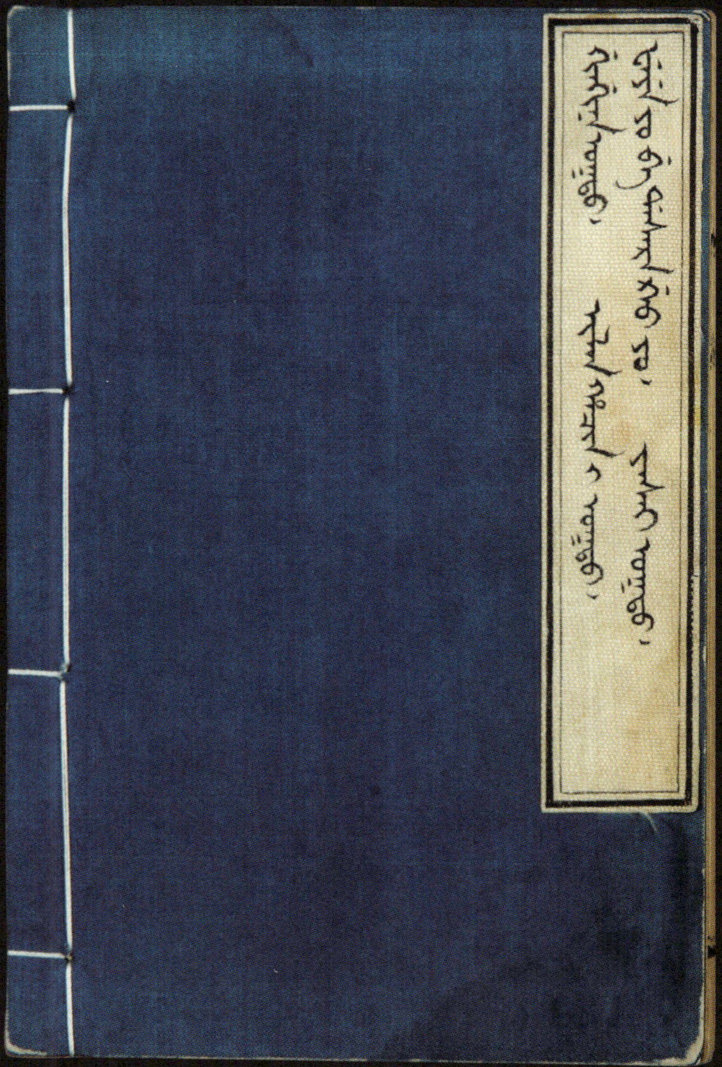

藍色素絹書面
Blue silk cover

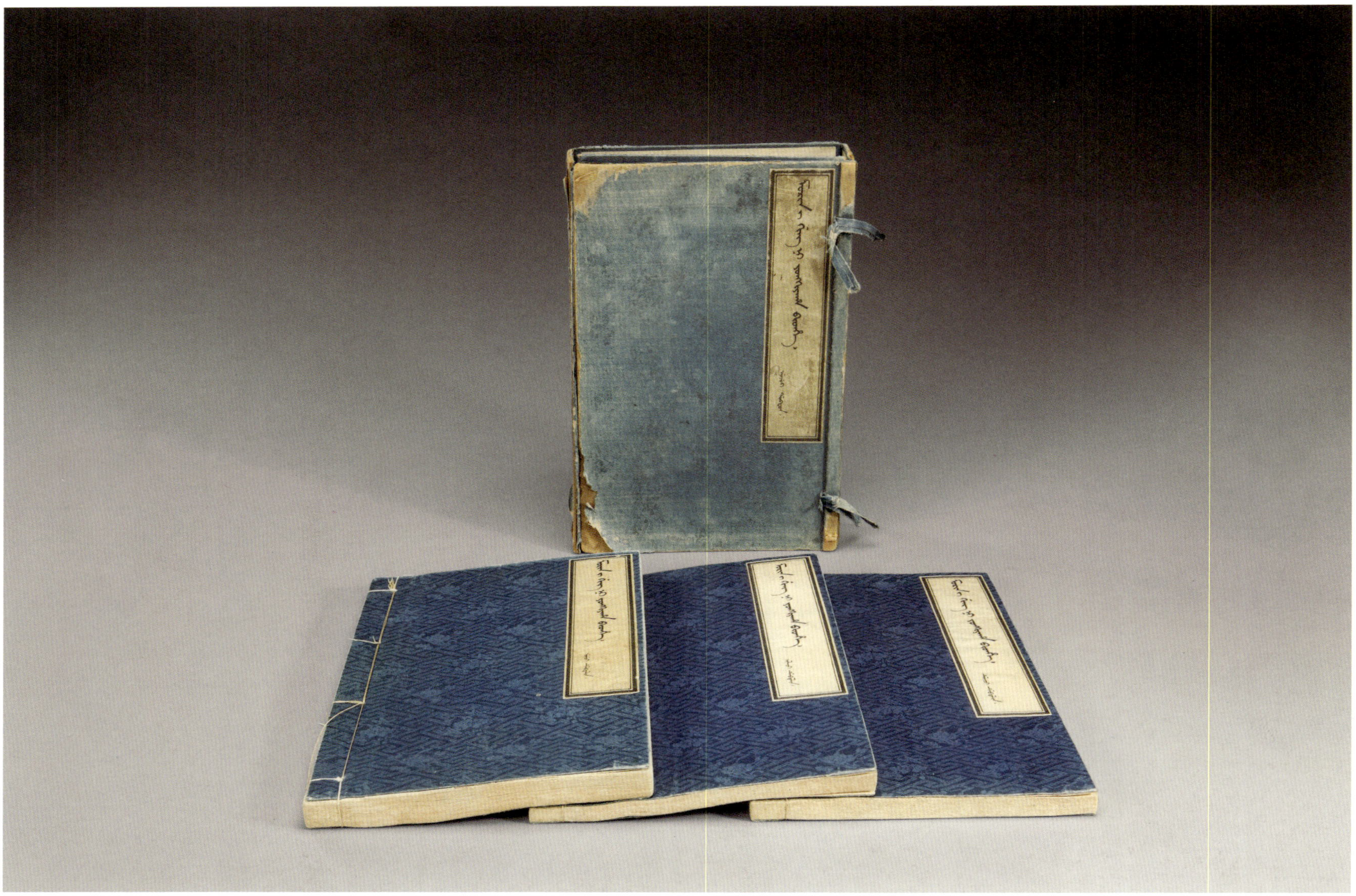

藍色曲水朵花紋暗花綾書函
Blue twill-weave silk case with veiled swastika and floral pattern

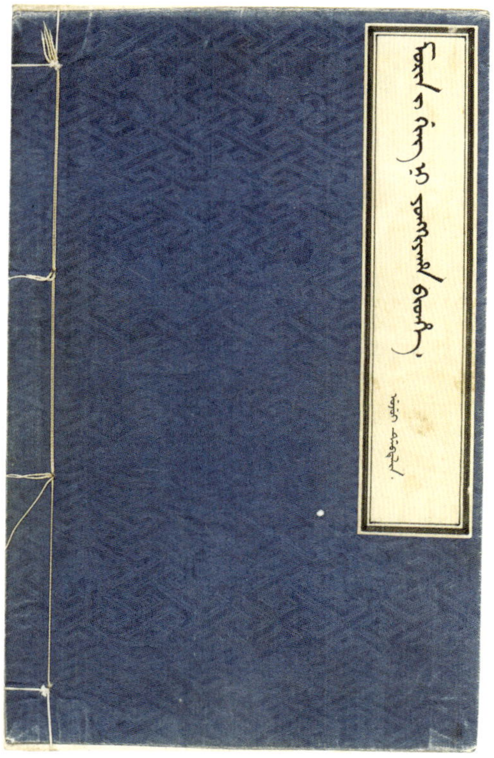

藍色曲水朵花紋暗花綾書面
Blue twill-weave silk cover with veiled swastika and floral pattern

91

書22245
《馬經全書八卷》
清　佚名輯
清初精寫繪圖滿文本
開本　縱31厘米　橫20厘米
版框　縱24.1厘米　橫15.5厘米
八冊　二函

Inventory number: Shu 22245
Complete Book of Horse Classics
Anonymous, Qing dynasty (1644-1911)
Transcribed in Manchu in the early Qing dynasty, with illustrations
Format: 31 × 20 cm
Frame: 24.1 × 15.5 cm
Eight volumes in two cases

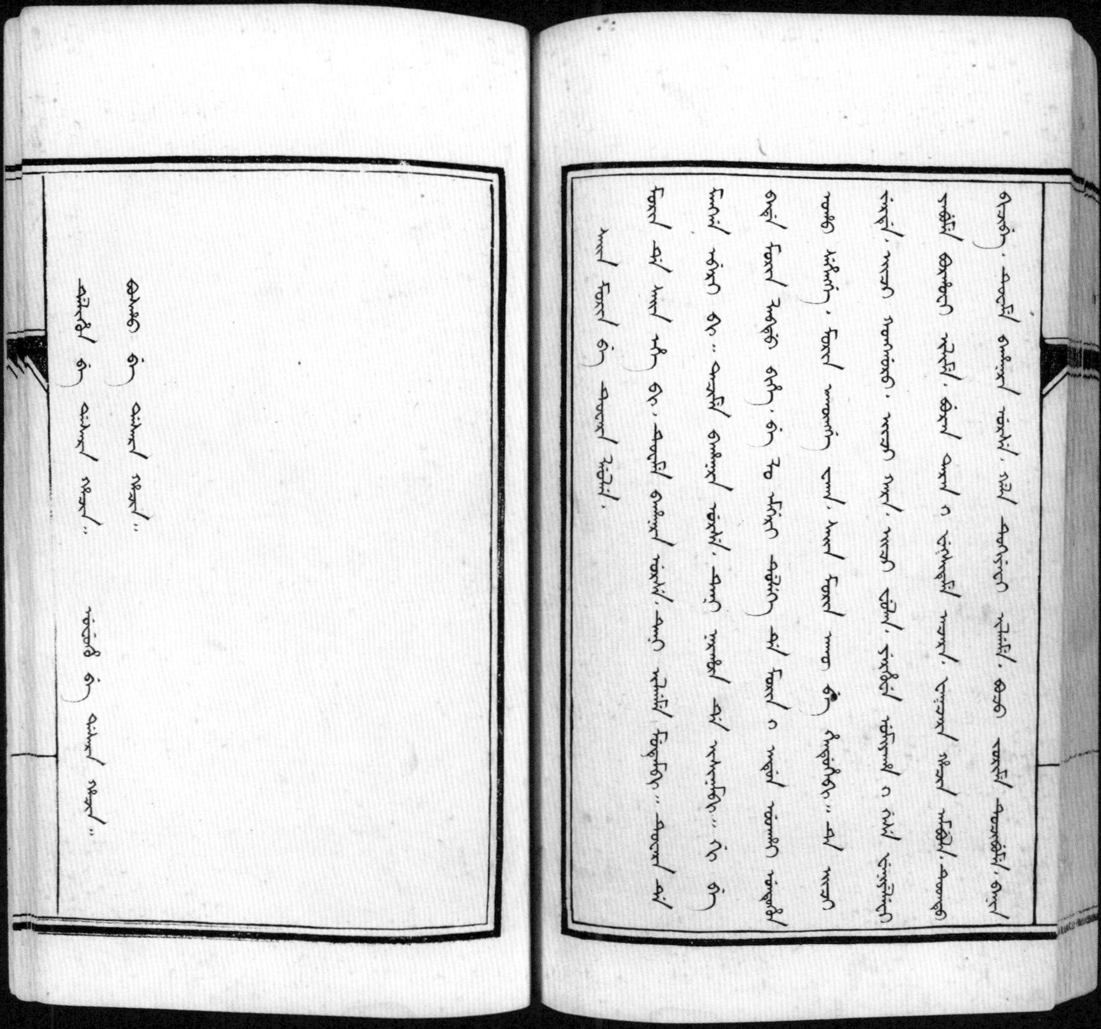

目録及卷端
Contents and Beginning

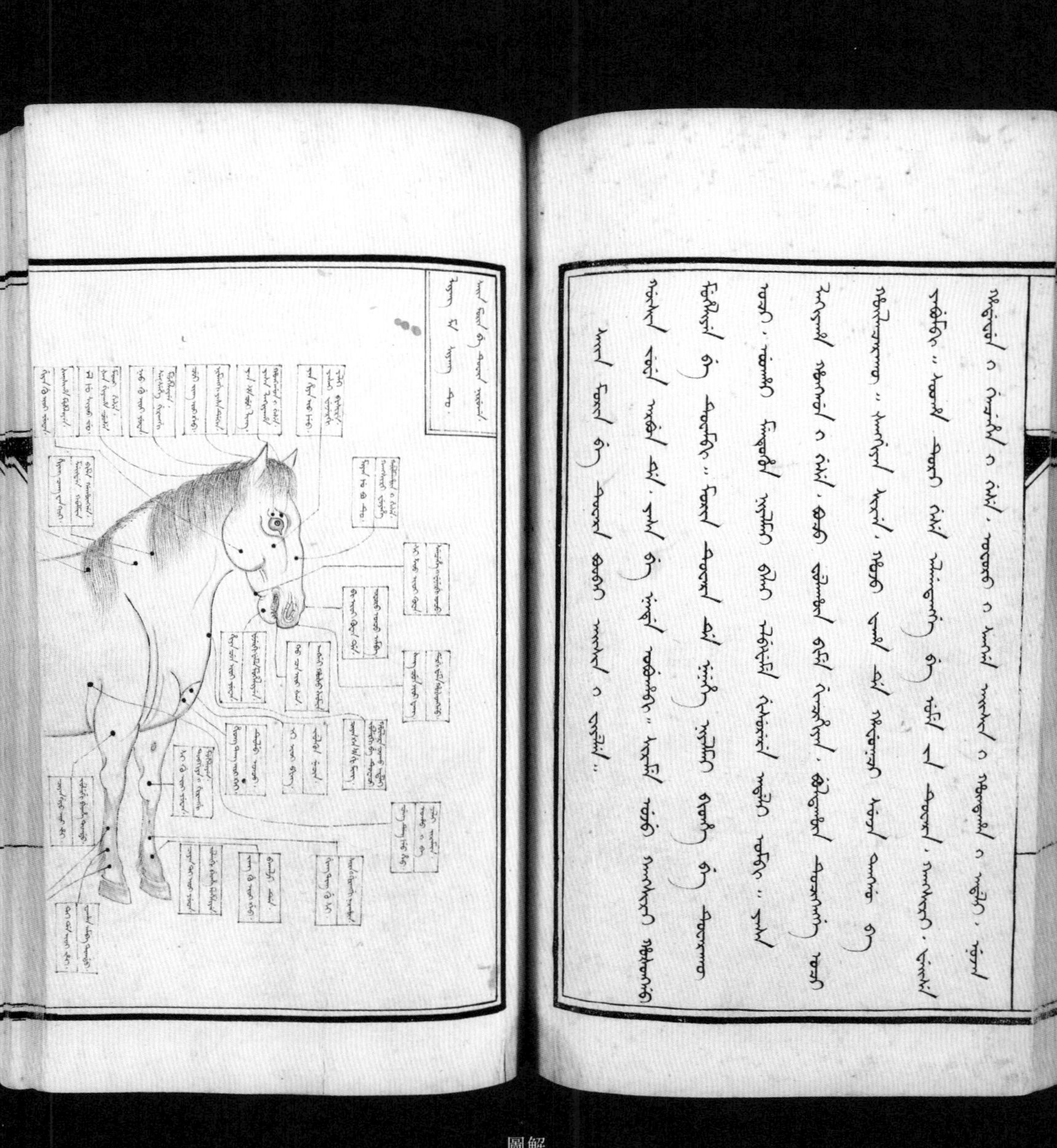

圖解
Illustrated explanation

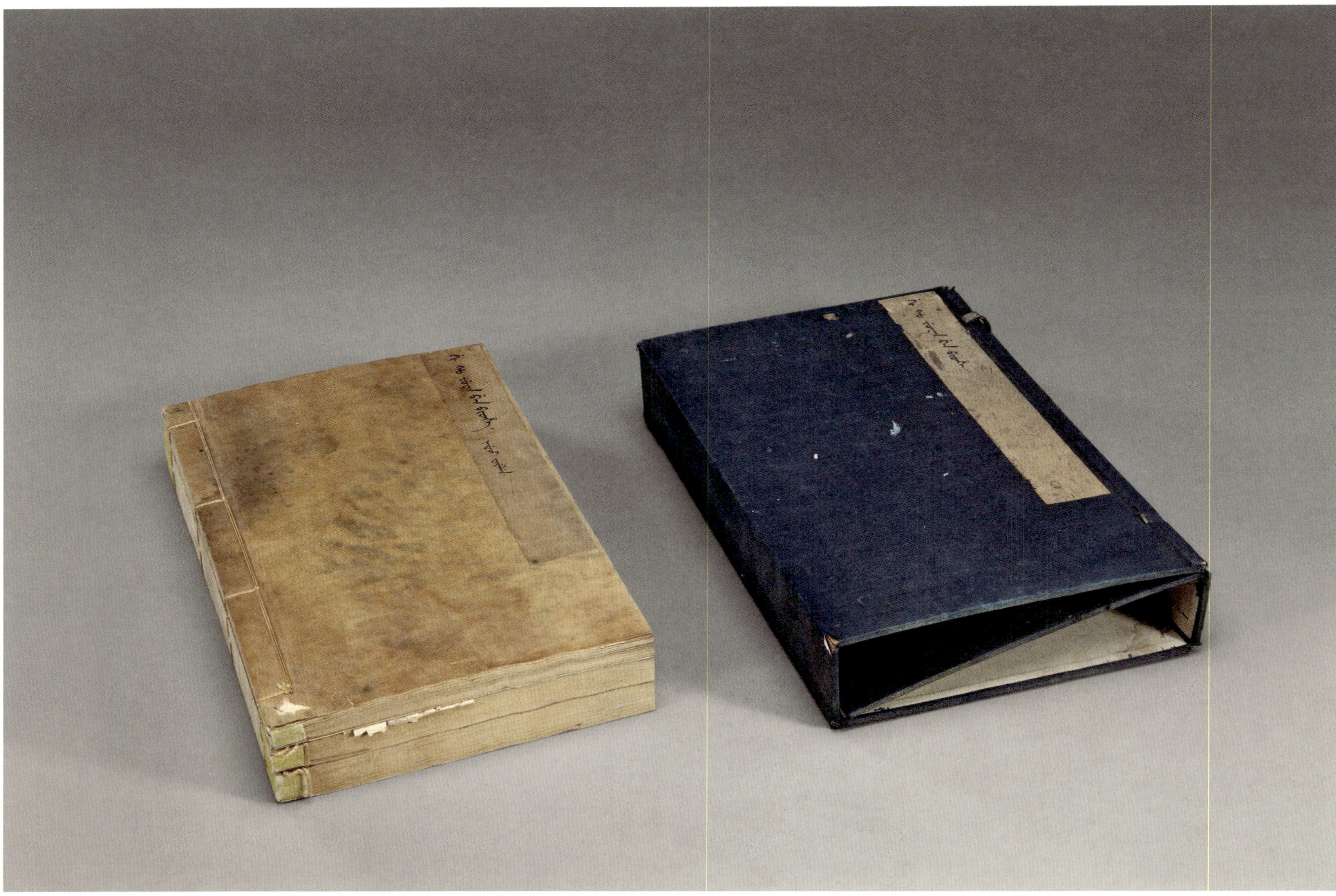

藍色素布書函
Blue cloth case

書22246
《幾何原本七卷》
清　佚名輯
清康熙年鈔繪滿文本
開本　縱29.1厘米　橫17.7厘米
三册　一函

92

Inventory number: Shu 22246
Elements
Seven chapters
Compiler unknown, Qing dynasty (1644-1911)
Transcribed in Manchu in the Kangxi period (r.1662-1722), with illustrations
Format: 29.1 × 17.7 cm
Three volumes in one case

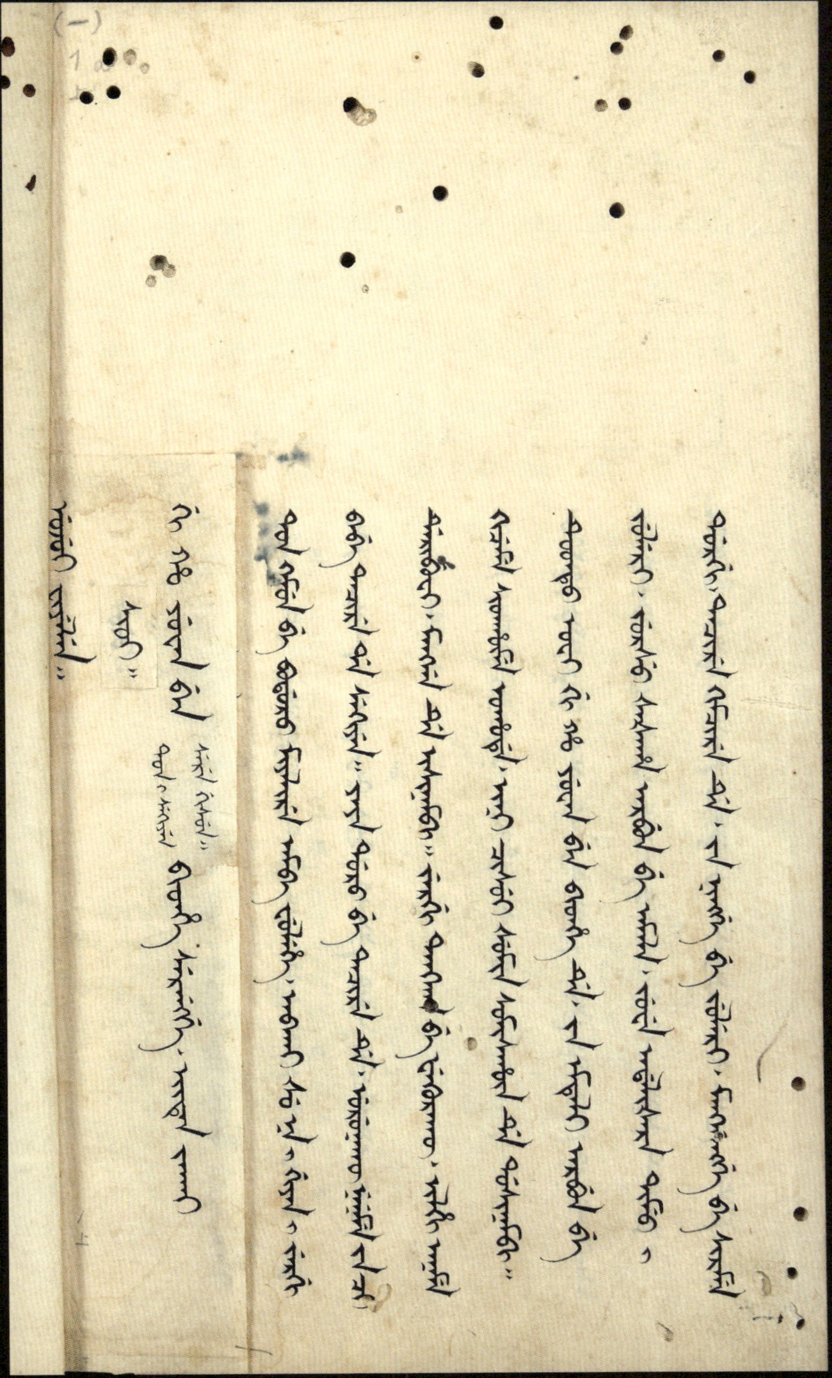

序
Preface

絳色紙書面
Brown paper cover

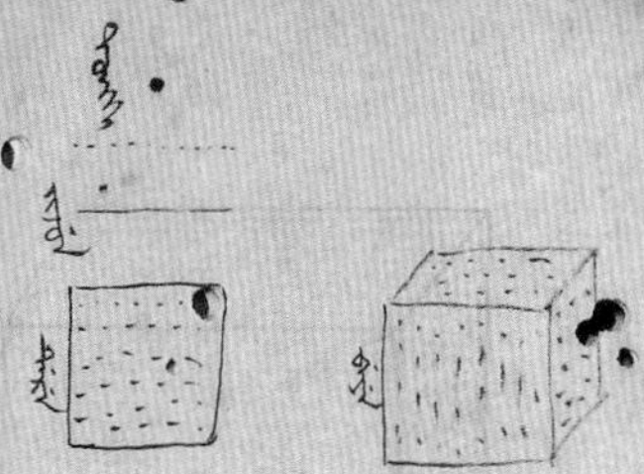

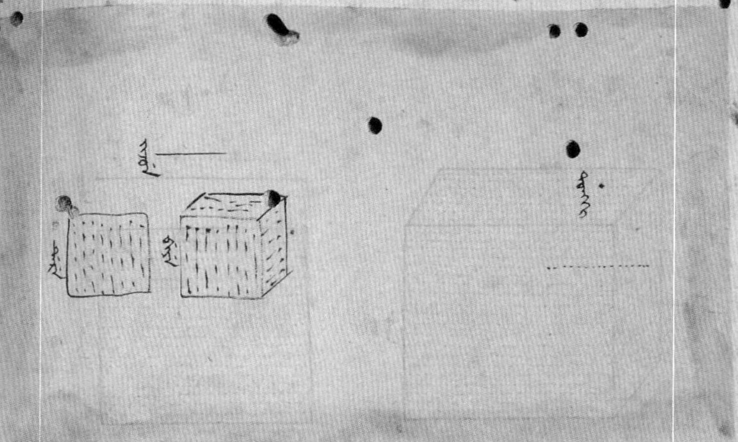

ᠵᡠᠸᡝ ᡳ ᡴᡝᠮᡠᠨ 度 ᡳᠯᡳᡥᠠ᠉

ᡨᠣᠩᡤᠣ ᡳ ᠪᡝᠶᡝ᠈ ᡳᠯᠠᡵᡠ ᡤᡝᡵᡳ ᡩᡝᡵᡝ᠉ ᡨᠣᠩᡤᠣ 線 ᠪᡝ ᡨᠣᠩᡴᡳ ᡩᡝ ᡳᠯᡳᠪᡠᡥᠠᡩᡝ᠈ ᠵᡠᠸᡝ ᡨᠣᠩᡤᠣ 線 ᠪᡝ ᠪᡠᡵᡠᠨ ᡨᡝᠨ ᠪᡝ ᡩᡝᡵᡝ ᡥᠠᠨᡳ᠉

ᠪᠣᡩᠣ᠈ 度

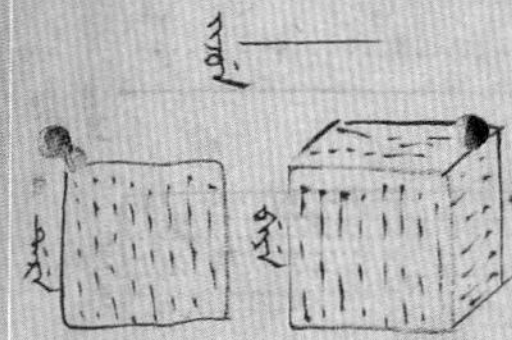

ᠪᡝᡩᡝᡵᡝᠮᡝ ᠪᡠᡩᡠᠨ᠈ ᡨᡝᡵᡝ ᡳ ᡨᡝᠨ ᡳ ᠵᡠᠸᡝ 度 ᡩᡠᠪᡝ ᡳ ᡨᠠᠴᡳᠨ᠉

ᡨᠣᠩᡤᠣ 線 ᡳ ᡩᡠᠪᡝ ᡨᡝᠨ ᡨᠣᠩᡴᡳ 點 ᡴᠠᡳ᠉ ᡨᠣᠩᡴᡳ 點 ᡳ ᡴᡝᠮᡠᠨ 度 ᡳᠯᡳ

ᠠᡴᡡ᠈ ᡤᡝᠮᡠᠨ ᡳᠰᡳᠨᠠᡵᠠ ᡨᠣᠩᡤᠣ ᡨᠣᠩᡴᡳ 點 ᠪᡝ ᡨᠣᠩᡴᡳ 點 ᡳ ᡨᠣᠩᡴᡳ ᡳᠯᡳᡥᠠ᠉ ᡨᠠᡴᠠ

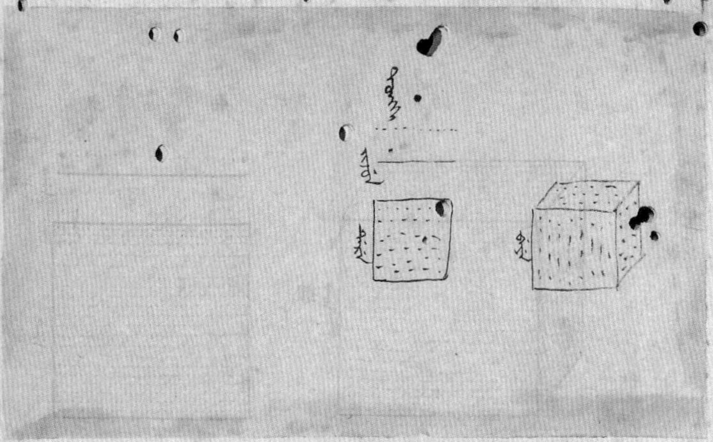

ᡴᠠᡵᠠᠨ 度 ᡳᠯᡳᡥᠠ᠈

ᡨᡠᡳᡨᡝ ᡨᡝᡵᡝ ᡨᡠᠪᡳᠰᡳ ᠪᡝ ᡩᡝᡵᡝ 體 ᡳᠯᡳᡥᠠ᠉

ᠪᡝᠶᡝᠯᡝᡵᡝ ᡨᡝᡵᡝ ᡨᠠᡴᠠᡵᠠ᠈ ᡨᡝᡵᡝ ᠠᡴᡡ ᠪᡝ ᡩᡝᡵᡝ 面 ᡳᠯᡳᡥᠠ᠉ ᠪᡝᠶᡝᠯᡝᡵᡝ

ᡩᡝᡵᡝ ᡨᡝᡵᡝ᠈ ᠪᡝᠶᡝᠯᡝᡵᡝ ᡨᠣᠩᡤᠣᡵᡝ᠈ ᡨᡝᡵᡝ ᡳᠰᡳᠨᠠᡵᠠ ᡨᠠᡴᠠ ᠪᡝ 線 ᡳᠯᡳᡥᠠ᠉

度 ᡨᡝᡵᡝ᠈

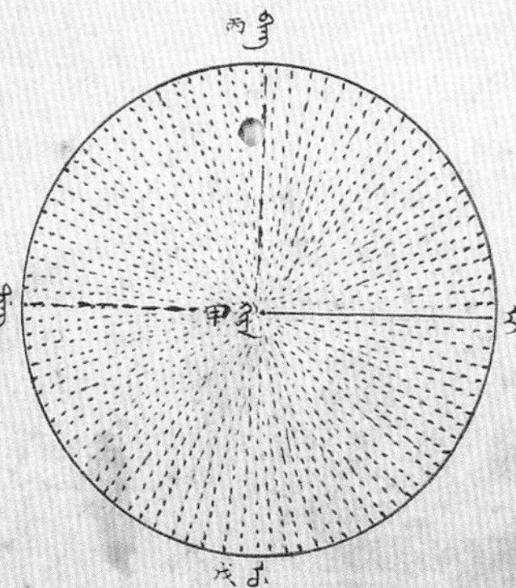

丙
丁
甲
戊

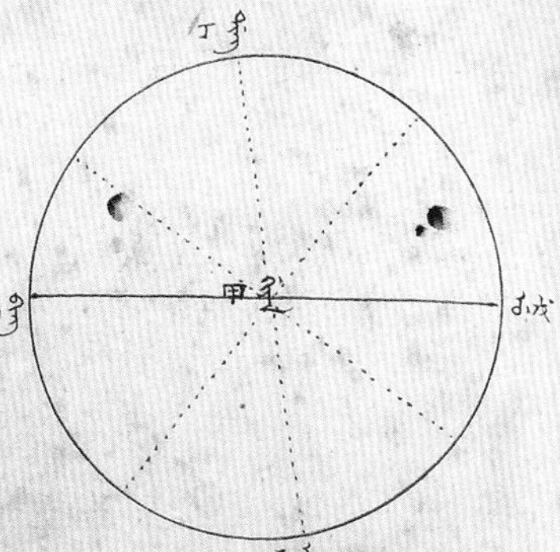

丁
丙
甲
戊
乙

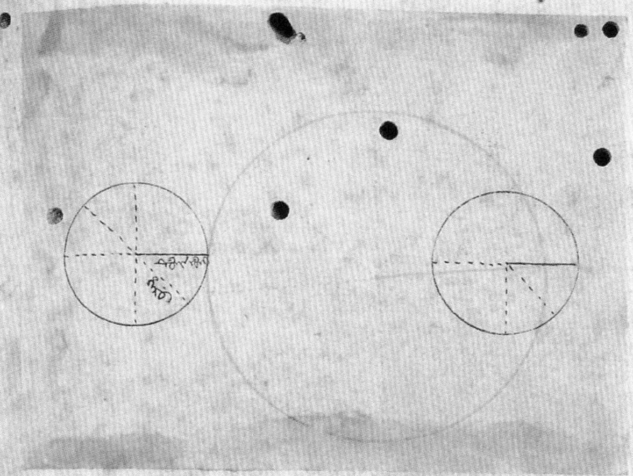

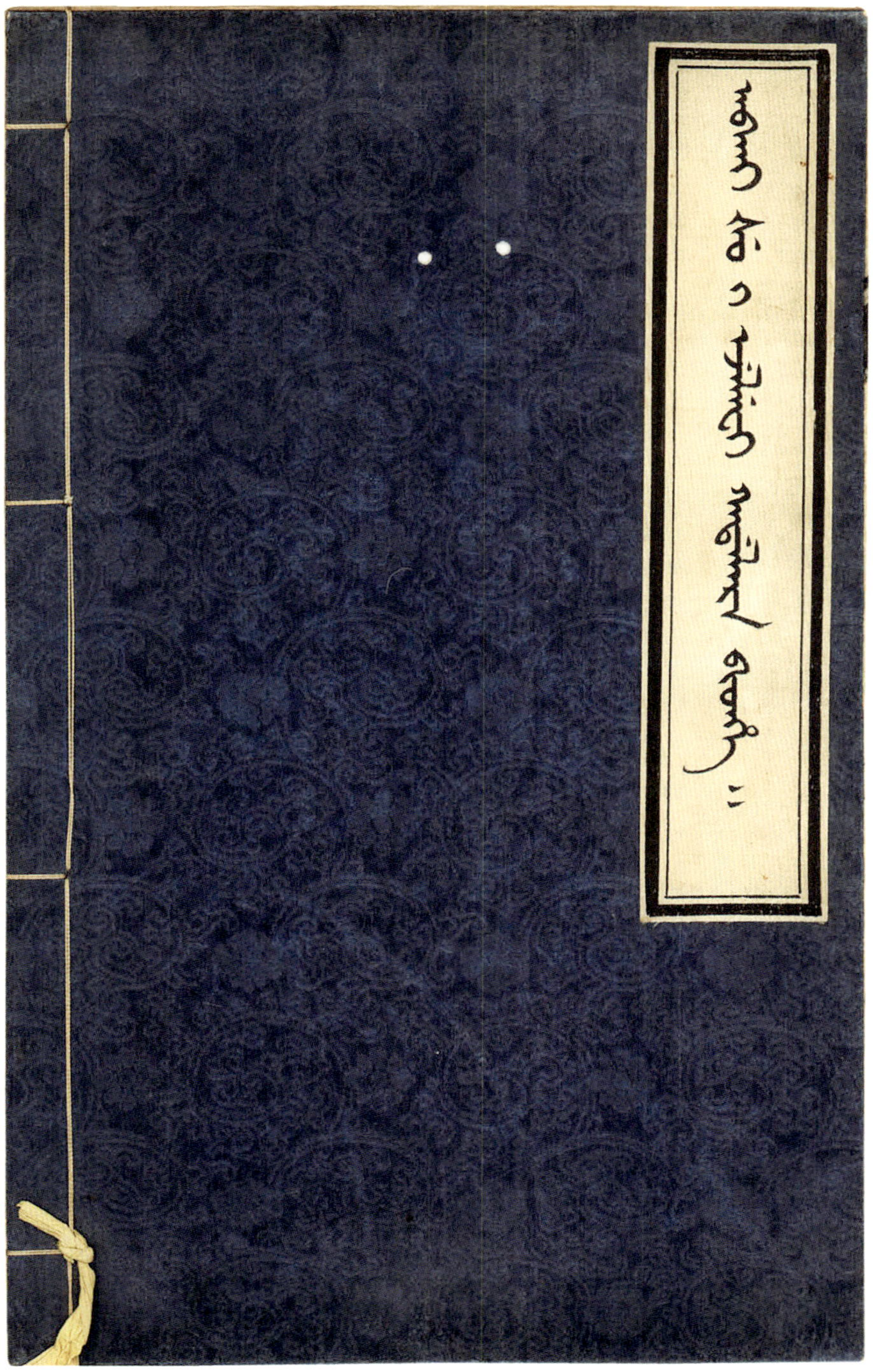

藍色纏枝花紋暗花綾書面
Blue twill-weave silk cover with veiled pattern of floral scrolls

書22248
《天文星宿記考一卷》
清　佚名輯
清康熙年内府精寫滿文本
開本　縱32.4厘米　橫20.7厘米
版框　縱23.8厘米　橫18厘米
一冊　一函

93

Inventory number: Shu 22248
Records on Astronomy and Constellations
One chapter
Anonymous, Qing dynasty (1644-1911)
Transcribed in Manchu by the Qing court in the Kangxi period (r.1662-1722)
Format: 32.4 × 20.7 cm
Frame: 23.8 × 18 cm
One volume in one case

ᠮᡠᡩᠠᠨ ᠪᡝ ᠠᠯᠠᠯᡳᠮᠪᡳ᠉ ᡤᡝᠯᡳ ᡝᠮᡠ ᠮᡠᡩᠠᠨ᠈ ᠮᡠᠰᡝᠯᡳ ᠠᡳᠰᡳᠯᠠᠮᡝ

ᠠᠯᡳᠮᠪᡳ᠉ ᡳᠰᡳ ᠵᡠ᠈ ᠵᡠᠸᡝ ᡩᡝ ᠮᡠᡩᠠᠨ ᠪᡝ ᠪᡳᠰᡳᡵᡝ ᡩᡝ ᠠᠯᠠᠩᡤᠠ ᠮᡠᠰᡝᠯᡳ

ᠮᡠᡩᠠᠨ ᠪᠠᡳᡨᠠ ᠪᡝ ᡨᡠᡨᡳᠯᡳ ᡤᡝᠨᡤᡝᠯᡳ ᡨᡠᠸᡝᠨ ᡳ ᡤᡝᠨᡤᡝᠯᡳ ᡩᡝ

ᠵᡳᠶᡝ ᠵᡳᠨ᠈ ᠪᡳᠨ᠈ ᠵᡠ᠈ ᠪᠠᠨ ᠵᡳ ᡩᡝ ᠪᡳᡨᡝᡥᡝᠪᡳ᠉ ᠠᠯᡳᡥᠠ ᡨᡠᠯᡳ᠈

ᠪᡳᡨᡝᡥᡝᡳᠩᡤᡝ ᡩᡝ᠈ ᠵᡠ᠈ ᠵᡠᠸᠠᠨ᠈ ᠵᠠᠨ᠈ ᠵᡠ᠈ ᡩᡝ ᠪᡳᡨᡝᡥᡝᠪᡳ᠉ ᡩᡝ ᡳ ᠪᡝ

ᠵᡳ ᠵᡳᠨ ᠪᡳᡨᡝᡥᡝᡳᠩᡤᡝ ᠮᡠᡩᠠᠨ᠈ ᠮᡠᡩᠠᠨ ᡳ ᠵᡠᠸᡝᡵᡳ᠉ ᠪᡳᡨᡝᡥᡝᡳ

ᠵᡳ ᠵᡳᠨ ᠮᡠᡩᠠᠨ᠈

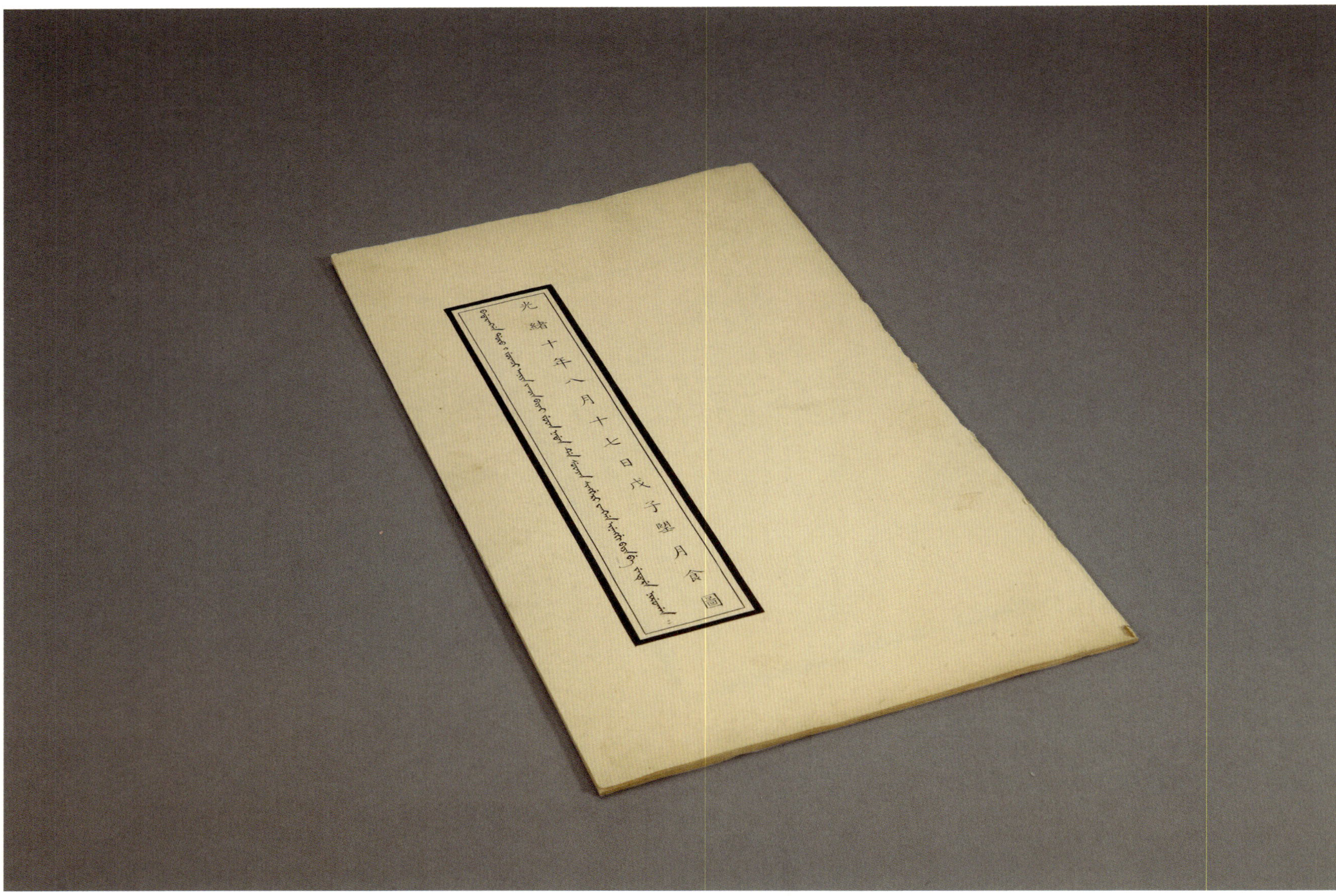

黄色紙書面
Yellow paper cover

書6481
《光緒十年八月十七日戊子望月食圖》
清　欽天監編
清光緒年内府寫繪滿漢合璧本
開本　縱32.9厘米　橫18.5厘米
版框　縱24.9厘米　橫29厘米
一冊

94

Inventory number: Shu 6481
Lunar Eclipse on August 17, 1884
Compiled by Imperial Board of Astronomy, Qing dynasty (1644-1911)
Transcribed in Manchu and illustrated by the Qing court in the Guangxu period (r.1875-1908)
Format: 32.9 × 18.5 cm
Frame: 24.9 × 29 cm
One volume

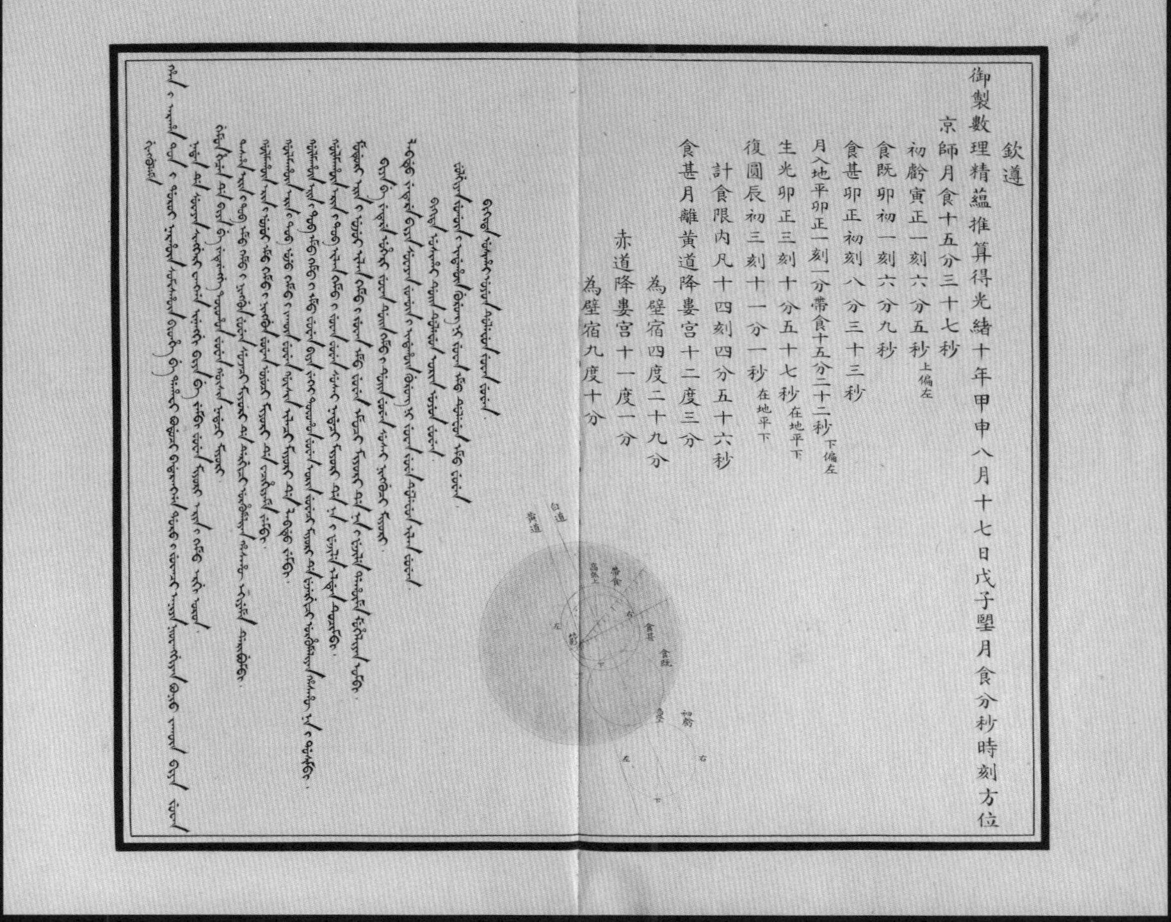

欽遵

御製數理精蘊推算得光緒十年甲申八月十七日戊子望月食分秒時刻方位

京師月食十五分三十七秒

初虧寅正一刻六分五秒 上偏左

食既卯初一刻六分九秒

食甚卯正初刻八分三十三秒

月入地平卯正一刻一分帶食十五分二十二秒 下偏左

生光卯正三刻十分五十七秒 在地平下

復圓辰初三刻十一分一秒 在地平下

計食限內凡十四刻四分五十六秒

食甚月離黃道降婁宮十二度三分

為壁宿四度二十九分

赤道降婁宮十一度一分

為壁宿九度十分

卷端
Beginning

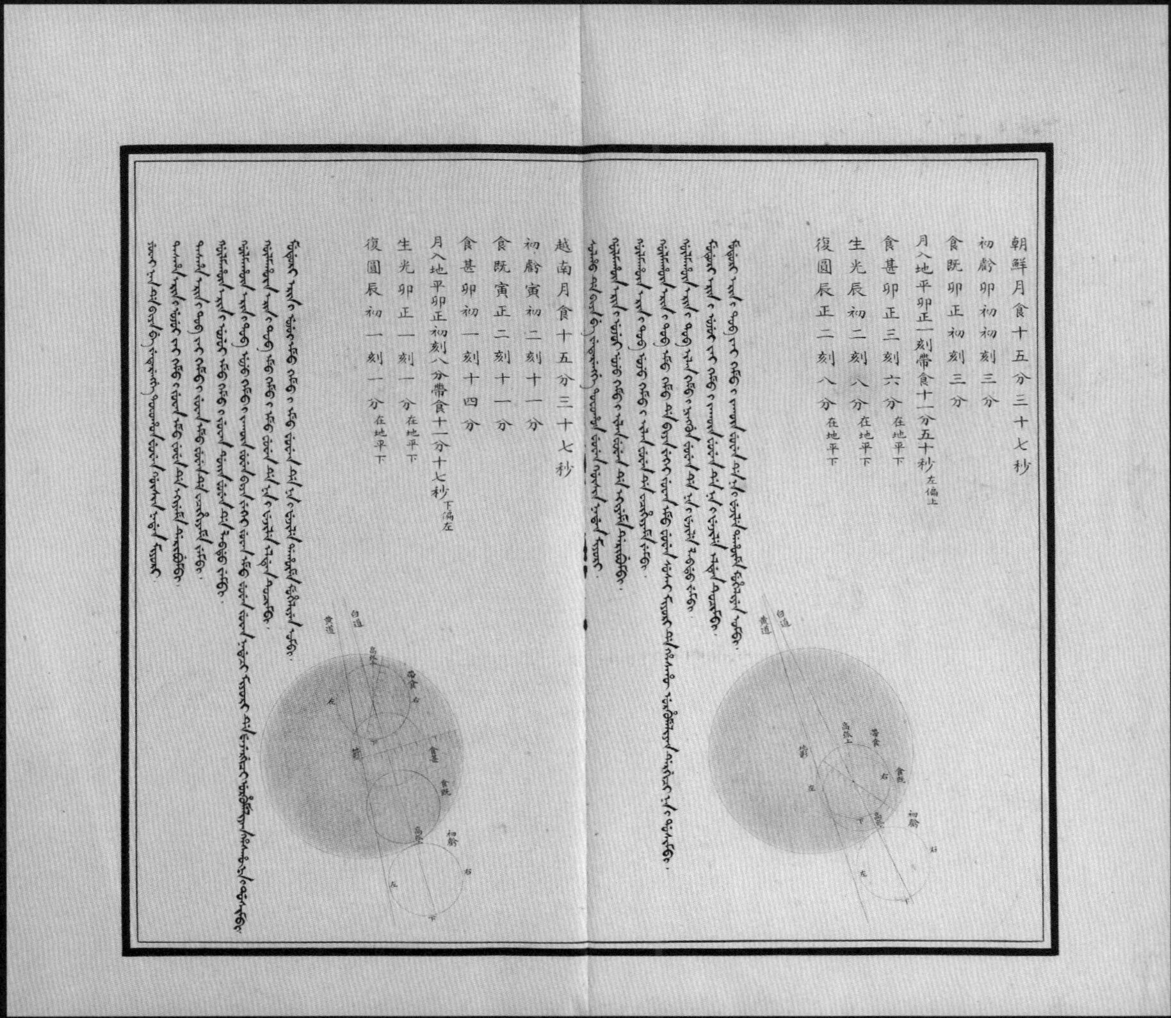

朝鮮月食十五分三十七秒

初虧卯初初刻三分

食既卯正初刻三分

月入地平卯正一刻帶食十一分五十秒 左偏上

食甚卯正三刻六分 在地平下

生光辰初二刻八分 在地平下

復圓辰正二刻八分 在地平下

越南月食十五分三十七秒

初虧寅初二刻十一分

食既寅正二刻十一分

食甚卯初一刻十四分

月入地平卯正初刻八分帶食十一分十七秒 下偏左

生光卯正一刻一分 在地平下

復圓辰初一刻一分 在地平下

正文
Text

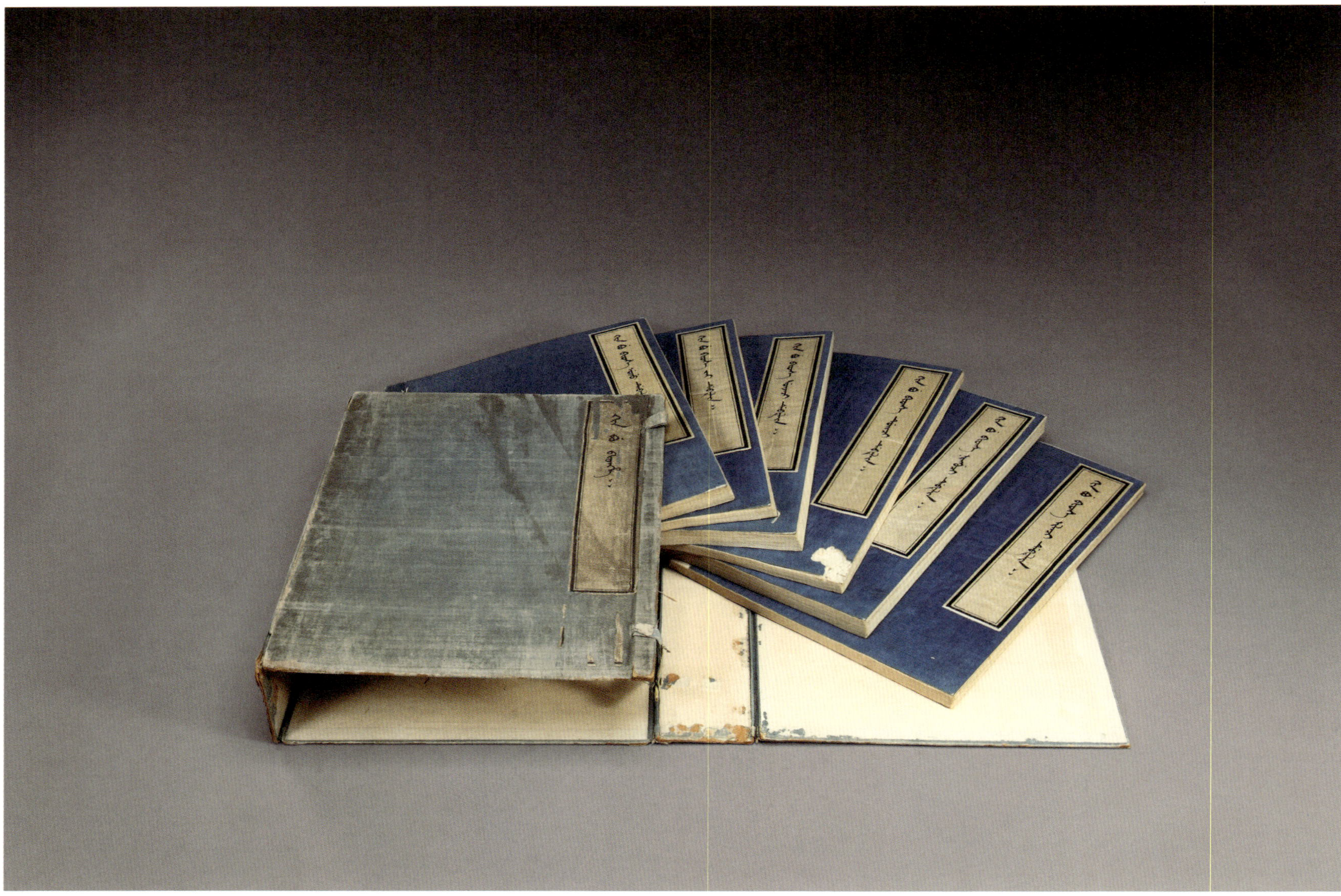

湖色素絹書函
Lake blue silk case

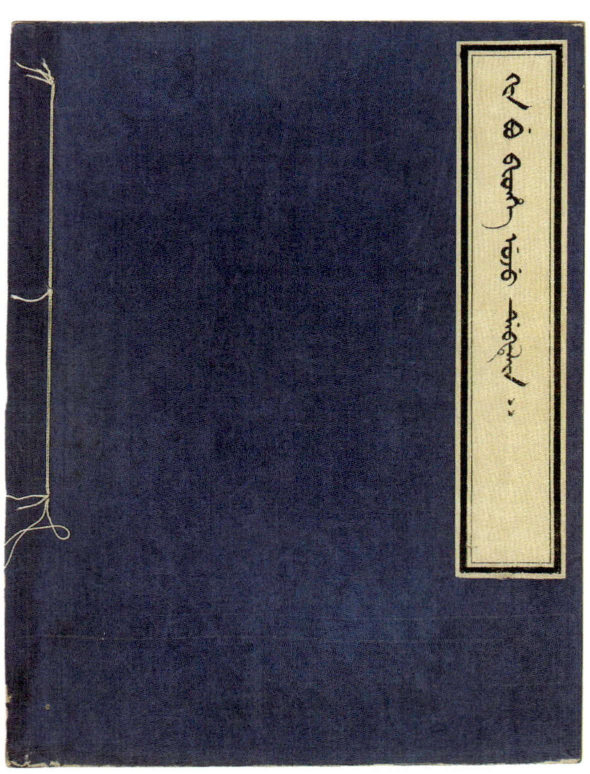

藍色素絹書面
Blue silk cover

書22491
《琴譜六卷》
清　佚名輯
清康熙年鈔滿文本
開本　縱29.5厘米　橫23厘米
六冊　一函

95

Inventory number: Shu 22491
Music Score for Qin
Six chapters
Anonymous, Qing dynasty (1644-1911)
Transcribed in Manchu in the Kangxi period (r.1662-1722)
Format: 29.5 × 23 cm
Six volumes in one case

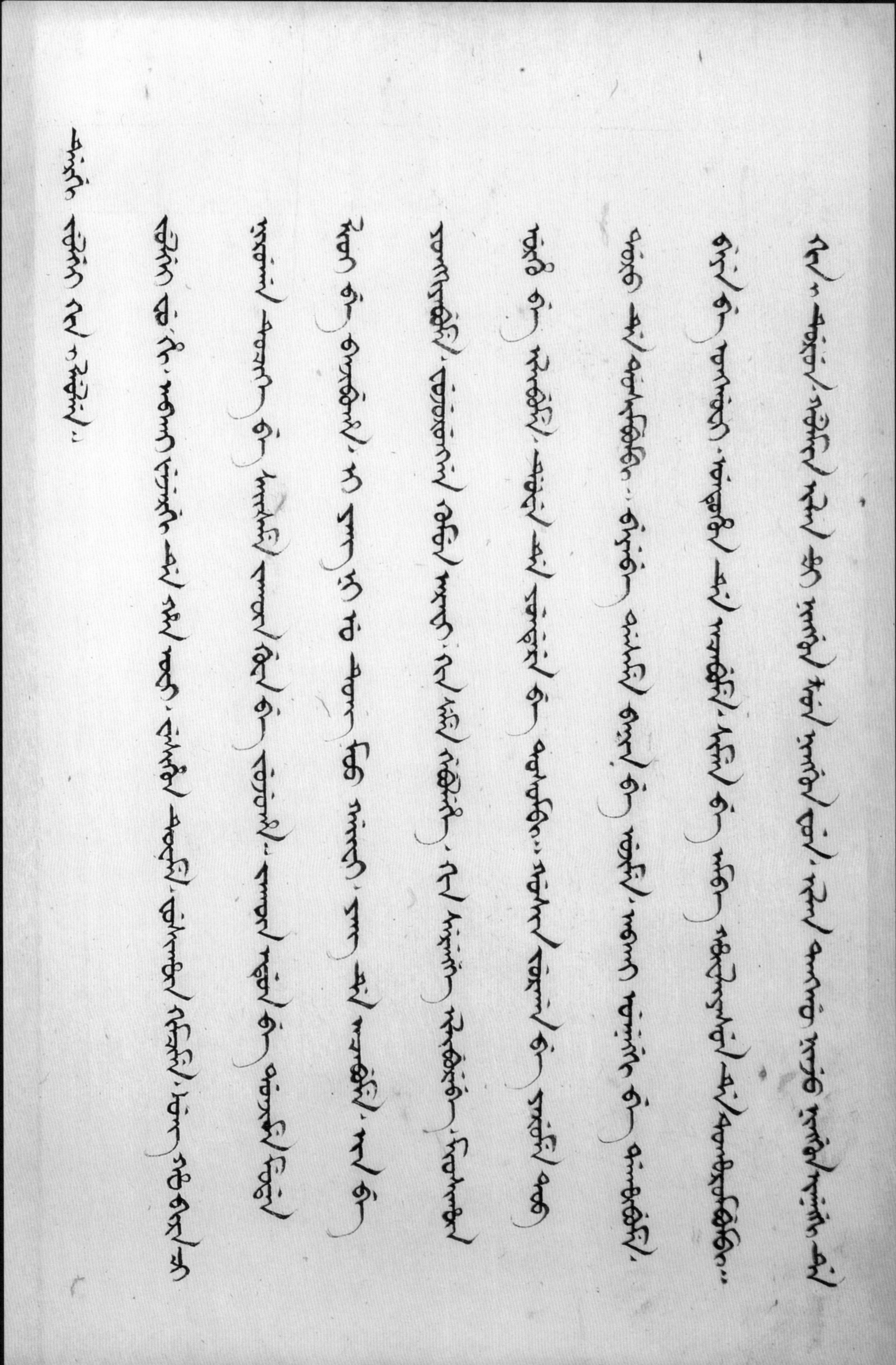

卷端
Beginning

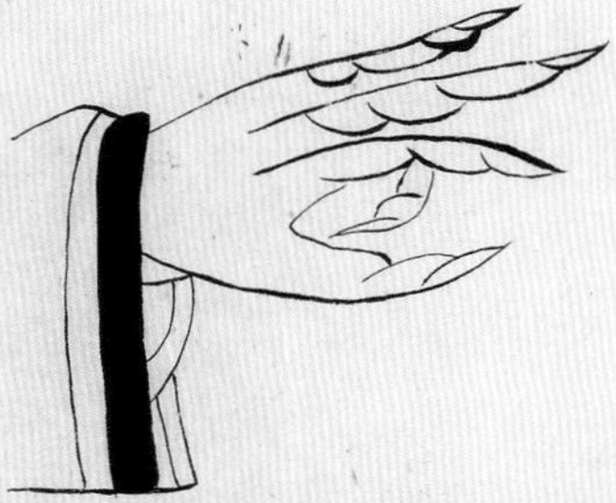

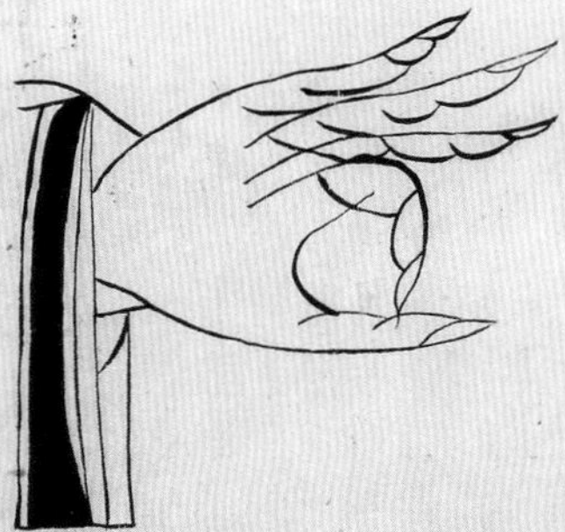

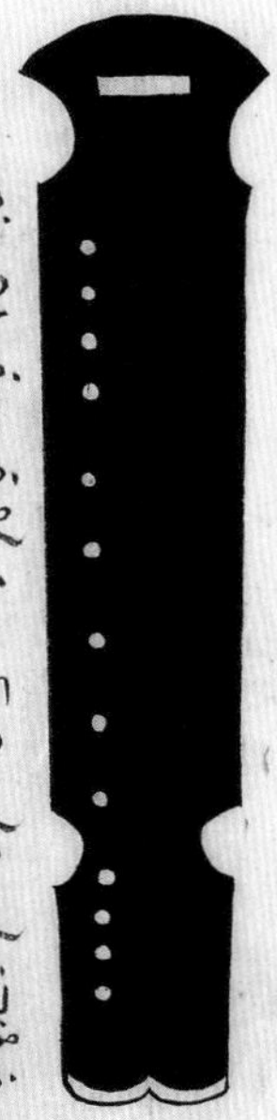

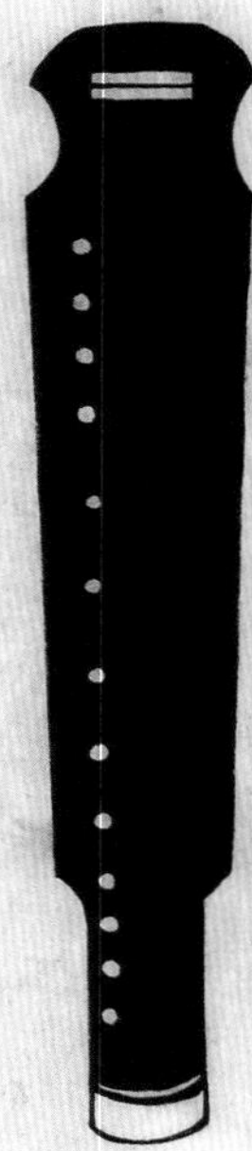

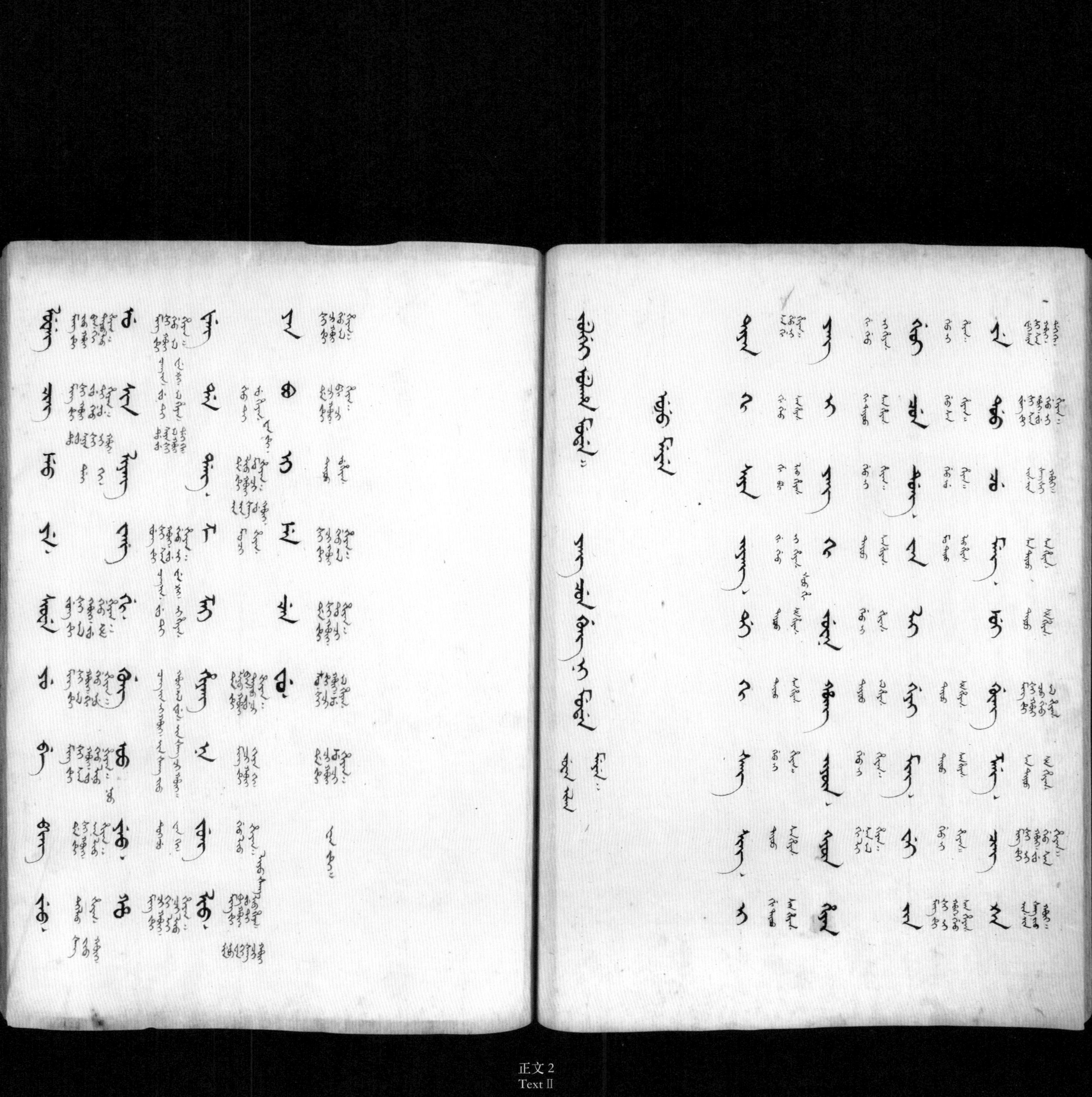

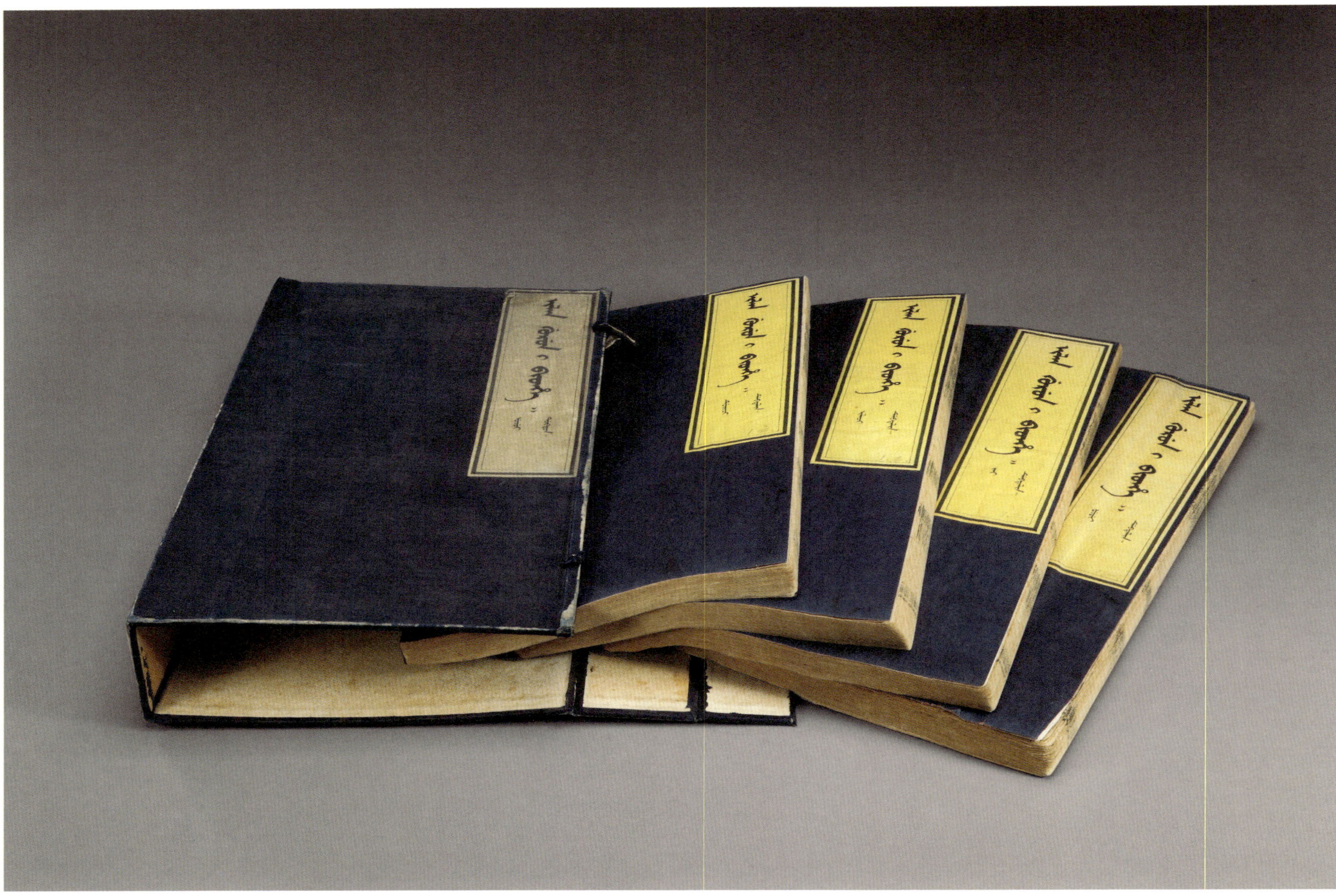

藍色素絹書函
Blue silk case

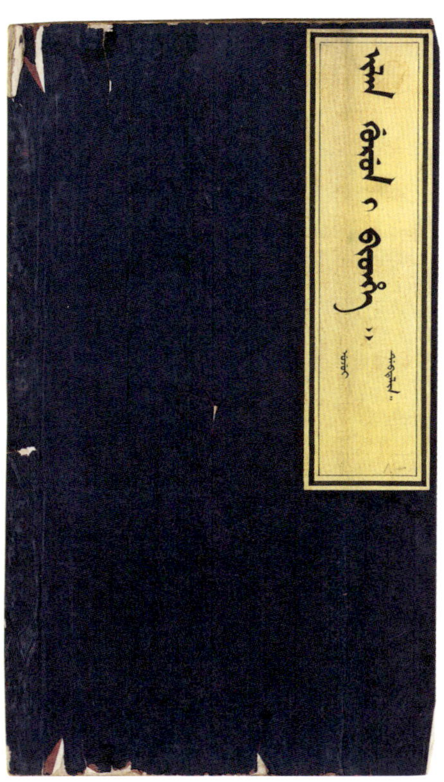

藍色紙書面
Blue paper cover

96

書22521
《三國志演義二十四卷》
元　羅貫中撰　清　達海等譯
清順治七年（1650）內府刻滿文本
開本　縱39.5厘米　橫22.6厘米
版框　縱28.8厘米　橫21厘米
二十四册　六函

Inventory number: Shu 22521
Romance of the Three Kingdoms
Twenty-four chapters
Written by Luo Guanzhong, Yuan dynasty (1271-1368)
Translated by Dahai et. al., Qing dynasty (1644-1911)
Printed in Manchu in 1650 by the Qing court
Format: 39.5 × 22.6 cm
Frame: 28.8 × 21 cm
Twenty-four volumes in six cases

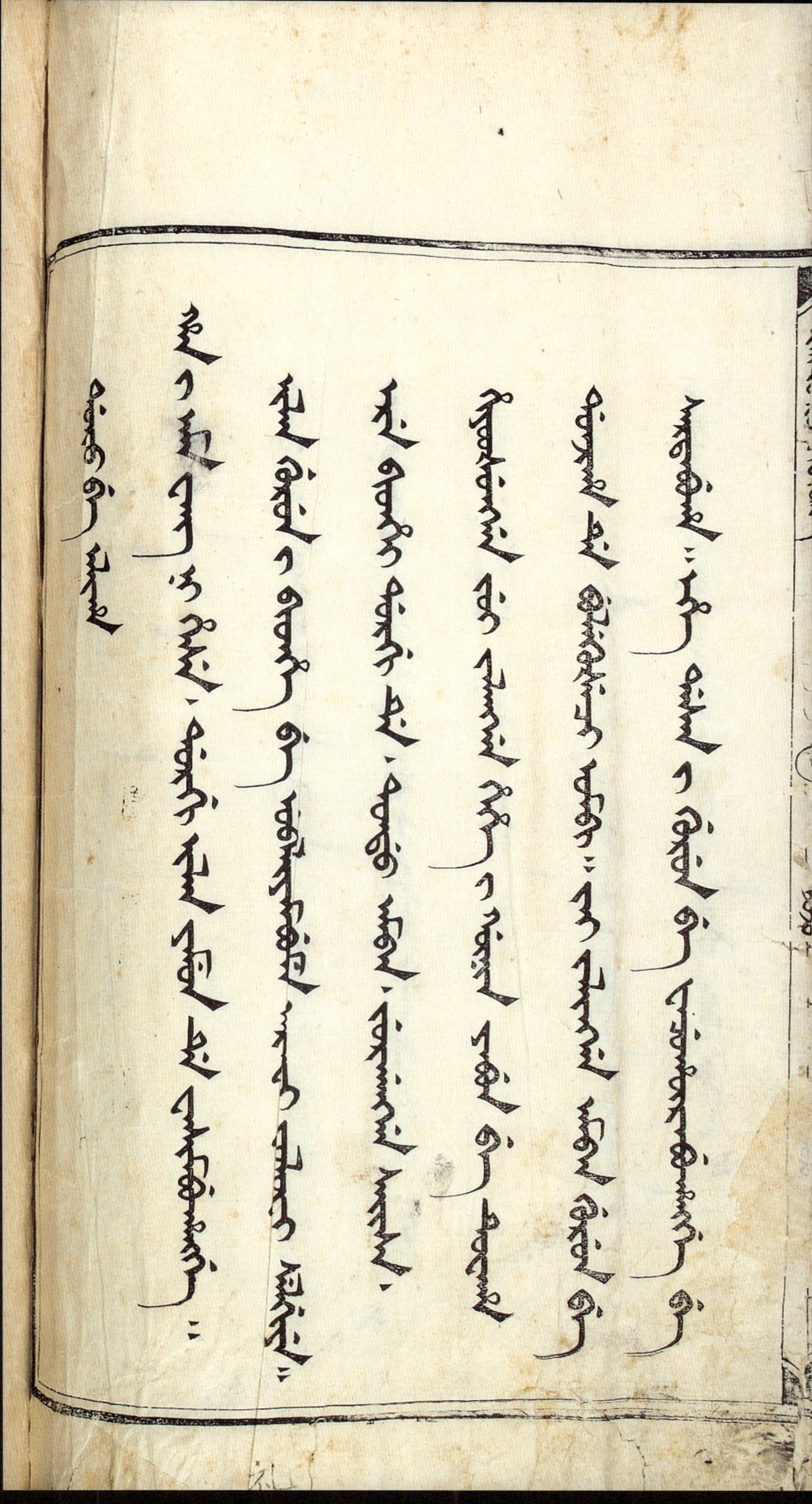

順治七年皇父攝政王上諭
Edict by the Imperial Father Prince Regent

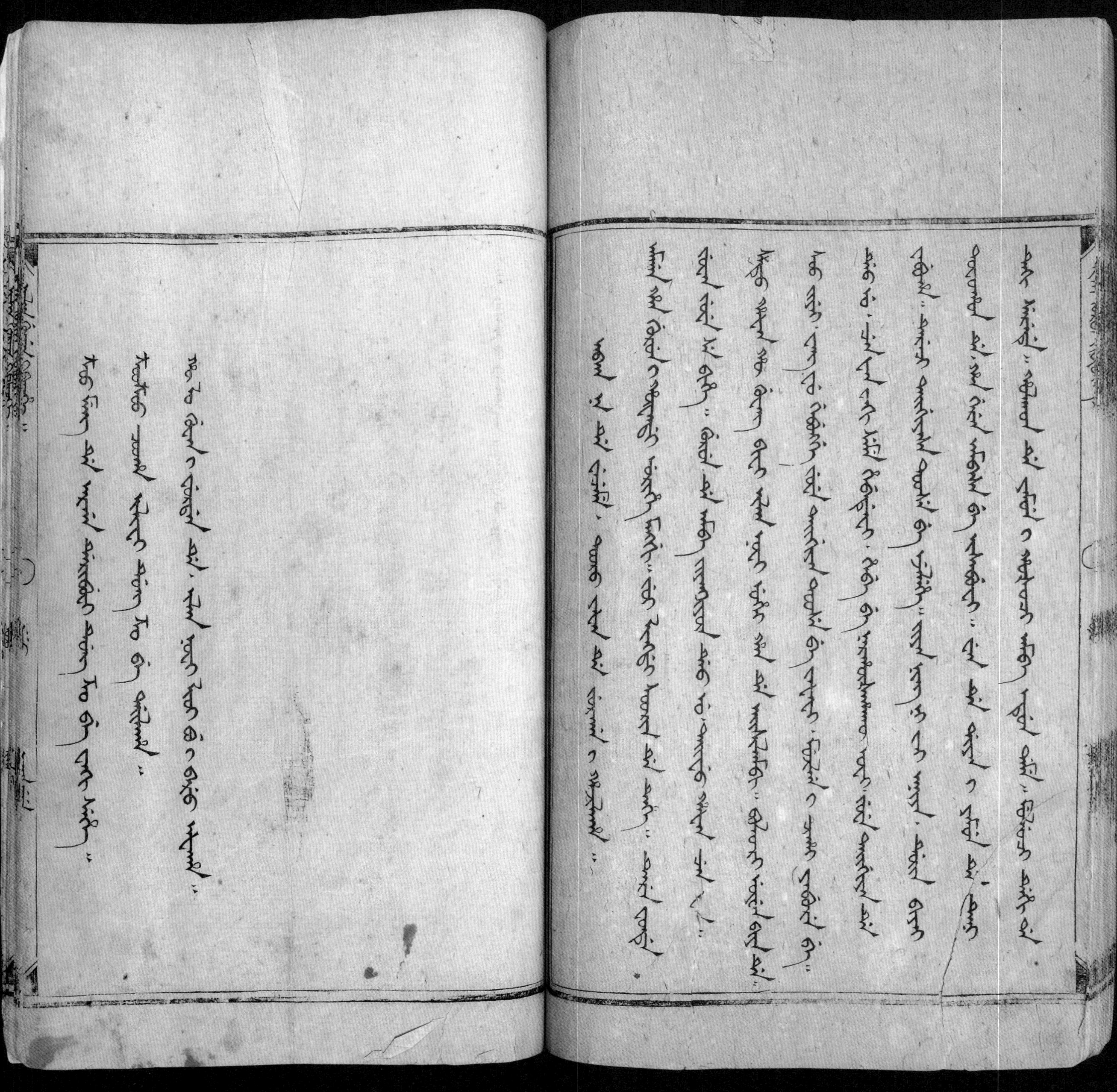

卷目及卷端
Contents and Beginning

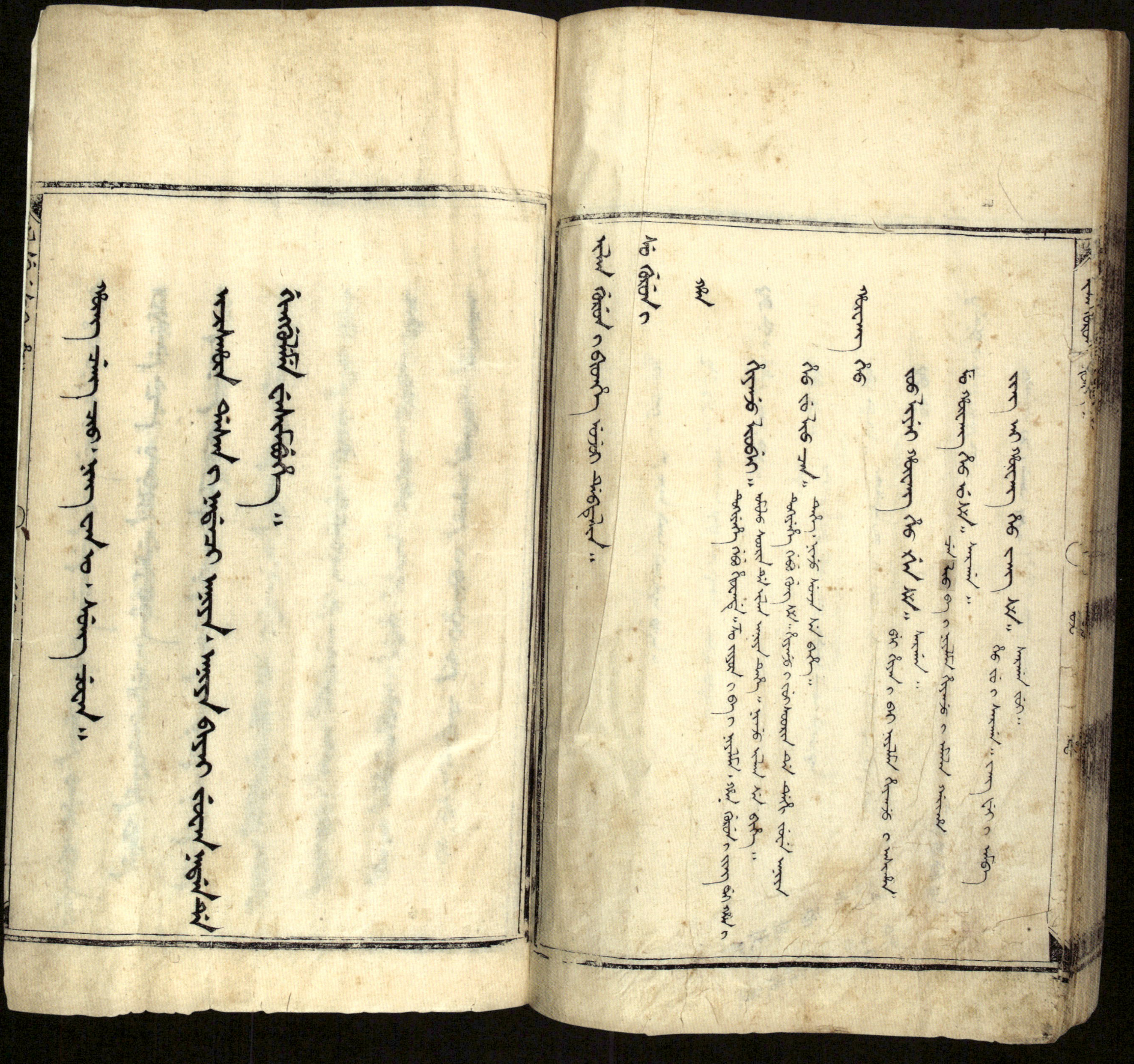

序及卷首人物簡介
Preface and a brief introduction to characters

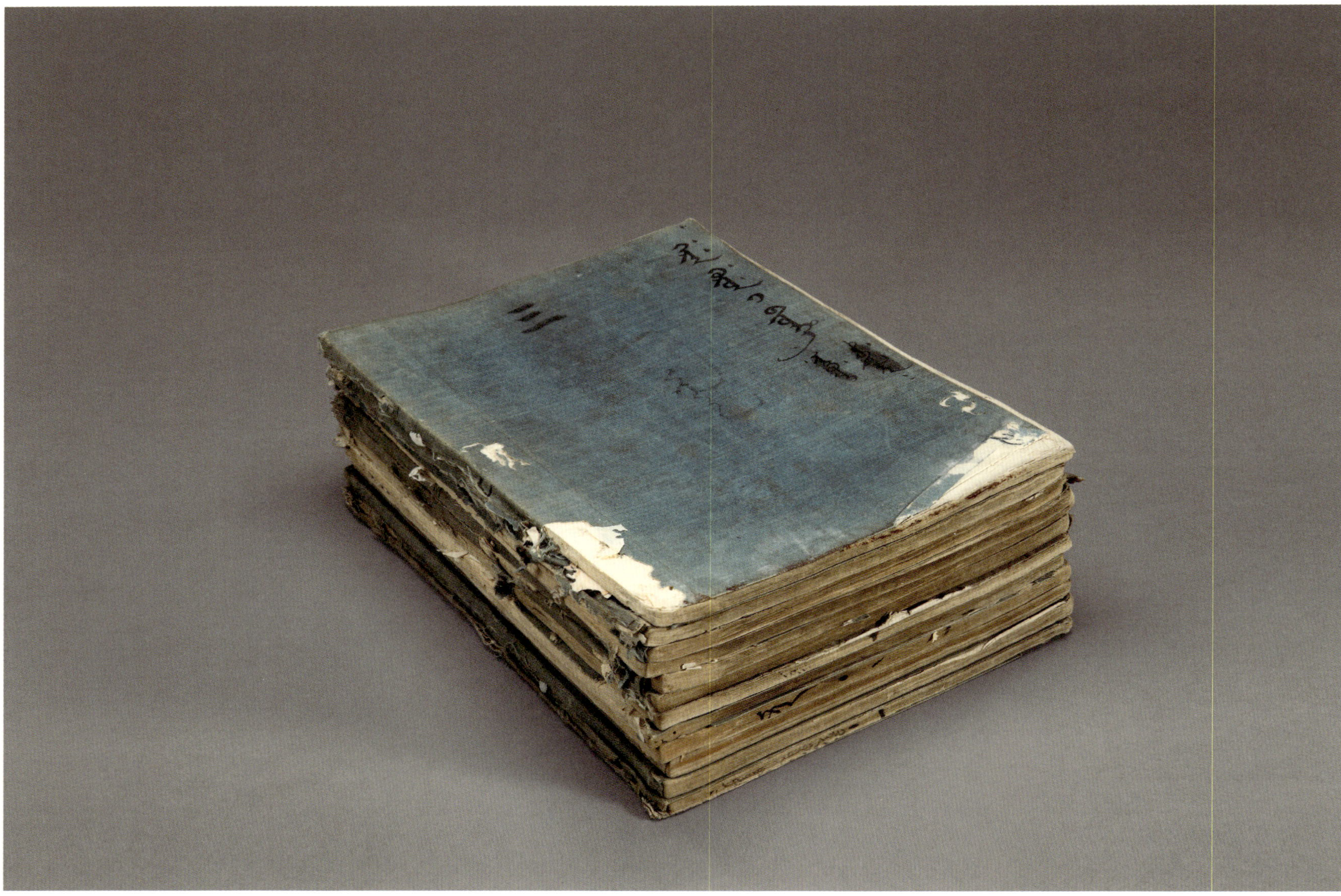

湖色素絹書面
Lake blue silk cover

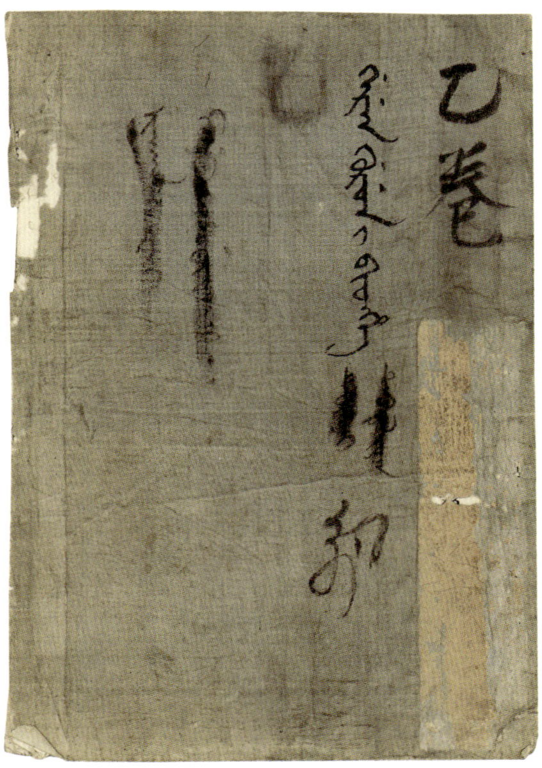

湖色素絹書面
Lake blue silk cover

97

書21981
《列國志一百八回》
明　馮夢龍撰　清　佚名譯
清初鈔滿文本
開本　縱32厘米　橫23厘米
存二十九册　二函

Inventory number: Shu 21981
Records of the States
108 chapters
Written by Feng Menglong, Ming dynasty (1368-1644)
Translator unknown, Qing dynasty (1644-1911)
Transcribed in Manchu in the early Qing dynasty
Format: 32 × 23 cm
Twenty-nine volumes in two cases extant today

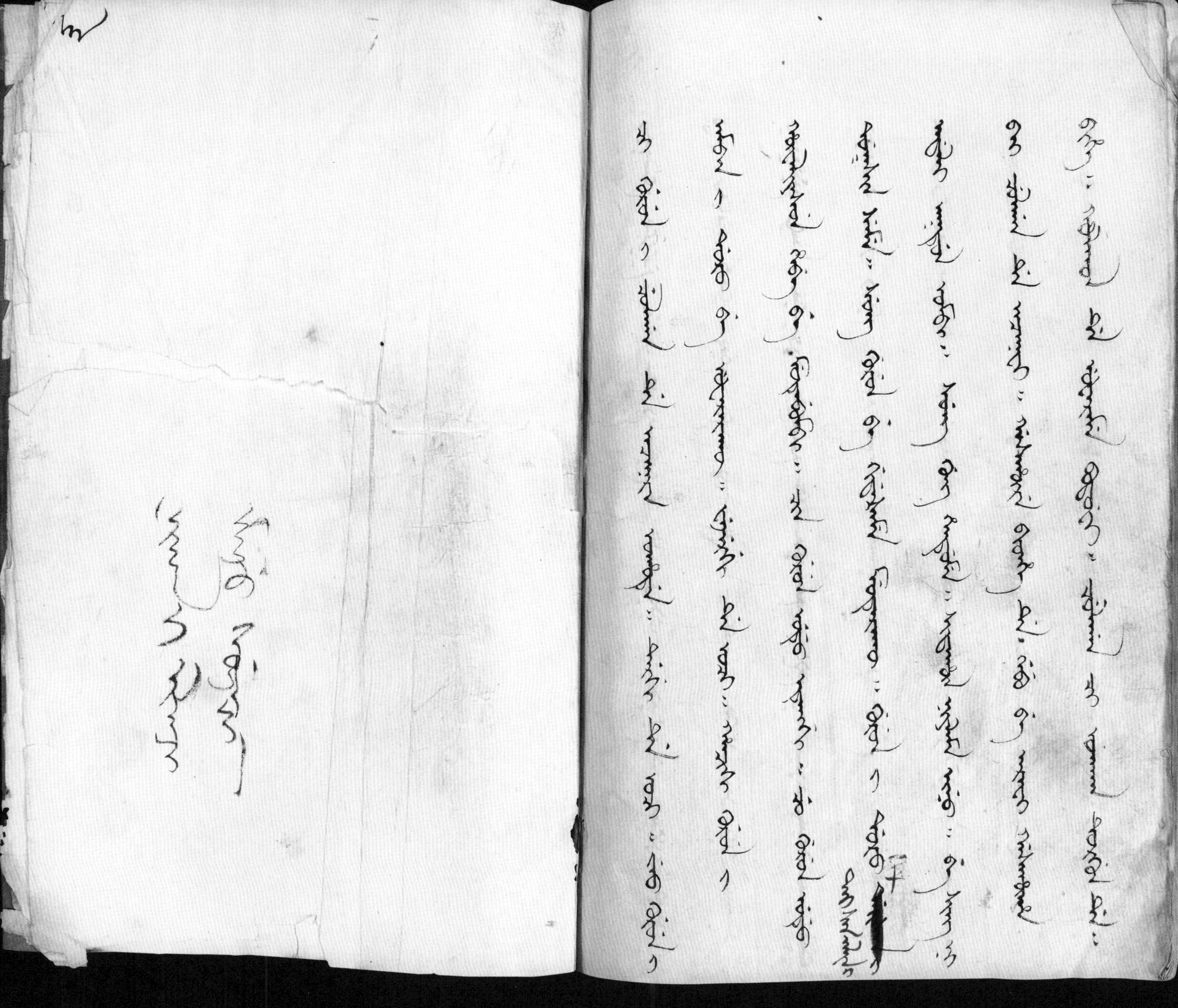

卷端
Beginning

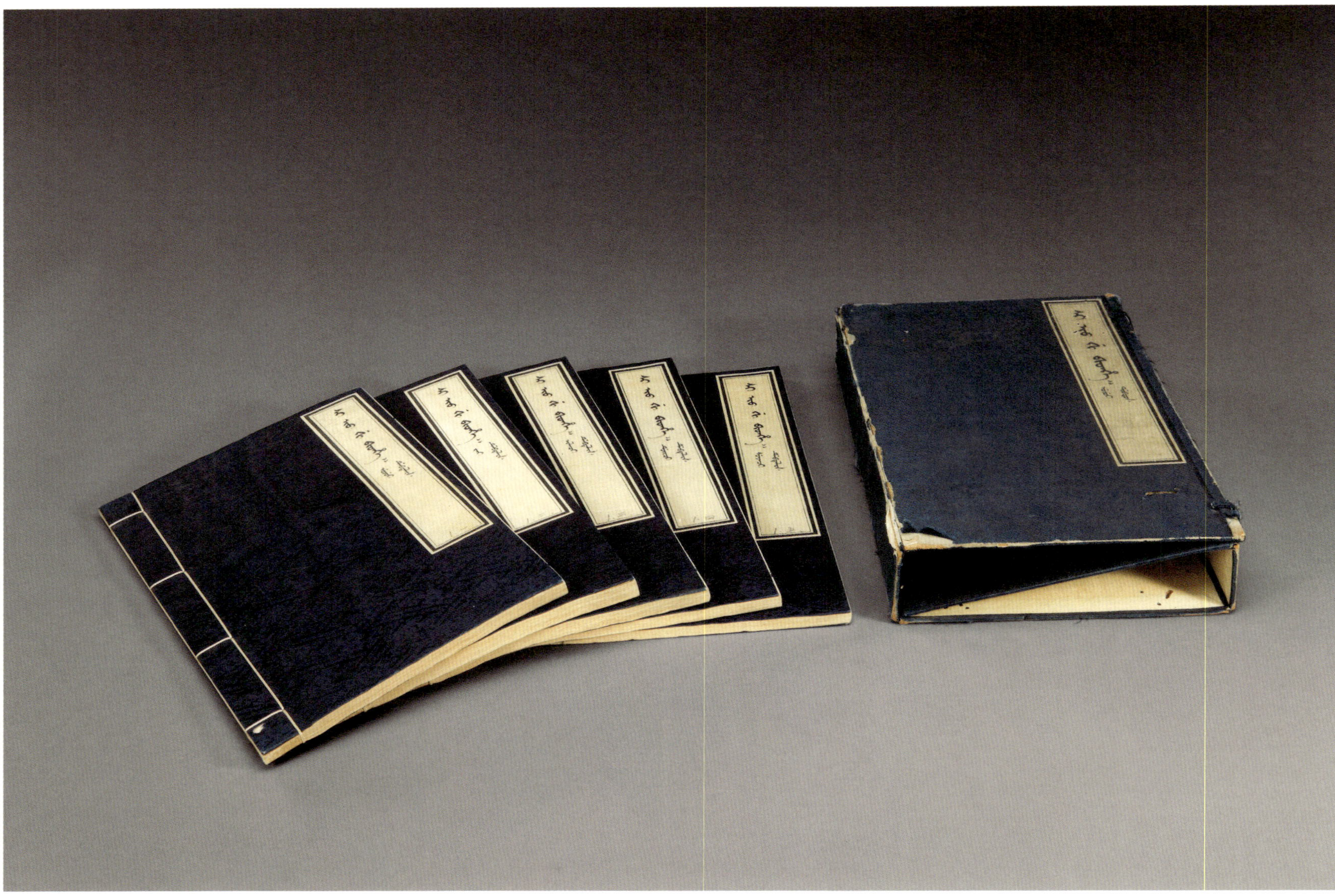

外觀
Exterior

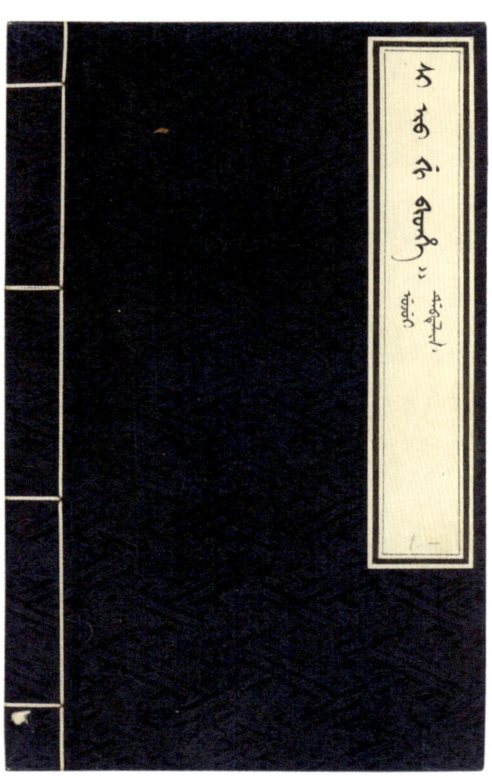

藍色曲水雜寶紋暗花綾書面
Blue twill-weave silk cover with veiled swastika and treasure pattern

98

書22531
《西游記一百則》
明 吴承恩撰 清 佚名譯
清内府精寫滿文本
開本 縱30.8厘米 橫20厘米
版框 縱23.2厘米 橫17厘米
五十册 十函

Inventory number: Shu 22531
Journey to the West
100 chapters
Written by Wu Cheng'en, Ming dynasty (1368-1644)
Translator unknown, Qing dynasty (1644-1911)
Transcribed in Manchu by the Qing court
Format: 30.8 × 20 cm
Frame: 23.2 × 17 cm
Fifty volumes in ten cases

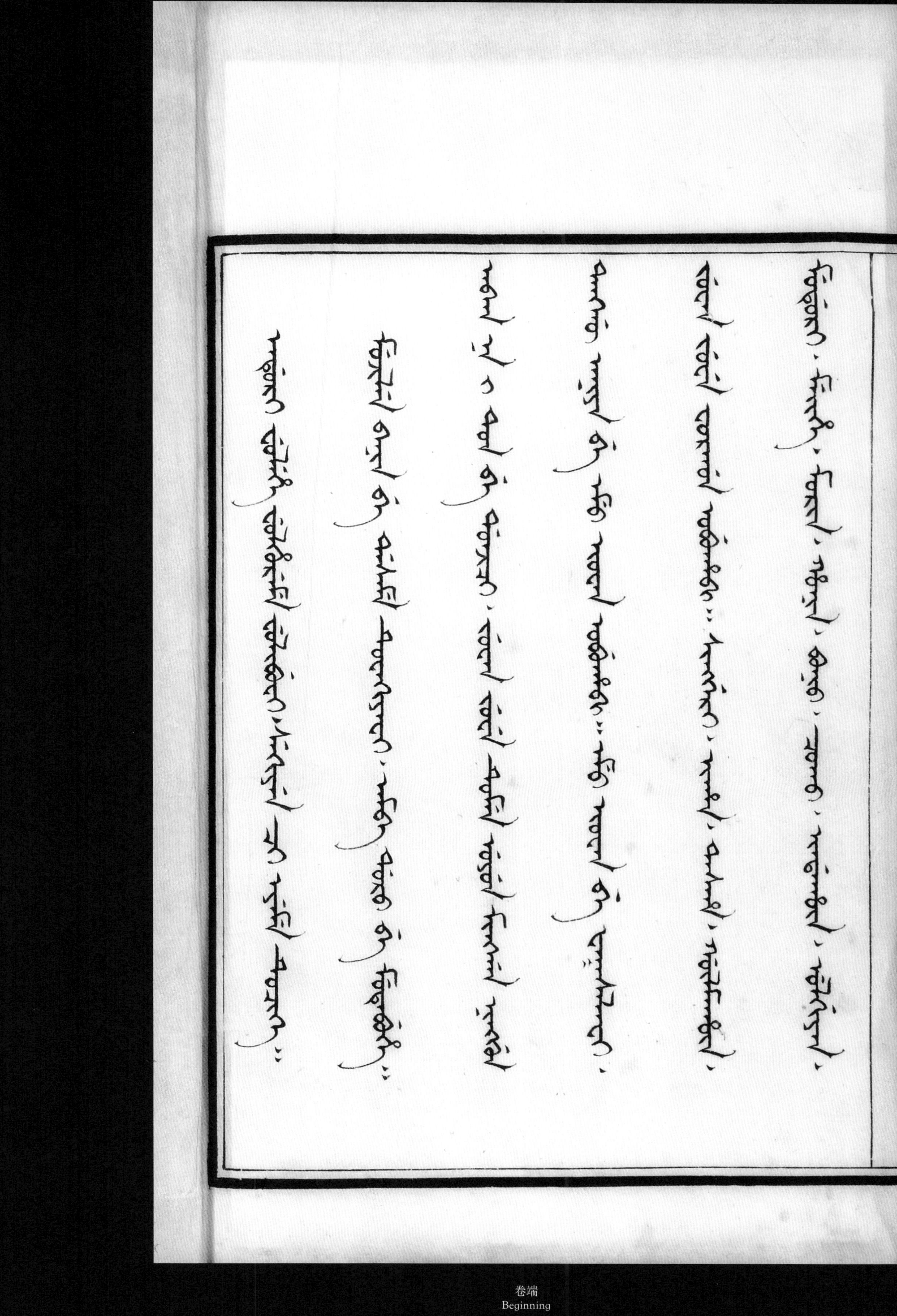

[illegible]

[illegible]

[illegible]

[illegible]

[illegible]

[illegible]

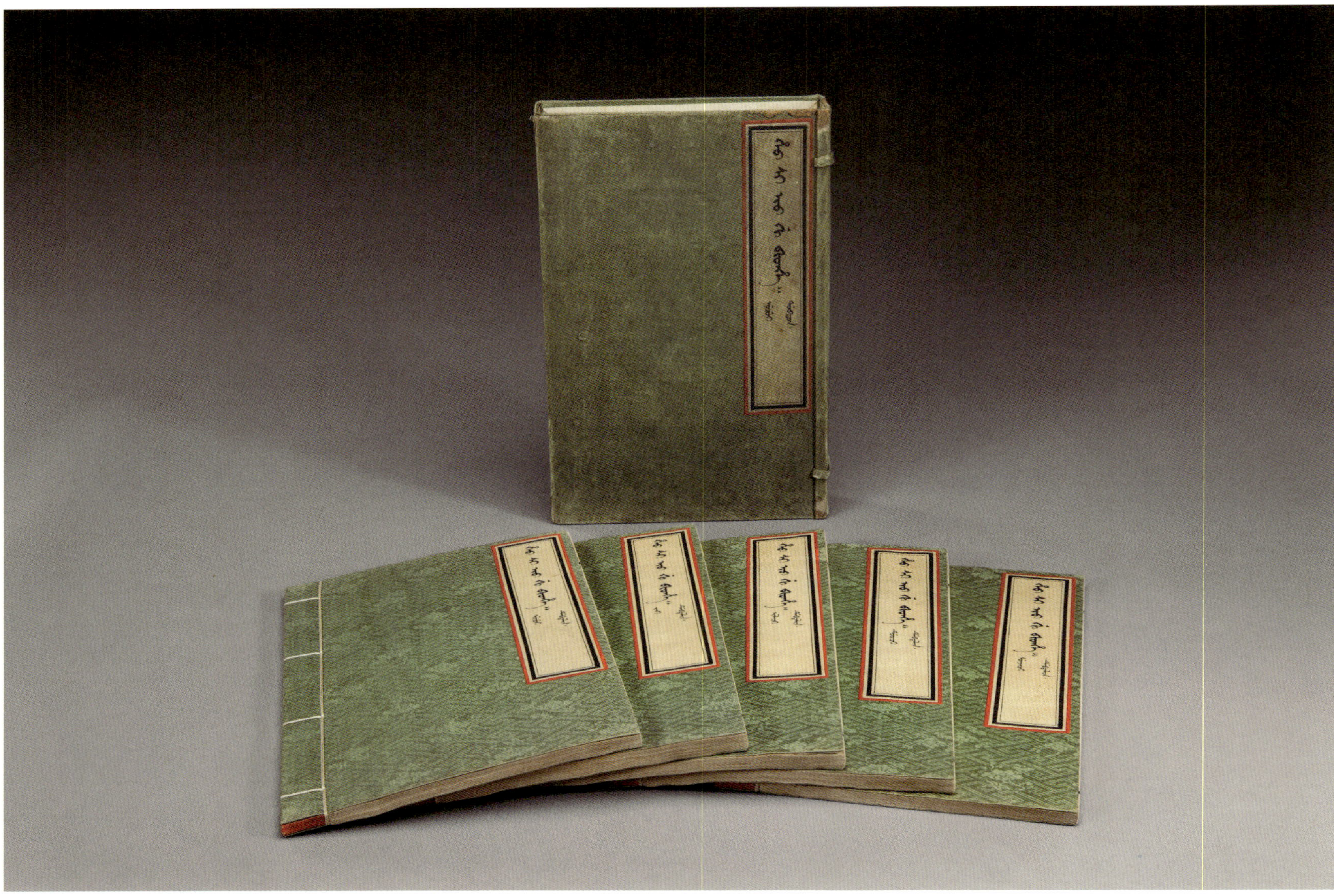

绿色曲水朵花紋暗花綾書函
Green twill-weave silk case with veiled swastika and floral pattern

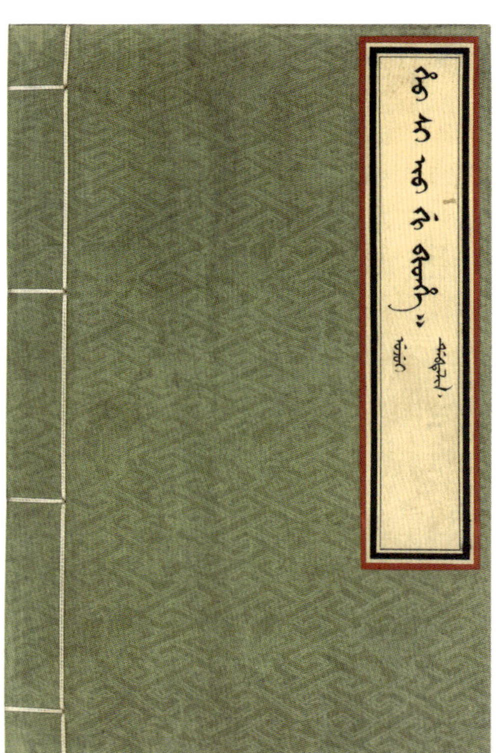

绿色曲水朵花紋暗花綾書面
Green twill-weave silk cover with veiled swastika and floral pattern

書22532
《後西游記四十回》
清　天花才子撰　佚名譯
清内府精寫滿文本
開本　縱31厘米　横22厘米
版框　縱23.2厘米　横17厘米
二十册　四函

99

Inventory number: Shu 22532
Sequel to "Journey to the West"
Forty chapters
Written by Tianhua Caizi, Qing dynasty (1644-1911)
Translator unknown, Qing dynasty (1644-1911)
Transcribed in Manchu by the Qing court
Format: 31 × 22 cm
Frame: 23.2 × 17 cm
Twenty volumes in four cases

卷端
Beginning

序
Preface

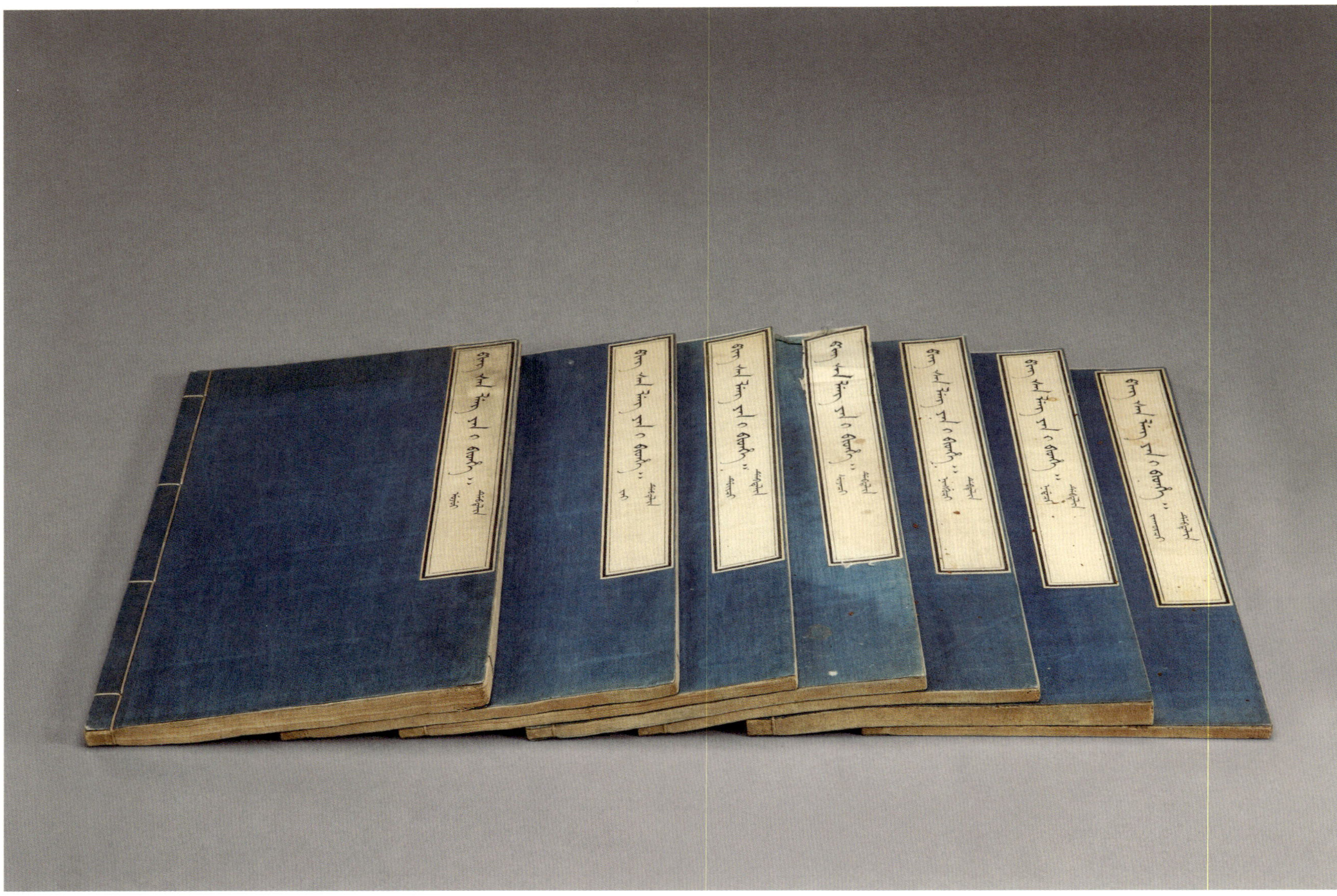

藍色素絹書面
Blue silk covers

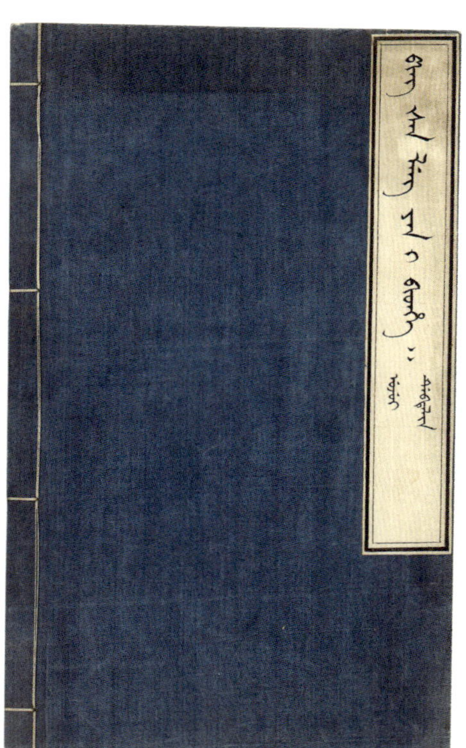

藍色素絹書面
Blue silk cover

100

書22542
《平山冷燕十六卷》
清　獲岸散人撰
清精寫滿文本
開本　縱28.4厘米　橫17.2厘米
版框　縱21.6厘米　橫15.1厘米
十六册　二函

Inventory number: Shu 22542
Ping Shan Leng Yan
Sixteen chapters
Written by Di'ansanren, Qing dynasty (1644-1911)
Transcribed in Manchu in the Qing dynasty
Format: 28.4 × 17.2 cm
Frame: 21.6 × 15.1 cm
Sixteen volumes in two cases

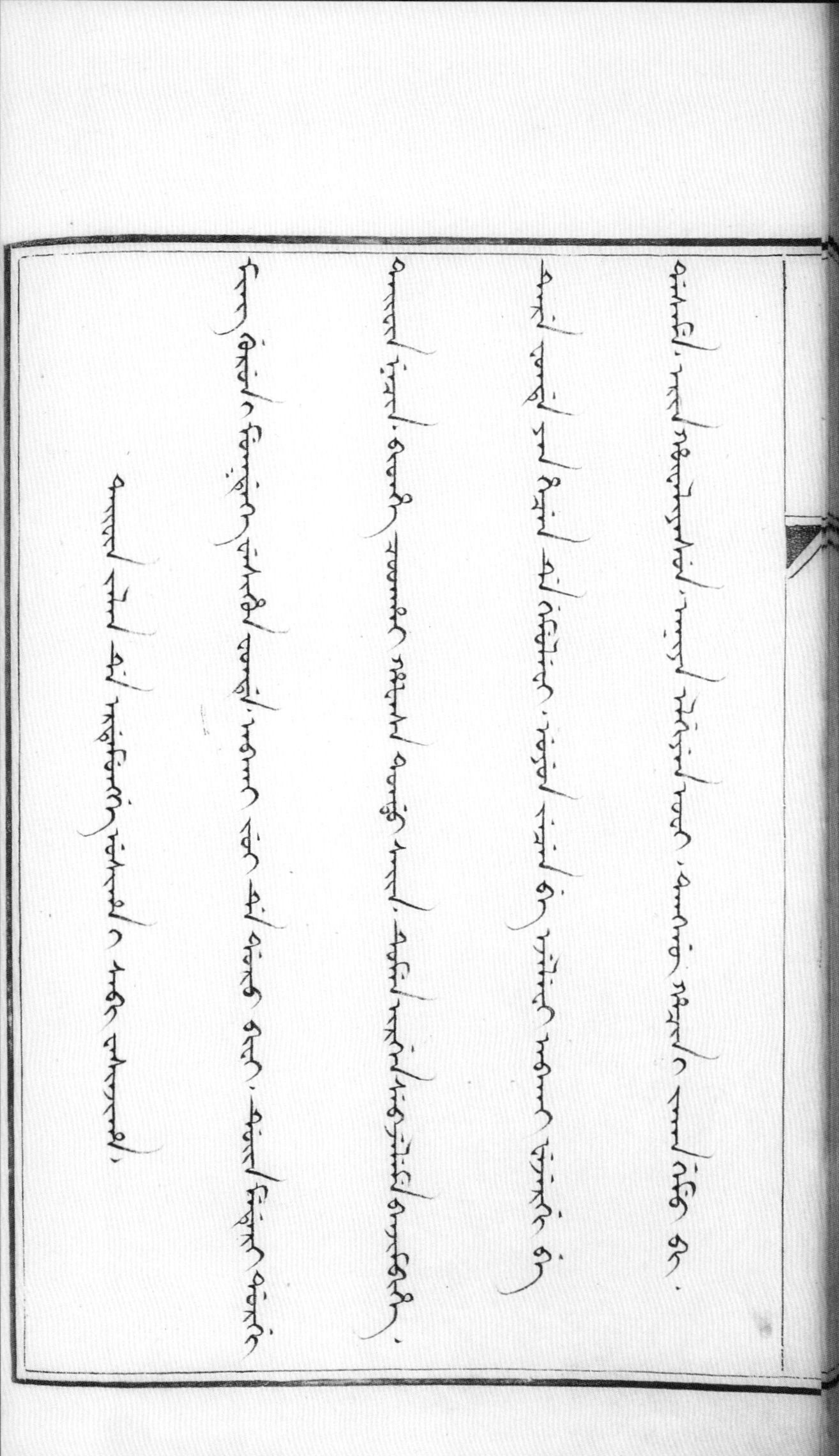

卷端
Beginning

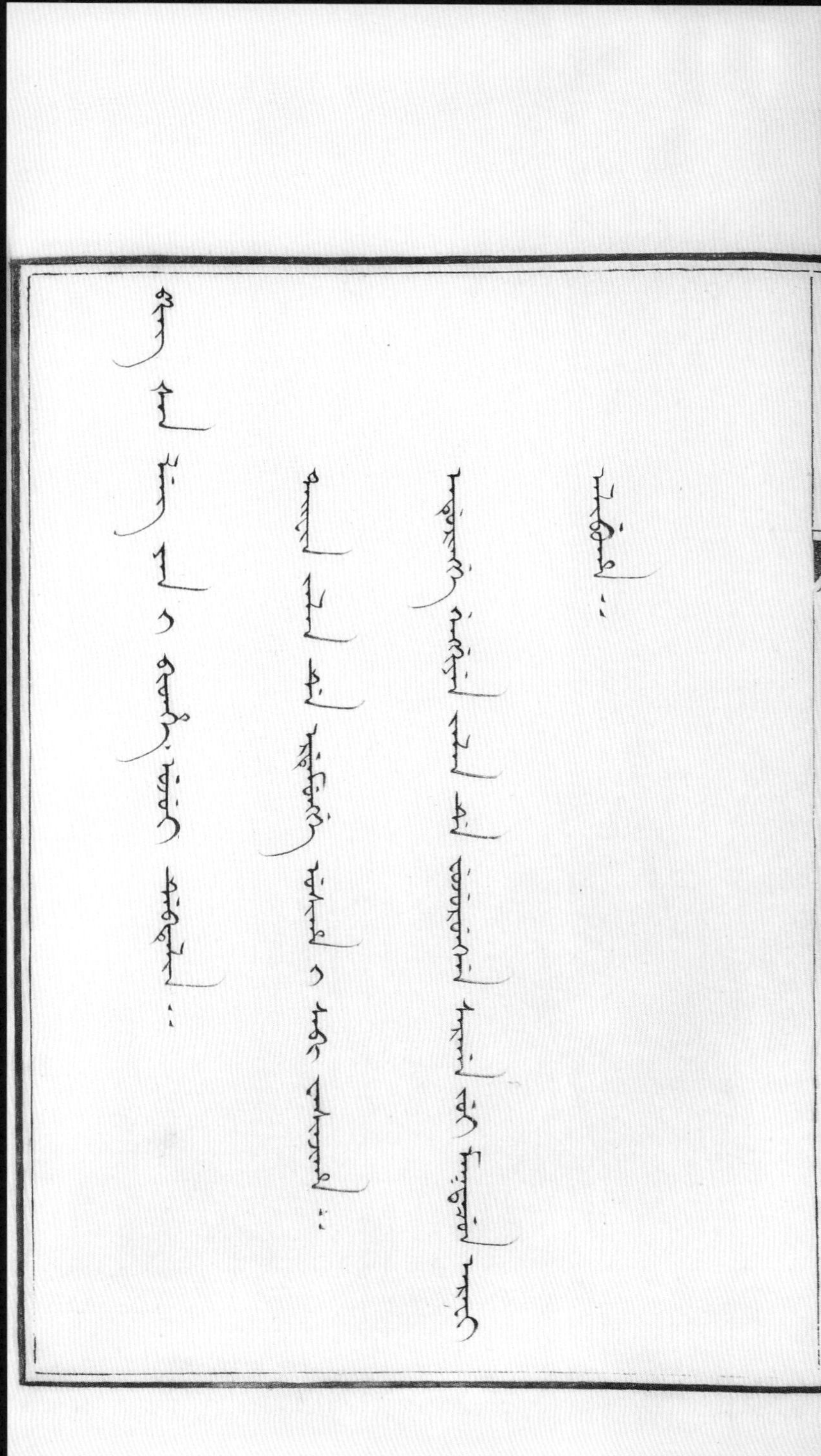

卷目
Contents

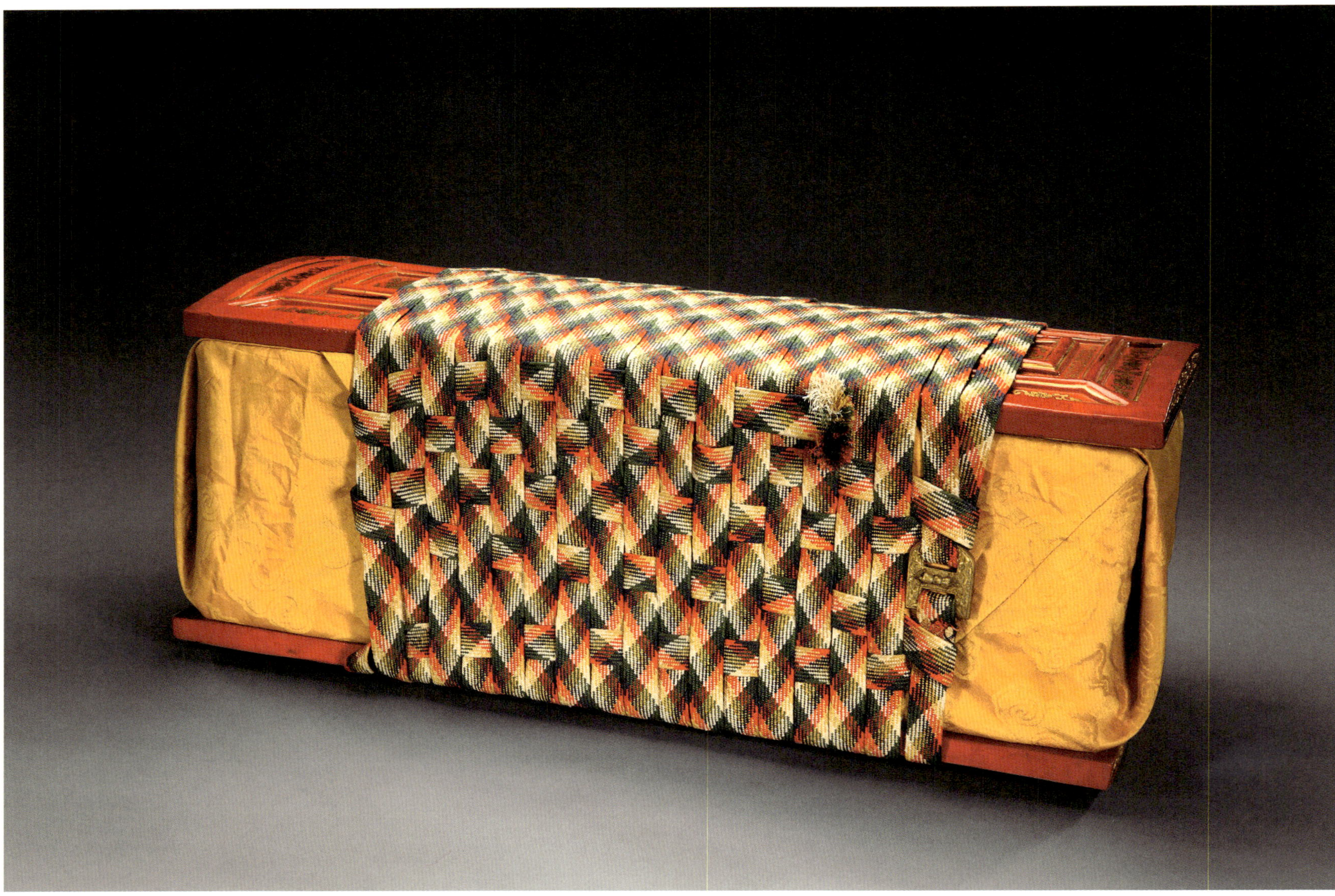

朱漆護經板外纏五彩絛帶
Red lacquer protective boards wrapped with five-colored cord

書27120
《清文翻譯全藏經一百八卷目録一卷》
清　章嘉三世若畢多吉等奉敕譯
乾隆五十九年（1794）武英殿刻朱印滿文本
開本　縱45厘米　橫24厘米
版框　縱35厘米　橫20.6厘米
存76册　76函

101

Inventory number: Shu 27120
Tripitaka in Manchu
108 chapters as text, one chapter as contents
Translated by imperial order by Icang-skya III et. al., Qing dynasty (1644-1911)
Printed in red in 1794 at the Hall of Martial Valour
Format: 45 × 24 cm
Frame: 35 × 20.6 cm
Seventy-six volumes in seventy-six cases extant today

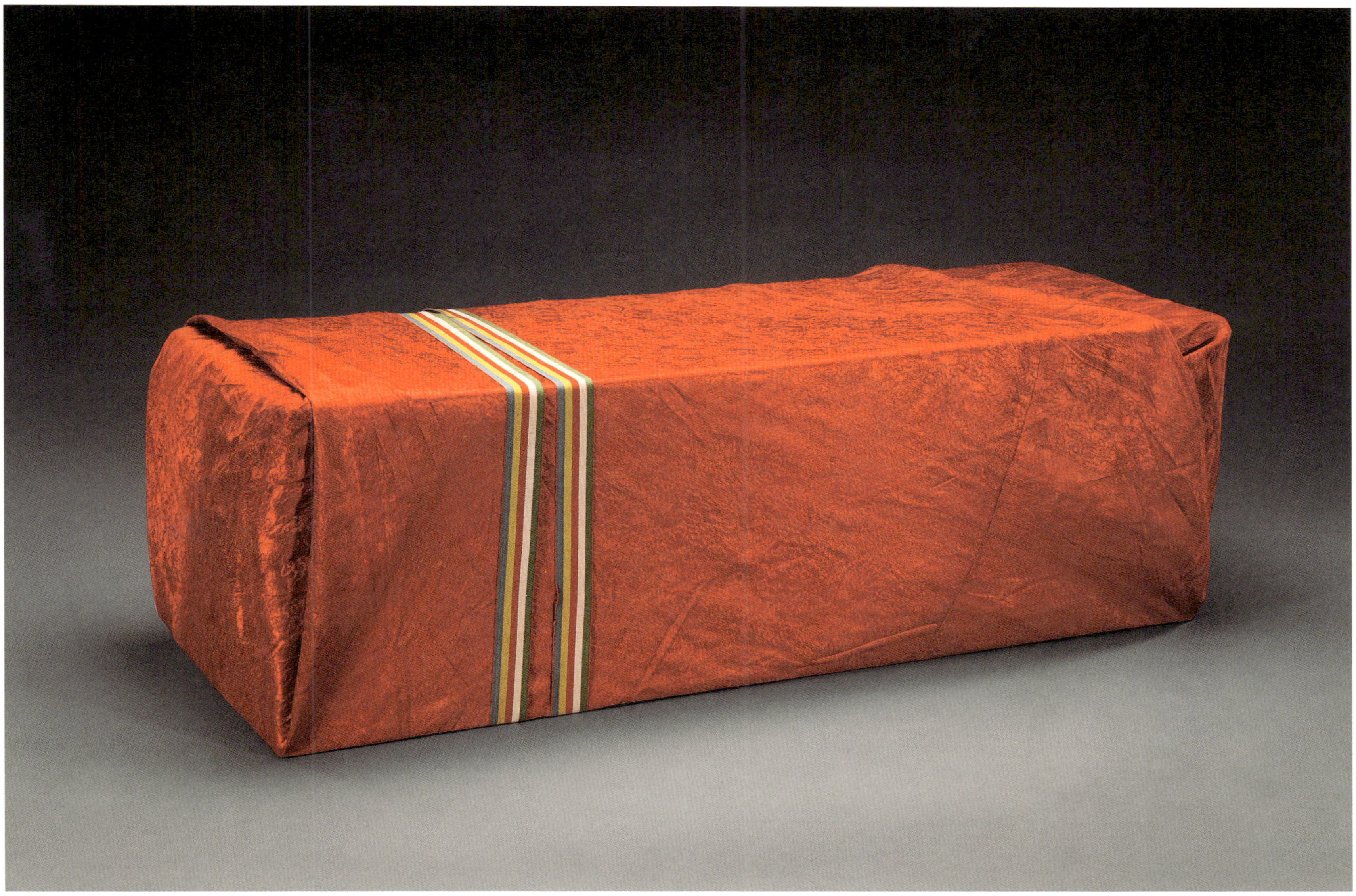

紅色暗花綢單袱
Red silk wrapping with veiled pattern

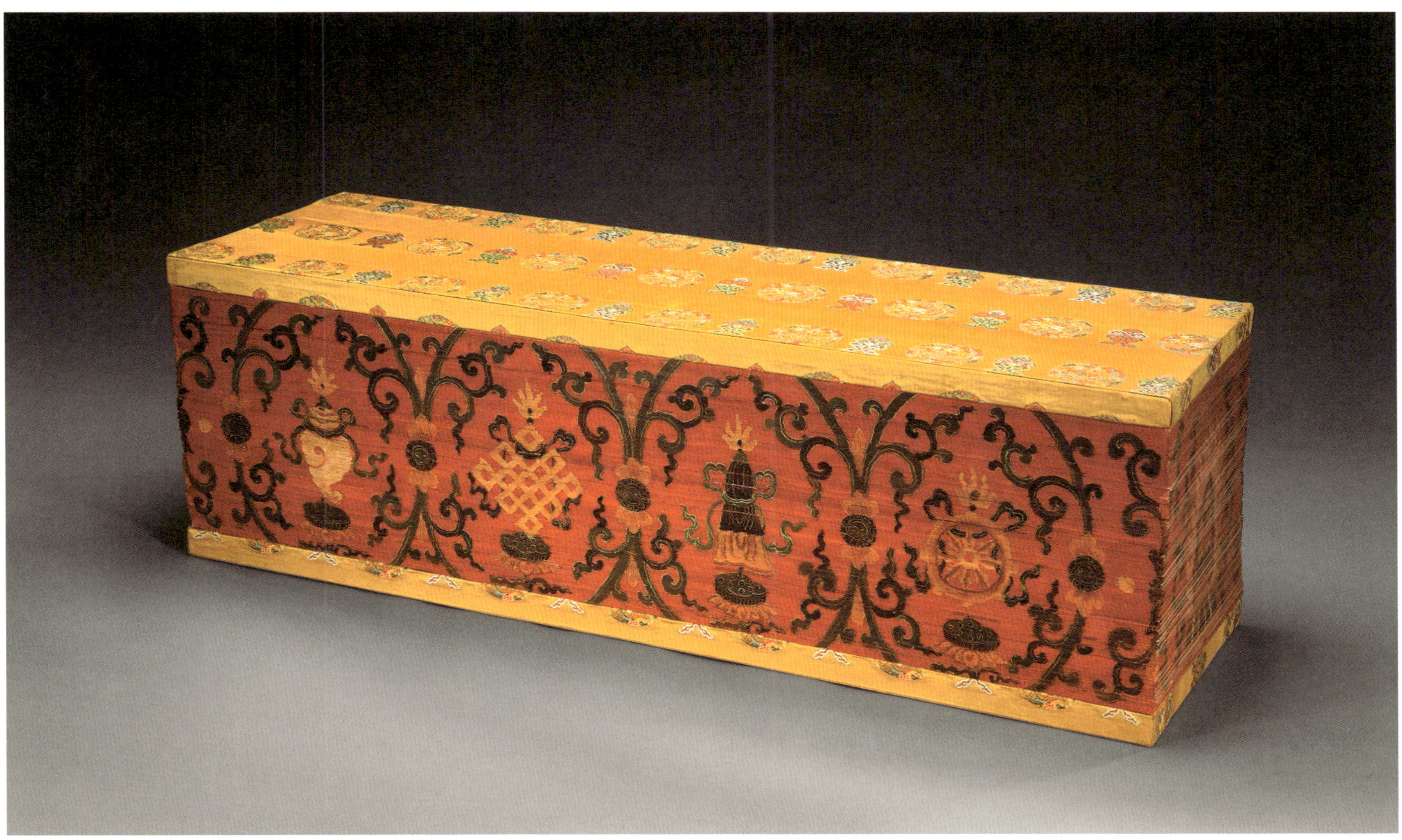

内護經板及經頁側面八寶圖
Inner protective board and the pattern of eight emblems on one side of the stacked sutra leaves

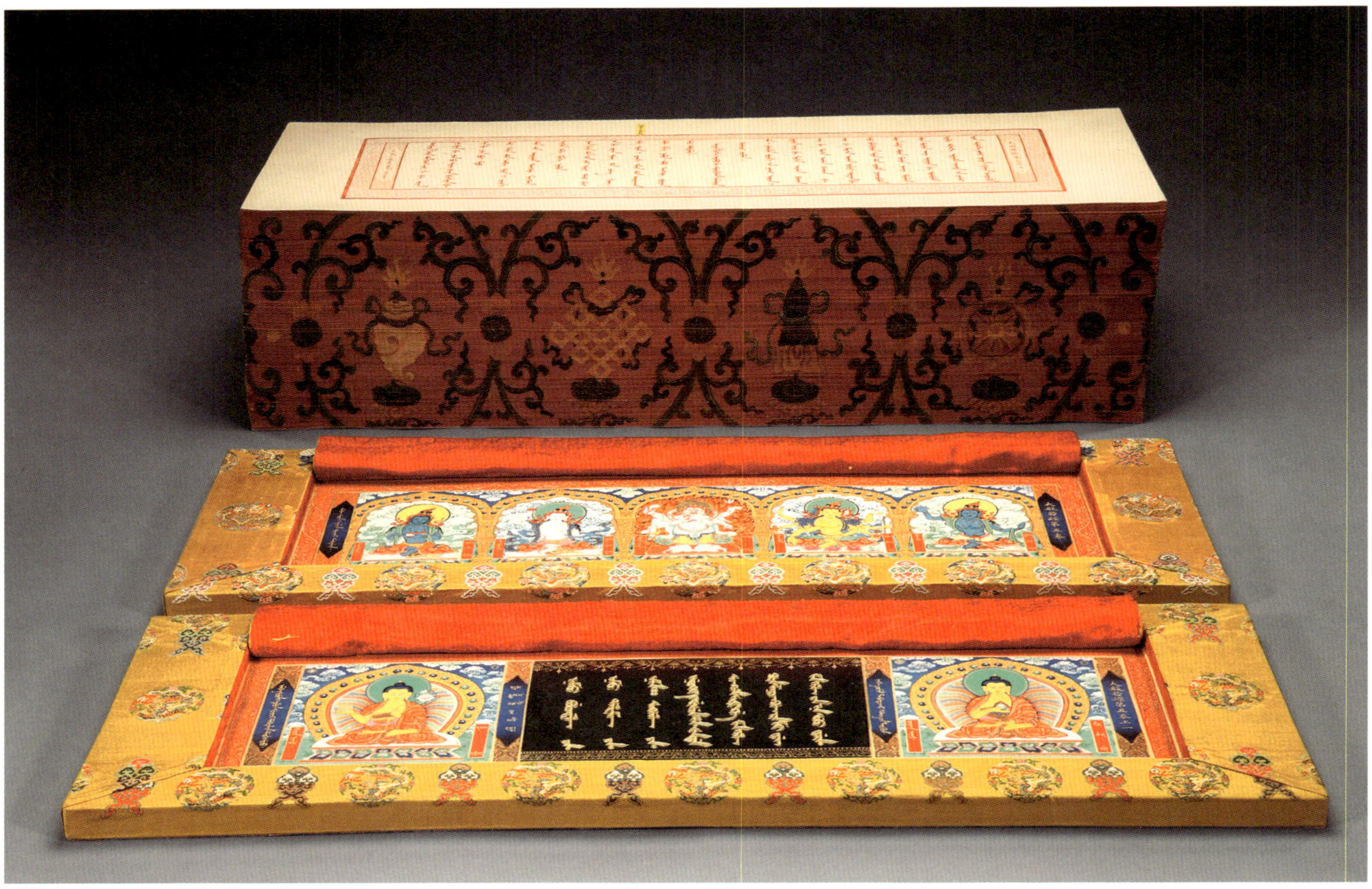

卷首、卷末佛像
Buddhist figures at beginning and end

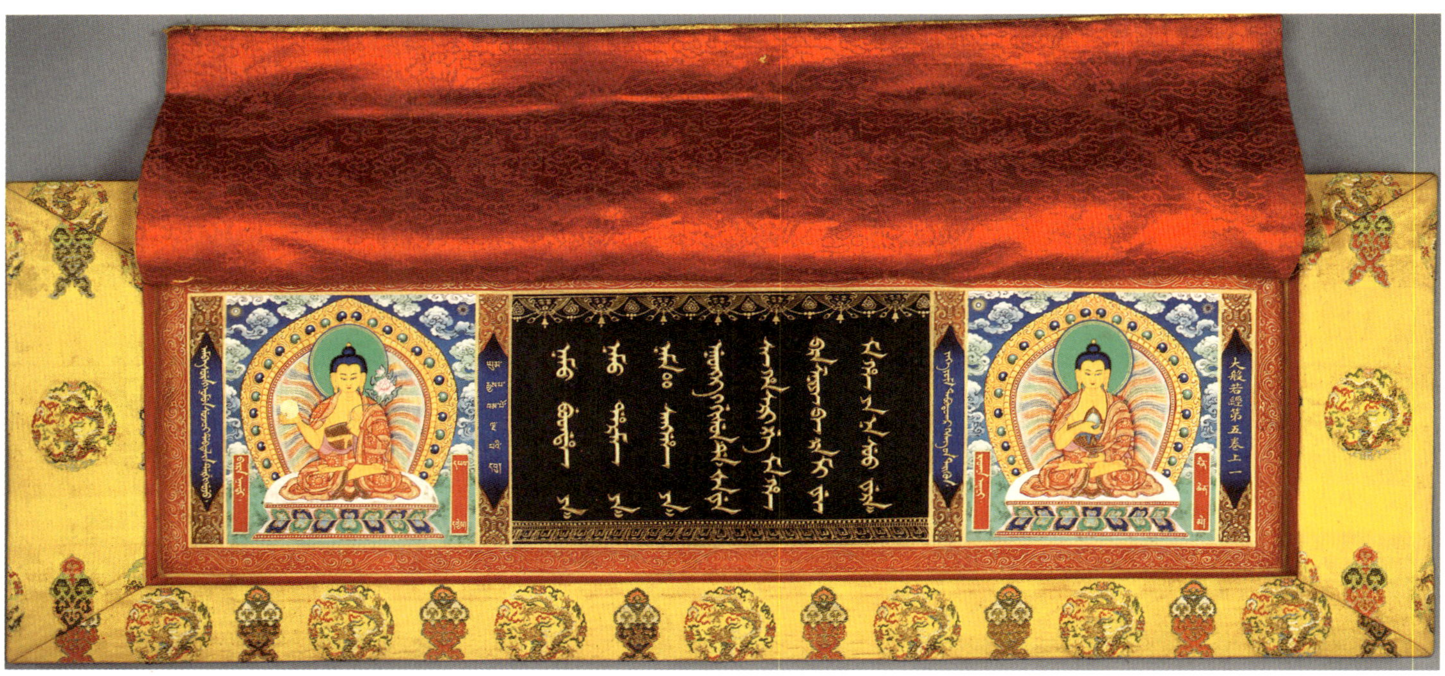

卷端
Beginning

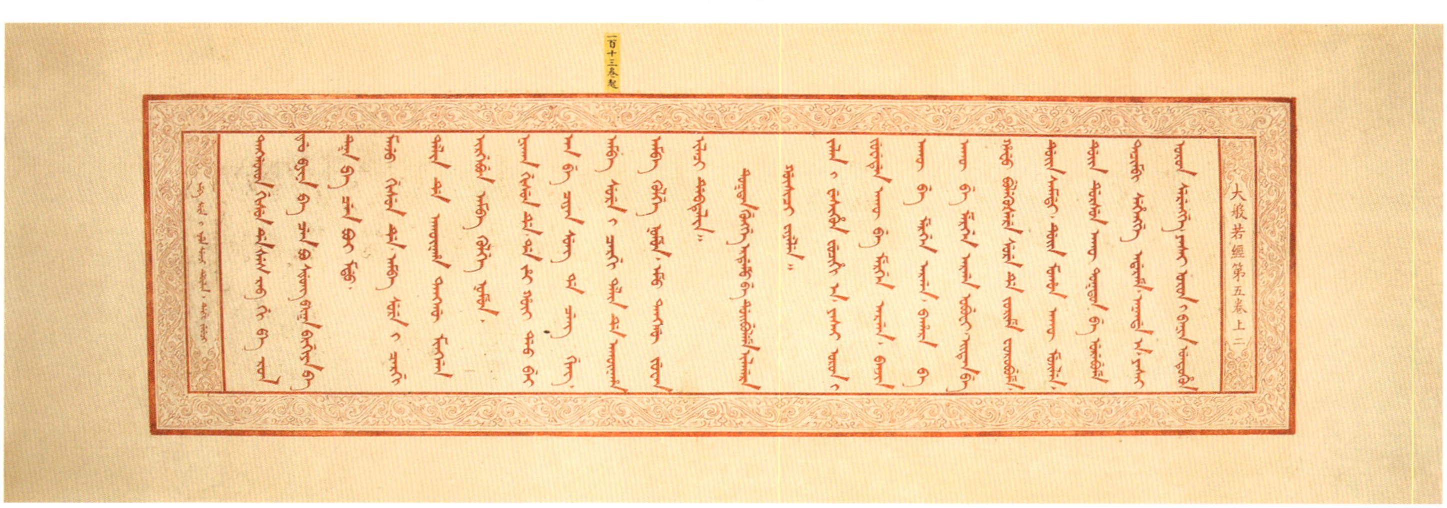

正文
Text

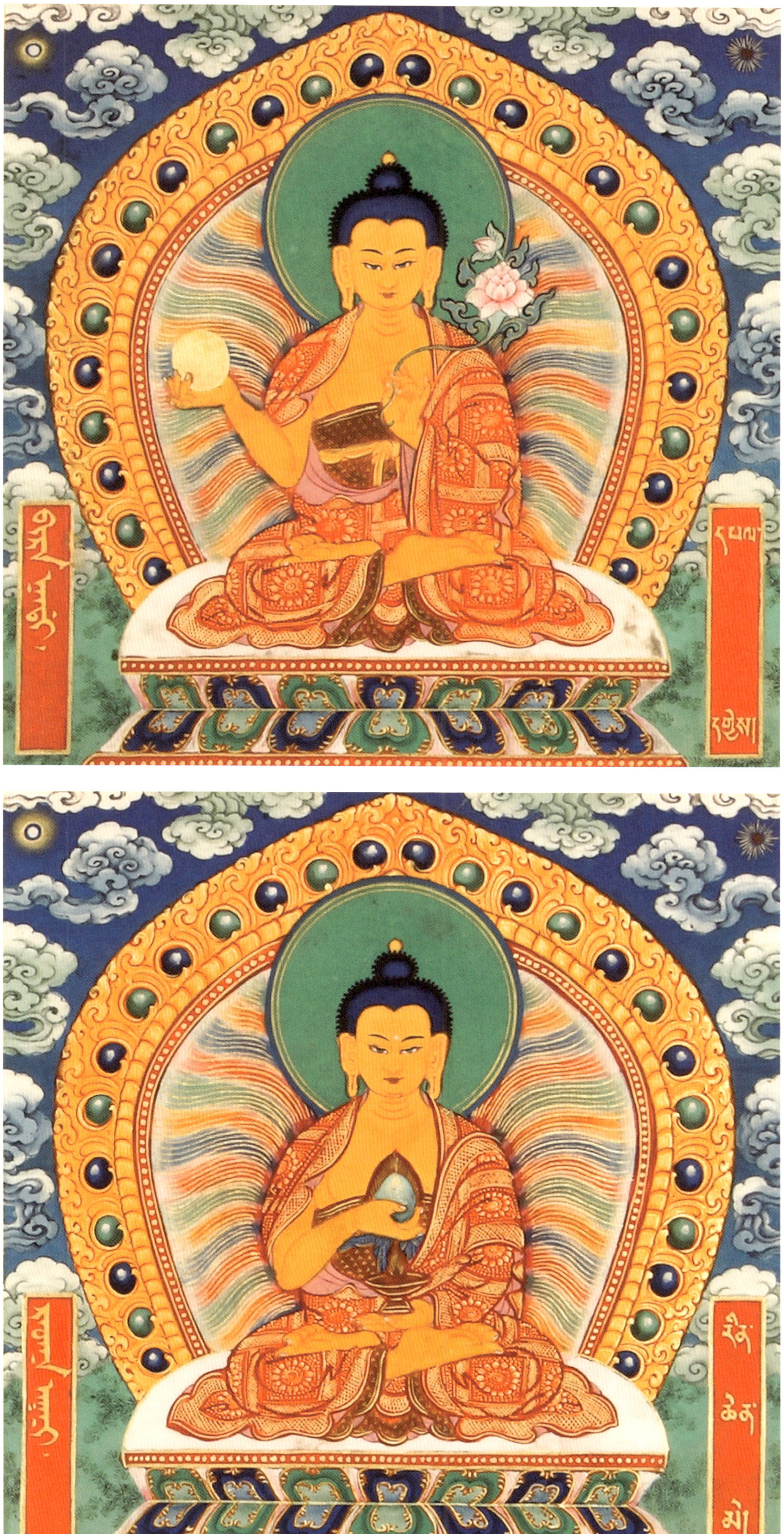

佛像
Buddhist figures

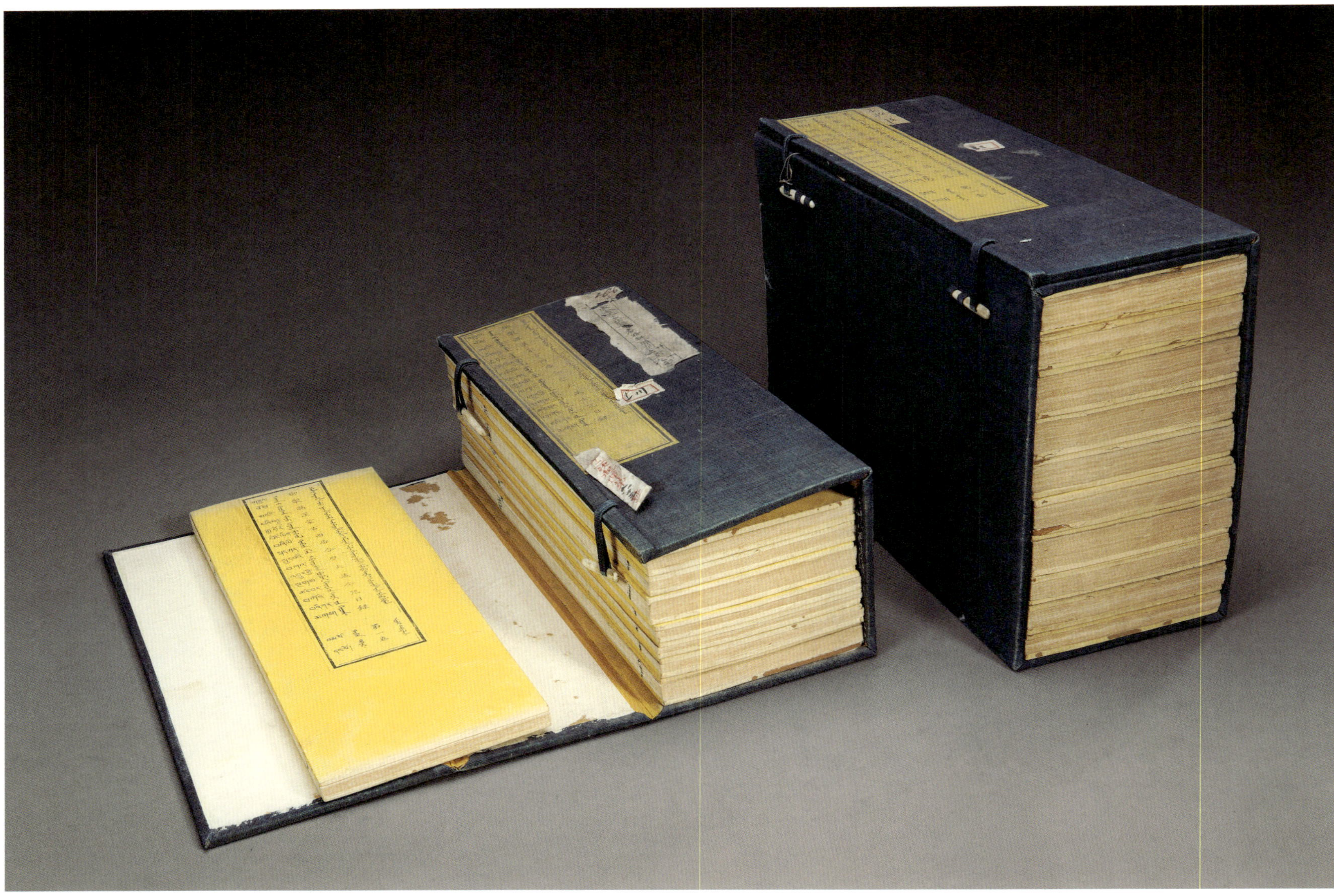

藍色素布經函
Blue cloth case

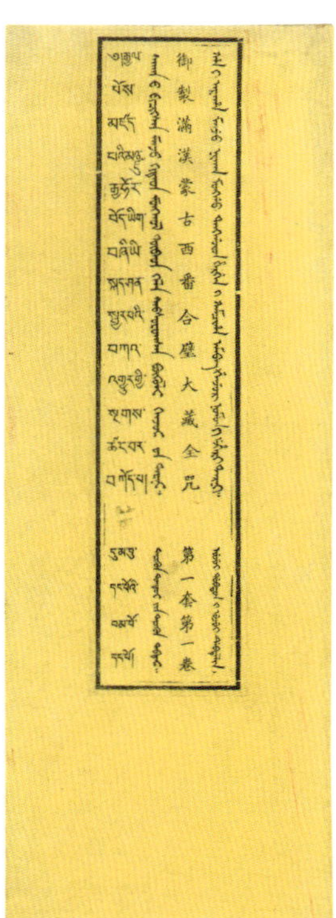

明黄色紙經面
Bright yellow paper cover

102

書27917

《御製滿漢蒙古西番合璧大藏全咒八十卷目录八卷》

清　允禄等奉敕撰　章嘉三世若畢多吉校

清乾隆三十九年（1774）武英殿刻藏滿蒙漢合璧本

開本　縱36.9厘米　横13厘米

版框　縱25.4厘米　横13厘米

八十八册　九夾

Inventory number: Shu 27917

Mantras of the Tripitaka

Eighty chapters as text, eight chapters as preliminary remarks
Compiled by imperial order by Yunlu et. al., Qing dynasty (1644-1911)
Proofread by Icang-skya Khutukhtu
Printed in Tibetan, Manchu, Mongolian and Chinese in 1774 at the Hall of Martial Valour
Format: 36.9 × 13 cm
Frame: 25.4 × 13 cm
Eighty-eight volumes, in nine cases

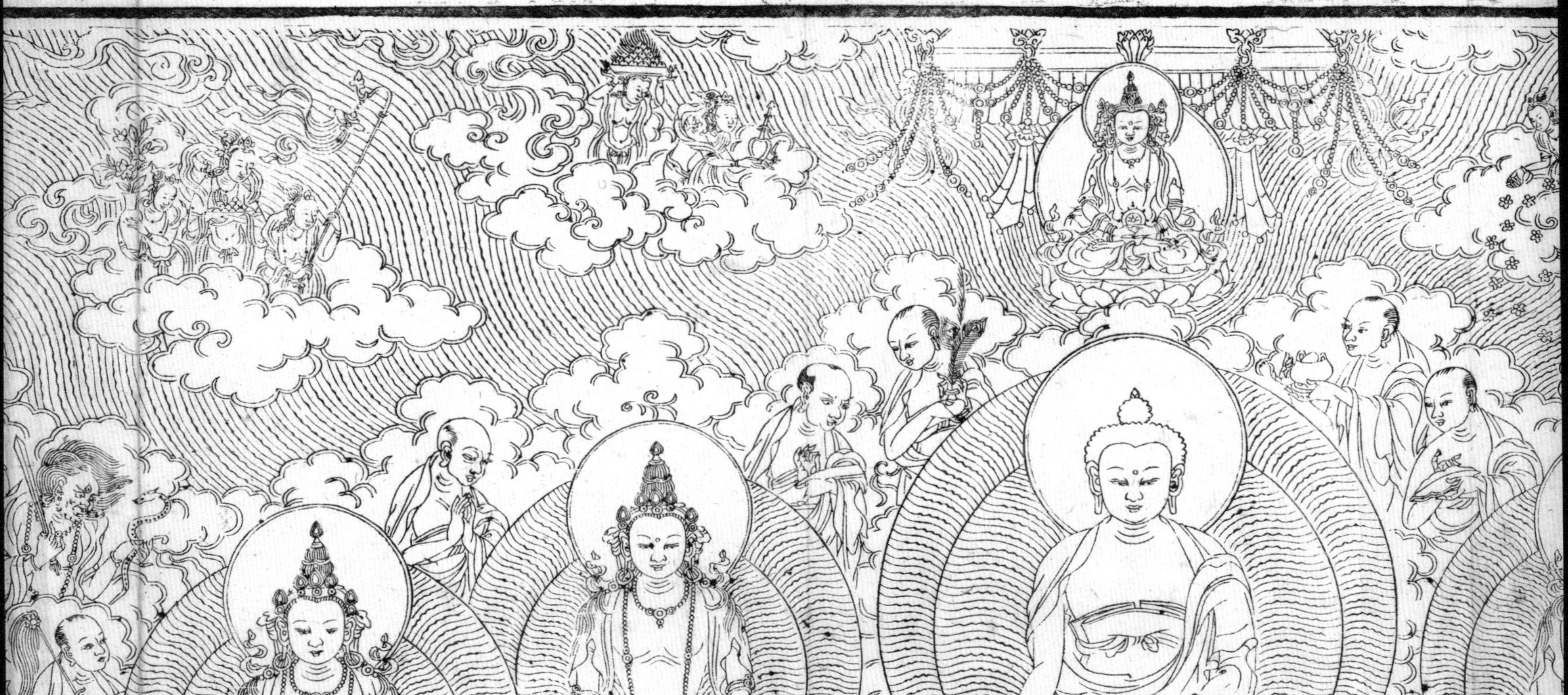

卷首扉畫
Illustrated title page

乾隆三十八年二月十五日奉

旨大藏經中呪語乃諸佛秘密心印非可以文義強求是以概不繙譯惟是呪中字樣當時譯經者僅依中華字母約畧對音與竺乾梵韻不啻毫釐千里之謬甚至同一漢字亦彼此參差即如納摩本音上為諾牙切下為模倭切而舊呪或作曩謨或

乾隆三十八年上諭

Imperial edict in 1773

御製

善哉調御具大雄力說無上咒普度衆生於轉輪中扶濟真教泰衍式煥玉燭常融品彙昭蘇陰陽和會鴻圖翊運龍域歸仁萬法同圓三塗並徹以慈功德不可思議諸天諦聽信受奉行

大清乾隆二十四年閏六月初四日

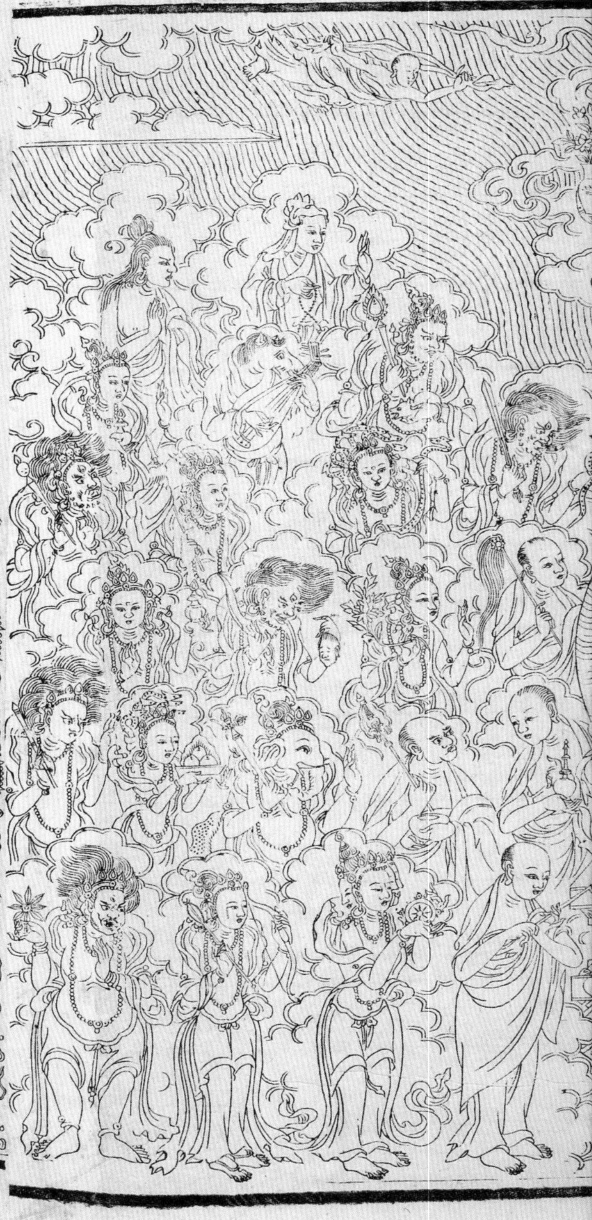

乾隆二十四年御製序

Preface by the Qianlong emperor in 1759

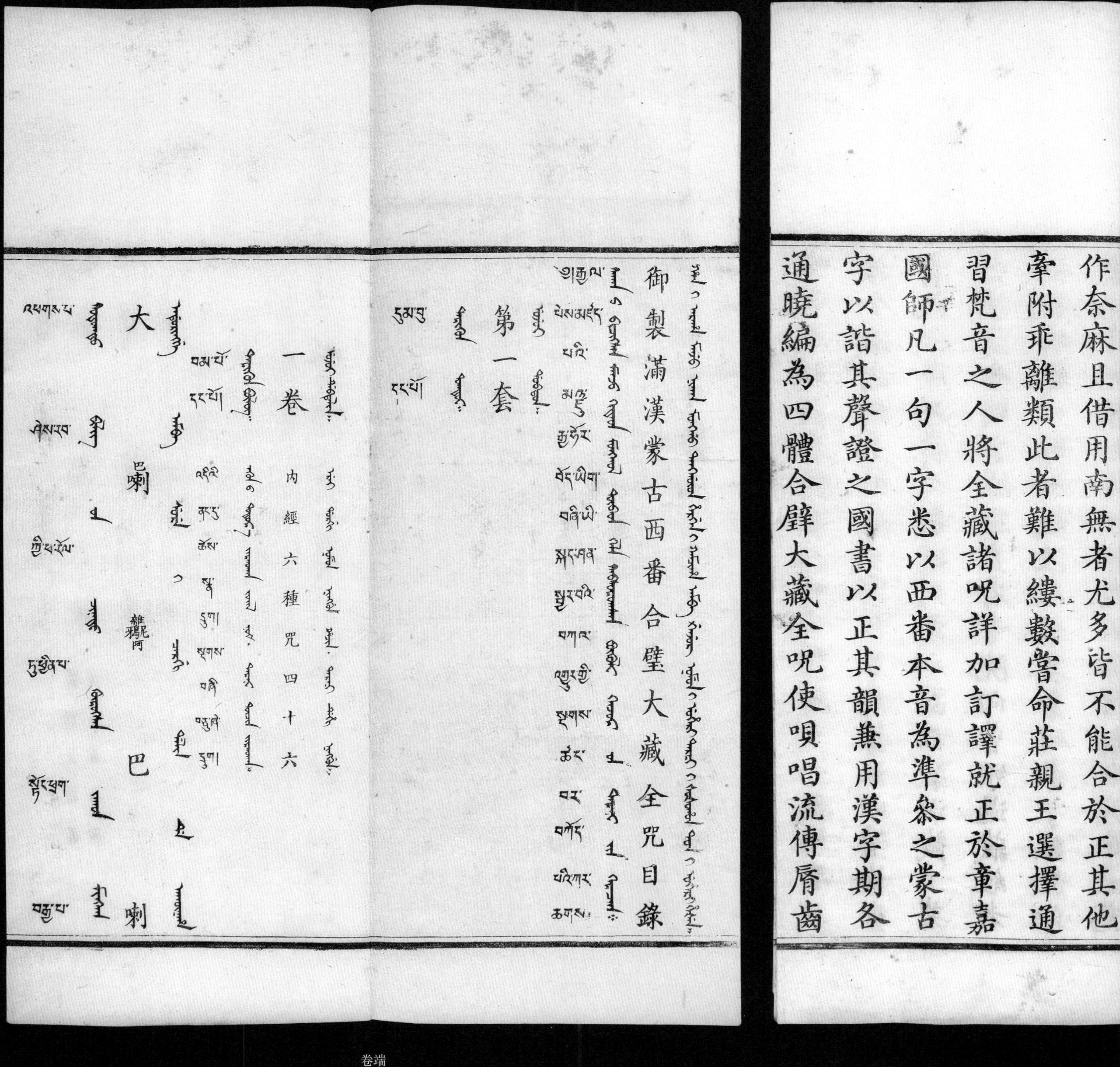

作奈麻且借用南無者尤多皆不能合於正其他牽附乖離類此者難以縷數嘗命莊親王選擇通習梵音之人將全藏諸呪詳加訂譯就正於章嘉國師凡一句一字悉以西番本音為準參之蒙古字以諧其聲證之國書以正其韻兼用漢字期各通曉編為四體合璧大藏全呪使唄唱流傳脣齒

御製滿漢蒙古西番合璧大藏全咒目錄

第一套

一卷　内經六種咒四十六

大巴喇雜鵝阿巴喇

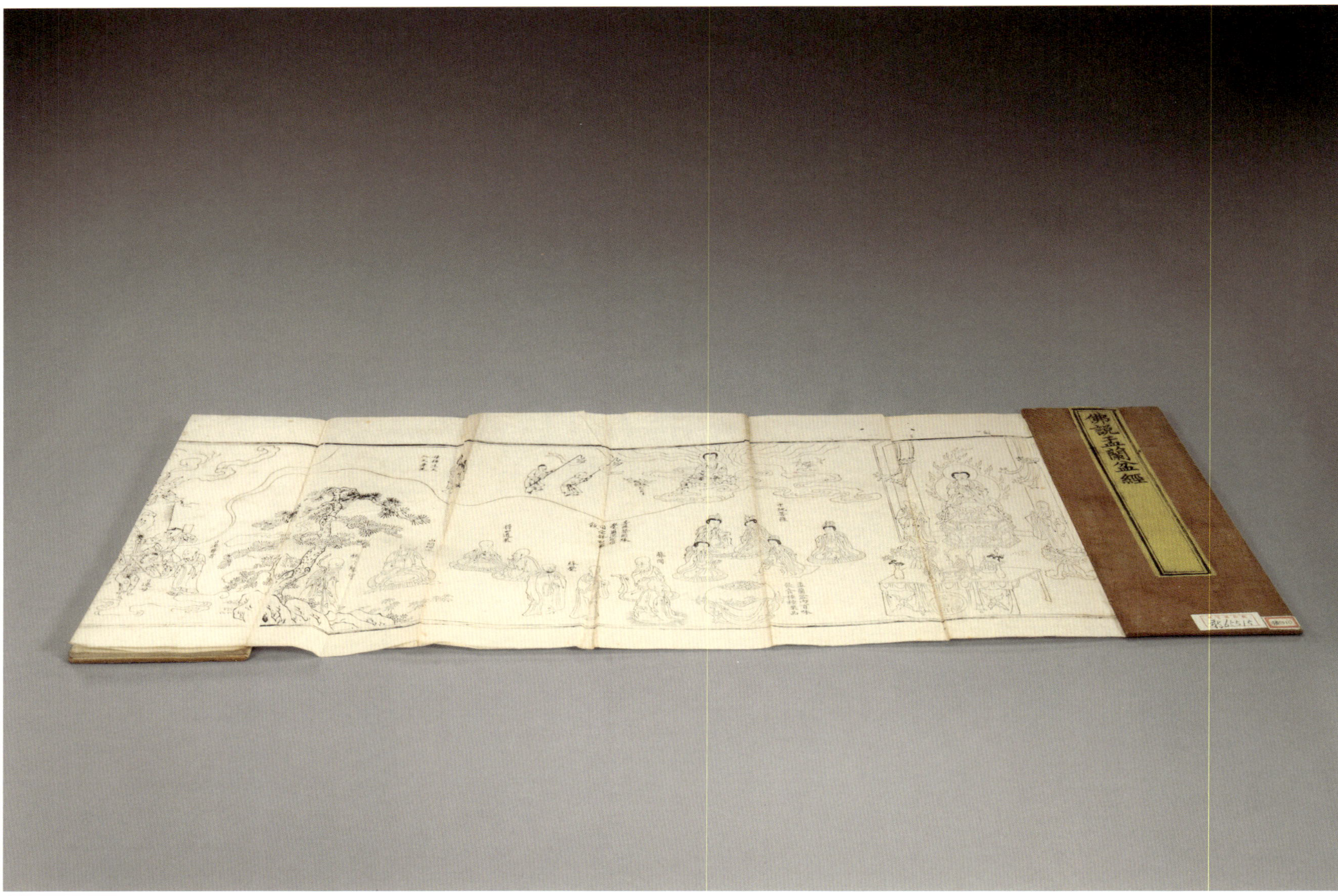

卷首扉畫
Illustrated title page

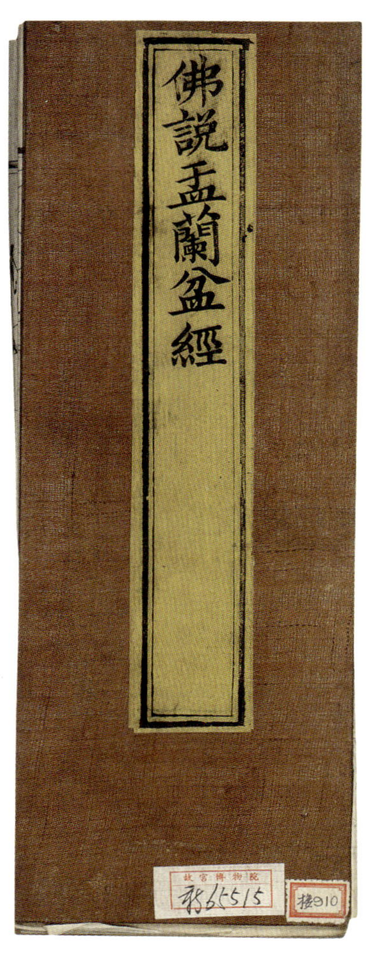

絳色素布經面
Brown cloth cover

書28240
《佛說盂蘭盆經》
西晉　三藏法師竺法護譯　清　劉養中輯
清康熙五十七年（1718）刻滿漢合璧本
開本　縱30.5厘米　橫11.6厘米
版框　縱24.2厘米　橫11.6厘米
一冊　一函
其滿文爲漢文的對音字

103

Inventory number: Shu 28240
Ullambana Sutra
Translated by Master Fahu, Western Jin dynasty (265-317)
Compiled by Liu Yangzhong, Qing dynasty (1644-1911)
Printed in Manchu and Chinese in 1718
Format: 30.5 × 11.6 cm
Frame: 24.2 × 11.6 cm
One volume in one case
Manchu text corresponding to Chinese text in pronunciation

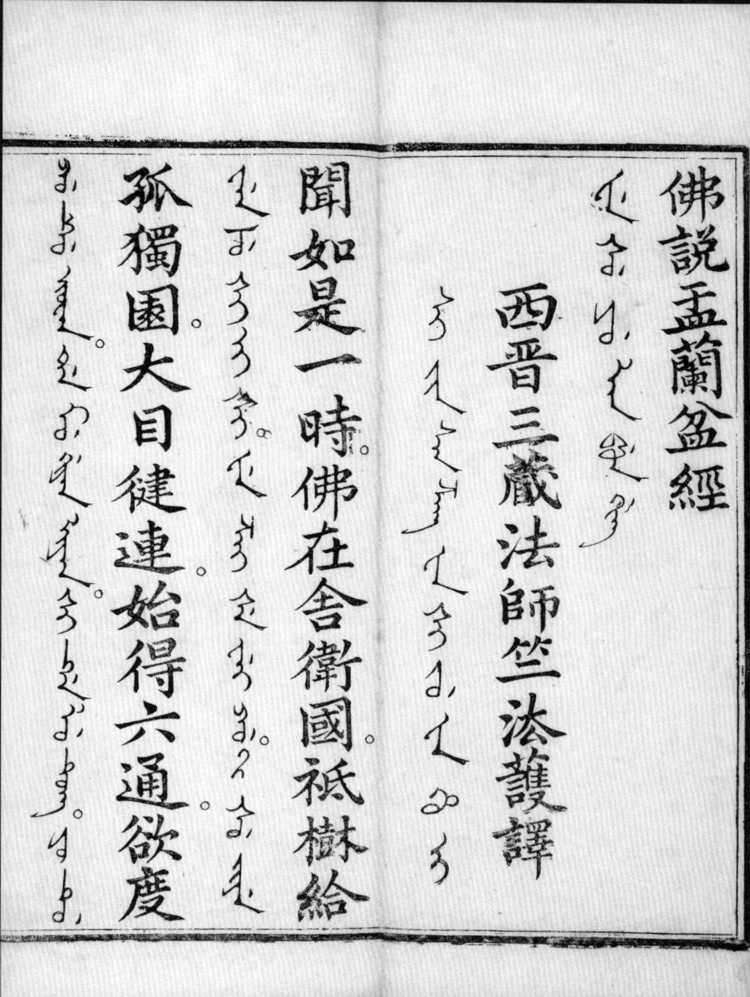

佛說盂蘭盆經

西晉三藏法師竺法護譯

聞如是一時佛在舍衛國祇樹給

孤獨園大目揵連始得六通欲度

卷端
Beginning

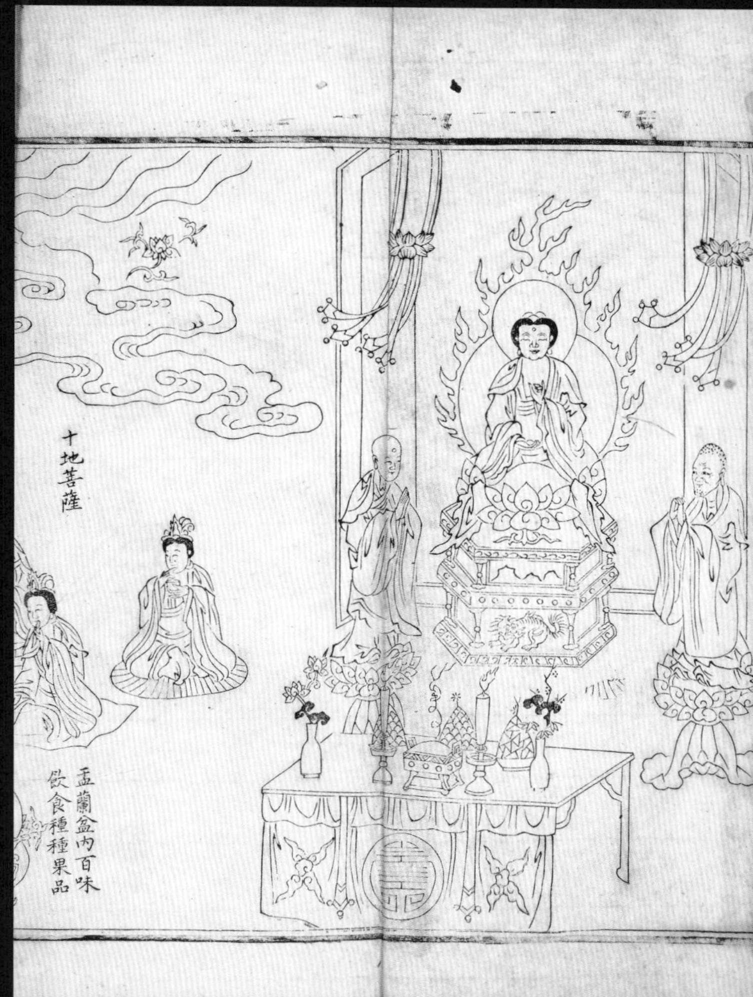

卷首扉畫
Illustrated title page

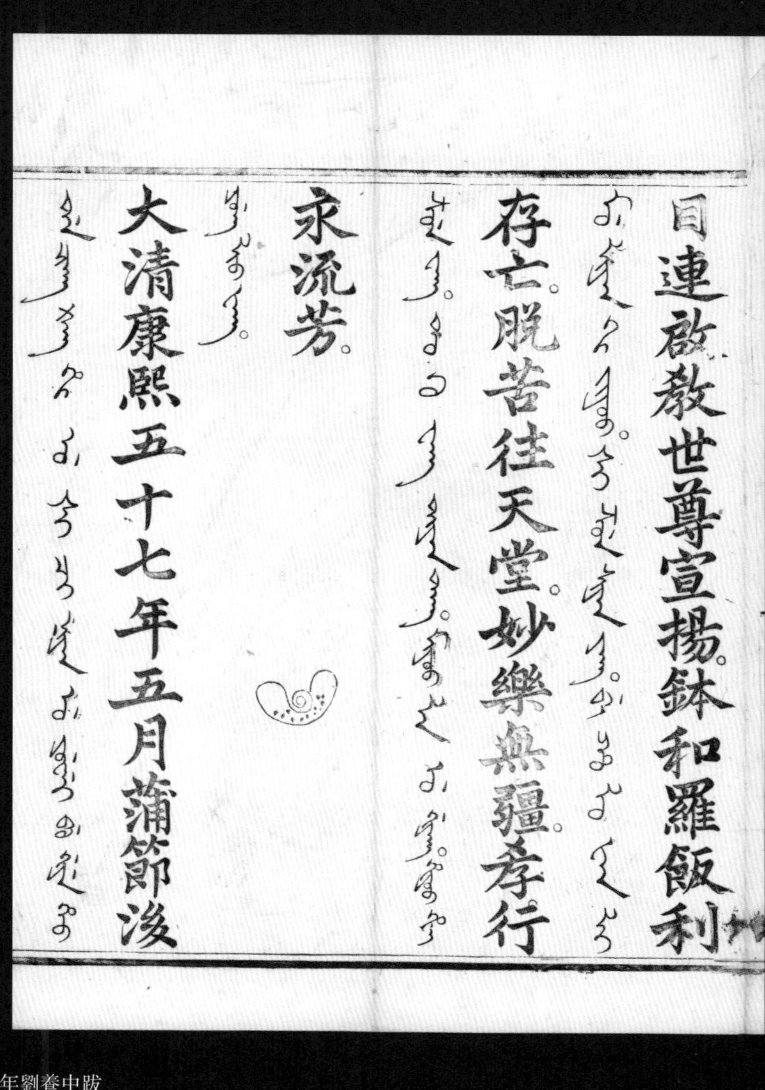

目連啟敎世尊宣揚鉢和羅飯利

存亡脫苦往天堂妙樂無疆孝行

永流芳

大清康熙五十七年五月蒲節後

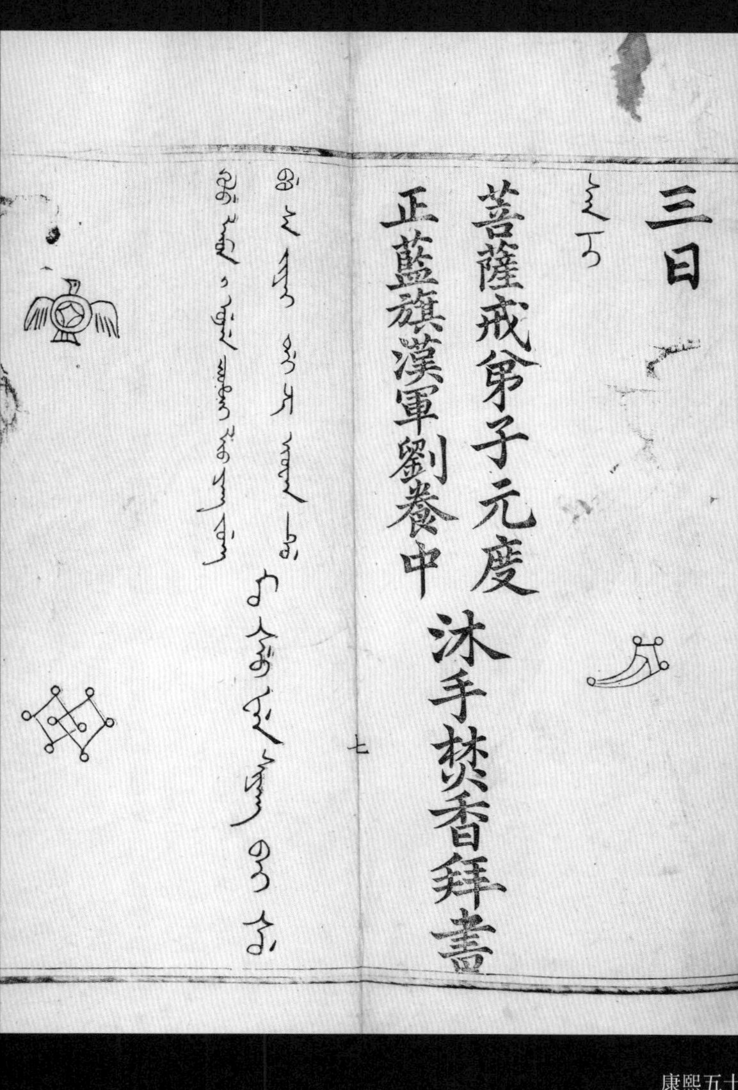

三日

菩薩戒弟子元度

正藍旗漢軍劉養中　沐手焚香拜書

七

康熙五十七年劉養中跋
Postscript by Liu Yangzhong in 1718

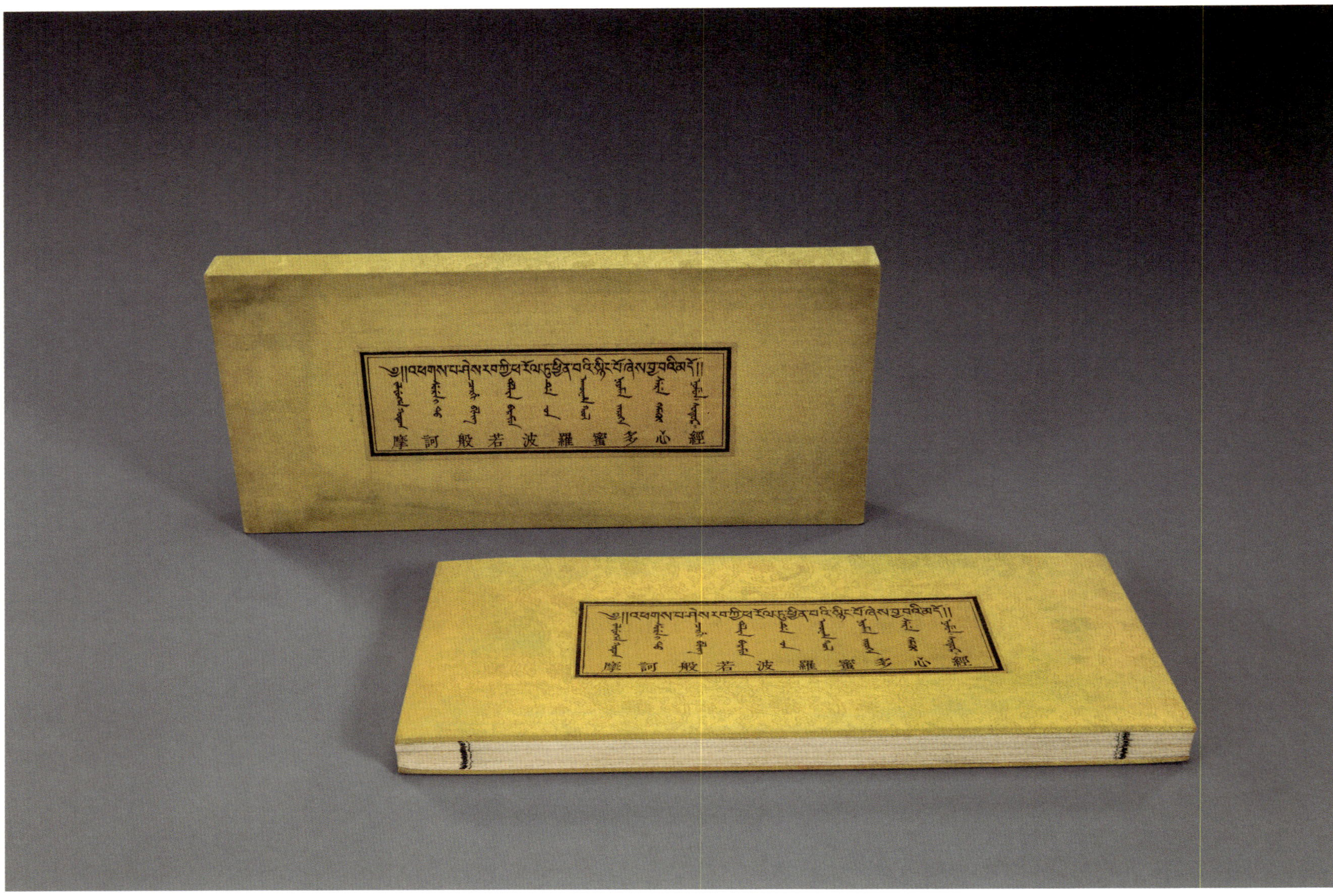

明黃色纏枝蓮花紋暗花綾經函
Bright yellow twill-weave silk case with veiled pattern of lotus scrolls

104

書27780
《摩訶般若波羅蜜多心經》
唐　三藏法師玄藏譯
清乾隆年武英殿刻藏滿蒙漢合璧本
開本　縱13.1厘米　橫31.1厘米
版框　縱13.1厘米　橫25.9厘米
一册　一函

Inventory number: Shu 27780
Prajnaparamita Heart Sutra
Translated by Master Xuanzang
Printed in Manchu, Mongolian and Chinese by the Qing court in the Qianlong period (r.1736-1795)
Format: 13.1 × 31.1 cm
Frame: 13.1 × 25.9 cm
One volume in one case

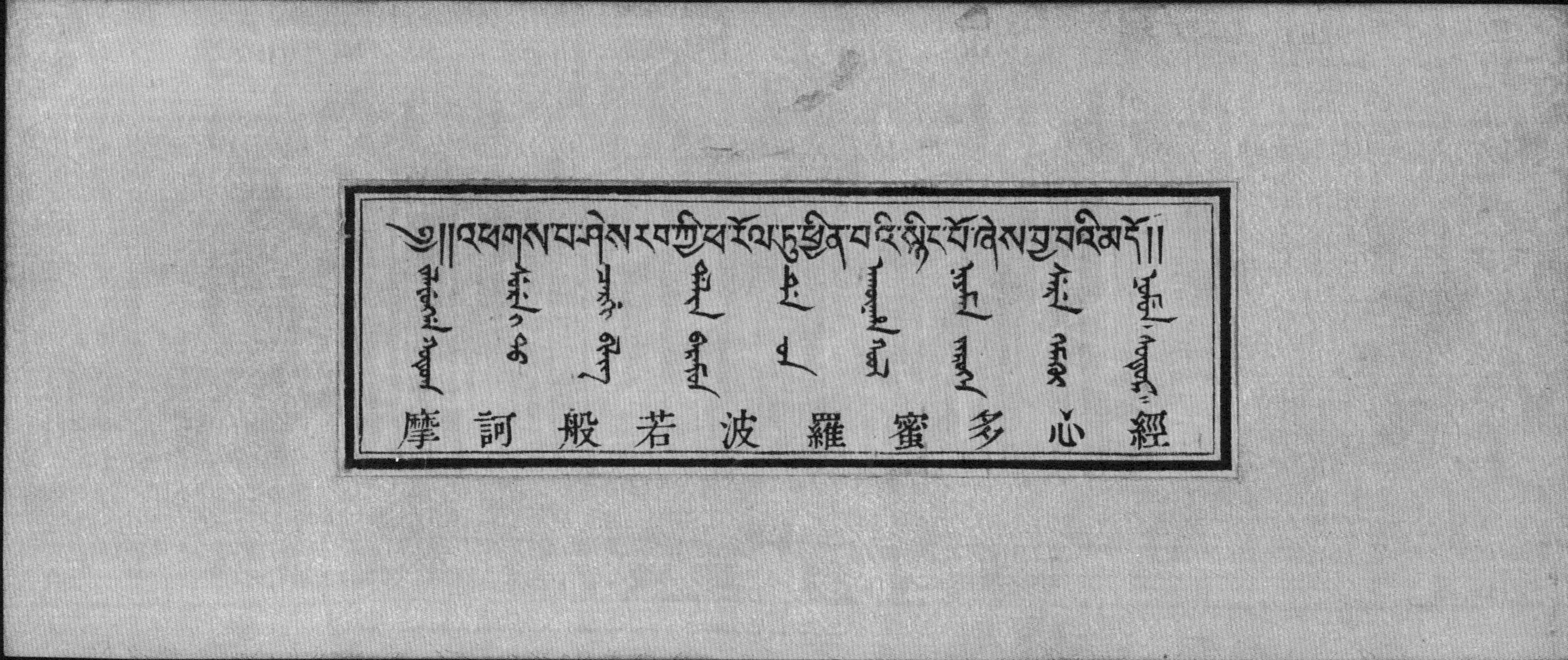

明黃色纏枝蓮花紋暗花綾經面
Bright yellow twill-weave silk cover with veiled pattern of lotus scrolls

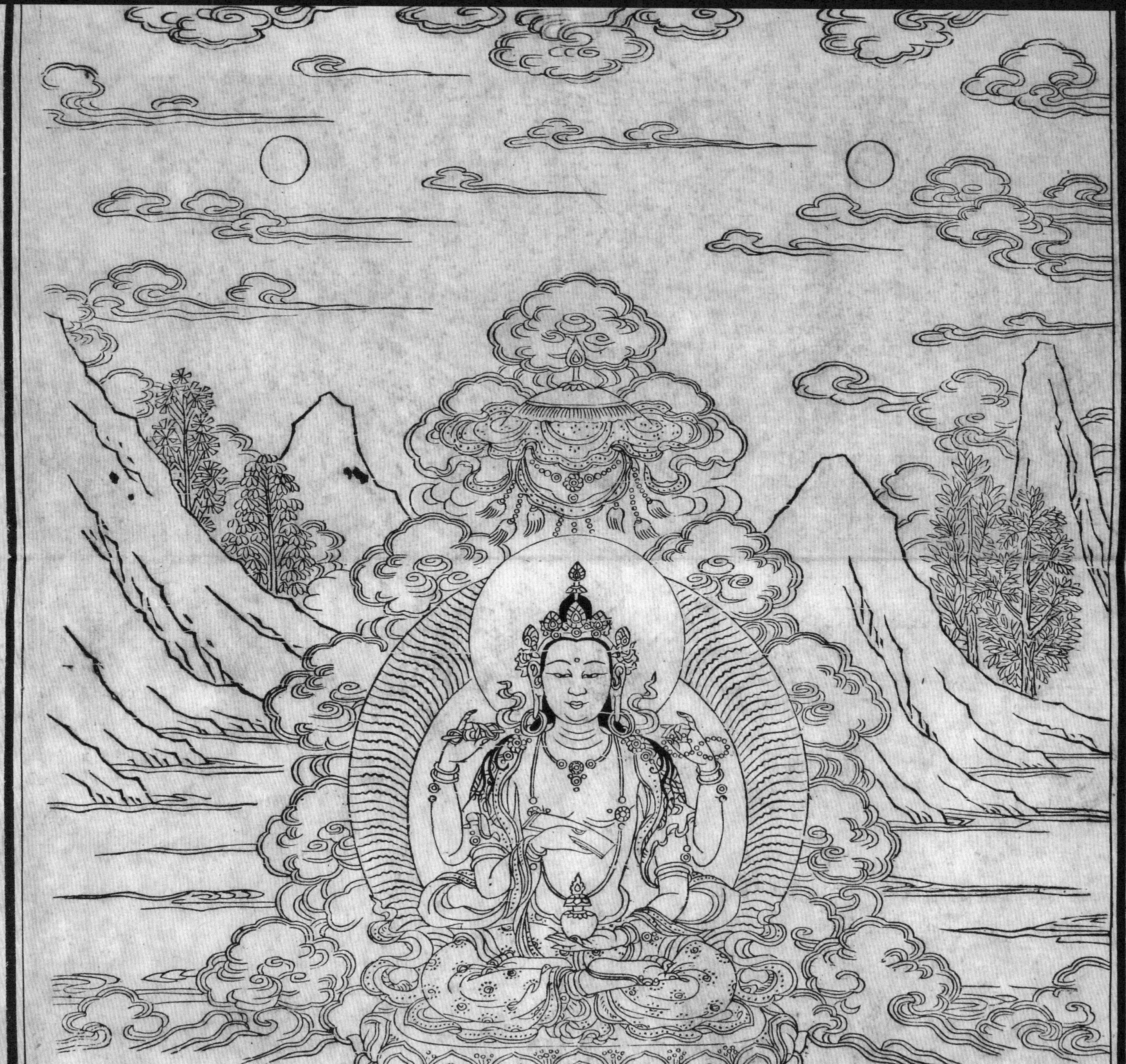

佛像
Buddhist figure

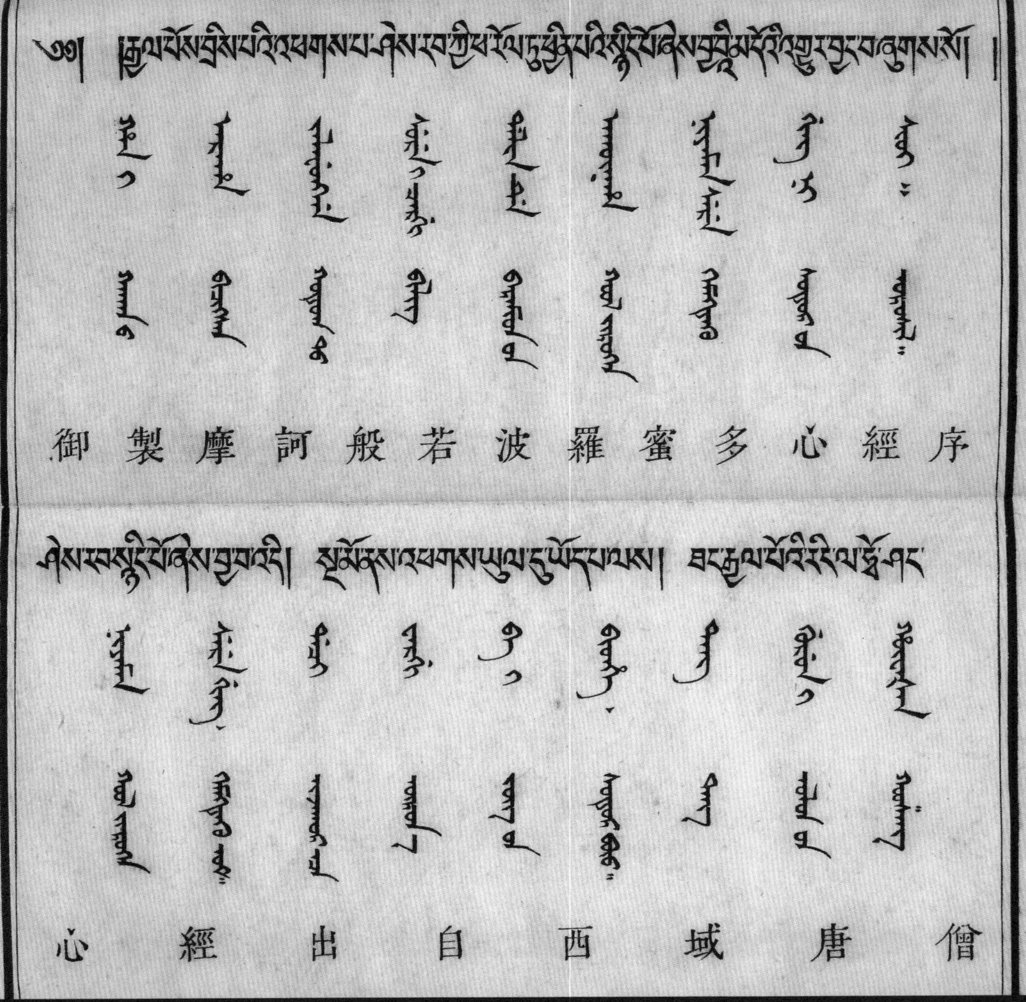

御製摩訶般若波羅蜜多心經序

心經出自西域唐僧

雍正元年御製序
Preface by the Yongzheng emperor in 1723

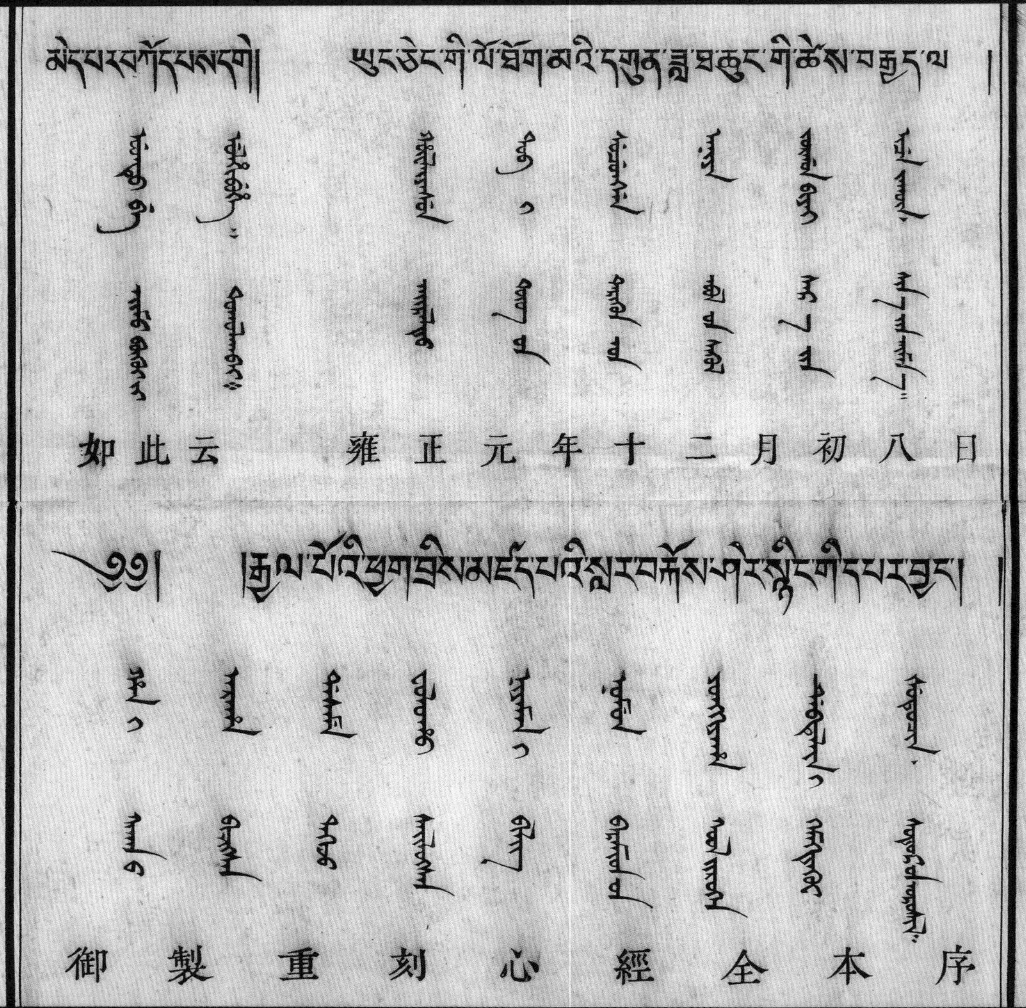

如此云 雍正元年十二月初八日

御製重刻心經全本序

乾隆年御製重刻序
Preface by the Qianlong emperor

བཅས་པའི་འཇིག་རྟེན་ཡིད་རངས་ཏེ། བཅོམ་ལྡན་འདས་ཀྱིས་གསུངས་པ་ལ་མངོན་པར་བསྟོད་དོ།།

一切世間皆大歡喜宣讚佛旨

འཕགས་པ་ཤེས་རབ་ཀྱི་ཕ་རོལ་ཏུ་ཕྱིན་པའི་སྙིང་པོ་ཞེས་བྱ་བའི་མདོ་རྫོགས་སོ།

摩訶般若波羅蜜多心經終

正文
Text

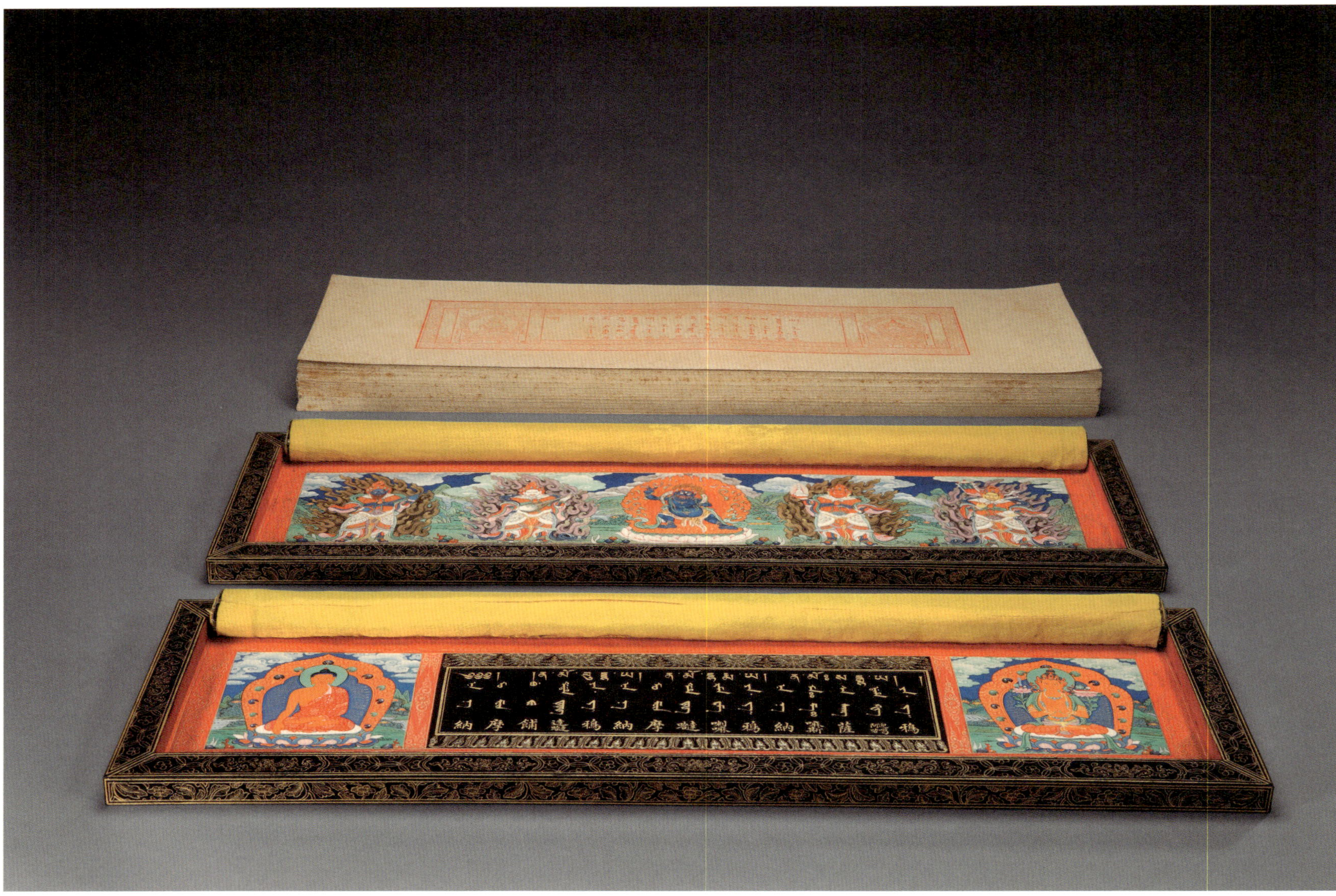

卷首及卷尾佛像
Buddhist figures

書28366
《大乘首楞嚴經十卷》
清　允祿　傅鼐等譯　章嘉三世若畢多吉校
清乾隆二十八年（1763）武英殿刻藏滿蒙漢合璧朱印本
開本　縱21.5厘米　橫66.6厘米
版框　縱17厘米　橫57.3厘米
十冊　十夾

105

Inventory number: Shu 28366
Surangama Sutra
Ten chapters
Translated by Yunlu, Funai et. al., proofread by Icang-skya Khutukhtu, Qing dynasty (1644-1911)
Red edition
Printed in Tibetan, Manchu, Mongolian and Chinese in 1763 at the Hall of Martial Valour
Format: 21.5 × 66.6 cm
Frame: 17 × 57.3 cm
Ten volumes, each protected with two boards

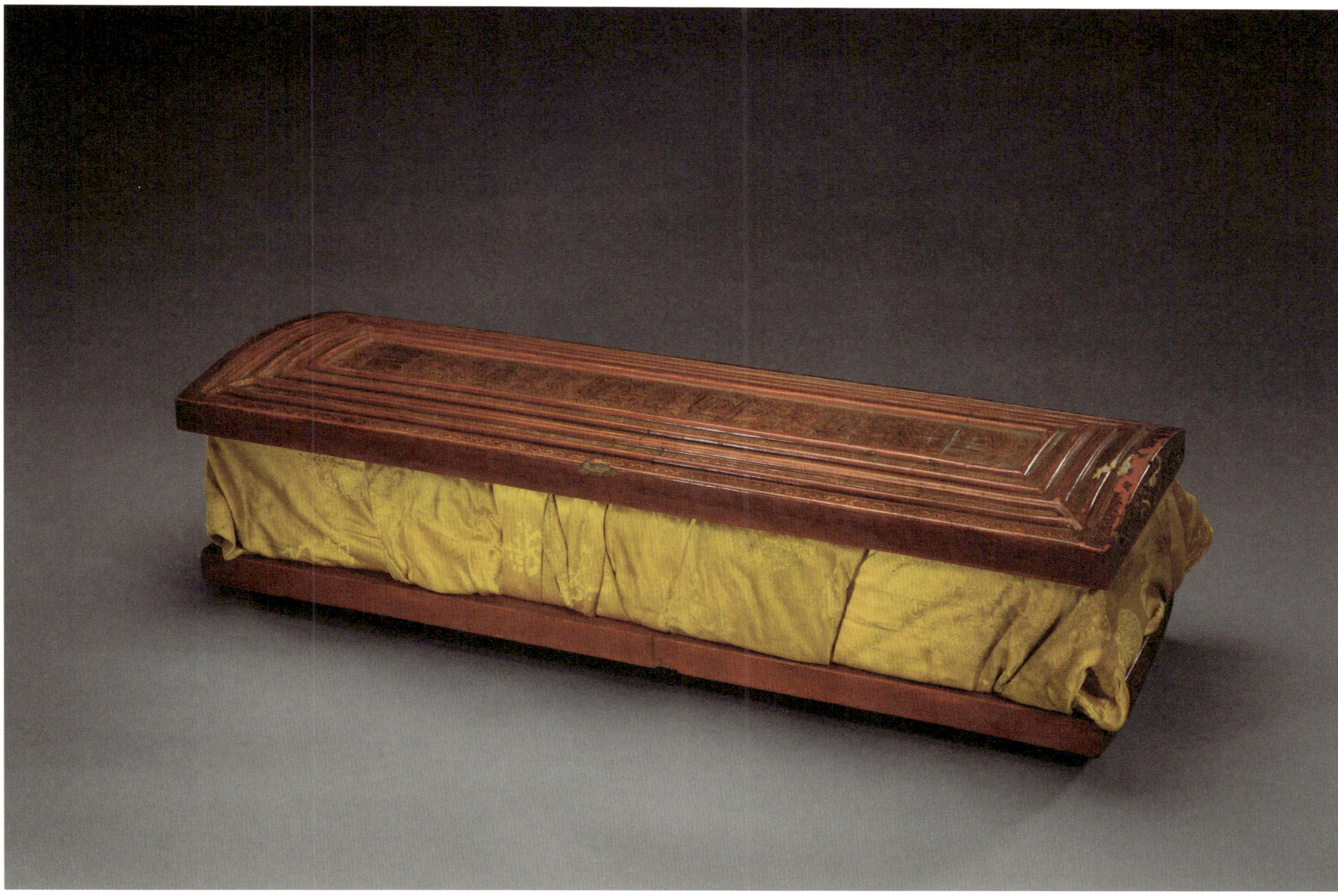

朱漆描金護經板
Red lacquer protective boards

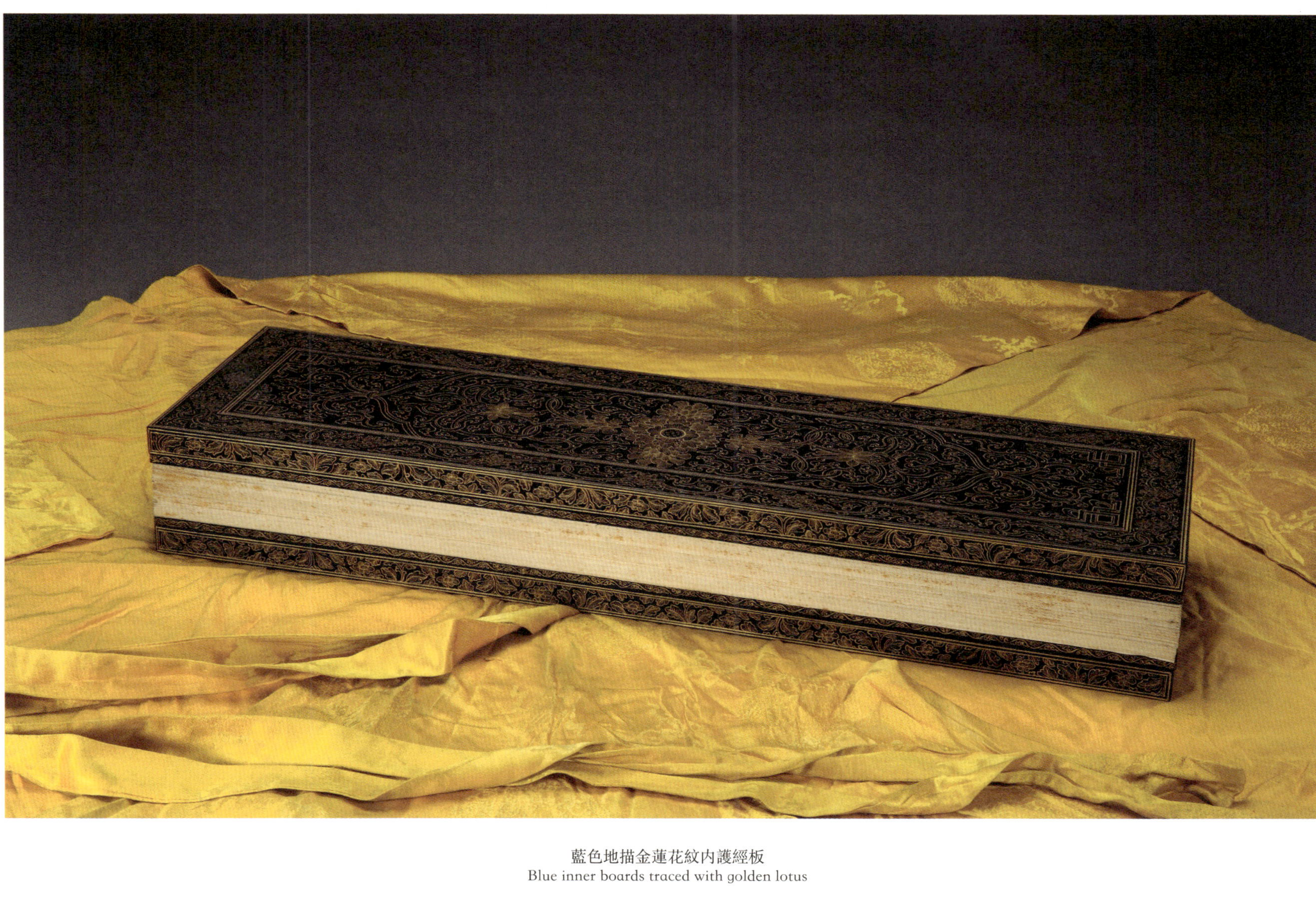

藍色地描金蓮花紋内護經板
Blue inner boards traced with golden lotus

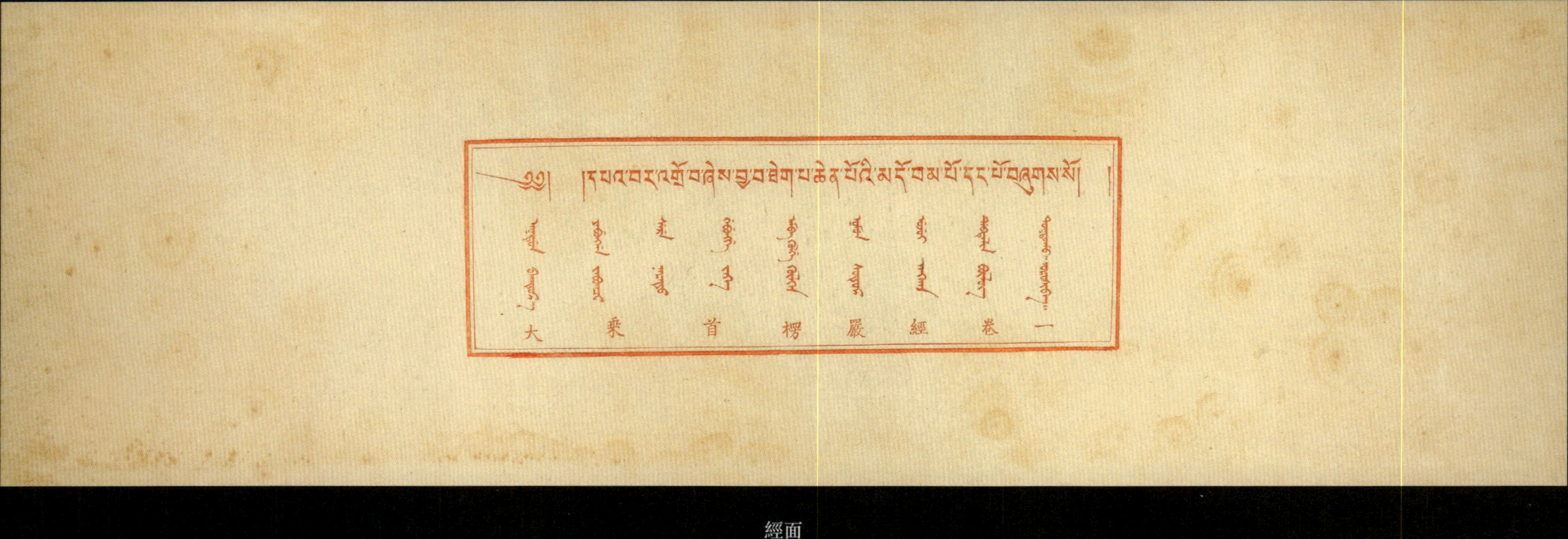

༄༅། །དཔའ་བར་འགྲོ་བ་ཞེས་བྱ་བ་ཐེག་པ་ཆེན་པོའི་མདོ་བམ་པོ་དང་པོ་བཞུགས་སོ། །

大乘首楞嚴經卷一

經面

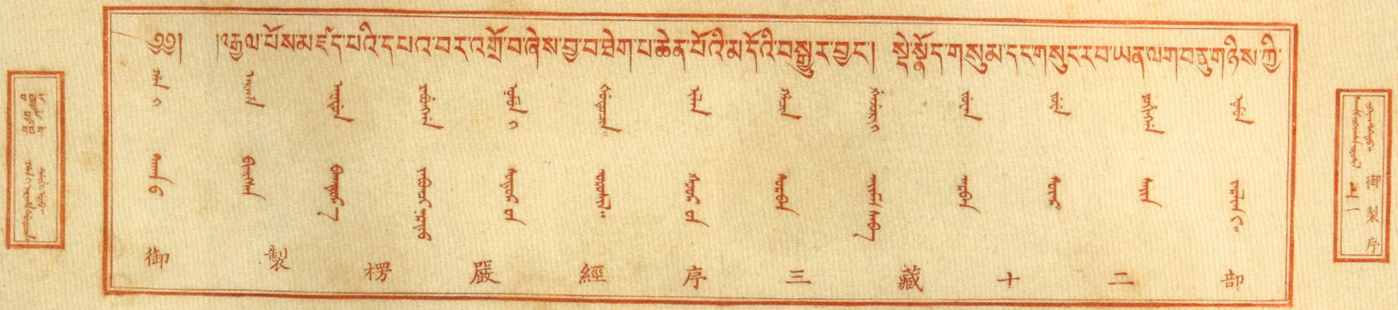

御製楞嚴經序三藏十二部

御製序 上一

乾隆二十八年序
Preface by the Qianlong emperor in 1763

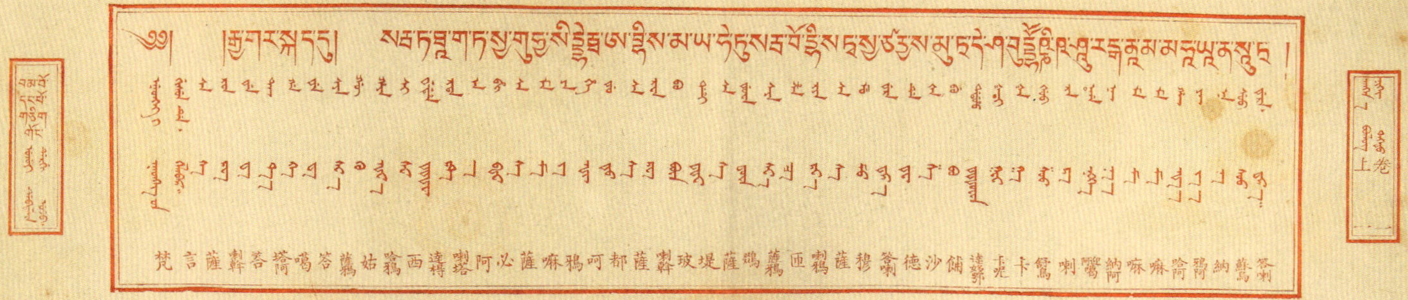

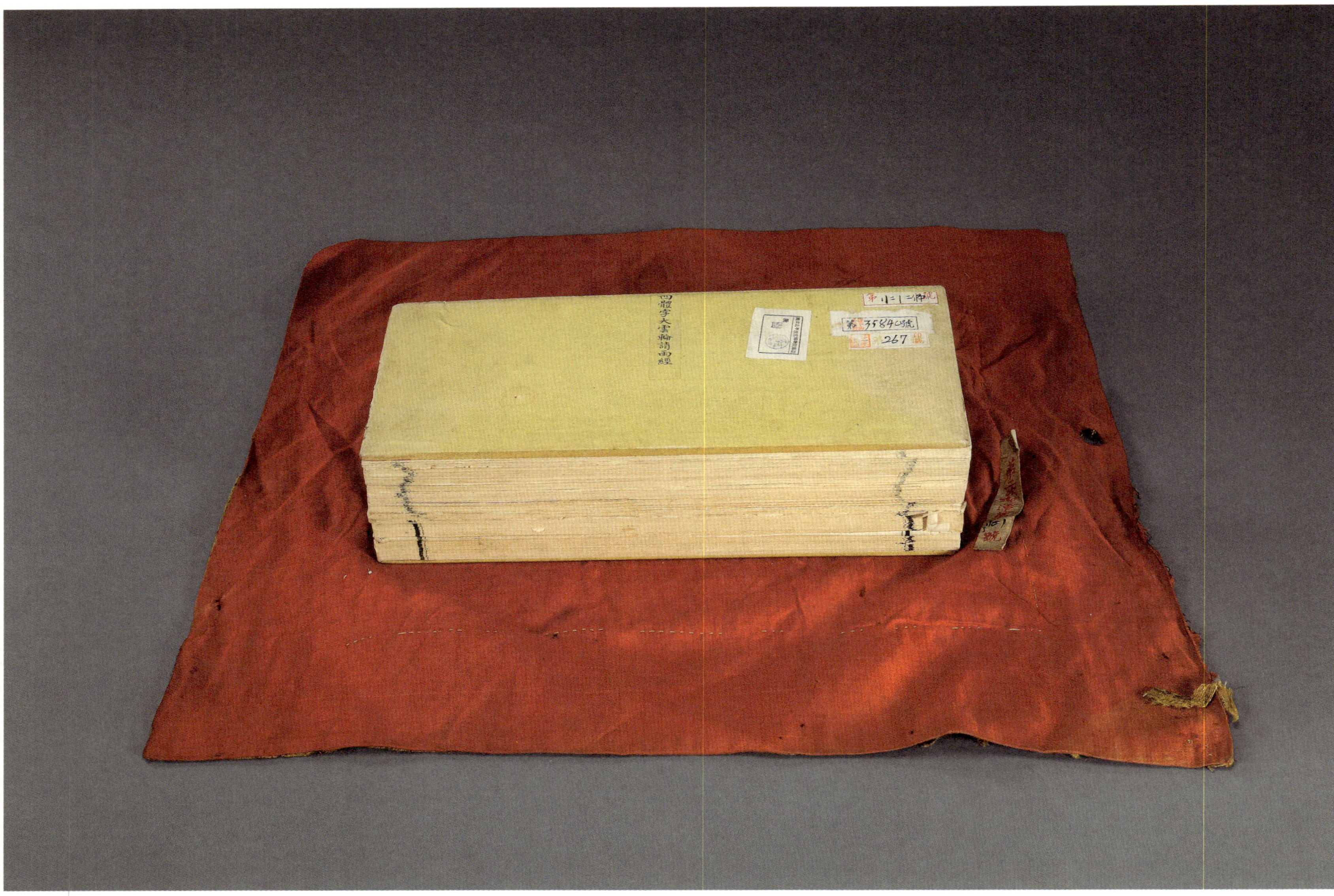

紅色素綾夾袱
Red twill-weave silk wrapping

書27213
《御譯大雲輪請雨經八卷》
清　高宗弘曆譯
清乾隆四十三年（1778）刻藏滿蒙漢合璧本
開本　縱12.8厘米　橫31.7厘米
版框　縱12.7厘米　橫25.3厘米
四册　一夾

106

Inventory number: Shu 27213
Sutra on Praying for Rain at the Hall of Grand Clouds
Eight chapters
Translated by Emperor Qianlong (r.1736-1795)
Printed in Tibetan, Manchu, Mongolian and Chinese in 1778
Format: 12.8 × 31.7 cm
Frame: 12.7 × 25.3 cm
Four volumes, protected with two boards

明黄色花卉紋暗花綾經面
Bright yellow twill-weave cover with veiled floral pattern

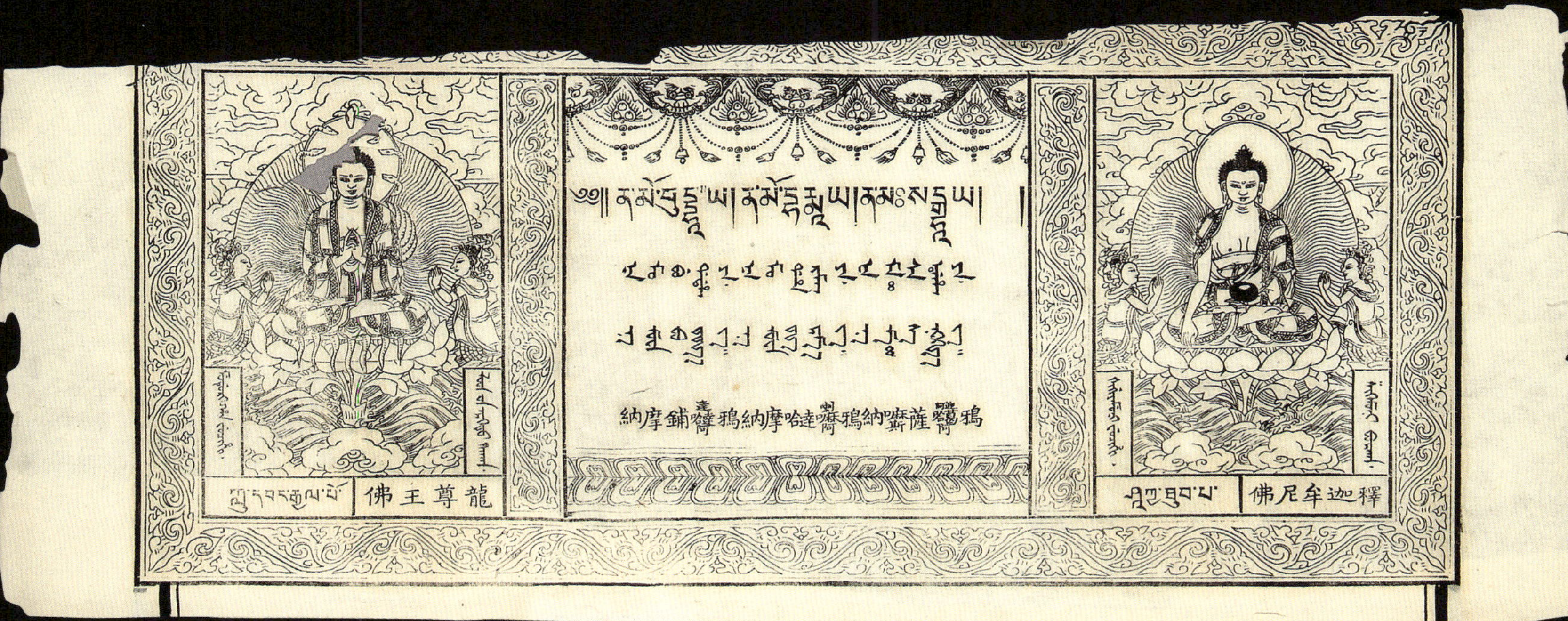

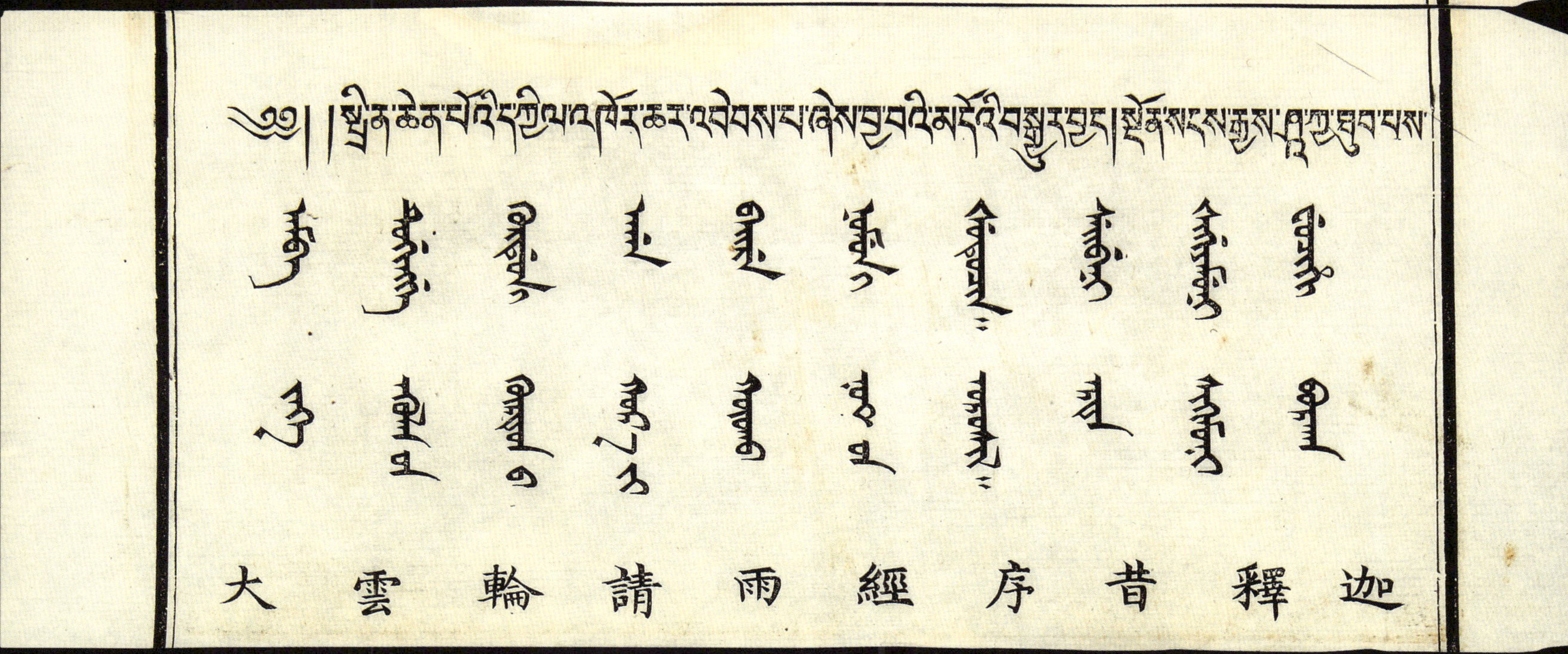

乾隆四十三年序
Preface by the Qianlong emperor in 1778

大雲輪請雨經終

總圖說

謹按結壇儀軌並依經文陳設擇潔淨地方廣十二步以為道場築壇其中東向高一尺方十步取潔淨黃土代犛牛糞塗壇四周攷犛字玉篇廣韻並云牛名字典引本草云北牛曰犛小於水牛今牛種無此稱未知所指又攷楞嚴經云白牛食雪山肥草飲雪山清水其糞微細可合梅檀疑此經所云犛牛亦即此類蓋北方得水之正位而白色則金行為水之母故可因以致雨取類而用之耳今亦依楞嚴經法穿地五尺取淨黃土和香末代之壇中設牀方廣二丈為高座覆以青幄經所云青蓋北方黑色亦取水德也幄中設主壇僧座一高桌一兩傍設誦經僧矮座并矮桌如其人數凡座褥桌幃皆以青色從高座東量三肘外按韻會云一尺五寸為一肘古尺當今尺七寸許今酌以一尺為一肘設青幃高桌一桌上設供器及乳糜雜果南西北並同供龍王一身三頭並諸眷屬西向經文云用牛糞汁畫今以白檀香水代之畫於揷屏上從高座南量五肘外供龍王一身五頭並諸眷屬北向從高座西量七肘外供龍王一身七頭並諸眷屬東向從高座北量九肘外供龍王一身九頭並諸眷屬南向壇四角各竪青旛七一旛下各燃酥油燈一燈前四角各設花缾插諸雜花壇之四周或一步或數步外以席為牆四面有門門各畫二行龍守護用代經所云或灰或水以為界畔者龍首皆向門而蜿蜒其尾互相鉤結門外有屏亦以席為之選高行持戒僧一人主壇兩序亦擇戒行清淨僧人唪經又選僧二人或四人入壇為侍者以供添香注水之役僧皆青衣薰沐齋祓悉如經儀晝夜嚴淨虔誠結願諷誦經文至一七日或二七日遠至三七日自然感召天和甘霖應禱矣

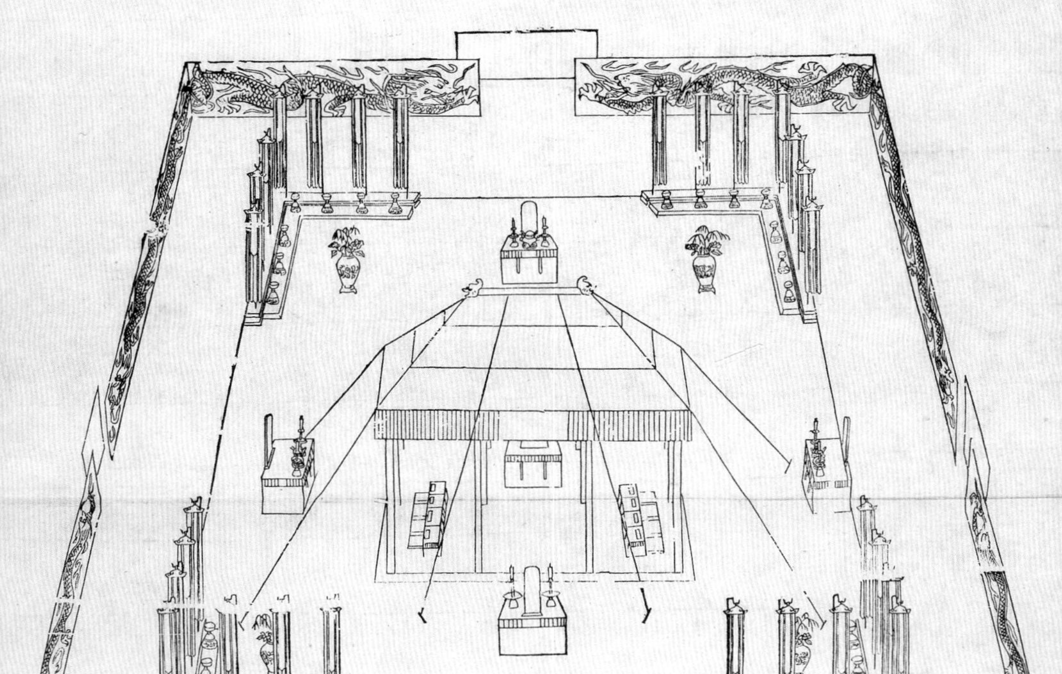

圖說
Illustrated text

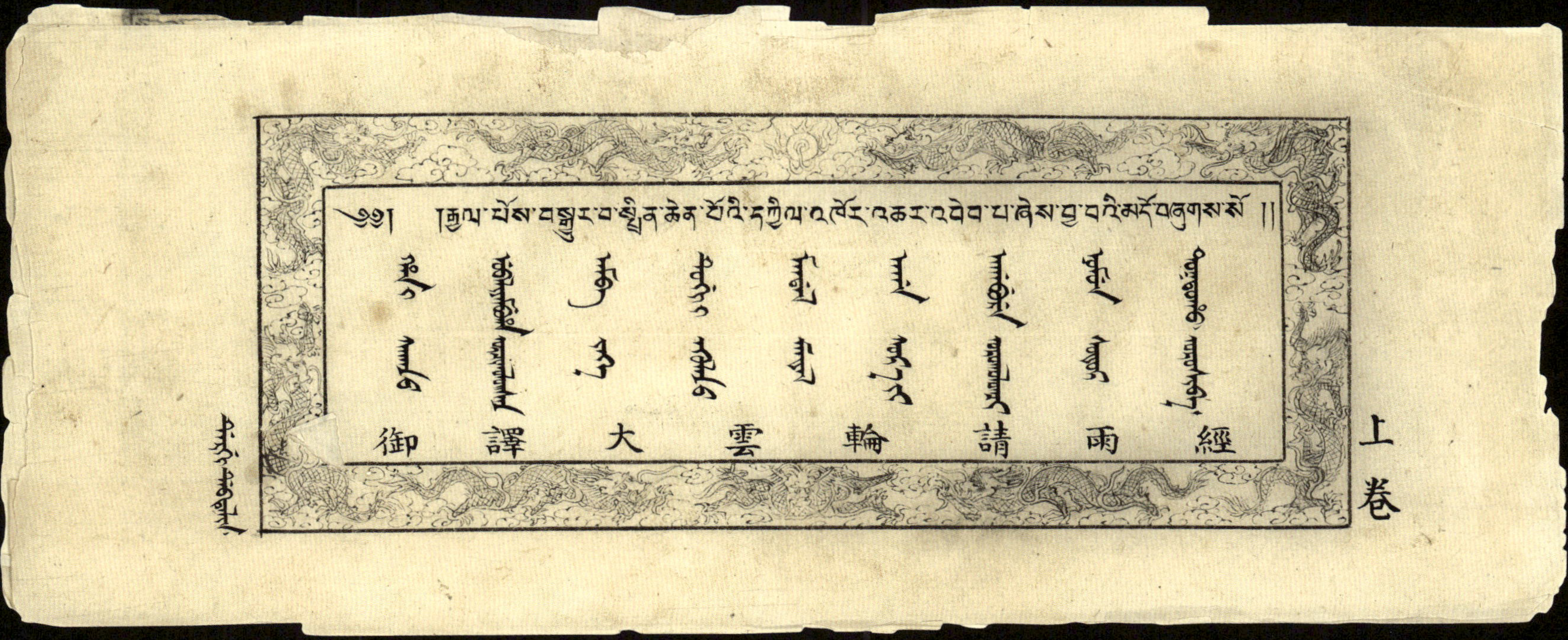
༄༅། །རྒྱལ་པོས་བསྒྱུར་བ་སྤྲིན་ཆེན་པོའི་དཀྱིལ་འཁོར་འཆར་འབེབ་པ་ཞེས་བྱ་བའི་མདོ་བཞུགས་སོ། །

御譯大雲輪請雨經

上卷

卷端
Beginning

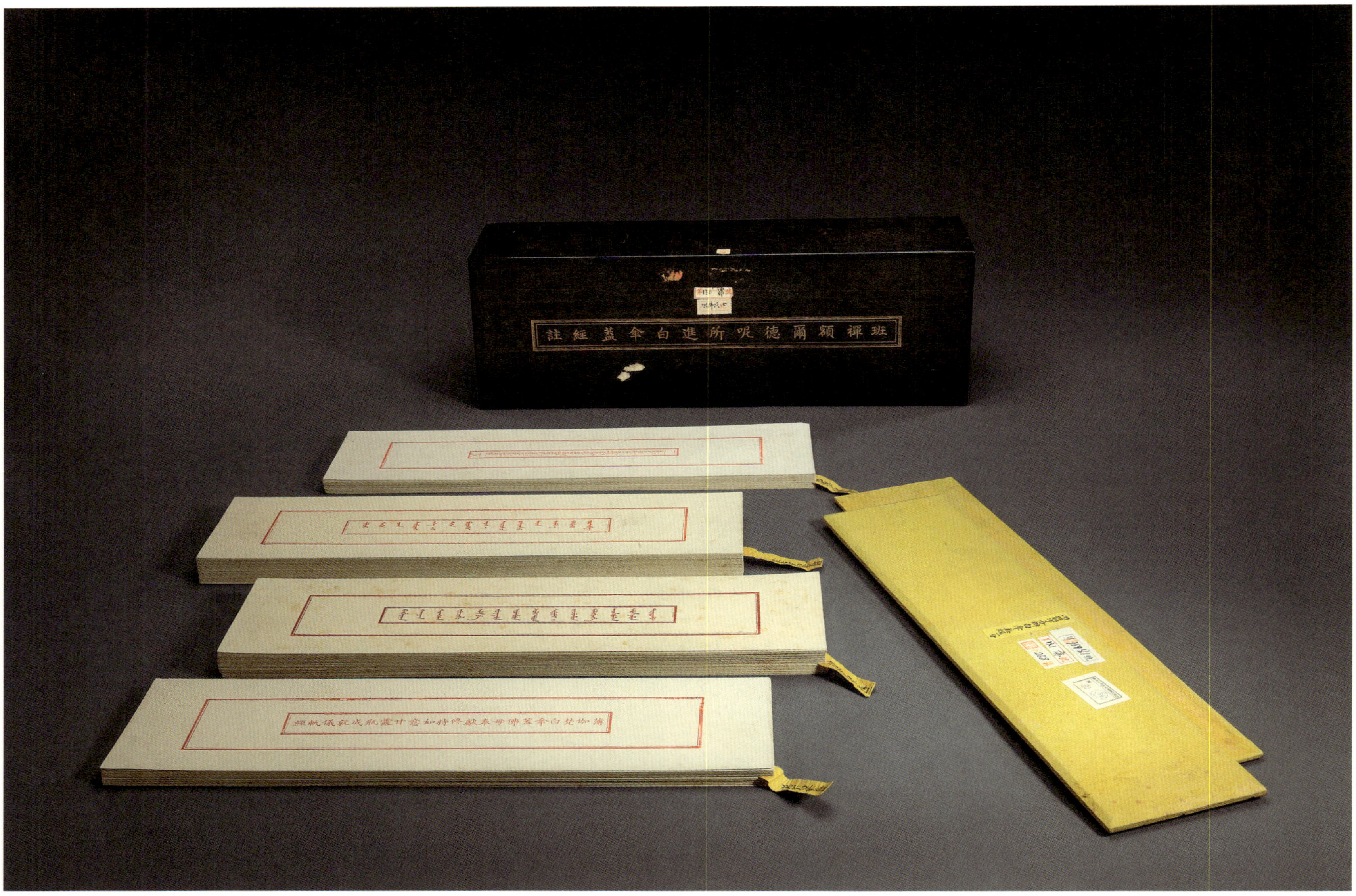

紫檀木經盒
Red sandalwood case

書27239
《白傘蓋儀軌經》(又名:《薄伽梵白傘蓋佛母成就發悉地甘露寶瓶》)
清　佚名譯
清乾隆四十五年(1780)武英殿刻漢藏滿蒙合璧本
開本　縱11.9厘米　橫48.5厘米
版框　縱6.6厘米　橫37.9厘米
四冊　一盒

107

Inventory number: Shu 27239
Sitatapatra Kalpa Sutra
Translator unknown, Qing dynasty (1644-1911)
Printed in Chinese, Tibetan, Manchu and Mongolian in 1780 at the Hall of Martial Valour
Format: 11.9 × 48.5 cm
Frame: 6.6 × 37.9 cm
Four volumes in one case

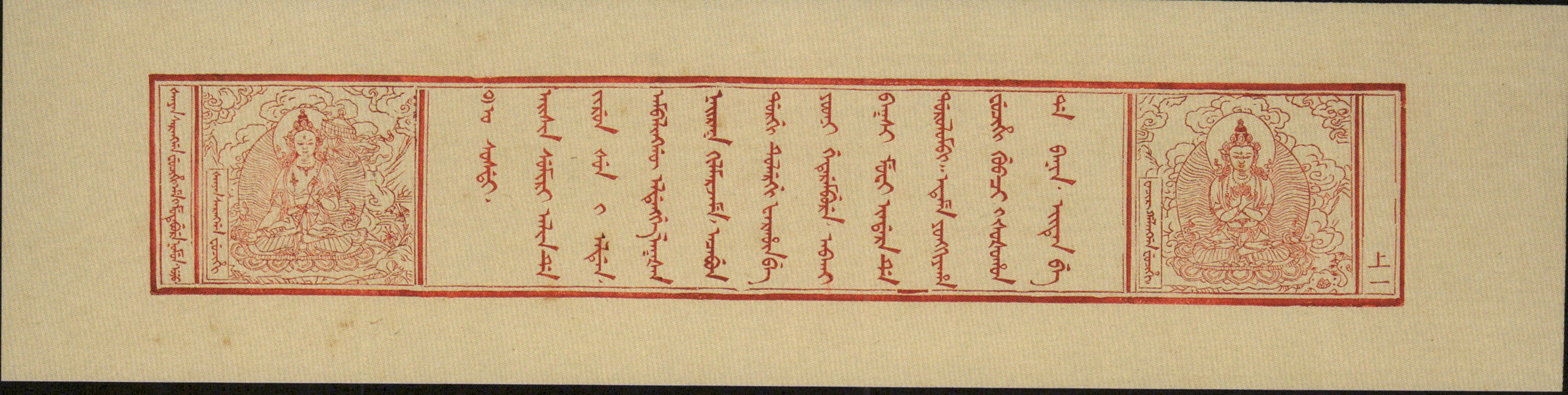

卷端
Beginning

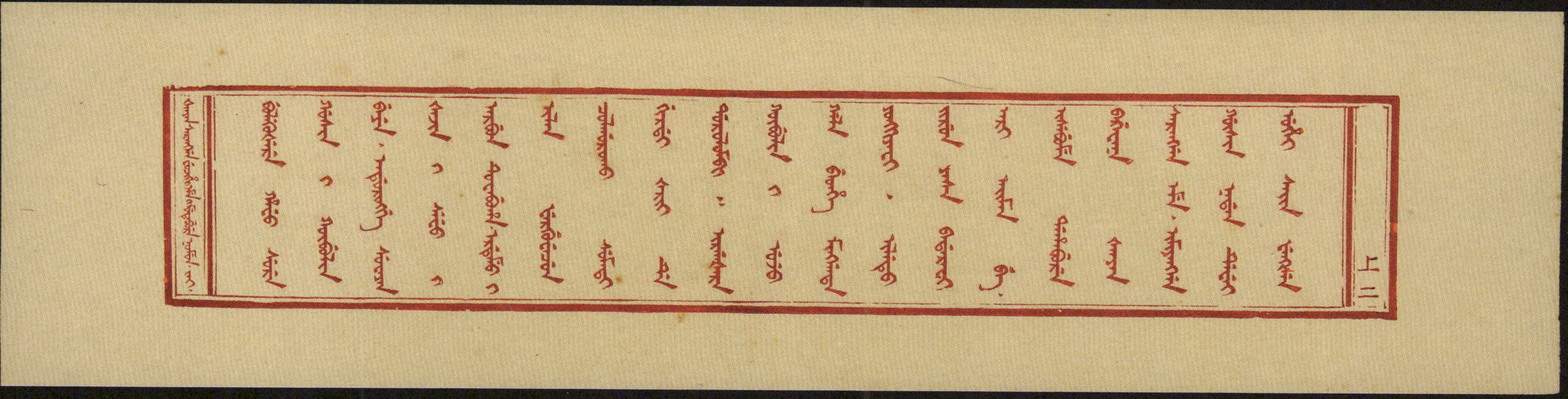

正文
Text

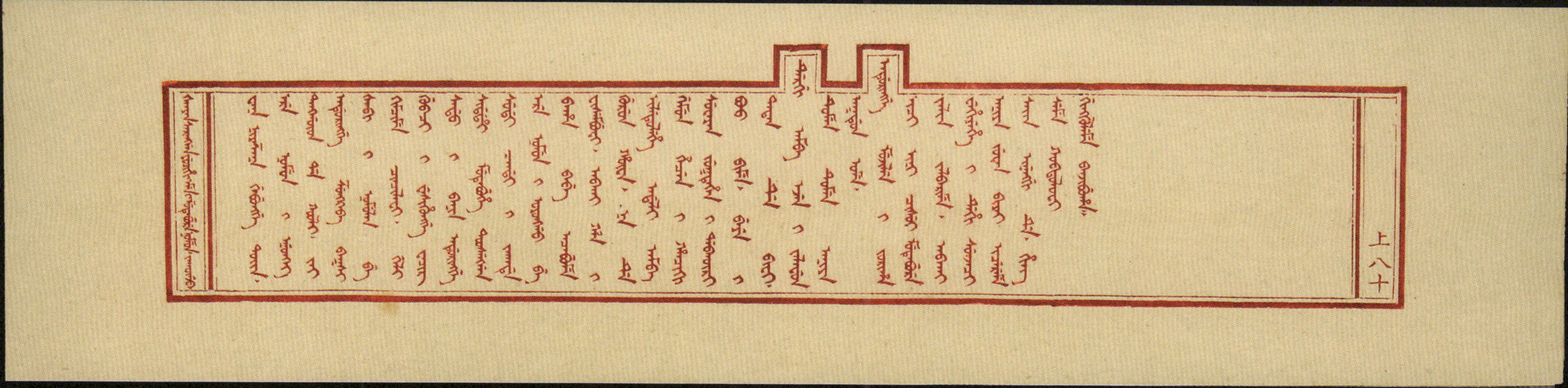

卷末
End

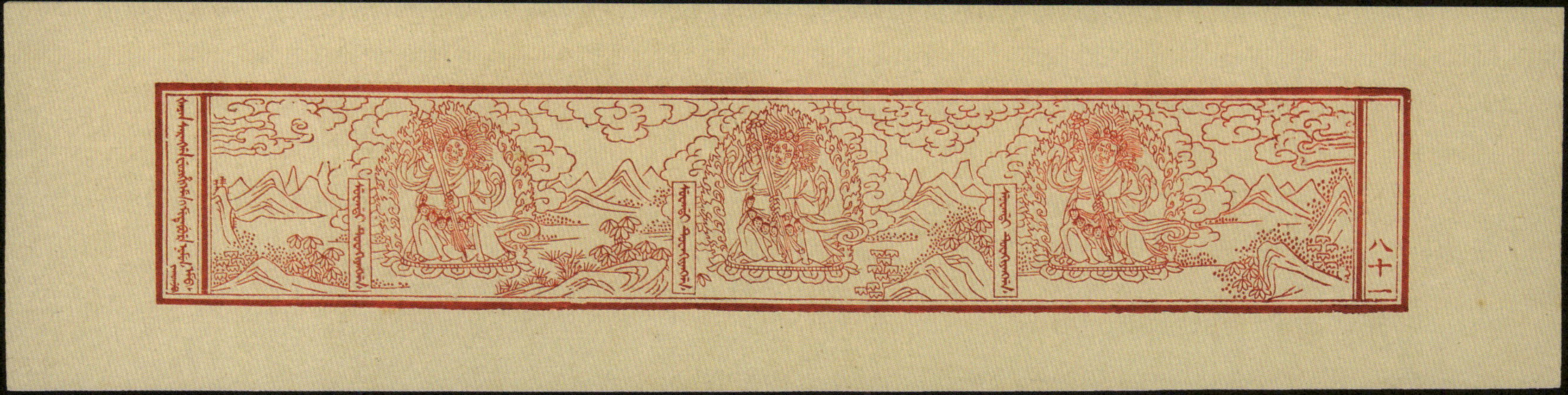

佛像
Buddhist figure

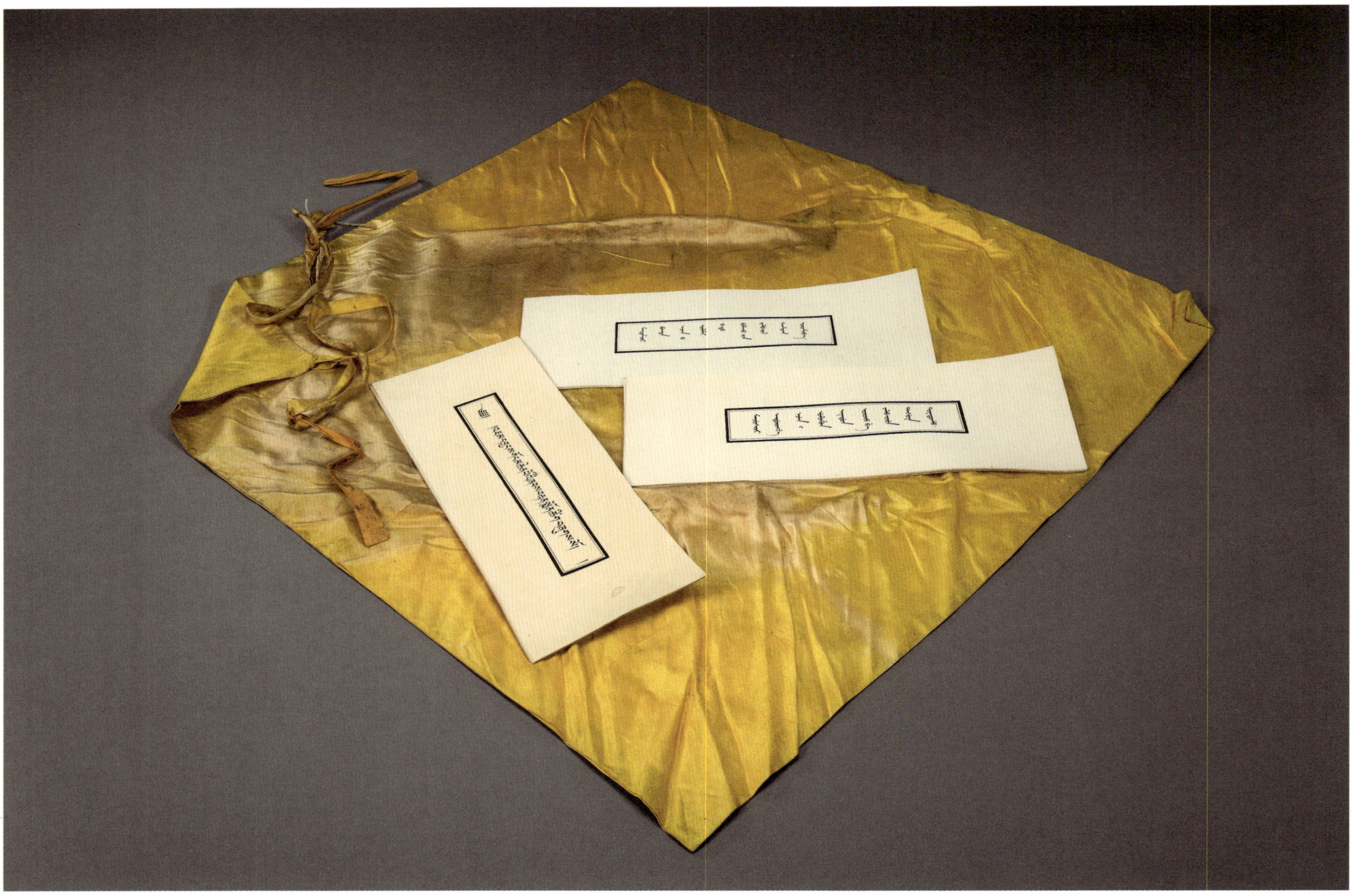

明黃色纏枝蓮紋暗花綾夾袱
Bright yellow twill-weave silk wrapping with veiled pattern of lotus scrolls

108

書27208
《丹書克經》
清　洞闊爾呼圖克圖著
清咸豐十一年（1861）寫滿文本
開本　縱12.2厘米　橫32.3厘米
版框　縱7.1厘米　橫23.1厘米
一册　一包

Inventory number: Shu 27208
Sutra Presented to the Court
Written by Donkhor Khutukhtu
Transcribed in Manchu in 1861
Format: 12.2 × 32.3 cm
Frame: 7.1 × 23.1 cm
One volume in one bundle

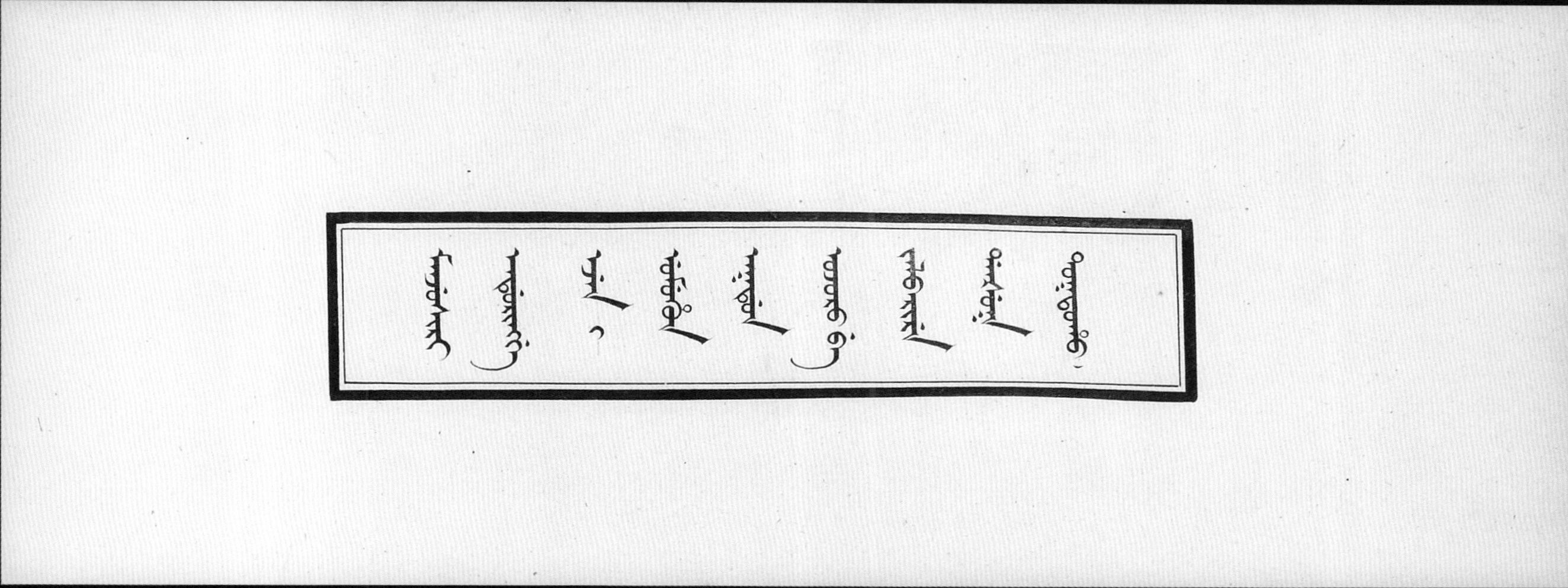

經面
Cover

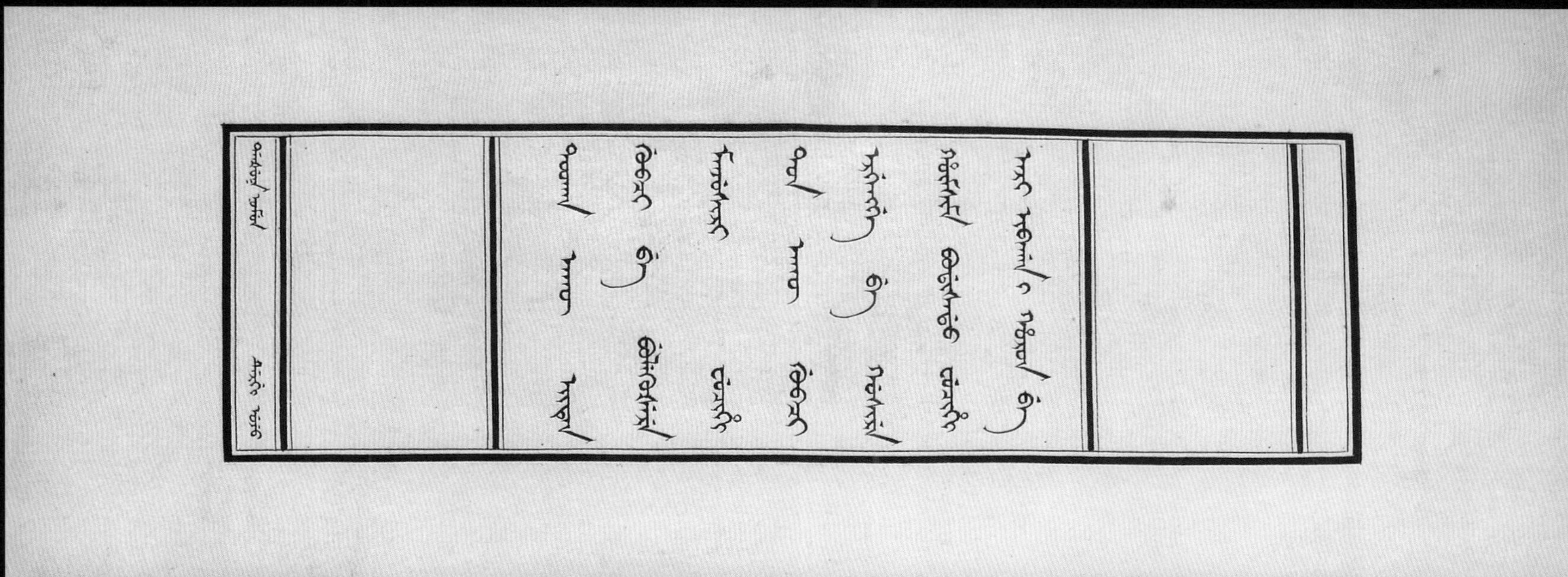

卷端

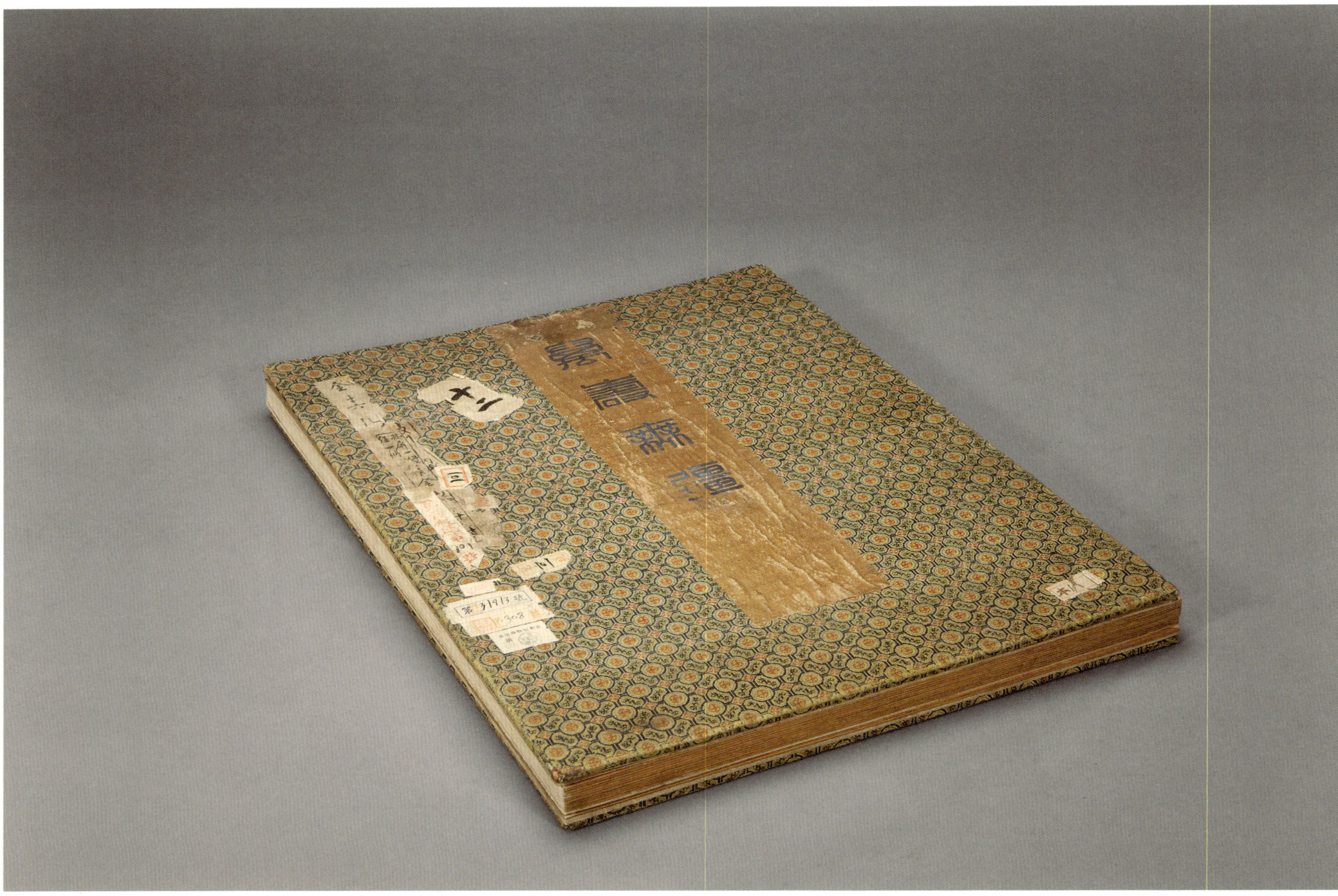

藍色萬字夔龍紋錦面
Blue brocade cover with swastikas and *kui*-dragons

書9927
《諸佛事略圖說》
清　佚名輯
清乾隆年泥金寫藏滿蒙漢合璧本
開本　縱47厘米　橫36.5厘米
版框　縱40.5厘米　橫31.8厘米
一冊　一函

109

Inventory number: Shu 9927
Illustrated Biographies of Various Buddhas
Anonymous, Qing dynasty (1644-1911)
Transcribed with powdered gold in Tibetan, Manchu, Mongolian and Chinese in the Qianlong period (r.1736-1795)
Format: 47 × 36.5 cm
Frame: 40.5 × 31.8 cm
One volume in one case

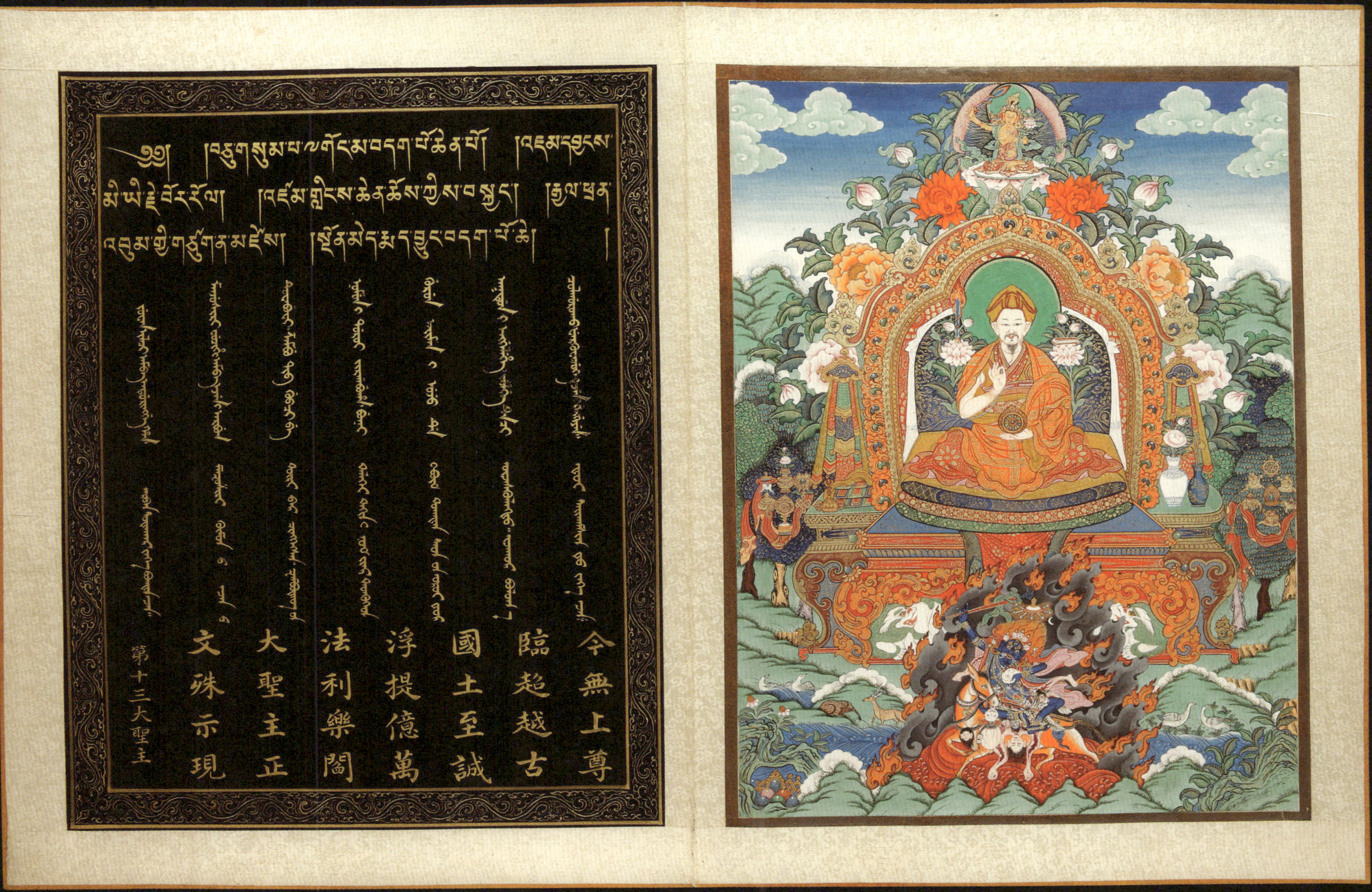

卷端
Beginning

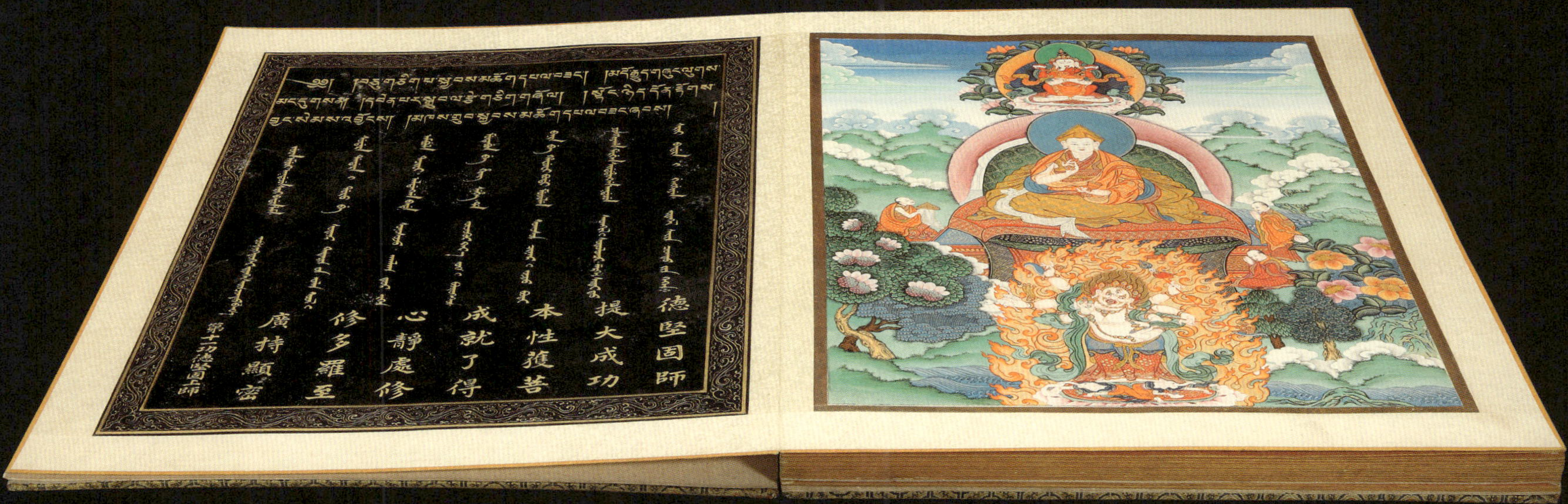

正文
Text

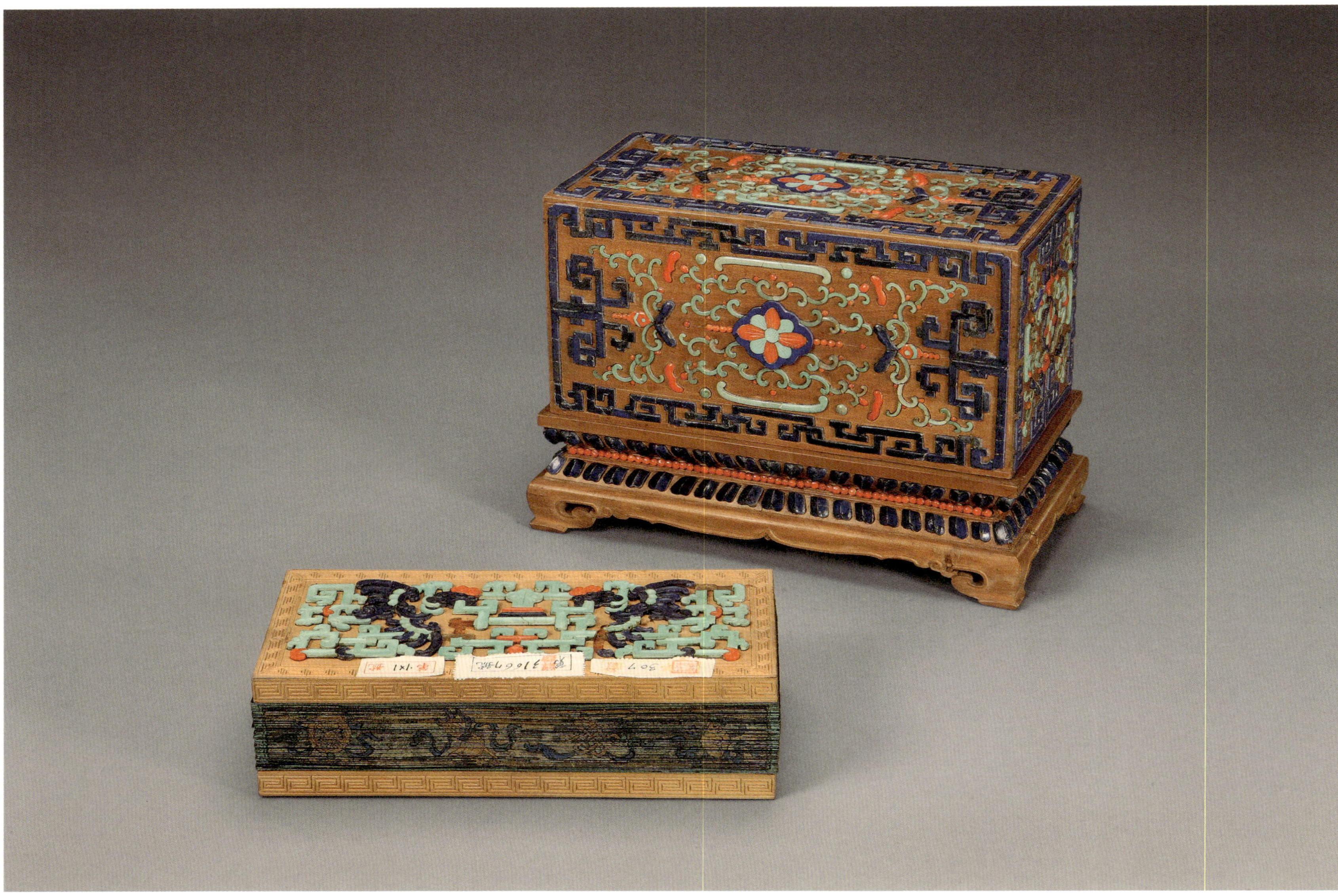

檀香木鑲百寶書盒
Sandalwood case inlaid with gems

書9755
《無量壽佛經》（又名《佛說大乘聖無量壽決定光明王如來陀羅尼經》）
清　佚名輯
清泥金寫藏滿蒙漢合璧本
開本　縱9.6厘米　橫21.5厘米
版框　縱8.9-9厘米　橫20.5-20.8厘米
一冊　一匣

110

Inventory number: Shu 9755
Amitayurdhyana Sutra
Anonymous, Qing dynasty (1644-1911)
Transcribed with powdered gold in Tibetan, Manchu, Mongolian and Chinese in the Qing dynasty
Format: 9.6 × 21.5 cm
Frame: height: 8.9-9 cm, width: 20.5-20.8 cm
One volume in one case

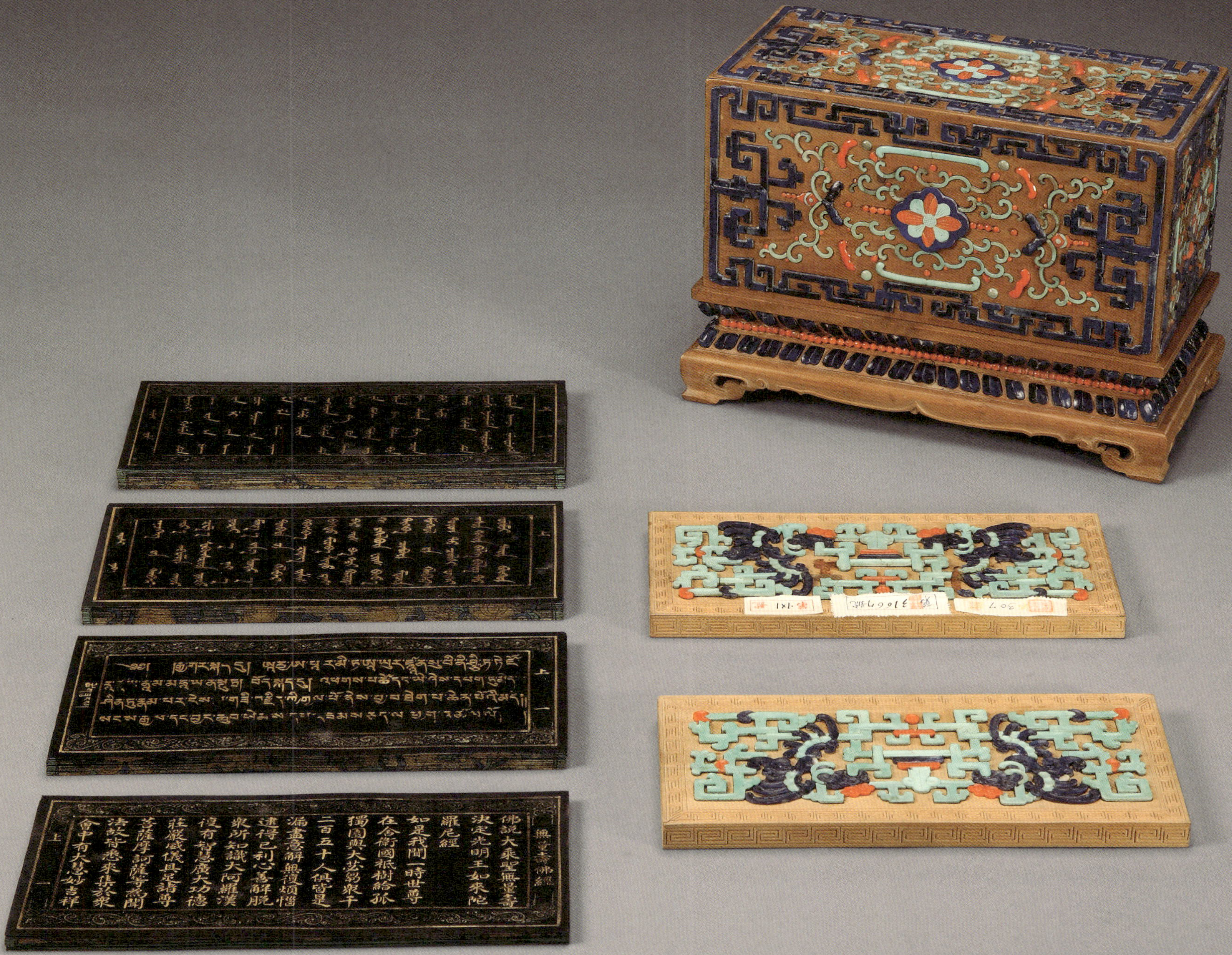

護經板及正文
Protective boards and text

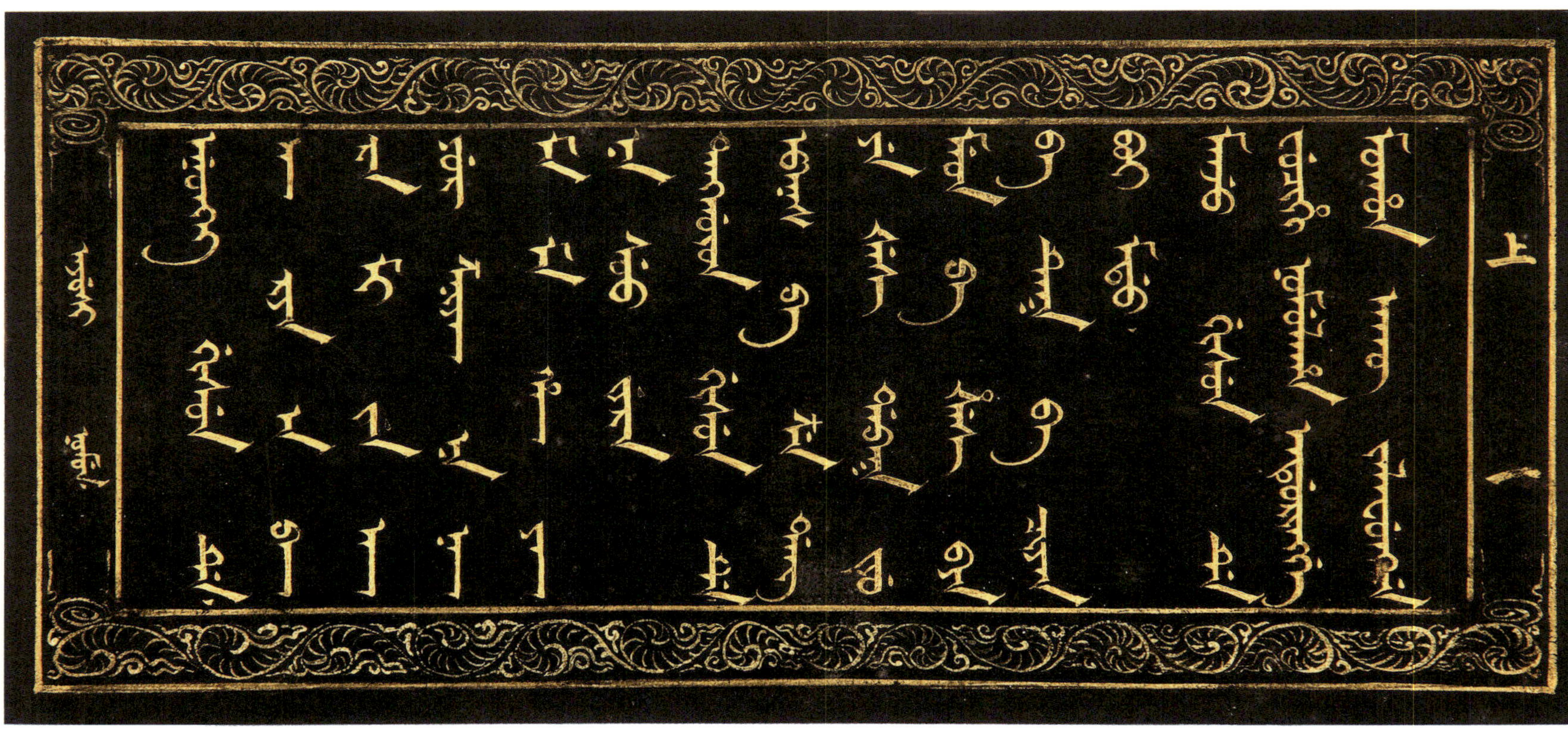

卷端
Beginning

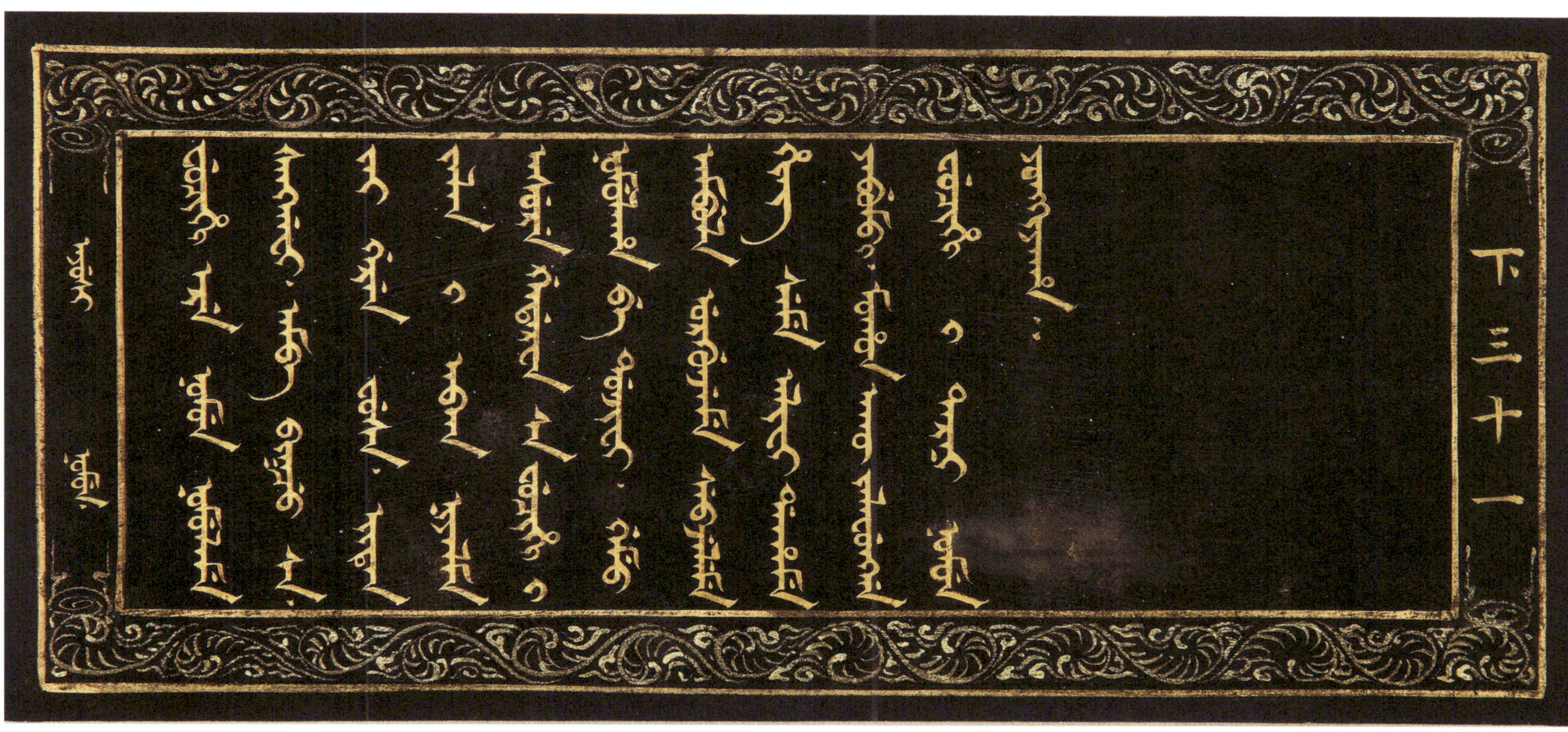

卷末
End

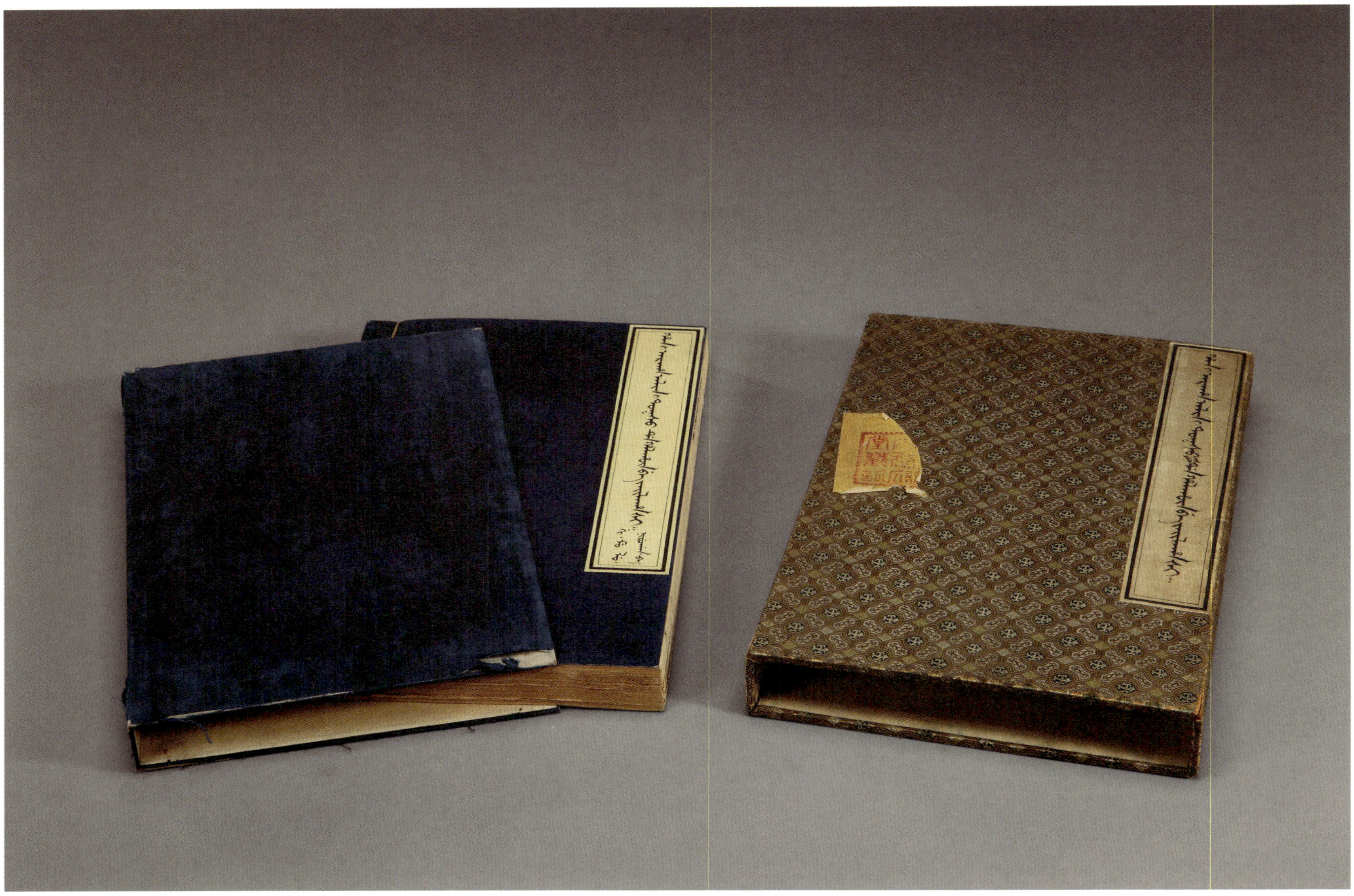

絳色萬字夔龍紋錦函
Brown brocade case decorated with swastikas and dragons

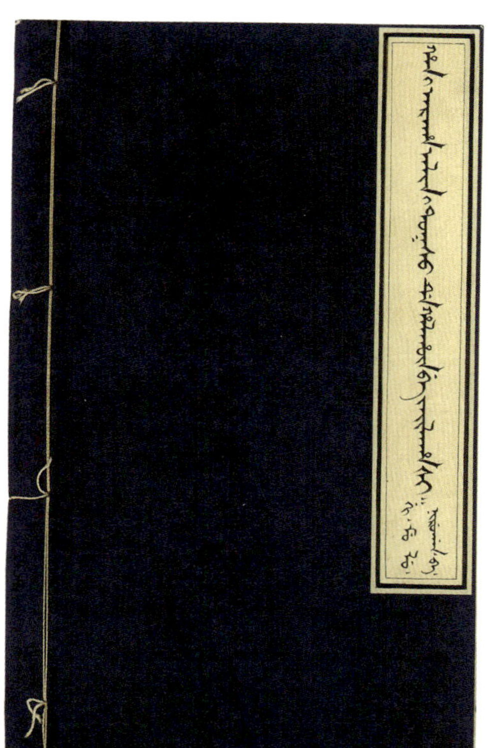

藍色素絹書面
Blue silk cover

書22514
《御製避暑山莊詩二卷》
清　聖祖玄燁撰　揆叙等恭注
清康熙五十年（1711）武英殿刻墨繪滿文本
開本　縱26.4厘米　橫16.6厘米
版框　縱19.7厘米　橫13.5厘米
一冊　一函

111

Inventory number: Shu 22514
Imperial Poems on the Mountain Resort for Summer Retreat
Two chapters
Written by the Kangxi emperor (r.1662-1722)
Annotated by Kuixu et. al., Qing dynasty (1644-1911)
Printed in Manchu in 1711 at the Hall of Martial Valour, with illustrations
Format: 26.4 × 16.6 cm
Frame: 19.7 × 13.5 cm
One volume in one case

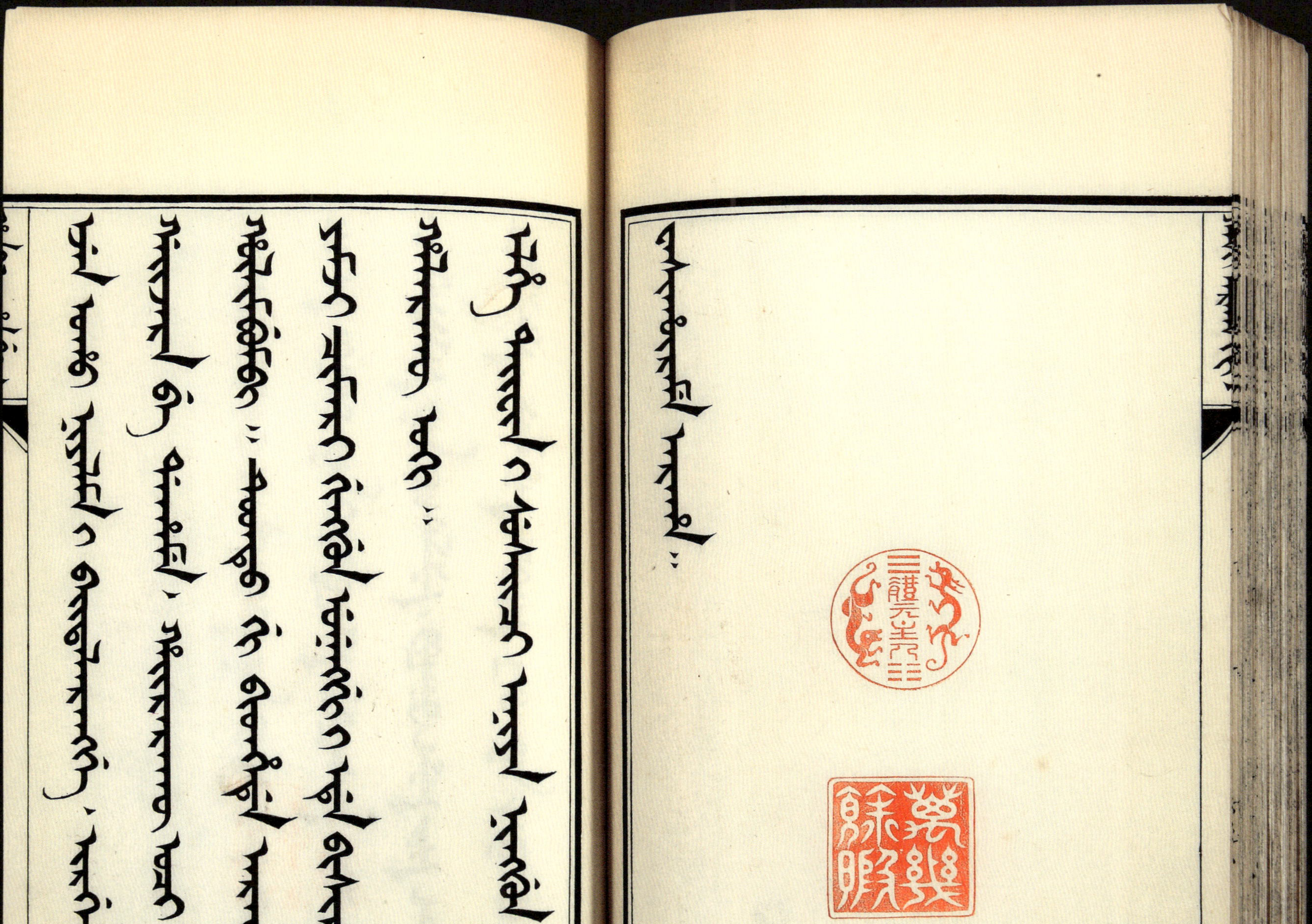

康熙五十年御製序
Preface by the Kangxi emperor in 1711

卷端
Beginning

[illegible]

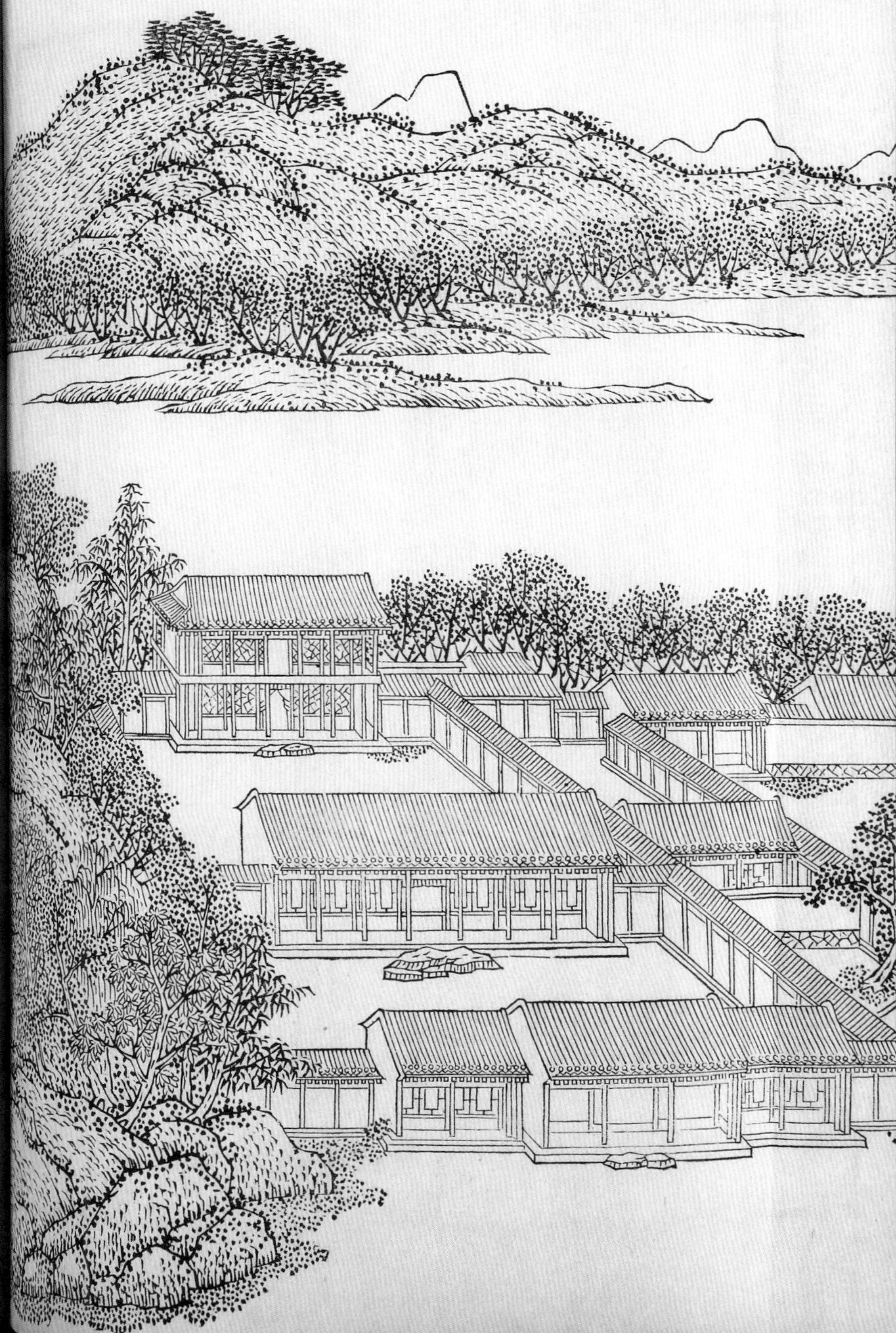

插圖
Illustration

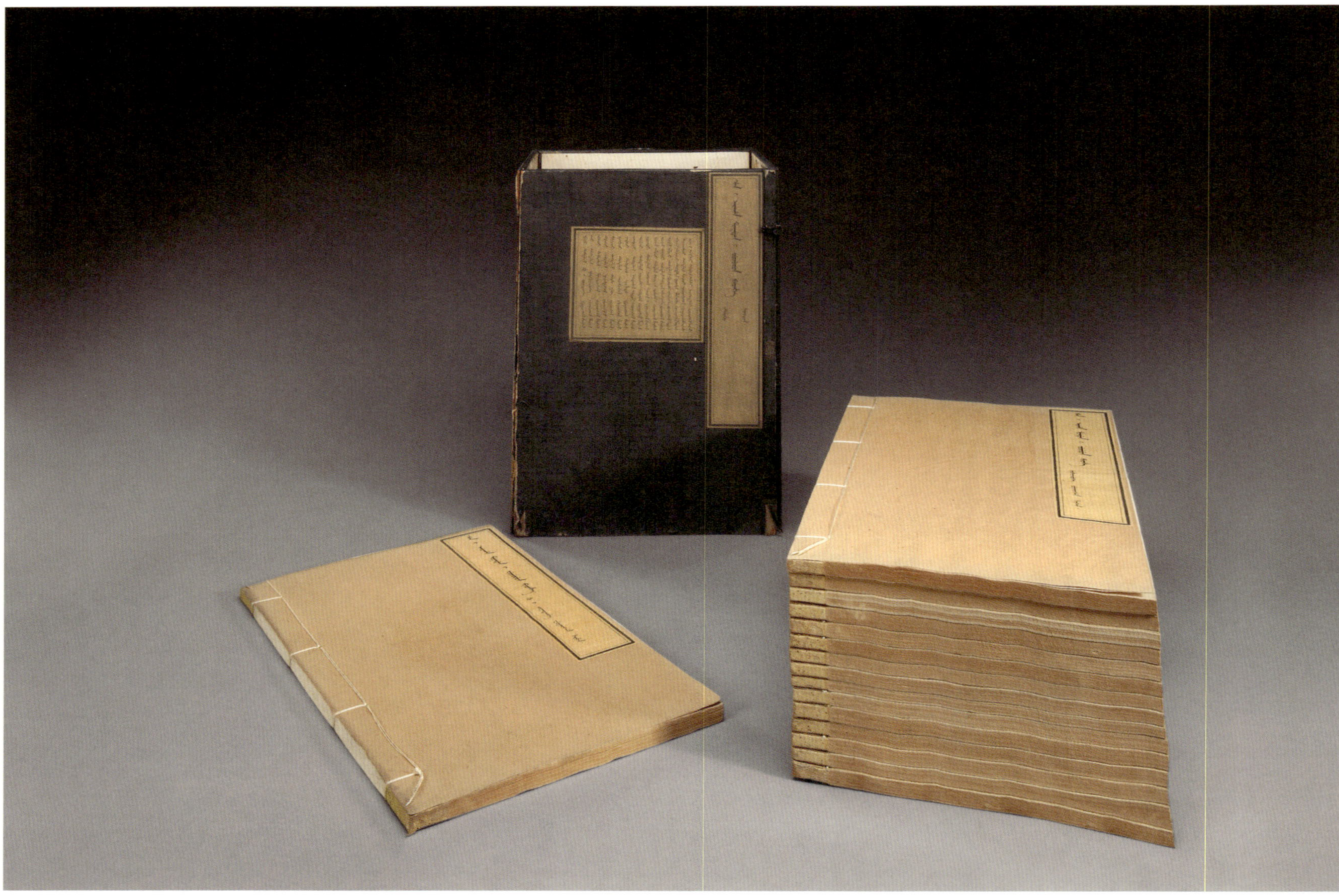

藍色素絹書函
Blue silk case

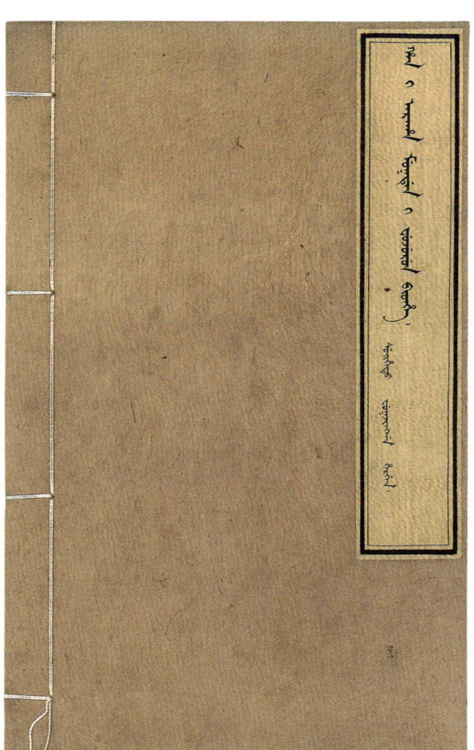

黄色紙書面
Yellow paper cover

書22508
《御製盛京賦三十二卷》
清　高宗弘曆撰　鄂爾泰等注　傅恒等校
清乾隆十三年（1748）武英殿刻滿文三十二體篆字本
開本　縱34.7厘米　橫21.5厘米
版框　縱22厘米　橫16.5厘米
三十二册　二函

112

Inventory number: Shu 22508
Imperial Rhapsody on Shengjing
Thirty-two chapters
Written by the Qianlong emperor (r.1736-1795)
Annotated by Ortai et. al., proofread by Fuheng et. al., Qing dynasty (1644-1911)
Thirty copies in Manchu seal script
Printed in 1748 at the Hall of Martial Valour
Format: 34.7 × 21.5 cm
Frame: 22 × 16.5 cm
Thirty-two volumes in two cases

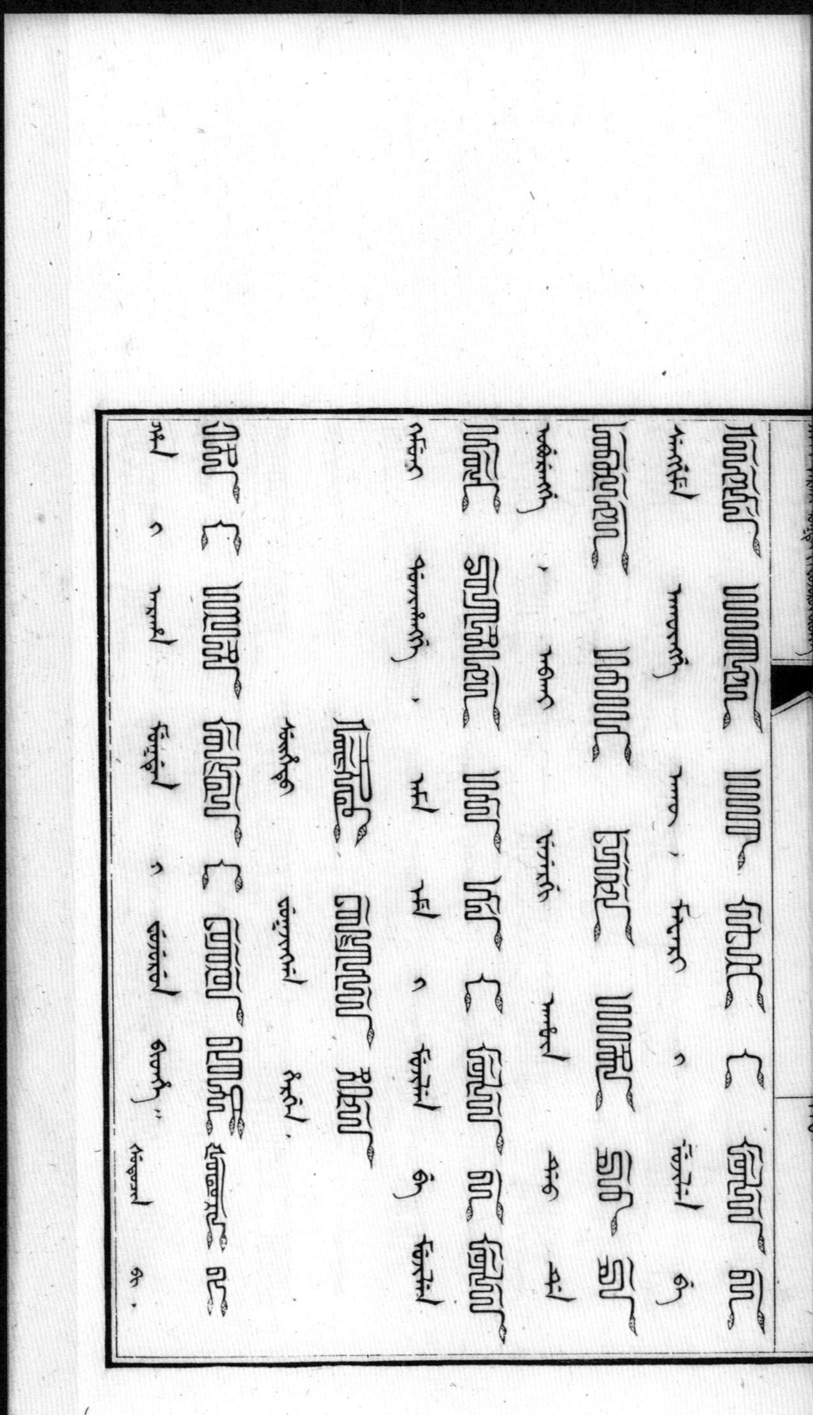

卷端
Beginning

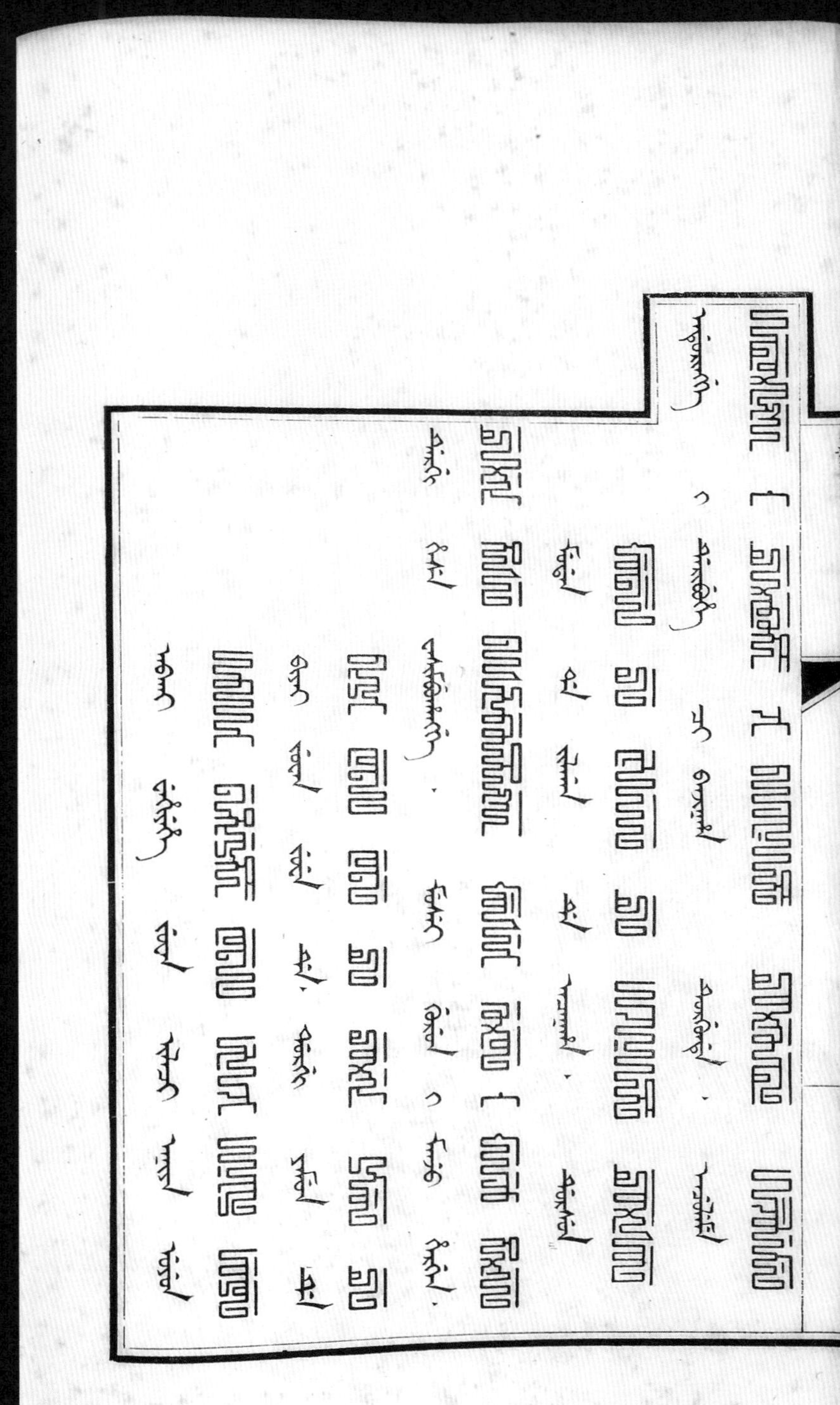

乾隆十三年上諭
Imperial edict in 1748

圖版索引

7

40

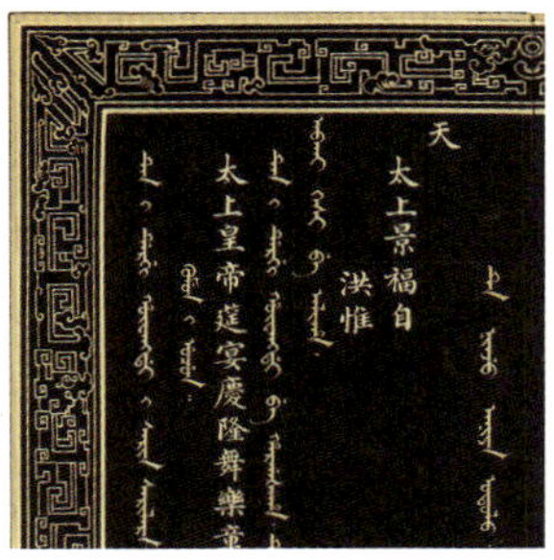

書6568

《太上皇帝筵宴慶隆舞樂章一卷》

Inventory number: Shu 6568

Music of Banquet Dance Presented to the Super-sovereign

8

42

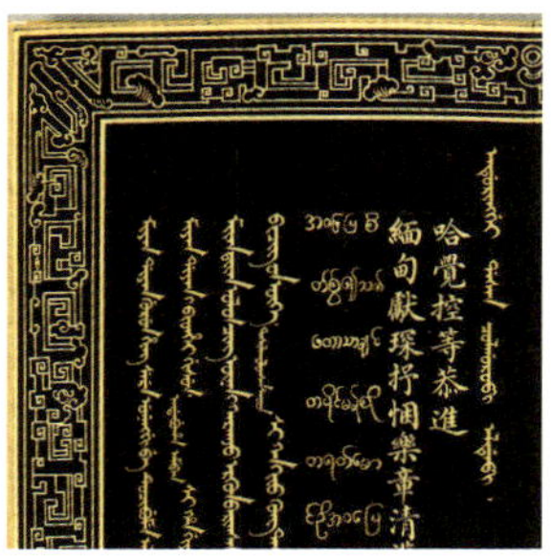

書6569

《緬甸獻琛抒悃樂章一卷》

Inventory number: Shu 6569

Music Respectfully Presented by Envoys of Burma

9

44

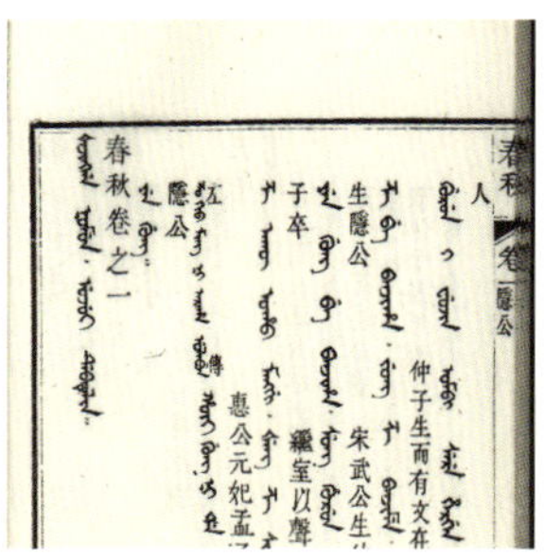

書21739

《御製翻譯春秋六十四卷綱領一卷》

Inventory number: Shu 21739

Translated Version of the Spring and Autumn Annals

Sixty-four chapters as text, one chapter as guiding principle

10

46

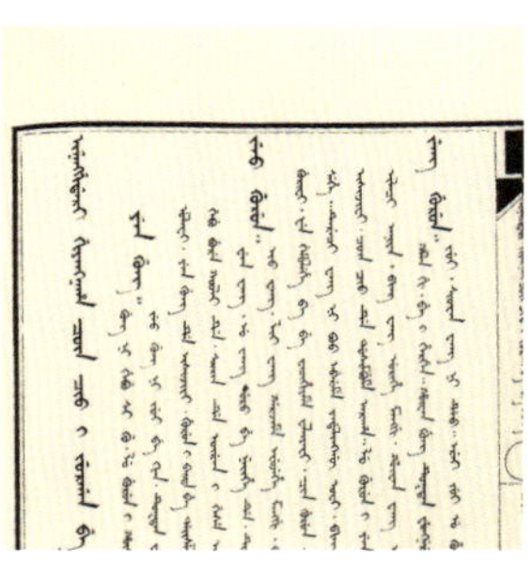

書21746

《日講春秋解義六十四卷總説一卷》

Inventory number: Shu 21746

Everyday Textbook: Interpretation of the Spring and Autumn Annals

Sixty-four chapters as text, one chapter as introduction

11

48

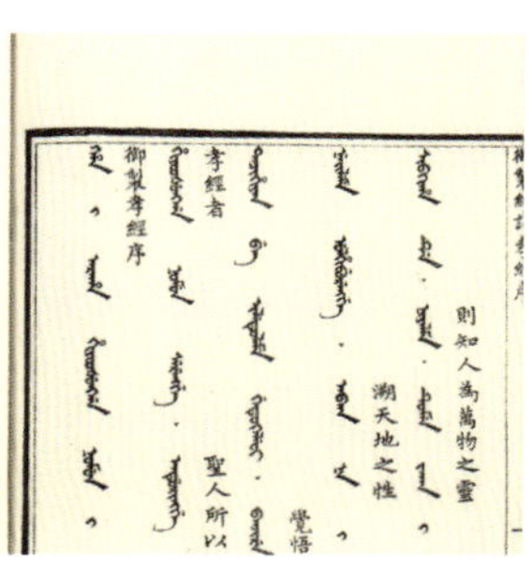

書21571

《翻譯孝經一卷》

Inventory number: Shu 21571

Translated Version of the Classic of Filial Piety

One chapter

12

52

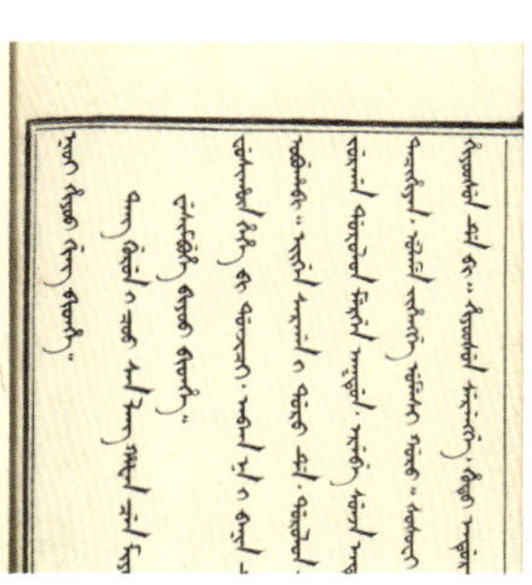

書21759

《女孝經一卷》

Inventory number: Shu 21759

Classic of Female Filial Piety

One chapter

1

22

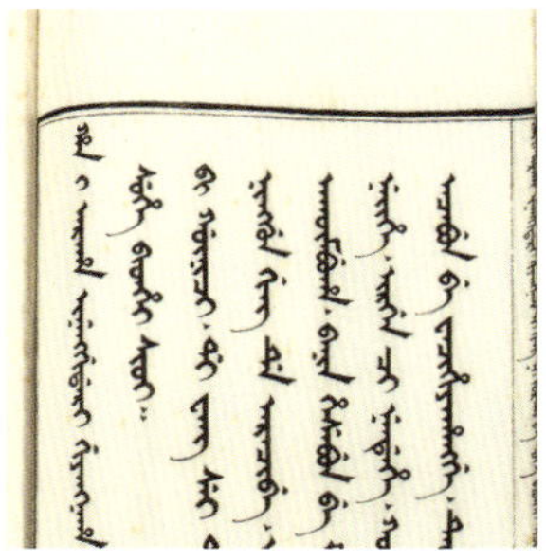

書21723

《日講易經解義十八卷》

Inventory number: Shu 21723

Everyday Textbook: Interpretation of the Book of Changes

Eighteen chapters

2

26

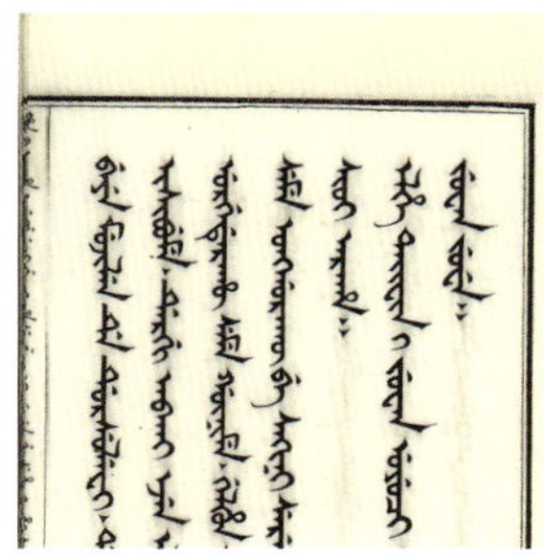

書21726

《日講書經解義十三卷》

Inventory number: Shu 21726

Everyday Textbook: Interpretation of the Book of History

Thirteen chapters

3

28

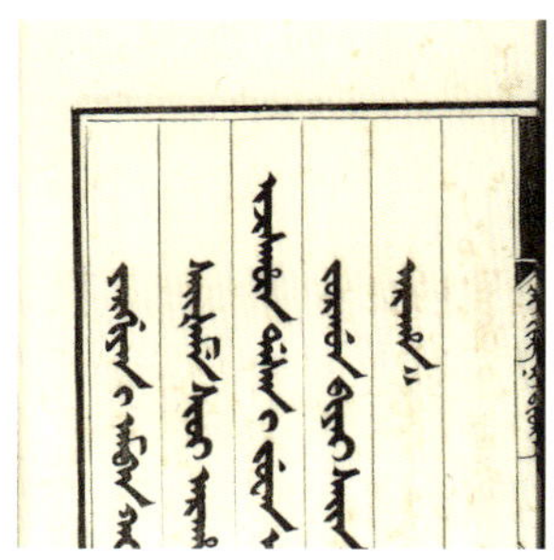

書21730

《詩經二十卷》

Inventory number: Shu 21730

Book of Odes

Twenty chapters

4

30

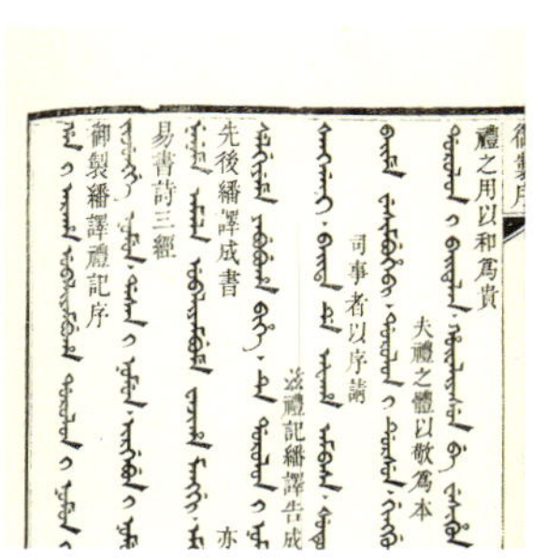

書21735

《御製翻譯禮記三十卷》

Inventory number: Shu 21735

Translated Version of the Book of Rites

Thirty chapters

5

34

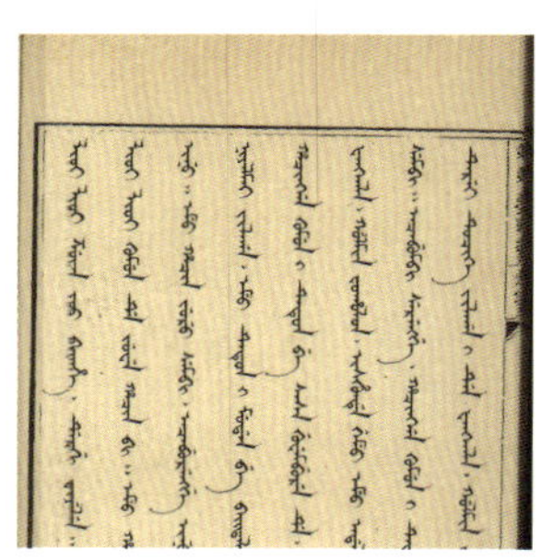

書21782

《律吕纂要二卷》

Inventory number: Shu 21782

Elements of Music

Two chapters

6

38

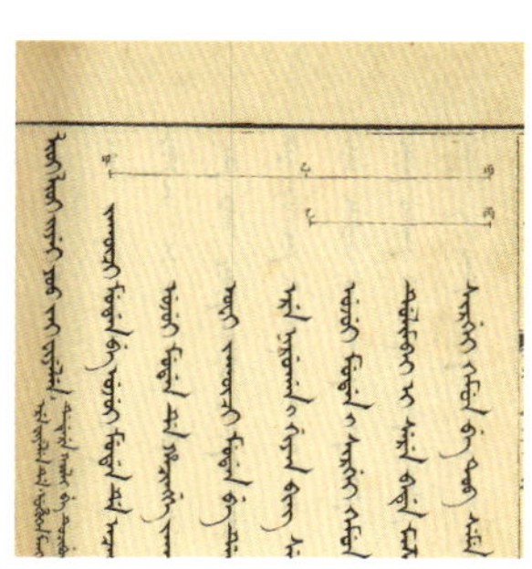

書21783

《律吕節要五卷》

Inventory number: Shu 21783

Essentials of Music

Five chapters

13 54

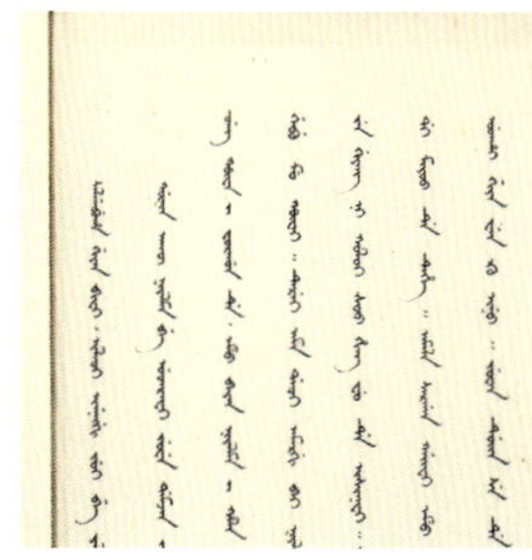

書21763
《聖孝鑒十卷》

Inventory number: Shu 21763
Mirror for Imperial Filial Piety
Ten chapters

14 56

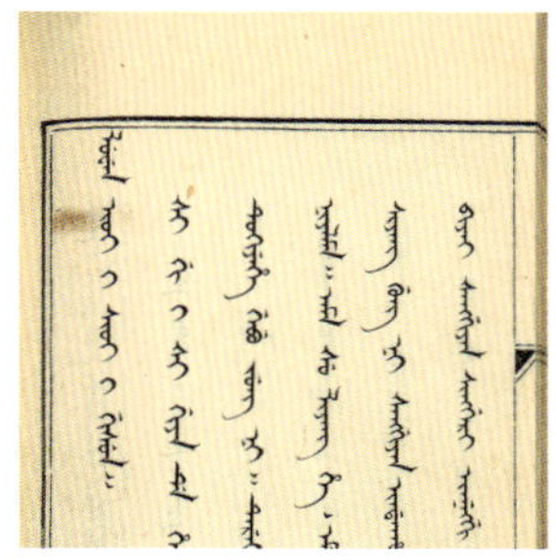

書21764
《四書十三卷》

Inventory number: Shu 21764
Four Books
Thirteen chapters

15 60

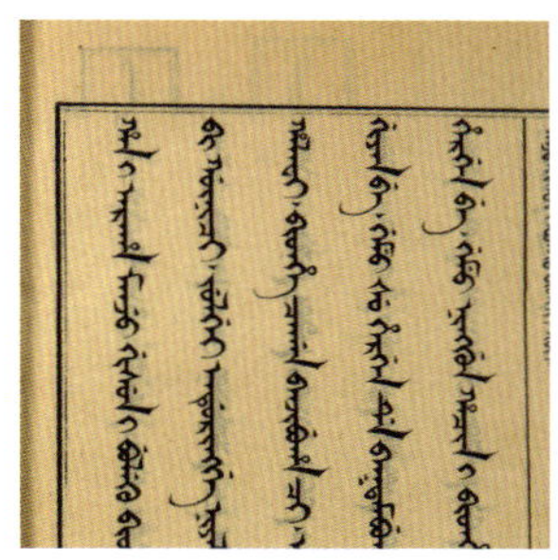

書21842
《御製清文鑒二十卷首一卷後序一卷總綱四卷》

Inventory number: Shu 21842
Dictionary of the Qing Language
Twenty chapters as text, one chapter as preliminary remarks, four chapters as general principles,
one chapter as postscript

16 64

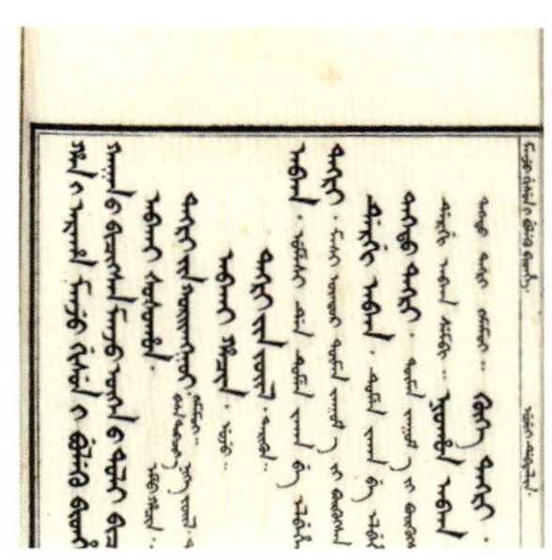

書21866
《御製滿蒙文鑒二十卷首一卷總綱八卷》

Inventory number: Shu 21866
Manchu-Mongolian Dictionary
Twenty chapters as text, one chapter as preliminary remarks

17 66

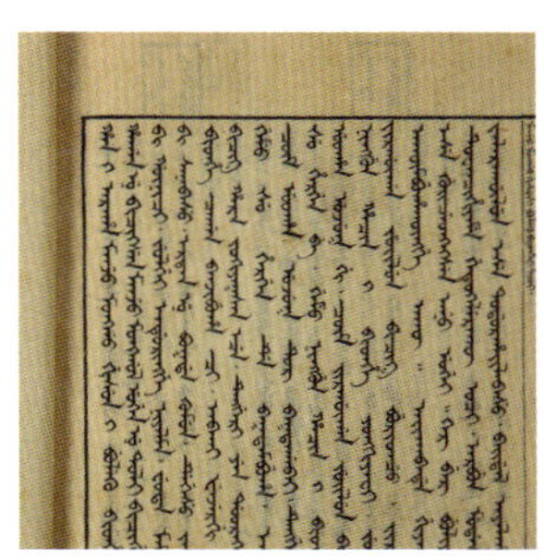

書21867
《御製滿蒙文鑒二十卷首一卷》

Inventory number: Shu 21867
Manchu-Mongolian Dictionary
Twenty chapters as text, one chapter as preliminary remarks

18 68

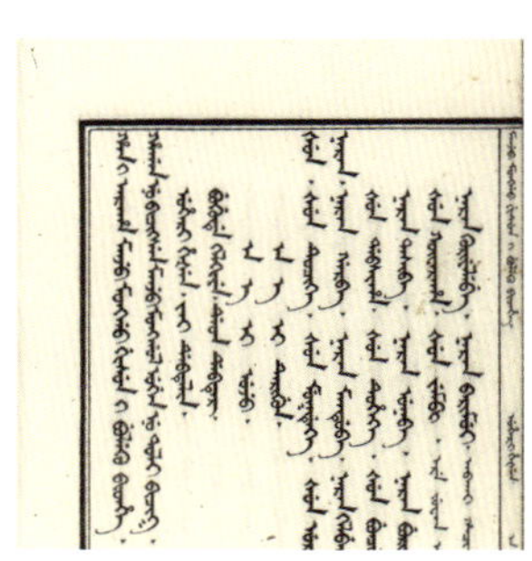

書21875
《御製滿蒙文鑒總綱八卷》

Inventory number: Shu 21875
General Principles of the Manchu-Mongolian Dictionary
Eight chapters

19 70

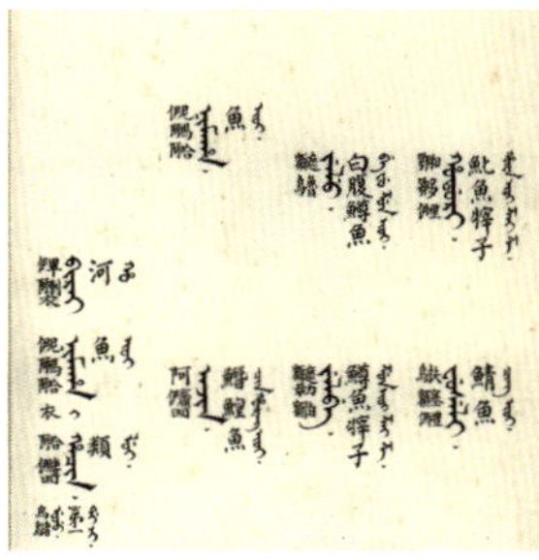

書21860
《御製兼漢清文鑒不分卷》

Inventory number: Shu 21860
Phonetically Transcribed Bilingual Dictionary of Chinese and the Official Language of the Qing

20 72

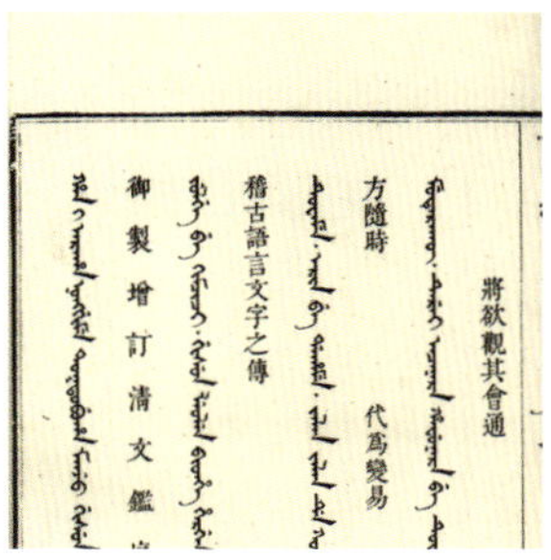

書21850
《御製增訂清文鑒三十二卷首二卷總綱八卷補編四卷補編總綱一卷》

Inventory number: Shu 21850
Supplement to the Dictionary of the Qing Language
Thirty-two chapters as text, two chapters as preliminary remarks, eight chapters as general principles, four chapters as supplement to the text, one chapter as supplement to the general principle

21 74

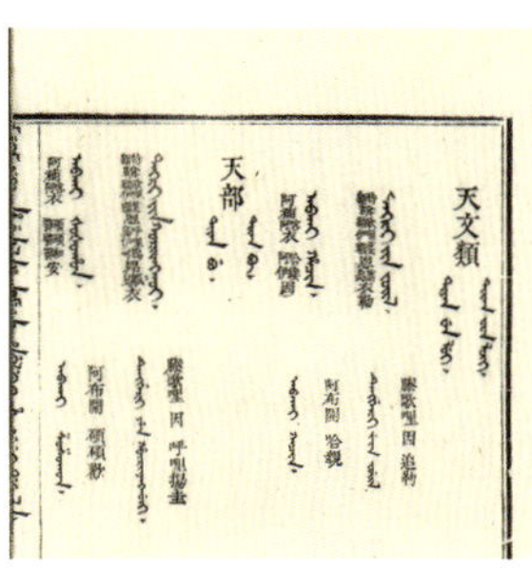

書21863
《御製滿州蒙古漢字三合切音清文鑒三十一卷首一卷》

Inventory number: Shu 21863
Trilingual Dictionary of Manchu, Mongolian and Chinese Phonetically Transcribed, Adopting the Method of Qieyin
Thirty-one chapters as text, one chapter as preliminary remarks

22 76

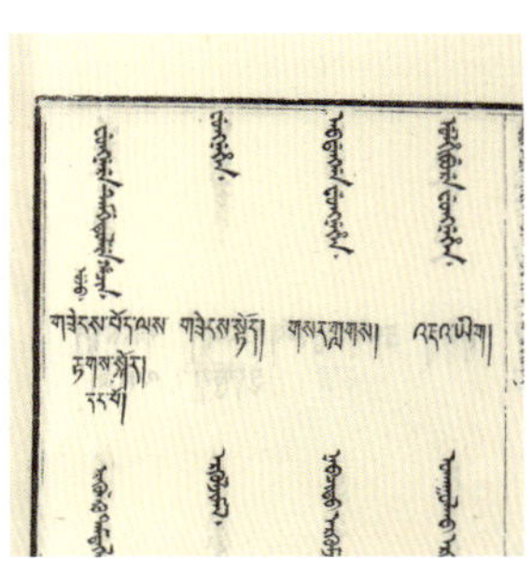

書55
《御製四體清文鑒三十二卷補編四卷》

Inventory number: Shu 55
Dictionary of the Four Languages in the Qing Dynasty
Thirty-two chapters as text, four chapters as supplement

23 78

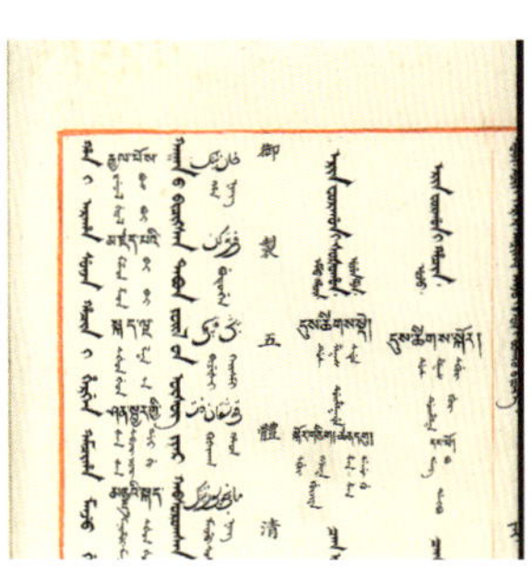

書21840
《御製五體清文鑒三十二卷補編四卷》

Inventory number: Shu 21840
Dictionary of the Five Languages in the Qing Dynasty
Thirty-two chapters as text, four chapters as supplement

24 80

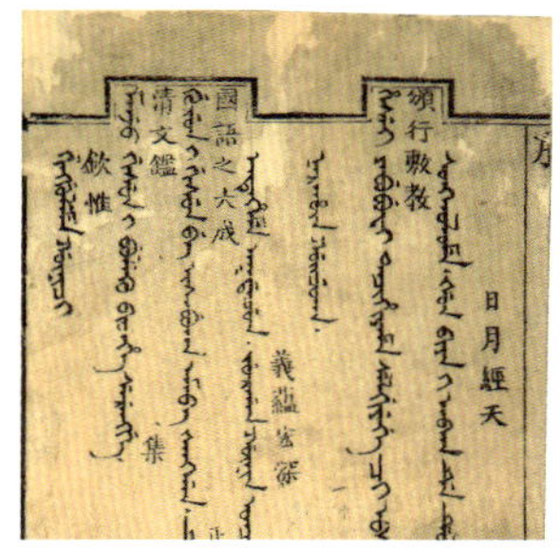

書21861

《音漢清文鑒二十卷》

Inventory number: Shu 21861

Manchu-Chinese Dictionary

Twenty chapters

25 84

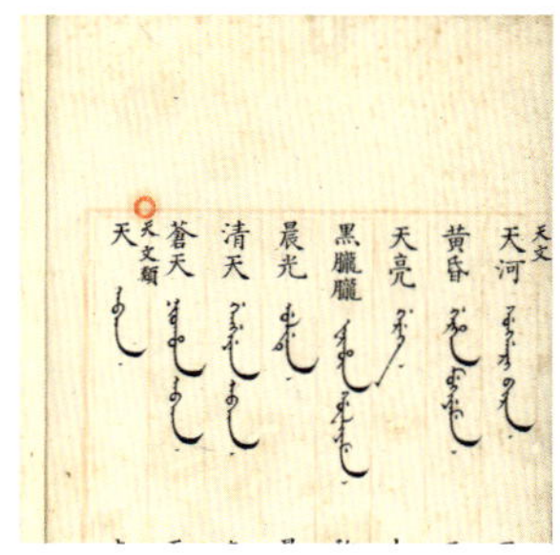

書21859

《清文鑒擇録八卷》

Inventory number: Shu 21859

Selections from the Dictionary of the Qing Language

Eight chapters

26 86

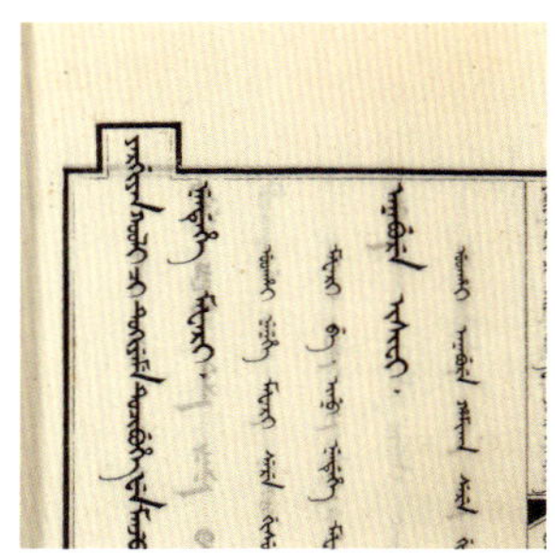

書21790

《實録内摘出舊清語十四卷》

Inventory number: Shu 21790

Old Qing Language Selected from Veritable Records

Fourteen chapters

27 88

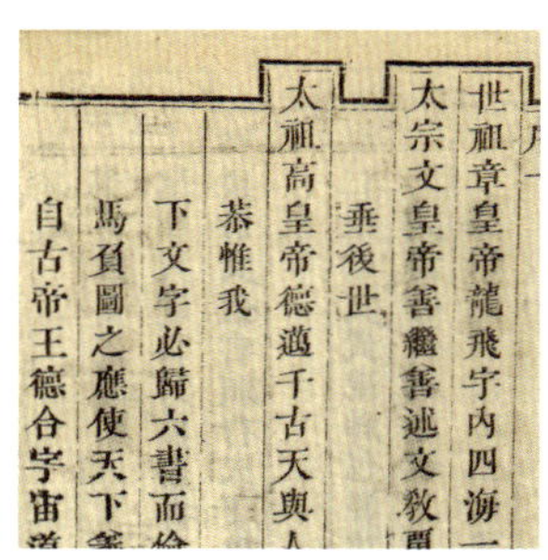

書21820

《清文彙書十二卷》

Inventory number: Shu 21820

Comprehensive Dictionary of the Qing Language

Twelve chapters

28 90

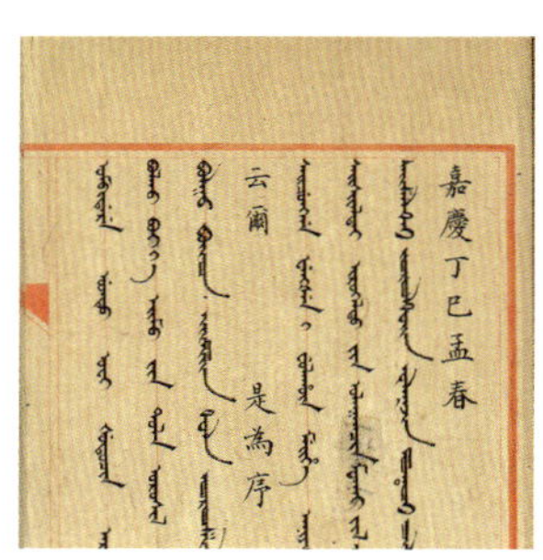

書21832

《蒙古托忒彙集八卷》

Inventory number: Shu 21832

Tuote Mongolian Dictionary

Eight chapters

29 92

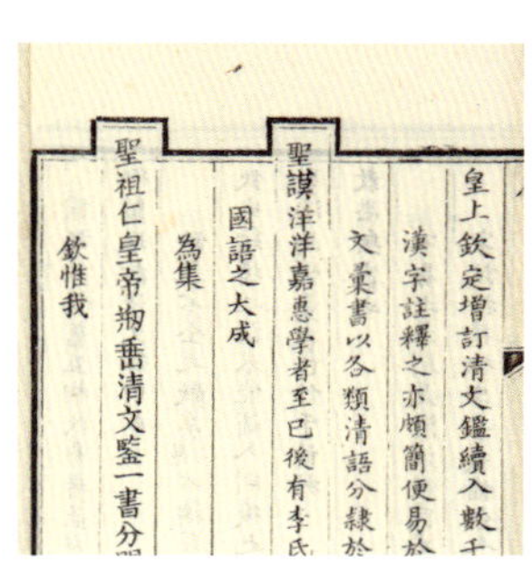

書21829

《清文補彙八卷》

Inventory number: Shu 21829

Supplemental Dictionary of the Qing Language

Eight chapters

30 94

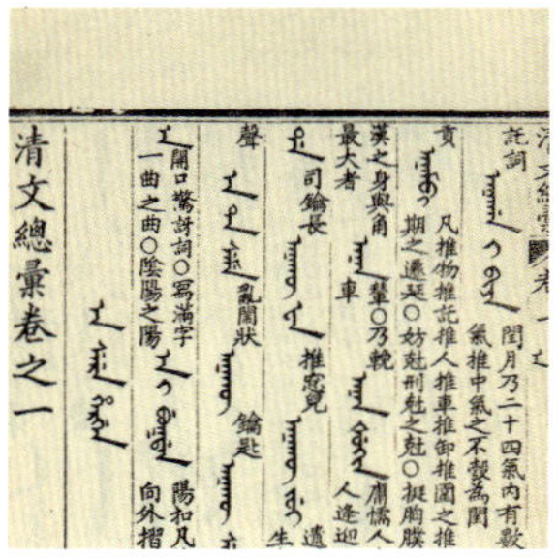

書21818

《清文總彙十二卷》

Inventory number: Shu 21818

Complete Dictionary of the Qing Language

Twelve chapters

31 98

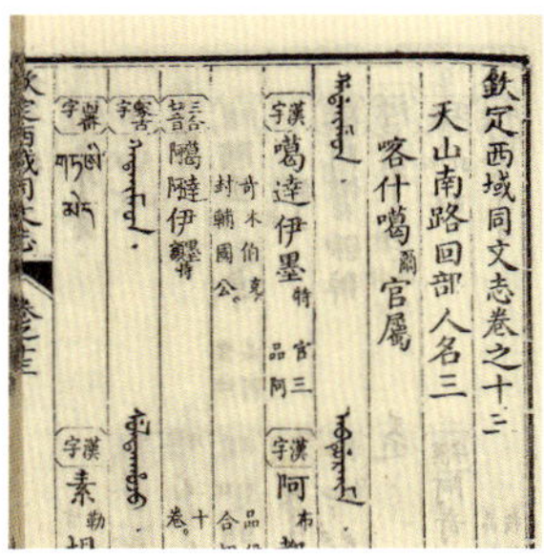

書59

《欽定西域同文志二十四卷》

Inventory number: Shu 59

Geographical Dictionary of Places and Names in the Western Region

Twenty-four chapters

32 100

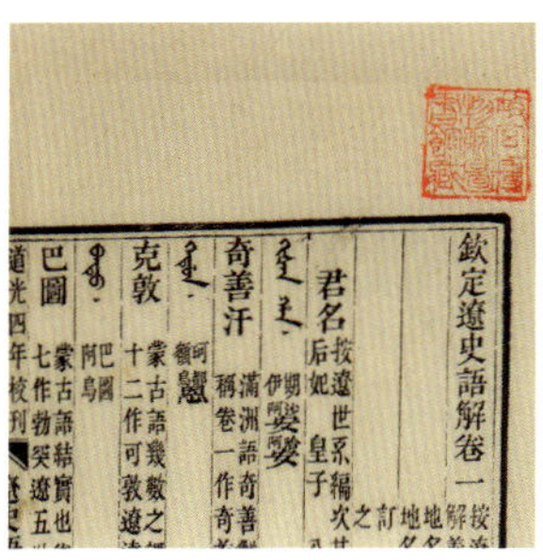

書74

《欽定遼金元三史語解四十六卷》

Inventory number: Shu 74

Dictionary for Terms in the Histories of Liao, Jin and Yuan

Forty-six chapters

33 104

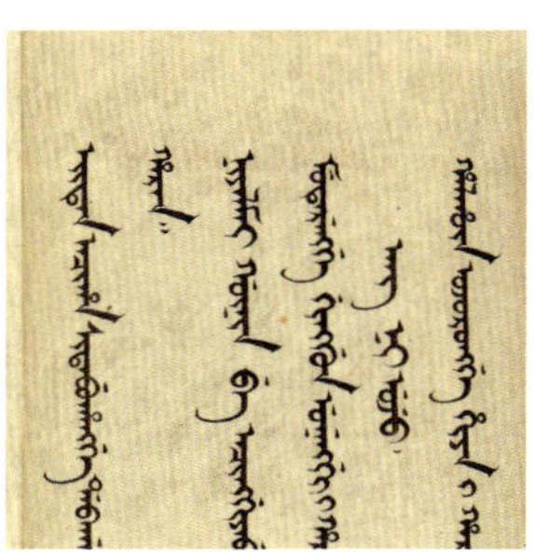

書21836

《滿蒙漢字書不分卷》

Inventory number: Shu 21336

Manchu-Mongolian-Chinese Dictionary

34 106

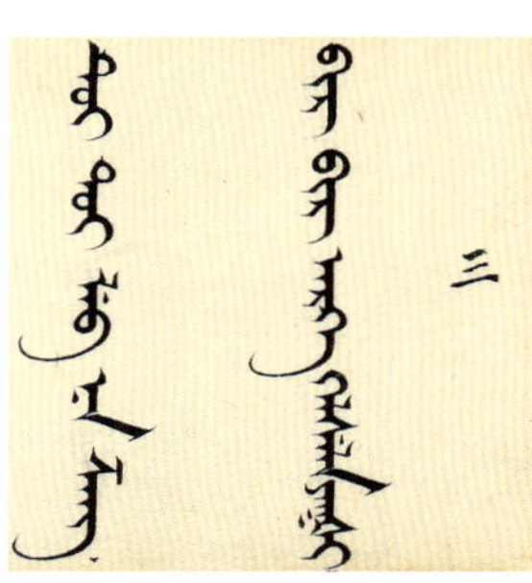

書27218

《滿蒙藏維四體字書一卷》

Inventory number: Shu 27218

Manchu-Mongolian-Tibetan-Uighur Dictionary

35 108

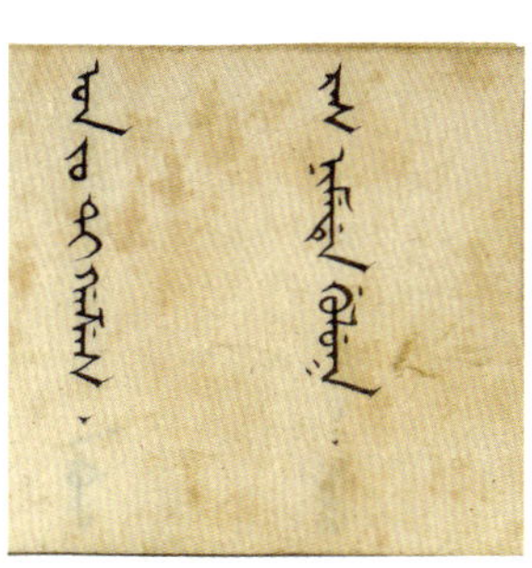

書21841

《滿蒙藏嘉戎維語五體字書不分卷》

Inventory number: Shu 21841

Manchu-Mongolian-Tibetan-Jiarong-Uighur Dictionary

42 128

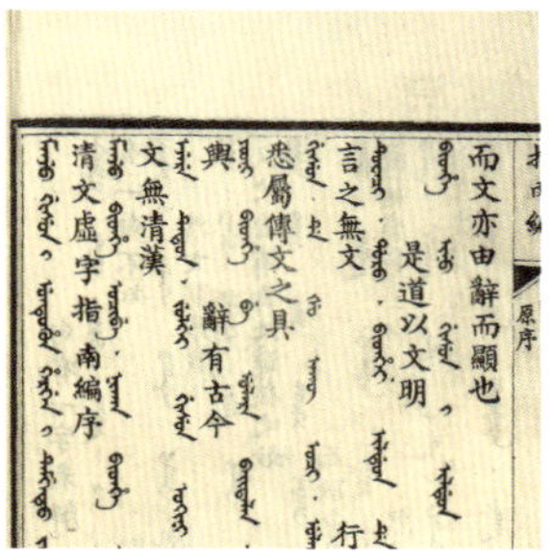

書21833
《重刻清文虛字指南编二卷》
Inventory number: Shu 21833
Reprinted Version of the Guidebook of Manchu Function Words
Two chapters

43 132

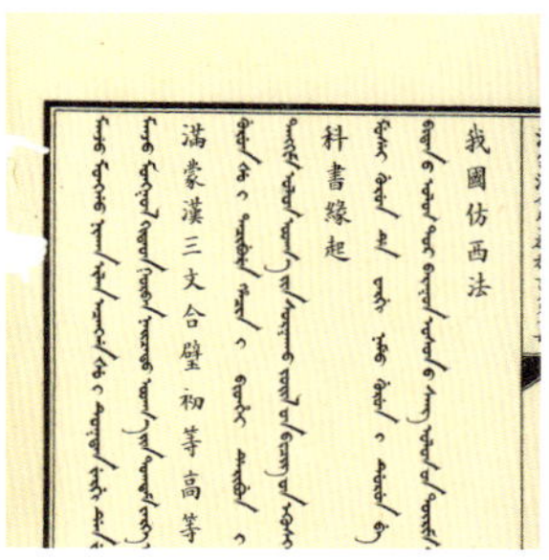

書21784
《滿蒙漢三文合璧教科書八卷》
Inventory number: Shu 21784
Manchu-Mongolian-Chinese Textbook
Eight chapters

44 134

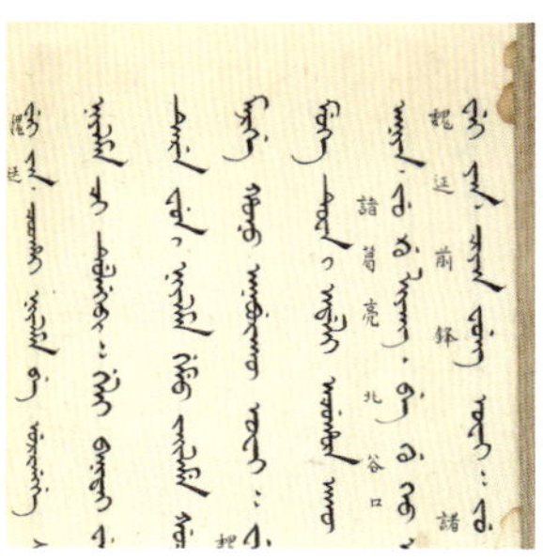

書21928
《三國志六十五卷》
Inventory number: Shu 21928
Records of the Three Kingdoms
Sixty-five chapters

45 136

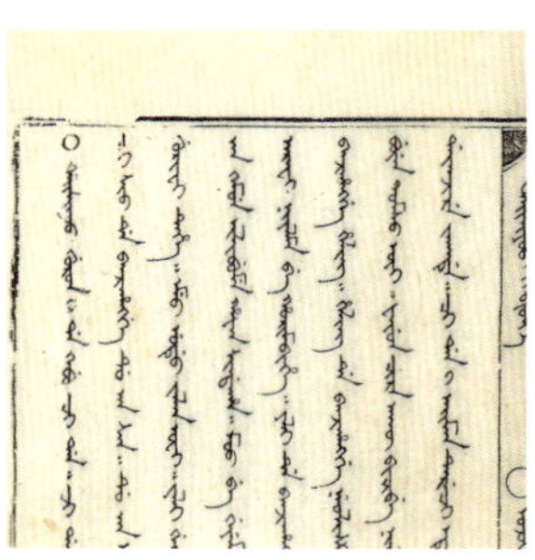

書21914
《遼史八卷》
Inventory number: Shu 21914
History of Liao
Eight chapters

46 138

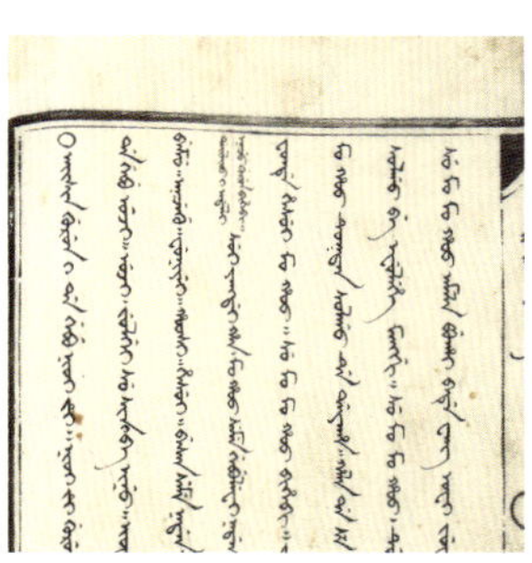

書21916
《金史八卷》
Inventory number: Shu 21916
History of Jin
Eight chapters

47 140

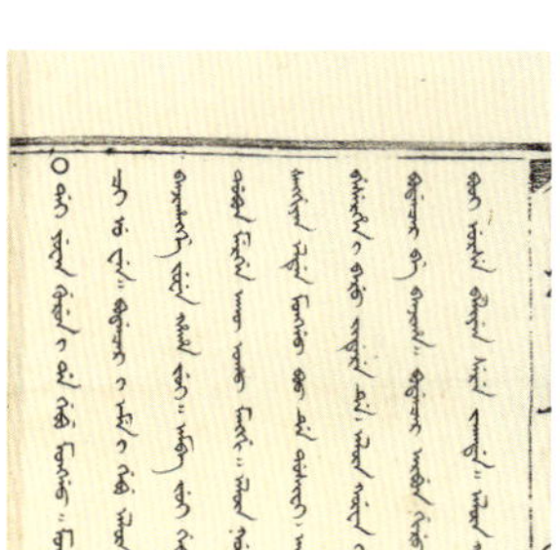

書21920
《元史十五卷》
Inventory number: Shu 21920
History of Yuan
Fifteen chapters

36 110

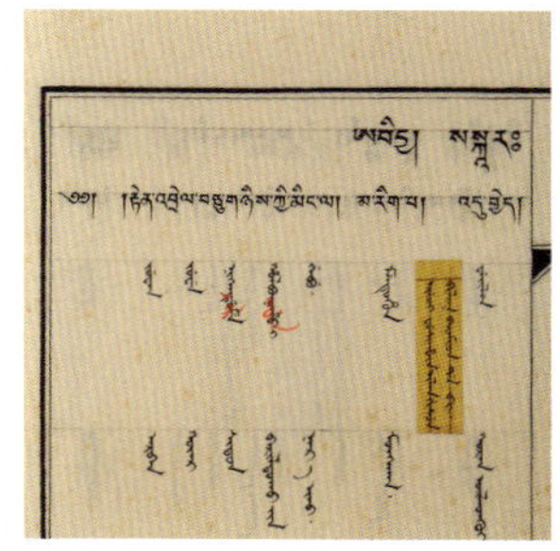

書21834
《集要二卷》
Inventory number: Shu 21834
Condensed Buddhist Dictionary in Five Languages
Two chapters

37 114

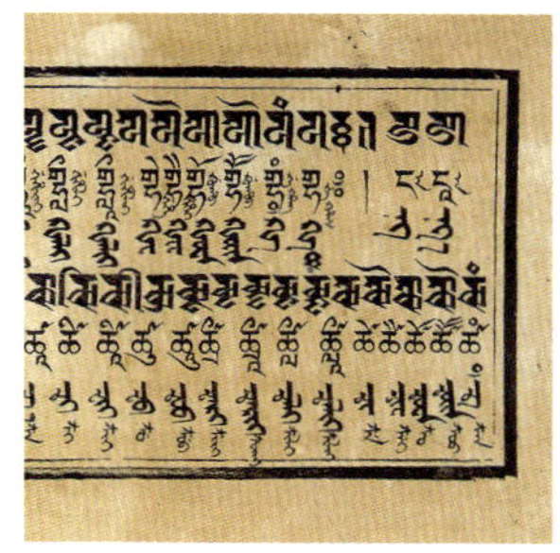

書27158
《四體阿禮嘎禮字一卷》
Inventory number: Shu 27158
The Ali Gali Transliterations of the Four Languages

38 116

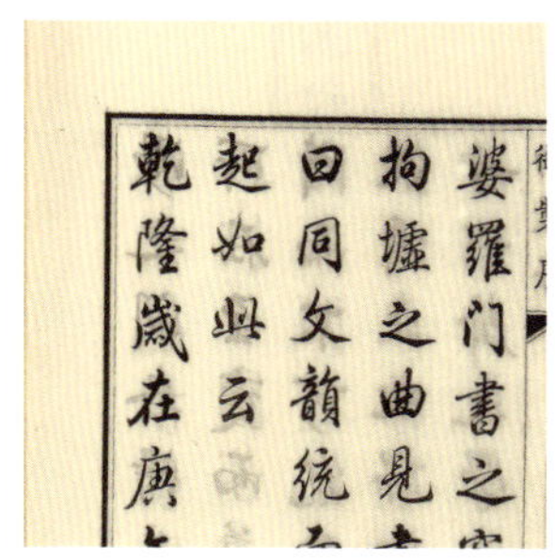

書62
《欽定同文韻統六卷》
Inventory number: Shu 62
Unified Syllables Imperially Commissioned
Six chapters

39 120

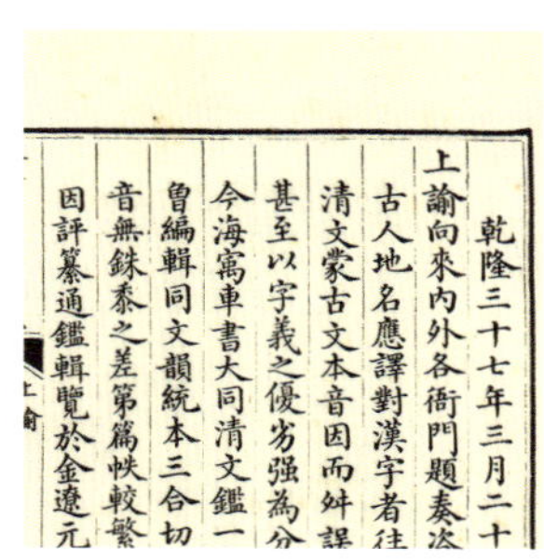

書21796
《欽定清漢對音字式一卷》
Inventory number: Shu 21796
Patterns of Manchu and Chinese Corresponding Phones
One chapter

40 122

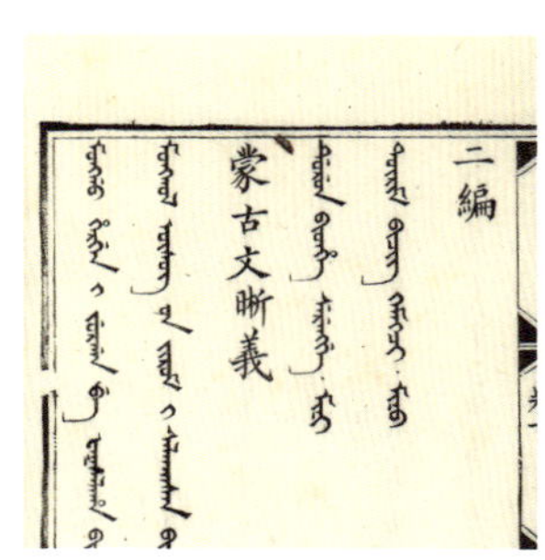

書21813
《蒙文指要四卷》
Inventory number: Shu 21813
Essentials of Mongolian
Four chapters

41 126

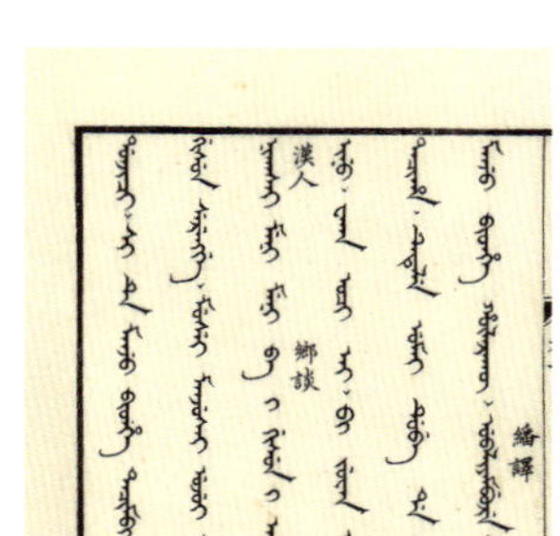

書21881
《一百條四卷》
Inventory number: Shu 21881
One Hundred Conversational Terms
Four chapters

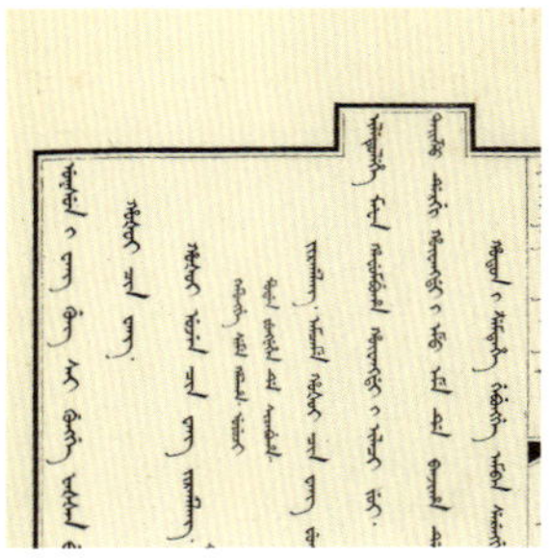

54 154

書22018

《宗室王公功績表傳五卷首二卷》

Inventory number: Shu 22018

Tables and Biographies of the Nobility's Achievements

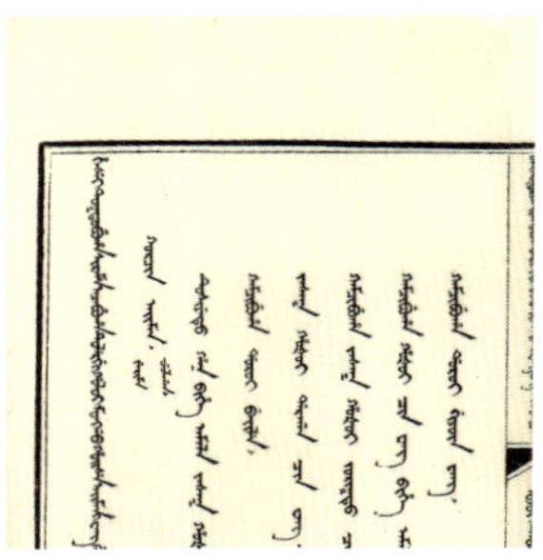

55 156

書22038

《欽定續纂外藩蒙古回部王公傳十二卷》

Inventory number: Shu 22038

Sequel to Biographies of Mongolian and Uigurian Princes

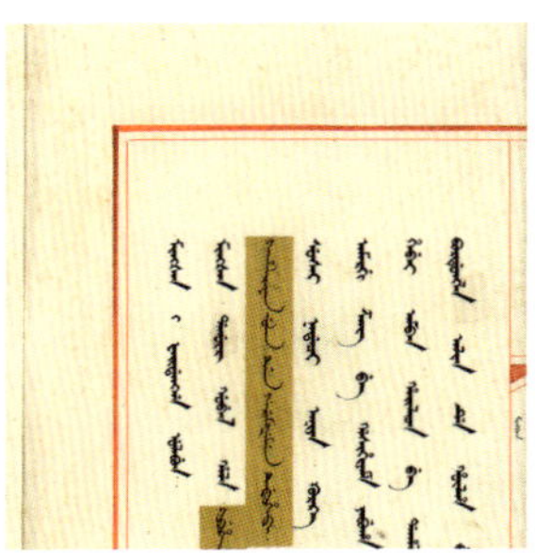

56 158

書22049

《大清國史大臣列傳》（擬訂）

Inventory number: Shu 22049

Biographies of the Qing Ministers

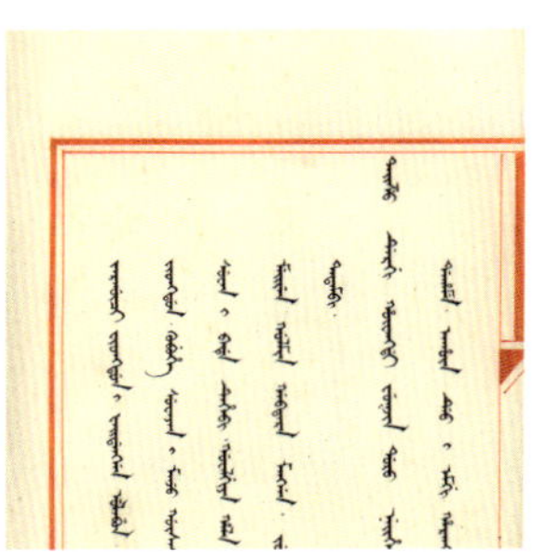

57 160

書22058

《大清國史功臣列傳》

Inventory number: Shu 22053

Biographies of the Meritorious Officials in the Qing History

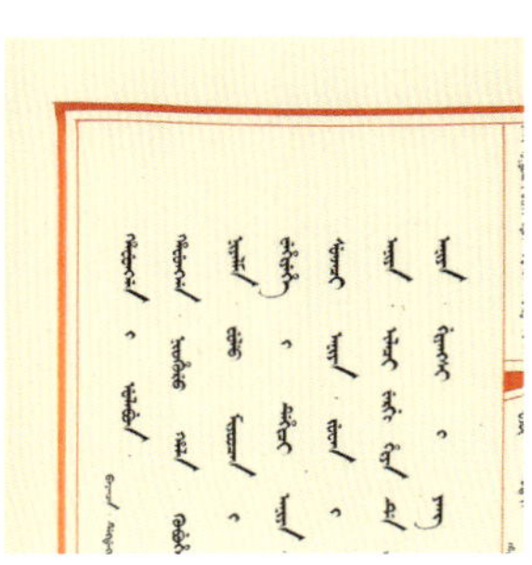

58 162

書22067

《欽定國史忠義列傳十九卷》

Inventory number: Shu 22067

Biographies of the Loyal and Righteous Subjects in the Qing History, Made by Imperial Order

Nineteen chapters

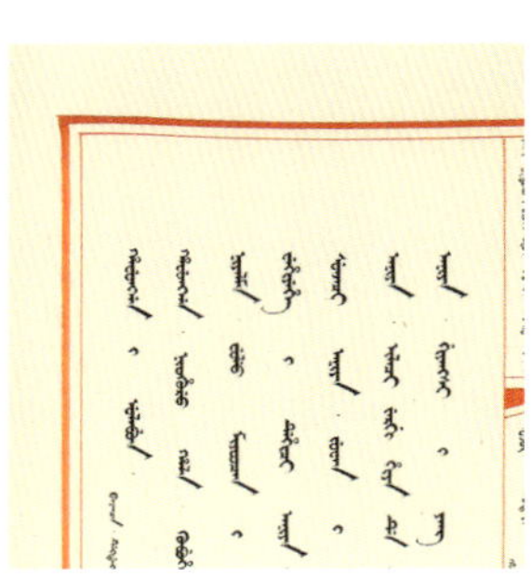

59 164

書22077

《昭忠祠列傳續編一百二十卷》

Inventory number: Shu 22377

Biographies of the Martyrs in the Shrine of Manifest Loyalty

120 chapters

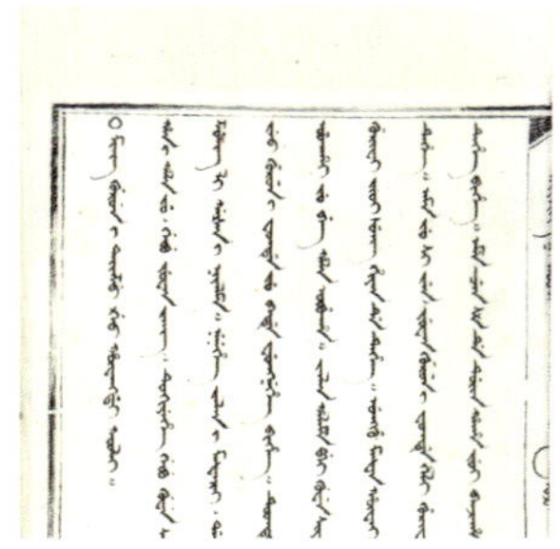

48 142

書21924

《明史九十七卷》

Inventory Number: Shu 21924

History Of Ming

Ninety-Seven Chapters

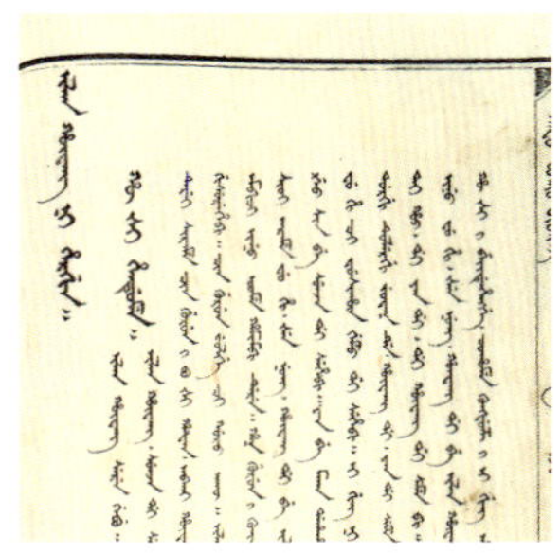

49 144

書21928

《通鑒彙纂八十卷》

Inventory number: Shu 21928

Collection of Brief History

Eighty chapters

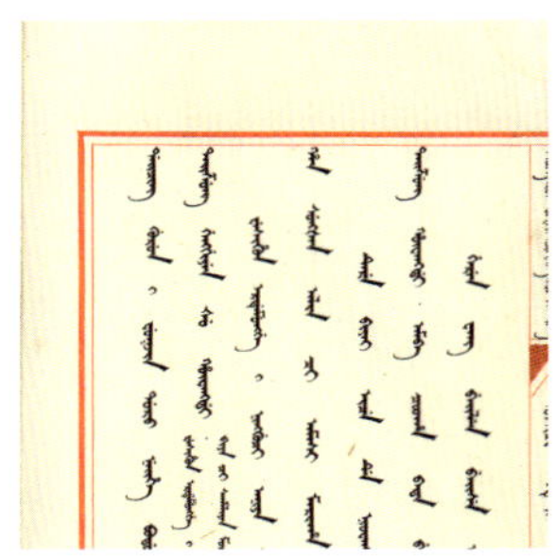

50 146

書21947

《大清開國方略三十二卷》

Inventory number: Shu 21947

The Qing Strategies on Establishing the State

Thirty-two chapters

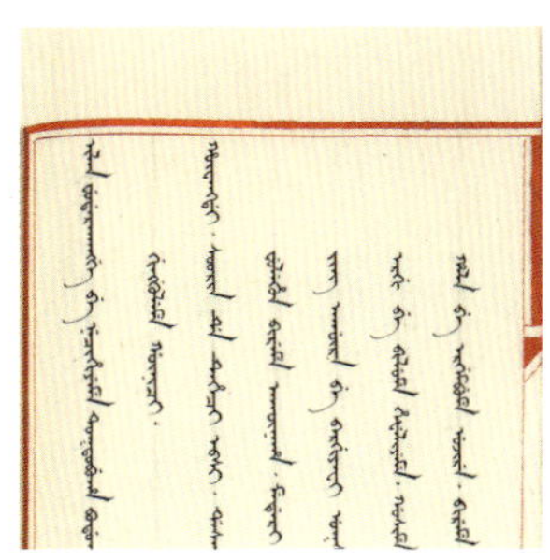

51 148

書21968

《平定三逆方略六十卷》

Inventory number: Shu 21968

The Qing Strategies on Suppressing the Three Rebels

Sixty chapters

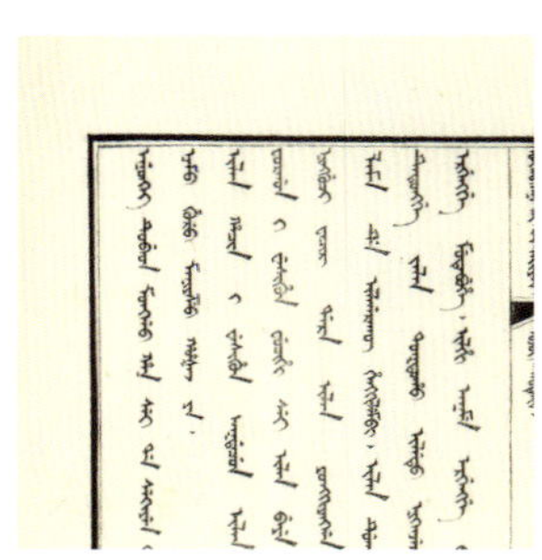

52 150

書21973

《蒙古源流八卷》

Inventory number: Shu 21973

Origin and Development of Mongolia

Eight chapters

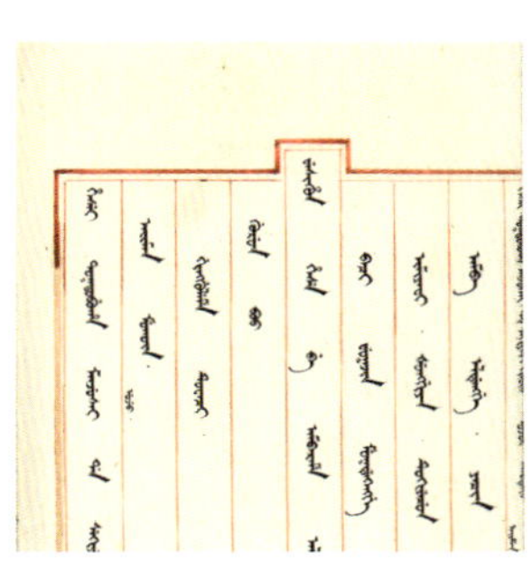

53 152

書21980

《欽定滿州源流考二十卷首一卷》

Inventory number: Shu 21980

A Study of the Origin and Development of Manchuria

Twenty chapters as text, one chapter as preliminary remarks

66 180

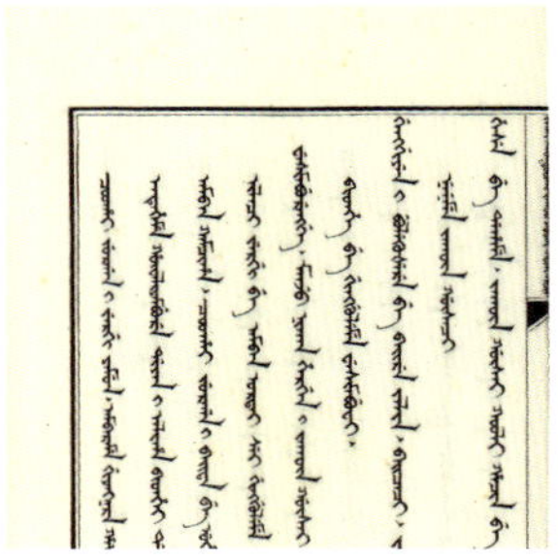

書22131
《欽定八旗則例十二卷》

Inventory number: Shu 22131
Rules and Regulations on Eight Banners
Twelve chapters

67 182

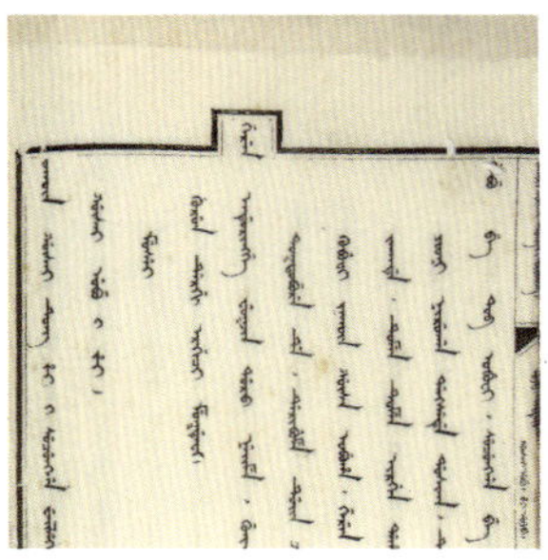

書22127
《八旗通志初集二百五十卷目録二卷》

Inventory number: Shu 22127
Comprehensive Records on the Eight Banners, First Compilation
250 chapters as text, two chapters as contents

68 184

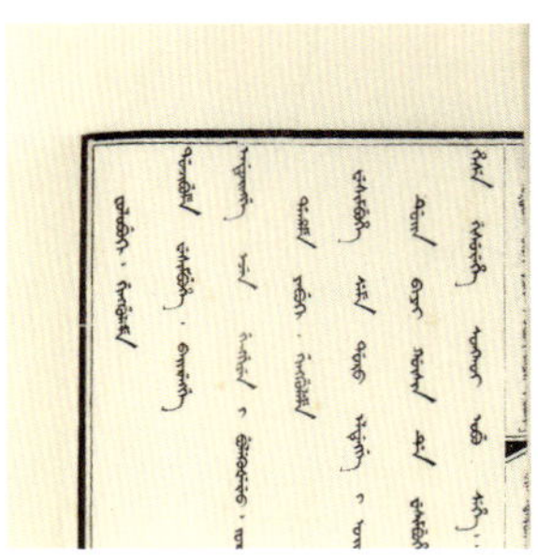

書22150
《欽定回疆則例八卷首一卷》

Inventory number: Shu 22150
Rules and Regulations on the Frontier of Uighur
Eight chapters as text, one chapter as preliminary remarks

69 186

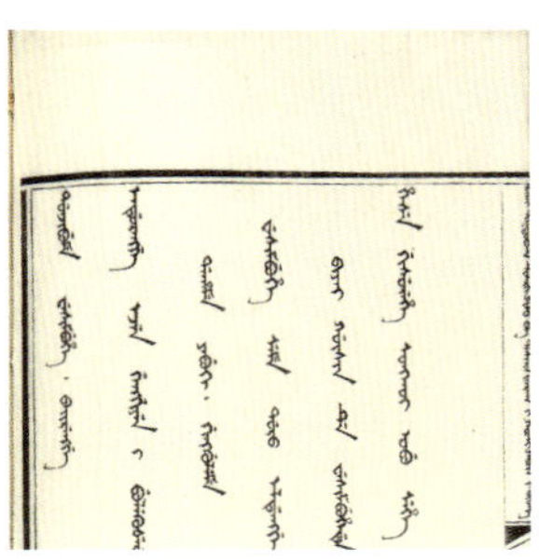

書22149、書23060
《欽定理藩院則例六十三卷首三卷》

Inventory number: Shu 22149, Shu 23060
Rules and Regulations on the Board for National Minority Affairs, Made by Imperial Order
Sixty-three chapters as text, three chapters as preliminary remarks

70 188

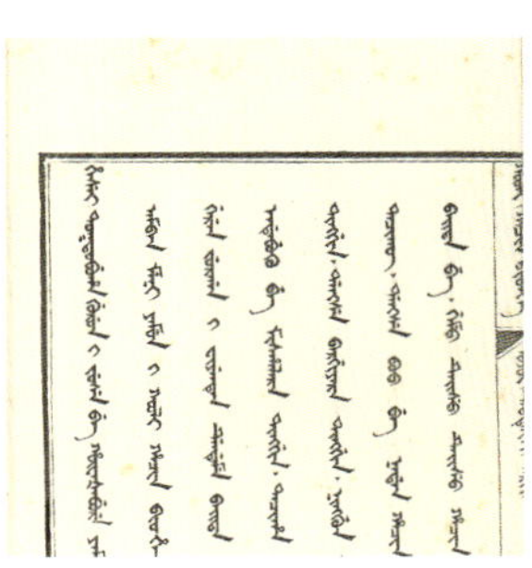

書22152
《欽定國子監則例三十卷首二卷》

Inventory number: Shu 22152
Rules and Regulations on the Imperial Academy
Thirty chapters as text, two chapters as preliminary remarks

71 190

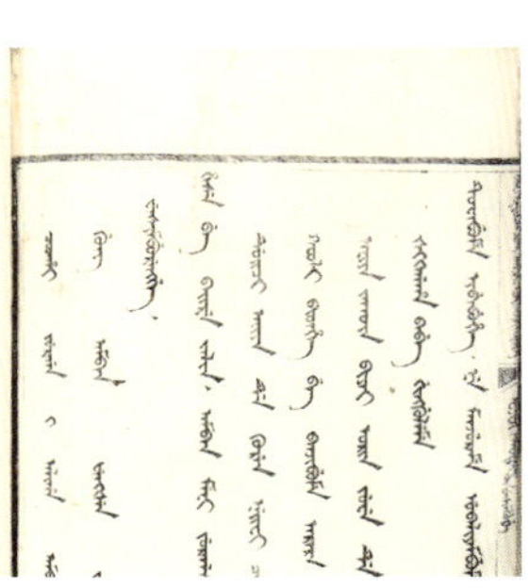

書22239
《欽定軍器則例十二卷》

Inventory number: Shu 22239
Rules and Regulations on Military Arms
Twelve chapters

60 166

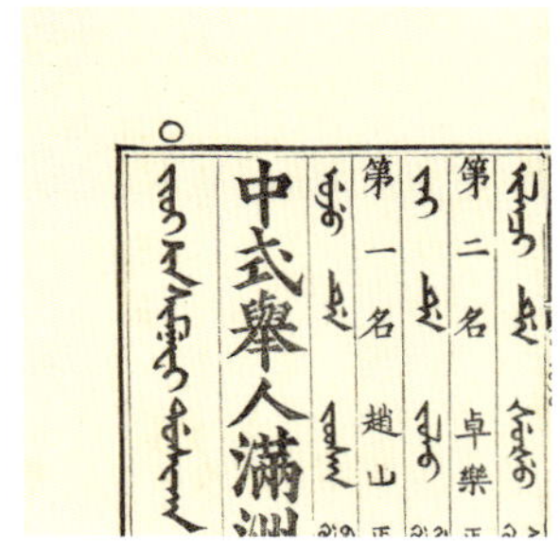

書22086
《順天鄉試題名一卷》

Inventory number: Shu 22086
Names of Juren (Successful Candidates at the Provincial-level Imperial Examination of Shuntian)
One chapter

61 168

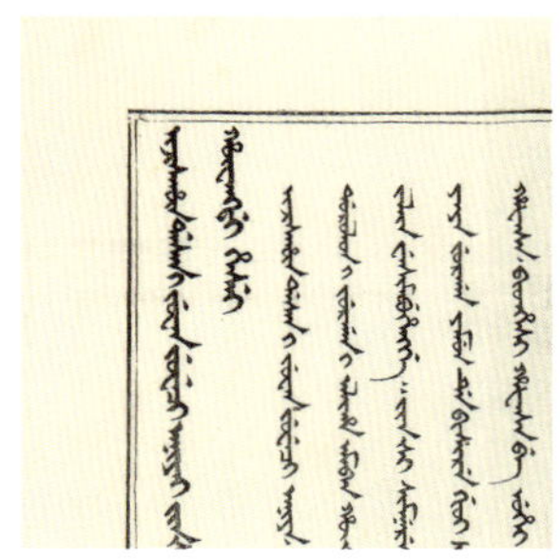

書22083
《進士登科録一卷》

Inventory number: Shu 22083
Records on Jinshi (Successful Candidates of the Highest-level Imperial Examination)
One chapter

62 170

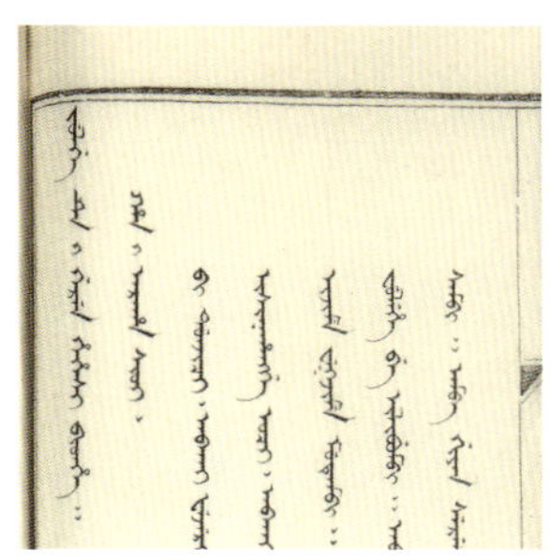

書22075
《古今列女傳六卷》

Inventory number: Shu 22075
Biographies of Exemplary Women of Past and Present
Six chapters

63 172

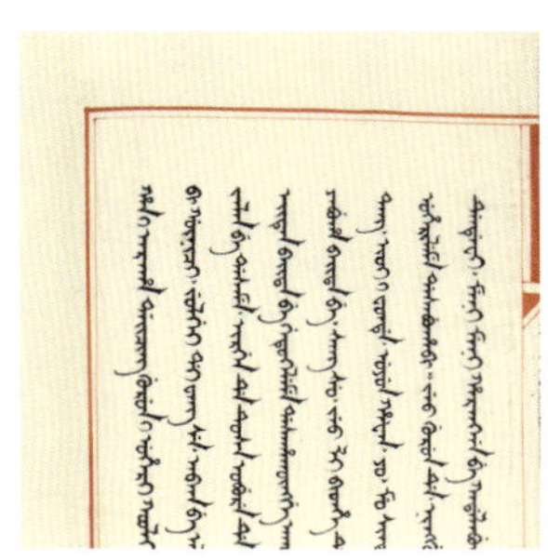

書22099
《大清會典一百六二卷首一卷》

Inventory number: Shu 22099
The Qing Institution
162 chapters as text, one chapter as preliminary remarks

64 176

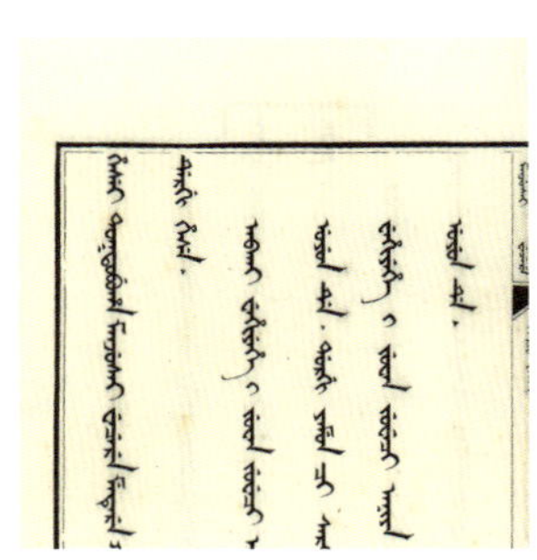

書22098
《欽定滿洲祭神祭天典禮六卷》

Inventory number: Shu 22098
Manchu Sacrificial Rites to Worship Heaven and Deities
Six chapters

65 178

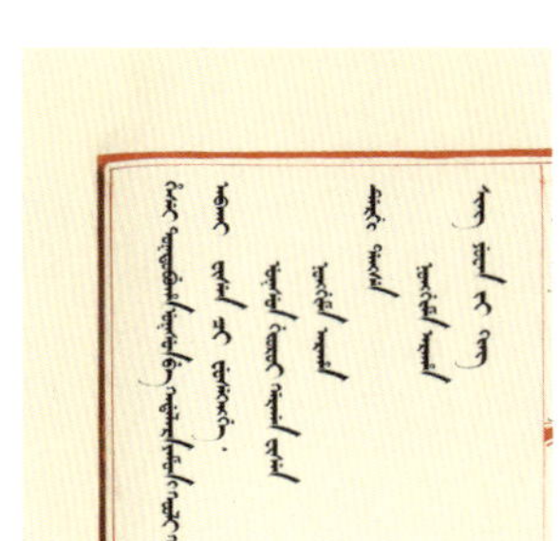

書22110
《欽定宗人府則例三十一卷首一卷》

Inventory number: Shu 22110
Rules and Regulations on Imperial Clan Court
Thirty-one chapters as text, one chapter as preliminary remarks

72 194

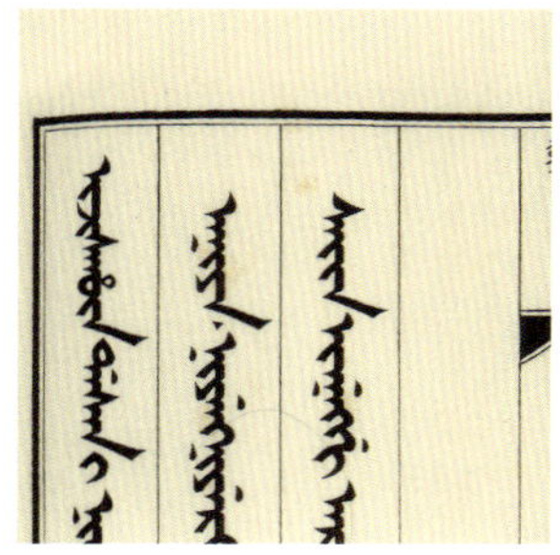

書22185

《御製人臣敬心録一卷》

Inventory number: Shu 22185

Collection of Political Essays on Mental Cultivation of Officials

One chapter

73 196

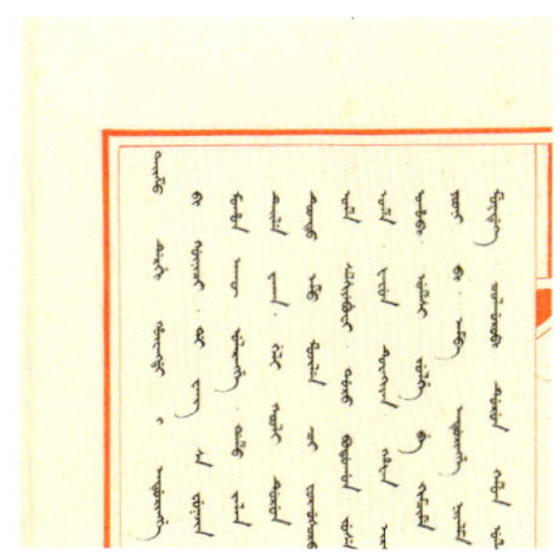

書21982

《大清太祖高皇帝聖訓四卷》

Inventory number: Shu 21982

Holy Teachings of the Taizu Emperor of the Qing

Four chapters

74 200

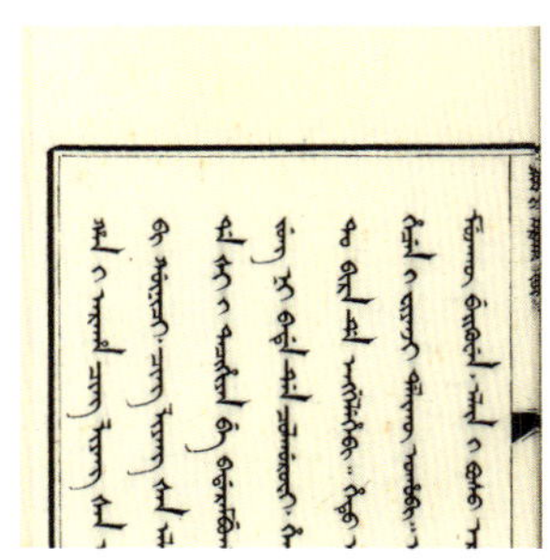

書22090

《清凉山志十卷》

Inventory number: Shu 22090

Records on Mount Wutai

Ten chapters

75 202

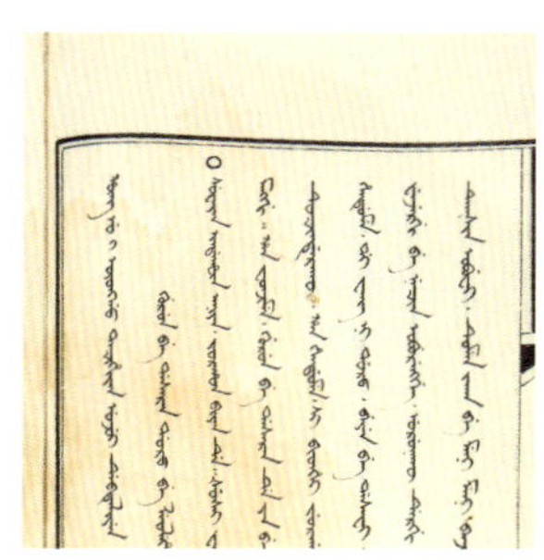

書22183

《明洪武寶訓六卷》

Inventory number: Shu 22183

Valuable Teachings of the Hongwu Emperor

Six chapters

76 204

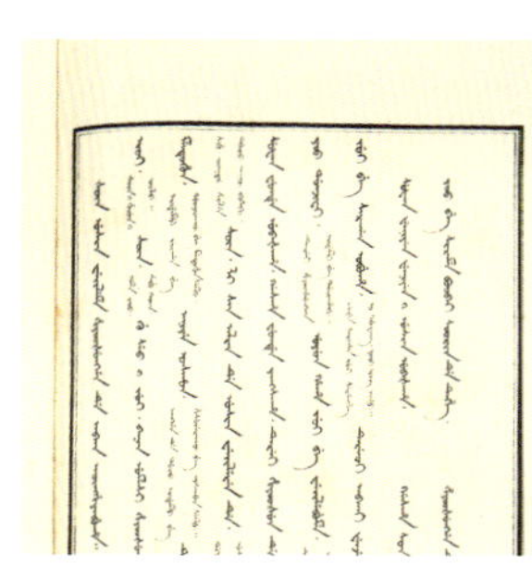

書22234

《二十四孝圖説不分卷》

Inventory number: Shu 22234

Twenty-four Filial Exemplars Illustrated

77 208

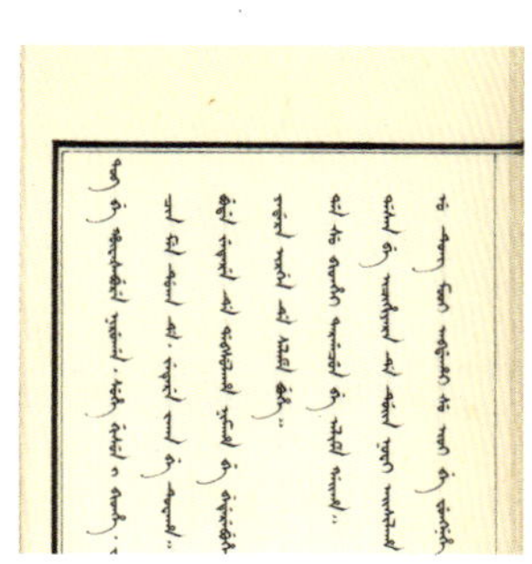

書22211

《養正圖解四卷》

Inventory number: Shu 22211

Illustrated Explanation on Cultivating Propriety

Four chapters

78 212

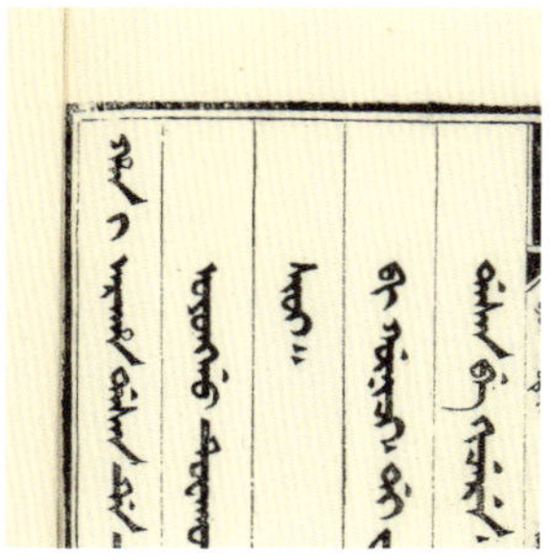

書22219

《御製資政要覽三卷後序一卷》

Inventory number: Shu 22219

Essential Principles to Aid in Politics

Three chapters as text, one chapter as postscript

79 214

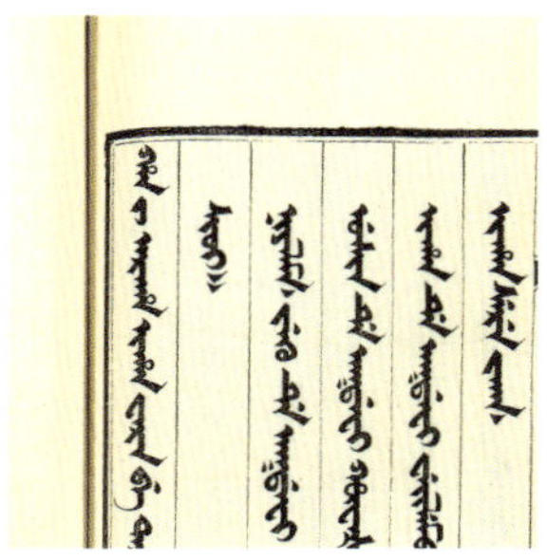

書22225

《御製牛戒一卷》

Inventory number: Shu 22225

Ox Commandment

One chapter

80 216

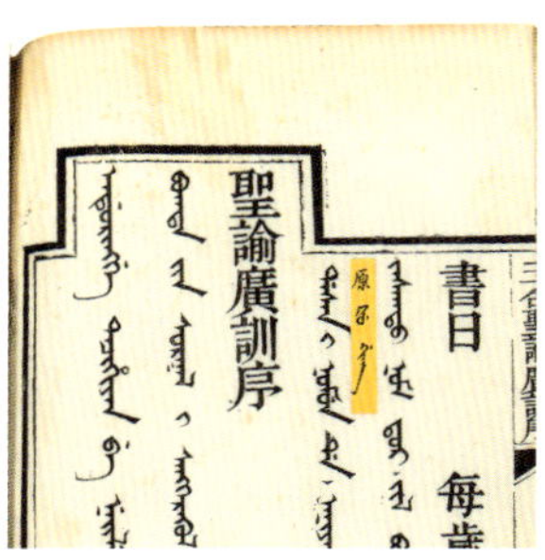

書22201

《三合聖諭廣訓四卷》

Inventory number: Shu 22201

Amplified Instructions on the Sacred Edicts in Three Languages

Four chapters

81 220

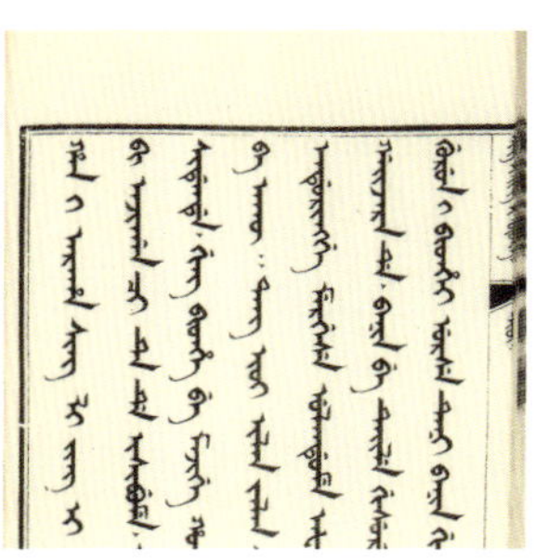

書13448

《御纂性理精義十二卷》

Inventory number: Shu 13448

Essence of Nature and Rationality

Twelve chapters

82 224

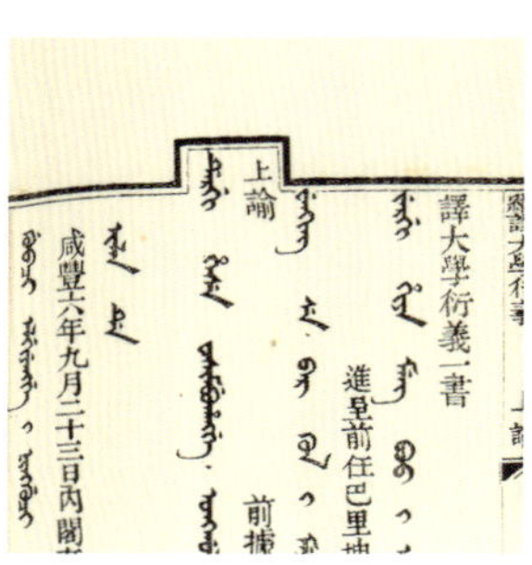

書22173

《翻譯大學衍義四十三卷首一卷》

Inventory number: Shu 22173

Exposition of the Great Learning

Forty-three chapters as text, one chapter as preliminary remarks

83 228

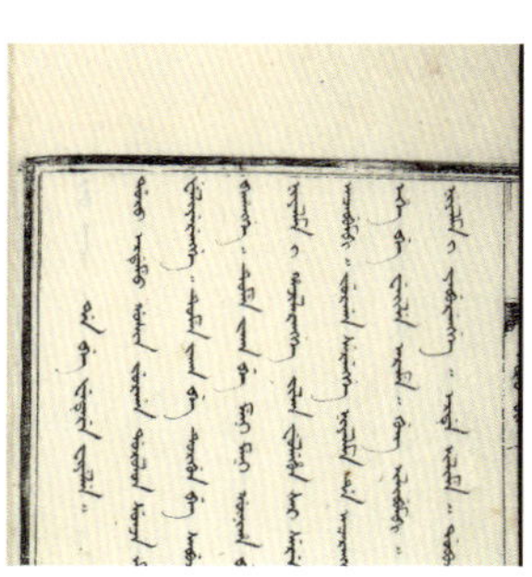

書22153

《素書一卷》

Inventory number: Shu 22153

Pure Book

One chapter

84 230

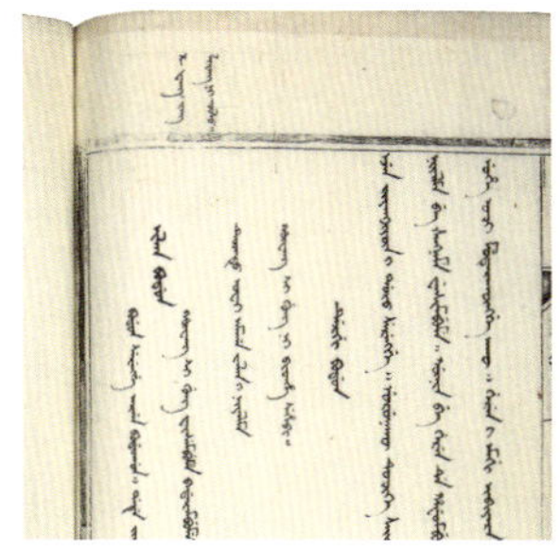

書22154
《三略一卷》
Inventory number: Shu 22154
Three Military Strategies
One chapter

85 232

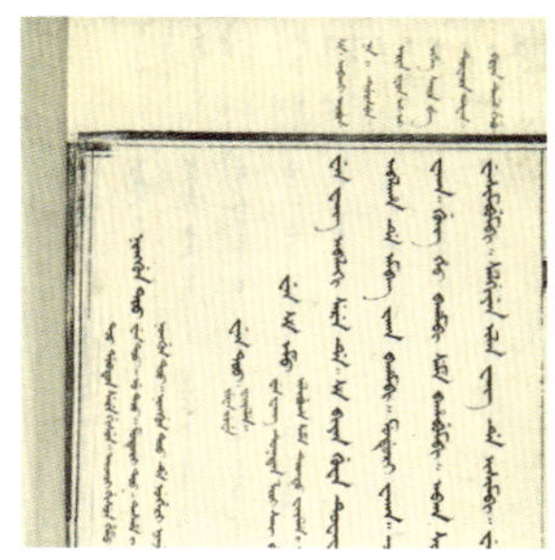

書22155
《六韬二卷》
Inventory number: Shu 22155
Six Military Principles
Two chapters

86 236

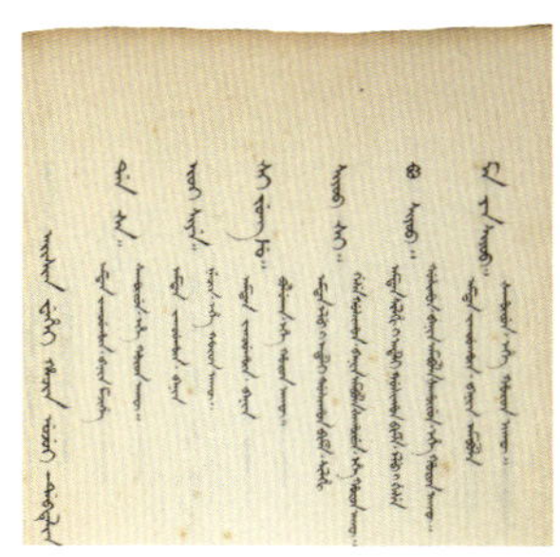

書22242
《雷公炮製書十六卷》
Inventory number: Shu 22242
Master Lei's Process of Preparing Chinese Medicine
Sixteen chapters

87 238

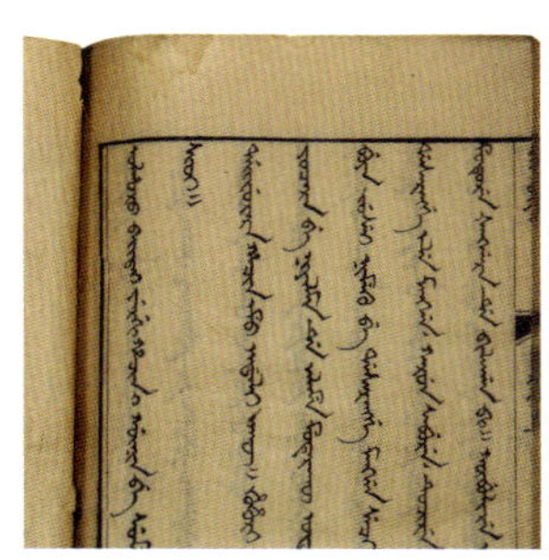

書22240
《醫藥治症通書三卷》
Inventory number: Shu 22240
General Book on Therapeutics of Chinese Medicine
Three chapters

88 242

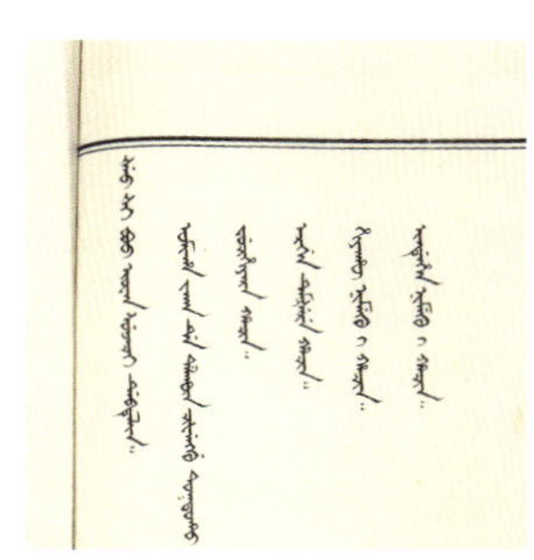

書22241
《壽世保元二十二卷》
Inventory number: Shu 22241
Longevity and Vitality Preservation
Twenty-two chapters

89 244

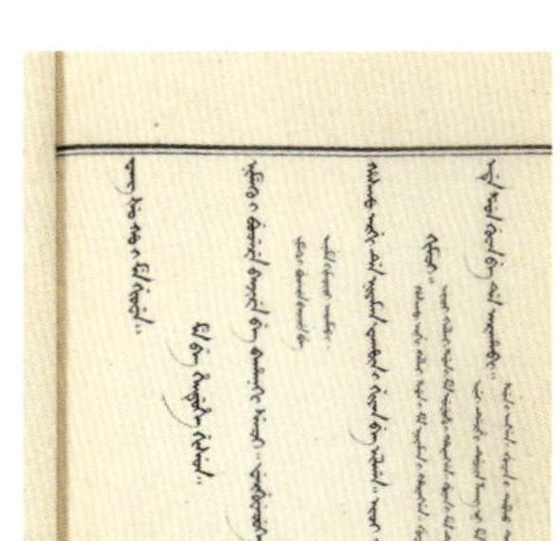

書22244
《王叔和脉訣四卷》
Inventory number: Shu 22244
Wang Shuhe's Pulse Classic
Four chapters

90 246

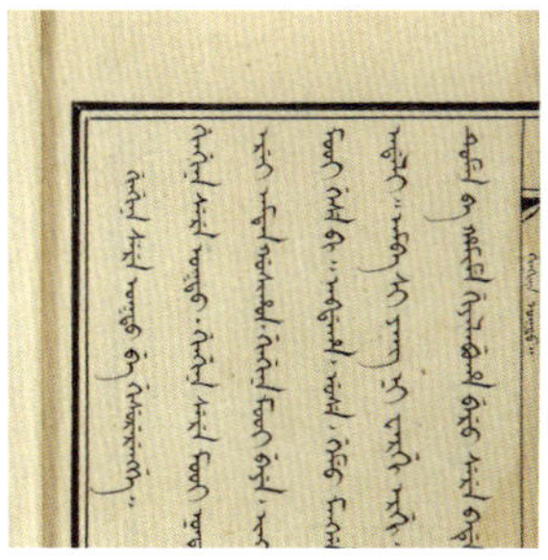

書22243
《西洋藥書不分卷》
Inventory number: Shu 22243
Western Medicine

91 248

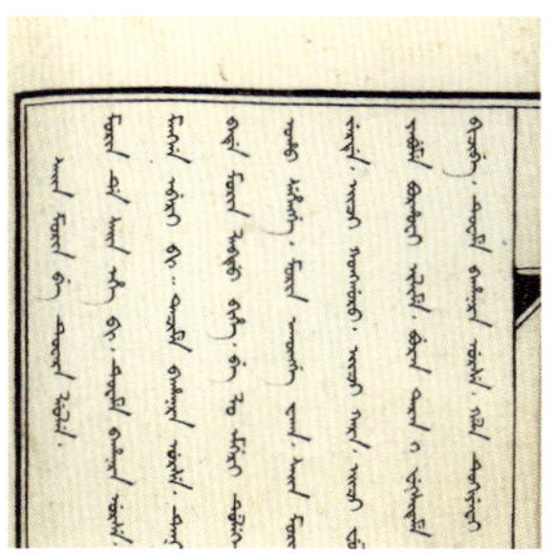

書22245
《馬經全書八卷》
Inventory number: Shu 22245
Complete Book of Horse Classics

92 250

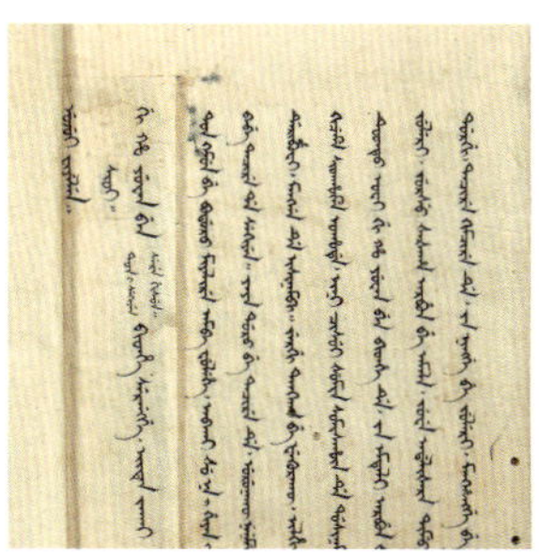

書22246
《幾何原本七卷》
Inventory number: Shu 22246
Elements
Seven chapters

93 254

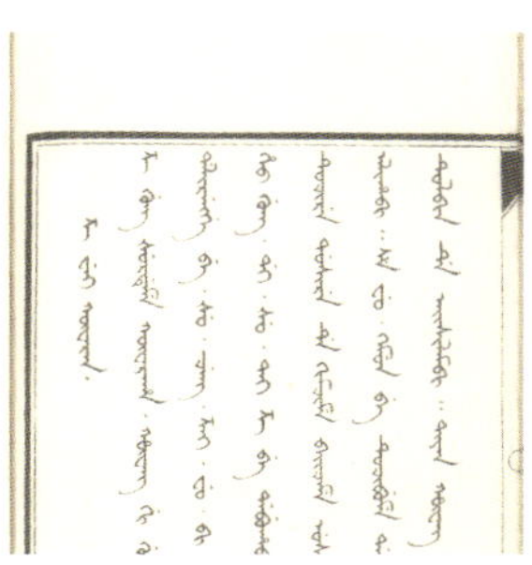

書22248
《天文星宿記考一卷》
Inventory number: Shu 22248
Records on Astronomy and Constellations
One chapter

94 256

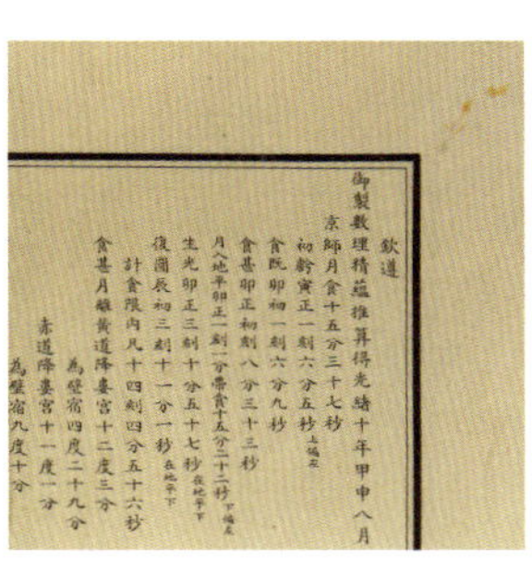

書6481
《光緒十年八月十七日戊子望月食圖》
Inventory number: Shu 6481
Lunar Eclipse on August 17, 1884

95 258

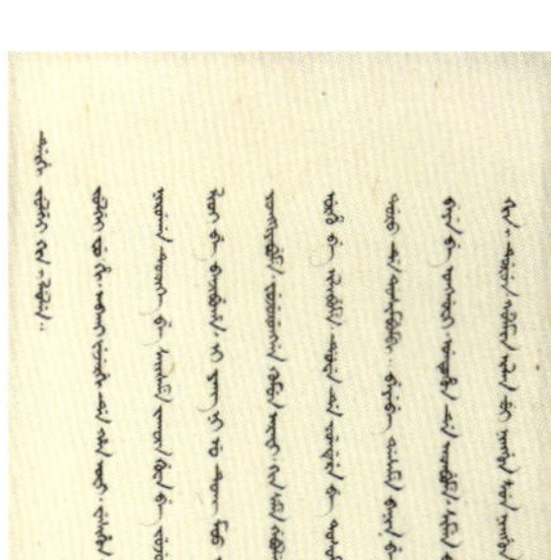

書22491
《琴譜六卷》
Inventory number: Shu 22491
Music Score for Qin
Six chapters

96 262

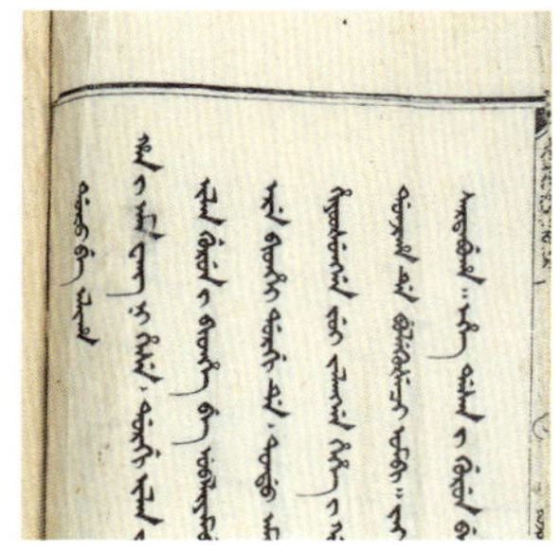

書22521
《三國志演義二十四卷》
Inventory number: Shu 22521
Romance of the Three Kingdoms
Twenty-four chapters

97 266

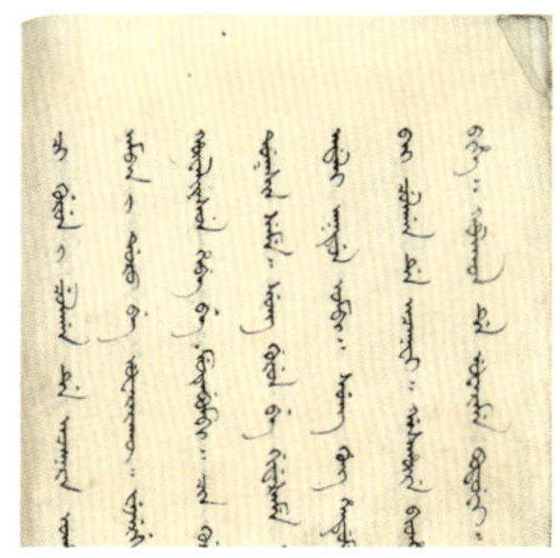

書21981
《列國志一百八回》
Inventory number: Shu 21981
Records of the States
108 chapters

98 268

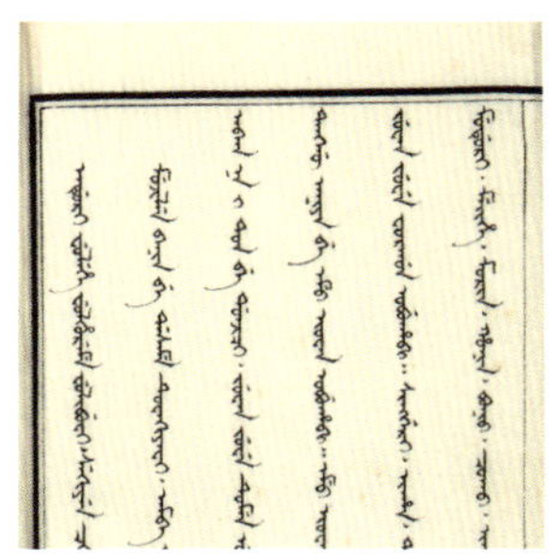

書22531
《西游記一百則》
Inventory number: Shu 22531
Journey to the West
100 chapters

99 270

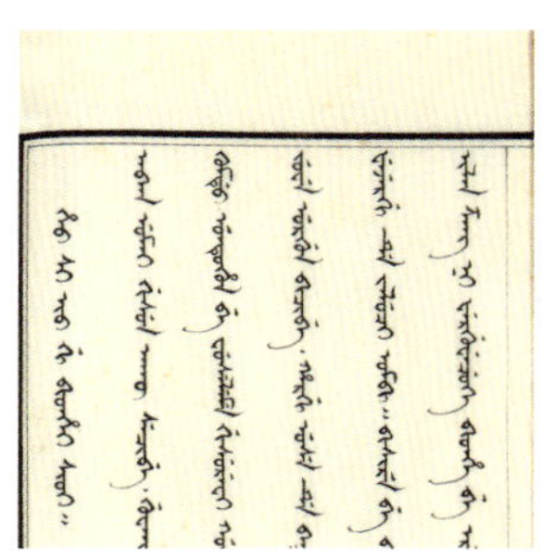

書22532
《後西游記四十回》
Inventory number: Shu 22532
Sequel to "Journey to the West"
Forty chapters

100 272

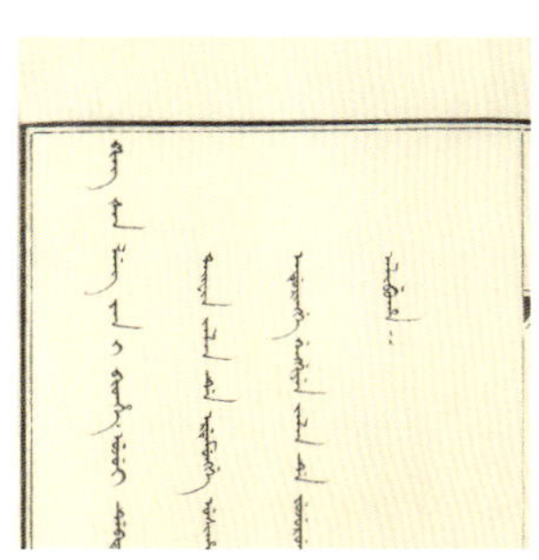

書22542
《平山冷燕十六卷》
Inventory number: Shu 22542
Ping Shan Leng Yan
Sixteen chapters

101 274

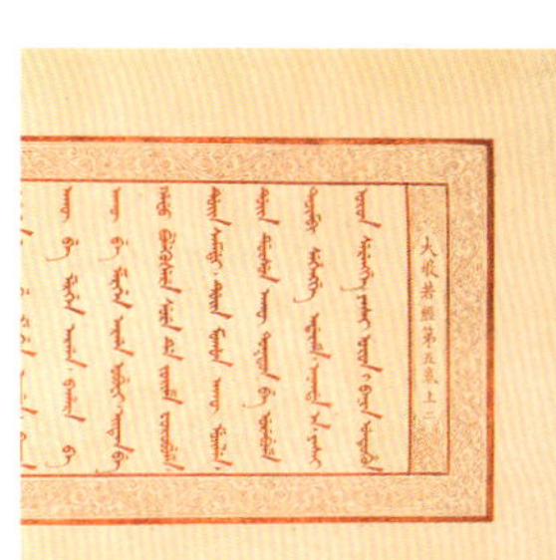

書27120
《清文翻譯全藏經一百八卷目録一卷》
Inventory number: Shu 27120
Tripitaka in Manchu
108 chapters as text, one chapter as contents

102 278

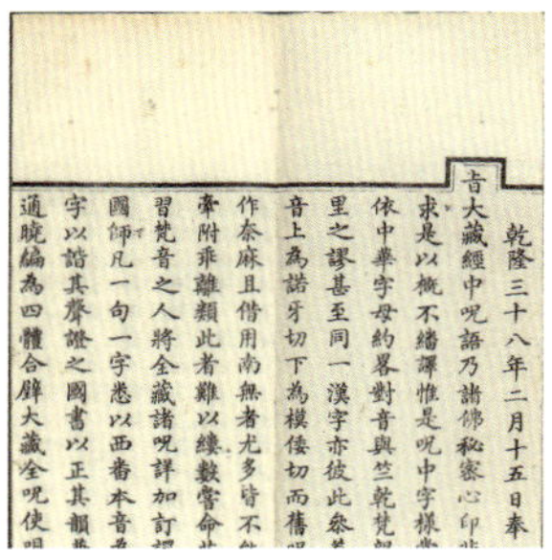

書27917
《御製滿漢蒙古西番合璧大藏全咒八十卷目录八卷》
Inventory number: Shu 27917
Mantras of the Tripitaka
Eighty chapters as text, eight chapters as preliminary remarks

103 282

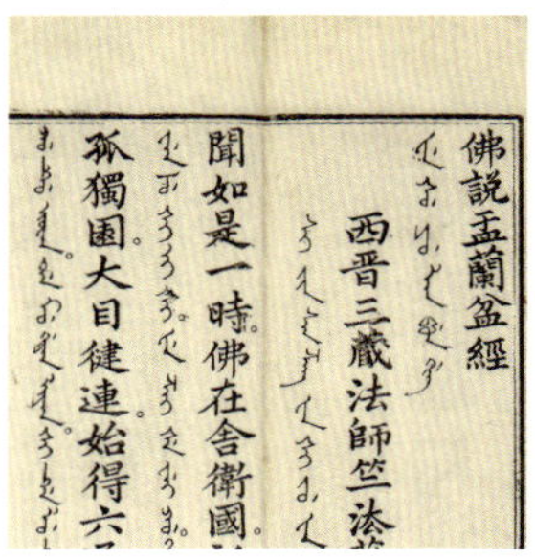

書28240
《佛說盂蘭盆經》
Inventory number: Shu 28240
Ullambana Sutra

104 284

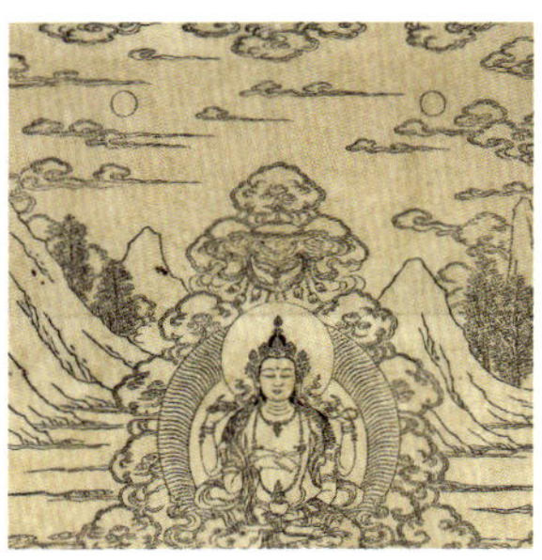

書27780
《摩訶般若波羅蜜多心經》
Inventory number: Shu 27780
Prajnaparamita Heart Sutra

105 288

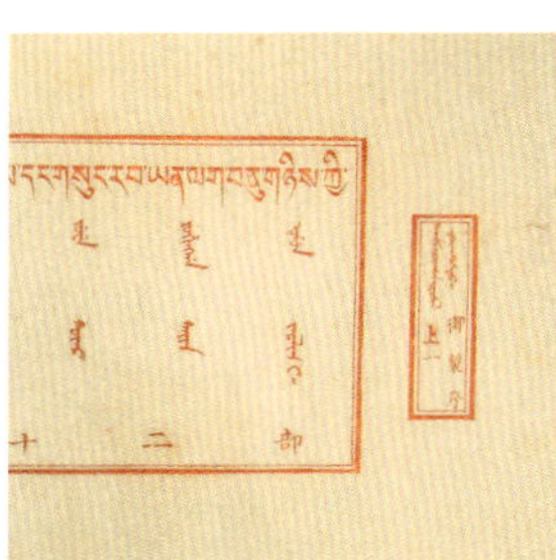

書28366
《大乘首楞嚴經十卷》
Inventory number: Shu 28366
Surangama Sutra
Ten chapters

106 292

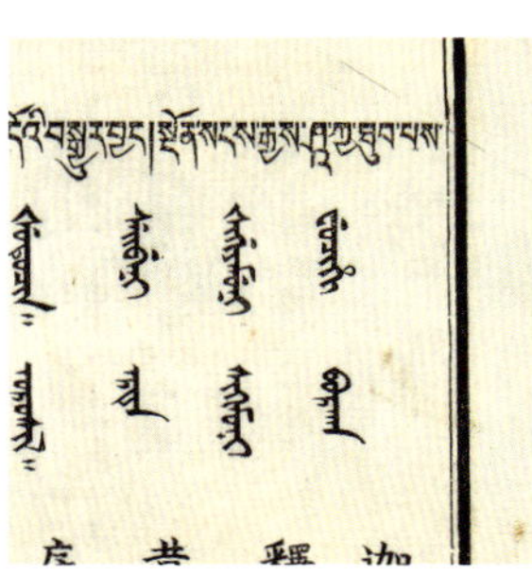

書27213
《御譯大雲輪請雨經八卷》
Inventory number: Shu 27213
Sutra on Praying for Rain at the Hall of Grand Clouds
Eight chapters

107 296

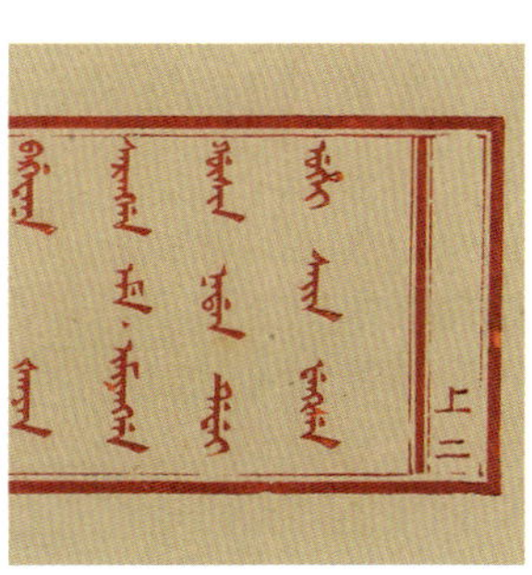

書27239
《白傘蓋儀軌經》（又名：《薄伽梵白傘蓋佛母成就發悉地甘露寶瓶》）
Inventory number: Shu 27239
Sitatapatra Kalpa Sutra

108 298

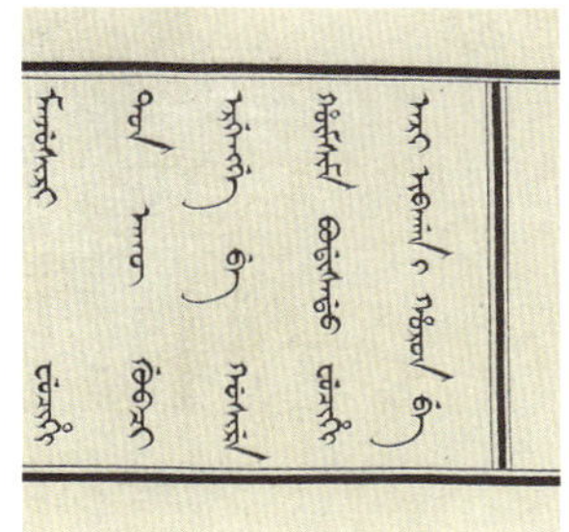

書27208
《丹書克經》
Inventory number: Shu 27208
Sutra Presented to the Court

109 300

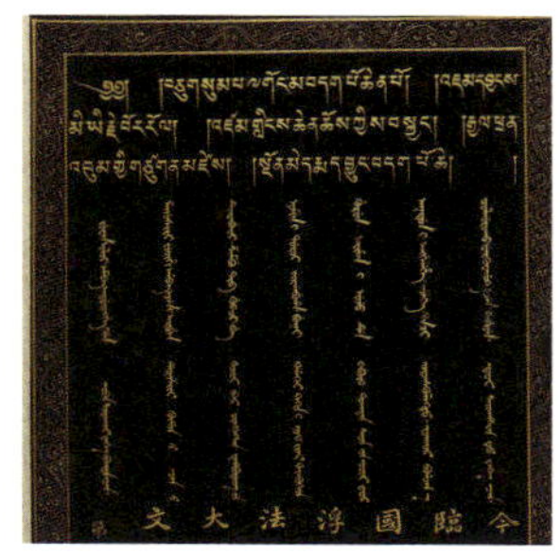

書9927
《諸佛事略圖說》
Inventory number: Shu 9927
Illustrated Biographies of Various Buddhas

110 302

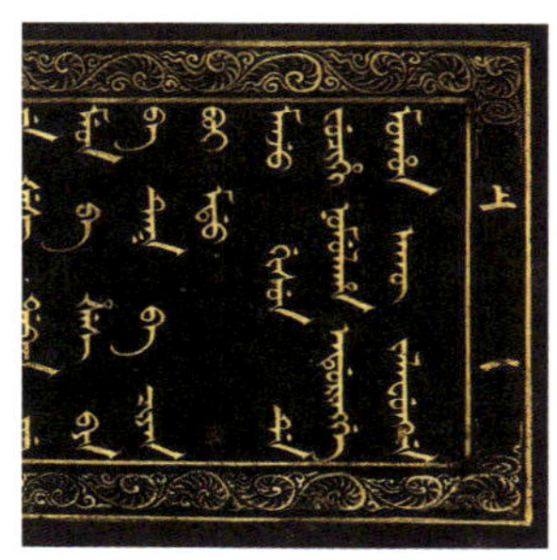

書9755
《無量壽佛經》（又名《佛説大乘聖無量壽决定光明王如來陀羅尼經》）
Inventory number: Shu 9755
Amitayurdhyana Sutra

111 306

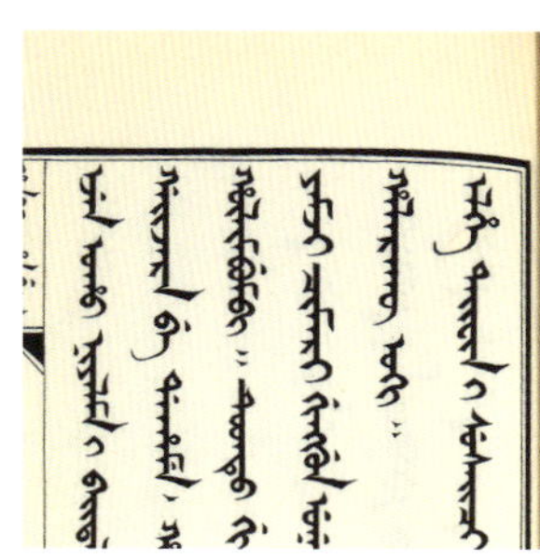

書22514
《御製避暑山莊詩二卷》
Inventory number: Shu 22514
Imperial Poems on the Mountain Resort for Summer Retreat
Two chapters

112 310

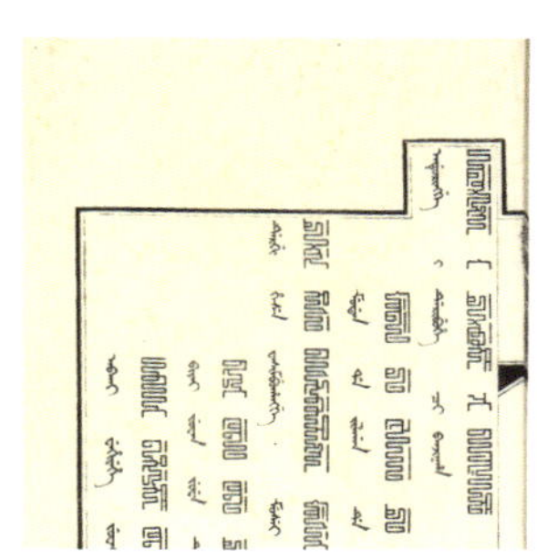

書22508
《御製盛京賦三十二卷》
Inventory number: Shu 22508
Imperial Rhapsody on Shengjing
Thirty-two chapters

Compendium of Collections in The Palace Museum

Rare Books and Special Archives

8

Books in Manchu

The Forbidden City Publishing House

Contents

iv/9 Introduction of Books in Manchu

x/14 Explanatory Notes

xii/17 List of Plates

21 Plates

313 Plate Index

Introduction of Books in Manchu

Chunhua, Li Ying

Preface

Qing Dynasty was a multi-national country established by Manchu noblemen. In 1599, the 27th year of Emperor Wanli of Ming Dynasty, Manchu was created. After Qing Dynasty was founded in 1644, Chinese classics were translated, and books on history, policy, and law were written in Manchu. To rule Mongols and Tibetans effectively, Qing emperors legalized their belief of Buddhism and translated many Buddhist scripts into Manchu. They also compiled some Manchu and multilingual dictionaries to facilitate the learning and translation of Buddhist scripts. In general, the Manchu books in Qing Dynasty covered the translated and created versions based on their sources.

Part One Translated Books

(1) **Translations of Han People's Classics.** Qing emperors worshipped Han People's culture. Before Manchu people unified China, they had translated some Chinese classics into Manchu, such as *Statute Book of Ming Dynasty*, *Sushu*, *The Book on the Art of War*, *History as a Mirror*, *Mencius*, *Romance of the Three Kingdoms*, and *History of Jin Dynasty*. After Manchu people unified China, Emperor Shunzhi worshipped Confucius, respected Confucianism, and learnt Han People's culture with zealous effort. He ordered to translate such Chinese classics into Manchu as *The Imperial Edicts of Emperor Hongwu*, *Models for Behavior and Speech*, *The Loyalty to the Court*, and *The Book of Songs*, which consolidated the Manchu-Han Alliance and established foundation for the cultural prosperity in Emperor Kangxi, Emperor Yongzheng, and Emperor Qianlong.

Emperor Kangxi valued the essence of Han people's culture, Confucianism, Cheng-Zhu School, etc. He also translated, noted, and printed with Manchu many Confucianist classics and other books, such as *Imperially Edited Commentaries to the Four Books*, *Imperially Compiled Notes on Character and Reason*, and *Imperially Noted Outline of History as a Mirror*. Besides, scholars translated some literary works into Manchu, including *Romance of the West Chamber*, *Romance of the Western Han Dynasty*, *Journey to the West*, *The Plum in the Golden Vase*, *Romance of Sui and Tang Dynasties*, and *History of Kingdoms in Eastern Zhou Dynasty*. As a result, Confucius and Zhu Xi's thoughts became the dominant ideology in Qing Dynasty.

Emperor Yongzheng also respected Confucianism. He founded many governmental schools to publicize education among the bannermen. Emperor Qianlong continued to popularize Confucianism. He re-edited Confucianist classics with standard Manchu and printed *The Four Books*, *The Five Classics*, etc.

(2) **Translations of Buddhist Scripts.** Before Manchu people unified China, Da Hai translated *Mahayana Sutra* into Manchu. After they unified China, Qing emperors carried out the policy that Mongols and Tibetans were allowed to believe in Buddhism and compiled many Buddhist scripts in Manchu, such as *Golden Light Sutra*, *Heart Sutra* (in the reign of Emperor Yongzheng), *Complete Tibetan Sutra in Manchu*, *Ode on Saving Mother Sutra*, *Infinite Life Pray Scripts*, *Sanskrit Texts* (in the reign of Emperor Qianlong), *Imperially Edited Sanskrit Texts in Mahayana Sutra*, *Imperially Translation of Pleading Rain Sutra*, and *Incantation Sutra* (in Manchu, Chinese, Mongolian, and Tibetan). In early Qing Dynasty, the emperor's belief in Buddhism and compilation of Manchu Buddhist scripts enhanced the influence of Buddhism among officials and princes. For instance, De Leke, Duck of Balin written *Ode on Manjusri* and *Manjusri Sutra*, and Yong Rong written *Diamond Longevity Sutra*, which were all written in Tibetan, Manchu, Mongolian, and Chinese, and presented to Emperor Qianlong.

In early Qing Dynasty, emperors valued and learnt Confucianism and translated Confucianist classics and Buddhist scripts into Manchu for more than 100 years, which contributed to implement the Manchu-Chinese Alliance and Manchu-Mongolian Alliance policies and promoted the production and prosperity of Manchu and multilingual dictionaries.

(3) **The Publication and Development of Dictionaries.** After Manchu people unified China, Emperor Kangxi ordered to compile *Imperially Edited Reference Book in Qing Dynasty* to meet the need of translation, which was printed in 1708, the 47th year of Emperor Kangxi. Later, it was translated into Mongolian and Chinese, and printed with the Manchu-Mongolian edition, with the Manchu-Chinese edition *Reference Book for Learning Phonetics in Manchu and Chinese* and *Reference Book for Learning Manchu*.

To standardize the transliteration of Chinese words, Emperor Qianlong ordered Imperial Household Department, ministries, and offices to compile I*mperially Edited Manchu*, *Newly Edited Manchu*, *New Manchu Words Borrowed from Other Languages*, *Imperially Edited Reference Book for Chinese and Manchu*, etc, in which borrowed words from Chinese in *Imperially Edited Reference Book in Qing Dynasty* were replaced with Manchu transliterated words. *Imperially Edited Reference Book in Qing Dynasty* was supplemented with new and out-of-date words, turning out to be *Supplemented Imperially Edited Reference Book in Qing Dynasty*. It was printed in 1771, the 36th year of Emperor Qianlong and became the model for the compilation of Manchu dictionary. To preserve, develop, and standardize the phonetics in other languages, Emperor Qianlong ordered to compile some multilingual dictionaries, such as *Imperially Edited Reference Book for Learning Phonetics in Manchu, Mongolian, and Chinese, Imperially Edited Manchu-Mongolian-Tibetan-Chinese Reference Book*, and *Imperially Edited Manchu-Mongolian-Tibetan-Uigur-Chinese Reference Book*, which were based on *Supplemented Imperially Edited Reference Book in Qing Dynasty*. In preface to *Supplemented Imperially Edited Reference Book in Qing Dynasty*, Emperor Qianlong took the histories of Liao, Jin, and Yuan dynasties as an example and emphasized the importance of transliteration. Meanwhile, he ordered to note with Manchu the names of people, place, and official's position in the histories of the three dynasties. In 1780, the 45th year of Emperor Qianlong, *Imperially Edited Notes on the Histories of Liao, Jin, and Yuan Dynasties* was printed.

In Qing Dynasty, the compilation of Manchu phonetic dictionary kept pace with that of governmental professional dictionary. In Manchu-Chinese *Encyclopedia of Qing Dynasty*, *Manchu-Chinese Encyclopedia*, and *Collections of Manchu Words*, the transliteration of Chinese was basically consistent with that in *Imperially Edited Reference Book in Qing Dynasty*.

After *Supplemented Imperially Edited Reference Book in Qing Dynasty* was published, Yi Xing, a member of royal clan, collected over 7,900 new Manchu words with the imperial approval. Sharing the stylistic rule of *Collections of Manchu Words*, he compiled *Supplementation of Manchu Words* and printed it in 1786, the 51st year of Emperor Qianlong. Later, Zhi Kuan and Pei Kuan, chief instructor of translation for the Eight-Banner troops in Jingzhou, organized students to integrate *Collections of Manchu Words* with *Supplementation of Manchu Words*, forming *An Overall Collection of Manchu Words*. It was printed in 1897, the 23rd year of Emperor Guangxu.

In short, the Manchu and multilingual dictionaries compiled in Qing Dynasty marked the unprecedented prosperity of Manchu words. They provided the most effective way to consolidate the Manchu-Chinese Alliance policy and promote the spread and communication of national cultures, and played an active role in perfecting Manchu and popularizing the national culture.

Part Two　Created Books

(1) The Compilation of Historical and Chorographical Books. In the reign of Emperor Kangxi, book-compilation organizations were established in National Strategy Academy, National History Academy, and Hall of Martial Valor Book Compilation Institute. Emperor Kangxi ordered to compile many historical and chorographical books of Qing Dynasty in Manchu, Chinese, and Mongolian.

Firstly, *The Memoir in the Reigns of Emperors in Qing Dynasty*, *The Imperial Edicts in Qing Dynasty*, *The Tactics of Emperors in Qing Dynasty*, and *The Biography of Emperors in Qing Dynasty* were compiled in National History Academy. In Qing Dynasty, when the emperor deceased, his successor immediately ordered to compile *The Memoir in the Reigns of Emperors in Qing Dynasty* and *The Imperial Edicts in Qing Dynasty*. From Emperor Taizu to Emperor Dezong in Qing Dynasty, there were 12 books on *The Memoir in the Reigns of Emperors in Qing Dynasty* and *The Imperial Edicts in Qing Dynasty* respectively. In the 9th year of Emperor Tiancong, *The Memoir in the Reigns of Emperor Hongwu* was compiled in Manchu, Mongolian, and Chinese. The Manchu edition of *The Memoir in the Reigns of Emperors in Qing Dynasty* and *The Imperial Edicts in Qing Dynasty* were all decorated with large and small red damask silk or small yellow damask silk. Some books on *The Imperial Edicts in Qing Dynasty* had Hall of Martial Valor Edition.

In addition, the compilation of *Imperially Edited History of Qing Dynasty and Biographies of Accomplished Persons* was started in 1710, the 49th year of Emperor Kangxi and completed in the reign of Emperor Qianlong by National History Academy. This ushered in the beginning of the compilation of biographies of outstanding officials and faithful generals. For instance, Emperor Yongzheng ordered to compile *A General Genealogy of Clans in the Eight-Banners* in 1735, the 13th year of his reign, which was printed in 1744, the 9th year of Emperor Qianlong. Emperor Qianlong re-edited *Imperially Edited History of Qing Dynasty and Biographies of Accomplished Persons*, and recounted in detail the accomplishments of members of royal clan and outstanding persons, such as in *Accomplishments and Biographies of Princes and Dukes*, *Records of Conferred Princes and Dukes*, *Imperially Edited Biographies of Princes and Dukes of Hui Tribes in Outer Mongolia*, *Imperially Edited History of Qing Dynasty and Biographies of Officials*, *Imperially Edited History of Qing Dynasty and Biographies of Accomplished Persons*, *Imperially Edited History of Qing Dynasty and Biographies of Faithful Generals*, and *Biographies of Persons with Shrines in Zhaozhong Temple*. These books were re-compiled by the successors of Emperor Qianlong.

Secondly, Emperor Kangxi set up National Strategy Academy that concentrated on the compilation of the history of war in Qing Dynasty. In the reign of Emperor Kangxi, some books recording the wars in the frontier among minorities were compiled in Manchu and Chinese, such as *Records of the Pacification of Revolt of the Three Feudatories*, *Records of the Pacification of the Rebels in the Northern Desert Led by the Emperor*, *Records of the Pacification of the Rebels of Dzungar People*, *Records of the Pacification of the Rebel of Tusi in Jinchuan*, and *Records of the Pacification of the Rebels of Tusi in Major and Minor Jinchuan*. Besides, Emperor Qianlong ordered to compile *Records of the Foundation of Qing Dynasty* to propagate the history of early Qing Dynasty.

Thirdly, there were numerous geographical books. However, few had been translated into Manchu, including *Imperially Edited Research of the Origin and Spread of Manchu*, *Imperially Edited Primary Collection of Records of the Eight Banners*, *Imperially Edited Chorography of Mount. Wutai*, and *Imperially Edited Records of the Imperial College*.

(2) The Collection of Policies and Statutes. To maintain social order and consolidate national unity, Qing emperors established National Law Academy and printed many books on the polices and statutes in Manchu and Chinese. In 1670, the 9th year of Emperor Kangxi, *Cases Attached to Laws in Qing Dynasty*, the earliest Manchu statute book, was printed. *Laws for Supervision and Arrest* had been printing in Qing Dynasty to settle the problem that peasants fled because of the enclosure done by the Eight Banners. In 1680, the 19th year of Emperor Kangxi, *The Imperially Edited Temporary Laws for the Six Ministries* was printed.

When Emperor Yongzheng ascended the throne, he ordered to reduce and standardize the laws. *Explanations for Qing-Dynasty Laws* was supplemented with notes and cases and renamed *Imperially Edited Qing-Dynasty Laws*. The form that cases attached to the laws ended the condition that laws and cases were separated or laws were replaced with cases since the reign of Emperor Kangxi. Emperor Qianlong conformed the original, supplemented, and imperially edited notes in the laws. With the supplemented cases, *Laws and Cases in Qing Dynasty* was compiled and printed in 1740, the 5th year of Emperor Qianlong, and became the model for statute books in Qing Dynasty. It was ruled that statute books should be re-edited in small scale after 5 years and in large scale after 10 years, based on the principle that laws were changed and supplemented while being passed down. In *The Edited Laws and Cases in Qing Dynasty*, there were more volumes and cases.

In addition, Qing emperors compiled *Rules in Imperial Clan Court* to maintain the royal privilege and *Temporary Rules in Imperial Household Department* to maintain the order in the court. Many specific rules were made, such as *Rules for the Eight Banners*, *Rules for Ordnance*, *Rules for the Examination in Ministry of Military*, *Rules for Barbette at Baita Mountain*, *Rules for Selecting Officials*, *Rules for Examining and Grading Officials*, *Rules for Punishment*, *Imperially Edited Rules for Banner Affairs in Ministry of Revenue*, *Imperially Edited Rules for Tai Chang Temple*, *Imperially Edited Rules for Imperial College*, etc. Their compilation and edition were also based on the rule that statute books should be re-edited in small scale after 5 years and in large scale after 10 years.

Qing emperors paid attention to the pacification and management of minorities in the frontier. To rule Mongolia, *Rules Made in Shengjing* was issued in 1633, the 7th year of Emperor Tiancong. It was the earliest national and regional law in Qing Dynasty. In 1636, the 1st year of Emperor Chongde, Office for Mongolian Affairs was established, which was renamed Board for National Minority Affairs in 1638, the 3rd year of Emperor Chongde. In 1643, the 8th year of

Emperor Chongde, *Books of Laws for Mongolia* was issued, which was printed with the edited version in 1657, the 14th year of Emperor Shunzhi and reprinted in 1667, the 6th year of Emperor Kangxi. With continuous edition, it was printed in Manchu, Mongolian, and Chinese in 1715, the 54th year of Emperor Qianlong, with the new name *Laws and Cases for Mongolia*. Since 1811, the 16th year of Emperor Jiaqing, Mongolian laws and cases had been edited. Supplemented with *A General History of Tibet*, *Rules for Huijiang*, and other rules for Lamaism and Russian affairs, *Laws and Cases for Mongolia* was renamed *Rules for Board for National Minority Affairs* in Manchu, Mongolian, and Chinese in 1814.

The laws and rules made in Qing Dynasty covered different fields and diverse types. Therefore, in 1684, the 23rd year of Emperor Kangxi, Law Collection Academy was established to collected the laws and rules. In 1690, the 29th years of Emperor Kangxi, *Collected Laws in Qing Dynasty* was printed. It was the first comprehensive law in Qing Dynasty and re-edited four times. In the 3rd edition in the reign of Emperor Qianlong, *Rules* and *Cases* were compiled. In the 4th edition in the reign of Emperor Jiaqing, illustrations were added.

In general, the laws and rules, such as *Collected Laws in Qing Dynasty*, *Rules,* and *Cases* constituted the complete administrative and legal system in Qing Dynasty. While maintaining the existence of royal privileges, they stabilized the multi-national country.

(3) Manchu Literary Works Created by Manchu People. With the Manchu-Chinese cultural communication and influence deepened, many Manchu writers emerged. However, few could write in Manchu and their works were in small amount such as *Imperial Poems on Chengde Mountain Resort*, *Imperial Ode on Shengjing*, *Imperially Composed Ancient Poems*, *Essay on Emperor Taizong's Defeat against Ming-Dynasty Troops at Songshan Mountain*, *Records on March with Army*, *Records of the Remote Area*, *Records in the Diplomatic Mission to Jiaozhi*, etc. Among them, *Imperial Poems on Chengde Mountain Resort* was the only Manchu poetry collection of Emperor Kangxi. *Imperial Ode on Shengjing* was composed in 1743, the 8th year of Emperor Qianlong, when Emperor Qianlong worshipped the ancestral temple in Shengjing. As the most famous ode of Emperor Qianlong, it was transcribed in 32 styles in Manchu seal character and printed in Manchu-Chinese seal character in 1748, the 13th year of Emperor Qianlong. Manchu-Chinese *Imperially Composed Ancient Poems* was a creative work of Emperor Qianlong and was printed in 1779, the 44th year of Emperor Qianlong. *Records on March with Army*, *Records of the Remote Area*, and *Records in the Diplomatic Mission to Jiaozhi* were essays recording journey and folks.

In conclusion, the Manchu works were later translated into Mongolian, and some into French, German, and English.

Explanatory Notes

Range of Collection: This series selects and introduces the collections in the Palace Museum, which are mainly valuable ancient books in Mongolian, Manchu, Chinese, Tibetan, and Uigur. Most are compiled in Manchu-Mongolian and Manchu-Chinese-Mongolian. Few are in Tibetan-Uigur.

Category and Structure: This series follows the traditional category in ancient Chinese books, *Jing* (Confucianist Classics), *Shi* (History), *Zi* (Philosophy), and *Ji* (Literature). In each category, we firstly edit the governmental edition, and then the non-governmental edition based on the chronological order.

Title: Some Manchu or plurilingual books have more than one titles which differ little from each other and lie in different places, like titles in title page, head page, copyright page, cover page, and bookmark, like the phrases "records in books," "title in the total catalogue," "alias," "planned name," and "translated name." This series mainly takes the title in head page, and that in title page, copyright page, or cover page if the book has no title in head page. In some cases, the title is chosen not completely based on the rule so long as it can fully represent the feature of the book. In some Mongolian and plurilingual books, such words as "Imperially Edited," "Imperially Printed," "Translated," "Manchu-Chinese," and "Multi-language" are reserved to present the real condition when the books were compiled. The titles are in Chinese and Mongolian.

Language and Genre: In Qing Dynasty, most Mongolian books were plurilingual, in two, three, four, or five languages and with diverse genre. For instance, *Collections of Words and Expressions Used in Life and Production in Tuote Mongolian* is a Mongolian-*Tuote*-Manchu-Chinese dictionary. As *Tuote* is a kind of Mongolian used by Oirats, the dictionary is actually a Mongolian-Chinese-Manchu edition. In addition, *Imperially Edited Reference Book for Manchu and Mongolian Learning, On Mongolian, Manchu-Mongolian-Uigur Characters, Manchu-Mongolian-Tibetan-Uigur Characters*, and *Manchu-Mongolian-Tibetan-Gyarung-Uigur Characters* are dictionary in two or more languages. The words in Mongolian, Tibetan, Gyarung, and Uigur are transliterated from Manchu letters. *Manchu-Mongolian-Chinese Characters* is a Manchu-Mongolian-Chinese dictionary, in which the Mongolian part is all transliterated from Manchu letters. The dictionary has only Chinese and Manchu editions. It can be concluded that plurilingual dictionaries have more languages than editions. In some plurilingual dictionaries, the words are transliterated from more than one language. For example, in *Imperially Edited Collections of Names in Translation*, Sanskrit words in Buddhism are transliterated from Manchu, Chinese, Mongolian, and Tibetan. In general, the language and genre in one book differ. This series mainly bases itself on the number of languages and edits on the order of them to present the multilingual books.

December 10, 2013

Explanatory Notes

I. Range of Collection: This series selects and introduces the collections in the Palace Museum, which are mainly valuable ancient books in Mongolian, Manchu, Chinese, Tibetan, and Uigur. Most are compiled in Manchu-Mongolian and Manchu-Chinese-Mongolian. Few are in Tibetan-Uigur.

II. Category and Structure: This series follows the traditional category in ancient Chinese books, *Jing* (Confucianist Classics), *Shi* (History), *Zi* (Philosophy), and *Ji* (Literature). In each category, we firstly edit the governmental edition, and then the non-governmental edition based on the chronological order.

III. Title: Some Manchu or plurilingual books have more than one titles which differ little from each other and lie in different places, like titles in title page, head page, copyright page, cover page, and bookmark, like the phrases "records in books," "title in the total catalogue," "alias," "planned name," and "translated name." This series mainly takes the title in head page, and that in title page, copyright page, or cover page if the book has no title in head page. In some cases, the title is chosen not completely based on the rule so long as it can fully represent the feature of the book. In some Mongolian and plurilingual books, such words as "Imperially Edited," "Imperially Printed," "Translated," "Manchu-Chinese," and "Multi-language" are reserved to present the real condition when the books were compiled. The titles are in Chinese and Mongolian.

IV. Language and Genre: In Qing Dynasty, most Mongolian books were plurilingual, in two, three, four, or five languages and with diverse genre. For instance, *Collections of Words and Expressions Used in Life and Production in Tuote Mongolian* is a Mongolian-*Tuote*-Manchu-Chinese dictionary. As *Tuote* is a kind of Mongolian used by Oirats, the dictionary is actually a Mongolian-Chinese-Manchu edition. In addition, *Imperially Edited Reference Book for Manchu and Mongolian Learning, On Mongolian, Manchu-Mongolian-Uigur Characters, Manchu-Mongolian-Tibetan-Uigur Characters,* and *Manchu-Mongolian-Tibetan-Gyarung-Uigur Characters* are dictionary in two or more languages. The words in Mongolian, Tibetan, Gyarung, and Uigur are transliterated from Manchu letters. *Manchu-Mongolian-Chinese Characters* is a Manchu-Mongolian-Chinese dictionary, in which the Mongolian part is all transliterated from Manchu letters. The dictionary has only Chinese and Manchu editions. It can be concluded that plurilingual dictionaries have more languages than editions. In some plurilingual dictionaries, the words are transliterated from more than one language. For example, in *Imperially Edited Collections of Names in Translation*, Sanskrit words in Buddhism are transliterated from Manchu, Chinese, Mongolian, and Tibetan. In general, the language and genre in one book differ. This series mainly bases itself on the number of languages and edits on the order of them to present the multilingual books.

List of Plates

1 *Everyday Textbook: Interpretation of the Book of Changes*
Eighteen chapters —— 22

2 *Everyday Textbook: Interpretation of the Book of History*
Thirteen chapter —— 26

3 *Book of Odes*
Twenty chapters —— 28

4 *Translated Version of the Book of Rites*
Thirty chapters —— 30

5 *Elements of Music*
Two chapters —— 34

6 *Essentials of Music*
Five chapters —— 38

7 *Music of Banquet Dance Presented to the Super-sovereign* —— 40

8 *Music Respectfully Presented by Envoys of Burma* —— 42

9 *Translated Version of the Spring and Autumn Annals*
Sixty-four chapters as text,
one chapter as guiding principle —— 44

10 *Everyday Textbook: Interpretation of the Spring and Autumn Annals*
Sixty-four chapters as text, one chapter as introduction —— 46

11 *Translated Version of the Classic of Filial Piety*
One chapter —— 48

12 *Classic of Female Filial Piety*
One chapter —— 52

13 *Mirror for Imperial Filial Piety*
Ten chapters —— 54

14 *Four Books*
Thirteen chapters —— 56

15 *Dictionary of the Qing Language*
Twenty chapters as text, one chapter as preliminary remarks,
four chapters as general principles,
one chapter as postscript —— 60

16 *Manchu-Mongolian Dictionary*
Twenty chapters as text,
one chapter as preliminary remarks —— 64

17 *Manchu-Mongolian Dictionary*
Twenty chapters as text,
one chapter as preliminary remarks —— 66

18 *General Principles of the Manchu-Mongolian Dictionary*
Eight chapters —— 68

19 *Phonetically Transcribed Bilingual Dictionary of Chinese and the Official Language of the Qing* —— 70

20 *Supplement to the Dictionary of the Qing Language*
Thirty-two chapters as text,
two chapters as preliminary remarks,
eight chapters as general principles,
four chapters as supplement to the text, one chapter as
supplement to the general principle —— 72

21 *Trilingual Dictionary of Manchu, Mongolian and Chinese Phonetically Transcribed, Adopting the Method of Qieyin*
Thirty-one chapters as text,
one chapter as preliminary remarks —— 74

22 *Dictionary of the Four Languages in the Qing Dynasty*
Thirty-two chapters as text,
four chapters as supplement —— 76

23 *Dictionary of the Five Languages in the Qing Dynasty*
Thirty-two chapters as text,
four chapters as supplement —— 78

24 *Manchu-Chinese Dictionary*
Twenty chapters —— 80

25 *Selections from the Dictionary of the Qing Language*
Eight chapters —— 84

26 *Old Qing Language Selected from Veritable Records*
Fourteen chapters —— 86

27 *Comprehensive Dictionary of the Qing Language*
Twelve chapters —— 88

28 *Tuote Mongolian Dictionary*
Eight chapters —— 90

29 *Supplemental Dictionary of the Qing Language*
Eight chapters —— 92

30 *Complete Dictionary of the Qing Language*
Twelve chapters —— 94

31 *Geographical Dictionary of Places and Names in the Western Region*
Twenty-four chapters —— 98

32 *Dictionary for Terms in the Histories of Liao, Jin and Yuan*
Forty-six chapters —— 100

33 *Manchu-Mongolian-Chinese Dictionary* —— 104

34 *Manchu-Mongolian-Tibetan-Uighur Dictionary* —— 106

35 *Manchu-Mongolian-Tibetan-Jiarong-Uighur Dictionary* —— 108

36 *Condensed Buddhist Dictionary in Five Languages*
Two chapters —— 110

37 *The Ali Gali Transliterations of the Four Languages* —— 114

38 *Unified Syllables Imperially Commissioned*
Six chapters —— 116

39 *Patterns of Manchu and Chinese Corresponding Phones*
One chapter —— 120

40 *Essentials of Mongolian*
Four chapters —— 122

41 *One Hundred Conversational Terms*
Four chapters —— 126

42 *Reprinted Version of the Guidebook of Manchu Function Words*
Two chapters —— 128

43 *Manchu-Mongolian-Chinese Textbook*
Eight chapters —— 132

44 *Records of the Three Kingdoms*
Sixty-five chapters —— 134

45 *History of Liao*
Eight chapters —— 136

46 *History of Jin*
Eight chapters —— 138

47 *History of Yuan*
Fifteen chapters —— 140

48 *History Of Ming*
Ninety-Seven Chapters —— 142

49 *Collection of Brief History*
Eighty chapters —— 144

50 *The Qing Strategies on Establishing the State*
Thirty-two chapters —— 146

51 *The Qing Strategies on Suppressing the Three Rebels*
Sixty chapters —— 148

52 *Origin and Development of Mongolia*
Eight chapters —— 150

53 *A Study of the Origin and Development of Manchuria*
Twenty chapters as text,
one chapter as preliminary remarks —— 152

54 *Tables and Biographies of the Nobility's Achievements* —— 154

55 *Sequel to Biographies of Mongolian and Uigurian Princes* —— 156

56 *Biographies of the Qing Ministers* —— 158

57 *Biographies of the Meritorious Officials in the Qing History* —— 160

58 *Biographies of the Loyal and Righteous Subjects in the Qing History, Made by Imperial Order*
Nineteen chapters —— 162

59 *Biographies of the Martyrs in the Shrine of Manifest Loyalty*
120 chapters —— 164

60 *Names of Juren (Successful Candidates at the Provincial-level Imperial Examination of Shuntian)*
One chapter —— 166

61 *Records on Jinshi (Successful Candidates of the Highest-level Imperial Examination)*
One chapter —— 168

62 *Biographies of Exemplary Women of Past and Present*
Six chapters —— 170

63 *The Qing Institution*
162 chapters as text, one chapter as preliminary remarks —— 172

64 *Manchu Sacrificial Rites to Worship Heaven and Deities*
Six chapters —— 176

65 *Rules and Regulations on Imperial Clan Court*
Thirty-one chapters as text,
one chapter as preliminary remarks —— 178

66 *Rules and Regulations on Eight Banners*
Twelve chapters —— 180

67 *Comprehensive Records on the Eight Banners, First Compilation*
250 chapters as text, two chapters as contents —— 182

68 *Rules and Regulations on the Frontier of Uighur*
Eight chapters as text,
one chapter as preliminary remarks —— 184

69 *Rules and Regulations on the Board for National Minority Affairs, Made by Imperial Order*
Sixty-three chapters as text,
three chapters as preliminary remarks —— 186

70 *Rules and Regulations on the Imperial Academy*
Thirty chapters as text,
two chapters as preliminary remarks —— 188

71 *Rules and Regulations on Military Arms*
Twelve chapters —— 190

72 *Collection of Political Essays on Mental Cultivation of Officials*
One chapter —— 194

73 *Holy Teachings of the Taizu Emperor of the Qing*
Four chapters —— 196

74 *Records on Mount Wutai*
Ten chapters —— 200

75 *Valuable Teachings of the Hongwu Emperor*
Six chapters —— 202

76 *Twenty-four Filial Exemplars Illustrated* —— 204

77 *Illustrated Explanation on Cultivating Propriety*
Four chapters —— 208

78 *Essential Principles to Aid in Politics*
Three chapters as text, one chapter as postscript —— 212

79 *Ox Commandment*
One chapter —— 214

80 *Amplified Instructions on the Sacred Edicts in Three Languages*
Four chapters —— 216

81 *Essence of Nature and Rationality*
Twelve chapters —— 220

82 *Exposition of the Great Learning*
Forty-three chapters as text,
one chapter as preliminary remarks — 224

83 *Pure Book*
One chapter — 228

84 *Three Military Strategies*
One chapter — 230

85 *Six Military Principles*
Two chapters — 232

86 *Master Lei's Process of Preparing Chinese Medicine*
Sixteen chapters — 236

87 *General Book on Therapeutics of Chinese Medicine*
Three chapters — 238

88 *Longevity and Vitality Preservation*
Twenty-two chapters — 242

89 *Wang Shuhe's Pulse Classic*
Four chapters — 244

90 *Western Medicine* — 246

91 *Complete Book of Horse Classics* — 248

92 *Elements*
Seven chapters — 250

93 *Records on Astronomy and Constellations*
One chapter — 254

94 *Lunar Eclipse on August 17, 1884* — 256

95 *Music Score for Qin*
Six chapters — 258

96 *Romance of the Three Kingdoms*
Twenty-four chapters — 262

97 *Records of the States*
108 chapters — 266

98 *Journey to the West*
100 chapters — 268

99 *Sequel to "Journey to the West"*
Forty chapters — 270

100 *Ping Shan Leng Yan*
Sixteen chapters — 272

101 *Tripitaka in Manchu*
108 chapters as text, one chapter as contents — 274

102 *Mantras of the Tripitaka*
Eighty chapters as text,
eight chapters as preliminary remarks — 278

103 *Ullambana Sutra* — 282

104 *Prajnaparamita Heart Sutra* — 284

105 *Surangama Sutra*
Ten chapters — 288

106 *Sutra on Praying for Rain*
at the Hall of Grand Clouds — 292

107 *Sitatapatra Kalpa Sutra* — 296

108 *Sutra Presented to the Court* — 298

109 *Illustrated Biographies of Various Buddhas* — 300

110 *Amitayurdhyana Sutra* — 302

111 *Imperial Poems on the Mountain Resort*
for Summer Retreat
Two chapters — 306

112 *Imperial Rhapsody on Shengjing* — 310